Regional Economics and Policy, Third Edition

To Sue and Lynnette

Regional Economics and Policy

third edition

Harvey Armstrong, University of Sheffield

and

Jim Taylor, Lancaster University

First published 1985
Second edition published by Harvester Wheatsheaf 1993

Third edition published by Blackwell Publishers 2000

2 4 6 8 10 9 7 5 3 1

Blackwell Publishers Ltd
108 Cowley Road
Oxford OX4 1JF
UK

Blackwell Publishers Inc.
350 Main Street
Malden, Massachusetts 02148
USA

British Library Cataloguing in Publication Data
A CIP catalogue record for this book is available from the British Library.

Library of Congress Cataloging-in-Publication Data
Armstrong, Harvey.
    Regional economics and policy / Harvey Armstrong and Jim Taylor.—3rd ed.
        p. cm.
    Includes bibliographical references and index.
    ISBN 0–631–21657–X (alk. paper)—ISBN 0–631–21713–4 (pb. : alk. paper)
    1. Regional economics.   2. Regional planning.   3. Regional planning—Great Britain.
    4. Regional planning—European Union countries.   I. Taylor, Jim.   II. Title.
    HT391.3.A76   2000
    338.9—dc21   00–028902

Typeset in 10/12pt Book Antique
by Graphicraft Limited, Hong Kong
Printed in Great Britain by MPG Books, Bodmin, Cornwall
This book is printed on acid-free paper.

Contents

Preface to the third edition

There have been immense changes in regional economics and policy since the first edition of this book was published in 1985. At that time, regional policy in Britain was under considerable threat and it seemed possible that it might not survive. The reverse has happened. Interest in regional economics and policy has flourished since the dark days of the early 1980s. Not only has interest in regional policy seen a remarkable revival in Britain, but more importantly, radical new policies have been introduced by the European Union. The 1990s therefore saw a reversal of the downgrading of regional policy witnessed in the previous decade. This resulted in a transformation of attitudes towards regional issues at all levels of government, from the local level to the supranational level.

In addition to this resurgence of interest in regional policy among policy makers, there was an equally remarkable change in attitudes among economists towards regional economics during the 1990s. Economists turned their attention to the study of regional economic disparities since they realized that spatially disaggregated data offer immense opportunities for studying economic behaviour. This intensification of interest in regional issues happened among economists drawn from several mainline areas such as economic growth, labour economics, the economics of small and medium firms, industrial economics, labour migration, input–output modelling and the construction of regional econometric models.

This growing interest in regional economic issues has meant that much new material has been published in recent years, and we have consequently had to make major changes from the contents of the second edition of this book in order to incorporate these many new and exciting developments. In making these changes, we have tried to show how the latest research ties in with earlier work. This inevitably means that the book is now longer and more comprehensive than earlier editions, but we feel that this is necessary in order to provide a reasonably balanced picture of this emerging and rapidly expanding subject. It will also become clear that the contents of the book have benefited greatly from research undertaken by economic geographers and other social science disciplines as well as by economists. This will be no great surprise to those who read the academic journals devoted to regional issues.

While doing our utmost to be as up to date as possible in covering recent research into regional economics and policy, we must frankly admit that we have only been able to do a partial job. This is inevitable given the fact that textbooks in subjects in which a lot of new research is being published are out of date even before they are published. We can do nothing about this other than try to provide a framework within which the latest and newest ideas can be placed. Since earlier editions of this book seem, according to our readers, to have provided such a framework we have deliberately left the broad structure of the book unchanged.

As in the previous edition, we have continued to treat regional economics and regional policy separately since we feel that this has been useful for teaching purposes. We have also continued with our previous policy of designing the book with students undertaking economics courses in mind. We do, however, know that students in other disciplines such as economic geography, regional planning and other subject areas with a spatial orientation have found the contents of some of the chapters in previous editions of interest. Hence, although we assume a basic training in the principles of economics, the chapters in part II will be readily accessible to a much wider audience than just economics students.

Those who have used this book in the past will find that the main changes are as follows. First, more attention has been paid to empirical studies conducted by researchers in many different parts of the world, but especially Europe and the USA. Second, there is now greater recognition of the importance of endogenous processes within regions, including endogenous growth and regional feedback mechanisms in product and labour markets. Third, the policy section has been expanded to incorporate major new policy developments that came on stream during the 1990s. These new developments include: the greater emphasis on the importance of small and medium firms, the increasing importance of regional policy in the EU, community economic development policies, and the devolution of economic and political power down to the regions. Fourth, the evaluation chapter has been completely revised in order to reflect the vast expansion in policy evaluation techniques and the developments in evaluation methodology that have occurred since the early 1990s.

We would like to thank our colleagues at many universities around the world for their generous comments and for providing access to working papers and ongoing research. Special thanks are due to Hervey Gibson of Glasgow Caledonian University and Cogent Strategies Ltd, Isobel Mills at the Government Office Yorkshire and Humberside, and Peter Wells at the University of Sheffield. We are also grateful to those at Blackwell Publishers who have been involved in the production of this edition of the book.

Harvey Armstrong and Jim Taylor

part one

Regional economics

Part I is concerned with regional economics. The purpose of this part of the book is to examine why regional economies behave as they do in order to gain a better understanding of how regional disparities arise and why they persist over time. An obvious reason for attempting to explain the economic behaviour of regions is that this may help us to find solutions to economic and social problems. Knowing more about why some regions perform well while others perform poorly is essential if policy makers are to receive sound advice about how they should tackle the economic and social problems associated with regional disparities in economic performance.

The first part of this book is therefore concerned with finding answers to the following questions. What factors determine regional output and regional employment? Why is regional income per capita higher in some regions than in others? Why does the growth of labour productivity vary between regions? What factors determine regional specialization and interregional trade? To what extent can the migration of people between regions be explained by economic factors? Why do some regions have higher unemployment rates than others?

Much of the analysis in this part of the book is derived directly from techniques and theories initially developed in order to understand the behaviour of national economies. This is an obvious way to proceed since individual regional economies are similar in many respects to national economies in their underlying structure and behaviour. After all, regional economies are nothing more than aggregations of individuals and institutions in the same way as national economies. Moreover, many regional economies within nations are far bigger in size than many national economies and they often have a far more diversified and more complex structure than many national economies. Indeed, the very term 'regional economy' raises the question of what is meant by 'region'. We take a very pragmatic approach in this book and adopt a definition that is most appropriate at the time. The term 'region' will therefore be used to refer to administrative areas and political jurisdictions as large as states or provinces; and 'region' will also be used to refer to areas as small as local authority areas. In theoretical discussions, 'region' is often treated vaguely and simply means that it is a geographical sub-unit of the national economy. In other places, such as labour market analysis, however, a region is normally defined as a local labour market in theoretical work but data availability often forces researchers to adopt a less rigorous definition. The term 'regional economy' is therefore likely to vary according to the topic under discussion and according to data availability.

The differences between regions and nations cannot, of course, be ignored. One of the most fundamental differences is that regional economies are normally far more open than the national economies in which they are located. Interregional trade within national economies, for example, is free from tariff and other barriers to trade, and all regions within the same country use the same currency. Moreover, labour and capital tend to be more mobile between regions than they are between nations. Legal, political, language and cultural barriers operate far more severely on international migration of labour and capital than on interregional migration. And the very high degree of economic interdependence that exists between regions within national boundaries plays a particularly important part in regional economic analysis. Not only are trade links very powerful between the regions of national economies, but the government's role in transferring income between regions plays a very important part in determining regional standards of living and the quality of life more generally.

There are four main themes in part I. First, chapters 1 and 2 are concerned primarily with the determination of income, output and employment. Chapter 1 discusses various models of income determination and shows how the economic fortunes of regions are highly dependent upon their performance in international markets. A primary purpose of this introductory chapter is to provide some insight into the underlying economic structure of the regional economy. This theme is pursued further in chapter 2. The purpose of chapter 2 is to show the advantages and drawbacks of using input–output models to provide a more detailed picture of the consequences of exogenous shocks on output and employment at industry level, as well as providing information about the effect of such shocks on household income.

The second major theme in part I is concerned with the long run. Chapters 3 and 4 investigate the causes of regional disparities in productivity and productivity growth from two entirely different perspectives. Chapter 3 focuses on the neoclassical growth model while chapter 4 discusses some alternative and quite different explanations of regional growth disparities to the neoclassical approach. Both chapters, however, stress the need to incorporate endogenous growth processes into any model of economic growth which aims to explain regional growth disparities in the real world.

Third, since the discussion of the behaviour of regional economies in the first four chapters stresses the importance of economic ties with other regions, chapters 5 and 6 examine these interregional linkages in greater detail. Chapter 5 investigates trade linkages and offers several explanations of why regions specialize in the production of particular commodities and services and why these specializations change over time. Chapter 6 discusses the extent and causes of interregional migration, a topic which turns out to be integrally linked to the

subject matter of the final chapter in part I since much migration occurs in response to disparate conditions in regional labour markets.

The final chapter in part I is devoted to a topic which has figured prominently
in the economic analysis of regions, namely, regional disparities in unemployment. It is the existence and persistence of high levels of unemployment which
have played such an important role in the development of regional policy over
the last half century and which will no doubt continue to dominate discussion of
regional policy issues over the foreseeable future.

chapter one

Regional income and employment determination

contents

Some regions have higher income levels and better job prospects than others. Why should this be so? What factors determine the income level and job prospects of regions? Why is it useful to be able to predict the future growth and development of regions, or the consequences of national business fluctuations for regional income and employment levels? Major new investments have large economic impacts on a region's income and employment and it is essential for policy makers to have accurate forecasts so that these effects are taken into account in the physical and economic plans for the region. It is also useful to be able to predict the impact of plant closures on the regional economy, especially if the plant is an important employer.

Numerous attempts have been made to model the underlying economic structure of regions in order to gain a better understanding of the factors determining regional economic variables such as income and employment. Regions differ considerably in their geographical and economic size, demographic characteristics, industry mix, labour force skills, age of plant and machinery, trading links with other regions, consumption patterns and many other fundamental economic characteristics. Nevertheless, it is possible to construct general models, which can be used to explain the determinants of income and employment in all types of region regardless of the vast differences between them. Two main routes have been taken, one based on the Keynesian income–expenditure approach to modelling the national economy, and the other based on input–output analysis. The present chapter focuses on the Keynesian income–expenditure model, which has been modified for use at local and regional level. In the second chapter, an entirely different approach, based upon the input–output model, is discussed and evaluated.

There are two main reasons why economists construct regional economic models. First, large organizations such as electricity generating companies and water authorities need forecasts of demand for their output for at least 15 years ahead because of the long-run nature of their investment projects. Power stations and water plants are expected to have lives of over 30 years, thus making it imperative that their investment plans dovetail with the economic and demographic developments of the region in which they operate. Regional forecasts play a critical role in such investment planning, and private forecasters provide long-run forecasts for companies needing such information. Second, regional models are constructed in order to estimate the impact of possible new industrial developments in particular locations. Opening up a new motor vehicle assembly plant or a new power station can be expected to have both short-run effects during the construction phase and long-run effects when the new plants become fully operational. The full economic impact of such large investments and their phasing over time need to be estimated so that the implications for public expenditure (on schools, houses, hospitals, recreational facilities and other social overheads) can be adequately addressed.

The present chapter is in seven sections. Section 1.1 introduces the notion of feedback. Any change in the demand for goods and services produced by a locality (or a region) will have further effects on the local economy over time through indirect effects on other industries and induced effects through the household sector. Section 1.2 explains how the Keynesian national income–expenditure model can be adapted and applied to localities and regions. Several contrasting applications of the regional multiplier model are then discussed and appraised in section 1.3, which is followed in section 1.4 by a discussion of the major weaknesses of the regional multiplier approach. Ways of overcoming these weaknesses are then examined in sections 1.5 and 1.6. Section 1.5 discusses the importance of a region's balance of trade position in determining its long-run equilibrium income level, and section 1.6 explains why it is crucial to take more care over modelling the supply side of the regional economy if accurate predictions are to be made. Finally, section 1.7 provides an introduction to a more comprehensive approach to modelling the regional economy.

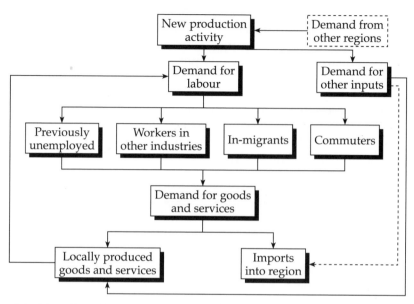

Figure 1.1 The effect of a new production activity on a region's employment, output and imports.

1.1 Impact analysis: indirect and induced effects

At the very heart of all regional economic models is the notion of internal feed-back through input–output linkages between economic agents such as firms and households. Firms are linked to other firms through the goods and services they buy from each other. Households sell their labour services to firms and buy goods from them. These linkages occur both within regions and between regions.

The way in which an injection of expenditure works its way through a regional economy can be demonstrated by considering the impact of a new productive activity. Suppose a new plant is to be built in a particular locality. A model can be constructed to estimate the effect of the new plant on local income and employ-ment. This includes not only the direct impact of the plant itself on local income and jobs, but the indirect and induced effects as well. Indirect effects occur in industries supplying components and other inputs, such as transport and com-mercial services, to the new plant. Induced effects occur as those employed in the new plant spend some of their income on locally produced goods and services.

A simplified illustration of the way in which a new production activity can be expected to affect the local economy is demonstrated in figure 1.1. The new plant requires labour. This may be obtained in various ways: by attracting existing workers from other industries in the locality; by employing unemployed workers; by inducing persons not currently in the labour force to join it; and by attracting labour from other localities. The impact of the new plant spreads to other local industries both through direct purchases from other industries in the locality and through additional purchases of locally produced goods and services, which result from the increase in income and employment. Further impacts occur due to feedback effects. Industries producing for local consumption require more labour and more inputs from the construction industry in order to expand capacity to meet the extra demand for their own output. This multiplier process continues until the initial injection (i.e. the additional output produced by the new plant) has worked its way through the local economy. It is useful to think of this happening as consecutive rounds of expenditure occurring through time until the multiplier effect works its way through the system, but in practice the expenditure effects are likely to be extremely complex with one round overlapping another (Sinclair and Sutcliffe 1978).

1.2   The Keynesian income–expenditure approach

The model

The Keynesian approach to modelling the regional economy is virtually identical to the simplest open economy version of the Keynesian income–expenditure model, the only difference being that all the expenditure variables refer to the regional (or local) economy instead of to the nation. The model begins with the familiar income–expenditure identity:

$$Y = C + I + G + X - M \qquad (1.1)$$

where Y is regional income, C is regional consumption, I is regional investment, G is government expenditure, X is regional exports and M is regional imports. Investment, government expenditure and exports are all assumed to be exogenously determined (denoted by a zero subscript):

$$I = I_0, \qquad G = G_0, \qquad X = X_0 \qquad (1.2)$$

Consumption and import expenditure are assumed to be partly exogenous and partly dependent on disposable income:

$$C = C_0 + cDY \qquad (1.3)$$

$$M = M_0 + mDY \qquad (1.4)$$

where DY is disposable income and is given by

$$DY = Y - tY \qquad (1.5)$$

where t is the rate of income tax. On substituting equations (1.2)–(1.5) into the regional income–expenditure identity (1.1), we obtain

$$Y = k \, (C_0 + I_0 + G_0 + X_0 - M_0) \qquad (1.6)$$

Table 1.1   Values of the regional multiplier from equation (1.7) for various combinations of the tax rate t and the marginal propensity to consume locally produced goods $(c - m)$

Marginal propensity to consume locally produced goods $(c - m)$	Tax rate, t		
	0.1	0.2	0.3
0.1	1.10	1.09	1.08
0.2	1.22	1.19	1.16
0.3	1.37	1.32	1.27
0.4	1.56	1.47	1.39

where k is the regional multiplier and is given by

$$k = \frac{1}{1 - (c - m)(1 - t)} \tag{1.7}$$

The multiplier

The critical variable in the Keynesian regional multiplier formula is the marginal propensity to consume locally produced goods $(c - m)$. The numerical importance of $c - m$ can be seen from table 1.1, which shows the effect on the regional multiplier of varying the tax rate and $c - m$. A low value for $c - m$ results in a multiplier that only just exceeds unity, and this is the case even with a tax rate as low as 10 per cent. The multiplier is clearly sensitive to changes in $c - m$, rising quite rapidly as it increases. Since the marginal propensity to consume locally produced goods $(c - m)$ has a crucial effect on the magnitude of the regional multiplier, it is worth exploring the factors that may be expected to affect it. Several factors are likely to be important. First, a region's size is likely to affect its $c - m$ since import leakages are likely to be large for small regions. The marginal propensity to import into the region is therefore likely to be large for small regions, thus reducing $c - m$. Some support for this negative relationship is offered in figure 1.2, which shows a significant negative relationship between a country's dependence on trade and its GDP across 105 countries for which data were available (from the World Bank's database).

Second, a region's marginal propensity to consume locally produced goods $(c - m)$ will be affected by its industry mix. Highly specialized regions will depend heavily on imports because of their specialization. In practice, even very large regions which have a highly diversified industry mix rely heavily on trade with the outside world because of intra-industry trade.

Third, a region's marginal propensity to import may be affected by its location, especially in relation to other local labour markets. If inward commuting into a region is high due to the region's nearness to other labour market areas (such as when a town is surrounded by other towns), this will lead to a smaller multiplier. The reason is obvious: commuters will tend to spend their earnings in the region where they live rather than in the region where they work. This will raise a

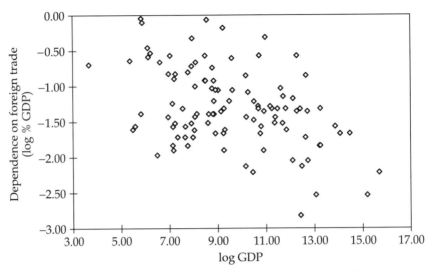

Figure 1.2   Dependence on foreign trade versus GDP, 105 countries, 1994.

region's marginal propensity to import. The geographical location of a region will also affect the propensity of its residents to spend locally, since the absence of shopping facilities in nearby regions will encourage local shopping, thus reducing the marginal propensity to import. We shall return to the question of the influence of geographical location on the size of the regional multiplier later in this chapter.

It is clear from the previous section that the magnitude of the regional multiplier will vary according to the characteristics of each individual region or locality for which it is being estimated. There is no single numerical value which can be used for all regions or all localities. Each case is unique and should be treated as such. Estimates of the regional multiplier are therefore region-specific. Indeed, regional multipliers are usually estimated for specific projects in specific locations and the multipliers are project-specific as well as region-specific. Different projects in the same region may well have different multiplier consequences (allowing for differences in the size of projects).

Early work on the estimation of regional multipliers concentrated upon obtaining broad estimates of the regional multiplier for 'typical' regions. Archibald (1967), for example, used the national Family Expenditure Survey to estimate the marginal propensity to consume locally produced goods for a typical region. Goods and services that are likely to be purchased locally (such as expenditure on car maintenance, retail services, local government services, cinemas, health care, education, etc.) were first identified, and total expenditure on these items was then summed. This exercise was repeated for a number of years to obtain an annual time series L_t, which is a measure of that part of national expenditure which is spent locally. Regressing this on personal disposable income produces an estimate of the marginal propensity to consume locally produced goods out of disposable income:

Table 1.2 The proportion of total expenditure on locally produced goods and services by staff and students at Nottingham University

Expenditure category	Academic and related staff		Students	
	% of total income	Proportion of income spent locally	% of total income	Proportion of income spent locally
Food	19	0.25	17	0.25
Housing, rent	17	0.15	28	0.85
Travel, vehicles	15	0.21	12	0.30
Durable goods, gifts	12	0.25	10	0.25
Drink, tobacco	7	0.25	15	0.30
Clothing, footwear	7	0.25	5	0.25
Fuel, light, power	5	0.10	2	0.10
Miscellaneous	18	0.27	11	0.25
Total	100	0.22	100	0.43

Source: Bleaney et al. (1991)

$$L_t = \alpha + \beta DY_t \tag{1.8}$$

where L is national expenditure on locally produced goods and services, DY is national disposable income, α is a constant reflecting that part of L which is independent of DY, β is an estimate of the marginal propensity to spend on locally produced goods and services, and t is time.

Since β is an estimate of the marginal propensity to spend on locally produced goods and services $(c - m)$, this can now be used to provide an estimate of the regional multiplier (such as that given by equation (1.7)). Using this method, Archibald estimated that $c - m$ was approximately 0.23 for the hypothetical region which he had in mind when identifying locally produced goods and services. With a tax rate of 0.2, this gives a multiplier value of around 1.2.

Most multiplier studies now use a similar basic methodology to that developed by Archibald, but derive specific estimates for the particular region being studied; that is, they are region-specific. Consider, for example, the approach used by Bleaney et al. (1992) to estimate the impact of Nottingham University on the economy of Nottingham. An estimate of the marginal propensity to spend on locally produced goods and services is obtained for students and staff separately, since students spend a far higher proportion of their income locally than do university staff. Students also have a different pattern of expenditure from staff, spending a far greater proportion of their income on housing and on drink and tobacco (see table 1.2). Moreover, a far higher proportion of expenditure on housing stays within the Nottingham economy than is the case for staff. One of the reasons for this is that students' rental payments flow to local landlords (including the university), whereas the mortgage repayments of staff flow to building society head offices outside Nottingham. At the foot of the second and fourth columns in table 1.2 are the propensities to spend locally by staff (0.22) and students (0.43) respectively. (The value of 0.22 for staff is obtained by multiplying the first column by the second and then summing across all categories of expenditure; and similarly for students.)

More complex regional multipliers can be constructed by adding more realism to the model. Two obvious modifications involve the treatment of the government sector. On the expenditure side, an allowance can be made for the effect of changes in income on transfer payments (such as unemployment benefit). As regional income declines, unemployment will increase and cause an increase in government expenditure. We therefore have

$$G = G_0 - gY \tag{1.9}$$

where G_0 is the autonomous component of government expenditure and gY is that part of government expenditure induced by changes in income in the region. For example, if $g = 0.1$, then government spending falls by £10 for every £100 increase in regional income. When equation (1.9) is incorporated into the model, regional income is given by the following formula:

$$Y = \frac{1}{1 - (c - m)(1 - t) + g}(C_0 + I_0 + G_0 + X_0 - M_0) \tag{1.10}$$

Further realism can be added to the regional multiplier by allowing for expenditure taxes as well as income taxes. An expenditure tax dependent on consumption expenditure, for example, could be incorporated into the model by a suitable modification to the consumption function. This is straightforward and need not be pursued here.

Another modification is to allow for the interaction between regions. One region's imports are another region's exports. Suppose region B increases its imports from region A. This additional demand for A's output will have multiplier effects in region A. The resultant increase in A's income will raise A's demand for B's exports and B's income will increase in turn. The initial increase in the demand for A's output therefore has feedback effects and the whole process begins again, continuing until the additional income generated in each round diminishes to zero. It is a simple task to modify the multiplier formula to take such interregional repercussions into account in a two-region economy. As more regions are added, however, the multiplier formula becomes increasingly complex. In practice, interregional feedback effects are likely to be very small provided that the region itself is small in relation to other regions. These interregional feedbacks are therefore ignored in applications of the regional multiplier model. This is fine provided that the region in question is small relative to the size of the national economy.

The multiplicand

The previous discussion of the regional multiplier emphasized the critical role of the leakages from regional expenditure which occur after the initial expenditure injection. In practical applications of the regional multiplier, however, it is found that the impact of an expenditure injection is far more likely to be influenced by leakages from the initial expenditure injection itself. It is extremely important to discover how much of the initial expenditure injection actually stays inside the region. In other words, the import content in the initial expenditure injection needs to be estimated in order to calculate the impact of this on the regional economy through the multiplier process.

There are two reasons why it is important to measure the first-round leakages as accurately as possible. First, the first round of expenditure is usually very large relative to the second and subsequent rounds of expenditure. Second, the leakages from the first round may be very large relative to the size of the initial expenditure injection. An example of the latter is provided by McGuire's (1983) estimates of the impact of nuclear power stations on regional income and employment in two Scottish towns, Dounreay and Torness. At the Dounreay plant, for example, 57 per cent of the inputs required to operate the plant each year were imported from other regions. The leakages in the construction phase were even larger: 90 per cent of the inputs were imported into the Torness region. It is clearly crucial to take these leakages into account when estimating the first round of the multiplier.

The significance of the first round in determining the multiplier consequences of any given expenditure injection into the regional economy can be demonstrated by considering an income–expenditure model (see Brownrigg 1971). To keep it simple, this model has no government sector and the only leakages are the import content embodied in consumption, investment and exports. Since the import content varies between different types of goods, however, the import function must allow for this explicitly. The model consists of the regional expenditure identity and two expenditure equations:

$$Y = C + I_0 + X_0 - M \tag{1.11}$$

$$C = C_0 + cY \tag{1.12}$$

$$M = M_0 + m_c C + m_i I_0 + m_x X_0 \tag{1.13}$$

The import equation argues that in addition to an increase in an autonomous element M_0, imports will increase whenever expenditure on C, I or X increases. The effect on M, however, will vary between C, I and X depending upon the numerical value of m_c, m_i and m_x, all of which are between 0 and 1.

The effect of any change in autonomous spending (C_0, I_0, X_0 or M_0) on regional income can be estimated from the above model once it has been solved for regional income. This is done by substituting equations (1.12) and (1.13) into the regional income–expenditure identity (1.11), from which we obtain

$$Y = k \left[(1 - m_c) C_0 + (1 - m_i) I_0 + (1 - m_x) X_0 - M_0 \right] \tag{1.14}$$

where

$$k = \frac{1}{1 - c(1 - m_c)} \tag{1.15}$$

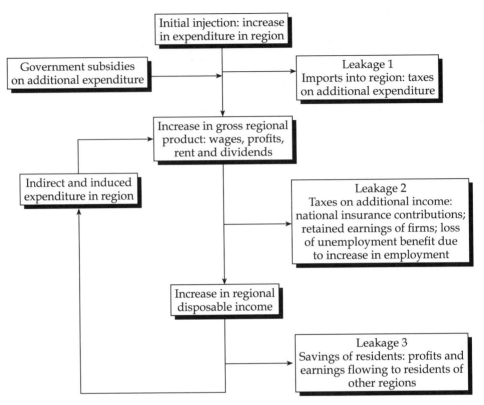

Figure 1.3   Leakages during the first round in the multiplier process: two measures of regional income.

To demonstrate the importance of the different leakages associated with different types of injection, suppose we have the following data:

$$c = 0.7, \qquad m_c = 0.6, \qquad m_i = 0.8, \qquad m_x = 0.7$$

Suppose also that $\Delta C_0 = 100$. By taking first differences of equation (1.14) and substituting the above values into the resulting equation, we obtain

$$\Delta Y = k\,(1 - m_c)\,\Delta C_0 = 1.39 \times 0.4 \times 100 = 55.6$$

If we now do the same for $\Delta I_0 = 100$ and $\Delta X_0 = 100$, we obtain

$$\Delta Y = k\,(1 - m_i)\,\Delta I_0 \ = 1.39 \times 0.2 \times 100 = 27.8$$

$$\Delta Y = k\,(1 - m_x)\,\Delta X_0 = 1.39 \times 0.3 \times 100 = 41.7$$

Notice that $k = 1.39$ is obtained by substituting $c = 0.7$ and $m_c = 0.6$ into equation (1.15).

A further important consideration when estimating the leakages from the first round of expenditure concerns the actual measure of regional income which is being used (Sinclair and Sutcliffe 1978; 1984). The two most commonly used measures of regional income are gross regional product (GRP) and regional disposable income (RDI). The difference between these two measures of regional income is simply that RDI is less than GRP because of the leakages that occur between earning an income and receiving it. Figure 1.3 shows these leakages together with the leakages that occur between the initial expenditure injection and the creation of GRP. It also shows the leakages that occur after income has been received by households. The multiplier effects of any given injection of expenditure will therefore depend upon the type of income change being investigated. Only after the definition of income has been specified can the multiplicand itself be calculated (by taking into account the appropriate leakages).

1.3   Applications of regional multiplier analysis

This section describes three quite different applications of the regional multiplier in order to demonstrate the wide variety of problems to which the concept has been applied. We turn first to the calculation of tourism multipliers for Malaga on the Costa del Sol.

Estimating the multiplier effects of tourist expenditure

An interesting application of regional multiplier analysis is the estimation of various tourist multipliers by Sinclair and Sutcliffe (1984). Their aim is to demonstrate the importance of estimating the first and second rounds of the multiplier process separately. They also stress that to obtain meaningful and accurate estimates of the regional multiplier it is first necessary to define the type of income under investigation. Only when this has been done is it possible to measure the leakages from the first and second rounds of expenditure accurately. This approach allows for separate multipliers to be calculated for two different definitions of regional income (i.e. disposable income and gross income) and to show how long it takes for the multiplier process to work itself through the regional economy. The main results of applying their method to tourist expenditure in Spain's resort area of Malaga can be used to demonstrate the potential value of regional multipliers, particularly to local and regional planners.

The two main findings of the Malaga study were as follows. First, the regional multiplier is substantially larger for gross income than for disposable income. For every £1 of expenditure by tourists in Malaga, for example, disposable income rises by £0.54 whereas gross income rises by £0.72 (see table 1.3). It is also shown that the multiplier effect varies enormously between different types of tourist expenditure, with tourists staying in flats and villas having the lowest multiplier effect on local income because rentals leak to owners who reside in other regions. Second, table 1.4 shows that the effect of an increase in tourist expenditure on

Table 1.3   Estimated multipliers for different types of tourist expenditure

Type of tourist expenditure	Effect of £1 of expenditure on	
	Disposable income	Gross income
Expenditure by tourists in flats and villas	0.36	0.47
Food, drink and entertainment	0.40	0.53
Accommodation	0.50	0.66
Miscellaneous	0.75	0.99
Total expenditure	0.54	0.72

Source: Sinclair and Sutcliffe (1984: 330–1)

Table 1.4   The effect of an increase in tourist expenditure on local disposable income: the pattern of income change over time

Year	% change in disposable income		
	First round	Second and subsequent rounds	Total effect
1	69.9	8.4	78.3
2	69.9	18.2	88.1
3	69.9	25.2	95.1
4	69.9	29.4	99.3
Long run	69.9	30.1	100.0

Source: Sinclair and Sutcliffe (1984: 334)

local income takes over four years to work its way through to its ultimate long-run level. This demonstrates the importance of time in the multiplier process.

The income and employment effects of local government financial assistance

Local government spends money on economic development initiatives such as providing factory premises, industrial sites, advisory services for small businesses and direct financial assistance to small firms (Armstrong 1988). Since the purpose of these initiatives is to increase local income and employment, it is important to assess their impact on the local economy. The purpose was to investigate the extent to which the multiplier effects of given expenditure injections vary between different types of firms in different local authority areas. Lancaster was selected as one of the areas because of its rural hinterland (and its relative remoteness from alternative major shopping areas); and Stockport was selected because of its location within the large Manchester conurbation.

The injection of expenditure into a locality's income stream is affected by (1) the wages and salaries paid to extra workers, and (2) the additional material inputs which a firm requires to increase production. For manufacturing firms, a large proportion of expenditure on material inputs can be expected to leak out of the locality in the form of goods and services imported from other localities. These will include the purchase of inputs such as energy, fixed assets and commercial services. There will therefore be a large leakage of expenditure out of the locality in the initial injection itself. Armstrong (1988), for example, shows that the propensity to import inputs into a locality varies enormously between different types of firm. The leakages from the initial injection are therefore potentially very important in determining the income and employment effects of any expenditure injection, particularly in small local economies. The import content in the expenditure injection can be incorporated into the impact model as follows:

$$\Delta Y = k\left[J_1 + (1-m)J_2\right] \tag{1.16}$$

where ΔY is the increase in local income, J_1 are the wages and salaries of the extra workers employed, J_2 are operating expenditures such as purchase of fixed assets and all indirect costs, and m is the propensity to import items (of type J_2) into the local area.

Import leakages play a large part not only in determining the size of the expenditure injection but also in determining the size of the local multiplier. This is typically small for assistance to manufacturing firms in local authority areas. There are two reasons for this:

1 Companies recruit part of their workforce from nearby localities. These commuters will spend very little of their income in the local area in which they work.
2 Those who work and live in the locality will spend part of their income in other localities, especially if shopping facilities in nearby towns are attractive.

The extent to which these two factors affect the multiplier will largely depend upon a locality's remoteness. The multiplier is likely to be smaller for localities situated within or near to a conurbation since inward commuting and outward shopping by local workers will be higher than for an area which is geographically remote from other localities. This point is clearly demonstrated by comparing Lancaster (a free-standing town surrounded by agricultural hinterland) and Stockport (part of the Greater Manchester conurbation). Only about 5 per cent of Lancaster's workers are inward commuters compared with 22 per cent for Stockport; and Stockport residents have twice as high a propensity to shop in nearby centres compared with Lancaster. In practice, the expenditure leakages from local districts are so large that the multiplier consequences of any expenditure injection are likely to be very small. Estimates of the multiplier for four manufacturing firms located in Lancaster, for example, range between 1.1 and 1.2.

The main lessons for local authorities which are planning to provide financial and other types of aid to firms in order to stimulate economic development in their own local area are as follows:

1   The multiplier impacts are likely to be small due to expenditure leakages into neighbouring localities.
2   Local councils have little power to influence the size of an individual company's multiplier effects other than through the provision of good shopping facilities in the local area.
3   If the local impact of financial assistance to firms is to be maximized, those administering such schemes need to take account of the extent to which a company employs inward commuters (rather that local residents) and the extent to which it purchases material inputs from within the locality. Small firms, for example, are likely to rely more heavily on local inputs (such as transport, banking and other services) than are branch plants of national and multinational firms.

From a wider policy viewpoint, the main lesson is that local authorities need to co-ordinate their economic development policies since the benefits of such policies will spill over into neighbouring localities. Acting independently will lead to under-funding of local economic development unless the free-rider problem is faced head on.

The impact of higher education on the regional economy

Universities have a substantial economic impact on the regions in which they are located. They employ many workers, occupy large areas of land and spend a substantial amount in the local economy. In addition to the effect they have on the local economy through the multiplier effects of their expenditure, universities can have much wider effects through the outputs they produce such as knowledge, skills and amenities. Traditionally, far greater emphasis has been placed upon the backward linkage effects of universities on their local economy through expenditures on inputs. Important though these effects may be, universities may have a wider role in determining a locality's economic development through forward linkages (Felsenstein 1996; Luger and Goldstein 1996).

How might universities contribute to local economic development? To answer this question, it is necessary to consider the potential backward and forward linkages between a university and its local economy (see figure 1.4). The backward linkages are well known. These include the demand for local output across a very wide range of service activities provided by the private and public sectors. In addition, universities employ workers who spend a proportion of their income locally, thereby having further multiplier effects. There positive effects on local income and employment will be offset to some extent by the displacement of some local service activities as a result of the provision of these services on the university campus. Furthermore, the additional pressure on local public services may lead to additional social costs such as congestion and pollution. It is not usual for multiplier studies to take such negative effects into account even though they may be substantial in some cases.

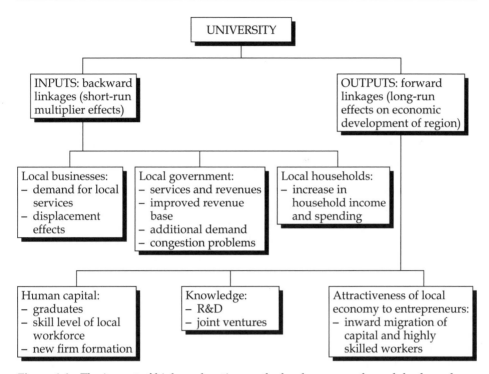

Figure 1.4 The impact of higher education on the local economy through backward and forward linkages.

The possible forward linkage effects of universities on the local economy are less well researched than the backward linkage effects. Universities not only produce highly skilled human capital but also employ highly skilled workers in a wide variety of disciplines and this high concentration of skills is likely to have several beneficial effects on the local economy. First, to the extent that a region is able to retain its graduates, a university will enhance the quality of the local workforce through the training these graduates acquire. Second, the existence of a university acts as an incentive for firms to expand their activities in the area in order to take advantage of its highly skilled graduates. Third, a university's highly skilled staff may provide expert advice to local development agencies as well as to local firms in a wide range of business-related activities, such as marketing, finance and product development. Economists, for example, are often involved in the evaluation of regional development projects in the area in which their university is located; business and management schools offer customized courses for the managers of firms located in their region; and engineering departments may be involved with local firms in developing new processes and new products. Finally, the presence of a university in an area enhances the cultural as well as the economic attractiveness of an area, thereby increasing the area's image not only to mobile firms but also to highly skilled workers.

1.4   Weaknesses of regional multiplier analysis

Despite the widespread use and popularity of regional multiplier analysis, this approach to measuring economic impacts does have several major weaknesses. First, regional multiplier analysis does not take capacity constraints into account. If a regional economy faces capacity constraints, an expenditure injection may have little, if any, effect on regional income. Producers may respond to an increase in demand by raising their prices rather than by increasing output, or they may contract out the extra work to other firms in other regions. Alternatively, the production bottlenecks may be in industries that supply households with goods and services, in which case the effect of an expenditure injection may be to increase the marginal propensity to import (thereby reducing the regional multiplier). Over the longer run, the existence of production bottlenecks will induce further investment in order to expand the region's productive capacity.

Second, regional multiplier analysis has been criticized for failing to allow for interregional feedback effects. According to the regional multiplier model described in section 1.2, an increase in regional income will result in an increase in imports. Since these imports are another region's exports, this will raise income in other regions, which in turn will increase their own imports. Such interregional feedback effects are not allowed for in regional multiplier analysis. This will not matter, however, in the case of small regions since feedback effects will be very small. Only where the region is relatively large in relation to the entire system of regions will the feedback effects be worth taking into account.

Third, the calculation of multiplier effects would be more useful if it were recognized that the multiplier effects of a given expenditure injection occur over time, and that it may take several years for the full multiplier effects to work through the local economy. Sinclair and Sutcliffe (1989) argue that insufficient attention has been paid to estimating the timing of income changes resulting from expenditure injections. Attention is usually focused on the long-run multiplier consequences.

Fourth, regional multiplier analysis provides only a very aggregative picture of the impact of expenditure injections. Planners and policy makers need to know the effect of these injections not only on the output and employment of the regional economy as a whole, but also on particular industries. Section 1.6 explains how the regional multiplier approach can be extended to provide more detailed information about the ways in which expenditure injections can affect a regional economy.

Fifth, the impact of expanding firms will depend heavily on the extent to which individual firms purchase inputs from the region rather than importing these inputs from other regions. This will vary between firms for many reasons, such as the ability of the region to provide the necessary inputs and the location of the region in relation to other potential suppliers. Collis and Roberts (1992), for example, estimate that foreign-owned companies investing in the West Midlands purchased 20 per cent of their material inputs from within the region, whereas the corresponding estimate for Wales is 14 per cent (Phelps 1997). The difference is probably a consequence of the West Midlands having a larger and more diversified industrial base.

Finally, apart from some notable exceptions, money has largely been ignored in regional modelling (Dow and Rodriguez-Fuentes 1997). More often than not, regional models do not include any reference to the effect of money on the regional economy. It is usual to assume that money is neutral so that regional economic analysis is conducted entirely in terms of real variables. Monetary changes are assumed to have no real effects on the variables of central importance, such as output and employment.

But is this assumption realistic? One of the reasons why money has been ignored in regional economic analysis is the lack of regional monetary data. This lack of data has probably been instrumental in diverting the attention of regional economists away from the role of money as a determinant of regional economic activity. In fact, money is assumed to respond to regional differences in economic activity rather than help to explain why such differences occur. The national monetary authority, for example, is assumed to determine monetary conditions which then affect the macroeconomy in various ways. These monetary effects are then transmitted to all regions by the linkages between regional and national variables rather than by any specific monetary changes within the regions themselves. There is no role for money within individual regions since the regions do not have their own monetary policy instruments. Moreover, regions are very open economies which means that money and goods flow freely across regional boundaries without any obvious constraints. The money supply is therefore assumed to respond to money demand at regional level. This is why regional models of income determination and economic growth have traditionally excluded monetary variables and focused almost exclusively on real variables.

It has been convincingly argued, however, that money will affect regional economic development through either the cost of credit or its availability (Dow 1987), both of which may vary between regions. Firms in peripheral regions, far away from central financial markets, may find it more difficult and more expensive to obtain credit for financing working capital and investment in new productive capacity. The constraint on credit availability may arise because of a lack of the information needed by financial institutions for assessing risk and potential profitability. Local branches of national banks may find it difficult to create credit in response to the demand for loans to finance investment, especially in less prosperous regions where loans are believed to be more risky, and hence more expensive.

We turn now to discuss some of the ways in which these weaknesses of the regional multiplier model have been addressed.

1.5 A multi-region model of income determination

A major weakness of the single-region model of income determination is that it fails to take interregional feedback effects into account. It is quite obvious, however, that one region's exports are another region's imports and this means that income changes in one region will be transmitted to other regions. Some insight into these interregional feedback effects can be obtained by considering a world in which there are only two regions. This may seem rather simplistic, but the general principles are the same as in a multi-regional model. A further advantage of developing a two-region model is that it allows us to take a region's balance of trade into account in determining its long-run equilibrium income level. Balance of trade deficits can only be sustained over the long run in very restrictive circumstances (i.e. if other regions are willing to finance such deficits indefinitely). The influence of a region's balance of trade on its equilibrium income level over the long run therefore needs to be carefully investigated.

The determination of equilibrium income in a two-region model

Suppose there are two regions, North and South, which trade with each other. For the time being, assume that there are no supply constraints. Each region's output is therefore determined by the demand for its output. Consider the demand for the North's output y_n. This will depend upon demand within the North itself (i.e. consumption, investment and government spending) and on the demand for its exports from the South. The South's demand for the North's output will depend upon its own income y_s. The demand for the North's output can therefore be expressed as follows:

$$y_n = \alpha + \beta y_s \tag{1.17}$$

where y_n is income (= output) in the North, y_s is income (= output) in the South, α is the autonomous demand for the North's output, and β is a measure of the responsiveness of the demand for the North's exports when the South's income increases. Since the coefficient β is likely to be a positive fraction, the North's demand function will be as shown in figure 1.5a.

A demand function for the South's output can be constructed in exactly the same way as for the North. The South's demand for goods and services is given by the following expression:

$$y_s = \gamma + \delta y_n \tag{1.18}$$

where γ is the autonomous demand for the South's output, and δ is a measure of the responsiveness of the demand for the South's exports when the North's income increases. The South's demand function is shown in figure 1.5a.

In order to find the equilibrium output levels in the North and the South, we now need to consider the two functions simultaneously. The reason for this is clear. We cannot determine the equilibrium income in the North unless we know the South's income; and we cannot determine the equilibrium income in the South unless we know the North's income. The joint equilibrium for the North and the South occurs at the intersection of the two functions at point A in figure 1.5a, which shows that equilibrium income is y_n^* in the North and y_s^* in the South.

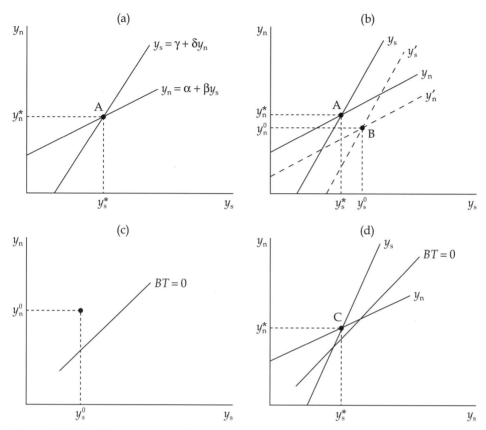

Figure 1.5 Equilibrium income levels in a two-region model.

We now need to ask what would happen if autonomous expenditures in either the North or the South change. For example, suppose that the North's wealth declines and the South's wealth increases (e.g. due to the South's assets increasing in value while the North's assets decline in value). This would result in a downward shift of the y_n function and a rightward shift in the y_s function if we assume that autonomous expenditure is positively related to wealth. Hence, in figure 1.5b a new joint equilibrium income level would be established at point B.

The balance of trade function

The balance of trade function now needs to be added to the model. The reason for this will become clear later. It can be shown that the North's balance of trade will improve as income in the South increases (since the South will import more from the North as its income increases) and the South's balance of trade will improve as income in the North increases (since the North will import more from the South as its income increases). In other words, for the balance of trade to be in equilibrium ($BT = 0$) in both regions simultaneously, the balance of trade function must slope upwards as shown in figure 1.5c. Thus, if income in the North is at y_n^0 (and income in the South is at y_s^0), the North will have a balance of trade deficit (and the South will have a corresponding surplus). Balance of trade equilibrium will be regained either if the South's income increases (thereby causing its imports from the North to increase) or if the North's income falls (causing it to reduce its imports from the South).

The effect of the balance of trade on equilibrium income in the North and South

The two income functions and the balance of trade function can now be combined in order to examine the effect of trade imbalances on equilibrium income in both regions. Figure 1.5d shows a situation in which the two regions are in simultaneous equilibrium with respect to their income levels but a balance of trade deficit exists in the North (offset exactly by a corresponding surplus in the South). What will happen as a result of this disequilibrium in the balance of trade between the two regions?

Before answering this question, it is necessary to consider the relationship between a region's balance of trade and its balance of payments. The first question to be answered is, 'Does a region have a balance of payments?' Although the flows of goods and money across regional borders are not recorded, this does not mean that regions do not have a balance of payments. A region must have a balance of payments in practice since these flows of goods and money are a reality. Interregional transactions are very substantial and the consequences of any structural imbalances in a region's transactions with the rest of the world therefore need to be carefully considered. In particular, these structural imbalances can have serious consequences for the 'real' regional economy, namely, output and employment. It is therefore necessary to describe very briefly the component parts of a region's balance of payments with the rest of the world.

A region's balance of payments is defined as follows:

balance of payments	=	balance on current account	+	balance on capital account

where:

balance on current account	=	balance of trade	+	net transfer payments
balance of trade	=	exports	–	imports
net transfer payments	=	net government transfers (e.g. taxes, income support)	+	net income from rest of world (e.g. dividends, interest on savings)

and where:

| balance on capital account | = | net long-term investment (e.g. inward direct investment) | + | net short-term investment (e.g. government bonds, equities, savings) |

Since regions do not have foreign exchange reserves and since the balance of payments must balance (by definition), it follows that the current account and the capital account must sum to zero. This means that any deficit on the trading account (i.e. imports exceed exports) must be offset somewhere else in the region's balance of payments. Hence, if a region suffers a loss of its export markets and its trade balance deteriorates as a result, the trade deficit balance has to be 'paid for' in one or more of the following ways (Dow 1986):

1 The government can increase transfer payments into the region. Indeed, this is automatically achieved through fiscal stabilizers such as unemployment benefit.
2 The region's residents may run down their stock of savings.
3 The region's residents may borrow from the banking system (which implies a net transfer of cash balances into the region from within the national banking system).
4 The region's residents may sell assets, such as bonds and securities, to residents in other regions in order to pay for the excess of imports over exports.
5 Firms outside the region may invest directly in the region.

These various ways of financing a trade deficit indicate that the deficit region will continuously lose assets unless the government is willing to finance the deficit indefinitely through income transfers into the region. The region's stock of wealth will be gradually depleted and this will reduce the ability of the region's residents to borrow on favourable terms from the banks. Expenditure by the region's residents will consequently be reduced as assets are sold off to pay for the excess of imports over exports. This will be reinforced by a decline in asset values since the fall in regional income will induce a corresponding fall in the value of the region's fixed assets, such as the housing stock, industrial plant and commercial property. Out-migration will induce further deflation in the region. Exactly the opposite will happen in the South since the North's persistent trade deficit is the South's persistent trade surplus.

The consequence of the fall in the North's wealth due to the persistent trade deficit is a downward shift in the North's income function (as already shown in figure 1.5b). The opposite will occur in the South, which will experience a rightward shift in its income function. The adjustment process will continue until a new equilibrium is established such that the y_n, y_s and balance of trade functions intersect at the same point (i.e. point C in figure 1.5d).

This analysis suggests that policies designed to increase income in low-income regions need to focus on increasing a region's export competitiveness, otherwise persistent trade deficits will lead to a continuous outflow of assets. If low-income regions are not to rely indefinitely on government income transfers, the supply side of the regional economy will have to be addressed. The range of supply-side policies available to policy makers will be discussed at length in part II of this book.

An example of a chronic regional trade deficit: eastern Germany

An excellent example of a regional balance of payments problem is provided by the recent experience of eastern Germany. In the immediate aftermath of the reunification of Germany in 1990, the output of the former East Germany fell by 45 per cent. Job losses were consequently severe and this resulted in substantial migration from east to west as people moved in search of a job and a higher standard of living. To stem this east–west migration, the German government had to prop up the economy of the depressed eastern regions through massive fiscal transfers, in the form of unemployment benefit and subsidies to state-owned industries, in order to prevent a catastrophic economic collapse. These massive fiscal transfers have been a major cause of Germany's economic problems in the 1990s.

In addition to the fiscal transfers to the eastern regions, private sector investors have been seeking out investment opportunities through mergers and acquisitions of former state-owned companies. Together with the fiscal transfers, the flow of investment funds has helped to plug the huge balance of trade deficit of the regions of eastern Germany.

Not surprisingly, this process has caused balance of payments problems for Germany as a whole. The way in which these regional transfers have caused problems for Germany's balance of trade as a whole can be explained most easily by considering the economy's expenditure and income identities. These are defined as follows:

$$\text{expenditure} = C + I + G + X - M$$

$$\text{income} \quad = C + S + T$$

where C is consumption, I is investment, G is government expenditure, X is exports, M is imports, S is saving and T is taxation.

In equilibrium, expenditure and income must be equal, and so

$$C + I + G + X - M = C + S + T$$

On rearranging this equation, we obtain

$$(I - S) + (G - T) + (X - M) = 0$$

Thus, if the economy starts initially from a situation where $I = S$ and $G = T$, then X and M must also be equal. An increase in investment relative to saving ($I > S$)

and an increase in the fiscal deficit $(G > T)$ will inevitably result in an increase in imports relative to exports $(M > X)$. This must be the case since the equality has to hold. The direct consequence of unification has therefore been a worsening in Germany's trade balance.

The ultimate intention of these fiscal transfers into the regions of eastern Germany, accompanied by inflows of private capital, is to improve industrial efficiency so that these depressed regions can compete in world markets. The alternative is mass migration from a jobless and derelict east to a prosperous and growing west, causing severe social and political problems as a consequence. These problems can only be averted if the German government continues with its policy of regenerating the eastern regions. Substantial fiscal transfers into eastern Germany will be required for years to come since the eastern regions will continue to run a chronic balance of trade deficit until they are able to compete effectively in both domestic and overseas markets. Massive capital transfers from west to east will be required to reduce the competitiveness gap.

1.6   Further developments in the economic modelling of regions

Regional multiplier models have proved to be a useful device for predicting the effects of investment projects on the aggregate income and employment levels of local and regional economies. A major weakness, however, is that they fail to take into account the effect of feedback effects emanating in the region's labour market. This is because the regional multiplier model assumes a perfectly elastic supply of labour (and indeed a perfectly elastic supply of all other factors of production). The factor markets are completely ignored. Any increase in the demand for labour, for example, is assumed to be met by a corresponding increase in supply at current wages.

More ambitious approaches to modelling regional economies deliberately take these feedback effects in the labour and other factor markets into account explicitly. We are interested not simply in estimating the effect of imports on aggregate income and employment but also on other key regional economic variables such as unemployment, net migration, participation rates and factor prices. How will the investment in new productive capacity in a region affect the job market? How will the closure of an existing plant affect the local unemployment rate and net outward migration from the region? What effect would a labour subsidy have on employment levels in the region? These are the sorts of questions that regional economic models are designed to address.

Regional models vary tremendously in detail and complexity. They range from very aggregative, demand-driven explanations based upon simplistic interpretations of the Keynesian macro-model to more sophisticated approaches which allow for the supply side to respond to changes in capital and labour markets. It is useful to provide an outline of these two approaches before discussing them in more detail.

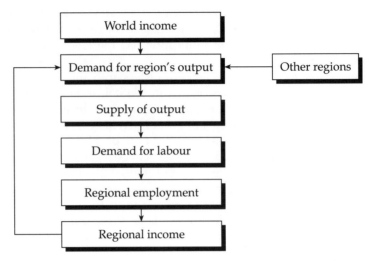

Figure 1.6   A simple demand-based model of regional income and employment determination.

Features of the model

1   Output and employment respond positively to an external demand 'shock' (e.g. an increase in the demand for the region's exports).
2   There are no capacity constraints on output or employment. The labour supply is perfectly elastic (e.g. the regional economy has high unemployment and a lot of excess capacity).
3   The wage rate is exogenously determined, i.e. it is determined by national wage setting arrangements.

Demand-based models

Models of the regional economy based on the simplest versions of the Keynesian model were developed to answer the question: 'What are the effects of demand shocks on regional economic activity?' The usual assumptions are made:

1   The supply of labour is perfectly elastic at the current market wage.
2   There is plenty of spare productive capacity in the economy so that output can be increased without affecting prices.
3   Regions are price-takers.

This approach is referred to as demand-based since it is assumed that the supply of factor inputs responds to increases in demand without this leading to any price effects either in factor markets or in product markets. Supply is entirely 'endogenous'. It is always available when needed and it is available without having to offer higher prices to purchase greater quantities of it.

   How would a demand shock affect the regional economy according to the demand-based model? The answer is provided in figure 1.6. An injection of demand (e.g. either from other regions in the same country or from other countries) will lead to

increased output and a higher demand for labour. Since the wage is not determined within the region (by assumption), the increased demand for labour has
no effect in the labour market apart from creating more jobs, thereby reducing
unemployment. Higher employment levels lead to an increase in regional income
(notice that the regional wage is exogenously determined and is given by the
national wage), and this increase in income leads to further increases in the
demand for regional output by way of the Keynesian multiplier.

The weakness of the demand-based model of regional economic activity is
clear: it ignores the fact that the impact of an increase in the demand for a region's
output is likely to affect the price of factor inputs. An increase in the demand for
labour, for example, may be expected to affect regional wage levels unless there is
an abundance of unemployed workers looking for jobs at the going wage. Under
normal circumstances, an increase in the demand for labour will lead to wage
increases, which in turn will lead to price increases and a consequent fall in
competitiveness. Regional wage levels may be strongly influenced by national
wage setting arrangements but they are unlikely to be entirely exogenous. Local
demand and supply conditions are likely to have some effect. Furthermore, an
increase in wages relative to other regions will have effects on net migration flows
and on the participation rate of the region's workforce. These potential effects on
the supply side of the regional economy suggest a need to construct a more comprehensive model than is offered by the demand-based approach.

Incorporating the supply side into the model

A more realistic approach to modelling the regional economy needs to allow for
the supply side to be active and responsive to regional demand shocks. An
extended model is sketched out in figure 1.7. This shows that a demand injection
can be expected to have secondary effects in the labour market. An increase in
employment, for example, will reduce unemployment which in turn will raise the
regional wage. This induces an increase in net inward migration and an increase
in the region's participation rate, both of which will raise the supply of labour
and dampen the upward pressure on wages. As wages rise, however, the region
will lose some of its competitiveness, which in turn will lead to a decline in
the demand for the region's output (as prices rise relative to the price of competing products). As in the demand-based approach, the combined effect of an
increase in employment and wages will stimulate the local demand for the
region's output.

This response from the supply side of the labour market to increased labour
demand means that an increase in employment will not be matched by an equal
reduction in unemployment. Net outward migration will fall as more jobs become
available and the participation rate will rise as more non-workers are induced
into the job market. The combined effect of these two responses will be that
employment will increase by more than the reduction in unemployment since the
unemployed have to compete with others for the new jobs being created.

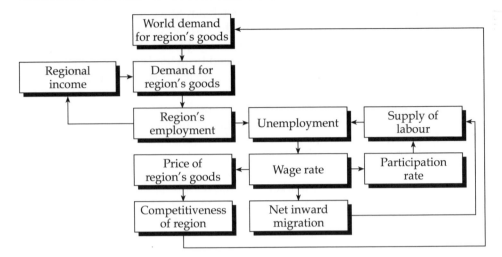

Figure 1.7   Regional income and employment determination assuming an active supply side.

Features of the model
1   The supply side is endogenous since an increase in the demand for the region's output will have effects in the labour market, which in turn will affect the supply of output.
2   The region's wage rate is determined within the region (by the excess demand for labour).
3   An increase in the regional wage will lead to an increase in the labour supply through: (a) inducing an increase in net inward migration; (b) inducing an increase in the region's participation rate.
4   An increase in the regional wage will reduce competitiveness by raising production costs.

1.7   Regional econometric models

Regional multiplier models are useful for providing estimates of the effects of expenditure changes on total regional income and employment. There is a need to construct models capable of providing more detailed predictions, however, if economic development policies are to be efficient and effective. Such models must be capable of providing forecasts for a wide range of economic variables so that the consequences of alternative policy strategies can be evaluated. If detailed forecasts of the likely consequences of any given policy action (such as changing the pattern or level of public expenditure) are provided, the policy maker will be able to select the policy with the most favourable outcome. It is the purpose of regional econometric models to assist the policy maker to achieve this objective by producing quantitative forecasts of a range of economic variables.

To be useful for planning purposes, regional models must possess several characteristics. First, the model must be sufficiently detailed so that relevant government departments at both national and local level (e.g. education, health, housing, industrial development, social services) can be provided with the sort of data needed to carry out their functions efficiently. A detailed industrial break-down of output and employment forecasts is required, for example, if local or regional authorities are to construct effective industrial development plans. A detailed age and gender breakdown of population forecasts is also needed if local authorities are to plan their public services efficiently. School enrolment rates, for example, have implications for staffing levels in schools and for school buildings, and a detailed occupational breakdown of workforce forecasts is needed if estab-lishments of further education are to develop appropriate training programmes.

Second, regional models must be constructed for geographical areas which correspond to administrative authorities if they are to be useful for planning pur-poses. Furthermore, it may be necessary to disaggregate the model spatially if the administrative area for which the model is being constructed has functions that are undertaken at different spatial levels. Educational planning, for instance, requires detailed demographic forecasts at district level. A further problem arises when different administrative functions require different levels of disaggregation. In such cases, it is necessary to construct the model such that it can be aggregated up into the set of spatial units that are required for planning each administrative function.

Third, it is essential that the model is internally consistent. This means that the region must be treated as a set of interdependent elements. Whenever one part of the regional economic system is affected by an exogenous shock (e.g. a sudden change in demand), this will have reverberations throughout the regional economy. The model must be capable to predicting the 'full system effects' of any such shocks.

Regional econometric models vary tremendously in detail and size. They vary for a number of reasons. First, different models are constructed for different purposes. Some models, for example, are constructed for the purpose of estim-ating the impact of alternative fiscal policies on employment and output in each main sector of the regional economy. Other models are more concerned with providing forecasts of the main economic and demographic variables.

A second and very important reason why regional econometric models differ from each other is that the models actually constructed by researchers are largely determined by data availability. It may not be possible to construct what the researcher believes to be the 'true' model simply because such a model may require data that do not exist.

Finally, modellers are often reduced to *ad hoc* devices in order to make their models work. According to economic theory, for example, private investment spending is determined, at least in part, by the rate of interest. But if the re-searcher finds that this determinant does not help to explain variations in the level of investments in practice, there is no alternative but to discard it from the investment function. The equations of econometric models do not always corres-pond with *a priori* theorizing.

A simple hypothetical model

Regional econometric models consist of a set of equations. Each equation deter-mines the numerical value of one of the region's economic variables. The deter-minants on the right-hand side of each equation may include exogenous variables

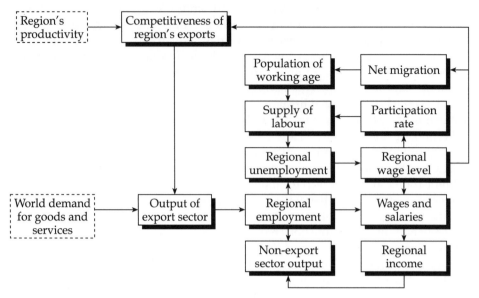

Figure 1.8   Illustration of the structure of an econometric model.

(such as national output, the national wage rate, autonomous government expenditure and taxation, and demographic variables such as birth rates and death rates) or endogenous variables (which are the variables determined by the model itself).

Such models attempt to measure the economic linkages that exist (1) within the region, and (2) between the region and the outside world. The link between each element of the model is estimated by econometric methods and is represented by an equation in the final model used for prediction purposes. The potential importance of such linkages is illustrated in figure 1.8. It can be most easily understood by considering the effect of an exogenous shock.

Suppose world income increases. This will lead to increased output in the region's export sector (assuming there exists spare capacity). Export sector employment will consequently increase and this will increase the wage bill on the one hand and reduce unemployment on the other. The fall in unemployment will exert pressure on the local labour market and push up the regional wage rate. Wages and salaries will therefore increase because employment increases and the wage rate increases. Gross income will increase, thus raising disposable income which in turn leads to an increase in the demand for the output of the non-export sector. The process just described is then reinforced by further feedback effects as the non-export sector employs more labour.

The increase in the regional wage can also be expected to have longer-term effects through inducing more in-migration, which will occur whenever the regional wage rises relative to the national wage. Tracing the effect of this through the labour market, we see that the inflow of workers from other regions will increase the labour supply and so raise the level of unemployment. This in turn will ease the pressure on the regional wage rate. The net inward migration there-fore acts as a safety valve by helping to satisfy the excess demand for labour which originated in an increased demand for the region's exports. Higher wages in the region will also induce an increase in the labour supply by raising the labour force participation rate. Working in the opposite direction is the adverse effect of increased wages on the competitiveness of the region's exports, thus deflating demand in this sector.

The model could be made more realistic in numerous ways:

1   Transfer payments into the region will fall since any reduction in unemploy-ment will automatically reduce the unemployment benefit flowing into the region.
2   Taxes could be made to depend partly on wages and salaries since tax revenue automatically increases as income increases.
3   The export sector could be disaggregated into several sectors, each of which may respond quite differently to changes in world income (and also to changes in their competitive position in world markets).
4   Other parts of the model besides the export sector could be disaggregated in order to provide more detailed forecasts. These might include: population change by age and gender, and employment by industry and occupation. No two regional models are therefore likely to be the same. Different models serve different purposes and their construction is very heavily influenced by data availability.

1.8   Conclusion

The primary concern of this first chapter has been to explain how regional income and employment are determined. Much of the discussion has been about how the simplest version of the Keynesian model of income determination has been adapted for application at regional level. Understanding how regional income and em-ployment are determined is an essential prerequisite not only for estimating the impact of exogenous shocks on the regional economy, but also for predicting the consequences of policy action aimed at reducing regional disparities in economic performance. Predictions about the likely consequences of policies designed to improve the economic performance of regions are likely to be more reliable if these are made within the context of a coherent theoretical model of the regional economy. We need to know how the regional economy 'works' before we can start to predict policy impacts.

A major aim of this chapter has therefore been to explain how a regional version of the Keynesian multiplier model can be used to estimate the effect of expenditure injections on local and regional economies. Lying at the very heart of this approach to estimating regional impacts is the income multiplier itself, which has been used extensively by economists to predict the impact of expenditure injections on local and regional economies. The basic elements of regional multiplier analysis have been explained and its potential usefulness has been illustrated by reference to particular applications. The critical feature of regional multipliers is the extent to which expenditure injections leak out of a region and special attention has therefore been paid to identifying the nature of these leakages. Not surprisingly, the marginal propensity to spend on locally produced goods plays a prominent role in determining the regional multiplier effects resulting from an expenditure injection.

The critical test of the value of regional multiplier analysis is whether it provides policy makers with useful information. The rapid growth in the use of regional multipliers to estimate the impact of a wide variety of different types of economic impact provides considerable support for the view that this technique has some value. One of the most important developments over recent years in the application of regional multiplier analysis is the calculation of several multipliers for the same region, where each multiplier refers to a specific type of expenditure injection. This is important because the multiplier consequences of an expenditure injection are very sensitive to leakages in the initial expenditure injection itself (i.e. leakages in the multiplicand).

Regional multiplier analysis has undoubtedly proved to be of substantial value, not only in impact analysis but also in providing an explanation of how regional economies actually function. But it does nevertheless have its weaknesses, one of the primary ones being that it does not provide sufficient detail of the economic effects of expenditure injections. The response to this criticism has been to construct regional econometric models, which provide far greater detail than regional multiplier models. Needless to say, regional econometric modelling also faces serious drawbacks since the data requirements are very demanding. Progress is, however, being made in this direction as more data become available. It seems inevitable that regional econometric modelling will become increasingly commonplace in the near future.

One type of regional economic model which has not been discussed in this chapter is the regional input–output model. This has been extensively used in local and regional planning, particularly in the United States. Local and regional applications of input–output models are the subject matter of the next chapter.

Further reading

Archibald (1967); Brownrigg (1971; 1973); Sinclair and Sutcliffe (1978; 1984); McGuire (1983); Dow (1986; 1987); Glasson et al. (1988); Love and McNicoll (1988); Armstrong (1988; 1993); Bayoumi and Rose (1993); Felsenstein (1996); Dow and Rodriguez-Fuentes (1997).

chapter two

The input–output approach to modelling the regional economy

contents

In the previous chapter, we saw how models of the regional economy could be constructed in order to identify the major determinants of income and employment. Although these models were initially simplistic and focused attention only on the major regional aggregates (such as regional income and employment), there has been a proliferation of far more detailed econometric models based upon time-series data. A major requirement of these models, however, is a data set which spans several years, preferably at least two decades. An alternative approach to modelling regional economies is to construct a detailed snapshot of the input–output linkages that exist within a region. This can then be used for predicting the consequences of any planned or potential changes in the demand for the region's output. The technique was developed by Leontief during the

Table 2.1   The transactions table for Scotland by main industry group, 1994 (£m)

	Purchases by industry group						
	Agriculture, forestry, fishing	Mining	Manufacturing	Energy and water	Construction	Transport, communications	Distribution and catering
Sales by industry group							
Agriculture, forestry, fishing	368	2	865	0	14	122	8
Mining	0	93	416	72	98	5	1
Manufacturing	626	49	2 151	104	1 048	980	386
Energy and water	42	8	334	1 211	38	123	82
Construction	31	51	1	1	1 234	50	24
Distribution and catering	168	175	1 397	80	309	478	272
Transport, communications	90	95	237	14	36	932	719
Finance, business services	99	249	1 124	113	335	1 580	925
Public administration	120	1	30	0	1	26	10
Other services	12	3	122	18	43	99	151
Total intermediate inputs	1 556	726	6 677	1 613	3 156	4 395	2 578
Payments							
Imports: rest of UK	210	446	5 858	294	1 201	728	578
Imports: rest of world	39	160	5 668	289	265	132	163
Taxes and subsidies	−295	−5	2 032	237	29	849	−113
Value added	1 333	1 035	10 985	1 320	2 141	6 595	3 293
Total primary inputs	1 287	1 635	24 542	2 141	3 637	8 305	3 921
Total inputs	2 842	2 362	31 218	3 753	6 793	12 698	6 498

Source: Industry Department for Scotland

1930s and has since been used in a wide range of applications, including regional impact analysis.

The input–output method is based on the simple but fundamental notion that the production of output requires inputs. These inputs may take the form of raw materials or semi-manufactured goods, or inputs of services supplied by households or the government. Households provide labour inputs, while the government supplies a wide range of services such as national security, social services and the road system. Having purchased inputs from other producing sectors, or primary inputs from households, an industry then produces output and sells this either to other industries or to final demanders, such as households or residents of other regions. In other words, a wide range of inputs is used to produce an equally wide range of outputs.

Exactly how input–output models are constructed, and the uses to which they can be put, is the subject matter of this chapter. The first section deals with the construction of input–output models in general, while the second section examines a number of interesting (and quite different) applications of regional input–output modelling. Some of the major limitations of the input–output approach are then discussed in section 2.3. The chapter ends with a brief look at new developments in regional modelling which treat the standard input–output model as a special case of a more general approach.

Table 2.1 *cont'd*

	Purchases by industry group			Final demand					Total domestic output
Finance, business services	Public administration	Other services	Intermediate demand	Consumer expenditure	Gross investment	Tourist expenditure	Exports (rest of UK)	Exports (rest of world)	
13	1	3	1 396	471	37	10	560	368	2 842
2	2	1	690	2	15	0	968	687	2 362
350	64	93	5 851	2 178	1 729	91	8 325	13 046	31 218
98	52	35	2 023	1 309	135	9	240	39	3 753
312	17	11	1 732	270	4 379	4	407	0	6 793
469	93	82	3 523	5 485	781	1 117	1 792	0	12 698
723	74	130	3 050	1 186	283	134	1 299	545	6 498
2 926	109	462	7 922	4 628	1 404	114	2 114	995	17 177
86	80	37	391	1 015	10 087	44	328	158	12 022
194	115	444	1 201	1 327	177	74	299	254	3 332
5 173	607	1 298	27 779	17 871	19 030	1 598	16 332	16 092	98 695
1 857	375	250	11 797	9 963	5 142	279	0	0	27 183
332	84	106	7 238	6 216	1 834	129	0	0	15 416
312	9	45	3 100	3 264	−1 085	272	3 320	787	9 660
9 504	10 950	1 632	48 788						
12 005	11 417	2 034	70 924	19 444	5 892	680	3 320	787	101 047
17 177	12 022	3 332	98 695	37 315	24 922	2 279	19 652	16 879	199 741

2.1 The input–output method

The transactions table

The input–output linkages that exist within an economy are clearly shown by the transactions table (or transactions matrix), which records all the production flows occurring within the regional economy during a given year. Input–output models vary enormously in their degree of industrial disaggregation, ranging from the 15-industry model constructed for the Western Isles in Scotland (McNicoll 1991) to the 123-industry model constructed for the Scottish economy (Scottish Office 1997a). A condensed version of the 1994 Scottish transactions table is given in table 2.1. Although only ten producing sectors are identified in this table, it provides us with all the information necessary for understanding transactions tables of any size.

The condensed version of the 1994 Scottish transactions table is very easy to understand. Consider agriculture, forestry and fishing. Reading along the first row, we see that this industry produced a gross output of £2842 million, of which £368 million was sold within the same industrial sector, £865 million was sold to manufacturing industries, £471 million was sold to consumers within Scotland for final demand purposes, and £928 million was exported to the rest of the UK and the rest of the world. Reading down the first column, the agriculture sector bought inputs from all other industrial sectors (including itself). For example, it purchased £626 million from manufacturing and £168 million from the distribution and catering sector. In addition, the agriculture sector purchased inputs from outside Scotland (£249 million), from the government sector (where subsidies exceeded taxes by £295 million), and from households within Scotland (value added by households = £1333 million). Note that the value-added row is primarily payment for labour services from the household sector. The corresponding rows and columns for each industry, it should be noted, sum to the same total. Thus, gross output in agriculture equals total inputs used up in producing this output (since total inputs equal total output by definition). In other words, the value of all output sold by each sector is accounted for by expenditures on all inputs including income flowing into the household sector (i.e. value added).

The transactions table therefore provides information about the structure of an economy during any given period of time, usually of one year duration. It describes where each industry's output goes to and where its inputs come from. It also provides information about the relative importance of the linkages not only within the economy itself but also between the economy and other economies. In the case of the Scottish economy, for example, imports by the manufacturing sector accounted for over one-third of the total inputs of the manufacturing sector. This tells us immediately that Scottish manufacturing relies very heavily on imports in order to produce its own output. Any increase in the demand for Scottish manufactured goods will therefore result in a substantial leakage because of the high import content. Much more information can be gleaned from the transactions table by careful perusal.

The main elements of the transactions table can be understood by considering a simple illustrative example. Table 2.2 describes the input–output linkages in a three-industry economy. Consider first the upper left-hand quadrant, which is referred to as the processing sector. This sector lies at the heart of the input–output system. It describes the flow of output from one producing activity to another. Reading down the first column (and ignoring the numbers in brackets), we see that agriculture requires £20 worth of agricultural inputs and £20 worth of manufacturing inputs in order to produce £100 of agricultural output (shown in the gross output column on the extreme right of the table). Agriculture also needs inputs, which it buys from households (labour services £40), from the government (£10) and from goods and services imported into the region. These inputs are recorded in the payments sector in the lower left-hand quadrant. Finally, by reading along the first row, we see that agriculture sells its output not only to itself (£20) and to other producing sectors (manufacturing £40) but also to 'final demanders' such as households (consumption £20), and to residents of other regions (exports £20).

Notice that the gross output of each industry is exactly equal to its gross inputs (i.e. the total outlay). This equality between gross output and gross inputs is a consequence of the fact that the transactions matrix is constructed on the principle of double-entry book-keeping. The entire output of each industry must be accounted for by the inputs used up during production. Any excess of the value

Table 2.2 The transactions table[a] (£)

	Inputs purchased by			Final demand sector				Gross output
	Agriculture	Manufacturing	Services	Households	Government	Exports	Investment	
Outputs purchased by:								
Agriculture	20 (0.2)	40 (0.2)	0 (0)	20	0	20	0	100
Manufacturing	20 (0.2)	20 (0.1)	10 (0.1)	75	10	55	10	200
Services	0 (0)	40 (0.2)	10 (0.1)	25	20	5	0	100
Payments for:								
Household services	40 (0.4)	45 (0.225)	70 (0.7)	5	0	0	0	160
Government services	10 (0.1)	15 (0.075)	5 (0.05)	0	0	0	0	30
Imports into regions	10 (0.1)	40 (0.2)	5 (0.05)	0	0	0	5	60
Gross inputs	100	200	100	125	30	80	15	650

[a] Values in parentheses ( ) are technical coefficients: see text for details.
Source: Yan (1969: 20)

of gross output over payments made for inputs is profit (or loss) and is included in the payments sector. The transactions table therefore tells us exactly where the inputs of an industry *come from* and where its output *goes to*. In doing this, the table focuses attention on the interdependent nature of economic activities.

Before explaining how the information in the transactions table can be used for predicting the effects of changes in the final demand for the region's output, several additional features of this table should be noted. In particular, it provides valuable information about the underlying economic structure of the region. This is indicated not only by the pattern of inter-industry linkages (which are examined in more detail below), but also by the relationship between the final demand sector and the payments sector. Table 2.2 shows that in this particular illustration the government expenditure of £30 in the region equals the payments to the government sector (i.e. taxation) while exports can be seen to exceed imports. Finally, the value added by the residents of the region during the production process is £160 (which is the total payment for household services). This is the region's GDP, as can be seen by subtracting payments to the government and to other regions from the total final demand for the region's output:

household consumption	125
government expenditure in region	30
regional exports	80
investment in region	15
payments for government services (taxation)	−30
imports into region	−60
regional GDP	160

It is worth noting that although this method of constructing an input–output table is the one most commonly used, it is not the only one available. So far, the inter-industry output flows have been measured *exclusive* of their import content. This is known as the domestic-flows approach. An alternative procedure is to measure output *inclusive* of any import content and then include an additional import column in the final demand sector (McGilvray 1965). Each entry in this column will, of course, have a negative sign. This is known as the total-flows approach since the inter-industry flows include *all* inputs and not just those originating in the region itself. The total-flows approach has the advantage that it is cheaper to collect the data needed for the transactions table provided that data for imports are readily available. This approach is cheaper since firms generally find it easier to supply total-flows data than domestic-flows data. This approach is used by McNicoll (1991) to construct an input–output model for the Western Isles.

The reason for constructing a transactions table for a regional economy is not simply to describe input–output flows. The primary purpose is to predict the consequences of exogenous demand shocks. Once the interdependencies between sectors have been quantified, it is possible to estimate the effect of any change in final demand on the entire system. Before showing how this is done, a few critical assumptions have to be made.

First, it is assumed that production technology is one of fixed proportions (sometimes known as Leontief technology after the inventor of input–output analysis). This means that an industry is assumed to have to double its inputs in order to double its output. Furthermore, this relationship is assumed to remain constant over the period for which any forecast is being made. The flow of output from industry i to industry j is given by the following equation:

$$x_{ij} = a_{ij}X_j \tag{2.1}$$

where x_{ij} is the flow of output from industry i to industry j, reading i as a row and j as a column (e.g. $x_{12} = 40$ in table 2.2); X_i is the gross output of industry j (e.g. $X_2 = 200$); and a_{ij} is the technical coefficient relating inputs to output (e.g. $a_{12} = x_{12}/X_2 = 40/200 = 0.2$).

Equation (2.1) simply assumes that the flow of output from industry i to industry j is a fixed proportion of industry j's gross output. If gross output increases by 1 unit in industry j, then a_{ij} extra inputs are required from industry i. The coefficient a_{ij} is obtained from the transactions table by simply dividing x_{ij} by X_j. The full set of these 'technical coefficients' is shown in parentheses in table 2.2. (The next section utilizes these technical coefficients for forecasting the impact of a given increase in final demand on the entire input–output system.)

A second major assumption used in input–output models is that there are no constraints on productive capacity, which is assumed to be able to 'deliver the goods' if there is any increase in final demand. The supply of factor inputs is assumed to be perfectly elastic.

To demonstrate the value of the input–output method in forecasting the consequences of an increase in final demand on each industry's inputs and output, it is helpful to take a specific numerical example. Suppose the final demand for agricultural output increases by £10 in table 2.2. In this case, we assume that the increased demand originates entirely in the export sector. Suppose also that spare productive capacity exists in all sectors and that any increase in labour income will have no effect on household purchases from within the region (i.e. households are 'exogenous'). The assumption that households are 'exogenous' is obviously unrealistic, especially for applications of the input–output method to regional economies, and it will be relaxed below. An increase in agricultural output of £10 means that the agricultural sector requires:

    $0.2 \times £10 = £2$ of additional agricultural output
    $0.2 \times £10 = £2$ of additional manufacturing output
    $0.0 \times £10 = £0$ of additional service sector output

and

    $0.4 \times £10 = £4$ of additional household services
    $0.1 \times £10 = £1$ of additional government services
    $0.1 \times £10 = £1$ of additional imports

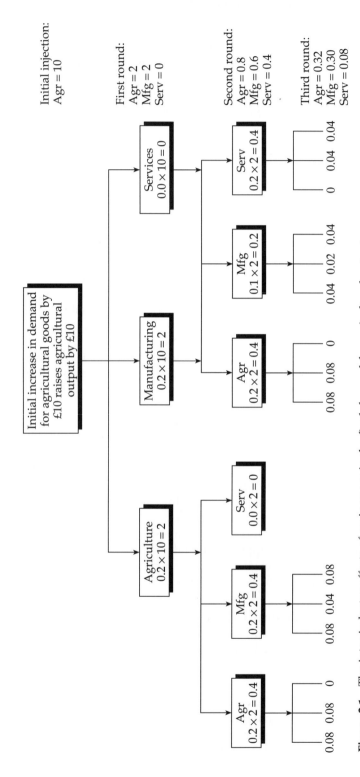

Figure 2.1 The inter-industry effects of an increase in the final demand for agricultural output.
Cumulative effect on each industry of an increase in agricultural output by £10: agriculture £13.26; manufacturing £3.02; services £0.67; total £16.95.

This is only the first round of expenditure, however, since extra output produced by any of the three industries will itself generate further output effects through inter-industry linkages. The inter-industry effects for the first, second and third rounds are shown in figure 2.1.

With each round, it can be seen from figure 2.1 that the net additions to output in each industry become smaller and smaller, eventually converging to zero. By adding the extra output produced in each round of expenditure, a cumulative total is obtained for each industry. In the present case, the cumulative effect on each industry of an increase in agricultural sales of £10 is as follows:

Industry	Additional output produced in each round of expenditure (£)					
	Initial injection	*1st round*	*2nd round*	*3rd round*	*nth round*	*Long run*
Agriculture	10	2	0.8	0.32	. . .	13.26
Manufacturing	–	2	0.6	0.30	. . .	3.02
Services	–	0	0.4	0.08	. . .	0.67

The effects of an increase in the demand for agricultural exports of £10 are shown in the final column of table 2.3. These are obtained by continued application of equation (2.1) as demonstrated in figure 2.1.

It is interesting to note that the additional income earned by the household sector shown in table 2.3 (i.e. £6.47) is not earned entirely by workers employed in the agricultural sector. Households supplying services to the manufacturing and service sectors also increase their income as a result of the indirect effects of the increase in output by these two sectors.

Output, income and employment multipliers

Input–output models are constructed primarily because they provide a detailed industry-by-industry breakdown of the predicted effects of changes in demand. It is sometimes useful, however, to provide a summary statement of these predictions. This can be done by constructing sectoral output multipliers and household income multipliers. We turn first to sectoral output multipliers.

These are obtained by calculating the inverse matrix. The inverse matrix shows exactly how the output of each sector will be affected when the final demand for a region's output increases by £1. For very small input–output models (such as the 3×3 model being discussed here), it is possible to calculate the inverse matrix 'by hand'. But as the model increases in size, the task becomes more complex. Fortunately, the calculation of the inverse is made easy by the existence of computers and standard statistical packages. In table 2.3, for instance, we saw that an increase in final demand for agricultural goods by £10 would increase the gross output of each sector as follows:

Table 2.3 The effects of an increase in the final demand for agricultural goods by £10

	Inputs purchased by			Final demand sector				Gross output
	Agriculture	Manufacturing	Services	Households	Government	Exports	Investment	
Outputs purchased by:								
Agriculture	2.652	0.604	0.000	0	0	10	0	13.256
Manufacturing	2.652	0.302	0.067	0	0	0	0	3.021
Services	0.000	0.604	0.067	0	0	0	0	0.671
Payments for:								
Household services	5.304	0.695	0.469	0	0	0	0	6.468
Government services	1.326	0.227	0.034	0	0	0	0	1.587
Imports into regions	1.326	0.604	0.034	0	0	0	0	1.964
Gross inputs	13.269	3.020	0.670	0	0	10	0	26.959

Table 2.4 The inverse matrix and sectoral output multipliers for each sector

	Matrix of multipliers (the inverse)		
	Agriculture	Manufacturing	Services
Agriculture	1.33	0.30	0.03
Manufacturing	0.30	1.21	0.13
Services	0.07	0.27	1.14
Sectoral output multiplier[a]	1.70	1.78	1.30

[a] The sectoral output multiplier k is defined as follows for the case where households are exogenous (see text for details): k = (direct effect + indirect effect)/(direct effect).
Source: Yan (1969: 37)

    agriculture   £13.26
    manufacturing   £3.02
    services   £0.67

This implies that an increase in the final demand for agricultural goods by £1 would increase the gross output of each sector as follows:

    agriculture   £1.326
    manufacturing   £0.302
    services   £0.067

Summing these we obtain a total (i.e. direct plus indirect) effect on gross output of £1.695. The number 1.695 is known as the sectoral output multiplier for the agricultural sector. A similar exercise can be undertaken for the other two sectors, the results for which are given in table 2.4. The set of numbers given in table 2.4 (excluding the column sums) is, in fact, the inverse matrix for the 3 × 3 model described in table 2.2. Thus, a £1 increase in the demand for manufactured goods would raise gross output in agriculture, manufacturing and services by £0.30, £1.21 and £0.27 respectively; and similarly a £1 increase in the demand for services would raise gross output in agriculture, manufacturing and services by £0.03, £0.13 and £1.14 respectively. The sums at the bottom of each column are referred to as type I output multipliers (for reasons to be explained below).

Output multipliers are not the only types of multiplier that can be obtained from the input–output model. Income multipliers for households, for example, can also be calculated. These household income multipliers differ from sectoral output multipliers since the latter refer to the direct and indirect effects on the output of the processing sector, whereas household income multipliers refer only to the effect of output changes on the income of the household sector. The simplest household income multiplier is obtained by first calculating the total increase in household income generated by an increase in the demand for any given sector's output by £1. The result is then divided by the increase in the household income of the sector experiencing the increase in demand. This is easily obtained for each sector by utilizing two pieces of information: (1) the inverse matrix (table 2.4); and (2) the purchase of household services per £1 of gross output (as given in table 2.2). Suppose, for example, that the demand for agricultural output increases by £1. This will lead to an increase in the gross output of each sector by the amounts shown in column 1 of table 2.4. Multiplying each number by the amount of household services needed to produce each unit of gross output (see the household row in table 2.2), we obtain:

$$
\begin{aligned}
£1.326 \times 0.4 \quad &= £0.530 \\
£0.302 \times 0.225 \quad &= £0.068 \\
£0.067 \times 0.7 \quad &= £0.047 \\[4pt]
\text{total effect on household income} \quad &= £0.645
\end{aligned}
$$

Dividing this by the amount of household services required to increase gross output in agriculture by £1 we obtain

$$
\text{type I household income multiplier} = \frac{\text{direct effect} + \text{indirect effect}}{\text{direct effect}}
$$

$$
= \frac{£0.645}{£0.4} = 1.61
$$

Performing similar calculations for the other two sectors, we obtain 2.58 for manufacturing and 1.20 for services. The calculation of household income multipliers represents an additional valuable piece of information that can be obtained from input–output models.

The other useful multiplier that can be derived from the input–output model is the employment multiplier. This is very easy to calculate from the output/employment ratios for each industry once the outputs themselves have been calculated. The employment multiplier converts the extra income received by households into direct and indirect jobs created and then expresses these extra jobs as a ratio of the jobs created in the industry experiencing the initial increase in final demand. The formula is as follows:

$$
\text{type I employment multiplier} = \frac{\text{direct jobs created} + \text{indirect jobs created}}{\text{direct jobs created}}
$$

This multiplier is particularly useful since it provides an estimate of the number of jobs likely to be generated in the region as a whole as a consequence of extra jobs being created in a particular industry.

Endogenizing the household sector

In all the examples considered so far, no allowance has been made for the possibility that an increase in household income may lead to an increase in household consumption of locally produced goods and services. We may ask, however,

Table 2.5   Sectoral output multipliers and the inverse matrix with households endogenous

	Matrix of multipliers (the inverse)		
	Agriculture	*Manufacturing*	*Services*
Agriculture	1.74	0.68	0.58
Manufacturing	1.13	1.96	1.22
Services	0.48	0.64	1.68
Sectoral output multiplier[a,b]	3.35 (1.70)	3.28 (1.78)	3.48 (1.30)

[a] The sectoral output multiplier k is defined as follows for the case where households are endogenous (see text for details): k = (direct effect + indirect effect + induced effects)/(direct effect).
[b] The multipliers for the exogenous case (see table 2.4) are shown in ( ) for comparison.

whether it is reasonable to assume that household consumption is unresponsive to changes in household income. When household income increases, household consumption is likely to increase as well.

This induced effect on household consumption can be taken into account by assuming that any extra income received by households due to an increase in output will be spent on goods produced both within the region and in other regions. To incorporate this induced effect into the prediction of the output and income changes resulting from an increase in final demand, we need simply to treat the household sector as if it were a producing sector rather than being part of the final demand sector. Households therefore consume inputs from 'other industries' in order to produce their own output of household services. The process described in figure 2.1 and table 2.3 would therefore be extended to cover the household sector as well as the three industries already included. Thus, a £10 increase in agricultural exports would require an extra £4 of household services in the first round. This would then lead to an increase in the demand for the output of all the other industries (which now include households) in the second round as follows:

$(20/160) \times £4 = £0.50$ extra agricultural output
$(75/160) \times £4 = £1.87$ extra manufacturing output
$(25/160) \times £4 = £0.62$ extra service industry output
$(5/160) \times £4 = £0.12$ extra household services

The full system effects of an increase in the demand for agricultural exports will therefore be different to the case where household expenditure is exogenous (i.e. unresponsive to changes in household income). An extra producing sector (i.e. households) has to be incorporated into figure 2.1 in order to allow for the endogeneity of the household sector. This increases the number of cells in the inter-industry sector of the transactions table from nine (3×3) to sixteen (4×4). When this is done, an entirely new set of sectoral output multipliers emerges. As might have been expected, the new sectoral multipliers are greater than in the case where households are assumed not to respond to an increase in their income (see table 2.5).

Table 2.6   Type I and type II household income multipliers

	Type I multiplier (households exogenous)	Type II multiplier (households endogenous)
Agriculture	1.61	3.33
Manufacturing	2.58	5.33
Services	1.20	2.48

The effect of 'converting' the household sector into an industry by making households endogenous (i.e. responding to an increase in income) results in a new multiplier referred to as a type II multiplier. In calculating type I multipliers above, households were treated as exogenous. They did not respond to changes in their income by increasing their purchases of local goods and services. A further set of multipliers (type II) can now be obtained which take these *induced* effects into account. These are obtained in the same way as for type I multipliers except that the numerator includes induced effects. In the case of household income, the type II multiplier (for agriculture) is as follows:

$$\text{type II household} \atop \text{income multiplier} = \frac{\text{direct effect} + \text{indirect effect} + \text{induced effect}}{\text{direct effect}}$$

$$= \frac{£1.33}{£0.4} = 3.33$$

The numerator in this case is obtained directly from the matrix of multipliers, which in the present illustrative example is as follows:

	Agriculture	Manufacturing	Services	Households
Agriculture	1.74	0.68	0.58	0.65
Manufacturing	1.13	1.96	1.22	1.29
Services	0.48	0.64	1.68	0.65
Households	1.33	1.20	1.79	2.07

Type II household income multipliers are therefore obtained (for each of the three industries separately) by dividing each cell in the fourth row of the above matrix by the respective direct technical coefficients for the household sector (0.4). Table 2.6 shows that the effect of treating households as endogenous is to increase the size of the household income multipliers.

The output, employment and income effects of any change in final demand will therefore be considerably greater when households are endogenous. When such feedback effects are taken into account, the multiplier effects of any given change in the demand for a region's output are said to include both *indirect* and *induced* effects. The indirect effects stem from the input–output relationships between the industrial sectors of the regional economy, whereas the induced effects stem from the response of household consumption to the increase in household income. An example of the way the total impact is divided between the direct, indirect and induced effects is provided in section 2.2.

Although type II household income multipliers may appear to be more appropriate than type I multipliers in so far as we can expect households to respond to increases in their income by spending more, estimates of both multipliers may be of value in practice. The type I multiplier is more appropriate, for example, if there is full employment of labour since it is more difficult in this case for the household sector to supply more labour services in response to a demand expansion. The type II multiplier is more appropriate for small open economies which can easily attract workers to migrate into the region from other localities. In practice, it is likely that type I multipliers will underestimate the impact of exogenous shocks whereas type II multipliers may well overestimate such impacts, particularly in the short run. A further reason why type II multipliers are likely to overestimate the induced effects through the household sector is that any increase in household income is assumed to be spent, whereas a proportion of any increase in income is likely to be saved.

The difference between type I and type II multipliers can be extremely wide. In calculating type I and type II multipliers for Portsmouth University, for example, Harris (1997) obtains the following results:

Type of expenditure	Estimated income multipliers	
	Type I	Type II
Students	1.18	1.70
Staff	1.12	1.61
University	1.15	1.65
Total	1.16	1.66

Harris (1997) suggests that the type II income multipliers are likely to provide more useful estimates of the impact of each type of spending in the case of Portsmouth University since the geographical size of the labour market is large in relation to the impact of the university's expenditure. A further example of the gap between type I and type II multipliers is provided by the Scottish input–output model. As can be seen from the household income multipliers in table 2.7, the differences can be very large at sector level. On average across all sectors, the type II income multipliers are 27 per cent larger than the type I multipliers. The corresponding differences for the output and employment multipliers are 26 per cent and 28 per cent respectively.

2.2   Regional applications of input–output analysis

The potential value of input–output analysis to regional policy making can best be appreciated by considering actual applications of its use. A very large number

Table 2.7 Type I and type II household income multipliers for Scotland, 1994

Sector	Household income multipliers	
	Type I	Type II
Agriculture, forestry, fishing	2.5	3.2
Mining, quarrying	1.6	2.0
Manufacturing	1.4	1.7
Energy and water	1.9	2.4
Construction	1.8	2.3
Transport and communications	1.5	1.9
Distribution and catering	1.4	1.7
Finance and business	1.5	1.9
Public administration	1.0	1.3
Other services	1.6	2.0

Source: Alexander and Martin (1997)

of regional input–output models have been constructed in many parts of the world over recent decades, and for many different reasons. The potential value of these models, and the major criticisms levelled against the input–output approach, can be illustrated by briefly reviewing a few models constructed for different purposes.

Models of island economies

We turn first to an interesting application of input–output analysis to small island economies off the north-west coast of Scotland. McNicoll (1991) constructs an input–output model for the Western Isles in order to assess the impact of tourism compared with other local industries, and a more recent model has been constructed for the Orkney Islands by McGregor et al. (1998). The input–output approach is ideally suited for this type of exercise since these island economies are sufficiently small to make data collection feasible. Moreover, island economies are very well defined by their coastline.

The purpose of the Western Isles model is primarily to estimate the impact of tourist expenditure on household income and employment compared with other economic activities. Instead of providing the actual income and employment multipliers, however, McNicoll calculates (for each sector of the Western Isles economy): (1) the income generated in the local economy per £1000 of additional output produced, and (2) the number of jobs created per £100 000 of additional output produced. All three of these multipliers vary substantially between sectors (see table 2.8). Fish processing, for example, has a very large output multiplier, which implies that this sector has close input–output linkages with other industries in the Western Isles economy. By contrast, hotels and catering has only a small output multiplier. As far as income and employment effects are concerned, however, the social services sector has by far the largest income and employment

Table 2.8   Estimated multiplier effects from the Western Isles model

Sector	Output multiplier	Total income generated per £1000 of additional demand for each sector's output	Employment generated per £100 000 of additional output
Fish catching	1.47	851	9.0
Fish processing	1.95	660	7.8
Textiles	1.23	386	8.9
Hotels and catering	1.06	343	6.5
Social services	1.68	1090	15.4
Local government	1.89	871	8.1

Source: McNicoll (1991)

Table 2.9   Output and employment multipliers estimated for the Orkney Islands, 1995

Sector[a]	Estimated multipliers	
	Output multiplier	Employment multiplier
Agriculture, forestry, fishing	1.7	1.3
Fish catching	1.7	1.2
Oil terminal	1.7	1.8
Food and drink	2.1	4.9
Crafts, textiles and clothing	2.0	1.3
Construction	2.0	1.5
Transport and communications	2.3	1.4
Distribution and catering	2.4	1.4
Hotels and catering	2.2	1.3
Finance and business	1.4	1.4
Public administration	2.7	1.1
Health and social work	2.6	1.4

[a] Only selected industries are included in this table.
Source: McGregor et al. (1998)

multipliers. This is because social services is extremely labour-intensive (compared, for example, with the highly capital-intensive textile sector). Hotels and catering has low income and employment multipliers as a result of the high import content in its total output.

The output and employment multipliers calculated for each sector of the Orkney Islands are shown in table 2.9. These can be seen to vary substantially between sectors. Finance and business, for example, has the lowest output multiplier and this is probably a result of large import leakages into this sector's output. By contrast, the food and drink sector has a much larger output multiplier and an extraordinarily large employment multiplier compared with all other sectors. This very large employment multiplier is a direct consequence of the fish processing industry being highly capital-intensive, which means that an increase in employment in this sector is associated with a very substantial increase in its output. Other industries such as transport which service the fish processing sector are therefore stimulated to increase employment substantially when more jobs become available in fish processing. A similar result was obtained for the Western Isles model. Some of the service sector industries, such as public administration and health services, also have high output multipliers and this is due to the large feedback effects into other industries when output is expanded.

The main lesson to be learned from the island economy applications of input–output is that the input–output method can be applied fairly easily to small regional economies. Information of immense value to local and regional planners can be provided once the transactions table has been constructed since it is then possible to estimate the impact of any new development on a range of variables. These include, for example, the workers needed by local industries, the housing needs of new in-migrants and the increased demand for local public services. Constructing input–output models for local economies where there is consider-able overlap in travel-to-work patterns, however, is far more complex and less likely to produce accurate estimates of multiplier impacts of changes in demand.

The impact of North Sea oil on the Shetland economy

A similar model was constructed for Shetland, another island economy in the North Sea (McNicoll 1984). The purpose of this model was to estimate the impact of North Sea oil on a predominantly rural community. It is an interesting model to examine since it has been used by local planners not only for monitoring changes in the structure of the Shetland economy, but also for evaluating existing policies as well as indicating where policy changes needed to be made.

The impact of North Sea oil on the Scottish economy has undoubtedly been substantial. It is therefore particularly interesting to examine the specific impact of developments such as the Sullom Voe oil terminal on the small, rural economy of Shetland. Not only has the structure of the Shetland economy changed dramatic-ally as a consequence of oil-related investment, but its absolute size has increased considerably as well.

To estimate the impact of oil-related developments on the Shetland economy, a distinction was made between three types of activities:

1   The onshore bases which supply the offshore oil rigs with essential materials and services.
2   The Sullom Voe oil terminal which provides landing and storage facilities for the oil and gas brought ashore.
3   The construction of the supply bases and oil terminal.

Since the aim of the exercise was to predict the consequences of these three activities on Shetland, it was necessary to construct a transactions table based in part on information obtained from other areas. This was necessary since the model was constructed in advance of the oil sector becoming fully operational in Shetland. The firms setting up activities in Shetland were therefore asked to provide information about their inputs and outputs at their oil terminals at Milford

Haven, Bantry Bay and Great Yarmouth so that an oil sector could be incorporated into the Shetland transactions table. This information was supplemented by obtaining forecasts from the oil firms of the proportion of their expenditure which was likely to be spent within the Shetland economy.

As expected, leakages from the initial injection were very high (over 85 per cent) because of the smallness of the Shetland economy. It was also estimated, however, that the pattern of direct expenditure on locally produced goods and services was likely to vary substantially between the three oil-related activities. Thus, households were expected to supply over 70 per cent of total inputs purchased by the supply bases, 28 per cent of total inputs for the oil terminal and zero inputs for construction activities (which were assumed to rely entirely on temporary in-migrants). Local government services, on the other hand, were expected to supply over 50 per cent of total inputs for the oil terminal whereas these were negligible for the supply bases and construction activities.

Having constructed the transactions table for Shetland, partly by a direct survey of establishments in the area and partly by surveying incoming oil companies, it was then possible to calculate sectoral multipliers for each of the three oil-related activities. These are as follows:

Sector	Income multiplier	Employment multiplier
Supply base	1.3	1.6
Sullom Voe oil terminal	2.6	3.9
Construction phase	1.3	1.7

The large employment multiplier obtained for the Sullom Voe terminal (i.e. 3.9) is explained by the fact that the terminal was highly capital-intensive. A large change in output was therefore associated with a small change in direct employment at the Sullom Voe terminal, thus resulting in a large employment multiplier. The increase in output at the Sullom Voe terminal generates a considerably greater increase in employment in other Shetland industries than it does at the terminal itself.

Direct, indirect and induced effects: the impact of forestry on other industries

In an application of regional input–output modelling, McGregor and McNicoll (1992) estimate the impact of the forestry industry on other industries in the United Kingdom. One of the motivating factors behind this study is the controversy surrounding the environmental impact of forestry. To demonstrate the importance of forestry to other industries, McGregor and McNicoll use the 1984 UK input–output table to estimate the consequences of reducing output in forestry to zero. Since forestry purchases inputs from several other industries as well as from households, and since its output is used by several other industries (see table 2.10), the input–output approach provides a useful framework for estimating the impact of forestry on other industries and on household income.

Table 2.10 Purchases and sales of forestry industry products

Major suppliers to forestry industry	%	Major purchasers of forestry output	%
Households	53	Timber and wood products	41
Forestry	18	Forestry	18
Electricity	4	Final markets	14
Business services	3	Investment	10
Construction	3	Wooden furniture	6
Other	19	Other	11
Total	100	Total	100

Source: McGregor and McNicoll (1992)

Two estimates of the effect of the complete eradication of the forestry industry are computed. The first is intended to be a lower limit on the estimated effect since it assumes that industries which *use* timber could substitute imports for domestic supplies. Perfect import substitution is therefore assumed in this case. The second estimate of the impact of forestry provides an upper limit on the estimated effect since it assumes that there is no international market in certain types of timber (i.e. roundwood). If domestic supplies of timber disappear, the industries using this particular type of timber are also assumed to cease producing that part of their output which requires this timber in the production process (i.e. paper, pulp and board; and timber processing). A regional breakdown of the effects on individual industries is provided for England, Scotland, Wales and Northern Ireland.

The estimated effects of reducing output in the timber industry to zero are given in table 2.11. Since the output of forestry in the base year was £383 million, the estimated loss across all sectors of £839 million (see simulation I) implies a multiplier of 2.2. This includes the direct, indirect and induced effects on aggregate output. The impact on household income is estimated to be £263 million. Comparing this with the household income of £161 million accruing to the forestry industry, this indicates an income multiplier of 1.63. These output and income multiplier effects more than double in simulation II (increasing to 5.1 and 3.4 respectively), when the disappearance of forestry is assumed to result in the collapse of parts of other industries which use domestic timber supplies.

The application of the input–output method therefore produces very useful estimates of the relative significance of the forestry industry in the United Kingdom in determining output in other sectors of the economy and as a contributor to household income. This particular application is also interesting because it demonstrates how constraints can be built into the estimation procedure. In this case, the first simulation assumes that timber imports can be substituted for domestic timber; the second simulation assumes that once domestic production of timber ceases, this will lead to reductions in output since certain types of timber are not traded internationally. Once domestic supplies end, the industries using this timber are assumed to lose their own markets to overseas competitors.

Table 2.11 The impact of forestry on the output of UK industries

Industry	Effect on output (£m at 1984 prices)	
	Simulation I[a]	Simulation II[b]
Agriculture, forestry and fishing	−394	−408
Energy and water	−74	−138
Extraction industries	−14	−63
Metals, engineering and vehicles	−61	−105
Other manufacturing	−80	−798
Construction	−18	−28
Distribution, hotels and catering	−44	−114
Transport and communications	−66	−115
Banking, finance and insurance	−76	−161
Other services	−12	−25
Total output	−839	−1954
Household income	−263	−552

[a] Simulation I assumes that only the forestry industry reduces its output to zero.
[b] Simulation II assumes that output in paper, pulp and board is reduced by 2 per cent and in timber processing by 21.6 per cent due to the complete absence of roundwood.
Source: McGregor and McNicoll (1992)

The impact of foreign students on regional income and employment

It may seem odd at first sight to regard higher education as an export industry but many countries are major international providers of higher education. The extent to which higher education contributes to export earnings, and the dependence of local and regional economies on foreign students, are therefore interesting questions to which input–output analysis can provide clear cut answers. Such an exercise has been undertaken for several regional economies, including Scotland (Love and McNicoll 1988), Wales (Hill et al. 1998) and Wollongong in Australia (McKay 1998).

The advantage of using the input–output approach to estimating the economic impact of foreign students is that it provides estimated impacts on each sector of the economy. Since higher education institutions are in a highly competitive environment and use some of their resources to attract students from abroad (in order to generate more income from fees), it would clearly be useful to know what the wider effects of this expenditure are likely to be on their local economy. This would then provide some indication of the return of such expenditure to the wider community in terms of extra income and extra jobs.

In the Welsh study, based on data for the academic year 1995–6, the aim was to estimate the impact of 8400 full-time overseas students, together with the impact of research and consultancy income undertaken for overseas organizations. The main findings of this exercise are that a spending injection of £56 million from these two sources led to a total spending of £92.5 million, a multiplier effect of 1.65. This total expenditure is estimated to have generated over 2500 jobs (full-time equivalents), with 40 per cent of these being in the higher education sector itself and the remaining 60 per cent in the rest of the Welsh economy. This study therefore provides a clear indication that the benefits to the wider economy of increasing the number of foreign students in Welsh universities and colleges would be substantial.

The use of input–output methods to estimate the impact of foreign students on the Wollongong economy yields somewhat higher estimates of the multiplier effects than were found in the Welsh study. An income multiplier of 1.8 and an employment multiplier of 2.1 were estimated for foreign students attending the University of Wollongong. Furthermore, each student was estimated to generate 0.57 full-time equivalent jobs (that is, 57 FTE jobs result from every 100 foreign students). This latter figure compares with a multiplier effect of 66 FTE jobs for every 100 foreign students in Love and McNicoll's estimate of their impact on jobs in Scotland.

2.3 Some limitations of the input–output approach

Although input–output analysis is a valuable technique, it is essential to realize that it is not problem-free. One serious obstacle is the high cost of collecting the necessary data to construct the transactions matrix, especially for large regions. In practice, it is often necessary to undertake a sample survey of firms. The construction of the original Scottish input–output model, for instance, involved a survey of around 650 firms over a period of 18 months. Between them, these firms employed about 25 per cent of total employees in Scotland. The Scottish model is now updated annually using sampling techniques. Even when direct surveys are undertaken, the transactions table will only be an approximation to the truth. Perfect accuracy cannot be attained in constructing the transactions table because of 'the hiding of information, lies, inadequate training of observers, poor question design, the difficulty of mass observations, definition and classification problems, instrumental error, passage of time and error-compensating processes' (Jensen 1980: 140).

It is because of the high costs involved in collecting data for the transactions table that non-survey methods have been used for 'filling in' the transactions table when a direct survey is either too costly or not possible due to lack of co-operation by firms. The most popular non-survey approach is to use technical relationships between industries calculated for national input–output models. The use of national technical coefficients in regional models, however, is fraught with difficulties. Production techniques, for instance, are likely to vary between regions. The reliability of forecasts will therefore depend upon the errors introduced into the model by the assumptions used to bypass the expensive task of collecting data directly from firms.

A more commonly used method of constructing regional input–output models is to use a combination of national input–output tables (which themselves use sampling techniques to construct the national transactions matrix) together with some regional-level data. Information may be available, for example, for gross output levels and household income at the regional level and this information can be used to modify the national technical coefficients matrix so that it provides an adequate approximation to the region's economic structure. This approach has been used extensively to overcome the problem of collecting primary data. An example is provided by an input–output model constructed for a proposed extension to an international airport in a major metropolitan area (Batey et al. 1993; Batey and Madden 1998).

Another alternative method is to use national coefficients for the inter-industry relationships which are small in magnitude and to collect primary data for the major inter-industry transactions. Jensen (1980) argues that provided that the major inter-industry transactions are accurately estimated (using survey methods), the remaining cells can be estimated by non-survey methods without seriously damaging the forecasting accuracy of the model. Recent work on the Scottish input–output table indicates that the partial approach to collecting primary data rapidly runs into diminishing returns as more data are collected (Dewhurst 1992). This suggests that once an input–output table has been constructed by survey methods, it can be updated at low cost by obtaining accurate information for the major inter-industry transactions.

One of the primary problems with using national input–output data to approximate inter-industry relationships at the regional level is that the dependence of a region on imports could be severely underestimated. It is well known that regions are far more dependent on external trade than national economies and it is crucial to make sure that these trade linkages (i.e. the export column in the final demand sector and the import row in the payments sector) are estimated reasonably accurately. The income multipliers estimated from using non-survey methods to construct the transactions matrix can differ considerably from those estimated using direct survey data (Harris and Liu 1998). Because non-survey methods tend to underestimate trade (and hence leakages from an initial injection of expenditure), the income multipliers tend to be overestimated when non-survey methods are used. The accuracy of the multipliers can be substantially improved, however, at relatively low cost by collecting some information on a region's exports and imports.

The great advantage of input–output models is their internal consistency. All the effects of any given change in final demand are taken into account. As shown in section 2.1, any change in output by one sector will have repercussions throughout the regional economy through the myriad of inter-industry linkages. This supreme advantage of input–output models is quickly eroded, however, if the inter-industry linkages change rapidly over time. Input–output tables are produced for a specific period of time, such as a calendar year. If production techniques are changing through time, or if the pattern of linkages is sensitive to changes in the relative price of inputs (such as oil prices rising relative to nuclear fuel), the model may quickly become redundant as a forecasting tool. Input–output analysts have consequently attempted to devise low-cost methods of updating the technical relationships between industries. If significant structural changes are known to be occurring, it may be possible to undertake additional survey work on specific parts of the processing sector. More generally, there is a need not only for updating the technical relationships between industries but also for forecasting these relationships into the future.

One way of improving the predictive performance of input–output models is to use specially selected data sets. If the impact of an increase in the demand for a specific industry's output is to be predicted for a number of years ahead, more accurate forecasts may be obtained by using the technical linkages between industries estimated for the most efficient (or 'best practice') firms. The assumption underlying this approach is that the technical linkages between firms in a few years' time are likely to be more accurately approximated by the current technical linkages of the most efficient firms in an industry rather than by the average for all firms.

A further drawback of the input–output approach is that the technical relationship between industries assumes that all industries exhibit constant returns to scale. A doubling of output requires a doubling of the inputs. This assumption is restrictive but is necessary in the absence of information on the returns to scale in individual industries.

Finally, input–output models usually ignore the existence of supply constraints. A rapid output expansion may not be possible in the short term because of a shortage of a necessary input, such as labour. Inward migration into the region may remove this obstacle to expansion over a period of time, but labour availability is likely to operate as a constraint in the short term. Similar constraints may exist on intermediate inputs with the result that local producers have to switch to outside suppliers in the short term if their output is to be increased. It should, however, be recognized that one of the main purposes of input–output modelling is to forecast bottlenecks, which may arise in the regional economy as a consequence of a growth in demand for the region's output.

2.4   New developments in regional modelling

The two main drawbacks of the input–output approach are: (1) that it assumes a proportional relationship between inputs and outputs (known as Leontief or fixed-coefficient technology); and (2) that it assumes excess supply in all factor markets. Since it is assumed that there are no supply constraints in factor markets, any increase in demand is met without any upward pressure on factor prices. Hence, as in a simplified Keynesian world, only demand matters.

Endogenizing the supply side of the regional economy

An alternative approach to input–output modelling is to incorporate supply-side constraints into a regional model. Incorporating supply-side constraints into the model means that any excess demand for a factor input will result in a change in factor prices. Thus, an increase in the demand for labour will result in wages increasing (relative to the price of capital). There will therefore be price adjustments as well as quantity adjustments. Furthermore, changes in income will affect

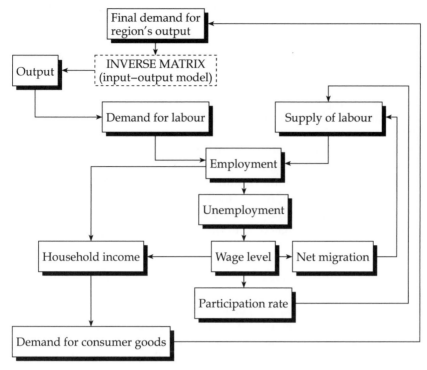

Figure 2.2 Integrating the input–output model into an econometric model.

the consumption pattern of households as well as affecting the inflow of government transfer payments into the region. Changes in the demand for a region's output will therefore have repercussions in the region's factor and product markets which need to be taken into account if the predictions are to be reasonably accurate. This can be done by expanding the input–output model in two directions: first, by adding factor (labour and capital) markets to the input–output model; and second, by adding a time dimension through combining the input–output model with an econometric (time-series) model.

An outline of the essential elements of an 'integrated input–output econometric model' is provided in figure 2.2. At the heart of this integrated model is the Leontief inverse matrix itself, which is the set of multipliers described earlier. Starting from some critical injection of final demand (at the top of the diagram), this is converted into changes in output via the inverse matrix. The increase in output leads to increased employment (through the output/labour ratio) which causes a reduction in unemployment. Several things may now occur. First, increased demand for labour will lead to an increase in the real wage, thereby raising both the participation rate and net inward migration. This increase in the labour supply may be necessary to provide producers with the extra workers if unemployment is low. Second, the increase in employment and in wages will mean that household income in the region has now increased and so a proportion of this will find its way into the demand for consumption goods. Some of these household consumption goods will be produced within the region and some will be imported into the region. The extra demand for the region's output will now generate yet another round of output and employment increases, provided that the region does not run into production bottlenecks.

The integrated model has several advantages over the static input–output model for predicting the impacts of changes in the final demand for a region's output. Its prime advantage is that it converts a static model into a dynamic model. For example, the output/employment ratio increases over time due to productivity improvements, and the effects on employment of an output change will consequently be over-predicted unless the trend over time in the output/employment ratio is taken into account. Another example is provided by the household sector's consumption pattern. As income levels increase over time, the pattern of consumption across commodities is likely to change. These changes in the pattern of consumption can be estimated from the econometric component of the model.

Allowing for alternatives to fixed-factor proportions technology

Dropping the assumption of a proportional relationship between inputs and outputs means that factors can be employed in variable proportions, the actual proportion depending upon relative factor prices (wages relative to capital costs). The most critical development of this new approach to regional modelling is that the price of inputs is no longer assumed to be determined exogenously (as when wages are set nationally and are then simultaneously transmitted to all regions). All factor prices are therefore assumed to be determined endogenously by each region's own labour market.

What difference does it make when the assumptions of the input–output model are modified by (1) allowing for different types of technology and (2) allowing factor markets to respond to excess demand and excess supply? This is exactly the question investigated by Harrigan et al. (1991). They construct a computable general equilibrium (CGE) model of the Scottish economy to examine the sensitivity of input–output multipliers to alternative assumptions about technology and factor markets.

They begin by producing a set of multipliers for a model of the Scottish economy which employs Leontief (or fixed-coefficient) technology and which assumes unlimited supplies of factor inputs (i.e. fixed factor prices no matter what the level of demand). The assumptions of fixed technology and unlimited factor supplies are then dropped. Various sets of multipliers are then estimated for different assumptions about the structure of technology in each sector. The consequences of changing the assumptions underlying the technology of each sector and of assuming that factor prices respond to market forces are demonstrated in table 2.12. This shows the estimated impact of increasing the demand for Scotland's manufactured exports by 10 per cent under three sets of assumptions. The first assumes fixed-coefficient technology and unlimited factor supplies; the second assumes a variable-input production function (e.g. a Cobb–Douglas production function)

Table 2.12   The impact of a 10 per cent increase in the demand for Scottish manufactured exports

Variable being predicted	% increase in each variable resulting from a 10% increase in the demand for exports		
	Input–output simulation[a]	Keynesian simulation[b]	Neoclassical simulation[c]
GDP	4.5	2.1	1.0
Value added in manufacturing	8.5	5.0	2.7
Employment	4.8	3.0	1.5
Price of commodities	0.0	1.2	2.2
Household disposable income	3.0	1.1	1.8

The following assumptions have been made:
[a] input–output simulation: fixed-coefficient technology + unlimited supplies of capital and labour + fixed factor prices.
[b] Keynesian simulation: variable factor proportions + fixed capital stock + unlimited supply of labour + fixed wages (determined nationally).
[c] neoclassical simulation: variable factor proportions + fixed capital stock + competitive labour market (flexible wages determined in region).
Source: Harrigan et al. (1991)

and unlimited supplies of labour with a fixed capital stock; and the third assumes a variable-input production function and a competitive labour market which determines Scottish wage rates. As expected, the estimated impact of an exogenous increase in demand on regional output and employment is considerably less when the assumptions about technology and factor markets are more realistic than in standard input–output models.

More recent work by the Fraser of Allander researchers compares the predictions of the input–output model with the predictions obtained from a neoclassical model over the long run. Their CGE model is used to predict the effects of a 10 per cent increase in the demand for Scottish exports on a range of Scottish variables (i.e. employment, value added, capital stock and exports). A crucial assumption of the neoclassical model is that capacity constraints are relieved over the longer run as the capital stock expands in response to the increased demand for output. The effect of allowing the economy to expand its productive capacity over the long run is that the predictions from the neoclassical model get closer and closer to the predictions of the input–output model (see table 2.13). What this simulation demonstrates is that the input–output approach actually produces identical predictions to the neoclassical model over the long run.

This recent research into regional modelling therefore indicates that input–output models may considerably overestimate the impact of demand shocks in the short term, when regions face capacity constraints. The reliability of input–output models for making short-term predictions is therefore questionable when regions face supply bottlenecks. The input–output approach is more suitable for making longer-term predictions since factor supplies are more elastic over the long run through interregional factor migration and through investment in capital stock.

Table 2.13   The predicted effects of a 10 per cent increase in the demand for manufactured exports

Variable affected	% change in each variable			
	Neoclassical model			Input–output model
	Period 1	Period 10	Period 20	
Effect on employment				
Manufacturing	3.5	8.1	8.5	8.5
Non-manufacturing (traded goods)	1.2	4.1	4.4	4.4
Non-manufacturing (non-traded goods)	2.8	1.9	1.9	1.9
Effect on value added				
Manufacturing	2.8	8.0	8.5	8.5
Non-manufacturing (traded goods)	0.9	4.1	4.4	4.4
Non-manufacturing (non-traded goods)	2.1	1.9	1.9	1.9

Source: McGregor et al. (1996: 485)

2.5   Conclusion

Input–output analysis has much to offer policy makers in spite of its many weak-nesses. The input–output method provides a considerable amount of detailed information about the regional economy which is of immense value to those involved in regional economic development. It not only is an excellent way of describing the multitude of interactions that exist between a region's industries but also provides us with an extremely valuable tool for making predictions of possible future outcomes. Under ideal conditions, regional input–output models can trace the impact on output, employment and income of exogenous 'shocks' to the regional economy with precision.

The input–output approach, however, is not the only method of estimating the impact of changes in the demand for a region's output. Neither is the input–output method necessarily the most appropriate approach in all circumstances. Keynesian multiplier models may be more useful in some cases, if only because they are less demanding of data and can therefore be constructed more quickly. These alternative approaches, however, do not provide the sectoral detail offered by input–output models. This criticism does not apply, of course, to the more sophisticated and more detailed regional econometric models, some of which have been integrated with the input–output approach.

The integration of econometric models into input–output models has meant that this joint approach to modelling regional economies has become the accepted practice. The primary reason for this integrated approach has been to build a time dimension into the previously static approach embodied in the input–output method. As explained in some detail in this chapter, input–output offers only a static picture of the regional economy, and combining the input–output model with an econometric model allows for the underlying input–output structure of the regional economy to change over time. The augmented input–output model explicitly predicts changes in the input–output structure of the regional economy so that the predictions of exogenous demand shocks are not based upon the assumption that the input–output structure remains static during the prediction period.

The first two chapters of this book have been concerned with explaining various approaches to gaining a better understanding of how regional output and employment are determined. These approaches vary from simplistic Keynesian-type models through to more sophisticated and detailed econometric models and input–output models of regions. Once the internal workings of regions have been modelled, it is a simple step to use these models for predictive purposes. This indeed has been the main motivating force behind the construction of regional (and in some cases interregional) models.

The techniques and models which have been described and evaluated in chapters 1 and 2 have stressed the interrelated nature of regional economies. Regions are persistently bombarded by 'shocks', which originate in other regional economies. The next two chapters explore the interdependent nature of regional economies from a somewhat longer-term perspective. They are concerned primarily with regional disparities in economic growth.

Further reading

Miernyk (1965); Yan (1969); McGregor and McNicoll (1992); McGregor et al. (1996); Harris (1997); Wisniewski (1996).

Regional growth disparities: neoclassical perspectives

contents

Recent developments in the theory of economic growth and the increasing avail-ability of regional data have together led to a strong revival of interest in regional growth disparities. The main impetus for this revived interest in economic growth has come from attempts to improve the predictive ability of the so-called neoclas-sical model of growth, which was initiated by the US economist, Robert Solow, in two path-breaking papers in 1956 and 1957. Several US economists have pion-eered further theoretical developments in the neoclassical approach to growth and some of these new theories have been tested on regional data. The main purpose of this chapter is to explain the basic elements of the neoclassical growth model and to assess its relevance for explaining regional growth disparities.

Although economic growth has been investigated by economists for generations, there is still disagreement about its underlying causes. This is well illustrated by recent research into regional growth disparities. Some researchers have followed the neoclassical route, emphasizing the role of factor supplies in the growth process. Technical progress is assumed to be the engine of growth and determines the rate at which output per worker increases over the long run. Given the importance of technical change in the neoclassical model of growth, recent developments have focused very heavily on explaining how technical change is determined. The proponents of the extended neoclassical growth model have developed what has become known as the endogenous growth model. This new growth theory argues that technical progress is both a cause and an effect of growth, and much effort has been expended in analysing the implications of this radical extension to the simple neoclassical growth model developed initially by Solow (1956).

Other researchers have taken a Keynesian route and stress the role of demand factors. This post-Keynesian approach places particular emphasis on the competitiveness of a region's export sector as the main generator of output growth. The approach stresses the significance of the price and income elasticities of the demand for a region's exports relative to its own demand for imports from other regions. But perhaps the most interesting development in regional growth theory has been the attempt to incorporate the principle of cumulative causation into demand-based explanations of regional growth disparities. According to this approach, once growth disparities occur, they tend to become cumulative and self-perpetuating. Although this idea was developed by Myrdal (1957) for explaining differences in growth between the world's rich and poor economies, it has been adapted to explain regional growth disparities within countries. The theory underlying these demand-based models is discussed in the next chapter. It might be noted at this point, however, that the neoclassical approach is concerned with the very long run, whereas the demand-based approach focuses more on the medium term.

It is tempting to regard these various explanations of regional growth disparities as complementary rather than competitive, especially since they are based upon different theoretical time periods. There may be a case for using the demand-based approach for explaining growth in the medium term while leaving an explanation of regional disparities in growth over the long term to the neoclassical model. No attempt is made here to fuse these two approaches. We have taken the more cautious route in this chapter and the next of discussing these two approaches separately.

It is useful to begin this chapter with a brief look at some facts about regional growth disparities. This is done in section 3.1. A brief introduction of the Solow growth model is then provided in section 3.2, which is followed in section 3.3 by two empirical applications of the model to US and UK regions. The extension of the basic model to cover endogenous technical progress and its role as the engine of growth is discussed in section 3.4. Section 3.5 examines the transfer of technology between regions and the potential for low-technology regions to benefit from the more advanced technology of high-technology regions. Section 3.6 reviews some recent empirical work on the regional convergence of per capita incomes. Finally, section 3.7 discusses extensions to the neoclassical model.

3.1   Regional growth disparities: some facts

Care is needed when discussing regional growth disparities since growth can be defined in different ways. The most commonly used measures of growth are: (1) growth of output, (2) growth of output per worker, and (3) growth of output per capita. It is important to be clear about which particular measure of growth is being used since these three measures may give quite different readings of a region's growth performance. A region may, for example, experience low output growth and rapid growth of output per capita simultaneously if there is significant net out-migration of non-workers. In general, there tends to be a high correlation between output growth and the growth in output per capita, but there is a much lower correlation between output per worker and the other two measures. Table 3.1 demonstrates that growth rates have diverged considerably between regions in the EU during 1975–96.

Which measure of growth is the most appropriate? This depends on the purpose for which the measure is to be used. Output growth is used as an indicator of the growth of productive capacity, which depends in part on the extent to which regions are attracting capital and labour from other regions. The growth of output per worker is often used as an indicator of changes in a region's competitiveness (since it measures productivity growth), while the growth of output per capita is used as an indicator of changes in economic welfare. There is therefore no 'best' measure of regional growth. All three are useful in their own right. In this chapter and the next, we shall focus on output growth and on the growth of output per worker.

3.2   The neoclassical growth model

The growth equation with no technical change

The aggregate production function lies at the heart of neoclassical growth models. In an economy in which there is no technical progress, output is determined entirely by capital and labour inputs. This relationship can be expressed in general form as follows:

$$Y = F(K, L) \tag{3.1}$$

where Y is real output, K is the stock of capital and L is the labour force.

A specific form of this general relationship is provided by the well-known Cobb–Douglas production function. Assuming constant returns to scale, we have

Table 3.1 Regional growth disparities in selected EU countries and regions, 1975–96

Country and region	Exponential annual growth rate (1975–96)		
	Output	Output per worker	Output per capita
Italy			
Valle d'Aosta	1.6	0.8	1.3
Sicilia	1.9	2.1	1.6
Lombardia	2.7	2.3	2.6
Emilia–Romagna	2.8	2.5	2.8
Campania	3.0	3.0	2.8
Portugal			
Alentejo	1.5	3.2	1.8
Algarve	2.1	1.9	1.3
Centro	2.2	2.2	2.2
Lisboa	2.3	2.9	1.8
Norte	2.9	2.9	2.3
Spain			
Asturias	1.3	2.8	1.4
Pais Vasco	1.5	2.0	1.6
Cantabria	1.6	2.9	1.2
Madrid	2.0	2.9	1.8
Cataluña	2.1	2.1	1.8
Rioja	3.2	3.5	2.6
Baleares	3.5	2.3	2.6
France			
Lorraine	1.0	1.5	1.0
Nord–Pas-de-Calais	1.4	1.8	1.3
Champagne–Ardennes	1.5	1.9	1.4
Île-de-France	2.5	2.4	1.9
Midi–Pyrénées	2.6	2.3	2.0
Languedoc	2.7	1.9	1.9
Basse-Normandie	2.8	2.7	2.3

Source: Cambridge Econometrics

$$Y = AK^\alpha L^{1-\alpha} \tag{3.2a}$$

where A and α are parameters to be estimated (usually by regression analysis). This relationship can also be expressed in per capita terms by dividing through by L to give

$$y = Ak^\alpha \tag{3.2b}$$

where $y = Y/L$ and $k = K/L$. Both these forms of the production function will be used here.

This per capita production function (3.2b) states that output per worker can only increase if capital per worker increases. In other words, capital must grow

Output per worker ($y = Y/L$)

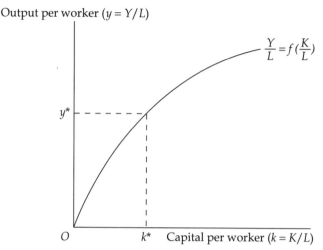

$$\frac{Y}{L}=f(\frac{K}{L})$$

y^*

O k^* Capital per worker ($k = K/L$)

Figure 3.1   Output per worker and the capital/labour ratio. $Y = F(K, L)$ implies $Y/L = f(K/L)$ provided that $F(K, L)$ is homogeneous of degree one. A Cobb–Douglas production function with constant returns to scale is such a function and is often used in growth models.

faster than the labour supply for output per worker to grow. This positive relationship between capital per worker and output per worker is shown in figure 3.1. Output per worker will increase as each worker is provided with more capital equipment – a process known as capital deepening – but the increase will be at a decreasing rate due to diminishing marginal returns. Furthermore, when the marginal product of labour has fallen to a sufficiently low level, net investment will fall to zero and gross investment will be just sufficient to maintain the existing stock of capital. The capital/labour ratio will then be at its long-run equilibrium level (k^* in figure 3.1). This equilibrium capital/labour ratio is associated with a corresponding equilibrium level of output per worker y^*. Once this equilibrium has been reached, there will be no incentive for producers to increase the capital/labour ratio any further. Since both the capital/labour ratio and the output/labour ratio are constant in this equilibrium situation, the economy must be in long-run equilibrium.

A more complete treatment of the neoclassical growth model would also show that the equilibrium capital/labour ratio k^* shown in figure 3.1 is determined partly by the production function and partly by another function referred to as the fundamental equation of growth. This latter function states that the capital/labour ratio will continue to grow while gross investment per worker exceeds the level required to (1) replace worn-out capital equipment and (2) provide the extra capital stock required by a growing workforce. A clear explanation of this crucial part of the neoclassical growth model can be found in Jones (1998).

In this simplest version of the neoclassical model, there can be no growth in per capita income in the long run since long-run equilibrium is defined as a situation in which output, capital and labour are all growing at the same rate. There is scope for an increase in output per worker, however, in the medium term, as can be seen by converting equation (3.2a) into a growth equation. By applying some mathematics to equation (3.2a) (i.e. taking logs and differentiating with respect to time), we can obtain the following function:

$$\frac{\Delta Y}{Y} = \alpha \frac{\Delta K}{K} + (1 - \alpha)\frac{\Delta L}{L} \qquad (3.2c)$$

where $\Delta Y/Y$ is output growth, $\Delta K/K$ is the growth of capital stock and $\Delta L/L$ is the growth of the labour force.

The constants α and $1 - \alpha$ are the respective contribution of capital and labour inputs to aggregate output. Hence, if the capital stock were to grow by 5 per cent per annum while the labour force expanded by 1 per cent per annum, output growth would be 2.6 per cent assuming a value of 0.4 for $\alpha([0.4 \times 5] + [0.6 \times 1]$ $= 2.6)$. Subtracting $\Delta L/L$ from both sides of equation (3.2c), we obtain an equation for the growth of output per worker:

$$\frac{\Delta Y}{Y} - \frac{\Delta L}{L} = \alpha\left(\frac{\Delta K}{K} - \frac{\Delta L}{L}\right) \qquad (3.3)$$

We can see from this equation that output per worker would increase by 1.6 per cent if the capital stock and the labour force were growing at 5 and 1 per cent respectively $(0.4 \times [5 - 1] = 1.6)$. But this growth in per capita income can only occur in the medium term given the long-run equilibrium condition that capital and labour must grow at the same rate.

What conclusions can be drawn so far?

1 Output grows without limit as the supplies of capital and labour increase.
2 Output per worker can increase only if there is capital deepening (i.e. if the capital/labour ratio increases).
3 When the capital/labour ratio reaches its long-run equilibrium level, there will be no further increase in output per worker. Growth in output per worker is at an end.

The growth equation with technical change

More realism can be built into the neoclassical model by allowing for the effect of technical progress on output growth. The most convenient way of allowing for technical progress is to regard technical knowledge as an additional and separate element in the production function. Capital and labour are assumed to benefit equally from any technical progress that may occur as in the following function:

$$Y = F(A, K, L) \qquad (3.4)$$

where A is technical knowledge. Technical progress is said to be disembodied in this model since it is independent of capital and labour inputs. If we assume that

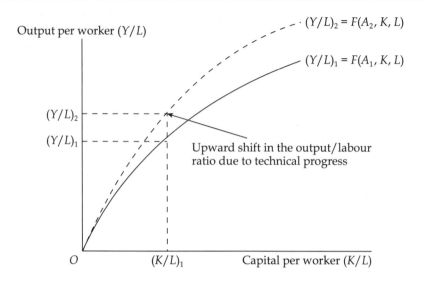

Figure 3.2   The influence of technical progress on output per worker.

technical progress increases smoothly over time (at a constant growth rate), we can extend the Cobb–Douglas production function, given in equation (3.2a), by adding an extra term to reflect the influence of technical progress:

$$Y = Ae^{gt}K^{\alpha}L^{1-\alpha} \tag{3.5}$$

where g is the constant rate of technical progress per time period t. This way of representing the impact of technical progress on output growth is grossly over-simplified since it ignores the possibility that technical progress is built into new additions to the capital stock through investment in the latest machines. The labour force will also acquire new knowledge and new skills, thereby increasing the efficiency of workers over time, in which case labour, like capital, needs to be adjusted for its 'quality'.

In spite of problems with modelling the way in which technical progress affects the growth of output and output per worker, there can be little doubt that technical progress is of crucial significance in the growth process. The effect of technical progress on output per worker is shown in figure 3.2. The upward shift in the output per worker function caused by technical progress results in an increase in output per worker at each level of the capital/labour ratio. If we again assume constant returns to scale, equation (3.5) can be used to obtain the following growth equation (with the application of a little mathematics):

$$\frac{\Delta Y}{Y} = g + \alpha \frac{\Delta K}{K} + (1 - \alpha) \frac{\Delta L}{L} \tag{3.6}$$

where g is the annual rate of technical progress. Hence, if the rate of technical progress were, say, 2 per cent, output would also grow by 2 per cent if both capital and labour exhibited zero growth. This extended version of the neoclassical model has the attraction that it allows for the possibility of a steady growth in output per worker over the long run. This is easily seen by subtracting $\Delta L/L$ from both sides of equation (3.6) to obtain

$$\frac{\Delta Y}{Y} - \frac{\Delta L}{L} = g + \alpha \left(\frac{\Delta K}{K} - \frac{\Delta L}{L} \right) \tag{3.7}$$

Thus, even if the capital stock and the labour force grow at the same rate, output per worker will increase provided that the rate of technical progress exceeds zero. In long-run equilibrium, it is assumed that output growth and the growth of the capital stock will be equal ($\Delta Y/Y = \Delta K/K$). By substituting $\Delta Y/Y$ for $\Delta K/K$ into equation (3.7), we obtain the long-run equilibrium growth rate of output per worker:

$$\frac{\Delta Y}{Y} - \frac{\Delta L}{L} = \frac{g}{1-\alpha} \tag{3.8}$$

Thus, if $g = 2$ per cent and $\alpha = 0.6$, the output per worker will grow at 5 per cent in long-run equilibrium.

This brief discussion of the neoclassical model of growth has covered enough ground to demonstrate its potential value for using it to explain regional growth disparities. Equation (3.6) is easily converted into a regional version of the neoclassical growth model:

$$\frac{\Delta Y_r}{Y_r} = g_r + \alpha \frac{\Delta K_r}{K_r} + (1-\alpha)\frac{\Delta L_r}{L_r} \tag{3.9}$$

where $\Delta Y/Y$, $\Delta K/K$ and $\Delta L/L$ are as given in equation (3.6), g is the rate of technical change and subscript r denotes region. We can see immediately from equation (3.9) that the neoclassical model identifies three reasons why regional growth disparities can occur:

1 Technical progress may vary between regions.
2 The growth of the capital stock may vary between regions.
3 The growth of the labour force may vary between regions.

The rate of technical progress g_r in region r may be expected to vary between regions (at least in the medium term). Subtracting the growth of the labour force $\Delta L_r/L_r$ from both sides of equation (3.9), we obtain

$$\frac{\Delta Y_r}{Y_r} - \frac{\Delta L_r}{L_r} = g_r + \alpha \left(\frac{\Delta K_r}{K_r} - \frac{\Delta L_r}{L_r} \right) \tag{3.10}$$

Thus, regional disparities in the growth of output per worker are explained by regional differences in the rate of technical progress and by regional differences in the growth of the capital/labour ratio.

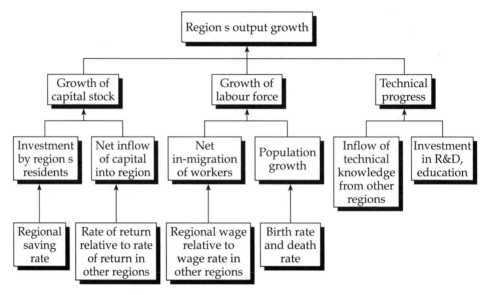

Figure 3.3   Factor supplies and the growth of regional output.

3.3   Identifying the components of economic growth in practice

The sources of output growth

The neoclassical model identifies three sources of output growth: the capital stock, the labour force and technology. A region's output growth will therefore depend upon the growth rate of these three factors of production. Before looking at attempts to identify the sources of growth, it will be useful to investigate the reasons why the rates of growth of capital, labour and technology might vary between regions.

A potentially important influence on regional growth disparities is interregional factor migration. According to the neoclassical model, capital and labour will move to those regions offering the highest rates of return. Producers will search for the most profitable locations for their plant and machinery while workers will be attracted to those regions in which wages are high. The neoclassical model assumes that there are no impediments to factor mobility between regions and that there is perfect knowledge about factor prices in all regions. Regional growth disparities therefore occur not only because of regional differences in the indigenous growth of capital and labour but also because of interregional factor migration.

An outline of this process is provided in figure 3.3, which demonstrates the range of factors that may be expected to influence the growth of capital, labour and technology within any individual region. The growth of the capital stock, for example, depends on investment by the region's residents and on the inflow of capital from other regions. These two factors are dependent, respectively, on the savings rate of the region's residents and the return on capital in the region compared with other regions. Hence, output growth will be faster if the savings rate increases since this will lead to a faster growth of the capital stock by raising the amount of investment per period. Similar arguments apply to the growth of the labour force, which will depend not only on the population growth rate but also on net in-migration from other regions.

Which regions are likely to grow the fastest, assuming that capital and labour are perfectly mobile? According to the neoclassical model, regions with a high capital/labour ratio will have high wages and a low yield on investment. This leads us to predict that capital and labour will move in opposite directions: regions with a high capital/labour ratio will have an inflow of labour and an outflow of capital, and conversely for regions with a low capital/labour ratio. In other words, low-wage regions will attract capital and lose labour, whereas high-wage regions will attract labour and lose capital. It is not possible to predict, however, whether output growth will be higher in low-wage regions than in high-wage regions since this will depend upon the speed at which capital is flowing into low-wage regions relative to the speed at which labour is flowing out of these regions. If capital is more mobile than labour (as seems very likely), the low-wage region will experience the fastest output growth because capital will be moving into these areas faster than labour is moving out.

Empirical studies of regional growth disparities

The United States

The first empirical test of the neoclassical growth model on regional data was undertaken in a seminal paper by Borts and Stein (1964). Their test of the neoclassical model was based upon the division of states into two groups: low-wage states and high-wage states. The model predicts that capital will move towards low-wage states and that labour will move towards high-wage states. These predictions were tested against what actually happened during the period 1919–57. The model was decisively rejected. Tests of the model by other researchers, however, turn out to be more favourable. In an econometric test, again using data for the US states, Ghali et al. (1981) found that both capital and labour responded to inter-state differences in factor prices. Capital moves to the states offering the highest rates of return and labour moves to the states offering the highest wages.

One of the first applications of the neoclassical growth equation to regional data was undertaken by Hulten and Schwab (1984) for the nine regional divisions of the USA. The relative importance of technical progress, capital stock growth and labour force growth in determining regional growth disparities was estimated for the period 1951–78, a period of generally rapid output growth in the USA. Using available data on output growth, capital growth and labour force growth, Hulten and Schwab attribute output growth in the manufacturing sector to three determinants: labour force growth, capital stock growth and a residual

Table 3.2   Sources of output[a] growth and labour productivity growth in US regions, 1951–78

Region	Output growth[b]	Output growth due to			Growth of output per worker[c]	Growth of output per worker due to	
		Capital stock growth	Labour force growth	Other factors[d]		Growth of capital/ labour ratio	Other factors[d]
Middle Atlantic	1.78	0.44	−0.35	1.70	2.25	0.56	1.70
New England	2.24	0.48	−0.06	1.82	2.26	0.45	1.82
East North Central	2.62	0.68	0.14	1.79	2.34	0.55	1.79
West North Central	4.19	1.20	0.97	2.02	2.70	0.68	2.02
Snowbelt regions	2.45	0.62	0.03	1.80	2.36	0.56	1.80
South Atlantic	4.49	1.42	1.39	1.69	2.31	0.62	1.69
Pacific	4.76	1..26	1.84	1.67	2.15	0.48	1.67
East South Central	5.09	1.90	1.58	1.61	2.45	0.83	1.61
West South Central	5.59	2.40	1.77	1.42	2.45	1.03	1.42
Mountain	5.87	1.90	2.58	1.39	1.91	0.52	1.39
Sunbelt regions	4.94	1.63	1.69	1.69	2.31	0.70	1.61

[a] Output = real value added in manufacturing.
[b] Output growth = growth of capital stock + growth of labour force + other causal factors.
[c] Growth of output per worker = growth of capital/labour ratio + other causal factors.
[d] 'Other factors' is commonly referred to as 'total factor productivity'.
Source: Hulten and Schwab (1984: 157)

component which includes technical progress. It should be noted that this exercise assumes that capital and labour are treated as if they were homogeneous throughout the period even though their productivity may have been enhanced substantially. The residual component is therefore only a very rough approximation to technical progress. The results given in table 3.2 therefore need to be interpreted cautiously.

One of the main findings of the Hulten and Schwab study is that while the Sunbelt regions experienced a much faster growth in output than the Snowbelt regions during 1951–78, there was virtually no difference in productivity growth between these regions. These results also indicate that the growth disparities between US regions were mainly due to differences in the growth of the labour force and (to a lesser extent) to differences in the growth of the capital stock. The residual category of 'other factors' played virtually no part in explaining regional growth disparities. This suggests that technical progress was diffused fairly evenly between regions in the USA.

The United Kingdom

The Solow equation of growth can also be used for investigating regional disparities in productivity growth. It is possible, for example, to rearrange the Solow equation in order to calculate total factor productivity (TFP) growth, which is

Table 3.3   Estimates of total factor productivity (TFP) growth in the manufacturing sector of UK regions

Region	TFP growth in manufacturing		Δ TFP growth
	1969–78	1979–91	
South East, East Anglia	2.1	3.2	1.1
South West	0.9	3.4	2.5
East Midlands	2.1	3.1	1.0
West Midlands	1.2	3.0	1.8
Yorkshire/Humberside	1.7	3.1	1.4
North West	2.4	2.7	0.4
North	1.3	3.2	1.9
Wales	0.2	5.3	4.1
Scotland	1.4	3.2	1.8
Northern Ireland	0.5	3.7	3.2
UK	1.7	3.2	1.5

Source: Harris and Trainor (1997)

simply the term g_r in equation (3.9). This is easily done since all that is required is to shift the terms containing $\Delta K/K$ and $\Delta L/L$ in equation (3.9) to the left-hand side, thereby solving for g_r as follows:

$$g_r = \frac{\Delta Y_r}{Y_r} - \alpha \frac{\Delta K_r}{K_r} - (1-\alpha)\frac{\Delta L_r}{L_r} \qquad (3.11)$$

The TFP growth g_r is therefore obtained as a residual once information about the growth rates of the variables Y, K and L has been obtained and once the parameter α has been estimated.

Calculations of TFP growth for the UK regions based upon a modified version of the above model are provided in table 3.3 for the manufacturing sector in the UK regions (Harris and Trainor 1997). Estimates are given for two sub-periods (1969–78 and 1979–91) since there are considerable differences in TFP growth over time. The annual growth of TFP was nearly twice as fast during 1979–91 as in the earlier period. Particularly striking is the fact that the peripheral regions (the North, Scotland, Wales and Northern Ireland) all experienced a massive surge in their TFP growth during the 1980s when UK regional policy was becoming less active. This could mean that regional policy is relatively ineffective in raising TFP growth. An alternative view is that the industrial restructuring that occurred as a consequence of regional policy in the 1960s and 1970s could have laid the foundations for faster productivity growth in the 1980s. Furthermore, the phenomenal increase in TFP growth in Wales during the 1980s is likely to have been caused, at least in part, by the massive industrial restructuring of the manufacturing sector as older industries disappeared and entirely new industries were established by foreign investors, such as Japanese electrical engineering companies.

We should also expect the growth of total factor productivity to vary not only between regions but also between industries. This point is made forcibly by Harris and Trainor (1997) in their study of TFP growth in the UK. It follows that any attempt to explain interregional differences in growth must also take into account the factors causing inter-industry differences in TFP growth since the industry mix varies between regions. The factors found to be significant determinants of regional (and industrial) disparities in TFP growth in the UK study are as follows:

1   The skill level of the region's workforce.
2   The flexibility of the region's workforce.
3   The proportion of small plants in a region (since scale economies have become less important in recent decades due to changes in production techniques).
4   A catch-up effect of productivity growth in the unionized sector due to better industrial relations compared to pre-1980.

Empirical studies of regional disparities in the growth of output per capita are still a rarity. This compares with a wealth of empirical studies of growth disparities between countries. As more data become available, however, it is inevitable that more work will be done in this important area of regional economics.

3.4   Endogenous technological progress: the engine of growth

The Solow growth model argues that the growth in output per capita is driven by the rate of technological progress. Without technological progress, there would be no growth in the long run. But since the causes of technological progress are not identified in the Solow model, this means that the underlying explanation of growth is not spelt out. Endogenous growth theory attempts to overcome this deficiency in the Solow model by providing an explanation of the causes of technological progress. This extension to the neoclassical model is referred to as endogenous growth theory since it argues that technological progress is itself determined by the growth process. Basically, entrepreneurs are looking for ways to make a profit and one way of doing this is to produce (and sell) new ideas. Since there is a profit incentive to produce new ideas, this means that economic growth is endogenous. The economy's technological frontier is automatically pushed outwards because of the profits to be earned in the knowledge-producing industry.

There are various approaches to explaining the rate of technological progress. Although modern growth theory is a highly complex field of economics, its elements can be explained most easily by considering a model developed originally by Romer (1986; 1990). This model begins with a slight amendment to the production function used by Solow. An economy's output is assumed to be determined by its capital stock, its labour force and the technological knowledge of its workers as in the Solow production function, but in this case the technological knowledge is assumed to be attached to the workers themselves. We therefore have a 'knowledge adjusted' workforce so that the production function is written as follows:

$$Y = K^{\alpha}(AL)^{1-\alpha} \tag{3.12}$$

Dividing by L to obtain output per worker:

$$y = k^{\alpha}A^{1-\alpha} \tag{3.13}$$

where $y = Y/L$ and $k = K/L$. This argues that output per worker is determined by the capital/labour ratio and the amount of technological knowledge in the economy. By applying some mathematics to this per capita production function we can express the model in growth terms:

$$\frac{\Delta y}{y} = \alpha\frac{\Delta k}{k} + (1-\alpha)\frac{\Delta A}{A} \tag{3.14}$$

where $\Delta y/y$ is the rate of growth of output per capita, $\Delta k/k$ is the rate of growth of capital per worker and $\Delta A/A$ is the rate of growth of technological knowledge.

If we now assume that the economy is in long-run equilibrium, this means that output per worker and capital per worker will be growing at the same rate. (This is necessary for 'balanced growth', which implies that the capital/output ratio is constant and so capital and output must be growing at the same rate.) If $\Delta y/y$ and $\Delta k/k$ are equal, it is easy to show that

$$\frac{\Delta y}{y} = \frac{\Delta k}{k} = \frac{\Delta A}{A} \tag{3.15}$$

In other words, output per worker must be growing at the same rate as technological knowledge, which is growing 'endogenously' due to the natural desire for profit by entrepreneurs in the knowledge-producing industry.

But what determines the rate of growth of technological knowledge? One explanation is based upon the following endogenous production function:

$$\Delta A = \delta L_A^{\lambda}A^{\phi} \tag{3.16}$$

where ΔA is the change in technological knowledge, L_A is the number of workers employed in the knowledge-producing industry, and δ, λ and ϕ are parameters of the production function. Equation (3.16) is the production function for new ideas. It argues that technological knowledge will increase over time and its rate of change will depend upon:

1   The number of workers L_A in the knowledge-producing industry.
2   The existing stock of knowledge A.

The influence of the number of workers in the knowledge-producing industry on the production of knowledge is clear, but the relationship is likely to suffer from diminishing returns due to the greater possibility of duplication of new ideas as more people are involved in producing them. The past discovery of ideas will also influence the amount of new ideas created today since existing knowledge is used to produce new ideas (e.g. calculus!). Isaac Newton, for example, said that he stood 'on the shoulders of giants'. If we also assume that the influence of the current stock of ideas on new ideas suffers from diminishing returns, then both λ and ϕ will be between 0 and 1.

We can now obtain the determinants of $\Delta A / A$ by rewriting the production function for new ideas as follows (dividing both sides of equation 3.16 by A):

$$\frac{\Delta A}{A} = \delta L_A^\lambda A^{\phi-1} \tag{3.17}$$

Now, since $\Delta A / A$ will be constant if there is balanced growth, we can again apply some mathematics to obtain

$$0 = \lambda \frac{\Delta L_A}{L_A} + (\phi - 1) \frac{\Delta A}{A} \tag{3.18}$$

Solving equation (3.18) for $\Delta A / A$, we obtain

$$\frac{\Delta A}{A} = \frac{\lambda}{1 - \phi} \left(\frac{\Delta L_A}{L_A} \right) \tag{3.19}$$

which argues that for given values of λ and ϕ (both greater than 0 but less than 1), the rate of growth of new ideas will be proportional to the rate of growth of the number of people employed in the knowledge-producing industry. This implies that the growth of the labour force (and hence the population growth rate) determines the rate of growth of technological knowledge in the long run. This is because L_A cannot keep on growing faster than the labour force for ever since at some point every worker would be in the knowledge-producing industry and no one would be producing anything else but knowledge! Hence, if the economy is in long-run equilibrium, then

$$\frac{\Delta A}{A} = \frac{\lambda}{1 - \phi} \eta \tag{3.20}$$

where η is the population growth rate. The growth of output per worker in the endogenous growth model is therefore determined by the equilibrium growth rate (together with the parameters λ and ϕ). In other words, the faster the world's population grows, the faster will new ideas be produced and the faster will output per worker grow.

3.5 Technology transfer between regions: catching up with the technology leaders

The endogenous growth model is not designed to explain why different economies (whether these are economic unions, countries or regions) grow at different rates. The model is designed to explain the growth of the world economy as a whole and not the growth of particular economies. The reason for this focus on the world economy as a whole is that technological progress diffuses across geographical space so that even small economies can benefit from technical progress without having to rely on knowledge created within their own frontiers. This diffusion of knowledge is likely to be particularly rapid across regions within countries, though the vast expansion of multinationals in recent decades, and the transmission of information across the world through vastly improved communication systems, mean that new ideas travel very quickly across international frontiers.

The catch-up model argues that technical progress in any given region will depend upon the extent to which its own technology A_r lags behind the technology of the most advanced region. This can be expressed algebraically as follows:

$$\frac{\Delta A_r}{A_r} = \lambda(A^* - A_r) \qquad \lambda > 0 \tag{3.21}$$

where A^* is the technology level in the most advanced region. This transfer of technology function argues that the further away a region's technology is from the technology of the most advanced region, the faster will be its technological progress.

The economics underlying this argument is straightforward. If a region has a long way to catch up technologically, it should be able to transfer technology into its economy fairly cheaply and so will have a fast rate of technical progress. Some technology transfers will be cheaper than others to acquire (e.g. they will be cheaper to copy). But if a region is already employing state-of-the-art technology, it will only be able to improve its technological knowledge by investing in new knowledge, which is likely to be more expensive than copying existing techniques of production.

The conclusion that we come to then is that regions with a relatively low level of technological knowledge will be able to benefit from catch-up, provided that other conditions such as the socio-political infrastructure are favourable to market forces. Low-technology regions will therefore experience the fastest growth in output per worker, which means that convergence is predicted to occur in the catch-up version of the endogenous growth model.

This rapid transfer of technological knowledge across regions and countries means that there is now less reason to expect spatial disparities in growth rates. There are two reasons, however, why growth rates are still likely to vary markedly between economies in the medium term. First, those economies with low per capita income levels have a lot of catching up to do and they can clearly benefit from the existing stock of technological knowledge by utilizing it more effectively. During the catch-up phase, their growth will consequently be faster than those economies which are already utilizing existing technical knowledge intensively. Growth rates are therefore likely to be faster in economies which are catching up in their use of existing knowledge.

Second, the incentives to invest and to use existing technical knowledge will vary between different economies. This may happen, for example, because some countries have more favourable economic and social infrastructure than others, or because the legal and political institutions are more favourable to the accumulation of capital. Countries in which there is social unrest, for example, will be less attractive to investors than countries in which there is a stable social and political environment.

Empirical work on the spatial diffusion of technology suggests that such diffusion between regions is far from being instantaneous as predicted by the neo-classical model (see chapter 10). Some regions appear to be innovation leaders. They are the sources of the basic inventions and take the lead in applying these inventions in the form of new products or more efficient ways of producing existing products. An example of the high geographical concentration of innovative activity is provided by Guerrero and Seró (1997) for Spain. Using the number of applications for a patent as a measure of innovative activity, they show that Madrid and Barcelona together accounted for over 50 per cent of Spain's innovative activity during 1989–92 while their share of national GDP was only 31 per cent. The only other very high concentration among Spain's 50 provinces was in Valencia with 6 per cent of the country's innovations. A statistical analysis of regional disparities in innovation in Spain reveals that government policy towards stimulating innovation has been highly biased in favour of the regions with the greatest innovation potential.

It should also be recognized that the geography of innovation can change dramatically over time, as has occurred in the USA (Suarez-Villa 1993; 1999). Using the number of registered patents as an indicator of innovative activity, Suarez-Villa shows that the Sunbelt states, particularly California and Texas, increased their share of total innovations in the USA from under 20 per cent in the 1940s to 50 per cent in 1995 (see table 3.4). The reasons for the increasing importance of the Sunbelt states as innovation leaders are varied and contain a mixture of market forces and government intervention. The new high-tech industries have clearly had a preference for the Sunbelt states and this has been backed up by substantial inward migration from the mid-western and north-eastern states. But federal and state governments have also had some influence on the rapid growth of the innovation capacity in the Sunbelt states through government expenditure on defence, infrastructure, higher education and research institutions.

Although technical knowledge diffuses outwards from source regions, the process is complex and is far from perfect. Information on new production processes, for example, appears to spread more rapidly to other regions than does information on entirely new products, which are often jealously guarded by innovating firms. Information also tends to diffuse along well-defined routes, from cities to small towns and from main plants to branch plants within firms. Until more is

Table 3.4 The regional distribution of innovations in the USA, 1940–94

Decade	% of newly patented inventions			
	Sunbelt	Northeast	Midwest	USA
1940–9	18.8	48.5	32.7	100
1950–9	21.6	46.7	31.7	100
1960–9	27.5	41.6	30.9	100
1970–9	32.8	38.6	28.6	100
1980–9	37.8	36.3	25.9	100
1990–4	42.7	33.4	23.9	100

Source: Suarez-Villa (1999)

known about the spatial diffusion of technical progress, the possibility that regional growth patterns are determined at least in part by regional differences in technical progress cannot be ruled out.

If the diffusion of technology between regions is an important determinant of productivity growth, we should expect those regions with 'low' technology to gain productivity improvements by exploiting the technology gap between themselves and the 'high'-technology regions. This suggests a positive relationship between productivity growth and the technology gap: the bigger the technology gap, the faster the productivity growth. McCombie (1982) has attempted to test this hypothesis using cross-section data for the US states. After allowing for other possible influences on the growth of labour productivity, he found no evidence that each state's technology gap had any effect on its productivity growth. He concludes that the diffusion of innovations has not been influential in determining inter-state differences in productivity growth in the United States. This result must, however, be regarded as only tentative since it is based upon highly aggregated data. More detailed empirical research is needed at the micro-level if the process of technological diffusion is to be more clearly understood.

3.6 The convergence of regional per capita incomes in practice

One of the key predictions of the neoclassical growth model is that spatial disparities in per capita incomes should converge over the long run. This will occur because capital will flow from high-wage to low-wage regions and labour will flow in the opposite direction until returns to capital and labour are equalized. In addition, poor regions can benefit from technology catch-up. To what extent has this catching-up process occurred? Some indication is provided by studies of the convergence of income per capita between regions.

It is important to distinguish between two different types of convergence. There is beta-convergence (or β-convergence) and sigma-convergence (or σ-convergence). These two types of convergence are defined as follows:

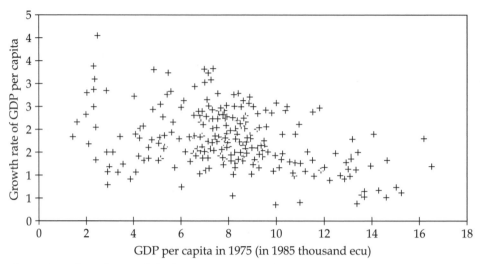

Figure 3.4   Growth rate of GDP per capita 1975–96 versus GDP per capita in 1975,
EU regions.
Source: Cambridge Econometrics

1 β-*convergence* occurs when poor regions grow faster than rich regions. This
   implies a negative relationship between the growth of per capita income (over
   several decades) and the level of per capita income at the start of the period.
2 σ-*convergence* is a more conventional measure of income inequality and is
   simply a measure of the dispersion of per capita income between regions at a
   given point in time. Convergence occurs in this case when the dispersion of
   per capita income between regions (though not necessarily between people
   within regions) falls over time.

Both these indicators of convergence have been employed in attempts to measure
the extent to which convergence has occurred in practice. The first major empirical
studies were undertaken by Barro and Sala-i-Martin (1991; 1992) for US and European regions. Using the β-convergence measure, they found a very strong negative
correlation between the growth of per capita income and the initial level of per
capita income over the very long run for US states. Those states with the lowest
levels of per capita income in 1880 grew the fastest over the subsequent century
(1880–1988), while those states with the highest per capita income in 1880 grew the
slowest. This suggests that regional levels of per capita income do tend to converge
over the long run, as predicted by the neoclassical growth model. Similar results are
obtained for European regions (see figure 3.4). The speed at which regional per
capita income levels converge, however, is a meagre 2 per cent per annum. This
implies a very slow process of convergence in per capita incomes. Using their results,
for example, to predict the speed at which East Germany's per capita income will
catch up with West Germany's, they conclude 'that East Germany's achieving
"parity" in the short run [with West Germany] is unimaginable' (1991: 154).

Table 3.5 Estimates of convergence of regional per capita income levels

Country	Number of regions	Time period	Estimated rate of convergence (β-convergence) % per annum	Regional income inequality (σ-convergence)			
				1940	1950	1970	1990
USA	48	1880–1990	1.7	0.35	0.24	0.17	0.17
Japan	47	1955–1990	1.9	0.63	0.29	0.23	0.15
Europe	90	1950–1990	1.5	–	–	–	–
Germany	11	1950–1990	1.4	–	0.31	0.20	0.19
Sweden[a]	24	1911–1993	2.4 (4.2)[b]	0.26	0.15	0.10	0.07
UK	11	1950–1990	3.0	–	0.17	0.10	0.12
France	21	1950–1990	1.6	–	0.21	0.17	0.14
Italy	20	1950–1990	1.0	–	0.43	0.33	0.27
Spain	17	1955–1987	2.3	–	0.34	0.27	0.22
Canada	10	1961–1991	2.4	–	–	–	–

[a] Data for Sweden obtained from Persson (1997).
[b] The figure in parentheses is estimated using per capita income data adjusted for regional differences in the cost of living.
Source: Sala-i-Martin (1996a; 1996b)

Recent international studies of convergence by Sali-i-Martin (1996a; 1996b) have indicated that regional convergence of per capita incomes has generally been very slow in the industrialized economies. Some of the results are given in table 3.5, from which we can see that both σ-convergence and β-convergence have occurred during the period 1950–90 in all countries. The measure of β-convergence, however, indicates that the convergence process has been very slow at around 2 per cent per annum. Armstrong (1995) finds a similarly slow rate of convergence across the regions of the EU. These results suggest that if current income per capita varies substantially between regions, such a low rate of convergence effectively means that regional per capita income levels will converge only very slowly over time. A similar picture emerges for σ-convergence, which indicates that the rate of convergence slowed down during 1970–90.

Several further attempts to measure the convergence of regional per capita income within countries give mixed results. A long-run study of regional convergence in Sweden indicates rapid β-convergence when the per capita income data are adjusted for cost of living disparities between regions (Persson 1997). Sweden also displays a sharp fall in σ-convergence, especially during 1940–70 (see table 3.5). In other countries, however, regional convergence has been found to be either extremely slow or even non-existent. This is the case, for example, in both Greece (Siriopoulos and Asteriou 1998) and Austria (Hofer and Wörgötter 1997). In the Austrian study, there is very weak evidence of convergence in regional per capita incomes during the 1970s but none during other periods for the nine major regions of Austria during 1961–89. The absence of convergence during the whole period is evident from the raw data of regional per capita income levels given in table 3.6. The evidence for spatial convergence in per capita incomes in Austria becomes stronger, however, when two modifications are made to the statistical

Table 3.6   Regional per capita income in Austrian regions, 1961–89

Region	GDP per capita		
	1961	*1989*	*Growth rate 1961–89*
Burgenland	44.5	125.7	3.7
Carinthia	63.6	150.0	3.1
Styria	66.2	141.2	2.7
Lower Austria	68.9	168.0	3.2
Tyrol	72.2	194.0	3.5
Upper Austria	74.0	194.1	3.4
Salzburg	78.4	211.0	3.5
Vorarlberg	82.1	199.4	3.2
Vienna	107.6	262.8	3.2
Measures of dispersion			
Standard deviation (%)	10.2	9.9	–
Coefficient of variation (%)	21.3	21.1	–

Source: Hofer and Wörgötter (1997)

analysis. The first modification is the use of 84 districts as the spatial units instead of just nine regions; and the second modification is when allowance is made for spatial disparities in the socio-economic structure of these 84 districts. This latter modification is referred to as conditional convergence since it measures convergence after other determinants of per capita income levels have been taken into account (as far as available data allow). These two major modifications lead to an estimated β-convergence rate of 2 per cent, which is in line with US estimates.

A completely different set of results is obtained for China. Estimates of β-convergence across the 27 provinces in China during 1986–95 indicate a very rapid rate of convergence in per capita incomes. Estimates by Wei et al. (2000a; 2000b) indicate a convergence rate of 13 per cent when other factors such as the diffusion of technology and technology transfer are taken into account. This is an extremely rapid rate of convergence and is clearly a result of the incredible speed at which the Chinese economy has been growing since the opening up of the country to foreign trade and to foreign direct investment. The prevailing economic conditions therefore appear to be a primary determinant of the speed at which regional per capita income levels are converging.

One of the problems with empirical studies of the rate of convergence in per capita incomes is that they fail to take spillover effects from neighbouring regions into account. Because of the strong trade and labour market linkages between contiguous regions, for example, a region's economy is likely to be affected by changes in per capita income occurring in neighbouring regions. One effect of these interregional linkages is that regions tend to display similar convergence trends to their near neighbours. This has been found to occur, for example, in the USA by Rey and Montouri (1999). They also show that allowing for these spillover effects reduces the estimated convergence rate, though only marginally for US states over the period 1929–94.

The general conclusion to be drawn from empirical studies of the convergence process is that convergence in per capita incomes between regions has certainly occurred but at a very slow rate. This is true even in the USA where factor flows between states are substantial. Labour migration between US states, for example, is far greater than between regions in the EU, which implies that the convergence process is likely to be even slower in Europe than in the USA (Bradley et al. 1995). The neoclassical model of growth therefore appears to predict correctly that there will be a convergence of per capita incomes over the long run, but empirical studies indicate that the convergence process is likely to be painfully slow.

The fact that empirical studies predict that convergence has been occurring in various groups of regions over different time periods offers some support for the neoclassical growth model. But as pointed out by Fingleton and McCombie (1998), this observed convergence is also consistent with other explanations of the convergence of regional per capita incomes. The observed β-convergence may be a result, for example, of technological diffusion and government policies to reduce regional disparities, including income support for low-income workers. The neoclassical adjustment mechanism may play a relatively minor role. In other words, β-convergence may be a very weak test of the neoclassical growth model since it is consistent with other plausible explanations of regional growth.

3.7   Extending the neoclassical growth model

A central weakness of the neoclassical explanation of regional disparities in economic development is the assumption that all factors of production are completely mobile between regions. According to the neoclassical model, regional disparities in labour productivity are a result of corresponding differences in the capital/labour ratio. Any such differences are predicted to disappear in the long run, however, as capital and labour move to the regions yielding the highest return. The neoclassical model therefore fails to explain why regional disparities in labour productivity persist over the long run. Moreover, although the neoclassical model also stresses the role of technology in determining economic growth, technology plays no part in explaining regional disparities in labour productivity. This is because it is assumed to be perfectly mobile between regions and so the latest technology will always be available to all regions simultaneously. But if capital, labour and technology are not completely mobile between regions, the neoclassical explanation breaks down and the predicted long-run convergence in labour productivity, between regions, will fail to occur.

The major strength of the neoclassical model is its emphasis on the crucial role of technical change in the growth process. Exactly how technical progress enters the economy and what factors determine the speed at which new technology is absorbed into the production system have been the subject of considerable debate. The most obvious and most direct way in which new technology enters the production system is through the embodiment of new production techniques and new products in the latest investment in capital stock. The vintage of a region's capital stock will therefore determine its level of technology.

But the embodiment of technogical progress in the newest capital goods is not the only way in which technology enters the production system. More recent developments of the neoclassical model recognize the importance of human capital as a critical factor in determining the productive capacity of the economy. Human capital is important for two reasons. First, a region's stock of human capital determines its ability to absorb and use new technology. As the stock of human capital increases, the economy will be more able to benefit from technological developments, thereby expanding the economy's productive capacity. Hence, although technology may be available everywhere, its efficient use requires an appropriately skilled workforce. Second, human capital is an important ingredient in determining the ability of a region to generate its own technical progress.

The capacity of a region to absorb or create technical progress is not simply a matter of investing in physical or human capital. A region's capacity to absorb or create technical progress is determined by its *institutional* environment. The creation of technical progress is determined by a collective learning process within which many individuals interact and exchange ideas and information, thereby providing a knowledge-rich environment. If such an environment exists, knowledge passes quickly from one economic agent to another, giving rise to the rapid creation of a wide variety of new ideas (Rauch 1993). There are therefore economies of scale to be gained from the geographical concentration of large numbers of highly educated people since their proximity to each other results in a more rapid transfer of knowledge and ideas. These ideas are then transformed into new products and new processes, thereby raising labour productivity. This means that technical progress is not simply an automatic outcome of investment in R&D, but requires an institutional environment which is conducive to the adoption and assimilation of new ideas into the production system. Regional disparities therefore occur in technical progress because the institutional environment varies between regions. In other words, some regions are more capable of using and producing technical progress than others (Fagerberg 1996).

Evidence of the external economic benefits to be gained from the geographical concentration of highly educated people is very hard to obtain. Indirect methods have therefore had to be used to test the basic hypothesis that the sharing of ideas has productivity-enhancing effects. Rauch (1993), for example, uses the average wage in a cross-section of 237 US cities as an indicator of labour productivity and regresses this on a number of explanatory variables including the average education level (i.e. years of schooling) of each city's residents. Since years of schooling is closely positively correlated with the wage variable (having controlled for a wide range of other determinants of each city's wage), Rauch concludes that there are substantial external economies to be gained from the geographical concentration of highly educated people. Rauch's estimated equations suggest that an extra year of schooling for a city's residents as a whole will raise its productivity by around 3 per cent.

Increasing emphasis on the importance of human capital in the growth process has led growth theorists to distinguish between embodied and disembodied technical progress. According to Castro and Jensen-Butler (1999), this distinction is essential for understanding regional disparities in productivity. Technology embodied in capital goods, for example, is *exogenous* in the sense that regions buying these capital goods will automatically acquire the embodied technology. A region's technology is therefore determined by the vintage of its capital stock.

Disembodied technical progress is quite different and is likely to make a substantial contribution to regional growth disparities. It is independent of the capital stock with which it is combined in order to produce output. The importance of disembodied technical progress for explaining regional disparities in productivity becomes apparent once it is realized that disembodied technical progress is more likely to be produced in the knowledge-rich and highly creative environments referred to above. Since some regions are more knowledge-rich and more creative than others, this suggests that disembodied technical progress is likely to vary between regions. Those regions which are knowledge-rich and which have relatively large quantities of human capital will specialize in creative activities such as R&D, scientific research institutions and high-level service activities. Such regions will generate new ideas which add to the region's technical knowledge which will be transformed into new products and new methods of production. Conversely, regions that are less well endowed with human capital will specialize in routine activities which rely on technical know-how embodied in the capital equipment available globally. Such regions will depend heavily upon being cost competitive in world markets.

This modern variant of the neoclassical model therefore explains why regional disparities in economic development can and do persist, even in the long run. The primary reason for long-term persistence is that some regions are more able to generate their own technical change. Knowledge-rich regions with an institutional environment conducive to the creation and transmission of new ideas will have a continuing advantage over less well-endowed regions which depend far more on acquiring technical change through purchasing capital equipment from other regions. Less well-endowed regions have no alternative but to rely on *exogenously* embodied technology since they are not capable of producing their own.

These modifications to the neoclassical growth model can be summarized as follows:

$$\frac{Y}{L} = f\left(\frac{K}{L}, EXOG, ENDOG, HUMCAP\right)$$

where Y/L is the output/labour ratio, K/L is the capital/labour ratio, $EXOG$ is the technology embodied in the capital stock (available to all regions), $ENDOG$ is the technology generated in the region (i.e. endogenous technology generated by the region's own highly skilled and innovative workforce) and $HUMCAP$ is the ability of a region to absorb and use new technology (determined by the stock of human capital). A highly simplistic outline of this model is sketched out in figure 3.5, which distinguishes between (exogenous) technical progress acquired through the purchase of new capital equipment from other regions and (endogenous) technical progress produced within the region itself.

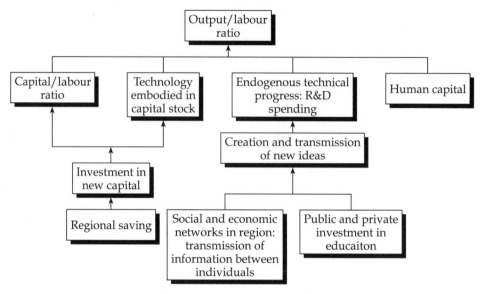

Figure 3.5   Determination of labour productivity.

3.8   Conclusion

This chapter began by demonstrating the vast disparities in economic growth that occur between regions within individual countries. Not only does output growth vary greatly between regions; there are also substantial regional variations in the growth of output per capita as well. Since output per capita is critically important in determining economic welfare, it is not surprising that policy makers have taken great interest in this variable. Thus, regional disparities in GDP per capita have figured strongly in defining regions in need of special assistance through the EU's Structural Funds. The increasing interest of policy makers in regional disparities in output per capita has been one of the primary motivating forces behind the recent spurt of empirical studies which attempt to explain these disparities. Policy makers want to know which factors are the most important determinants of regional per capita income levels and how low-income regions can best be helped to catch up to high-income regions over time.

A further reason for the increasing interest in regional disparities in output per capita is the revival of the neoclassical growth model. There are two reasons for this revival. First, the availability of regional output and employment data has encouraged economists to test one of the primary predictions of the neoclassical model, namely that regional per capita incomes will converge over the long run. Regional data provide an excellent opportunity to test this prediction since the conditions necessary for convergence to occur (i.e. free movement of goods and factors) are more likely to be present between regions within national borders than between countries. Economists have therefore attempted not only to discover whether convergence is occurring but also to measure the speed of convergence over time.

The second reason for the revival of interest in the neoclassical growth model is the emergence of endogenous growth theory, the aim of which is to rectify a fundamental weakness of the original neoclassical model. Instead of assuming that technical progress descends on the economy 'like manna from heaven', the new endogenous growth theory attempts to explain how technical progress is determined and whether governments can do anything to speed up technological change.

This chapter has shown that while the original neoclassical growth model offers some valuable insights into why economic growth varies between regions, recent modifications to the model have added to its potential value. The greatest of these insights is the role of technical progress as the primary determinant of growth. The central problem is that the new endogenous growth models have still not been widely tested. There is a long way to go before we can be confident that the new theories will offer policy makers the key to speeding up the convergence of regional per capita income levels.

It must be recognized, however, that the neoclassical approach still suffers from serious weaknesses despite the many recent improvements and modifications. Investors and workers are assumed to be perfectly informed about factor prices in all regions and to respond to any regional differentials by migrating to the region offering the most lucrative rewards. But neither investors nor workers are perfectly informed and there are significant impediments to this market response to factor price differences between regions. Neoclassical models also assume perfect flexibility of factor prices so that interregional movements of capital and labour will automatically remove factor price differences between regions. Factor prices are often far from perfectly flexible in practice, with the result that the neoclassical adjustment mechanism simply fails to work, except in the very long run.

The lack of realism of many of the fundamental assumptions of neoclassical models of regional growth has induced some researchers to reject the neoclassical approach and to search for entirely different explanations of why regions grow at different rates. These alternative approaches focus attention on the demand side of the regional economy instead of the supply side as in neoclassical models. This focus on the demand side of the regional economy means a change in the time scale since the neoclassical approach focuses very definitely on the long run, whereas models taking the demand side into account have a much nearer time horizon. In addition, it has been argued that the growth process is cumulative and self-perpetuating. Growth models based upon the cumulative causation approach to explaining regional disparities in economic growth are the subject matter of the next chapter.

Further reading

Solow (1957); Borts and Stein (1964); Richardson (1978); McCombie (1988a; 1988b); Barro and Sala-i-Martin (1991); Armstrong (1995); Bradley et al. (1995); Sali-i-Martin (1996a; 1996b); Jones (1998); Wei et al. (2000b).

chapter four

Export demand models, agglomeration and cumulative growth processes

contents

The discussion of regional growth disparities in the previous chapter was confined to the neoclassical approach, which stresses the influence of supply factors such as labour force growth, the growth of the capital stock and technical change. A major drawback of the neoclassical approach to explaining regional growth disparities, however, is that it ignores the potential contribution of factors on the demand side of the economy. To remedy this weakness, attempts have been made to modify the neoclassical approach by allowing regions to trade with other regions (Borts and Stein 1964). This opens up the possibility that regional growth differences may be explained, at least in part, by regional differences in the growth of a region's exports.

Once attention is focused on the influence of a region's export sector in determining its output growth, this takes us towards explanations of regional growth disparities which differ fundamentally from the neoclassical approach. Indeed, those researchers who have stressed the importance of a region's export sector in determining regional growth have specifically rejected explanations based on the neoclassical model (Kaldor 1970).

It is the purpose of this chapter to examine a range of growth models which depart significantly from the neoclassical approach. We begin, in section 4.1, with an explanation of the export-base approach. This emphasizes the potentially crucial role of the external demand for a region's output in determining its growth rate. The way in which the region responds to changes in the demand for its exports, and the influence that this has upon its growth rate, are also considered. Section 4.2 examines a model of regional growth based upon views originally expressed by Kaldor (1970). This model shows how an increase in regional output growth can trigger a cumulative expansion of a region's output through its effect on labour productivity. An extension to the Kaldorian approach, which emphasizes the constraint on a region's growth imposed by its balance of trade position, is discussed in section 4.3. This is followed, in section 4.4, by a more detailed examination of the process of cumulative causation, paying particular attention to the role of localization and agglomeration economies which arise as a result of the geographical concentration of industries. Section 4.5 discusses the potential effects of removing trade barriers on the geographical clustering of industry, and some evidence that firms regard geographical concentration as advantageous is provided in section 4.6. This evidence is based upon the locational choice of Japanese manufacturing plants in the USA and the UK since the early 1980s. Section 4.7 discusses the powerful tendency for financial services to concentrate their activities in core regions to the detriment of regions on the geographical periphery of an economy. Finally, examples of how various explanations of regional growth disparities can be tested are provided in section 4.8.

4.1   The demand for a region's output: the export-base approach

The potential significance of the export sector in explaining a region's growth was first investigated in depth by economic historians. Several historical studies of the growth and development of resource-based regions in North America (Innis 1920; North 1955) led to the emergence of the export-base model of regional growth. The early work on the model stressed that many regions, particularly in northwestern North America, were developed from 'without' rather than from 'within'.

Capital and labour flowed into these regions in order to exploit their rich natural resource base. As world demand for these natural resources expanded, the necessary transport links were forged with the outside world, leading to the integration of these regions into world markets. Shipping lines and railroads were therefore brought into these regions for the purpose of exploiting their natural resources.

The central proposition of the export-base model is that the initial stimulus to a region's economic development can be traced, at least for some regions, to the exploitation and export of its natural resources. The geographical distribution of natural resources may therefore help to explain why regions grow at different rates. But the analysis cannot stop here if the export-base model is to explain the continuing and sustained expansion of a region, or indeed its decline. If the export-base model is to prove useful, it must do two things. First, it must explain why regional specialization occurs. Second, export-base theory must concern itself with the circumstances under which a regional economy will continue to grow and under what circumstances it will decline.

Explanations of why regions specialize in certain export commodities have been sought in theories of comparative advantage. These theories attempt to explain regional patterns of production and export specialization. The Heckscher–Ohlin theorem, for instance, argues that regions will specialize in the production and export of commodities that use their relatively abundant factors intensively. Regions with abundant supplies of raw materials will therefore specialize in raw-material-intensive commodities (e.g. primary and semi-processed goods); labour-abundant regions will specialize in labour-intensive commodities; and capital-abundant regions will specialize in capital-intensive commodities.

It is now recognized, however, that the Heckscher–Ohlin explanation of regional export specialization is oversimplified and a variety of alternative theories now exist, as the next chapter shows. In addition, the Heckscher–Ohlin theorem assumes that factors of production do not migrate between regions, for otherwise 'regional factor abundance' has no meaning. This assumption of immobility is reasonable for raw materials but less so for labour (especially in the longer term) and very unreasonable for capital, which is highly mobile between regions. Regions favourably endowed with raw materials will therefore specialize in the production of raw materials for export as this is their relatively abundant factor. This will induce factor migration since capital will flow into these regions in order to exploit the natural resource base.

Once specialization has been established, the external demand for a region's output X^d will have a dominating effect on its growth. The influence of external demand on the growth of a region's exports, however, depends on a number of factors. These will include the price of the region's exports P_x, the income level of other regions Z, and the price of substitute goods in external markets P_s. The export demand function summarizes the influence of these determinants:

$$X^d = f(P_x, Z, P_s)$$

Factors such as the quality of the product and after-sales service will also affect demand and ought to be incorporated into the export demand function. The competitiveness of a region's export sector in world markets will also influence the growth of the export sector through its effect not only on price but also on the quality of the product being produced.

On the supply side, all factors having a significant effect on production costs can be expected to affect the region's competitive position in world markets. These will include wage costs W, capital costs P_k, raw material costs R, intermediate input costs C and the state of technology T. The export supply function X^s summarizes the influence of these determinants:

$$X^s = f(P_x, W, P_k, R, C, T)$$

If the demand and supply factors listed above are favourable to a region's export growth, this will lead to an expansion in the demand for factor supplies, the price of which will be bid up relative to other regions. This in turn will induce in-migration from other regions, leading to growth disparities between regions. How long this growth differential will continue will depend upon a range of factors. Two likely to be of some importance are the appearance of factor shortages (resulting in a rise in production costs) and the emergence of competing regions. On the supply side, the region may therefore face rising production costs which impair its competitiveness; and on the demand side, the region may find its customers turning to suppliers in other regions. This does not necessarily mean that the region will decline. But the emergence of strong competition from other regions will require the region either to improve its competitiveness (through reducing costs or improving productivity), or to switch into new lines of production in order to develop new markets.

A further reason why a region may be able to survive competition from elsewhere is that the growth process tends to become cumulative. The stimulus to export demand has both a multiplier effect on regional income and perhaps even an induced (accelerator) effect on investment as well (Hartman and Seckler 1967). In addition, higher factor prices will attract labour and capital from other regions. The inflow of labour will raise the demand for those goods that are produced and consumed locally, such as transportation, personal services and government services. Subsidiary industries supplying specialist services to the export sector will also emerge as growth proceeds. These will stimulate a full range of agglomeration and localization economies, which, alongside any internal economies of scale existing in the export industries, will give further stimulus to the export sector by reducing production and distribution costs. Over time, we may see subsidiary industries become less dependent on the original export sector and they may begin to export in their own right.

The original export activity does not necessarily continue to grow indefinitely. Indeed, anything is possible. Low-cost locations can, for a wide variety of reasons, become high-cost locations. The pattern of demand may change and swing away from the export commodity in question. A cumulative reversal of the growth process outlined above may rapidly set in. Provided that factor prices are flexible, however, and provided that factors are sufficiently mobile between industries, the law of comparative advantage will allow the region to survive through the reallocation of productive factors to more viable export commodities. During this period of reallocation, the region may also lose labour and capital to faster grow-ing regions.

The export-base theory, in its more extended form, is a seductive one. Its advantage over the neoclassical approach is that it stresses the role of demand factors without ignoring the supply side of the regional economy. Yet it was severely criticized soon after its appearance, mainly because, in its simplest form, it merely describes the historical development of regions dependent on raw mater-ial exports. It offered little insight into the conditions likely to have a dominant effect on growth. The role of factors internal to a region, for instance, such as local entrepreneurial activity and government development programmes, are entirely ignored. While the more naive export-base model is guilty of such omissions, however, those that incorporate induced investment effects, factor supply influ-ences and the effects of external economies of scale are less open to criticism. Perhaps the greatest weakness of the theory is that beyond the occasional men-tion of income elasticity of demand, no systematic explanation of the determin-ants of the demand for a region's exports is attempted, and without this it is impossible to predict regional growth differences. In its simplest form, the model is less rigorous than the neoclassical approach.

4.2   Regional exports and cumulative causation: a model of regional growth

The first section of this chapter discussed in very general terms the potential significance of a region's export base in determining its growth. The present section builds on the previous section and discusses a more carefully specified model which emphasizes the cumulative nature of the growth process. This model was initially proposed by Kaldor (1970), and was subsequently developed further by Dixon and Thirlwall (1975).

Kaldor argued that a region's growth of per capita output is determined by the extent to which regions are able to exploit scale economies and to reap the bene-fits that accrue from greater specialization. These benefits vary according to the type of productive activity in which a region specializes. Some sectors are more susceptible to productivity gains than others. In particular, the manufacturing sector is able to reap substantially greater benefits from growth than accrue from land-based activities, such as mining and agriculture. This means that regions specializing in manufacturing activities are likely to benefit far more from pro-ductivity gains than are regions which rely heavily on land-based activities.

This sectoral bias in the benefits to be gained from greater specialization leads to the prediction that regions specializing in processing activities are likely to grow faster than those specializing in land-based activities. Furthermore, the process is cumulative since those regions able to steal a march on other regions will gain a competitive advantage. This will reinforce regional specialization since the region with the competitive advantage expands its export sector (importing more land-based commodities from other regions).

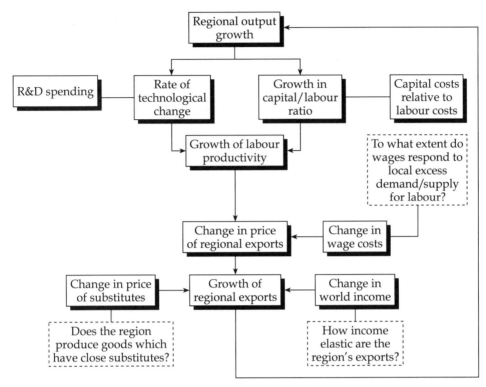

Figure 4.1   A schematic illustration of the Dixon–Thirlwall model of regional growth.

A more detailed specification of Kaldor's thesis has been developed by Dixon and Thirlwall (1975). Their major concern is to construct a rigorous presentation of Kaldor's explanation of regional growth disparities, paying particular attention to the way in which the process of cumulative causation may affect a region's growth. The process of cumulative causation is incorporated into the model by allowing for the feedback effect of a region's growth on the competitiveness of its export sector. This in turn affects output growth in the region, which has further beneficial effects on productivity and competitiveness in the export sector. This is the process of cumulative causation at work.

The key features of the Dixon–Thirlwall model can be demonstrated with the aid of figure 4.1. Since the focal point of the model is the growth in labour productivity, it is useful to begin by considering the factors that determine it. According to Kaldor, productivity growth is dependent upon two factors: the rate of technical change and the growth of the capital/labour ratio. Productivity will rise if technical progress increases, or if the capital/labour ratio increases (through investment in new plant and equipment). These in turn depend in part on output growth, which is itself determined by the growth of the export sector (using a simple export-base model of regional growth). Since the growth of the export sector depends upon its competitiveness relative to regions producing substitutes, this means that the price of the region's exports relative to the price of substitutes produced in other regions will affect the growth of the region's export sector. It is at this point that the process of circular causation is completed since the price of the region's exports is determined in part by productivity gains. Hence, productivity growth determines competitiveness, which leads to an increase in regional exports, which causes further output growth, which itself leads to further productivity growth, which generates further increases in competitiveness. And so the cycle goes on indefinitely, leading to cumulative growth.

The model

The model is set out formally by Dixon and Thirlwall (1975). It consists of four functional relationships, the first one being the relationship between output growth y and productivity growth q:

$$q = \alpha + \lambda y_{-1} \tag{4.1}$$

where α is autonomous productivity growth and λ is a constant known as the Verdoorn coefficient. This relationship is commonly referred to as the Verdoorn Law (following Verdoorn 1949). It argues that productivity growth is determined partly by output growth lagged one period y_{-1} and partly by other unspecified factors α. The faster the growth in output, the faster will labour productivity increase. The significance of the numerical value of λ will become clear below.

This takes us to the second part of the model, which argues that any increase in production costs will feed through directly into the region's rate of inflation, and that any productivity gains will reduce the inflation rate:

$$p = w - q \tag{4.2}$$

where p is price inflation in the region and w is cost inflation in the region. Thus, if productivity growth and cost inflation are equal, there will be no increase in the region's prices. The assumption that cost inflation is determined outside the model can be defended on the grounds that it is likely to be determined by national rather than regional factors.

The third component of the model argues that the growth of exports x depends upon the region's price inflation p, the inflation rate of the region's main competitors p_f and the growth of world income z, where 'world' could be interpreted as the region's main export markets:

$$x = b_0 p + b_1 p_f + b_2 z \tag{4.3}$$

where b_0 and b_1 are price elasticities of demand and b_2 is the income elasticity of world demand for the region's exports. The faster the growth of world income, and the lower the region's inflation rate relative to the inflation rate of the region's main competitors, the faster will the region's exports grow. The importance of the relative magnitude of the three elasticities is discussed below.

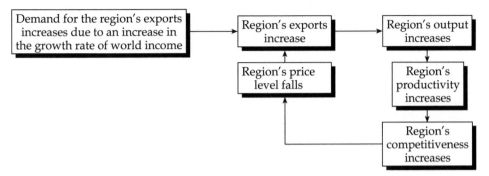

Figure 4.2 Cumulative growth induced by an increase in the growth of world income.

Finally, a simple export-base relationship is used to link output growth y and the growth of exports x:

$$y = \gamma x \tag{4.4}$$

where γ is the responsiveness of a region's output growth to the growth in its exports. The interesting feature of this model is that it contains a feedback mechanism because of the Verdoorn relationship (4.1). This is most easily seen by grouping the equations together:

$$q = \alpha + \lambda y_{-1} \tag{4.1}$$

$$p = w - q \tag{4.2}$$

$$x = -b_0 p + b_1 p_f + b_2 z \tag{4.3}$$

$$y = \gamma x \tag{4.4}$$

The link between these equations should be carefully noted. Provided that λ (the Verdoorn coefficient) is greater than zero, any output growth will create further output growth by making the region more competitive. This in turn increases export sales which boosts regional output. The system is cumulative and self-perpetuating.

To see how the model works, consider the effect of an increase in world income (z in equation 4.3). As world income increases ($z > 0$), exports grow and this leads to an increase in the region's output growth. The effect of the increase in output growth is to raise the growth of labour productivity which subsequently results in an increase in the region's export competitiveness by reducing domestic price inflation. Cost inflation is assumed to remain constant. It is at this point that the second-round effects begin. The improvement in the region's competitive position induces a further increase in its exports; and so the process continues. Figure 4.2 traces out the pattern of first-round effects of an increase in world income. The second and subsequent rounds will be the same except for the fact that the additional increase in exports induced during each round will become smaller and smaller (similar to the multiplier process).

Equilibrium growth

The equilibrium rate of output growth can be obtained by substituting equations (4.1), (4.2) and (4.3) into equation (4.4) as follows:

$$y = \gamma[-b_0(w - \alpha - \lambda y_{-1}) + b_1 p_f + b_2 z] \tag{4.5}$$

By rearranging the terms in equation (4.5), we obtain

$$y = \gamma[-b_0(w - \alpha) + b_1 p_f + b_2 z] + \gamma b_0 \lambda y_{-1} \tag{4.6}$$

or, more simply,

$$y = \alpha_0 + \alpha_1 y_{-1} \tag{4.7}$$

where

$$\alpha_0 = \gamma[-b_0(w - \alpha) + b_1 p_f + b_2 z] \tag{4.8}$$

$$\alpha_1 = \gamma b_0 \lambda \tag{4.9}$$

In long-run equilibrium, the growth rate will be constant ($y = y_{-1}$), in which case equation (4.7) becomes

$$y = \frac{\alpha_0}{1 - \alpha_1} \tag{4.10}$$

This is the equilibrium growth rate in the Dixon–Thirlwall model.

Since we now have a growth equation, we should be able to estimate a region's equilibrium growth rate provided that we know the actual values of all of the *coefficients* (α, λ, b_0, b_1, b_2 and γ) and the *exogenous* variables (w, p_f and z). For illustrative purposes, consider a region with the following characteristics:

coefficients: $\alpha = 2, \quad \lambda = 0.5, \quad b_0 = b_1 = b_2 = \gamma = 1$

exogenous variables: $p_f = 3, \quad z = 2, \quad w = 4$

Substituting these numerical values into equations (4.8) and (4.9), we obtain

$$\alpha_0 = 1[-1(4 - 2) + 1(3) + 1(2)] = 3$$

$$\alpha_1 = 1(1)(0.5) = 0.5$$

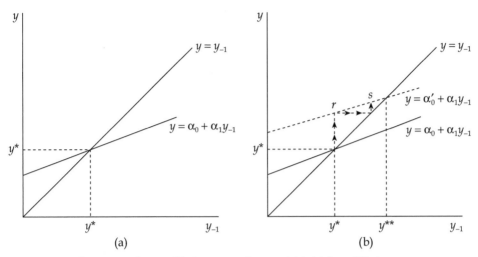

Figure 4.3 Changes in the equilibrium growth rate: (a) initial equilibrium;
(b) movement to a new equilibrium.

From equation (4.10), we obtain the equilibrium growth rate:

$$y = \frac{3}{1 - 0.5} = 6$$

Substituting $y = 6$ into the productivity equation (4.1):

$$q = 2 + 0.5(6) = 5$$

This is the equilibrium growth in labour productivity. Finally, subtracting labour productivity growth (5 per cent per year) from output growth (6 per cent per year) gives us the growth of employment (1 per cent per year).

It is interesting to note that equation (4.7) tells us whether the equilibrium growth rate is itself stable or unstable. So far, we have simply shown that a region will have an equilibrium growth rate provided that α_0 is positive and provided that α_1 is a positive fraction (in equation (4.7)). We can use equation (4.7), however, to show what will happen if a region's actual growth departs from its equilibrium growth rate. Figure 4.3 shows the relationship between current output growth y and output growth in the previous period y_{-1}.

We start from a situation where $y = y_{-1} = y^*$ in figure 4.3a. This equilibrium is now disturbed (e.g. by an increase in world income growth). The function shifts upwards (α_0 increases in value to α_0') and y^* is no longer the equilibrium growth rate since a growth of y^* in period 1 leads to an output growth of r in period 2 (figure 4.3b). This output growth of r in period 2 leads to an output growth of s in period 3; and so on until the new equilibrium growth rate is reached at y^{**}. The process is stable (or convergent) in the sense that any disturbance to equilibrium leads automatically to a return to a new equilibrium. A fuller discussion of the question of stability is provided by Swales (1983).

Evaluation of the model

As might be expected, this model suffers from several drawbacks. First, it fails to explain the type of exports in which a region will specialize. The export demand equation simply shows how a given set of export commodities will respond to changes in factors such as world income growth, but it says nothing about how the region acquired its export specialization in the first place. This may be explained by factor endowment or even by chance factors. Whatever the causes of a region's export specialization, these are not specified by the model as it stands.

Second, the model assumes that the export sector is the only source of regional output growth. In practice, it is conceivable that regional output may grow as a consequence of an expansion in trade within the region. There is no reason why productivity improvements due to increasing specialization should be restricted to the production of exports. The service sector may also benefit from productivity growth. It may change in size and form quite independently of events in the export sector.

Third, the Verdoorn Law conceals an exceedingly complex process. The ways in which an expansion of output in a region leads to an improvement of productivity growth (as shown in equation 4.1) are poorly understood, and are grossly oversimplified by the Verdoorn Law. Verdoorn (1949) himself argued that rapid output growth creates opportunities for greater division and specialization of labour. Other contributory factors have also been identified, such as the tendency for technical progress to be stimulated when output grows rapidly. The Verdoorn Law therefore encompasses a variety of processes by which output growth triggers productivity gains.

Fourth, the empirical evidence offered in support of the Verdoorn relationship is controversial. Some researchers have argued that the statistical tests of the Verdoorn Law have been theoretically unsound and no inferences can be drawn from the empirical results (Boulier 1984). There has, in fact, been a considerable debate on the appropriate specification to be used for testing the relationship between output growth and productivity growth (McCombie and De Ridder 1984). Statistical estimates of the Verdoorn Law must therefore be treated with caution and alternative specifications have had to be developed for testing whether such a relationship exists in practice. Using US data, McCombie and De Ridder find firm statistical support for the Verdoorn Law. More recently, Fingleton and McCombie (1998) have estimated the Verdoorn coefficient in a detailed investigation of productivity growth across 178 regions in the EU. This econometric investigation suggests that the Verdoorn coefficient lies between 0.5 and 0.6, which indicates that output growth has very strong effects on productivity growth and is very close to estimates obtained in earlier studies. A coefficient of 0.5, for example, suggests that a 1 per cent increase in a region's output growth leads to a 0.5 per cent increase in the growth of labour productivity. This result indicates

Table 4.1 Estimated returns to scale in UK regions (manufacturing industries only)

Region	Estimated returns to scale: weighted average based on	
	Region's own industry mix	National industry mix
South East, East Anglia	1.6	1.5
South West	2.1	2.4
East Midlands	1.5	1.3
West Midlands	1.6	1.5
Yorkshire/Humberside	1.6	1.4
North West	1.6	1.3
North	2.1	1.7
Wales	2.0	1.7
Scotland	1.6	1.5
Northern Ireland	1.6	1.9

Source: Harris and Lau (1998)

the presence of substantial increasing returns to scale. The EU study also finds evidence that technology is diffused from high-productivity to low-productivity regions, though this effect is found to be rather weak.

Further support for the presence of a Verdoorn effect is provided by Harris and Lau (1998) for UK regions. They show that the Verdoorn coefficient is determined by the combined returns to capital and labour and argue that the Verdoorn Law will be in operation only if there are increasing returns. In other words, increasing returns to scale are a necessary condition for a positive Verdoorn coefficient. Empirical estimates of the returns to capital and labour for UK regions indicate the presence of increasing returns. The estimates obtained by Harris and Lau are given in table 4.1. These suggest that returns to scale (and hence the strength of the Verdoorn effect on productivity growth) were greatest in the peripheral regions of the UK during 1968–91. The reasons why returns to scale have been greater in the peripheral regions of the UK have not yet been discovered, though part of the differential is accounted for in some regions by differences in the industry mix. Wales, for example, had an industry mix which resulted in relatively high returns to scale.

Finally, the model discussed in this section is deficient in one major respect. It ignores the consequences of output growth on a region's balance of payments. The relationship between a region's growth and its balance of payments is examined in the next section.

4.3   A constraint on regional growth: the balance of payments

According to Thirlwall (1980), a region's growth rate is constrained by its balance of payments position. It may seem strange that a region can suffer from a balance of payments problem since statistics are not collected on interregional trade and capital flows, nor do regions face currency crises since they share the same currency as all other regions within national borders. Regions do, nevertheless, have balance of payments problems even though they may be hidden.

Consider a region which initially exports as much as it imports. Its exports suddenly become uncompetitive due to the appearance of a better, cheaper substitute produced in another region. The consequent loss of jobs and fall in income lead to a fall in imports to offset the fall in exports. But imports are likely to fall less than exports since imports will be maintained to some extent because of the inflow of unemployment benefit into the region. The region's balance of trade deficit is therefore partially financed by an inflow of government transfer payments to the unemployed.

But other regions in the same country may not be willing to continue to finance a region's trade deficit indefinitely. If a region is to achieve a trade balance in the long run, this means that its imports must be covered by its exports. In other words, exports must equal imports in the long run:

value of exports = value of imports

or

$$P_x X = P_m M$$

Converting these levels into rates of change, we obtain

$$p_x + x = p_m + m$$

This argues that the rate of change in the value of exports must equal the rate of change in the value of imports over the long run. If we now assume that export prices change at the same rate as import prices over the long run (i.e. purchasing power parity holds over the long run), then $p_x = p_m$. This means that $m = x$ in long-run equilibrium.

If we now assume (1) that the growth of regional exports x is determined only by the growth of world income z, and (2) the growth of regional imports m is determined only by the growth of regional income y in the long run, then we have the following relationships:

$$x = \alpha z$$

$$m = \beta y$$

where α is the income elasticity of demand for the region's exports and β is the income elasticity of demand for the region's imports. Since $m = x$ over the long run (by assumption), this means that

$$\beta y = \alpha z$$

or

$$y = \frac{\alpha z}{\beta} = \frac{x}{\beta} \tag{4.11}$$

which argues that the growth of a region's output is determined by the growth of world income and the two income elasticities of demand.

The policy implications to be drawn from this model are clear. To raise long-run growth, a region must either switch into export industries which have a high income elasticity of demand α, or reduce the income elasticity of demand for imports β. Implementing such a policy, however, will be extremely difficult, especially in regions with a heavy concentration of industries which suffer from a low income elasticity of demand for their exports. The problem over the long run, therefore, is basically a structural one. Depressed regions need to encourage the growth of the right kind of industries.

One of the weaknesses of Thirlwall's growth model (4.11) is that it concentrates entirely on the influence of demand factors on a region's growth. The performance of a region's exports in world markets will also depend on the competitiveness of its products. If the region's costs rise too quickly or if its productivity growth is sluggish, this will worsen the region's competitive position in world markets and reduce the demand for its exports. The supply side cannot be ignored.

Empirical tests of Thirlwall's 'law' of growth have so far been restricted to international growth differences due to data limitations at the regional level. The various tests which have been carried out have yielded mixed results. McGregor and Swales (1983), for example, use regression methods to test the relationship between output growth, export growth and the elasticity of demand for imports in an international cross-sectional study. They conclude from their empirical analysis that Thirlwall's 'law' does not hold. They find, for example, that the actual growth rate is less than the equilibrium growth rate in virtually all countries for the period 1953–76, which suggests that the model provides an incomplete explanation of growth. Bairam (1988) obtains the opposite result: actual growth exceeds predicted growth for the majority of countries in his study.

An alternative interpretation of Thirlwall's law

An alternative interpretation of the relationship between output growth and the ratio of export to import elasticities has been suggested by Krugman (1989), who argues that the causal relationship flows in the opposite direction to that proposed by Thirlwall. Krugman argues that output growth determines export and import elasticities, and that an increase in the supply of factor inputs will cause output growth to rise. As output grows more quickly, the region will be able to increase its product range with the result that exports will also grow more quickly since the region will be in position to sell to a wider market because it has diversified its product range. The region's export growth will consequently increase relative to world income growth and so the export elasticity of demand will rise. In this interpretation, the elasticity of demand for exports is endogenous: that is, it is simply a consequence of the region growing faster than the growth of world income, and this occurs through the region widening its export base. This begs the question, 'Why has the export base of the region widened?'

Krugman's explanation of the empirical relationship between output growth and the ratio of export to import elasticities can be challenged on two counts. First, it fails to explain why output growth increases. He simply assumes that an increases in the growth rate of factor inputs automatically leads to an increase in output. This is the basic assumption underlying the neoclassical growth model (which is 'supply-based' as shown in chapter 3). The argument may hold over the long run but an increase in factor supplies may have little effect on output growth over the medium term. Second, Krugman ignores the obvious importance of the demand for exports in export growth.

The view that Thirlwall's 'law' does not hold and should be disregarded has been vigorously challenged by McCombie (1992) and by McCombie and Thirlwall (1997). The debate over Thirlwall's 'law' will no doubt continue.

4.4   Some alternative explanations of cumulative growth

The most interesting and useful feature of the Kaldorian explanation of regional growth disparities is the process of cumulative causation. The Verdoorn relationship is used to incorporate a cumulative growth process into what is essentially an export-led model of regional growth. Although a cumulative causation mechanism is introduced explicitly into Kaldor's explanation of regional growth disparities, the Verdoorn relationship masks a complex set of economic processes which deserve a more detailed investigation.

To the extent that the Verdoorn relationship captures the influence of economies of scale in generating cumulative growth, it overlaps with the ideas of growth-pole theorists such as Perroux (1950), Myrdal (1957) and Hirschman (1958). If an industry is subject to significant internal economies of scale, the firms that grow quickly will gain a competitive advantage over rivals and growth will become cumulative. Internal economies of scale, however, play only a minor role in growth-pole explanations of regional growth. A more convincing explanation of cumulative regional growth, and one stressed by development economists and more recently by trade theorists (Krugman 1991a; 1991b), incorporates the effect of external economies of scale into the explanation of regional growth disparities.

External economies arise as a result of the spatial proximity of related activities. Two sources of external economies of scale have been identified, both of which depend on the geographical clustering of economic activity. *Localization economies* result from the geographical concentration of plants in the same industry. They include transfer or linkage economies, which occur because of the geographical proximity of plants that have input–output ties with each other. These linkage economies deserve special mention because they reveal some of the reasons why the nodal points of transport networks are locations where distribution and assembly costs can be minimized for certain types of industry. An example is provided by the location of a large number of US-owned assembly plants in the border region of Mexico. US firms have taken advantage of low-cost labour in

Mexico while locating as near as possible to the US market so that transport costs are minimized. The forward and backward linkages to buyers and suppliers located in the USA exert a strong economic pull on the location of these assembly plants.

As was pointed out so clearly by Marshall (1920), economies of localization occur because firms in the same industry find it advantageous to cluster in the same geographical area. Several factors lead to clustering. First, clustering allows individual plants to specialize more than they would if firms in the same industry were widely dispersed. This increase in specialization leads to increased efficiency in production, with specialization taking several organizational forms. Separate firms may, for example, be established as specialist plants within an industrial complex, or groups of firms may come together to set up joint facilities, subcontracting being a typical feature of production.

Second, clustering strongly facilitates research and innovation in an industry. Physical proximity enhances the exchange of information, ideas and knowledge between firms. These technical spillovers may also occur through highly skilled workers changing firms as well as through flows of intermediate inputs between firms. Little is known, however, about how these technological spillovers actually occur. They are more likely to occur, however, in areas where there are a lot of small, high-tech firms and where highly educated workers move freely between firms, carrying their expert knowledge with them. Silicon Valley in California is the often quoted example of this rapid transmission of knowledge between high-tech firms. Protecting knowledge can be extremely difficult in such circumstances.

Third, the clustering of firms in the same industry will reduce risks for both workers and employers. Workers with industry-specific skills will be potentially more mobile between firms if firms in the same industry are geographically concentrated since changing jobs will not necessarily mean moving out of the region. Moreover, workers will be more willing to acquire industry-specific skills if they are more confident about their future job prospects in the same industry. This will reduce the risk premium that employers have to pay, thus reducing production costs. Firms will also have greater access to workers with relevant skills.

Agglomeration economies arise from the geographical association of a large number of economic activities. These may not be in the same industry. They arise because of the concentration of many facilities jointly serving different industries. These include:

- urban transportation and commuting facilities
- well-organized labour markets and large pools of workers with different types of skill
- the provision of social overheads and government services
- legal and commercial services such as lawyers, accountants, consultants, freight-forwarding agencies and financial institutions
- market-oriented activities such as service trades, attracted by the large concentrations of population
- cultural and recreational activities which attract highly skilled managers and professional workers

Table 4.2   Correlation[a] between research activity, education level and population in US cities, 1992

	Number of patents 1988–92	Patents per capita	Number of research centres	Education level
Patents per capita	0.58*	–	–	–
Number of research centres	0.74*	0.09	–	–
Education level (% with degree)	0.42*	0.46*	0.41*	–
Population	0.64*	0.04	0.83*	0.17

[a] Correlation coefficients indicated by an asterisk * are highly statistically significant ($n = 58$).
Source: data obtained from Audretsch (1998)

- the clustering of organizations which invest heavily in the search for new products and new processes

The tendency for innovative activity to be geographically concentrated, at least in the USA, can be seen from data on the distribution of patents between the major US cities. In a study of 59 major cities, Audretsch (1998) shows that the number of patents registered by firms located within each city is significantly positively correlated with three variables: the number of research centres, the number of patents per head of population, and the percentage of the population with degrees (see table 4.2). These results suggest that innovative activity and the educational level of the population are intimately related. Firms at the forefront of innovative activity are likely to attract the most highly skilled, who then provide the inputs necessary to support further investment in innovation. The cumulative growth process is therefore reinforced.

The attractiveness of existing growth centres may lead to *backwash* effects, which operate to the detriment of the economy's less developed regions. The efficiency of growth centres as locations for investment makes them a magnet for mobile capital. In addition, growth centres tend to drain the less developed regions of their most efficient and most enterprising workers.

The cumulative causation process may also be reinforced by the tendency for rich regions to trade with other rich regions rather than with poor regions. Developing countries frequently exhibit the well-known phenomenon of dualism whereby one part of the economy is highly capital-intensive, while the remainder is highly labour-intensive. Growth centres are typically dominated by rapidly growing, capital-intensive and technologically advanced industries. At first, the rapidly growing regions may simply bypass the less developed regions and trade predominantly with the rapidly growing regions of other countries. Over time, however, the less developed regions will gradually be drawn into the market economy, bringing many economic benefits to these regions. The opening up of poor regions to trade, however, is unlikely to be entirely costless since less efficient firms, which had formerly survived by virtue of their isolation, may simply be overwhelmed by the more efficient industries of the growth centres once interregional trade begins to occur. Reversing the cumulative causation process may not, therefore, be easy.

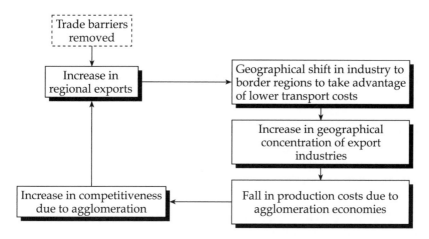

Figure 4.4   Agglomeration economies and cumulative causation.

It should also be realized that the process of polarization may work in reverse. Excessive growth can result in external diseconomies, such as urban congestion, pollution and the bidding-up of factor prices, particularly land values and wages. Firms may therefore begin to search out lower-cost locations. Economically backward regions may also benefit from 'trickle-down' effects which emanate from the centres of growth. As a nation develops, transport links between regions are likely to improve with the result that enterprising firms will begin to search for new investment opportunities in underdeveloped regions. Finally, the government may not stand idly by. It may deliberately attempt to stimulate growth in the less developed regions through regionally discriminating expenditure on economic development.

4.5   Trade costs, industrial clusters and regional growth

Trade theorists have recently turned their attention to regional growth disparities by arguing that the interaction between trade costs and the agglomeration of economic activity helps to explain why some regions grow faster than others. This 'new' trade theory approach draws heavily on the cumulative causation mechanisms discussed above.

The starting point for new trade theorists is the widely held view that the theory of comparative advantage fails to explain the patterns of interregional trade. Regions do not specialize in a very narrow range of goods based upon their factor endowment and then trade these goods for entirely different goods. In practice, regions import and export very similar types of goods. The strongest trade linkages are therefore between regions with very similar industrial structures, not between economies with very different industrial structures. This intra-industry trade has led to the development of new trade theories, which emphasize the interaction between internal scale economies, market access and agglomeration economies in determining interregional trade flows. Since regional exports play a critical role in the growth process, these new trade theories may help to explain why regions grow at different rates.

The new trade theory approach to explaining regional growth is based on three propositions:

- the existence of scale economies encourages firms to choose a single location
- barriers to trade (which include transport costs) encourage firms to locate near to their main markets
- agglomeration economies encourage firms to cluster in particular locations

How do these three factors interact to determine the geographical distribution of industry? Suppose that trade barriers between two regions are initially high and that these barriers severely restrict trade between them. Initially, their industrial structures are assumed to be similar because they do not specialize in exports. Suddenly, trade barriers are removed (due to improved communication, for example, or due to the removal of tariffs between the two regions). One of the regions decides to specialize in manufacturing and so increases its output and exports to the other region. Costs fall as manufacturing output increases and so the region specializing in manufacturing gains a competitive advantage through scale economies (Kaldor 1970). Alternatively, if one region was initially bigger than the other, then it will be in a better position to expand its manufacturing exports when trade barriers are reduced since it will already be benefiting from scale economies.

Reaping the benefits from these internal economies of scale is not, however, the end of the story. These internal economies will be reinforced by external economies in industries which are highly vertically integrated (Venables 1998). The clustering of firms which buy from each other may result in significant cost reductions. Being in close physical proximity to firms supplying intermediate inputs will reduce production costs not only because of lower transport costs but also because of the wide range of agglomeration economies offered by industrial clusters.

Reducing trade barriers may therefore have profound effects on the location decisions of firms and hence on the growth of regions. But which regions will grow and which regions will decline as a consequence of reducing trade barriers will depend on a number of factors. These include:

- the costs of transporting inputs from suppliers
- the costs of transporting the final product to the market
- the advantages of locating in areas with low labour costs
- the agglomeration economies resulting from a concentration of economic activity
- the congestion and land costs of locating in areas with large concentrations of economic activity

4.6   Evidence of the economic benefits of industrial agglomeration

To what extent do firms in the same industry cluster in order to take advantage of external economies of scale? There is undoubtedly considerable *prima facie* evidence that firms in the same industry cluster together. But it is not clear that this clustering is to take advantage of external economies of scale. An equally plausible explanation is that location decisions are determined by factor endowments. Some locations offer efficient transport links, for example, while others offer plentiful supplies of cheap labour or cheap land. Two examples of geographical clustering are provided here. The first is based on the clustering of US-owned assembly plants in the border region of Mexico. The second examines the clustering of Japanese inward investors in particular locations in the USA and the UK.

The clustering of assembly plants in the border region of Mexico

A large number of US-owned assembly plants have moved into the border region of Mexico since the Mexican government abandoned its policy of import substitution and joined the North American Free Trade Area in the mid 1980s. The creation of the North American Free Trade Area led directly to the virtual abolition of tariff and other trade barriers in Mexico, the effect of which was an increase in US imports from Mexico from $18 billion to $48 billion (at constant 1987 dollars) between 1980 and 1995 (Hanson 1998). The gravitational pull of the US economy on the location of industry in Mexico has been immense. This is evident from table 4.3. Previous to the liberalization of trade, manufacturing industries had been very heavily concentrated in the Mexico City region, but the opening up of the US market led to a remarkable shift of industry to locations in the border region. This geographical shift in manufacturing therefore occurred because of the attractiveness of the border region to US investors.

   Three location-specific factors have had a powerful influence on this clustering of US assembly plants (known as *maquiladoras*) in this border region of Mexico:

Table 4.3   The geographical concentration of manufacturing employment in Mexico

Region	Regional share of manufacturing employment (%)			
	1970	1980	1985	1993
Border	18.6	21.0	23.5	29.8
North	5.5	5.1	5.4	6.0
Centre	21.8	22.9	27.6	27.4
Mexico City	47.3	46.4	37.4	28.7
South	6.8	6.2	6.1	8.1

Source: Hanson (1998)

- US firms have taken advantage of low-cost labour in Mexico
- the assembly plants have been located with access to the US market a primary consideration so that transport costs are minimized
- backward linkages to suppliers located in the USA have exerted a strong economic pull on the location of these assembly plants

One of the consequences of the creation of assembly plants in Mexico's border region is a substantial intensification of the supply linkages between the US and Mexican economies during the 1990s (Hanson 1998). It is worth noting, however, that Mexico has not had the same effect on the location of industry in the USA. The Mexican market is still too small relative to the US market to have much influence on the location of US firms. This suggests that the economic integration of nations can have very large effects on the geographical distribution of industry of the smallest partners in new customs unions.

The clustering of Japanese inward investors

The high geographical concentration of Japanese manufacturing plants in particular regions (e.g. in both the USA and the UK) provides an ideal opportunity to investigate the extent to which the location decisions of these plants have been influenced by external economies due to clustering (Head et al. 1995). The aim is to discover the extent to which Japanese plants have been attracted to specific states by:

1   The number of US-owned plants in the same industry as the incoming Japanese plant.
2   The number of Japanese-owned plants already established in the same state.

The main findings of this research are that Japanese inward investors have indeed been attracted to locations which already have an existing concentration of plants in the same industry. The pull of states with a high concentration of *Japanese* firms in the same industry is even stronger. There are sound reasons for this. Japanese companies tend to establish long-term relationships with their suppliers and operate 'just-in-time' production methods in order to keep production costs down by reducing the need for inventories. Both these factors encourage suppliers to locate near to their buyers. There has therefore been a distinct 'follow-the-leader' effect in the choice of locations by Japanese manufacturing firms.

This is also confirmed by the high geographical concentration of Japanese inward investors in the UK. Table 4.4 shows the concentration of plants in the two largest Japanese-owned manufacturing industries in the UK, electrical engineering and motor vehicles. In the motor industry, for example, 10 of the 42 motor vehicle plants are located in just one county (out of 65 counties); and in the electrical engineering industry, 44 of the 107 plants are located in just seven counties. This high degree of clustering indicates that once a location decision has been made, other firms are attracted into the same location, possibly to take advantage of external economies of scale.

Table 4.4 The clustering of Japanese plants in the same industry, UK experience, 1996

County	Number of plants	Estimated number of employees
Electrical engineering		
Shropshire	11	4 693
Mid-Glamorgan	7	5 075
Strathclyde	7	1 568
Clwyd	6	2 105
Gwent	5	2 126
Devon	4	1 691
Durham	4	1 385
Subtotal for seven counties	44	18 643
Total for all 65 counties	107	33 316
Motor industry		
Tyneside	10	6 948
West Midlands	3	3 230
Wiltshire	3	1 960
West Yorkshire	3	1 665
Hereford and Worcester	3	1 345
Subtotal for 5 counties	22	15 148
Total for all 65 counties	42	23 456

Source: Invest in Britain Bureau, Department of Trade and Industry, London

4.7 The spatial concentration of the financial sector in core regions

An aspect of regional economic development which has received increasing attention in recent years is the role of financial institutions in the growth process. Financial institutions are major players in determining the availability of investment funds, which is the driving force behind regional growth disparities.

Financial institutions are very reluctant to supply credit to regions in which confidence is low due to economic stagnation. Credit shortages in depressed regions are likely to be particularly severe if the financial sector is highly integrated, since it will then be easier to direct capital flows to the regions where confidence is high (as in the core region). Since the financial services sector benefits from both scale and agglomeration economies, there is a powerful centripetal force in operation which leads to a high concentration of the financial sector in a nation's core region. Savings from peripheral regions therefore flow into financial institutions located in the core region and these financial institutions then decide where to invest. There is certainly no guarantee that the peripheral regions will attract sufficient investment to counterbalance the outflow of savings.

Evidence that capital flows are highly mobile between UK regions is provided by Bayoumi and Rose (1993). They argue that if capital flows were highly mobile, there would be no correlation between a region's savings rate and its investment rate. Capital will flow from regions with a high savings rate into regions with the highest expected returns on investment. This means that we should expect no correlation between the savings rate and the investment rate in a cross-section of regions. The zero correlation between the savings/GDP ratio and the investment/ GDP ratio across the regions of the UK confirms the view that capital is highly mobile between regions within the same country. This contrasts with a high positive correlation between the savings and investment rates at national level, which indicates that capital is far more mobile between regions within countries than it is between countries.

If peripheral regions suffer from a lack of perceived investment opportunities, the savings of these regions are likely to exceed the availability of investment funds in peripheral regions, thus having a detrimental effect on their economic development. Furthermore, the process may be cumulative since the lack of investment in local assets in peripheral regions will depress asset prices and encourage a further outflow of funds into the financial institutions in the core region. A highly integrated financial system will therefore fuel the process of uneven economic development between the core region and peripheral regions by causing savings to exceed investment in those regions suffering from poor investment opportunities.

There are several reasons why the peripheral regions might lose out to the core regions in the distribution of investment funds from financial intermediaries such as banks, pension funds and venture capital agencies:

- Lower income levels in the peripheral regions result in a higher demand for more liquid assets and these tend to be provided by national capital markets rather than by local financial institutions. Hence, savings flow to regions with a higher demand for investment capital.
- Financial institutions have extremely efficient networks for attracting savings away from the low-income/low-wealth regions into the centre.
- Low-growth regions have fewer opportunities for investment than high-growth regions. To the extent that the low-growth regions are also 'peripheral' regions, this means that savings are attracted towards the high-growth core region.
- Venture capital firms exhibit a powerful tendency to invest in small and medium enterprises (SMEs) which are located in fairly close proximity to the core region (Martin 1989b). This is partly due to the more rapid growth of SMEs in the high-income/high-growth areas and partly due to the preference of the venture capital funds to maintain regular contact with the SMEs in which they invest. Distance between investor and borrower is therefore a significant factor in determining the spatial allocation of investment in SMEs.
- The financial institutions themselves are located disproportionately in the core region, thus generating high-quality jobs and income in the core region.
- The continuing process towards further economic and monetary integration in the EU is likely to increase the spatial concentration of the financial and banking sector in the core regions of Europe. The peripheral regions of the EU could therefore find themselves at an increasing disadvantage in attracting investment funds in the absence of countervailing forces.

Since the structure of the financial system leads to a very strong centripetal tendency for savings to be sucked into the core region from all regions, it has been forcefully argued that banks should be required to reinvest a proportion of their deposits in the regions of origin. This is the case in Germany, for example, where local and regional banks are required by law to reinvest a proportion of their deposits in the region in which they are located. Local and regional banks in Germany are major supporters of locally based small firms and this is a powerful way of decentralizing financial power to the regions. Similar regulations are in place in France and Belgium, both of which have locally based investment agencies to raise capital for local investment (Martin and Minns 1995).

4.8   Empirical studies of cumulative growth processes

Research into identifying the processes of cumulative causation has been far less in evidence than empirical studies to test the neoclassical growth model. This is mainly because research into regional growth disparities during the past decade has been dominated by efforts to test the neoclassical growth model and to measure the long-run convergence of regional per capita income levels within national economies.

This focus on long-run equilibrium in neoclassical growth models has inevitably meant that the demand side of the regional economy has been ignored. Once it is admitted that the demand side of the regional economy has a role to play in the process of growth, the time dimension becomes critical. We are no longer in the very long-run world of neoclassical economics, but in the medium-term world of the policy maker and of those economists who stress the role of cumulative causation in determining regional disparities in economic growth. Unfortunately, there is still a severe shortage of empirical work on how the demand side and the supply side of the regional economy interact with each other in the growth process. Efforts have been made to address this deficiency by investigating regional growth disparities over the medium term, which usually means one or two decades in empirical analyses of economic growth.

Two medium-term empirical analyses of regional growth disparities are discussed here. The first is concerned with disparities in per capita GDP growth between the EU's major cities during 1979–90. The second investigates disparities in economic growth between the eastern and the western regions of China in the period following the economic reforms in 1979 which opened up the Chinese economy to world trade and capital flows.

Disparities in economic growth between cities in the EU

A detailed empirical analysis of disparities in the growth of GDP per capita between the major cities of the EU has been carried out by Cheshire and Carbonaro (1996). The motivation behind the Cheshire and Carbonaro study is to establish whether the EU's regional policy is consistent with what we know about the causes of regional growth disparities in Europe. The aim is to identify the main causes of regional growth disparities in the EU in order to discover whether concerns over the effect of economic and monetary integration on these disparities are justified.

Several potential determinants of regional growth disparities are identified:

1 *Industry mix*   The particular mix of industries in which a region specializes is expected to have some effect on a region's growth performance since some industries have more growth potential than others.

2 *National factors*   Regions located in rapidly growing countries are likely to benefit from their more favourable location compared with regions located in slow growing countries.

3 *The location of the region in relation to market potential*   The increasing economic integration within the EU through the reduction of tariff barriers and through enlargement as new member states have been admitted has led to an increase in the size of the European market. But this has been more beneficial to some regions than others depending upon their location in relation to the geographical distribution of the population. Those regions on the geographical periphery of Europe may have been disadvantaged by their geographical location compared with those regions nearer to the centre.

4 *Agglomeration economies and diseconomies*   Regions vary considerably in size and population density and these differences may have some effect on growth. Larger regions, for example, may benefit from agglomeration economies, but as the density of population increases and economic activity intensifies, congestion will occur and the land costs will increase.

5 *Endogenous growth through technological innovations*   Regions with more R&D activities will benefit from knowledge creation provided that this new knowledge does not rapidly transfer to other regions, as assumed in neoclassical growth models. One constraint, for example, is the use of new knowledge within existing organizations which are able to protect their discoveries, at least temporarily. The high concentration of R&D workers in specific regions may therefore be expected to generate advantages which result in faster growth for these regions.

6 *Spillover effects from other regions*   If regions within commuting distance are growing rapidly, this could have a detrimental effect on the growth performance of the region since its production costs will be forced up as workers are attracted by jobs being created in neighbouring regions. But longer-distance migration will alleviate the labour shortage over the medium term. Moreover, regions in close proximity to each other may benefit from trading relationships, which means that growth will spill over into contiguous regions.

To test their regional growth model, Cheshire and Carbonaro construct a database for 118 urban regions in the EU. Each region has a population of at least one-third of a million residents and the dependent variable in the statistical analysis is the growth rate of GDP per capita between 1979 and 1990. The explanatory variables were found to explain 60 per cent of the variation in growth between these urban regions. Several variables were found to be significantly positively correlated with the growth in GDP per capita in a multiple regression analysis of urban growth disparities. These were as follows:

- the growth rate of the national economy in which a region is located
- the growth of neighbouring regions
- the population of a region
- the number of R&D establishments (per capita)

These results suggest that growth is indeed cumulative since there appears to be a spatial clustering of rapidly growing regions. Moreover, the largest regions tend to be growing more rapidly than smaller regions, indicating that there may be significant scale economies to be gained from the growth process. Finally, the positive relationship between the number of R&D establishments and the growth of per capita income is consistent with the predictions of endogenous growth theory. The extent to which R&D determines growth and the extent to which it is a consequence of growth, however, are still open questions.

From a policy viewpoint, there does appear to have been a cumulative causation process at work in the regions of the EU, at least during the relatively short time period covered by the Cheshire and Carbonaro study. The fact that larger regions have a high endowment of R&D establishments and are in close proximity to other rapidly growing regions indicates a role for regional policy at EU level if regional growth disparities are to be controlled. Cheshire and Carbonaro conclude that their empirical analysis of regional growth disparities in the EU supports an interventionist strategy.

Spatial dualism in China

China has traditionally been characterized by regional dualism, with the provinces on the eastern seaboard experiencing higher levels of economic development than the inland provinces due to their proximity to world trade routes. It is therefore not surprising to find that the gap between the eastern and western regions of China has widened in the period since the 1979 economic reforms opened up China to world trade after the closed economy policy of the Maoist period (1949–76). This regional dualism has been investigated by Sun (1995; 1998), who shows that the coastal provinces in the east have benefited far more from the opening up of the Chinese economy than the inland provinces in the west.

The economic disparities between the eastern and western regions of China are clearly apparent from table 4.5. This shows that the gap between these two parts of China has widened substantially during the past two decades. The eastern region has increased its share of national GDP from 73 per cent to nearly 79 per cent, and the per capita income gap has increase from 85 per cent to over 140 per cent. On investigating the reasons for the widening gap between the eastern and the western regions, Sun (1998) identifies a number of explanatory factors. These include the following:

Table 4.5   Regional economic disparities in China, 1978–96

Socio-economic characteristic	Eastern region[a]	Western region[b]	Ratio of east to west
Population (% of total)			
1978	59.7	40.3	1.48
1995	60.1	39.9	1.51
GDP (% of total)			
1978	73.2	26.8	2.73
1995	78.8	21.2	3.72
GDP per capita (1978 prices)			
1978	488	264	1.85
1996	2483	1023	2.43
Growth rate of GDP per capita			
1978–96	9.3	7.0	1.33
Openness of economy (%, (exports + imports)/GDP)			
1978	10.7	0.9	–
1995	30.2	6.4	–
Dependence on primary sector (%)			
1980	23.7	36.0	–
1996	16.1	27.0	–
Foreign direct investment (%)			
1983–96	88.8	11.2	–

[a] The eastern region includes the 11 coastal provinces.
[b] The western region includes the 9 provinces in the interior of China.
Source: Sun (1998)

- there is a more favourable mix of industries in the eastern region, which has been far less dependent on agriculture than the western region
- the eastern region has much easier access to international trade than the western region due to its coastal location
- the eastern coastal provinces have found it much easier to attract foreign direct investment
- the eastern region has had much higher rates of domestic investment than the western region
- the Chinese government has promoted the economic development of specific growth zones in the eastern provinces

The Chinese government has consciously encouraged the concentration of both domestic and foreign investment in the eastern coastal provinces due to the growth potential of this region compared with elsewhere in China. The government's aim has been to concentrate both private and public investment so that the gains from a growth-pole strategy could be used as a foundation for further growth. This policy is based explicitly on the notion that growth is a cumulative process, as discussed earlier in this chapter. Scarce resources have therefore been deliberately geographically concentrated in order to exploit the internal and external economies of scale that are so crucial to determining economic growth. The preference of inward investors for locations along the coast has been allowed to override any longer-term regional development considerations in order to shift the Chinese economy into a new economic era. The expectation is that this will have spillover effects on the economically backward western provinces over the longer term.

Although regional growth disparities may be inevitable for developing economies because of the need to concentrate scarce resources in the regions with the greatest potential for growth, Sun (1995) argues that action is needed in China to reduce the rapidly growing gap between the eastern and the western regions. Such action is needed not only to prevent serious economic and social problems arising, such as increasing congestion in the coastal provinces and the further demise of the western provinces due to the selective nature of migration, but also to exploit the growth potential of China's vast interior.

The way to do this is to create greater economic linkages between these two regions so that the growth of the eastern region stimulates economic development in the western region. The domestic market needs to be much more integrated and one of the ways of achieving this is to improve transport links to the western provinces so that transport costs are reduced. The western provinces would then become more attractive to domestic and foreign investors as locations for new productive capacity, especially since labour costs are likely to be much lower in these economically depressed parts of China. Other infrastructure investment on a par with the investment in infrastructure in the coastal regon is also required in order to improve the competitiveness of these isolated regions. Unless serious attempts are made to divert investment and growth to the western provinces, there is little evidence that the gap between these two regions will stop widening. In other words, there is a powerful case for a policy specifically designed to induce the western provinces to catch up with the eastern coastal provinces. Regional priorities need to be changed in China if the potentially serious problems arising from unbalanced regional growth are to be avoided.

4.9 Conclusion

There is still no consensus among economists about the causes of regional growth disparities in spite of several noteworthy attempts to construct models of regional growth during recent decades. This lack of consensus is not surprising, however, in view of the immensely difficult task faced by researchers in the field of economic growth.

Recent developments in regional growth theory divide roughly into three categories: neoclassical models stress supply-side influences on growth; Keynesian-type models stress the importance of the demand for regional exports in the growth process; and cumulative causation models stress the self-perpetuating nature of the growth process. Attempts have been made to incorporate the principle of self-perpetuation into all growth theories, including the new growth theory based upon endogenous growth. But these models are still in their infancy and require further development if they are to prove successful in explaining regional growth disparities and in identifying the major determinants of growth. Regional growth theory still has a long way to go and therefore a long future lies ahead of it.

This does not mean that no progress has been made. Indeed, there has been a re-emergence of interest in the potential significance of external economies of scale resulting from the geographical clustering of industry and the role of these economies in the growth process. There has also been more interest in undertaking empirical work on regional disparities in growth, particularly since the recognition by the member states of the EU that greater economic integration has implications for regional disparities in economic welfare. Without the continual testing of theoretical models, regional growth theory will become sterile and academic.

It is clear that much more work needs to be done if growth theory is to become a useful device not only for explaining historical disparities in regional economies but also for providing policy makers with reliable guidelines for constructing policies capable of influencing regional disparities in economic welfare. Growth policy is very much on the agenda of policy makers, who have realized that regional policy has a major part to play in influencing future economic outcomes at local, regional and national levels.

Further reading

North (1955); Myrdal (1957); Kaldor (1970); Dixon and Thirlwall (1975); Thirlwall (1980; 1983); Swales (1983); McGregor and Swales (1985); McCombie (1988a; 1988b; 1992); Cheshire and Carbonaro (1996); McCombie and Thirlwall (1997); Audretsch (1998); Hanson (1998); Krugman (1998).

chapter five

Interregional trade

contents

A thorough understanding of why regions specialize in the production and export of particular commodities would be a major step forward. Regions, like nations, must actively trade if they are to be prosperous and successful. As with nations, more prosperous regions tend to run balance of payments surpluses while less competitive regions experience deficits. In the United Kingdom, for example, there is evidence that only the relatively prosperous South East and East Midlands regions routinely run balance of payments surpluses, with the remainder in deficit (PA Cambridge Economic Consultants 1990). Much work still needs to be undertaken, however, if the determinants of regional trade and specialization are to be fully understood. Research is particularly hampered by the lack of regional trade statistics. In addition, *interregional* trade differs in one very important respect from *international* trade: a region trades with other regions within the nation as well as with the rest of the world.

The distinguishing feature of interregional trade is that it is much freer than international trade. To begin with, geographical distances between regions are usually smaller than distances between nations. But this provides only part of the answer. The great distances between many of the US states, for example, do not prevent close trading links between them. Of more importance is the institutional and monetary framework. Interregional trade enjoys the advantage of a single currency with none of the uncertainties of exchange rate fluctuations. An

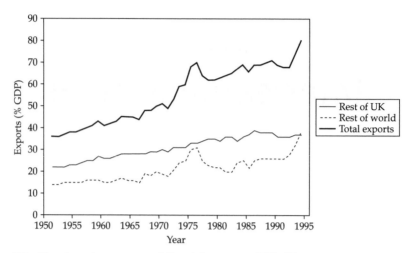

Figure 5.1   The changing pattern of Scottish exports, 1951–95.
Note: Total exports comprise exports to the rest of the UK and rest of the world (shown on figure), together with oil and gas exports from the Continental Shelf (not shown). The latter comprise the vertical difference between the total exports line and the sum of the other two lines.
Source: Gibson et al. (1997), tables 1.1A and 10. Reproduced with the permission of Glasgow Caledonian University and Cogent Strategies International Ltd

integrated national capital market and banking system also facilitates trade. Few of the many tariff and non-tariff barriers that impede international trade exist between regions. Of course, frictions to trade exist even at the regional level. Regional policy itself, for example, distorts trade through the subsidies it provides to industries in assisted areas. Barriers to trade are nevertheless still much lower between regions than between nations.

The openness of regional economies can be illustrated by drawing on data from the Scottish input–output table (Henderson 1984; Gibson et al. 1997), one of the few sources of reliable trade data at a sub-national level in the UK. In 1995, Scotland's exports were equivalent to 80 per cent of its GDP (up from the equivalent 1979 figure of 69 per cent). Half of these exports went to the rest of the UK and the other half to the rest of the world, though these proportions varied from commodity to commodity. Over time, this degree of openness of the Scottish economy has steadily increased. Figure 5.1, for example, which sets out Scottish exports from 1951 to 1995 (expressed as a percentage of GDP), shows the inexorable growth of Scottish exports. Total exports include oil and gas exports from the offshore Continental Shelf of Scotland, which accounts for part of the surge in exports from the late 1970s. However, exports to the rest of the UK and exports to the rest of the world, both of which exclude offshore oil and gas, indicate that the degree of openness of the Scottish economy has steadily increased. The fact that exports to the rest of the world from Scotland have recently overtaken exports to the rest of the UK is an indication of the growing importance of trade between UK regions and member states of the EU. It should be noted, however, that the *interregional* component of Scottish trade (i.e. trade with other regions of the UK)

Table 5.1 The increasing 'openness' of EU[a] member states' economies, 1960–96

Member state	Percentage of GDP			
	Exports of goods and services		Imports of goods and services	
	1960	1996	1960	1996
Belgium	38	75	39	69
Denmark	32	36	33	33
Germany	9	28	17	25
Greece	7	16	14	24
Spain	9	30	7	28
France	15	27	12	23
Ireland	30	82	36	65
Italy	13	28	14	23
Luxembourg	86	93	72	80
Netherlands	46	57	44	50
Austria	24	45	24	44
Portugal	16	36	21	45
Finland	23	41	23	32
Sweden	23	45	23	38
United Kingdom	21	32	22	29
EUR15	20	32	19	30
USA	5	12	5	14
Japan	11	12	10	10

[a] The EU refers to post-1996 membership of 15 member states (EUR15).
Source: European Commission, *European Economy: Convergence Report 1998*, Directorate-General for Economic and Financial Affairs, no. 65, 1998, Statistical Annex, tables 36, 40

continued to grow as a percentage of GDP, both before and after UK entry into the EU in 1973. Increased openness is therefore apparent in all of the main component elements of trade.

There is no doubt that a combination of freer world trade and EU integration is increasing the degree of openness of UK regions. Indeed, the removal of remaining trade barriers under the Single Market legislation, and the emergence of a single EU currency in 2002, suggest that EU member states will soon more closely resemble regions rather than nations in their trading relationships. This is strongly borne out by table 5.1, which shows how rapidly exports (as a percentage of GDP) have grown over time for EU member states. In the case of the United Kingdom, for example, exports of goods and services rose from the equivalent of 21 per cent of GDP to 32 per cent between 1960 and 1996. Other member states showed even more radical increases. Notice how some of the smaller member states, such as Ireland and the Netherlands, are already as open, or more open, to trade as the regions of larger member states such as the UK. Luxembourg, for example, had a level of exports equivalent to 93 per cent of its GDP in 1996.

The evidence presented above, fragmentary though it is, shows that regional economies rely heavily on trade for their economic wellbeing. Understanding why some regions are more successful exporters than others, and why different regions specialize in the production and export of different commodities, is therefore vital. Attempts to understand regional trade specialization inevitably begin with international trade theorems. Since regions trade directly with the rest of the world, the determinants of international trade have immediate relevance for a region. There are good grounds, in fact, for believing that most international trade theorems are appropriate not only for the international component of a region's trade but for the interregional component as well. Indeed, traditional trade theory was initially developed with interregional as well as international trade in mind.

While international trade theory throws some light on the determinants of regional trade, it does not tell the whole story. There is no single explanation of regional trade specialization, nor is it likely that a single explanation awaits discovery. Instead, we are faced with a rich and interesting pot-pourri of theories and ideas. To add to the fascination, the international trading system of which regions are a part is itself undergoing rapid change.

The present chapter examines the main explanations of regional trade specialization, beginning with traditional Ricardian and factor proportions explanations. This is followed by a discussion of how interregional movements of capital and labour require modifications to be made to traditional trade theory to make it relevant for explaining regional trade and specialization. More modern theories, such as those which examine the phenomenon of *intra-industry* trade, and those emanating from *competitive advantage* and *new economic geography* models, are examined in the final section.

5.1   The basis of regional trade specialization

The Ricardian explanation

Ricardian trade theory is an obvious starting point since it is the basis of more elaborate explanations discussed later in this chapter. Consider an economy with only two regions, East and West. In the initial pre-trade (or autarky) position, each region produces two commodities for its own consumption – textiles and steel (see table 5.2). The East is more efficient than the West in the production of *both* commodities. It takes two workers to produce a unit of textiles and

Table 5.2   Ricardian comparative advantage: an hypothetical example

Commodity	Number of workers required per day to produce one unit of each commodity[a]	
	East	West
Textiles	2	5
Steel	20	125

[a] Each number in the table is the inverse of the average product of labour. If it takes 2 person-days to produce one unit of textiles, 1 person-day will produce half a unit of textiles.

20 workers to produce a unit of steel in the East, whereas it takes five workers to produce a unit of textiles and 125 workers to produce a unit of steel in the West. The East has an *absolute* advantage in the production of *both* commodities.

Absolute differences in efficiency, however, are irrelevant as far as trade is concerned. Provided that a region has a *relative* advantage in the production of a commodity, trade will be advantageous. The East, for example, is relatively more efficient at producing steel while the West is relatively more efficient at producing textiles. To see why this should be so, we must look at the opportunity cost of producing steel and textiles. If the East were to produce one more unit of steel, it would have to transfer 20 workers from the production of textiles, thereby losing 10 units of textiles (since each unit of textiles requires two workers for its production). The opportunity cost of a unit of steel in the East is 10 units of textiles. In the West, 125 workers must be transferred from textiles to produce an extra unit of steel, which means that 25 units of textiles will have to be forgone (since each unit of textiles requires five workers for its production). It follows that the East is relatively more efficient in steel production. On the other hand, to produce one more unit of textiles the East must give up 1/10th of a unit of steel while the West must give up only 1/25th of a unit of steel. The West is therefore relatively more efficient in textile production.

The existence of *comparative advantage* creates the possibility of mutually advantageous trade between the East and the West, provided that barriers to trade are low. We have seen that one extra unit of steel 'costs' 10 units of textiles in the East, whereas an extra unit of steel 'costs' 25 units of textiles in the West. With these internal exchange ratios of 1 : 10 in the East and 1 : 25 in the West, it is clear that the East can obtain more textiles per unit of steel by trading steel for textiles with the West than by transferring resources into textile production at home. The East will therefore specialize in steel and export it to the West. The West will do the opposite.

With steel flowing from East to West, and with textiles flowing from West to East, both regions will be better off. Suppose the new 'world' exchange ratio settles at 1 : 15. The gains from trade to both the East and the West can be seen by comparing the initial exchange ratios with the newly established 'world' exchange ratio. The East can buy 15 units of textiles from the West for each unit of steel it exports whereas it can only produce 10 units of textiles by giving up the production of one unit of steel. The West reaps similar gains. To produce an extra unit of steel, the West must give up 25 units of textiles, whereas it can obtain an extra unit of steel by selling only 15 units of textiles to the East.

That trade is based on comparative advantage and not absolute advantage is universally accepted and rarely tested. Much more controversial is whether Ricardian theory offers a convincing explanation of what causes a region to have a comparative advantage in a commodity. In table 5.2 it can be seen that the underlying cause of the comparative advantage is regional differences in labour productivity, shown in the table as the number of workers required to produce a unit of output. Why labour productivity should vary between regions is not exactly clear. In view of the many restrictive assumptions on which the Ricardian model is based the only possible explanation is differences in regional technology.

As might be expected of such a simple theory of regional trade specialization, it does not seem to explain much when confronted with actual patterns of regional specialization (Dixon 1973).

The factor proportions explanation

The failure of regional differences in unit labour costs to explain much, if any, of the observed pattern of regional output specialization is not surprising. Labour, after all, is not the only factor of production, and a more realistic explanation would give other factors of production a role to play. This is precisely the aim of the factor proportions theory developed by Heckscher and Ohlin. Not only does it improve on the Ricardian explanation by introducing other factors of production such as capital, it also attempts a succinct explanation of the causes of comparative advantage.

We begin with the simplest version of the Heckscher–Ohlin theorem. Only two factors of production exist, labour and capital. The underlying *cause* of comparative advantage is the initial endowment of labour and capital within each region. A region endowed with a lot of labour, for example, will specialize in commodities which require a lot of labour (relative to capital) in their production. Consider a simple two-region economy in which the East is capital-abundant whilst the West is labour-abundant. There are two goods – steel and textiles. In the pre-trade situation, both regions produce both commodities. Production of steel is capital-intensive and production of textiles is labour-intensive in both regions. The Heckscher–Ohlin theorem predicts that the capital-abundant East will specialize in the production and export of steel, the capital-intensive commodity. Similarly, the labour-abundant West will specialize in the production and export of textiles, the labour-intensive commodity.

To see why this should be so, it is necessary to set out the basic elements of the Heckscher–Ohlin theorem in a little more detail. In the East, the price of labour is high compared with the price of capital since labour is the scarce factor. The East will therefore use less labour and more capital in producing a unit of steel than is the case in the West. Since the price of labour is high relative to the price of capital in the East (say at F_e in figure 5.2), this region will have an incentive to use a production method requiring a low labour/capital ratio to produce steel (R_e^s). The opposite argument applies to the West.

A similar argument relates to the production of textiles. To produce one unit of textiles, the East selects a labour/capital ratio of R_e^t whereas the West selects the higher ratio of R_w^t (see figure 5.3). Notice that textile production remains more labour-intensive than steel in both regions. The function relating relative factor prices (P_L/P_K) and factor combinations (L/K) is therefore further from the origin for textiles than for steel. In other words, textile production is assumed to require a higher labour/capital ratio than steel at all possible prices of labour relative to capital.

A relationship between factor prices and product prices can now be established, as figure 5.4 shows. Consider the labour-abundant West. Labour is cheap relative to capital (at F_w) and so the price of the labour-intensive commodity

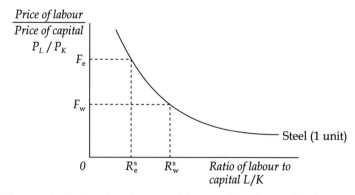

Figure 5.2 Factor abundance and factor prices: the steel industry.

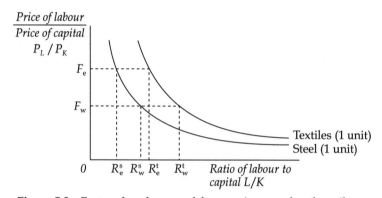

Figure 5.3 Factor abundance and factor prices: steel and textiles.

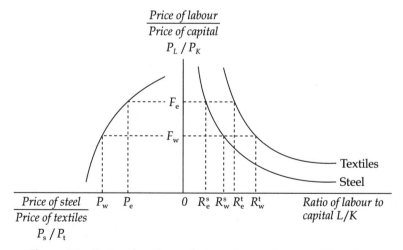

Figure 5.4 Factor abundance, factor prices and commodity prices.

(textiles) will be low relative to the price of the capital-intensive commodity (steel). The opposite situation pertains in the East: capital is the relatively cheap factor and so the price of steel can be expected to be low relative to the price of textiles. The price of steel relative to the price of textiles is therefore low in the East (P_e) and high in the West (P_w).

In a world of two regions, two factors of production and two commodities, the labour-abundant region has a comparative advantage in the production of labour-intensive commodities, and the capital-abundant region has a comparative advantage in the production of capital-intensive commodities. In our example, the labour-abundant West emerges with a high price of steel relative to the price of textiles; and the capital-abundant East ends up with a low price of steel relative to the price of textiles. It is precisely this difference between the pre-trade price ratios that creates the possibility of gains from trade, as indeed is the case in the earlier one-factor Ricardian model of comparative advantage.

The Heckscher–Ohlin theorem has a powerful intuitive appeal. One would expect the capital-abundant East to have low capital prices as the result of its endowment of capital. This in turn should give it a comparative advantage in steel. An identical argument would lead us to expect the West to specialize in textile production. This seductive logic, however, rests on the following highly restrictive assumptions:

1 There are only two factors of production – labour and capital.
2 Factors of production are qualitatively identical in both regions.
3 Each region's endowment of capital and labour is fixed.
4 Production functions are identical in both regions. (This assumption removes the possibility that comparative advantage will arise from regional differences in technology.)
5 Production functions exhibit constant returns to scale.
6 Perfect competition exists in the commodity and factor markets of both regions.
7 Trade is free from all obstructions – such as tariffs or transport costs.
8 Production of steel is capital-intensive and production of textiles is labour-intensive at all possible sets of factor prices (i.e. there exists 'strong factor intensity').
9 Tastes are identical in all regions and do not vary with regional income levels.

Some of these assumptions are obviously more restrictive than others in a regional setting. Most restrictive of all are the assumptions of perfect competition, constant returns to scale, fixed supplies of labour and capital, and only two factors of production. Relaxing these assumptions is not always fatal to the Heckscher–Ohlin theorem (see Deardorff 1979; Helpman and Krugman 1985; Staiger 1987). Nevertheless, the unreality of many of the assumptions remains a great weakness of the model. Before relaxing some of these restrictive assumptions (and thus introducing a range of additional determinants of trade specialization), we shall look at the evidence which has been accumulated on the relevance of the endowments of the two basic factors of production (labour and capital) for regional specialization.

There are two distinct ways in which the basic Heckscher–Ohlin theorem has been tested at regional level. The first, the 'factor content' approach, was pioneered by Leontief (1953; 1956). It involves measuring the amounts of labour and capital required to produce (i.e. embodied in) the exports of the region. These are then compared with the amounts of labour and capital required by local producers were they to replace the regional imports by their own import-substituting production. If the Heckscher–Ohlin theorem is correct, a labour-abundant region's exports will embody more labour and less capital than import substitution would require.

The second, and more popular, method of testing the Heckscher–Ohlin theorem at regional level is the 'commodity version'. In this approach, a direct check is made on whether a region does in fact specialize in the *production and export* of commodities which intensively use the locally abundant factor. The pioneering work for this test was undertaken by Moroney and Walker (1966) for the labour-abundant southern states of the United States. Subsequent studies in both the UK and the United States provide an excellent example of the rewards and difficulties of testing economic theorems using regional data.

Attempts to test the validity for regional trade of the two-factor Heckscher–Ohlin theorem have faced enormous problems. Lack of regional trade data has meant that tests have had to concentrate on patterns of *production* specialization rather than actual *exports*. Testing has posed severe problems for researchers (Swales 1979). Despite the problems, repeated testing of the Heckscher–Ohlin theorem over the years at regional level has provided evidence that initial factor endowment can account for a significant part of regional trade patterns. In the United States, for example, a series of studies in the 1960s, 1970s and 1980s using 'commodity version' methods have shown that initial factor endowments are important. This is particularly so when natural resource endowments are introduced alongside capital and labour (Moroney and Walker 1966; Estle 1967; Klaasen 1973; Coughlin and Fabel 1988). The US studies also included 'factor content' tests. Horiba and Kirkpatrick (1981), in a 'factor content' study, were able to demonstrate that regions of the United States can effectively export their surplus capital or labour through their exports of commodities to other regions. The north of the United States, for example, a capital-abundant region, showed a net loss of capital embodied in trade. That is, the goods which it exported utilized far more capital in their production than was used in the production (by other regions) of the goods imported into the north. The north also exhibited a net gain of natural resources embodied in goods imported from other regions. The results of tests on UK data have been much less convincing (Dixon 1973; Smith 1975; Swales 1979; Harrigan 1982; 1983).

Relaxing the assumptions of the model

The evidence of these earlier empirical studies therefore suggests that neither the Ricardian model nor the simple Heckscher–Ohlin explanation based on only two factor inputs (capital and labour) can hope to explain the *whole* of the pattern of regional specialization. The Heckscher–Ohlin model, however, does explain a significant part of trade at the regional level.

One obvious way of bringing much needed realism into the analysis of regional trade is to relax the assumption of only two factors of production, labour and capital. This assumption is a travesty not only of reality but also of the original work of Heckscher and Ohlin. The importance of natural resources in the production process is self-evident. Allowing for natural resources, as we have seen, almost always improves the predictive power of the Heckscher–Ohlin theorem, particularly where resources are incorporated as factors of production in their own right (Harrigan 1982).

Next there is the assumption that labour and capital are qualitatively similar in all regions. This is obviously unrealistic. Labour skills, for instance, may differ significantly between regions and access to skilled labour may well be an important influence in the location decisions of firms. There is a need to incorporate human capital explicitly into the tests. An obvious approach is to regard human capital (i.e. skills) as an additional factor of production. As with natural resources, this frequently improves the ability of the Heckscher–Ohlin theorem to explain patterns of regional specialization. There does seem to be a tendency for regions well endowed with *skilled* labour to specialize in *skill-intensive* industries.

There is now universal agreement that tests of the factor proportions explanation of regional trade need to acknowledge the existence of a wider set of factors of production, particularly natural resources and human capital. Indeed, analyses of regional trade in the 1990s, using more realistic sets of factors of production than earlier studies, have shown that the factor proportions explanation can be relied upon to explain a surprisingly high proportion of regional trade. These are important findings, for they reinforce the view expressed earlier that the Heckscher–Ohlin theorem may be better adapted to the freer trade which occurs between regions than to the more regulated *international* trade system.

Davis et al. (1997), for example, have drawn upon Japanese data to examine whether the Heckscher–Ohlin model (with ten separate factors of production identified) is better at explaining Japan's *regional* trade or its trade with the wider *international* community. The results are striking. The model performs poorly as an explanation of Japan's *international* trade, but is significantly better when applied to Japanese *regions*. The weaknesses of the Heckscher–Ohlin theorem at the international level have long been known (Bowen et al. 1987) and, as well as explaining only part of the trade observed, the model has also been shown to have other serious deficiencies. These difficulties include a large amount of 'missing trade'. Trefler (1995), for example, finds that the levels of relative factor abundance found in different countries are often 10 to 50 times higher than the levels of the same factors embodied in a country's exports. In other words, countries are simply not exporting anywhere near as much of the types of goods predicted by the Heckscher–Ohlin theorem. These problems are not found on anything like the same scale when regional trade is analysed.

Nor are these findings of the continuing success of the Heckscher–Ohlin model confined to Japanese regions. Kim (1995; 1999) has examined patterns of regional production specialization for 20 manufacturing sectors in a sample of US states for the period 1880–1987. A 'commodity version' test of factor proportions theory is applied. The results are again striking, for 'factor endowments explain a large amount of the geographic variation in US manufacturing over time... The geographic distribution of manufacturing activities between 1880 and 1987 is explained by a relatively short list of factor endowments' (1999: 28). The key factor endowments explaining US regional trade are labour, capital and natural resources. It is true, however, that there has been a small decline over time in the explanatory power of the factor proportions explanation. Kim argues that this is probably the result of regional differences in factor endowments in the USA getting smaller as a result of factor mobility between states and as a result of resource exhaustion leading to a switch to imported natural resources. Nevertheless, within the USA it is clear that the Heckscher–Ohlin theorem still remains an important explanation of regional trade specialization.

In order to understand why the factor proportions explanation remains a valid one for at least part of regional trade, it is necessary to look again at the main assumptions of the Heckscher–Ohlin model. An assumption that is vital for the model's success is 'strong factor intensities'. This asserts that an industry which is, say, capital-intensive at one factor price ratio will also be capital-intensive at all other factor price ratios (i.e. in all different regions). The 'strong factor intensities' assumption is rarely violated at regional level because factor prices differ less between regions than between nations. Hence factor reversals are much less likely to occur in the case of regional trade.

Similar comments also apply to two other key assumptions. The first is the assumption of identical technologies in the Heckscher–Ohlin model. Regions within a single country are much more likely to share the same fundamental technology than different countries. This being so, one would expect the model to perform better for regional trade than for international trade. The second is that tastes are identical and do not vary with income levels. Regions are much more likely to be similar in their consumption habits and patterns than are different nations, a feature which has been confirmed by empirical research (Davis et al. 1997).

The relative success of the Heckscher–Ohlin model in explaining regional patterns of trade and specialization should not, however, blind us to the fact that not all regional trade can be explained. Not all of the assumptions of the model hold perfectly at regional level. Two in particular are weak: zero factor mobility and constant returns to scale.

Taking factor mobility first, the assumption that factors are in fixed and inelastic supply in each region is particularly unrealistic in the context of regional trade because it implies that there can be no interregional migration of capital and labour. The basic *cause* of comparative advantage in the theorem is local labour or capital abundance. If labour and capital are mobile, local factor supplies can be augmented by attracting extra supplies from other regions. With factor mobility, therefore, the Heckscher–Ohlin theory has greater difficulty in predicting which region will specialize in which products. This may be the reason for the difficulties of the Heckscher–Ohlin theory in predicting trade specialization in the United Kingdom, where the distance between regions is relatively small, with large-scale factor mobility being the norm (Smith 1975).

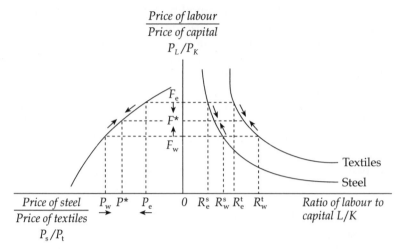

Figure 5.5   Regional trade and factor price equalization.

Regional trade and factor migration are linked in another way. The factor price equalization theorem predicts that free trade will tend to equalize regional factor prices. In our earlier example, the labour-abundant West has a comparative advantage in the production of textiles, while the capital-abundant East has a comparative advantage in the production of steel. This is reflected in figure 5.5 by the high price of steel relative to textiles in the West (P_w) and by the opposite situation in the East (P_e).

Once trading begins between these two regions, we find that the East concentrates on the production and export of steel whilst the West concentrates on the production and export of textiles. The effects of this are far-reaching. The rundown of steel production in the West releases more capital than labour, steel production being capital-intensive. The growing textile industry in the West, however, requires relatively more labour than capital. Since we have assumed both factors of production are in fixed supply in both regions, the West is forced to substitute capital for labour in its production. This is indicated in figure 5.5 by a fall in the labour/capital ratio. The switch to textile production in the West increases the demand for labour, leading to an increase in the price of labour (relative to the price of capital). The reverse process occurs in the East. The result is an equalization of the factor price ratio in both regions at F^*. Similarly, the commodity price ratios are equalized at P^*. It can be shown that *absolute* factor prices will also tend towards equality between regions.

The relationship between trade and regional factor prices is an important one. In each region, specialization of production for export effectively increases the derived demand for the previously abundant factors, and simultaneously decreases the derived demand for scarce factors. The result is a tendency, *even in the absence of factor migration*, for regional factor price differences to narrow. 'Commodity trade thus serves as a perfect substitute for factor mobility, since such trade implies the equalization of factor prices even under conditions when factors of production are immobile' (Krauss and Johnson 1974: 199).

Looking at this from a slightly different perspective, a region with abundant labour and low wages effectively exports the surplus labour in two ways: directly through out-migration, and indirectly in the form of labour services embodied in the goods in which it specializes for export. Trade therefore acts as a substitute for migration in allowing regions to use their abundant factor intensively. This is beneficial in two ways: (1) factor prices are equalized between regions; and (2) the economy as a whole is better off because trade and specialization are more efficient than autarky. All regions gain from trade.

We should not expect too much of the factor price equalization theorem. Its assumptions are many and restrictive. Nevertheless, free trade acts as a powerful equilibrating mechanism, and one which has been shown to be far more effective than factor migration in equalizing factor prices.

Finally, it must be acknowledged that the assumption of constant returns to scale is also extremely unrealistic at regional level. Even if there are no internal plant economies, the existence of external and agglomeration economies has long been recognized. For some industries, highly populated and highly industrialized areas may be the best locations irrespective of their factor endowment. It is extremely difficult to measure external and agglomeration economies or to allow for them in tests of trade theory, yet this does not mean that they have insignificant effects on regional trade specialization. Relaxing the assumption of constant returns to scale has led to the emergence of radical new explanations for regional trade, and it is to these that we now turn.

5.2   More modern theories of regional trade

Extended versions of the Heckscher–Ohlin theorem, particularly those incorporating natural resources and human capital as additional factors, have an important role to play in explaining patterns of regional specialization. It is clear, however, that these extended versions are not in themselves sufficient. Following the lead set in the field of international trade, attention is now increasingly switching to more radical explanations.

Three explanations radically different from the Heckscher–Ohlin model are examined here. The first is the possibility that regional trade exhibits the kind of *intra-industry trade* revealed at the international level (Grubel and Lloyd 1973). The second is the view that regional trade is based upon *competitive advantage* rather than *comparative advantage*. The third is the set of explanations for trade emanating from *new economic geography* models.

Intra-industry trade

The phenomenon of intra-industry trade has received much attention in recent years. In the various theories of trade so far examined, regions are assumed to concentrate on their own distinctive products which they export in exchange for *different* products ('inter-industry trade'). It has become apparent, however, that there is a substantial amount of intra-industry trade between regions (i.e. the exchange of virtually identical products) in addition to inter-industry trade. Regions, like their national counterparts, sometimes exchange very similar products.

The origins of intra-industry trade lie in the failure of perfect competition (an important assumption of the Heckscher–Ohlin theorem) to emerge in trade situations. The apparently rapid growth of intra-industry trade has led to a large literature on trade where imperfect competition exists. Intra-industry trade is essentially the result of two forces: the desire of modern consumers for a wide *diversity in the choice* of products; and *economies of scale* at the level of the firm. (See Greenaway and Milner 1986 and Greenaway et al. 1995 for some alternative variants of the basic model.) The result of these forces is the gradual loss of share in the domestic market as imports of close substitutes flood in to meet local consumers' desire for choice. Simultaneously, however, the local producers can invade markets elsewhere with their own distinctive brands of what is essentially the same commodity, and thereby maintain output at a high enough level to enjoy economies of scale.

There seems to be a close relationship between how closely integrated economies are, and the amount of intra-industry trade which takes place. This is certainly the case within the European Union. Neven (1990) has shown that the more highly integrated northern member states (e.g. the United Kingdom, Germany, Belgium, France and the Netherlands) show a high volume of intra-industry trade with one another. More recent EU members (e.g. Greece, Portugal) tend to have less intra-industry trade and more of the traditional inter-industry trade typical of the Heckscher–Ohlin model.

Some care must be exercised in analysing intra-industry trade. There are actually two distinctive types (Greenaway et al. 1995). *Horizontal* intra-industry trade occurs when regions or countries exchange goods which are slightly differentiated from one another, but of roughly similar quality. This is the type discussed above. There is, however, a second type. *Vertical* intra-industry trade occurs when regions or countries exchange goods within the same industry sector, but where the goods are of differing quality and are drawn from different stages in the production chain. It is thought that this latter type of intra-industry trade may well be determined by factor endowments in the traditional manner.

It has recently been shown that anywhere between 25 and 40 per cent (depending on which country is considered) of trade between the EU and Eastern Europe is intra-industry trade (Aturupane et al. 1999). However, only 10–20 per cent is horizontal intra-industry trade. The rest is vertical intra-industry trade, with Eastern Europe providing cheaper intermediate goods for Western European industries. A similar phenomenon has been noted among US border regions, with US manufacturers trading intermediate inputs with Mexican assembly plants in regions on the other side of the border (Hanson 1998).

Lack of trade data prevents a thorough *regional-level* analysis in Europe, but the much greater degree of integration among regions within each EU member state suggests that intra-industry trade is likely to be well established already at sub-national level. It would be interesting to know if more prosperous regions (e.g. the South East and East Midlands) have developed a large volume of intra-industry trade while more depressed regions (e.g. the North East of England and Scotland) have preserved more of the inter-commodity type of trade. What type of intra-industry trade exists between regions would also be very interesting. No data exist, however, to examine this.

Competitive advantage and regional trade

Perhaps the most welcome development in theories of regional trade in the 1990s has been the renewal of a long-standing tradition in regional economics: that in some circumstances firms can get competitive advantages which mutually reinforce one another. The tradition that firms in one region can gain competitive cost (and hence trade) advantages over their rivals in other regions by forming a geographical cluster goes back to Alfred Marshall's original work on agglomeration economies. These kinds of effects are, however, excluded by the constant returns to scale assumption within the Heckscher–Ohlin model.

Interest in the advantages which regions and countries can gain from the clustering of industries revived dramatically with the work of Porter (1990). The emphasis here is on competitive advantage for firms faced with fierce international competition, rather than on comparative advantage. The key insight of Porter has been to show that the most successful competitive advantages have been achieved when *four* sets of key competitiveness-enhancing elements are in place. These four elements mutually reinforce one another and generate a situation of *cumulative causation*.

Good examples of this are the widely researched Italian manufacturing industrial clusters in textiles and apparel, food and beverages and household goods. These are very traditional types of manufacturing and yet have been very successfully developed in the context of clusters of firms in a number of northern Italian regions. Figure 5.6 summarizes Porter's explanation of why industrial clusters of this type are able to develop and sustain strong internationally competitive advantages. The reason, Porter argues, lies in the interaction between four essential elements which must be present for strong competitive advantage. The first is the presence of favourable *demand conditions*. A strong home market demand encourages the exploitation of economies of scale. More importantly,

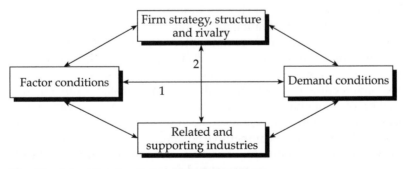

Figure 5.6 The determinants of competitive advantage.
Source: Porter (1990), figure 3–1 (2nd edn, 1998). Reproduced with the permission of The Free Press, a Division of Simon & Schuster, and Macmillan Press Ltd. Copyright © 1990, 1998 Michael E. Porter

however, are the dynamic pressures which a strong and sophisticated market of home consumers can place on local firms to ensure that they are innovative and quick to respond to changes in tastes. The second component necessary for competitive advantage is *factor conditions* (the left-hand box in figure 5.6). Again, however, this is a wider concept than the simple factor abundance of the Heckscher–Ohlin model. Factors of production are not just inherited in the Porter model. They can be actively developed and refined over time, with specialized factors (e.g. labour with highly specific skills) being distinguished from general-ized factors. The third key element in Porter's model of competitive advantage is *firm strategy, structure and rivalry*. As well as the need for strong competition between firms, this part of the Porter model stresses the need for society to create the best possible context in which firms can be created, organized and managed. It is as much to do with corporate governance as industrial structure. The final element is *related and supporting industries*. There are many advantages in firms having ready access to supply chain industries and close proximity to related industries.

The key to the Porter model is the interactions existing within a region (shown by the two-way arrows linking the boxes in figure 5.6). It is these interactions which establish and sustain competitive advantage. Take, for example, arrow 1 on the diagram. This links demand conditions and factor conditions. A strong home demand for particular commodities is likely to stimulate firms or the government to set in place training methods which rapidly lead to a buildup of a uniquely skilled local workforce. This will help to maintain the competitive advantage of the region. Another example is provided by arrow 2 in figure 5.6. This links the 'firm strategy, structure and rivalry' box with 'related and supporting industries'. Here the presence of a group of local rival firms encourages specialist supplier firms to set up in the same region. Once again competitive advantage is enhanced. Similar examples can be shown for all of the linking arrows in figure 5.6.

Although initially designed to try to explain the competitive advantages of *nations*, it was quickly realized that Porter's approach offered equally powerful insights into how *regions* can develop mutually reinforcing competitive advant-ages. The Porter model is not a formalized one, unlike the other theories set out in this chapter. It does, however, draw upon a large case study research literature which has examined industrial clusters in many nations. Not all successful clus-ters have the same set of advantages or, indeed, all four elements in figure 5.6. Other researchers also have sometimes stressed different fundamental factors underpinning competitive advantage. Kay (1996), for example, stresses a combina-tion of strategic assets (e.g. control of a resource), innovativeness, reputation and industry 'architecture' (e.g. subcontracting and franchising arrangements) as key determinants of competitive advantage. Nevertheless, whatever variant is adopted, it is clear that attention has once more been focused on forces which can give a region mutually reinforcing competitive advantages in a world of ever more open trade. This concept of cumulative causation in regional trading systems has been taken forward in a much more formalized manner through new trade and new economic geography theories, to which we now turn.

New economic geography models of trade

New economic geography models have grown out of a set of *new trade theories* developed in the late 1970s and 1980s (Ethier 1982; Krugman 1979; 1980). These new trade theories were initially developed to try to explain intra-industry trade and also the phenomenon of the predominance of trade flows between the larger, developed countries of the world, neither of which can be adequately accounted for in the Heckscher–Ohlin model. By focusing on industries characterized by economies of scale and imperfect competition, the new trade theories were able to highlight the competitive advantages enjoyed by regions and countries with the biggest local markets (or best access to wider markets such as those at the geographical centre of the EU).

Many manufacturing industries exhibit the kind of economies of scale and array of differentiated products which allow them to benefit from this *home market effect*. These industries can enjoy large competitive advantages (in the form of economies of scale) by setting up production at those few locations best placed to serve the home market. Hence, 'in equilibrium, we expect to see regions with good market access experiencing some combination of higher wages (as firms . . . bid up the wage rate) and net export of manufacturing products (since they have disproportionately much manufacturing)' (Venables 1998: 3). There is now evidence for strong 'home market effects' for manufacturing industries in regional trade (Davis et al. 1997; Davis and Weinstein 1999).

New economic geography (NEG) theory has taken the 'home market effect' analysis and extended it to produce explanations for the geographical clustering of industries. In NEG models, market access itself is no longer regarded simply as given. Instead, regions getting a head start find that their market size advantage is enhanced by forces which give rise to a process of *cumulative causation*. There are differing variants of the NEG model. In the *footloose labour* models pioneered by Krugman (1989; 1991a; 1991b), once a region gets a head start and manufacturing firms begin to congregate there to enjoy the fruits of a strong 'home market effect', mobile labour is also drawn in to work in the firms. The influx of labour stimulates the home market further (a process known as 'expenditure shifting'), encouraging yet more firms to come in. With mobile labour (a feature more characteristic of regional trading systems than international trade), there is a further benefit for the growing region. Normally wages will be bid up in the region enjoying the 'home market effect'. As footloose labour floods in, however, upward pressure on wages will be kept in check. Moreover, workers in the growing region may be able to buy some of the differentiated manufactured goods at lower prices than other regions, to the extent that these goods are free of transport cost charges since they are produced locally. Since migration equalizes *real wages* between the regions, and since prices are lower in the growing region, it follows that *nominal wages* will be lower in the growing region. This is known as the 'cost-shifting effect' and adds to 'expenditure shifting' in reinforcing the competitive advantages of firms in the growing region.

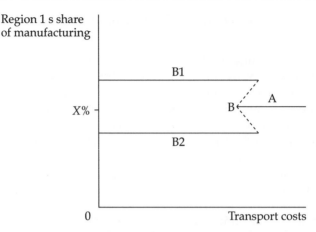

Figure 5.7   New economic geography and the concentration of manufacturing industries. *Source*: Reprinted from Krugman and Elizondo (1996), figure 4, with permission from Elsevier Science

The main alternative to the *footloose industries* version of NEG theory is the *vertically linked industries model* developed by Krugman and Venables (1995) and Venables (1996). Here the process of cumulative causation is driven not by footloose labour, but rather by intermediate goods producers gravitating to the growing region to create a cluster of firms. Close input–output linkages help to cut assembly and distribution costs, reinforcing the competitive advantages of the region with the head start.

NEG models also allow predictions to be made of how patterns of regional competitive advantage are likely *to alter over time*. In doing so, they highlight just how quickly a region's competitive advantage can be reversed. Dynamic change is introduced by allowing transport costs to steadily fall over time – a realistic assumption given improvements to transport technology and infrastructure. Falling tariffs and other non-tariff barriers will also have a similar effect. Historically, transport costs and other trade barriers were so high that the volume of trade was very low and each region was forced, even for industries with strong economies of scale, to have its own suppliers. At stage A in figure 5.7, transport costs are high and hence (in a simple two-region model) region 1 has only part (X per cent) of the manufacturing industry of the nation. Region 2 will have the remainder ($100 - X$ per cent). The solid line at stage A in figure 5.7 indicates a stable equilibrium. Broken lines indicate an unstable situation. As transport costs fall over time, the separation of production and consumption becomes feasible and concentration of manufacturing firms in one of the two regions is now very likely. Precisely which region gets the head start is often determined by very small differences between the two regions. Once a region gets a head start, great instability sets in. The onset of instability is shown at point B in figure 5.7. If it is region 1 which has the head start then a rapid shift in manufacturing firms to the region occurs (shown by the shift upwards to B1 in figure 5.7). The situation for region 2 is shown by B2 on figure 5.7. Companies in region 1 will be able to start exporting

Table 5.3 The main categories of forces affecting industrial concentration

Centripetal forces	Centrifugal forces
Market-size effects	Immobile factors of production
Thick labour markets	Land rents
Pure external economies	Pure external diseconomies

Source: Krugman (1998), table 1. Reproduced with the permission of the author and Oxford University Press

to region 2 and develop the kinds of cumulative advantages discussed earlier. The suddenness of the shift in competitive advantage between the two regions is well illustrated by figure 5.7. In some models there is a further final stage at which transport costs become so trivially low that dispersal of industry away from region 1 begins to occur (Krugman and Venables 1995). The result is not a return to autarky and a uniform distribution of manufacturing (i.e. stage A), but rather a continuation of trade but with a less agglomerated pattern of industrial location.

Perhaps the biggest problem facing NEG approaches to regional trade is that, as formalized models, they have been forced to home in on only one or two of the bewildering variety of forces which are thought to encourage industrial agglomeration. Moreover, no one is so naive as to think that there are merely agglomerative (i.e. centripetal) forces at work. There are also countervailing centrifugal forces bearing down on industries trading between regions. Krugman (1998), for example, distinguishes three main types of centripetal forces and three main sets of centrifugal forces (table 5.3). Taking the centripetal forces first, *market-size effects* refer to the advantages an industry can attain through backward and forward linkages. Locations with good access to large markets are excellent for industries with large internal economies of scale (backward linkage effects). Big markets also favour the establishment of local suppliers of intermediate goods and hence supply chain effects (forward linkages). *Thick labour markets* refer to the advantages that arise when an industrial cluster leads to the development of a large and appropriately skilled local labour force into which all of the firms can tap. *Pure external economies* are the web of additional external economies arising from informational spillovers (e.g. exchange of technological expertise). Turning to the centrifugal forces, *immobile factors* refer to those which are wholly immobile (e.g. land and some natural resources) and those where barriers to mobility are high (e.g. labour). *Land rents* deter agglomeration because increased economic activity tends to lead to them being rapidly bid upwards. Finally, *pure external diseconomies* are those spillovers such as congestion and pollution which emerge in urban and industrial agglomerations.

Most NEG models of trade have followed Krugman's initial decision to focus on only one type of centripetal force (the 'market-size effects' in table 5.3) and one set of centrifugal forces (the 'immobile factors' in table 5.3). The reasons for doing this have been widely misunderstood for 'these choices are dictated less by empirical judgement than by . . . strategic modelling considerations' (Krugman 1998: 9). The other centripetal and centrifugal forces which are omitted may or may not prove to be more important than those forces included within NEG models. Only rigorous empirical testing and future generations of NEG models will be able to resolve the question of which of the many centripetal and centrifugal forces really matter in regional trade.

There is growing empirical evidence that NEG models are correct in arguing that 'geography still matters' when it comes to trade, despite the decline over time of transport costs and other barriers to trade. Researchers such as Quah (1996), Markusen (1996a; 1996b) and Krugman and Venables (1996) continue to turn up evidence that industry remains highly clustered at the regional level within Europe and North America. Economic processes of some kind *must* be providing a competitive incentive for certain industries to agglomerate. Formal testing of NEG models is in its infancy, but some evidence in their favour is beginning to emerge. Davis and Weinstein (1999), for example, find that NEG explanations can account for the regional specialization of 8 of 19 Japanese manufacturing sectors including important industries such as steel, chemicals and electrical machinery.

NEG models also offer possible explanations of observed differences between the EU and the USA in manufacturing trade patterns. Regions in the USA exhibit greater geographical concentration of industries than do the member states of the EU. NEG models explain this by arguing that the longer history and greater degree of economic integration of US states have resulted in industrial agglomeration being much more advanced at a continent-wide scale than in the EU. That is, the USA is further along in stage B of figure 5.7 than the EU. On the other hand, the rapid recent integration of EU member states appears to be leading to increased industrial concentration at EU level (Amiti 1998; Krugman and Venables 1996).

5.3   Conclusion

This chapter has examined the causes of regional specialization in the production and export of particular commodities. The simple Heckscher–Ohlin theorem predicts that it is local factor abundance that lies at the heart of regional specialization. Detailed empirical tests of this theory indicate that the model continues to perform well as an explanation of regional trade, particularly where the trade is of an inter-industry kind (rather than intra-industry). However, it is also clear that the Heckscher–Ohlin theorem cannot adequately explain everything. In view of this, there has been a move towards the development of more radical alternative explanations.

The search for additional explanations of regional trade and production specialization has led to a focus on explanations for intra-industry trade, a rapidly growing part of total trade. In addition, there has been a welcome return to models which stress that 'geography matters' in trade. Competitive advantage theories such as those of Porter and Kay have focused attention on the possibility that the trade advantages which firms enjoy may mutually reinforce one another. New trade theories and NEG models have taken this further and restored transport costs and mutually reinforcing advantages to the heart of the explanation of why some regions attract and maintain clusters of competitive industries.

The available evidence suggests that the traditional Heckscher–Ohlin theorem can still explain a significant part of regional trade and production specialization. It cannot, however, account for the whole picture. Intra-industry trade models also play a role in explaining what is observed. So too do NEG models, which appear to perform better at the regional level than for international trade. This has led some researchers to conclude that the 'contrast in the ... significance of economic geography effects across regions versus internationally is a strong caution against accepting the view that the boundary between international and interregional economics is on the verge of vanishing due to reductions in border barriers' (Davis and Weinstein 1999: 402).

Further reading

Davis and Weinstein (1999); Helpman (1998); Kim (1999); Moroney and Walker (1966); Venables (1998).

chapter six

Interregional migration

contents

We have already seen in earlier chapters that interregional movements of capital and labour play a critical role in theories of regional development and growth. There has been little discussion so far, however, about the precise factors that determine these interregional factor flows. The assumption of neoclassical growth theory is that capital and labour respond to regional differences in factor prices. Capital is assumed to move to regions yielding the highest rates of return and labour moves to regions offering the highest real wages.

Reality turns out to be more complicated. It is the purpose of the present chapter to show that a wide range of factors influence interregional factor flows and that regional differences in factor prices are only one influence among many in determining these flows. Our discussion concentrates on labour migration in this chapter, primarily because labour migration is a more complex phenomenon than capital mobility between regions, and has therefore been the subject of a much greater volume of research.

Despite its limitations, it is useful to begin with the simple classical model of factor migration. Recent trends in migration between British regions are then examined and are shown to provide convincing evidence of the need to relax the restrictive assumptions of the classical migration model. This is followed by a discussion of alternative and in many ways more satisfactory theories of migration. The final two sections of the chapter discuss, first, the effect of economic cyclical downturns on interregional migration and, second, the extent to which migration is likely to be equilibrating in its effects on regional income inequalities and regional differences in job opportunities.

6.1   The classical theory of labour migration

The theory rests upon a number of restrictive assumptions:

- perfect competition exists in all markets
- production functions exhibit constant returns to scale
- factor migration is costless and there are no other barriers to migration
- factor prices are perfectly flexible
- factors of production are homogeneous
- owners of labour and capital are completely informed about factor returns in all regions

The theory is best illustrated with an elementary example. The economy is assumed to consist of two regions, East and West. For simplicity, each region is assumed to produce the same commodity and to use the same production technology. Each region is assumed to have an identical capital stock which is wholly immobile. Given that the labour market is perfectly competitive, the real wage must equal the marginal revenue product of labour for employers to be maximizing profits. Since the marginal product of labour declines as the level of employment increases (because of diminishing returns), more labour will be employed only if the real wage falls. This provides us with the demand for labour, which is identical in the two regions since identical production functions have been assumed. On the supply side of the labour market, more labour will be supplied as the real wage increases. Initially, the supply functions for labour are assumed to be identical in both regions. Since both the demand for labour and the supply of labour are identical in the two regions, it follows that the wage differential will be zero.

The power of labour migration to bring about factor price convergence can now be shown. To do this, it is necessary to disturb the idyllic situation shown in figure 6.1a. In a changing world, regions will experience fluctuations in both the demand and supply for labour. Consider, for example, the effect of a decrease in the supply of labour in the East. This could occur gradually as a result of natural population change, or more suddenly through, for example, the raising of the

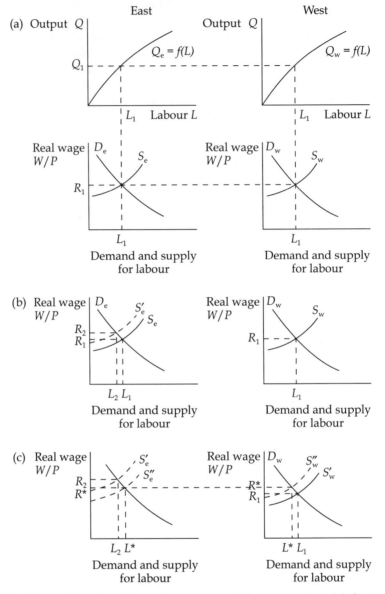

Figure 6.1   The equilibrating effects of interregional labour migration: (a) the initial position; (b) the supply of labour falls in the East and a real wage differential emerges; (c) labour migration removes the real wage differential.

school-leaving age or the reduction of the retirement age. This labour supply function shifts from S_e to S'_e in the East, as in figure 6.1b. Under the assumption of wage flexibility this results in an increase in the real wage in the East from R_1 to R_2. A regional wage differential R_1R_2 has thus emerged.

Given perfect information and the lack of costs or other barriers to migration, there will be a movement of labour from the West to the East in response to this real wage differential. In-migration into the East leads to an outward shift in the labour supply function in that region, while out-migration has the opposite effect in the West, as in figure 6.1c. Labour migration will continue until identical wage rates are re-established in both regions. The new equilibrium will be established at R^*, at which point the motivation for further migration vanishes. In addition to eliminating the real wage disparity, the migration also gives rise to a real allocative gain to the nation. Workers have migrated from the West, where the marginal product is low, to the East, where it is high.

The classical model of migration has been constructed under the most extreme assumptions. It should be no surprise, therefore, to find that its predictive performance is poor. The next section examines the actual behaviour of migrants and highlights the many serious flaws in the classical model. It also points the way to a more realistic analysis of labour migration.

6.2   Interregional migration in Great Britain, 1961–96

Table 6.1 sets out the pattern of regional population change in each British region during 1961–71, 1971–81, 1981–91 and 1991–6. The overall population change is subdivided into that part due to natural change (i.e. the difference between births and deaths) and that part due to other changes (principally net migration). The historically disadvantaged parts of Britain such as the North and North West have suffered net migration losses throughout the entire 1961–96 period. This provides some superficial support for the simple classical model of labour migration. Indeed, had it not been for the jobs created by regional policy over the long period covered by table 6.1, net migration out of these disadvantaged regions would have been even greater.

The experience of other regions, however, has not been in accord with the classical theory of migration, particularly during 1971–81 when the South East experienced substantial out-migration. Moreover, Wales and the South West experienced substantial in-migration during 1971–96. Since large parts of the South West and Wales were designated as assisted areas during this period, the net inflow of migrants into these two regions may be somewhat surprising. Part of the explanation lies in the fact that both regions are attractive locations for retired persons. The net outward movement of migrants from the South East during 1961–81 is rather more difficult to explain. Closer examination of the demographic data reveals that regions dominated by large conurbations have tended to lose population, suggesting that an understanding of interregional migration is more likely to be obtained from a more detailed spatial analysis of population movements than is provided by regional data.

The out-migration from the South East for some of the sub-periods and from the West Midlands over the whole period 1961–96 may be more easily explained in terms of the out-migration from Greater London and Birmingham respectively, rather than out-migration from the South East and West Midlands *per se*. The

Table 6.1 Components of regional population change, 1961–96

Standard regions	1961–71[a,b]			1971–81[a,b]			1981–91[a,b]			Government Office regions	1991–6[a,b]		
	Popn change[c]	Natural change	Net migration[d]	Popn change[c]	Natural change	Net migration[d]	Popn change[c]	Natural change	Net migration[d]		Popn change[c]	Natural change	Net migration[d]
South East	+0.56	+0.58	−0.02	−0.07	+0.15	−0.22	+0.31	+0.26	+0.05	London/South East	+0.55	+0.36	+0.19
East Anglia	+1.22	+0.50	+0.72	+1.09	+0.17	+0.92	+0.94	+0.14	+0.80	Eastern	+0.55	+0.26	+0.29
South West	+0.99	+0.40	+0.59	+0.61	−0.08	+0.69	+0.72	−0.02	+0.74	South West	+0.52	−0.01	+0.53
West Midlands	+0.75	+0.78	−0.03	+0.08	+0.25	−0.17	+0.13	+0.26	−0.13	West Midlands	+0.19	+0.24	−0.05
East Midlands	+0.87	+0.66	+0.21	+0.52	+0.18	+0.34	+0.43	+0.19	+0.24	East Midlands	+0.53	+0.18	+0.34
Yorkshire/Humberside	+0.40	+0.55	−0.15	+0.03	+0.07	−0.04	+0.07	+0.13	−0.06	Yorkshire/Humber	+0.21	+0.17	+0.04
North West	+0.33	+0.50	−0.17	−0.27	+0.05	−0.32	−0.13	+0.14	−0.27	NW/Merseyside	+0.02	+0.12	−0.10
North	+0.20	+0.53	−0.33	−0.11	+0.04	−0.15	−0.11	+0.06	−0.17	North East	−0.02	+0.05	−0.07
Wales	+0.34	+0.36	−0.02	+0.26	+0.01	+0.25	+0.25	+0.09	+0.16	Wales	+0.20	+0.05	+0.15
Scotland	+0.04	+0.66	−0.62	−0.19	+0.11	−0.30	−0.16	+0.05	−0.21	Scotland	+0.08	+0.04	+0.04

[a] Figures are average annual changes expressed as a percentage of the regional population as at mid 1971 (for 1961–71), mid 1981 (for 1971–81), mid 1991 (for 1981–91) and mid 1996 (for 1991–6).

[b] The 1961–71 estimates refer to standard regions as defined at 31 March 1974. Estimates for 1971–91 refer to the standard regions as defined at 1 April 1974. Estimates for 1991–6 refer to Government Office regions. The principal differences of these from the standard regions are the reallocation of Cumbria from the North to the North West, and the expansion of East Anglia to incorporate parts of the South East in a larger Eastern region.

[c] Population change is the sum of natural change and net migration.

[d] The column 'net migration' also includes a number of other changes in addition to migration (notably movements in the armed forces and changes in numbers at residential establishments and prisons).

Sources: Population Monitors PP1 (various), Office of Population Censuses and Surveys; *Annual Reports* (various), Registrar General Scotland; *Regional Trends* (various), Office of National Statistics; *Key Population and Vital Statistics: Local and Health Authority Areas*, series PP1 no. 19, Office for National Statistics, The Stationery Office, 1998; Office for National Statistics © Crown Copyright

Table 6.2 Gross and net migration for metropolitan and other areas of England and Wales, 1996

Government office regions[a]	Gross in-migration (000s)	Gross out-migration (000s)	Net inflow (000s)	Net migration rate per 1000 population
Tyne & Wear MA	21.5	26.0	−4.5	−4.0
Rest of North East	28.4	30.1	−1.8	−1.2
Merseyside MA	23.9	29.2	−5.4	−3.8
Greater Manchester MA	49.1	56.8	−7.8	−3.0
Rest of North West	69.6	66.6	+3.0	+1.0
South Yorkshire MA	26.2	29.7	−3.5	−2.7
West Yorkshire MA	41.9	48.6	−6.8	−3.2
Rest of Yorkshire and Humber	45.2	42.6	+2.5	+1.6
London	158.3	204.9	−46.6	−6.6
Rest of South East	217.9	190.2	+27.8	+3.5
West Midlands MA	48.2	66.8	−18.6	−7.0
Rest of West Midlands	76.2	68.3	+7.9	+3.0
East Midlands	97.6	90.8	+6.8	+1.6
Eastern	133.5	116.0	+17.6	+3.3
South West	133.0	105.6	+27.4	+5.7
Wales	53.1	51.3	+1.8	+0.6

[a] MA: Metropolitan Area.
Source: Key Population and Vital Statistics: Local and Health Authority Areas, series PP1, no. 19, table 3.1, Office for National Statistics, The Stationery Office, 1998, Office for National Statistics
© Crown Copyright 1998

other side of the picture is one of a movement of people into the rural areas and small towns of East Anglia, the East Midlands and the South West. Two distinct processes therefore appear to be at work. There is a north–south drift of migrants from less prosperous to more prosperous regions, and there is a drift of people away from large cities and towards smaller towns and rural areas. These two regional processes are also accompanied by an intra-urban phenomenon: the large long-term flows of migrants from central city areas to the suburbs.

Just how serious the migration losses are from the big cities of England is revealed by table 6.2. In 1996, all seven of the major metropolitan areas of England experienced large-scale net outward migration. With the exception of the North East, the rural and semi-rural remainders of the regions all experienced large-scale net inward migration. Moreover, the East Midlands, the Eastern region, the South West and Wales (all characterized by the absence of a large metropolitan area) experienced net inward migration. The coexistence of long-distance inter-regional migration and short-distance urban–rural migration (much of which occurs within the boundaries of individual regions) represents a phenomenon which any theory worth its salt has to be capable of explaining.

Once allowance is made for the movement of retired persons and for urban–rural shifts of the population, the pattern of interregional migration in Britain appears to offer some support for the classical theory of migration. There has been a distinct net drift of population away from the traditionally less prosperous regions in the north to the traditionally more prosperous regions in the south. An

Table 6.3 Interregional gross migration in Great Britain, 1996 (thousands)

Destination region[a]	Origin region[a]									
	North East	North West	Yorkshire/ Humber	East Midlands	West Midlands	Eastern	London/ South East	South West	Wales	Scotland
North East	–	6	8	3	2	3	9	2	1	4
North West	7	–	18	10	13	7	23	8	9	8
Yorkshire/Humber	10	19	–	15	8	8	18	6	3	5
East Midlands	4	10	18	–	15	15	25	7	3	4
West Midlands	3	13	8	13	–	8	23	12	8	3
Eastern	3	7	8	13	8	–	79	10	4	5
London/South East	10	29	23	25	27	59	–	51	14	17
South West	3	11	7	9	16	13	64	–	10	5
Wales	1	11	3	3	9	3	13	9	–	2
Scotland	4	7	5	3	3	4	13	4	2	–
Balance of inward and outward movements[b]	–7	–10	–6	7	–10	17	–12	29	0	–8

[a] Government office (GO) regions used throughout, except for the North West (which combines Merseyside and North West GO regions) and London and South East (which combines the London and South East GO regions).

[b] Balance of inward and outward movements is obtained by subtracting the region's row total from its column total. The balance ignores net migration associated with movements to and from Northern Ireland and the rest of the world.

Source: Regional Trends 1998, table 3.12, Office for National Statistics, London, Office for National Statistics © Crown Copyright 1998

examination of gross migration flows between regions, however, throws considerable doubt on just how effective the classical migration process is in reality. Net migration statistics conceal the important fact that gross migration between regions far exceeds net migration. In particular, a substantial amount of apparently perverse migration occurs. Thus London and the South East simultaneously attracted 29 000 migrants from the North West and lost 23 000 migrants to the North West during 1996 (see table 6.3). Focusing solely on interregional movements (i.e. ignoring flows to and from overseas countries), net out-migration in 1996 was 106 000 for GB regions as a whole, whereas gross out-migration flows amounted to 1 224 000 persons.

The existence of what are apparently perverse migration flows can be explained in part by the fact that labour is not homogeneous. As well as including non-workers, the migration data also include workers with many different skills. Regions which are on average low-wage regions may be high-wage locations for particular types of workers or for particular migrants. There are, however, a variety of other explanations of these perverse migration flows which are not so favourable to the classical model. A substantial number of migrants are return migrants who move back to their region of origin because of disappointed expectations. Others are moving for individual advancement, even though their destination may be a low-wage area for the majority of workers (Creedy 1974). Many may be moving as part of a career plan or because of a company transfer policy (Vanderkamp 1971; Salt 1990). The closer one gets to the interregional migration data, the more complex and varied the determinants of migration appear to become. Relying on the classical approach as the sole model for explaining interregional migration flows must therefore be rejected in favour of a more complex set of determinants.

6.3 The determinants of migration: relaxing the assumptions of the classical model

Regional wage disparities and migration

Interregional migration in Britain indicates that the determinants of migration are more complex than the explanation offered by the classical model. Regional wage differences undoubtedly play a part in determining interregional migration flows, but the real world is more complicated. A migrant is more likely to be concerned with the time stream of expected earnings over the remainder of his or her working life than with current wage differences. Human capital models of migration, such as those discussed in the next section, take expected lifetime earnings into account.

The classical model of migration oversimplifies the role of income differences in migration in other ways. Typically, it is assumed that it is the income of the head of household or principal wage earner in a household which determines whether or not migration occurs. Yet many households include two or more wage earners, which suggests that the relevant income variable is household income (Cooke and Bailey 1996).

One should also distinguish between different types of migrants since each type may have different reasons for moving. Thus, new migrants are more likely to be influenced by regional income differences than return migrants (i.e. those returning to their region of origin). Migrants who move as part of a career plan (*autonomous migrants*) often move at the request of their employer rather than in response to observed income differences between regions. There is also a difference between anticipatory moves, where no job offer has been received (*speculative migrants*), and job-in-hand moves (*contracted migrants*). The former are likely to require a larger interregional income difference than the latter.

Even when only new migrants are considered, the influence of income is far from simple. The classical model implies that it is the difference in income between destination and origin regions $(Y_j - Y_i)$ which is the main determinant of migration. It can be argued, however, that while Y_j indicates only the attractiveness of the destination region, Y_i reflects two distinct influences. It reflects the attractiveness of the origin region and also indicates whether migrants are able to finance the costs of a move. There is also some evidence that regional income differences have a greater effect on the choice of a specific destination once migrants have decided to move than they have on the initial decision to move, which seems to be influenced much less by income considerations.

A further weakness of the classical model is its inability to recognize that income gains are not the only benefit sought by migrants. The non-pecuniary benefits of a job such as climate and amenity considerations also have an important role to play (Cushing 1987; Graves 1983). There is now a considerable amount of empirical evidence in the USA that amenity differences (including environmental quality and climate) play a powerful role in interregional migration decisions, and that these regional amenity differences give rise to persistent equilibrium wage differences (Schachter and Althaus 1989; Greenwood et al. 1991; Treyz et al. 1993). Indeed, there is evidence that climate and other amenity influences on migration may be so powerful that manufacturing companies may be following the locational preferences of their key employees when making location decisions (Kohler 1997).

Regional disparities in employment opportunities

One of the major deficiencies of the classical migration model is that it fails to allow for regional differences in employment opportunities. This stems from the assumption that wages are perfectly flexible and that labour markets adjust automatically to situations of disequilibrium. In reality, wage rates are very sticky in a downwards direction and predictions of the classical model are affected accordingly.

Consider a simple example. Suppose regional wages are initially equal in our hypothetical economy, but that an excess supply of labour suddenly appears in the West and this is exactly matched by the appearance of excess demand in the

East. (Note that in a more realistic situation there would be no guarantee that the total demand for labour in all regions would equal its supply.) Since wages are flexible only in an upwards direction, the excess supply of labour in the West will not lead to a fall in the real wage in that region with the result that unemployment will appear. The excess demand for labour in the East may or may not lead to an increase in the real wage in that region, depending on the speed at which labour migrates from the West to the East to fill the new jobs that have appeared. In view of the many real-world frictions to labour mobility, it is likely that migration from the West to the East will be so desultory that it will be only partially successful in eliminating the excess demand. We therefore find ourselves in the position where the East has a higher real wage than the West and where there is also a persistent unemployment differential between the two regions. By relaxing the assumption of flexible real wages, regional unemployment differentials are given a central role alongside regional wage differences as a determinant of labour migration.

Simply to assume that wage rates are downwardly inflexible may not be sufficient. There is evidence of a tendency towards wage equality across regions despite substantial regional differences in the excess supply of labour. There are several possible explanations for this. National collective bargaining by trades unions or the protection by unions of established wage differentials go some way towards explaining wage equality in different regions. This phenomenon is augmented by firms which have plants in several regions and which negotiate wages for the firm as a whole, rather than for different parts of the firm located in different regions. It has also been shown that where wages are negotiated at plant level, wages are determined by the profitability of the individual plant irrespective of local unemployment rates (Walsh and Brown 1991). Situations such as this indicate the irrelevance of the assumption of perfect competition in regional labour markets. To the extent that the necessary wage 'signals' to migration fail to appear, it is regional differences in unemployment and job opportunities which become the main determinants of migration.

There is no doubt that employment opportunities have a strong influence on migration. The relationship, however, is far from simple. The unemployment rate is not always a good indicator of job prospects in regional labour markets. Furthermore, migration, employment and unemployment are mutually interdependent variables. Indeed, migration should be ideally modelled as part of a labour market system where each part comes to simultaneous equilibrium (Muth 1971; Vanderkamp 1989). Migration into a region occurs because of the employment opportunities located there and will also affect those employment opportunities through the multiplier consequences of increased spending on locally provided goods and services. This, in turn, will have further effects on migration. Migration and employment opportunities are therefore simultaneously related.

Nor should the mistake be made that unemployment always increases migration by inducing the unemployed themselves to migrate. It is true that unemployment (or the threat of it) will trigger job search activity and hence greater migration for those directly affected (Pissarides and Wadsworth 1989; Kitching 1990; Jackman and Savouri 1992a). Research has shown that in Britain the unemployed are about 1.8 times more likely to migrate than those in jobs (Hughes and McCormick 1990).

However, the relationship is a complex one. Manual workers, for example, are those most likely to experience high unemployment and yet this group has some of the lowest migration rates in Britain (McCormick 1997). In addition, increases in the overall unemployment rate, notably in recessions, tend to deter rather than stimulate mobility by the much larger group of people currently in a job. Overall, therefore, we observe that migration rates actually fall in recessions. (See section 6.5 for a more detailed discussion.)

The costs of migration

Two further weaknesses of the classical migration model are the assumptions that migration is costless and that migrants have perfect information. Migrants incur many costs, some pecuniary and others distinctly non-pecuniary or *psychic* (Sjaastad 1962). Sheer inaccessibility and the 'friction of distance' appear to be important barriers to migration (Molho 1995). The pecuniary costs include those resulting from the cost of buying and selling non-movable assets, such as houses and other property, and the costs of transporting movable assets. In addition, the migrant may have to forgo income temporarily while searching for a job in a new location. The non-pecuniary costs result from the uprooting of families and from the difficulties of settling into an unfamiliar location.

Although these non-pecuniary costs are extremely difficult to quantify, a rough measure of the total (pecuniary and non-pecuniary) costs of migration can be obtained by estimating the implied cost of distance. This is obtained by seeking an answer to the following question: by how much would a migrant's income have to be raised to induce the migrant to move one more mile? The answer is obtained by comparing (1) the responsiveness of migration to a £1 increase in the income of the destination region with (2) the responsiveness of migration to a 1 mile increase in distance. The results are interesting. Grant and Vanderkamp (1976), for example, discovered that interregional migrants in Canada of average income and moving average distances would require additional income greatly in excess of the *pecuniary* marginal cost of migrating to induce them to migrate an additional mile. The implication is either that non-pecuniary costs predominate or that lack of information poses a serious barrier to migration. It is highly probable that the non-pecuniary costs of migration are so formidable that many households will often prefer to engage in long-distance daily commuting rather than have to bear the full costs of migration (Jackman and Savouri 1992b; Cameron and Muellbauer 1998). It has recently been shown for the UK (Green et al. 1999) that this tendency to substitute long-distance commuting for migration is increasing over time, affects regions such as the South East much more than others, and is particularly prevalent among males in high-status non-manual occupations (see table 6.4).

Since both the pecuniary costs and the non-pecuniary costs of migration can be expected to increase with distance moved, and since migrants will be less well informed about distant regions, one would expect interregional exchanges of

Table 6.4 Some selected characteristics of long-distance weekly commuters in the UK

Characteristic	Group	% of commuters[a]
Gender	Male	77.7
	Female	22.3
Full-time/part-time status	Full-time	86.8
	Part-time	13.2
Permanent/temporary job	Permanent	87.9
	Non-permanent	12.1
Major occupational group	Managerial and administrative	21.8
	Professional	15.9
	Associate professional	12.5
	Clerical and secretarial	7.1
	Craft and related	11.2
	Personal and protective services	12.1
	Sales occupations	3.8
	Plant and machine occupations	9.4
	Other occupations	6.2
Job-related move in last year?	Take up new job	1.3
	Job relocated	1.7
	Some other reason	9.0
	Not moved	88.0

[a] Each characteristic sums to 100%.
Source: Green et al. (1999), table 4. Reproduced with the permission of John Wiley and Sons Ltd

labour to diminish as distance increases. This is precisely what happens: for Britain as a whole in a typical year around 85 per cent of migrants moving for employment reasons are *intraregional* migrants. Only 15 per cent of moves cross a regional boundary. Over two-thirds of all household relocations in Britain are over distances of less than 10 km.

Further complexities of the migration process

Another interesting feature of migration is that migration between prosperous regions is often greater than migration from depressed to prosperous regions. Thus, migration from the South East to the Eastern region and to the South West is substantially greater than to all other regions in the United Kingdom (see table 6.3). There are a number of possible explanations for this. First, those persons with the higher incomes typical of prosperous regions are more likely to be able to meet the pecuniary costs of migration. Second, prosperous regions tend to be contiguous and there is a powerful tendency for migration to occur between nearby regions rather than between non-contiguous regions. Third, prosperous regions are likely to have a larger stock of people who have already migrated at least once. Having migrated before, and having broken social and family ties, the non-pecuniary costs of *further* migration will be much lower than the initial migration. Individuals who already have experience of migration are more likely to migrate a second time.

Repeat migration of this type has received considerable attention (Da Vanzo 1983; Greenwood 1985). Migrating for a second or subsequent time is made easier by lower psychic costs since family ties and the like have already been broken. Many repeat moves, however, are the result of the first move being made on the basis of inadequate information. In a world of inadequate information, it is inevitable that many migrants will experience disappointed expectations and will choose to re-migrate. Migration becomes an act of information gathering, of learning by doing, and the costs of gathering information for subsequent moves are therefore reduced (Herzog and Schlottmann 1983).

Some re-migration will be to entirely new regions. Many migrants, however, choose to go back to their region of origin (Bell and Kirwan 1979). Although some return migrants are retired persons and others are moving as part of deliberate company transfers, the majority are *discouraged migrants* who originally migrated on the basis of inadequate information. An interesting issue is why so many discouraged migrants choose to return home rather than move on to other locations. Information again is probably the key. The migrant's home region is attractive because the discouraged migrant has better information about it and may even have *location-specific capital* there, such as job contacts or cheap accommodation with family or friends (Da Vanzo 1983).

The complexity of the migration process should not be underestimated. Regional wage differences of the type stressed by the simple classical model do play a role, though this is rarely as strong an influence as is often thought (Jackman and Savouri 1992a; Hughes and McCormick 1994). Traditionally it was thought that it was the *characteristics of the origin and destination regions* which were the main determinants of migration (e.g. wages, employment opportunities, climate and environment). More recent research has stressed two further groups of determinants:

- the institutional framework within which migration takes place
- the personal and family characteristics of migrants

The importance of the institutional framework in affecting migration reflects the failure of labour and other (e.g. housing) markets to operate in a perfectly competitive manner. The behaviour of institutions can have a profound impact on migration. Staffing and promotion policies of employers affect the behaviour of significant numbers of migrants, particularly within-firm career moves or 'autonomous' migrants (Sell 1990; Salt 1990). Other institutional factors which affect migration are those operating in the *housing market* (e.g. local authorities and financial institutions); those operating in the *labour market* (e.g. recruitment agencies and government Jobcentres); and the *government* itself through its taxation and unemployment benefit policies. The effect of these institutional factors can be very great. In Britain, for example, waiting lists and other restrictions on access to local council housing are known to have hindered migration (Hughes and McCormick 1981; 1987; McCormick 1997). Regional differences in property prices in the private sector, again arising from market imperfections, can also act as significant barriers to interregional migration (Bover et al. 1989; Jackman and Savouri 1992a; Cameron and Muellbauer 1998; Henley 1998). Similarly, unemployment benefits can deter job search by unemployed persons and hence reduce their likelihood of migrating (Goss and Paul 1990).

The personal and family characteristics of migrants are also now recognized as strongly influencing migration flows. Family ties, the need to consider the career of one's partner as well as one's own career, the effects of divorce, and lifecycle effects such as migration at retirement, are all important determinants of the decision to migrate (Mincer 1978; Snaith 1990; Green 1997; King et al. 1998). Migration is also highly selective at a personal level, with younger and more highly educated individuals being more likely to leave their home region (Antolin and Bover 1997). Lastly, there is the *migrant stock effect*. Migrants tend to follow in the footsteps of previous generations of migrants. A community of earlier migrants in a destination region opens up a channel of reliable information for friends and relatives 'back home' and can also reduce migration costs, both pecuniary and non-pecuniary.

6.4 Alternatives to the classical theory of migration

The human capital model

Migration is clearly a more complex phenomenon than is suggested by the classical model. An array of alternative models of migration now exist. One of the most enduring of the alternative theories has been human capital theory (Sjaastad 1962; Cooke and Bailey 1996). This is far richer in its predictions than the classical approach, though it does have the disadvantage of requiring a much greater amount of information before predictions can be made.

The supreme advantage of the human capital model is that it does not assume the existence of a timeless world in which workers respond instantaneously to current regional wage differences. Instead, the migrant is assumed to respond to the higher earnings that can be expected from migration over his remaining working life. Migrants, like other members of society, exhibit a positive time preference. The sooner the benefits of migration accrue, the more attractive will be the move. For this reason, the higher earnings which the migrant can expect to enjoy are expressed as a present value, with a discount rate being used to incorporate the influence of a migrant's time preference. This can be written as follows:

$$R_{ij} = \sum_{t=1}^{T} \frac{y_{jt} - y_{it}}{(1 + d)^t}$$

where R_{ij} is the gross present value of the lifetime increment to earnings expected to result from the migration from region i to region j; T is the number of years of working life remaining; $1/(1 + d)^t$ is a discount factor, where d, the discount rate, measures the time preference of migrants; y_{jt} is the expected earnings of the migrant in region j (the destination region) in year t; and y_{it} is the expected earnings of the migrant in region i (the origin region) in year t.

More rigorous human capital models also allow for risk and uncertainty, factors that undoubtedly play a crucial role in migration decisions. The existence of risk and uncertainty stems partly from poor information about economic and social conditions in other regions, and partly from the dangers of subsequently becoming unemployed. The greater the uncertainty, the less attractive a proposition will migration become (Pickles and Rogerson 1984). Human capital models have been successfully extended into a *risk-theoretical framework*, with adjustments being made to allow for the way a migrant's *expectations of the future* are formed – the terms y_j and y_i in the above equation (Brennan 1967; Molho 1986).

Another enormous advantage of the human capital approach over classical migration theory is its ability to incorporate all the costs and benefits of migration. There is no attempt to assume away any of the costs of migration. Potential migrants are assumed to weigh *all* the costs and benefits of migration, and the net present value of migrating from one region to another is expressed as follows:

$$PV_{ij} = R_{ij} - C_{ij}$$

where PV_{ij} is the net present value of migrating from region i to region j; R_{ij} is the gross present value of the time stream of expected benefits (pecuniary and non-pecuniary) of migrating from region i to region j; and C_{ij} is the gross present value of the expected costs (pecuniary and non-pecuniary) of migrating from region i to region j. If PV_{ij} is positive, the discounted value of the benefits exceeds the discounted value of the costs, thus making migration a worthwhile venture. The benefits of migration, as we have seen, consist principally of a time stream of higher earnings, but they may also include non-pecuniary benefits such as better working conditions in the destination region, or a superior social and environmental milieu. The costs of migration comprise both cash outlays and 'psychic' costs.

The greater realism of the assumptions underlying human capital models means that they offer a more acceptable explanation of a whole range of migration behaviour. Consider two examples. Perverse migration from prosperous to depressed regions can be accounted for in several ways by the human capital approach. As well as allowing for the fact that depressed regions may be high-wage regions for some occupations or individuals, it is also possible that the *expectations* of migrants may favour what is currently a depressed region. The human capital approach is even capable of explaining situations where migrants in the same occupational category, and receiving the same wage, move in opposite directions. This will occur if different migrants attach different weights to the non-pecuniary costs and benefits of migration.

A final example of the explanatory power of the human capital approach is its ability to account for the observed selective nature of migration. Migrants are typically drawn disproportionately from the ranks of younger workers, the skilled, and the highly educated. Figure 6.2, for example, shows that in 1996 the highest

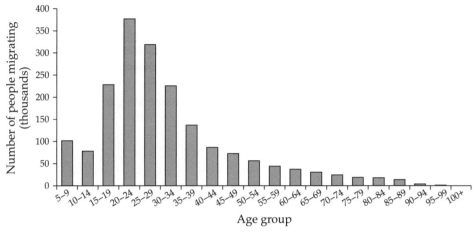

Figure 6.2   Internal migration by age group within the UK, 1996.
Source: Vickers (1998), figure 6, Office for National Statistics © Crown Copyright 1998

mobility rates in Britain were among 20- to 30-year-olds, and thereafter mobility declined sharply with age. This bias towards younger workers is explained by the longer remaining working lifetime over which the costs of migrating can be recovered. Younger workers have more time to recoup any additional costs that have to be borne, for example, when a change of job necessitates an element of retraining.

Workers in managerial, professional and non-manual occupations also exhibit far greater mobility than manual workers. Highly educated and professional workers are particularly mobile. There may be several reasons for this, one being the existence of greater earnings differentials between regions for this specific group. Another reason is that these workers have better access to information about job prospects and living conditions in other regions. Their higher incomes also enable them to meet the costs of migration more easily.

The human capital model does, however, have its problems. The primary criticism is that the model is *too successful* at explaining migration flows. Since all the costs and benefits associated with migration are included in the model, it is possible to explain *all* migration flows provided that the migrant behaves rationally. In practice, the model will include only a selection of what are believed to be the most critical explanatory variables. Migrants will not be able to consider all the 'pros' and 'cons' of migration in reality because of incomplete information.

The job search model

The failure of the human capital model to show adequately how migrants seek out and find information is a crucial weakness. Much research has therefore focused on the theory and techniques of *labour market job search analysis* (Rossi

1980; Rogerson 1982; Maier 1985; Hughes and McCormick 1990; Jackman and Savouri 1992a). In this approach, migration is viewed as the outcome of a series of search decisions (i.e. a *decision tree*), where probabilities can be estimated for each choice situation. In the approach developed by Hughes and McCormick (1994), for example, migration is modelled as a two-stage process:

1   *Top level of the decision tree*   To stay or leave the origin region.
2   *Lower level of the decision tree*   Which of the many alternative destination regions to choose.

The latter decision is an immensely complex one since many hundreds of alternative destinations are possible and each individual will have a different likelihood of choosing any one of them. Thus, the probability of individual h migrating from the origin region i to destination region j is given as

$$P_{hij} = A/B$$

Here A refers to the pulling power of region j: this in turn is expressed as a function of (1) the personal characteristics of the migrant (e.g. age, education) and (2) the characteristics of region j (e.g. employment opportunities). By contrast, B reflects the countervailing pull of all of the other possible destination regions: once again, B is seen to depend on the personal characteristics of the migrant and the characteristics of the regions themselves.

Job search models tend to be mathematically more complex than earlier migration models, but offer greater realism for the researcher. The determinants of the probability of an individual beginning a job search can be separated in job search models from those influencing the final choice of region (which itself will depend on whether the resulting job will meet the 'reservation wage' of the migrant). This is a great advance on previous theories. Nor is it just the search behaviour of the migrant which matters. The hiring behaviour of employers is also important and can be allowed for in job search models.

In job search models of migration, the distinction between *speculative migration* and *contracted migration* becomes a matter of crucial importance. For speculative migrants, migration is an integral part of the information gathering and job search process. For migrants who already have a contract for a job in the new region, migration is the *outcome* of the process and not part of the job search.

Job search models of migration have also deliberately incorporated an important feature of migration, and one which greatly reduces the ability of migration to reduce regional disparities: namely, response lags. Migration is notoriously slow in its response to the opening up of wage differentials or job opportunities between regions. At least three types of response lags exist. These are, first, lags in the flow of information from prosperous regions to potential migrants elsewhere; second, lags which arise as migrants respond to the information they receive and form expectations of what they can obtain elsewhere; and third, adjustment lags in their reaction to the expectations they have formed.

The gravity model

A discussion of migration theory would not be complete without reference to alternative theories which have been developed by disciplines other than economics. The analysis of migration is an area which has benefited greatly from the cross-fertilization of ideas between many disciplines. A migration model initially developed by geographers and which has exhibited remarkable durability has been the *gravity model*. Gravity models of migration take the general form

$$M_{ij} = f(A_i, B_j, D_{ij})$$

where M_{ij} is gross migration from region i to region j; A_i is a group of origin-specific determinants of migration flows (e.g. population level in region of origin); B_j is a group of destination-specific variables (e.g. population level in destination region); and D_{ij} is distance decay (reflecting the costs of migrating from i to j, including information search).

The gravity model is essentially based on an analogy with Newtonian physics, yet has proved very successful in forecasting many types of movement behaviour (e.g. shopping trips, interregional migration). There have been repeated attempts to show that gravity models can be reconciled with economic theory (Sheppard 1978; Anderson 1979). It has also been argued that while economic theory is best for understanding the decisions of individual migrants, the gravity model has a useful role in the statistical modelling of broad aggregate flows of migrants (Molho 1986).

A distinct advantage of the gravity model approach to explaining migration flows between regions is that it can be extended to incorporate economic variables. It was argued earlier, for example, that workers will tend to move from high-unemployment regions to low-unemployment regions, and from low-wage regions to high-wage regions. The gravity model can take variables such as these explicitly into account. An empirical test of the determinants of migration could therefore be based upon the following general model:

$$M_{ij} = f(P_i, P_j, D_{ij}, U_j - U_i, W_j - W_i)$$

where P_i is the population in region i, P_j is the population in region j, D_{ij} is the economic distance (e.g. transport cost) between i and j, U_i is the unemployment rate in i, U_j is the unemployment rate in j, W_i is the wage rate in region i and W_j is the wage rate in region j.

It is important to understand that economic theory may well have its limitations and that a certain part of migration behaviour may never be fully explained by economic concepts. Psychologists, for example, have suggested that some migration may be a response to stress in the lives of individuals, in which case some moves may be irrational in an economic sense. Something similar to this can be found in Gordon and Vickerman's (1982) view that migration may partly be the result of a logical attempt to increase utility and partly be subject to random, idiosyncratic influences. Such thoughts should not deter us from seeking the economic determinants of migration, which are clearly important influences on migrants and which are also tractable to analysis. We must, however, remain aware of the limitations of economic analysis in this field.

6.5   Migration during periods of recession

Migration is severely affected by national recessions, the most significant effect being a reduction in the gross flows of people between regions (Pissarides and Wadsworth 1989; Hughes and McCormick 1990). This can be demonstrated by examining gross migration rates during the period from the late 1970s through to the early 1990s. This period is noteworthy in that it contains within it the two most serious of the post-war British cyclical downturns: those of the early 1980s and the early 1990s. Data collected by the National Health Service (based on patients changing doctors when they migrate) allow a detailed picture of migrant flows within England and Wales to be built up for the two recessions (Ogilvy 1982; Rosenbaum and Bailey 1991). Despite quite a lot of year-on-year variability in migration rates, the lowest gross migration rates are in 1982 and 1991. These correspond to low points in the two successive recessions (see figure 6.3). The gross migration rates have continued to rise steadily since the low point in 1991 as the national economy has recovered. By 1996, for example, the gross number of moves in England and Wales had climbed by a quarter above the lowest point in the depths of the early 1990s recession (Vickers 1998).

There are numerous reasons why gross migration flows tend to fall during recessions. The human capital model points to lower rates of return from migration

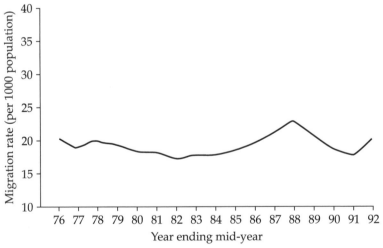

Figure 6.3   Interregional migration rates in the UK, 1976–92
Source: Stillwell et al. (1995), figure 2. Reproduced with the permission of the Regional Science Association International

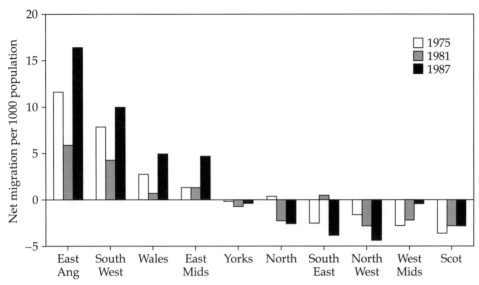

Figure 6.4 Net migration rates in the regions of Great Britain, 1975, 1981 and 1987.
Source: Office for National Statistics, *Regional Trends* (various), Office for National Statistics © Crown Copyright 1999; NHS registration data used

because of a fall in the probability of getting a job or because of lower expected earnings in previously attractive destination regions. In addition, the migrant is faced with greater uncertainty because of the difficulty of finding and holding on to a job in other regions where jobs are generally harder to find. Migrants may also be less able to finance the immediate costs of a move during a recession and may suffer greater liquidity problems (Gordon 1985; Molho 1986). Finally, there is considerable evidence that the character of migration changes during a recession: uncertain economic conditions lead to a greater number of disappointed migrants and an increase in return migration is the inevitable conclusion (Gordon 1985).

One would expect that with falling levels of gross migration during cyclical downturns there would also be a decline in *net* migration rates. There is some evidence that this is indeed normally the case. Take, for example, the very heavy recession in Britain in the early 1980s. This unusually deep recession was typical in the sense that the regions most seriously affected were those with a heavy concentration of manufacturing industries. Figure 6.4 shows net migration rates for the trough year of 1981, together with the years 1975 and 1987 on either side of the trough year. As can be seen, for several regions the net migration rates are significantly lower during the recession year of 1981. This is especially the case for those regions experiencing net in-migration. The effect of this recession was therefore to choke off a large part of the equilibrating flow of persons from the disadvantaged regions to the more prosperous regions.

The relationship between net migration and gross migration is not, however, a simple one. Even though gross migration tends to fall in recessions, this does not

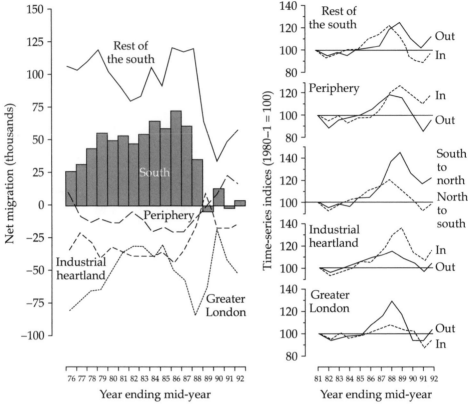

Figure 6.5   Net migration rates and gross migration indices for broad groups of UK regions, 1975–92
Source: Stillwell et al. (1995), figure 5. Reproduced with the permission of the Regional Science Association International

necessarily mean that net migration also falls. Take for example the North West region between 1975 and 1981 (see figure 6.4). Net outward migration from the North West actually increased between 1975 and 1981 despite a large fall in the gross migration rates. This was because gross out-migration fell more slowly than did gross in-migration to the North West. In summary, the effect of a recession is not only to depress the overall volume of migration, but also to trigger quite complex changes in the spatial pattern of net migration among regions.

Just how complex these effects can be has been starkly revealed by the 1990–3 recession in Britain. This was a very unusual recession in that it had its greatest effects via the property market and the financial services sector. These sectors had witnessed an unprecedented boom in the late 1980s in the South East of England. Figure 6.5 presents the results of a regional analysis of both gross and net migration in the UK between 1976 and 1992 (Stillwell et al. 1995). This analysis shows just how complex the migration effects can be of a business cycle as unusual as that of the early 1990s. Figure 6.5 shows the *net* migration estimates for the north and the south of the UK. The north comprises the periphery (North region, Scotland and Northern Ireland) and the industrial heartland (Yorkshire and Humberside, North West and West Midlands). The south comprises Greater London and the rest of the south (remainder of South East, South West, East Anglia and East Midlands). Alongside the net migration rates are the *gross* migration rates for these same broad regions (with in-migration and out-migration rates shown separately). As can be seen from figure 6.5, the low gross migration rates of the recession in the early 1980s were also accompanied by a (small) drop in net migration rates. This can be seen on figure 6.5 by the tendency of the net migration rates to move closer to the zero axis during 1979–82. It is also shown by the small fall in the volume of net in-migration to the south in figure 6.5.

The recession of the early 1990s had a dramatically different pattern of net migration changes compared with earlier years (see figure 6.5). Gross migration rates rose rapidly as the late 1980s boom ran its course, only to collapse again as the boom turned to recession in 1990–1. This was the case for both in-migration and out-migration and for all of the main regional groups. The effect on *net* migration was both startling and complex. Net migration to the south fell sharply in 1989 (i.e. at the height of the boom) and then remained unusually low through the subsequent recession. The reason for this complex shift in net migration was the surge in gross migration from south to north in 1989 and these trends continued to exceed north to south gross migration in the subsequent downturn. It is thought that this complex shift in the traditional pattern of net migration was the result of the unusual property market conditions of the late 1980s (Johnes and Hyclak 1994). The large gap in house prices made migration from north to south much harder and encouraged more moves from the south to the north (i.e. the reverse of the normal direction of movement). The subsequent recession in the early 1990s had a much greater impact on the south because of the collapse of property prices there. Negative equity reduced consumption spending in the south, leading to a sharp increase in unemployment (Taylor and Bradley 1994). The north remained relatively unscathed by the recession and this is probably the reason why net migration rates continued to remain so low. It should be noted, however, that the post-1993 recovery has again been associated with an increase in net migration and the general flow towards the south has resumed its long-run pattern (see table 6.3).

The relationship between migration flows and business cycle recessions is therefore consistent but complex. Recessions are invariably accompanied by a substantial fall in *gross* migration and are usually, but not always, accompanied by a drop in *net* migration. As has been shown, however, macroeconomic conditions are by no means the only influence on migration flows. Each cyclical upturn and downturn has its own distinctive impact on the spatial patterns of migration flows. The evidence for the late 1980s and early 1990s suggests that conditions in the housing market had a considerable impact on migration in Britain. The very low *net* migration to the south since 1988 (see figure 6.5) has reflected the deterrent effect of the historically unusual north–south difference in house prices which developed in the late 1980s.

6.6   The effects of migration: Is migration equilibrating?

Having examined in some detail the determinants of migration and the effects of recession on migration, it is appropriate to end the chapter with a brief examination of the wider impact of migration itself. It is important to distinguish between the effects of migration on the migrants themselves and the effects of migration on regional economic differentials.

As far as the migrants themselves are concerned, there is evidence that migration is beneficial and yields income gains, though these may sometimes be small (Grant and Vanderkamp 1980; Van Dijk et al. 1989). Eventually, long-distance movers do reap income gains in excess of income earned either by short-distance migrants or by those who do not move at all. The initial experience, however, and especially in the first year, is not so economically beneficial. Initially, most migrants suffer small income losses (or low income gains) and also experience higher rates of unemployment. It is these initial economic disappointments, together with the high psychic costs in the first year or two after migration, which probably account for the high volume of return migration.

Turning to the effects of factor mobility on regional income inequalities, the classical model predicts that labour migration will reduce regional differences in factor prices. The simple example used in section 6.1 assumed that capital was in fixed supply and was immobile between regions. If capital is now allowed to move freely, it can be shown that labour and capital movements will reinforce one another in equalizing factor prices between regions. In figure 6.1 we saw that a fall in the labour supply in the East led to the emergence of a higher real wage in that region. Capital can now be expected to flow towards the low-wage West since the capital owner will expect a higher rate of return on capital in regions where wages are lower (assuming a simple two-factor model). The real wage differential in favour of the East is therefore mirrored by a capital productivity differential in favour of the West. Labour flows from West to East, capital from East to West, and the combined effect of these movements is to eliminate regional disparities in wages *and* the return to capital.

In the case of labour migration there is some evidence that the net interregional flows of labour are in the expected direction: that is, towards prosperous regions. Moreover, flows are fairly substantial. This may well have had some immediate beneficial effects in reducing regional income differentials. Regional income differentials do seem to have narrowed over time. The effect of labour migration on regional disparities remains an issue fraught with controversy, and it is by no means certain that migration is the main cause of the long-term narrowing of regional disparities observed in Europe and the USA. On the contrary, research on per capita income differentials in the USA suggests that migration can account for only a small part of the observed narrowing of differentials over time (Barro and Sala-i-Martin 1991).

Some effects of migration may be less desirable. To begin with, the selective nature of labour migration not only may make it harder for depressed regions to attract the investment necessary for their regeneration, but will simultaneously improve the prospects of the more prosperous destination regions. Second, and perhaps more importantly, inflows of migrants into prosperous regions will have a cumulative expansionary effect on output, employment and incomes, while simultaneously having the opposite effects in depressed regions. By contributing to the growth of market demand in the prosperous regions, migrants enhance the attractiveness of those areas for further expansion of productive capacity. This process can sometimes be a cumulative one. Those employed by the new market-oriented industries themselves add to the demand for locally produced goods and services.

Moreover, new workers and their families will require accommodation, schooling, medical services, transport facilities and a whole range of other locally produced goods and services. Such demand is likely to be high in the first instance, the demand for housing being an obvious example. This 'lumpiness' of the migrants' initial expenditure and the consequent multiplier effects may lead to an increase in the demand for labour far greater than the increase in supply resulting from the in-migration. The immediate consequence of inward migration may therefore be the precise opposite of that predicted by the classical model: inward migration may actually stimulate further wage increases rather than reduce them.

Turning from regional wage and income disparities to differences in unemployment rates, there has again been considerable controversy on the issue of how beneficial migration has been. The fact that migration tends to fall in recessions (as section 6.5 has shown) is a strong indication that interregional migration is a very imperfect mechanism for eliminating regional unemployment problems. Opinion remains divided, however, on whether migration flows respond to regional unemployment differentials. Some researchers have found that migration between regions in the UK responds to regional unemployment differences (Jackman and Savouri 1992a; Pissarides and McMaster 1990). Others find no evidence of such an effect and argue that migration has had little impact on narrowing Britain's north–south divide (Hughes and McCormick 1994; McCormick 1997). Moreover, it has been shown that migration is a poor mechanism for reducing unemployment in geographically isolated regions which have high unemployment rates (Molho 1995). On the other hand, migration does seem to work better for many non-manual occupations (McCormick 1997), although these are unfortunately the very groups for which unemployment levels are lowest. Among manual workers, where regional differences in unemployment are the greatest, the migration mechanism appears to function worst of all.

The finding that the response of migrants to regional unemployment disparities is supported by Antolin and Bover's (1997) detailed investigation of interregional migration in Spain. Using data for a large sample of individuals of working age from Spain's Labour Force Survey, they conclude that individuals respond neither to their own unemployment nor to high unemployment in the regions in which they live. Hence, people do not move from high-unemployment regions such as Andalusia or Extremadura and into more prosperous regions. Migration is not therefore working as a mechanism for alleviating very high levels of unemployment in Spanish regions. They also find that the response of migrants to regional unemployment disparities varies between different types of workers.

The probability of a person migrating from a high-unemployment region to a low-unemployment region is heavily dependent upon their family situation and their educational qualifications. People are less likely to migrate from a high-unemployment region to a low-unemployment region, for example, if they have children and if they are not heads of households. And they are more likely to migrate from a high-unemployment region to a low-unemployment region if they are highly qualified. The personal characteristics of the unemployed therefore have a significant effect on the migration response to regional unemployment disparities.

Evidence that interregional migration is a slow and relatively ineffective process for the reduction of regional unemployment differences is widespread for many countries (Antolin and Bover 1997; Bentolila 1997; Faini et al. 1997; Groenewold 1997). The lack of responsiveness of migration to regional unemployment disparities is therefore by no means a UK phenomenon.

6.7   Conclusion

The migration of factors of production between regions plays a potentially important role in regional development and growth. Migration patterns do not, however, conform to the simple classical explanation, which argues that workers move to those regions offering the highest wages. In reality, we see workers moving *into* the traditionally depressed regions as well as *out* of them, and similarly for the traditionally prosperous regions. If interregional migration is to be explained, it is necessary to consider the effect of a wider range of determinants on migration than is allowed for in the classical model.

A major weakness of the classical model is that it assumes a perfectly competitive environment with free movement of factors of production between regions. The existence of considerable barriers to the free working of the labour market, however, together with impediments to factor mobility such as poor information flows, mean that the classical model has poor explanatory and predictive powers. More success is achieved by the human capital approach. This has a similar starting point to the classical model in that it assumes that potential migrants aim to maximize their economic welfare. It has the distinct advantage over the simple classical approach, however, that in principle it takes *all* factors affecting the costs and benefits of migration (to the migrant) into account explicitly. Even the human capital model has its weaknesses and a whole array of alternative migration models now exist.

One of the central questions raised in the analysis of migration is whether the migration process is equilibrating. Although net migration from high-unemployment regions to low-unemployment regions can be expected to help towards the reduction of regional disparities in unemployment, experience indicates that labour market adjustment via migration is very sluggish. There is the further problem that migration is itself sensitive to changes in national unemployment. As unemployment rises, job opportunities for potential migrants dry up and migration falls. It should also be obvious that interregional migration can only be expected to help to reduce regional *differences* in unemployment. It is most unlikely to be a useful device for reducing the national *level* of unemployment except when labour shortages exist in particular localities.

Further reading

Antolin and Bover (1997); Boyle et al. (1998); Jackman and Savouri (1992a); McCormick (1997); Molho (1986); Sjaastad (1962); Vickers (1998).

chapter seven

Regional unemployment disparities

contents

Regional policy exists primarily because of the persistence of regional unemployment disparities. The designation of assisted areas in the EU, for example, is strongly influenced by regional disparities in the unemployment rate, and unemployment has been the main criterion for designating assisted areas in the United Kingdom since the early 1930s. It is unemployment disparities which dominate discussions of the 'regional problem'.

Although the unemployment rate is an extremely important variable in its own right, since it is an indication of the extent to which a potentially valuable resource is being under-utilized, it is also a very important indicator of spatial disparities in social exclusion. This is clearly indicated by the high correlation between unemployment and variables such as income levels, educational attainment, the quality of jobs available, housing conditions and the quality of life more

Table 7.1 Correlation between unemployment rate and selected socio-economic variables across local authority areas in England and Wales

Variable	Correlation between unemployment rate and selected socio-economic variables[a]
% lone parent families	0.85
% of pupils eligible for free school meals	0.90
% of residents with higher qualifications	−0.67
% of pupils with five or more A*–C GCSEs[b]	−0.69
% of pupils with zero GCSEs	0.53
Truancy rate (% half days unauthorized absence)	0.56

[a] All the correlation coefficients are highly statistically significant.
[b] GCSE is the General Certificate of Secondary Education, awarded for exams usually taken by pupils aged 15–16.
Sources: Census of Population, 1991; School Performance Tables, Department for Education and Employment, London, 1996

generally. The use of the unemployment rate as an indicator of social exclusion can easily be justified. Table 7.1 shows the correlation coefficients between the unemployment rate and several key socio-economic variables in a cross-sectional analysis of local authority areas in England and Wales. Thus, the localities with the highest unemployment rates also have the highest proportion of lone parent families, the highest truancy rates and the highest proportion of pupils eligible for free school meals, which is an indication of poverty. There is also evidence of a positive relationship between regional unemployment disparities and crime rates. By contrast, the localities with the lowest unemployment rates have the highest proportion of pupils obtaining good exam results and the highest proportion of residents with higher educational qualifications.

It is therefore important on social as well as economic grounds to discover why regional unemployment disparities occur and persist. If a better understanding of the causes of regional unemployment disparities can be obtained, this should help policy makers to devise more appropriate and more effective policy instruments to reduce unemployment in high-unemployment areas.

Our aim in this chapter is therefore to explain why regional unemployment disparities occur and why they persist. Why do some regions have persistently lower unemployment rates than others? Why is the unemployment rate persistently higher in the cities than in their suburbs? Why do some towns and cities always have higher unemployment rates than other towns and cities even within the same region? Do these persistent geographical disparities in unemployment occur because markets are not working efficiently? Obtaining answers to such questions is not an easy task, but answers need to be found if effective and efficient policy instruments are to be devised for reducing these geographical disparities in unemployment.

This chapter is in six sections. The chapter begins, in section 7.1, with a brief discussion of the persistence of regional unemployment disparities in Europe and the USA. Section 7.2 outlines the conventional approach to identifying different types of unemployment, the aim being to allocate the unemployed between various causal categories. This is followed in section 7.3 by a discussion of the various approaches which have been used to estimate the various types of unemployment. Several explanations of the regional disparities in unemployment in the member states of the EU and in the USA are then discussed in section 7.4, and section 7.5 looks at socio-demographic causes of unemployment. Finally, section 7.6 draws attention to the inadequacy of regional unemployment data and suggests that participation rates need to be considered alongside unemployment rates in policy discussions.

7.1   Regional unemployment disparities: Why do they persist?

Unemployment varies tremendously between countries. Spain, for example, has had an unemployment rate in excess of 20 per cent for over a decade while its neighbour, Portugal, has experienced unemployment rates of around 7 per cent. Exactly why unemployment is consistently higher in some countries than in others is still an open and intriguing question and much research is needed to find answers to it. These international disparities, however, conceal even greater disparities between regions within countries (see table 7.2), and still greater disparities are evident between local labour market areas within regions. These spatial unemployment disparities within and between regions are of great interest to regional economists, since they provide an excellent opportunity for identifying the causes of unemployment. Before investigating these causes, it will be useful to examine the extent to which these spatial unemployment disparities are persistent over time and space.

If wages were perfectly flexible and workers could move quickly between different labour markets, labour markets would be in continuous equilibrium. This does not necessarily mean that unemployment disparities would not exist, however, since some areas may offer a more attractive living environment than others, due to better local amenities or better weather. This could lead to permanent

Table 7.2   Regional unemployment disparities in selected EU countries, 1995

Country	Number of regions	Average unemployment rate	Lowest unemployment rate	Highest unemployment rate
Spain	7	22.7	18.5	31.8
Finland	2	18.1	18.2	6.2
Italy	11	12.0	6.0	25.9
France	8	11.2	8.7	15.3
Belgium	3	9.4	6.9	13.3
Greece	4	9.1	7.4	11.0
UK	11	8.8	6.7	13.0
Germany	16	8.2	4.9	16.7
Netherlands	4	7.3	6.9	8.9
Portugal	3	7.1	4.6	7.8

Source: Regional Trends, 1997, table 2.3, 30–1

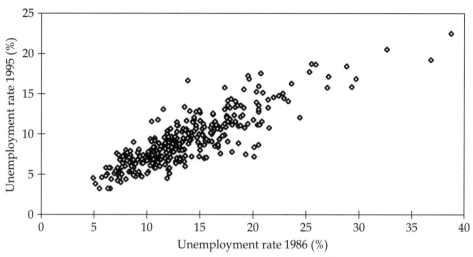

Figure 7.1 Unemployment rates in travel-to-work areas in Great Britain, 1995 versus 1986.

differences in wage rates and in the unemployment rate (Marston 1985; Carlsen 2000). These differences would then be consistent with equilibrium in each labour market area. Hence, we might expect wages to be lower and unemployment rates to be higher in areas well endowed with favourable local amenities. Divergence from these equilibrium unemployment rates would then occur only if labour markets did not clear in response to negative shocks. There is substantial empirical evidence which supports the view that persistent spatial disparities in the unemployment rate cannot be explained by corresponding disparities in the underlying equilibrium unemployment rate.

If labour markets responded quickly to demand shocks, a fall in labour demand would lead to a fall in wages (relative to other regions) and to outward migration to regions where wages were higher. In addition, capital would flow into low-wage regions as producers took advantage of lower labour costs. Indeed, there is plenty of evidence to suggest that such market adjustments do take place. The problem is that labour markets often adjust very slowly, with the adjustment process often being long and tortuous. In the meantime, unemployment disparities occur as a result of negative demand shocks affecting some regions more than others.

There is considerable evidence to support the view that labour market adjustment to demand shocks is very slow. This is true, for example, of the United Kingdom, which has had an extremely stable spatial pattern of unemployment rates over several decades. This is reflected in figure 7.1, which shows a very high correlation between travel-to-work area unemployment rates in 1986 and 1995. Similar results are obtained for local labour market areas in Germany over the period 1980–95 (Büttner 1999). There is also a high correlation over time in unemployment rates across the regions of the EU, as indicated in figure 7.2. Furthermore,

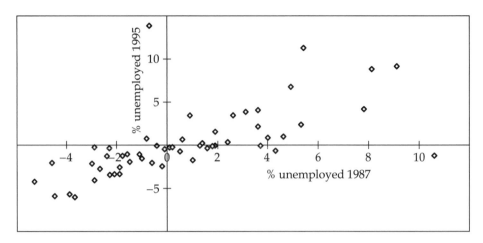

Figure 7.2   Regional unemployment differentials in the EU, 1995 versus 1987 (difference from national mean).

Table 7.3   The persistence of regional unemployment disparities in selected EU member states and the USA, 1980–94 (rank order correlations)

Country	Correlation between regional unemployment rates in each year with corresponding unemployment rates in 1980		
	1985	*1990*	*1994*
Germany	0.88	0.89	0.85
France	0.78	0.68	0.66
Italy	0.96	0.91	0.88
Spain	0.95	0.71	0.74
UK	0.88	0.82	0.77
USA	0.67	0.52	0.39

Source: Martin (1998)

detailed statistical analysis of the spatial structure of unemployment rates across the 394 regions of the EU indicates that regional disparities in unemployment have been neither converging nor diverging over the period 1983–95 (Baddeley et al. 1998a; 1998b). The spatial pattern of unemployment rates has tended to be more stable in Europe, however, than in the USA, a fact which has been interpreted as indicating greater flexibility in the US labour market. This is indicated by the higher correlation over time between regional unemployment rates in the EU than in the USA, as shown in table 7.3.

   These international comparisons suggest that the forces bringing about regional unemployment equality are weaker in Europe than in the USA (Nickell 1997). Why do European labour markets adjust only very slowly to disequilibrium situations? Several reasons have been suggested.

1   Wages are notoriously unresponsive to excess supply in European labour
    markets (Bean 1994). Trades unions resist wage cuts since they represent those
    with jobs and not the unemployed; and employers are often reluctant to
    impose wage cuts since this can adversely affect morale and therefore labour
    productivity. Wage cuts may therefore be self-defeating. Employers are also
    tied down by wage contracts – at least for the contract period – and this will
    prevent a quick response to changes in demand conditions.

2   Wages are negotiated nationally in many industries and these are then ac-
    cepted by workers and employers in all regions. This is the case, for example,
    for a substantial section of manufacturing workers in Germany (Büttner 1999).
    Acceptance of national pay scales does not necessarily mean that wages will
    be unresponsive to local labour market conditions, since actual wages diverge
    from nationally set wage rates through local adjustments such as incentive
    payments and bonuses. But the widespread acceptance of nationally negoti-
    ated wages does nevertheless induce some rigidity into the wage structure.

3   Many firms have decentralized their wage negotiating procedures to profit
    centres so that wages are tied more closely to the performance of individual
    production units within organizations (Walsh and Brown 1991). Highly profit-
    able units will therefore pay high wages regardless of the local level of unem-
    ployment. High levels of local unemployment may therefore have little impact
    on local wage levels in such cases.

4   The movement of workers from one occupation to another and from one local
    labour market to another is a costly process since such mobility will often
    involve either retraining or relocation of residence. These costs act as a deter-
    rent to inter-occupational and inter-locality labour mobility, thus slowing
    down the process of adjustment. Whether the government can do anything to
    speed up the adjustment process in local and regional labour markets is an
    interesting and important question to which we shall return in later chapters.

5   It has been argued that hiring and firing costs are particularly high in the EU,
    partly as a consequence of the EU's Social Chapter (negotiated at Maastricht)
    which aims to improve employment security and working conditions for
    employees. Employers can be expected to take considerable care over filling a
    vacancy where the costs of doing so may be very high. The existence of these
    fixed costs may have caused employers to be more selective in the recruitment
    process with the result that certain groups of unemployed workers have faced
    grave problems into trying to get back into the labour market.

Regional disparities in the flexibility of labour markets

The explanation of spatial disparities in labour market flexibility stems originally
from interest in the determinants of wage inflation. The basic hypothesis is very
simple: excess labour demand causes wages to rise, and excess labour supply
causes wages to fall. This suggests a negative relationship between wage change
and the unemployment rate. It is argued that wages will rise more quickly when
unemployment is low; and wages will rise more slowly when unemployment is

high. The degree of responsiveness of wages to the unemployment rate is measured in empirical studies by estimating the statistical relationship between wage
change and the unemployment rate. This is the well-known Phillips curve.

This basic hypothesis of wage change has been tested at national level in a vast
number of quantitative studies since the initial work by Phillips in 1958. There
have been far fewer tests, however, at regional level. One reason for this is that
inflation is often regarded as a national phenomenon, even though there may be
good reasons to believe that inflation is more likely to be generated in some
regions than in others. Labour-scarce regions, for example, can be expected to be
more likely to generate inflationary pressures than labour-abundant regions. If
this is the case, learning more about how regional labour markets operate may
help us to gain a better understanding of how inflation itself is generated.

Regional economists have been very interested in the relationship between
wage change and unemployment, however, for somewhat different reasons. They
tend to be more interested in the effect of wages on unemployment (known as the
Fisher curve) than the effect of unemployment on wages. In particular, we need to
discover whether regions in which wages are responsive to increases in unemployment have lower unemployment rates than regions in which wages are inflexible.
Hyclak and Johnes (1992a) develop a model which determines a region's unemployment rate and its rate of wage inflation jointly. Put simply, they argue (1) that
wage inflation is determined by unemployment (the Phillips curve) and (2) that
unemployment is determined by wages (the Fisher curve). They also assume that
regional labour markets are exogenous, which means that wages are determined
by labour market conditions in each region independently of labour market conditions in other regions. This joint determination of unemployment and wage
inflation is referred to as the Phillips–Fisher curve after the originators of the two
fundamental relationships in the model, which can be summarized as follows:

$$w = f(U, p^e) \tag{7.1}$$

$$\Delta U = g(w, y) \tag{7.2}$$

where w is the rate of change in the wage rate, ΔU is the change in the unemployment rate U, p^e is the expected price inflation and y is the growth in demand for
goods and services. The interaction between unemployment and wage inflation is
demonstrated in figure 7.3.

In a statistical analysis for UK regions, Hyclak and Johnes (1992b) show that the
change in the unemployment rate is (1) positively related to wage increases and
(2) negatively related to output growth. These results are not surprising since
employees are likely to decrease their demand for labour if either wages rise or
the demand for goods falls. There is also some evidence that the regions with the
highest unemployment rates are likely to be the most adversely affected by any
given increase in the wage rate. This result is consistent with the view that high-
unemployment regions are less competitive than low-unemployment regions since
any given increase in wage costs has a larger negative impact on the employment
level of high-unemployment regions.

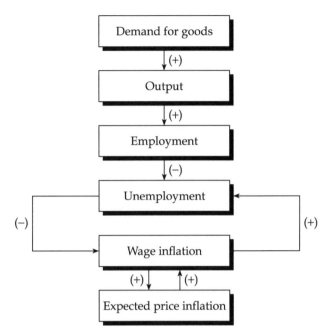

Figure 7.3   Interaction between unemployment and wage inflation.

In a similar empirical analysis of the flexibility of *real* wages in US states, Johnes and Hyclak (1995) estimate the relationship between the rate of change in wages and the unemployment rate over time for each state separately. They show that although it is usually assumed that wage flexibility is relatively high in the USA, the available evidence indicates that it varies considerably between states. The estimates of wage flexibility for the 48 contiguous states of the USA provided in table 7.4 indicate a high degree of wage flexibility in states such as North and South Dakota, Nebraska, Utah and Maryland. This compares with very little wage flexibility in Massachusetts, Connecticut, New York, New Jersey, Delaware and New Mexico. Similar results are obtained by Baddeley et al. (1998a) in a more recent study of wage flexibility of US states. Their main finding is that wage flexibility is much lower in the older industrial states in north-eastern USA than in most other parts of the USA. In other words, the slope of the Phillips curve is much flatter in the north-eastern states than in most of the mid-western and western states.

Why does the degree of wage flexibility vary between states? Several factors have been identified in empirical work which together explain over 80 per cent of the variation in wage flexibility between US states. These are as follows:

1   *The efficiency wage*   There is an extensive literature which argues that employers use the wage for inducing their employees to be more efficient. It is recognized that reducing wages during periods of slack demand can harmfully affect worker morale and hence productivity. States in which employers are more sensitive to these adverse effects on morale were found to have a lower degree of wage flexibility.

Table 7.4   The degree of wage flexibility in US states[a]

Very low	Low	High	Very high
Alabama	Arizona	Arkansas	Iowa
Connecticut	Illinois	California	Kansas
Delaware	Kentucky	Colorado	Maryland
Georgia	Louisiana	Florida	Montana
Maine	Michigan	Idaho	Nebraska
Massachusetts	Missouri	Indiana	North Dakota
Mississippi	Nevada	Minnesota	Oregon
New Hampshire	Ohio	North Carolina	South Dakota
New Jersey	Pennsylvania	Oklahoma	Texas
New Mexico	Vermont	South Carolina	Utah
New York	West Virginia	Virginia	Washington
Rhode Island	Wyoming	Wisconsin	
Tennessee			

[a] States were grouped according to the responsiveness of their wage change to the unemployment rate in time-series regressions. The expected change in price inflation was also included as an explanatory variable. The estimated coefficient on the unemployment rate is the measure of *real* wage flexibility.
Source: Johnes and Hyclak (1995: 178)

2   *The proportion of small firms*   Wage flexibility is likely to be greater in small firms (establishments with under 20 employees) than in large firms for two reasons. First, it is easier to monitor work effort in small firms and so wages will reflect the efficiency of workers more closely than in large firms. Second, small firms are more likely to be on the edge of competitiveness and will therefore monitor their wage costs very closely.

3   *Union activity*   Strong unions can prevent wage cuts during recessions, thereby reducing wage flexibility. Those workers who feel that their jobs are safe ('insiders') will therefore demand that wage levels are maintained during recessions even if this means reduced demand for labour and higher levels of unemployment as a consequence. States with the highest proportion of workers in unions will consequently have lower wage flexibility.

4   *Involuntary layoffs*   If the chances of being laid off involuntarily are high, wages will tend to be more flexible downwards since individual workers will presumably prefer a wage cut to losing their job.

5   *Minimum wages*   The imposition of a minimum wage will reduce wage flexibility since wages will be prevented from falling below the legal minimum even in the face of high unemployment. Moreover, even though the minimum wage affects only those with the lowest skill level, the need to maintain wage relativities between different groups of workers could introduce an element of wage rigidity at wage levels above the legal minimum wage.

All of the above potential determinants of wage flexibility are shown to be statistically significant in the empirical analysis of differences in wage flexibility between US states (Johnes and Hyclak 1995).

7.2 The causes of unemployment: the conventional approach

Unemployment occurs for a multiplicity of reasons. There is no single cause. This point is easily demonstrated by considering the potential effect of a region's industry mix on its unemployment rate. It might be expected that regions with a high proportion of 'high-unemployment industries' will have a higher unemployment rate than regions with a high proportion of 'low-unemployment industries'.

It is possible to measure the extent to which regional differences in industry mix account for regional differences in unemployment by constructing an expected unemployment rate for each region based upon (1) a region's industry mix and (2) national unemployment in each industry. This *expected* unemployment rate can then be compared with the *actual* unemployment rate to measure the extent to which a region's actual unemployment rate can be accounted for by its industry mix. Applications of this technique have indicated that regional disparities in unemployment cannot be explained by corresponding variations in the industry mix of regions. When national unemployment rates are applied to each region's industry mix, this results in a set of regional unemployment rates which are very similar to the national average. This result is obtained not only at regional level but also for travel-to-work areas (Taylor and Bradley 1983). This research therefore indicates that regional disparities in the unemployment rate cannot be explained by corresponding disparities in the industry mix of regions.

The finding that spatial disparities in unemployment are not accounted for by corresponding spatial variations in industry mix implies that the same industry experiences different unemployment rates in different regions. The unemployment rate tends to be high in *all* industries in high-unemployment regions and low in *all* industries in low-unemployment regions. The explanation for this appears to be that labour is far more mobile between industries (within travel-to-work areas) than it is between travel-to-work areas (within industries). There is apparently a strong tendency for unemployment to equalize between industries within travel-to-work areas; and there is a weak tendency for unemployment to become equalized within industries between travel-to-work areas. There is a very strong tendency for substantial unemployment rate disparities between travel-to-work areas to be sustained even within the same region. Travel-to-work areas which are near neighbours can have very different unemployment rates which persist for decades.

Types of unemployment

The absence of any simple explanation of spatial disparities in unemployment based upon a region's industry mix suggests that it may be more helpful to begin by identifying the underlying causes of unemployment. A simple, but useful, approach is to divide unemployment into separate categories. The following four categories are the ones most commonly used:

1 Frictional unemployment.
2 Structural unemployment.

3   Neoclassical unemployment.
4   Demand-deficient (or Keynesian) unemployment.

Although this classification is useful for distinguishing between the different underlying causes of unemployment, it should be stressed that *actual* unemployment cannot easily be divided into such categories despite several attempts to do so (see Thirlwall 1969; 1974; Armstrong and Taylor 1981). Moreover, the distinction between the various types of unemployment is fuzzy, as we shall show.

Frictional unemployment occurs when jobs exist for unemployed workers who possess the right skills and who want a job in the same area as the job vacancies, but it takes time for workers to find the right job and for employers to find the right worker for the job. Why is there a delay in matching unemployed workers to job vacancies? Workers do not necessarily accept the first job offer that comes along; they want to make sure that the job they take matches up to their expectations as far as possible. This search process takes time. A similar argument applies to employers, especially if training and recruitment costs are high. They search for workers who are expected to be a good investment over the longer term and will therefore take care, and hence time, in selecting the 'right' workers.

Two factors influence the level of frictional unemployment. First, frictional unemployment is likely to be higher during periods of economic boom since the number of workers voluntarily quitting their job tends to increase in booms and decline in slumps. The number of new entrants and re-entrants into the workforce also tends to increase during booms since there will be more job vacancies becoming available. Second, the industry mix may have an effect on frictional unemployment since the turnover rate of workers is higher in some industries than in others. Tourism, for example, has a far higher turnover rate than industries in the manufacturing sector. Areas heavily dependent on tourism can therefore be expected to have more frictional unemployment than areas dependent on the chemical industry (taking size into account).

Structural unemployment is similar to frictional unemployment in so far as unemployment and vacancies coexist. It differs from frictional unemployment, however, in that it occurs because of a fundamental *mismatch* between the unemployed workers and job vacancies. The problem with structural unemployment is that the unemployed either have the wrong skills or live in the wrong place to fill the vacant jobs. Structural unemployment can result from changes on either the demand or the supply side of the product market. On the demand side, changes in consumption lead to changes in the geographical pattern of demand as consumers switch into some products and out of others. On the supply side, technological changes result in changes in the methods of production and in the types of products being produced, and these changes affect the labour market; more labour is needed in some activities while less labour is needed in others. There may also be changes in the location of economic activity as some new locations become more attractive relative to existing locations. This happened in the 1980s in the Aberdeen region following the discovery and extraction of North Sea oil.

Once structural unemployment occurs, it tends to persist. This is because unemployed workers cannot easily acquire new skills or move to areas where there

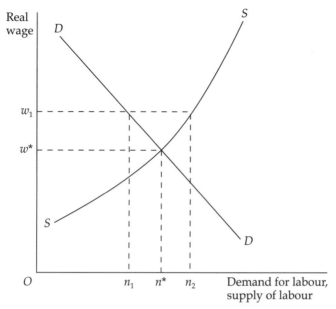

Figure 7.4   The neoclassical labour market.

is a demand for their existing skills. The costs of acquiring new skills or moving to other areas are often beyond the reach of the unemployed. Structural unemployment tends to be worse when major structural change in the economy is accompanied by slow growth and generally slack labour markets. When structural change is accompanied by rapid growth and labour scarcity, employers are far more willing to train workers, thereby reducing the skill mismatch.

The *neoclassical* view of unemployment argues that unemployment exists because real wages are too high. If the real wage is raised above its market clearing level (for example, by strong trades unions), this will inevitably result in unemployment. A typical situation is shown in figure 7.4. Unemployment of $n_1 n_2$ will persist as long as the wage remains above its market clearing level of w^*. Over the longer term, the labour market may adjust towards equilibrium as a result of outward migration as unemployed workers seek jobs in other areas. If this happens, the labour supply S shifts to the left, which raises the market clearing wage from w^* to w_1.

The neoclassical explanation of regional disparities in unemployment argues that real wages are held above their equilibrium level because high unemployment benefits and over-powerful trades unions have combined to prevent a realistic market equilibrium wage being reached. According to this argument, the best way to reduce high unemployment is to remove these labour market distortions so that lower wages will induce an increase in the amount of labour demanded (a movement down the demand curve D). In addition, lower labour costs will encourage firms to invest in new capacity, thereby shifting the demand for labour function to the right.

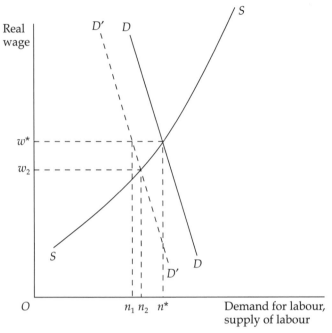

Figure 7.5   The effect on employment of reducing the real wage: the case of inelastic labour demand.

Demand-deficient (or Keynesian) unemployment occurs when there is a decline in the national level of demand. A national demand deficiency is then transformed into corresponding demand deficiencies in all regions of the economy, particularly if the decline in demand is severe. By its very nature, demand-deficient unemployment is widely dispersed throughout all regions. This inevitably results in unemployment rates in different regions being very highly correlated over time: regional unemployment rates rise and fall together. The explanation for this togetherness is very simple: no regions are immune from *national* fluctuations in economic activity because they are highly dependent on other regions for the demand for their output.

The neoclassical labour market model can be augmented to incorporate demand-deficient unemployment. We begin again at full employment where employment is n^* and the real wage is at its market clearing level of w^* (see figure 7.5). Product demand now falls and so producers reduce their demand for labour at each wage level. The labour demand function D therefore shifts left to D'. With the real wage unchanged at w^*, employment falls from n^* to n_1, resulting in a corresponding increase in unemployment. In principle, unemployment would disappear if the real wage fell to w_2. This fall in unemployment will be less than the original increase, however, since it will occur partly as a result of the fall in the supply of labour S. The original level of employment could only be achieved if product demand were to be restored to its former level. In the case of a demand deficiency, the most effective way of reducing unemployment in areas of high unemployment may therefore be to shift the labour demand function to the right by stimulating the demand for labour directly.

This discussion of the four main types of unemployment suggests that unemployment occurs for the following reasons:

1   The search for jobs by unemployed workers and the search for workers by employers take time. This results in frictional unemployment.
2   Unemployed workers may not be able to fill existing job vacancies because they have the wrong skills or live in the wrong place. This mismatch between labour demand and labour supply results in structural unemployment.
3   The labour market may be prevented from clearing because powerful unions keep the wage above its equilibrium level or because the government provides over-generous unemployment benefits. This results in neoclassical unemployment.
4   Jobs may be in short supply because of a low level of aggregate economic activity. This results in demand-deficient unemployment.

7.3   Estimating the relative importance of the various types of unemployment

Attempts to estimate the relative importance of these various types of unemployment have met with varying degrees of success. Two main approaches have been used, one based upon cross-sectional data and the other on time-series data. The cross-sectional approach utilizes unemployment and vacancy data to produce a snapshot of each region's unemployment problem at a specific point in time. The time-series approach is based upon the relationship between unemployment and vacancies over time.

Cross-sectional unemployment–vacancies (u–v) analysis

This method utilizes detailed unemployment and vacancy data for any given set of labour market areas. Provided that unemployment and vacancy data are available by occupation and by region, it is possible to identify the following three categories of unemployment.

Demand-deficient unemployment

Demand-deficient unemployment is defined as existing when the total number of unemployed in the economy as a whole exceeds the total number of job vacancies. According to UK data, this situation has occurred continuously since the early 1960s. But this is a direct consequence of the severe under-recording of job vacancies since there is no legal requirement for employers to notify job vacancies. Vacancy data therefore seriously underestimate the true level of vacancies, and by an unknown amount. The gap between total unemployment and total vacancies cannot therefore be used as a measure of demand-deficient unemployment at either national or regional level.

Frictional unemployment

Frictional unemployment can be estimated from the unemployment and job vacancies which coexist within the same occupational and geographical labour markets. Within any given geographical area at least some of the unemployed are likely to have the same occupation as some of the job vacancies.

Structural unemployment

After matching as many of the unemployed with coexisting vacancies within each geographical area as possible, the next step is to match the unemployed and job vacancies across labour markets. This provides estimates of structural unemployment. Unemployment can be reduced *within* a region, for example, if unemployed workers in occupations for which vacancies do not exist are retrained for occupations in which vacancies do exist. Similarly, unemployment can be reduced *within* occupations if unemployed workers in regions for which vacancies do not exist move to regions in which vacancies do exist (or if firms can be induced to move into high-unemployment regions). Retraining and the geographical movement of labour (or capital) are therefore ways of eliminating an occupational or a geographical mismatch between labour demand and labour supply. These two structural components of unemployment can therefore be estimated by matching unemployment to vacancies between occupations and between regions (Armstrong and Taylor 1981). Structural unemployment can therefore be subdivided into three sub-categories:

1   Unemployment due to a skill (or occupational) mismatch.
2   Unemployment due to a geographical mismatch.
3   Unemployment due to a simultaneous skill and geographical mismatch.

Although this method of estimating the various components of unemployment is attractive at first sight, serious problems arise in its implementation. The most significant of these problems is that for it to produce useful information for policy makers, far more detailed vacancy data (both by occupation and by labour market area) would be required than are currently available. This alone rules out the use of the simple matching process described above for identifying the various components of unemployment. The only advantage of this approach is that it focuses upon the two main dimensions of structural unemployment: occupational mismatching and geographical mismatching.

The matching process: placing the unemployed into jobs

An alternative way of finding out more about the matching process between the unemployed and job vacancies is to identify the determinants of the rate at which the unemployed are placed into jobs. This has been done for all travel-to-work areas in England and Wales (Coles and Smith 1996). The main object of the exercise is to examine the responsiveness of unemployment to the number of unemployed and the number of vacancies. Several other potential determinants of placings are also included in the empirical analysis. Not surprisingly, as the number of unemployed people and job vacancies increase in a locality, the rate at which the unemployed are placed into jobs will increase. This is only to be expected since the number of placings will be determined primarily by the absolute size of the labour market as measured by the number of unemployed searching for jobs and the number of jobs available.

Of greater importance for an understanding of the matching process, however, is the finding that the rate at which the unemployed are placed into jobs is negatively related to the geographical size of the labour market. This result makes sense since the larger the area, the more difficult it is for the unemployed to make contact with job vacancies. Information flows therefore appear to be a significant barrier to matching the unemployed with job vacancies in geographically large areas.

A further result is that the matching rate is negatively related to the proportion of people over 30. The result that the matching rate is lower in areas with a high proportion of older people indicates that it is easier to match younger unemployed workers with job vacancies. This may reflect the greater flexibility of younger workers. Matching unemployed workers to jobs is therefore likely to be more difficult in labour markets with a high proportion of older workers.

The only other significant determinant of placing unemployed workers into jobs is the proportion of workers employed in manufacturing in each area. This variable is positively related to the placement rate, perhaps because a larger manufacturing base provides a greater variety of jobs, and a greater quantity of semi-skilled jobs, both of which would help the matching process.

The u–v relation over time

The u–v relation traces out those combinations of unemployment and job vacancies which occur at each level of excess demand (and excess supply) in the labour market. This relation is intuitively easy to understand since it simply implies that as the demand for workers increases (relative to their supply), job vacancies will increase and unemployment will fall. Furthermore, the relationship is likely to be non-linear since there are always likely to be some workers searching for a job no matter how high the demand for labour, and there are always likely to be some employers searching for workers no matter how low the demand for labour.

This intuition can be formalized by deriving the u–v relationship from a formal treatment of the labour market. A more rigorous derivation of the u–v relation is provided by Jackman et al. (1990). Employment and the real wage are determined by the interaction between labour demand and labour supply. Suppose the real wage is above its equilibrium level w^* as shown in figure 7.6. This represents a situation of excess supply and in this case the level of employment is constrained

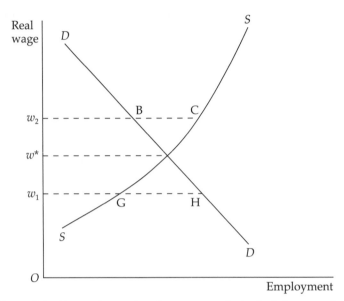

Figure 7.6   Excess demand and excess supply in the labour market.

by the demand for labour function. Unemployment will be BC, for example, when the wage is w_2. There will be no vacancies. Alternatively, suppose the real wage is below its equilibrium level at w_1. There is now an excess demand for labour, with vacancies at GH and zero unemployment. We have therefore obtained the result that vacancies and unemployment do not coexist. This does not match up with real-world experience, which tells us that vacancies and unemployment exist simultaneously. This is because of the existence of frictions in the labour market which give rise to a situation in which vacancies exist when there is an excess supply of labour ($w > w^*$) and unemployment exists when there is an excess demand for labour ($w < w^*$). In figure 7.6, for example, if the wage is w_2 then employment will be less than that shown by the demand for labour function because some employers will still be looking to fill vacant jobs in spite of the *excess supply* of labour. Similarly, if the wage is w_1 employment will be less than the supply of labour since some workers will still be searching for a job in spite of the *excess demand* for labour. This means that the actual level of employment will be less than the demand for labour when the real wage is above its equilibrium level; and employment will be less than the supply of labour when the wage is below its equilibrium level. The actual level of employment at each wage level is shown by the curve EE in figure 7.7a.

The employment curve EE can now be used to derive a relationship between unemployment and vacancies. We can see from figure 7.7a that

if $w = w_2$,   vacancies = AB and unemployment = AC (combination I)
if $w = w^*$,   vacancies = DE and unemployment = DE (combination II)
if $w = w_1$,   vacancies = FH and unemployment = FG (combination III)

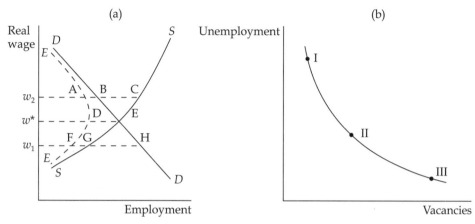

Figure 7.7   Deriving the unemployment/vacancies relationship.

These three combinations of vacancies and unemployment are plotted in figure 7.7b. Thus, the economy will move down the u–v relation (e.g. from I to II) whenever the demand for labour increases relative to the supply of labour. This will occur whenever the demand for goods and services increases (at given wage levels) or whenever the real wage falls (at given levels of the demand for goods and services) since both situations give rise to a fall in unemployment and an increase in job vacancies.

But how stable is the u–v relation? Under what circumstances will the u–v relationship shift? According to figure 7.7a, any leftward shift in the *EE* function would result in an increase in *both* vacancies *and* unemployment at each wage level. The u–v curve will therefore shift upwards and to the right in figure 7.7b whenever the *EE* function shifts to the left (assuming no change in the labour demand and labour supply functions). Conversely, the u–v relation will shift downwards and to the left whenever the *EE* function shifts to the right (with fixed labour demand and labour supply functions). Recent experience indicates that the u–v relation experienced substantial shifts (predominantly upward and rightward) in the majority of the world's industrialized nations during the 1970s and 1980s (Jackman et al. 1990). As might be expected, substantial shifts have also occurred at regional level.

What are the reasons for these shifts? Three main reasons have been suggested and investigated by researchers. First, structural shocks (such as a shake-out of labour, changes in the geographical pattern of the demand for goods and services, and changes in the types of skills required) have resulted in a severe mismatch between labour demand and labour supply. All of these factors would result in an upward shift in the u–v relation since any increase in either the geographical or the occupational mismatch between labour demand and labour supply will result in a higher level of unemployment at each level of vacancies.

Second, more favourable unemployment benefits may have caused the unemployed to search less intensively for jobs since higher benefits reduce the costs of job search (relative to benefits) by reducing the opportunity cost of being unemployed. In addition, any lengthening of the duration of benefits will have the same effect. Both will cause an upward shift in the u–v relation.

Third, an increase in long-term unemployment will shift the u–v relation upwards for several reasons. Experience indicates that the long-term unemployed are less attractive to employers than those who have been unemployed for only a short time, mainly because employers regard the long-term unemployed as having already been rejected by other employers. In addition, the unemployed lose confidence as their unemployment duration lengthens. This reduces their enthusiasm for finding a job and the search for work becomes less intense. One reason for this loss of confidence is that the skill gap between the employed and the unemployed widens as the time spent unemployed increases. This is because the employed regularly upgrade their skills as new products and new processes are introduced. This process whereby the probability of remaining unemployed increases the longer a person is unemployed is referred to as 'hysteresis'. Severe demand shocks will result in an increase in long-term unemployment, which in turn results in an increase in the underlying unemployment rate because the long-term unemployed find it increasingly more difficult to get back into employment the longer they are out of a job.

Recent work on the u–v relationship in UK regions by Jones and Manning (1992) shows that these upward shifts in the regional u–v relation are strongly positively correlated with an increase in long-term unemployment. The link between an increase in long-term unemployment and the upward shift in the u–v relation is consistent with the mismatch hypothesis since an increase in the duration of unemployment will make it increasingly difficult for the unemployed to get job offers (for the reasons discussed above).

7.4   Empirical studies of regional disparities in unemployment

We have already observed the strong tendency for regional disparities in the unemployment rate to persist over many years. There is a powerful tendency for some regions to have a persistently high unemployment rate while other regions have a persistently low unemployment rate. This section summarizes some of the recent studies that have attempted to explain this persistence in regional unemployment disparities. We begin with a study of regional unemployment disparities in Finland which attempts to estimate the equilibrium unemployment rate in each region and to show how this has been changing over time. This is followed by attempts to identify the determinants of regional disparities in the unemployment rate in the UK, the USA and the EU.

Regional unemployment rate disparities in Finland and Norway

Regions that adjust slowly to a demand shock can be expected to have a higher equilibrium unemployment rate than regions which adjust quickly. This degree of persistence has been estimated for individual regions in Finland, using time-

Table 7.5 Estimated equilibrium unemployment rates in the regions of Finland

Region	1963–75	1976–90	1991–3
Helsinki	1.0	3.0	8.9
Turku	1.5	4.5	14.8
Vaasa	1.6	4.0	12.0
Tampere	1.9	6.3	12.6
Kouvola	2.0	5.3	17.2
Jyväskylä	2.6	6.2	13.4
Kuopio	2.7	6.4	18.7
Joensuu	3.4	7.8	25.2
Oulu	3.5	8.0	18.1
Rovaniemi	4.8	11.3	25.0
Finland	2.2	4.8	14.5

Source: Pehkonen and Turvo (1998)

series data of the unemployment rate, by Pehkonen and Turvo (1998). They use the following simple regression model to estimate the equilibrium unemployment rate U^* for the ten regions of Finland and also for 359 municipalities:

$$U_t = \alpha + \beta U_{t-1} + \text{error} \tag{7.3}$$

where t is time and α and β are coefficients. It is expected that the coefficient β will lie between 0 and 1. A high value of β indicates that the unemployment rate in the current period will be highly correlated with the unemployment rate in the previous year. A low value of β indicates that the current unemployment rate is not highly correlated with the unemployment rate in the previous year. (In fact, if $\beta = 0$ then U_t will fluctuate randomly about its mean value which in this case would be α since the error term is assumed to be normally distributed with a mean value of zero.)

Once α and β have been estimated, the equilibrium unemployment rate can be calculated for each region. This is easily done since equilibrium implies that the unemployment rate is constant (i.e. $U_t = U_{t-1} = U^*$, where U^* is the equilibrium unemployment rate) and the error is assumed to be zero in the long run. Hence, substituting U^* into equation (7.3) for U_t and U_{t-1}:

$$U^* = \frac{\alpha}{1 - \beta} \tag{7.4}$$

Estimates of U^* for the regions of Finland are obtained for three separate sub-periods since the equilibrium unemployment rate is estimated to have risen substantially during recent decades. The estimates shown in table 7.5 indicate that the equilibrium unemployment rate has increased considerably during 1963–93 in all Finnish regions. Moreover, the high correlation between these equilibrium unemployment rates over time suggests that unemployment disparities between regions are 'equilibrium' disparities. Some regions in Finland are apparently able to adjust to demand shocks more quickly than other regions. The factors underlying regional variations in the degree of responsiveness to demand shocks, however, are not investigated by Pehkonen and Turvo.

The equilibrium approach to regional unemployment disparities argues that these disparities exist because of compensating variations in living conditions. Regions with a pleasant climate which are well endowed with local amenities, such as good public services, are more likely to have a higher unemployment rate than regions with a poor climate and poor public services. This is because a pleasant living environment will partially compensate for a higher probability of being unemployed. In equilibrium, regional disparities in unemployment will therefore reflect regional disparities in climate and locally available amenities. It is important to examine the validity of this view of regional unemployment disparities in order to inform the construction of policies that aim to reduce these disparities.

This hypothesis has been investigated empirically for over 300 Norwegian municipalities by Carlsen (2000). Each municipality's 'permanent' unemployment rate is calculated and then regressed on a set of community characteristics based upon a sample survey of residents in each locality. Two indicators of average weather conditions (summer temperature and winter snow) are also included. Residents were asked to rate their satisfaction with each of seven community characteristics, which were as follows:

- satisfaction with daycare services for children
- satisfaction with primary education
- satisfaction with cultural activities
- satisfaction with care for the elderly
- satisfaction with primary health care
- satisfaction with living conditions for children
- satisfaction with public transport

The main conclusion from this study is that regional unemployment disparities in Norway are unrelated to living conditions as indicated by a community's satisfaction with the above community characteristics. There is no evidence that regions with good living conditions have higher unemployment rates than regions with poor living conditions. The predictions of the equilibrium explanation of spatial disparities in unemployment do not hold in this case.

Regional unemployment rate disparities in the UK

Regional disparities in the unemployment rate widened considerably in the UK during the 1980s, leading to the popular notion of a north–south divide. This disparity suddenly went into reverse in the late 1980s and continued through until the late 1990s. Historically, the unemployment gap between north and south had widened during recessions and then narrowed during booms, so the experience of the 1990s contradicted trends which have existed since at least the 1920s. The narrowing of north–south unemployment disparities, however, hides the fact that spatial unemployment disparities have shown no tendency to decrease *within* regions despite their tendency to decrease *between* regions (Green 1998; Green et al. 1998).

To gain a better understanding of why unemployment rates vary between different geographical areas, Green examines unemployment rates for a sample of 10,000 small areas (referred to as 'wards') in Great Britain using data from the *Census of Population*. The intention is not to identify the underlying causes of unemployment but simply to see to what extent spatial disparities in unemployment can be accounted for by a set of socio-economic and demographic variables. The problem is not, therefore, to identify the causes of spatial unemployment disparities but to see which factors are most closely correlated with these disparities. An additional issue is to identify those factors which are most closely associated with the spatial disparities in the *change* in unemployment over time. The aim is therefore to describe rather than to explain.

The main findings of this statistical analysis are that between 50 per cent and 60 per cent of the variation in unemployment rates between small areas in Great Britain can be accounted for by the following factors:

% of households in rented housing	positive effect
% of adults with higher qualifications	negative effect
% of workers skilled	positive effect
% of workers semi-skilled or unskilled	positive effect
population of city, town or rural area in which area is located	positive effect
region in which an area is located	positive effect

These results are not particularly surprising since they simply say that the areas of high unemployment are also areas with a high proportion of people on low incomes (i.e. those in rented accommodation) who are poorly qualified and live in large cities. There is therefore a distinct geographical concentration of those most at risk of becoming unemployed. This suggests the need for spatially discriminating policies aimed at reducing unemployment.

Regional unemployment rate disparities in the United States

The US labour market is often characterized as being flexible compared with European labour markets. This is usually attributed to the freedom from government regulations, plant-level wage bargaining, and high rates of labour mobility between jobs and between states. Greater labour market flexibility in the USA is assumed to lead to a lower 'natural' rate of unemployment than in Europe.

There are considerable differences in the unemployment rate, however, between US states. Moreover, these unemployment disparities are persistent over time, which suggests that the 'natural' or 'equilibrium' unemployment rate varies between states. Before examining this possibility, it is useful to note that state unemployment rates are positively correlated over time. This is demonstrated for several pairs of years as follows:

state unemployment rates in 1992 versus 1972: $r = 0.55$
state unemployment rates in 1992 versus 1977: $r = 0.74$
state unemployment rates in 1992 versus 1982: $r = 0.56$
state unemployment rates in 1992 versus 1987: $r = 0.27$

Further tests on 1996 data reveal a correlation of 0.42 between the 1996 and 1980 state unemployment rates for males (and 0.34 for females).

These positive correlations between state unemployment rates over time suggest that the equilibrium unemployment rates are persistently higher in some states than in others. For example, West Virginia has had persistently high unemployment rates for several decades whereas Nebraska has experienced persistently low unemployment rates (relative to the national average). This raises an obvious question: why do residents of persistently high-unemployment regions not move to regions with persistently low levels of unemployment? The fact that migration does not equalize unemployment rates suggests that inter-state mobility is inadequate, perhaps because out-migration from high-unemployment areas is constrained.

Since states vary considerably in their labour market characteristics, there would seem to be good reason to expect the equilibrium unemployment rate to vary between states. Furthermore, since the labour market characteristics of states change over time, we should not expect the equilibrium unemployment rate to be constant. It would clearly be useful to know what the equilibrium unemployment rate is for all labour market areas since this would have important implications for the formulation of unemployment policies. Equilibrium unemployment cannot, however, be observed directly since the actual unemployment rate in any labour market must (by definition) be the sum of its equilibrium and disequilibrium components. Only if a labour market is in equilibrium (which it may never be in practice) will the actual unemployment rate equal its equilibrium level. It is therefore necessary to construct a model which is capable of predicting both the equilibrium and the disequilibrium components simultaneously.

This has been done for US states by Partridge and Rickman (1997). Although states are far too large to be regarded as labour market areas (indeed some states such as California contain several hundred labour market areas), the Partridge and Rickman study is valuable for developing a useful approach which could be applied at a much finer level of spatial disaggregation. Disequilibrium unemployment is assumed to be caused by national business fluctuations. Since cyclical sensitivity varies between industries during national cycles, it is necessary to take each region's industry mix into account when estimating the disequilibrium of unemployment in each region. The estimation of the equilibrium unemployment rates for US states is undertaken in two parts. A theoretical model is first proposed which identifies the main determinants of a state's equilibrium unemployment

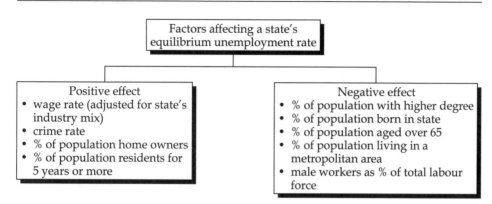

Figure 7.8   Factors affecting the equilibrium unemployment rate in US states.

rate. The second part of the analysis attempts to estimate the equilibrium unemployment rate by using regression analysis.

The equilibrium component is assumed to be determined by a wide range of economic and social factors. For example, the equilibrium unemployment rate may be higher in region A than in region B because of compensating differentials in variables such as the wage rate, local amenities, demographic factors and the climate. On the other hand, it may be higher in region A than in region B because there are a greater proportion of unskilled, low-income workers who either cannot afford to move or have little information about the probability of getting a job in other regions. Moreover, some regions have a higher proportion of workers who would suffer psychologically if they moved to another region (such as long-time residents and home owners). Such factors are taken into account by Partridge and Rickman in their attempt to estimate the equilibrium unemployment rate for each US state during 1973–91. The main findings are shown in figure 7.8.

The estimated equilibrium unemployment rate is given for several states in table 7.6. These estimates show that states such as California, Michigan and West Virginia have had persistently higher equilibrium unemployment rates than the USA as a whole, whereas the opposite is the case for Nebraska, South Dakota, Iowa and Wyoming.

Regional unemployment disparities in the European Union

We have already seen that unemployment rates vary considerably between the member states of the EU and between regions within member states. Taking the EU as a whole, one of the reasons for regional disparities in the unemployment rate is that national unemployment rates vary considerably. Regions in member states with high unemployment rates, such as Spain, are likely to have higher unemployment rates than regions in member states which have much lower unemployment rates, such as the UK. Country-specific factors may therefore be expected to exert a powerful influence on regional unemployment disparities

Table 7.6   The estimated equilibrium unemployment rate in selected US states

Selected US states	Difference between each state's equilibrium unemployment rate and the equilibrium unemployment rate in the USA as a whole		
	1973	1981	1991
Washington	4.3	3.1	1.9
California	3.0	1.9	1.8
Michigan	2.5	3.4	3.3
Oregon	2.4	2.2	1.0
Louisiana	2.3	1.6	3.3
West Virginia	1.5	3.5	4.6
Alabama	1.4	2.9	2.5
New Jersey	1.2	−0.6	−1.6
Mississippi	0.9	1.7	2.2
Connecticut	−0.9	−1.2	−1.6
Wyoming	−1.9	−3.1	−0.4
North Carolina	−1.9	−1.4	−1.3
Kansas	−1.9	−2.1	−1.9
Iowa	−2.3	−1.8	−2.1
South Dakota	−2.9	−2.9	−3.9
Nebraska	−3.7	−3.6	−3.3

Source: Partridge and Rickman (1997)

taking the EU as a whole. The unemployment rate for individual regions, for example, is very highly correlated with the corresponding national unemployment rate over time. Indeed, the correlation between regional unemployment rates and the unemployment rate for the EU as a whole is over 0.90 in the majority of EU regions (Decressin and Fatás 1995). Regional unemployment rates therefore tend to fluctuate together over the international business cycle.

Empirical studies of regional unemployment disparities in the EU have primarily been undertaken for individual member states rather than for the EU as a whole despite the importance of the unemployment rate in determining the geographical distribution of EU funding. An exception is the investigation of the effect of demand shocks on employment, unemployment, labour force participation and net migration by Decressin and Fatás (1995). The aim of this study is to compare the responsiveness of regional labour markets to demand shocks in the USA and in the EU. A distinction is made between (1) demand shocks originating in the economy as a whole (i.e. in the USA and EU respectively); and (2) demand shocks originating within each region separately. The purpose of the research is to examine the response to this second type of demand shock, namely region-specific demand shocks.

A demand shock may affect not only a region's employment and unemployment rates but also its participation rate and its net migration rate (see figure 7.9). It is therefore necessary to examine the effect of a demand shock on these variables separately. This is done in two stages. First, it is necessary to estimate region-specific demand shocks for a given time period (1975–90 in the Decressin and

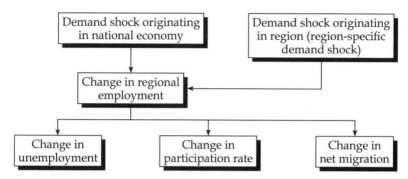

Figure 7.9   The effect of demand shocks on the regional labour market.

Fatás study) for each region separately. Second, the effects of these demand shocks on a region's employment, unemployment and labour force participation are then estimated. The main findings of this research are as follows:

1   Region-specific demand shocks have very similar effects on a region's unemployment rate in US states and EU regions.
2   The effects of region-specific demand shocks on the participation rate are much greater in EU regions than in US states.
3   Unemployed workers in the US are more likely to respond to negative demand shocks by migrating to other regions than is the case in the EU.

Negative demand shocks therefore affect the US and the EU labour markets quite differently, with US workers being more likely to respond by moving to other regions whereas EU workers are more likely to leave the labour force.

Other research work into regional unemployment disparities in the EU includes an investigation into regional unemployment disparities in Germany, Italy and the UK (Taylor and Bradley 1997). The results of this research indicate that three factors have had a substantial influence on regional unemployment disparities in these countries. First, unemployment is higher in regions with high labour costs. This result is consistent with a large body of empirical results obtained in national studies of unemployment (Bean 1994; Cameron and Muellbauer 1999). These national-level investigations of the unemployment rate indicate that one of the causes of the persistence of high unemployment rates in the EU since the early 1980s is that real wages have been too high and have failed to respond to slack labour demand. This compares with much greater responsiveness in the USA. Between 1970 and 1993, for example, employment in the USA increased by 50 per cent while real wages increased by 10 per cent, whereas in the EU employment increased by only 15 per cent while real wages increased by 50 per cent (Martin 1998).

Attempts to explain the persistence of regional disparities in the unemployment rate have therefore included the real wage as a key explanatory variable. This is supported by research into wage rigidity in the regions of Germany. Büttner (1999) shows that wages are particularly unresponsive to unemployment in those regions with the highest unemployment rates. This lack of flexibility, together with a low migration response to wage and unemployment differentials, is therefore likely to be a primary cause of the persistence of regional unemployment disparities in Germany.

Employers are concerned, however, not with the real wage *per se* but with the real wage relative to labour productivity (i.e. unit labour costs). Competitiveness will not be eroded when the real wage increases provided that labour productivity rises in proportion to the increase in the real wage. It is therefore not surprising to find that unit labour costs are strongly positively related to regional unemployment disparities in Germany, Italy and the UK (Taylor and Bradley 1997).

Second, a region's export base is likely to have a dominant effect on its economic performance, as suggested earlier in this book. A region's demand for labour will therefore depend, in part, on its industry mix. Regions highly dependent on industries in long-term employment decline such as agriculture and heavy manufacturing, for example, are likely to have higher unemployment rates than regions specializing in rapidly growing service sector activities such as business services and finance. Not surprisingly, empirical evidence supports this view. Regions such as Sicily and Sardinia, for example, in southern Italy have been severely adversely affected by their high dependence on agriculture, while regions such as Lombardy in northern Italy have benefited tremendously from their high dependence on services and from the growth of consumer goods industries. A similar story can be told for the UK except that it is the regions of southern England that have benefited most from a fast growing export base while the regions of the north have been less fortunate.

Finally, regional disparities in unemployment also appear to be affected by job density. Regions in which job density is high tend to have a high unemployment rate. It has been argued that this positive relationship between job density and the unemployment rate is due to a long-term trend in the preference of firms for a less congested, and hence less costly, location (Fothergill and Gudgin 1982).

7.5   Socio-demographic causes of unemployment: evidence from the UK

So far in this chapter, we have focused almost entirely on spatial disparities in the unemployment rate. But it is very clear from the results of a considerable body of economic research into the causes of unemployment that the probability of becoming unemployed varies tremendously between individuals with different socio-demographic backgrounds (Brown and Sessions 1997). Individuals in the labour market are not homogeneous in terms of their socio-economic characteristics. In fact, they are extremely heterogeneous. This means that individual participants in the labour market possess characteristics which differ widely between each other. Each person is defined by a set of characteristics such as: age, gender, marital status, ethnic origin, family background, place of residence, educational qualifications, occupation, income, wealth and so on. This heterogeneity in the labour market suggests that at least some of these personal characteristics may have an effect upon the probability of any individual becoming unemployed.

A question of great interest to regional economists is: to what extent can spatial disparities in unemployment be explained by corresponding disparities in the socio-demographic mix of regions? Are spatial unemployment disparities due simply to corresponding spatial disparities in the socio-demographic character-istics of regions or are these unemployment disparities due to a fundamental spatial mismatch between labour demand and labour supply? An answer to this question is important for policy makers since we need to know whether policies to deal with the problem of unemployment should be people-based or place-based. In other words, do policy makers need to be concerned with spatial un-employment disparities or can they afford to ignore the spatial dimension of unemployment?

The problem with trying to explain spatial unemployment disparities in terms of the socio-demographic characteristics of the workforce is that the latter are a consequence as well as a cause of the former. For example, a fall in the demand for labour in a particular area will induce an outward migration of the most mobile workers, who will tend to be young, well-qualified workers with high skill levels. The area will not only be left with a workforce which is more vulnerable to unemployment but will also be a less attractive location for employers. The supply-side explanation of unemployment may therefore be only part of the story since supply and demand are interdependent. What may begin as a negative demand shock could lead to significant adverse effects on the supply side of the labour market.

Nevertheless, there is no doubt that socio-demographic factors are very import-ant in determining an individual's chances of becoming unemployed. Some idea of the potential significance of socio-demographic factors on unemployment prob-abilities is vividly illustrated in table 7.7. The chances of becoming unemployed are over three times higher for persons with no qualifications than those with qualifications up to GCSE level (taken normally by pupils aged 15–16), and 18 times higher than for those with a degree. The chances of becoming un-employed are particularly high for young, unskilled, non-white males who have no qualifications, whereas middle-aged males with a degree who are profession-ally qualified have very little chance of becoming unemployed. But the question which interests us here is whether these socio-demographic factors alone explain spatial disparities in unemployment or whether location has an independent effect on the chances of becoming unemployed. This is exactly the question posed by Brown and Sessions (1997) in their UK study of interpersonal variations in the chances of becoming unemployed.

In order to discover whether location has any effect upon a person's unemploy-ment probability after taking into account their socio-demographic characterist-ics, Brown and Sessions use multiple regression techniques on data obtained from the British Social Attitudes Survey, which provides detailed data for over 15 000 individuals. They show that even after controlling for the effect of a large number of socio-demographic variables, a person's region of residence is a significant determinant of the chances of becoming unemployed. In particular, those living

Table 7.7   Unemployment rates by socio-demographic group

Socio-demographic group	Variable	% unemployed	
		Males	Females
Education	No qualifications	18.2	6.5
	GCSE O level	5.4	4.7
	Degree	1.8	3.6
Occupation	Unskilled	18.7	8.9
	Semi-skilled	12.7	6.1
	Clerical	9.3	4.3
	Professional	3.6	4.1
Age	18–24	15.5	11.5
	25–34	10.1	7.3
	35–44	7.0	4.6
	45–54	9.0	4.5
	55–59	10.6	4.7
	60–65	12.3	–
Marital status	Single	16.3	10.4
	Married	7.7	3.8
Spouse	Spouse works	3.3	3.6
	Spouse does not work	14.9	8.7
Colour	White	10.2	7.1
	Non-white	14.4	5.8
Housing	Owner occupier	5.1	3.8
	Private tenant	12.8	8.4
	Public sector tenant	27.6	11.0

Source: Brown and Sessions (1997: 354): data derived from the British Social Attitudes Survey

in Northern Ireland, the North West, Wales, the North and the West Midlands have a substantially greater chance of becoming unemployed than those living in other UK regions. If a similar analysis were undertaken at the travel-to-work area level rather than for regions, the effect of location on the probability of becoming unemployed is likely to be even more powerful since spatial disparities in unemployment are substantially larger for travel-to-work areas than they are for regions.

The broad policy implication of the results of these various empirical studies of spatial unemployment disparities is quite clear. Policies to reduce unemployment need to be directed at both people and places. While there is no doubt that an individual person's chances of becoming unemployed are far greater if they possess certain socio-demographic characteristics, it is also the case that their chances of becoming unemployed are far greater if they live in certain well-defined locations. Their personal characteristics are therefore important but so also are conditions in their local labour market area. This suggests that government policy should aim to increase the demand for labour in areas where it is persistently low.

7.6   Hidden unemployment

Official unemployment rates do not provide a complete picture of spatial disparities in the utilization of labour resource. To complete the picture we also need to consider spatial disparities in the participation rate. The participation rate is simply the proportion of people of working age who are economically active (though it is sometimes approximated in practice by the employment/population ratio). The fact that there are considerable spatial disparities in the participation rate suggests that there exists under-employment of labour in those regions where the participation rate is low. In other words, the unemployment rate may need to be supplemented by information about the participation rate if an accurate picture of the extent to which a region's labour force is being utilized is to be obtained.

There are two reasons why the official unemployment data may give a misleading picture of the true unemployment position of a region. First, not all persons who are actively searching for a job will be recorded as unemployed. Some may not have any entitlement to unemployment benefits and so will not be counted in the unemployment totals. Second, there may be a substantial number of persons who are not recorded as unemployed and who are not currently active in seeking a job but who would nevertheless do so if the prospects of getting a job offer were better. When the job market is slack, there is a strong tendency for the workforce to contract due to a 'discouraged worker effect'. This is particularly marked for married women workers, many of whom withdraw from the registered workforce when there is little chance of finding work. The existence of poor job prospects also encourages more earlier retirements, for males as well as females, than would otherwise occur.

The existence of a slack labour market may therefore be expected to lead to a lower participation rate than would exist if more jobs were available. Regions with high unemployment rates can therefore be expected to have low participation rates. This expected negative relationship is confirmed at regional level for most European countries and for the states of the USA. The correlation coefficients given in table 7.8 show that regional unemployment rates and regional participation rates are negatively related in all countries except Germany. The correlations were particularly strong in Italy, Belgium and the USA (see figure 7.10).

The negative correlation between the unemployment rate and the participation rate across regions in so many countries provides strong support for the view that labour force participation is strongly influenced by the availability of jobs. Factors on the supply side of the labour market are also likely to be important in determining a region's participation rate but there can be little doubt that the demand side plays a significant role as well. This is confirmed in empirical work by Molho and Elias (1984) for the UK. This shows that two of the main reasons for the sharp increase in the activity rate of married women since the 1960s have been the improvement in job prospects and the increase in wages paid to females following the introduction of equal pay for men and women.

Although factors on the supply side of the labour market are undoubtedly important in explaining spatial variations in the participation rate, empirical research indicates that socio-demographic factors account for less than 25 per cent of the

Table 7.8 Correlation between the regional unemployment rate and the regional labour force participation rate across regions in selected countries in Europe (1994) and in the USA (1996)

Country[a]	Number of regions	Correlation[b] between unemployment rate and participation rate[c]
Germany	36	0.35*
France	33	−0.31
Italy	30	−0.88**
Netherlands	23	−0.62**
Belgium	23	−0.87**
UK	35	−0.46**
Greece	13	−0.24
Spain	18	−0.28
Portugal	7	−0.27
Austria	9	−0.33
Sweden	24	−0.45**
Finland	11	−0.59**
Norway	19	−0.64**
USA (females only)	49	−0.66**
USA (males only)	49	−0.68**

[a] The correlations for US states are for 1996. The correlations for European countries are for 1994.
[b] * = statistically significant at 5 per cent; ** = statistically significant at 1 per cent.
[c] The participation rate is the employment/population ratio.
Sources: *Regional Trends 32*, 1997; US Bureau of Labor Statistics, *Employment and Earnings*, 1997

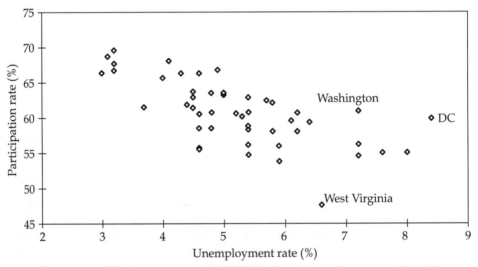

Figure 7.10 Participation rate versus unemployment rate in US states, females, 1996.
Source: US Department of Labor

variation in the female participation rate between US metropolitan areas (Odland and Ellis 1998). By contrast, over 60 per cent of the variation in participation rates between metropolitan areas is accounted for by differences in labour market experience for females with the same characteristics. In other words, metropolitan areas with very similar socio-demographic characteristics, such as educational attainment and marital status, can have very different female participation rates. One reason for this result may be that job opportunities are more abundant in some regions than they are in others, so that females with the same socio-demographic characteristics find it easier to get a job in some areas than in others.

This focus on hidden *female* unemployment is a direct consequence of the high response of the female participation rate to changes in the demand for labour. This does not, however, mean that hidden *male* unemployment is negligible. The sharp decline in the UK coal industry during the 1980s provides an excellent example of how job losses can lead to hidden unemployment among males. The closure of coal mines in England and Wales between 1981 and 1991 led to the loss of 160 000 coal mining jobs for males, yet the unemployment total was virtually unchanged in coal mining areas (Beatty and Fothergill 1998). The discrepancy between job losses in coal mining and the change in unemployment is accounted for by several factors, one of the main ones being a substantial decline in the participation rate of males (due to a sharp increase in early retirements and in the number claiming sickness benefit).

The observation that the severe job losses in coal mining areas were accompanied by sharp increases in early retirements and long-term sickness led Beatty and Fothergill to produce estimates of the *real* unemployment rate for all GB regions, counties and districts. Their basic premise is that the proportion of the population of working age taking early retirement or claiming long-term sickness benefit will be higher when jobs are scarce. Beatty and Fothergill therefore use the rates of early retirement and sickness benefit prevailing at times of 'full employment' as benchmarks. The South East region is used for obtaining these benchmarks and it is assumed that full employment was achieved in this region in 1991. Hence, the actual rates of early retirement and long-term sickness in each region are subtracted from the rates prevailing in the South East in 1991 in order to obtain estimates of hidden unemployment. This exercise is carried out for GB regions, counties and districts (for 1997). Two additional sources of hidden unemployment are added to the estimates of real unemployment. First, the claimant count of the unemployed is shown to understate the number of people seeking work and so the unemployment recorded in the Labour Force Survey is used instead of the claimant count. Second, those on government employment and training schemes need to be added in since these people would otherwise be unemployed. They show that on average over the economy as a whole the real unemployment rate is twice the unemployment rate obtained from the claimant count. The overall results for GB are shown in table 7.9. Figures 7.11 and 7.12 plot the estimated real unemployment rate against the claimant count unemployment rate for males and females separately at county level.

Two main criticisms can be levelled against this method of estimating the hidden unemployed. First, using the South East as the benchmark for estimating

Table 7.9   Estimates of the real level of unemployment in Great Britain, January 1997[a]

Classification of unemployment	Male	Female	Total
Claimant count	1 407 000	429 000	1 837 000
Hidden unemployment			
Extra unemployed (Labour Force Survey)	60 000	270 000	340 000
Government schemes	260 000	150 000	400 000
Excess of early retirements	80 000	30 000	100 000
Excess of long-term sick	820 000	450 000	1 260 000
Real unemployment	2 620 000	1 330 000	3 950 000
Unemployment rates (%)			
Claimant count	9.4	3.9	7.1
Real unemployment	16.4	10.9	14.2

[a] Numbers are rounded to nearest thousand.
Source: Beatty et al. (1997: 23)

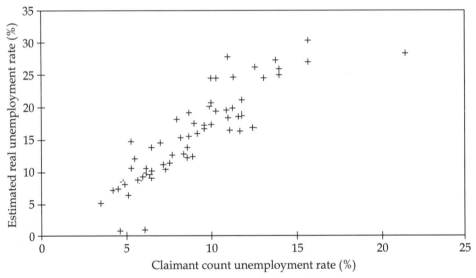

Figure 7.11   Real unemployment versus claimant count unemployment for males by county in Great Britain, January 1997.
Source: Beatty et al. (1997)

what would occur if all regions attained the South East's full employment levels of early retirements and long-term sickness fails to recognize that there may be substantial differences in the full employment levels of these two variables between different areas. The 'real' rate of long-term sickness, for example, may be substantially higher in some parts of the country than in others. It may be particularly high, for example, in areas of high unemployment since long-term

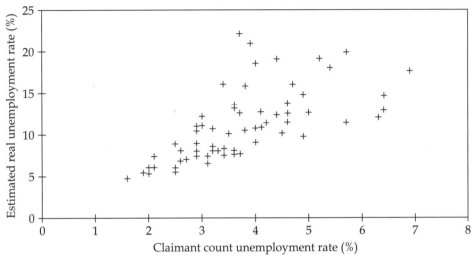

Figure 7.12 Real unemployment versus claimant count unemployment for females by county in Great Britain, January 1997.
Source: Beatty et al. (1997)

unemployment may itself be a cause of long-term sickness. There is ample evidence that long-term unemployment can lead to a deterioration in mental health (Warr 1987). Long-term sickness may therefore be caused to some extent by experience of long periods of unemployment. Second, using the situation prevailing in the South East in 1991 as a benchmark for a fully employed economy implies that this should be set as a target for all regions. But this ignores the possibility that different regions may have different equilibrium unemployment rates due to structural differences in their workforces. Ideally, it would be more appropriate to construct an economic model which explains spatial variations in the labour force participation rate. This could then be used to estimate the extent to which spatial disparities in labour force participation (and hence hidden unemployment) can be attributed to lack of demand rather than to factors on the supply side of the labour market.

Further estimates of the *real* unemployment rate, again based upon the notion of a benchmark for long-term sickness, are provided for Northern Ireland by Armstrong (1999), who estimate the *true* sickness rate for each local labour market area. After showing that there is a strong positive correlation between the long-term sickness rate and unemployment across the local labour market areas in Northern Ireland ($r = 0.7$ for 1991), Armstrong then estimates the proportion of those classified as long-term sick who would be more appropriately classified as long-term unemployed. Using this method, the *real* unemployment rate is estimated to be one-third higher than the official unemployment rate. Once again, however, the critical question is whether the benchmark is accurate. The problem of estimating an appropriate and accurate benchmark remains unresolved.

7.7   Conclusion

This chapter has shown that spatial disparities in the unemployment rate are substantial and persistent in both Europe and the USA. Some regions have persistently high levels of unemployment over very long periods of time, while other regions have persistently low levels of unemployment. There are, of course, many exceptions to these trends, but it is unemployment persistence that is the central focus of the present chapter since this is the primary reason for the existence of regional policies in many countries.

Although research into the causes of these spatial unemployment disparities has improved our understanding of why they occur, there is still much work to be done. Attempts to discover the underlying causes of spatial disparities in unemployment have taken two quite different routes. First, several attempts have been made to identify the factors determining the unemployment rate of entire regions (including regions as large as US states as well as much smaller regions such as travel-to-work areas, counties and metropolitan areas). These macro-level studies have attempted to measure the effect on regional unemployment disparities of factors such as the wage level, the mismatch between the demand and supply for labour, and the industry mix of regions. At the opposite end of the spectrum are micro-level investigations, which have been based on large-sample surveys of individual participants in the labour market. Both these approaches have yielded some useful findings.

What exactly has been discovered about the causes of spatial unemployment disparities? First, it is perhaps worth emphasizing the obvious: there is no single or simple explanation of spatial disparities in unemployment. Empirical studies have identified several primary determinants. These include the following: real wages are too high in high-unemployment regions; there is a substantial spatial mismatch in the demand and supply for labour; some regions have a more favourable industry mix than others; the socio-demographic structure is more favourable in some regions than in others; the underlying natural rate of unemployment is higher in some regions than in others; and some regions are more sensitive to national business cycles than others.

Do these results have any clear implications for regional policy? As with much economic research, the results are given different weight by different people. Some economists argue that the answer lies in improving labour market flexibility. According to this view, regional unemployment disparities would be significantly less if wages were more responsive to conditions in the labour market. Wages need to fall where unemployment is persistently high. Others argue that it is simply impossible to obtain the degree of wage flexibility required to significantly reduce unemployment through wage cuts. Moreover, wage reductions could have negative multiplier effects on high-unemployment regions, making the situation even worse. The other option open to policy makers is to increase labour demand directly. An alternative view is that the most effective way to reduce unemployment is by people-based policies which aim to get the long-term unemployed back into the labour market through policies such as wage subsidies, retraining and counselling. Finally, there are place-based policies which aim to create jobs in the worst affected areas. It is to such policies that we now turn in part II of this book.

Further reading

Hasluck (1987); McCormick (1991); Coles and Smith (1996); Brown and Sessions (1997); Partridge and Rickman (1997); Baddeley et al. (1998a; 1998b); Martin (1998); Pehkonen and Turvo (1998); Carlsen (2000).

part two

Regional policy

Part I of this book was concerned primarily with how regional economies function. Some of the questions which we sought to answer were: what determines regional income and output? Why do some regions grow faster than others? What factors determine the pattern of interregional trade? Why do net migration rates differ between regions? Why do unemployment rates differ between regions?

Although finding answers to such questions may be interesting for its own sake, there are more urgent reasons for discovering more about the economic behaviour of regional economies. First, regional economic disparities are generally regarded as being undesirable if they are chronic, that is persisting over long periods of time. Second, a thorough understanding of how regional economies behave is needed if economically efficient policies are to be devised for reducing regional economic disparities. In particular, it is crucially important to be able to evaluate the consequences of alternative policy instruments. Regional policy is the subject matter of part II of this book.

Regional policy exists because of the persistence of regional disparities in a wide range of variables, which have a profound effect on the economic welfare of a nation's regions. It should be said immediately, however, that the presence of regional disparities in economic welfare is not sufficient *per se* to justify the existence of regional policy. We need to know why regional policy is desirable and how the nation will benefit from it. It is now widely recognized that regional disparities cause problems since they prevent the attainment of national policy objectives – such as providing adequate job opportunities, achieving a satisfactory rate of growth and distributing income and wealth more equitably. It is therefore the purpose of regional policies to achieve specified national policy objectives. In this sense, we can regard regional policy as an important component of a broader and more comprehensive economic policy embracing the whole economy.

Part II has three broad themes. The first is concerned with the case for regional policy. This is discussed in chapter 8 alongside an overview of the development of regional policy in the United Kingdom since its introduction in the late 1920s. The second major theme covers the various regional policy instruments available to governments. These include not only the traditional instruments (discussed in chapter 9) but also more radical approaches including proposals to stimulate the formation of new firms, new products and new methods of production (discussed in chapter 10). Attempts to organize and implement a regional policy for the European Union as a whole are discussed in chapter 11, which is followed by an investigation of the various ways in which economic regeneration powers might be devolved to regional authorities (chapter 12).

In the third and final theme various methods of evaluating regional policy are described and appraised. Chapter 13 discusses the main methods which have been used to estimate the effects of regional policy on variables such as employment, investment and the movement of industry. This final chapter also discusses the broader issues involved in evaluating regional policy, such as the range of costs and benefits which ideally should be taken into account in policy evaluation.

chapter eight

The case for regional policy: British experience

contents

Regional economic policy in Britain has shown surprising tenacity. Economic fashions have waxed and waned, yet regional policy has remained on the statute books for over 70 years. In spite of persistent attacks on its very foundations, it is likely to remain a feature of economic policy making in one form or another for many years to come. The continuing expansion of EU regional policy in the member states (including Britain), discussed in chapter 11, provides an excellent example of the importance that policy makers continue to attach to reducing regional disparities in living standards.

This chapter explains why regional policy is a necessary component of the British government's economic policy. There would be little point in continuing with the second part of this book if we did not believe that a regional policy is beneficial to the national economy. We therefore begin (in section 8.1) by discussing the economic case for reducing regional disparities, primary attention being focused upon reducing regional *unemployment* disparities. Two diametrically opposed approaches to achieving this objective are then discussed in section 8.2, the first being the free market approach and the second the government interventionist approach.

Section 8.3 summarizes the main phases of regional policy since its inception in 1928, ending with the ascent to prominence in the 1990s of indigenous development initiatives. The chapter concludes, in section 8.4, with a discussion of whether regional policy should be reoriented towards the attainment of *social* objectives rather than *economic* objectives. As shall be shown, the debate on the balance between economic and social objectives is as old as regional policy itself. The 1990s, however, witnessed another of the periodic swings back towards social objectives. Urban policy in Britain has now been almost completely redirected towards the reduction of *social exclusion*. A similar swing in fashion is now being experienced in regional policy. A strong campaign is under way to 'bend' regional policy away from its traditional role as a component of the nation's industrial policy towards the social exclusion agenda.

8.1   The case for reducing regional economic disparities

Since the 1930s, a succession of policy makers have believed that there are sound reasons for having a regional policy. It is widely recognized that regional economic disparities (e.g. in unemployment rates and per capita incomes) which persist for long periods of time have harmful effects on the efficient operation of the *national* economy. In addition, such disparities may have harmful political and social consequences. The most significant of the harmful effects are as follows.

First, the existence of substantial regional disparities in living standards causes dissatisfaction and resentment. This is most strongly felt by those whose job prospects and living standards are poor through no fault of their own. School leavers in Liverpool and Glasgow, for example, have far poorer employment prospects than their counterparts in the suburban areas of south-east England. This is particularly true for those with poor educational qualifications. These arguments lie at the heart of the *equity* case for regional policy. Inequities in the distribution of income also underpin most of the *social* arguments for regional policy.

Second, persistently high levels of unemployment in the disadvantaged regions have harmful economic consequences. If unemployment could be permanently reduced in high-unemployment areas without leading to a loss of jobs in areas of low unemployment, the whole nation would be better off. The previously unemployed would be producing output and taxpayers would not have to support the unemployed. Lower unemployment also means lower crime rates and less social hardship, especially for those who would otherwise be long-term unemployed, and there is therefore also a social dimension to the problem of unemployment. A similar argument applies to the utilization of industrial and commercial land. There is a large amount of currently disused and derelict land available for economic development in the disadvantaged regions which could be brought into productive use or made available for housing. This would improve the urban environment as well as increasing national GDP.

Third, regional disparities in economic growth can inflict severe economic costs on rapidly growing urban areas through the excess demand for social infrastructure and public services – exactly the opposite situation to that prevailing in the areas losing their population, where social infrastructure is often under-utilized. Buildings, roads, rail networks and airports in the south-east of England, for example, are continuously under intense pressure. The severe congestion resulting from this pressure wastes an immense amount of time for travellers and freight transport users. It has been estimated, for example, that traffic congestion imposes costs on the British economy of some £15 billion per annum (Confederation of British Industry 1995).

The classic response to congestion is to relieve it by further investment to enlarge the existing facilities. Instead of trying to relieve congestion by reducing the *demand* for social infrastructure, the government consistently responds by increasing its *supply*. This inevitably results in a never-ending spiral in which demand and supply chase each other. Breaking this spiral is an immensely difficult task since the government is under enormous political pressure to relieve congestion wherever it occurs. Yet regional policy offers a feasible alternative, at least in the longer term, by diverting demand for social infrastructure away from the south-east towards less congested areas in the north and west. If other parts of Britain could be made economically more attractive, the relentless increase in the demand for social infrastructure would slow down. Both north and south would benefit.

Fourth, reducing regional disparities in the excess demand for labour would reap benefits to the whole economy by reducing inflationary pressures. Persistent disparities in the unemployment rate between regions mean that whenever a significant business upturn occurs, as it did during 1985–8 when the United Kingdom's real output growth averaged over 4 per cent per year, inflationary pressures build up very quickly in the low-unemployment regions. Inflationary pressures were slower to emerge in the late 1990s, perhaps because the upturn was a longer-drawn-out one, with GDP rising in 27 successive quarters from its low point in 1992.

Inflationary pressures arise because of the intense competition for skilled labour, which becomes extremely scarce during booms. The consequence is a sharp increase in wage inflation as firms raise wages in order to attract more labour (or to retain their existing workers). Wage increases are then transmitted to other regions through inter-plant bargaining within firms and through national wage agreements.

Since the economy runs into supply bottlenecks very quickly during booms because of labour shortages in particular geographical areas, it follows that inflationary pressure would build up less quickly if regional disparities in unemployment were less severe. Moreover, the inflationary pressures in the labour market spill over into other markets during booms. The transmission of inflationary pressures from the labour market to the housing market in the south-east in the late 1980s and again in the late 1990s provide excellent examples of these inter-market linkages.

The escalation of house prices in the late 1980s was unprecedented in its speed and intensity and was triggered by excess demand for property in London and the south-east. In 1988 alone average house prices rose by 34 per cent. Evidence that the British economy has once again entered a period of property-market-led inflation, with the south setting the pace, is also accumulating. Once property market inflation is triggered in the south-east it tends to 'ripple out' to the other regions, hence raising the national inflation rate (MacDonald and Taylor 1993; Alexander and Barrow 1994; Johnes and Hyclak 1994; Ashworth and Parker 1997). Property market inflation also triggers complex feedback effects on the labour market by encouraging workers in the south-east to demand yet higher wages so that they can meet their higher mortgage payments (Blackaby and Manning 1992; Manning 1995). Reversals in this process can also have drastic effects for the national economy. The collapse of the house price boom in the south of England in the late 1980s, for example, is thought to have been a major factor in triggering the 1990–2 recession in the UK. The result was that this recession impacted most severely on the southern regions rather than, as is usually the case, on the northern regions (Taylor and Bradley 1994).

In summary, low unemployment leads to higher wages, which in turn lead to an increased demand for housing and hence higher house prices. Higher house prices are then, in turn, used to justify higher wage demands. The regional disparities in unemployment are further aggravated by the fact that house prices in the low-unemployment regions are a barrier to net inward migration. The inducement of unfilled jobs and higher wages is therefore offset by the disincentive of high housing costs. Relieving tight labour markets through inward migration is consequently stifled.

The way in which a reduction in regional unemployment disparities could benefit the national economy (in terms of either reducing inflation or reducing national unemployment or some combination of both) is demonstrated in figure 8.1a. It is assumed (in the upper part of the figure) that national wage inflation is determined by the labour-scarce south. An unemployment rate of U_1^s in the south is associated with a corresponding rate of U_1^n in the north. This relationship between unemployment rates in the north and south is shown by the line R_1, which lies to the left of the 45° line because of the existence of regional problems in the north.

Suppose now that regional unemployment disparities are reduced (e.g. by inward investment from abroad, which creates new jobs in the assisted areas). The relationship between unemployment in the north and the south shifts rightwards (see figure 8.1b), so that the same unemployment rate of U_1^s is now associated with the lower unemployment of U_2^n in the north (on line R_2). Effectively, this implies that the unemployment rate in the south can be increased in order to reduce inflationary pressures while keeping the national unemployment rate at its initial level. (Note that the national unemployment rate is a weighted average of U^s and U^n.) Unemployment in the north would then lie between U_2^n and U_1^n. Alternatively, both inflation and the national unemployment rate could be lower than before the reduction in regional disparities in unemployment. This effectively means that the *national* trade-off between wage inflation and unemployment has improved. The national Phillips curve (which shows the relationship between unemployment and wage inflation) has shifted to the left.

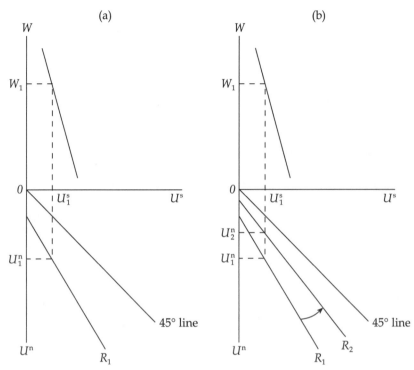

W = per cent annual change in wage
U^s = per cent unemployed in the south
U^n = per cent unemployed in the north
R = relationship between unemployment in the north and the south

Figure 8.1 Improving the inflation/unemployment trade-off.

8.2 Policy action: alternative approaches

If markets were efficient, regional unemployment disparities would be automatically eliminated. Markets would clear. The three main mechanisms that would ensure market clearing are as follows:

1 Wages would fall in areas of high unemployment and rise in areas of low unemployment, with corresponding impacts on numbers employed.
2 Workers would migrate from low-wage to high-wage areas.
3 Firms and mobile capital investment would move from high-wage to low-wage areas.

In a perfectly competitive world with no frictions to labour and capital mobility, the outcome would be an equality of wages and full employment in all regions.

This scenario does not accord with reality. Wages do respond to a limited extent to geographical variations in unemployment, and migration does respond to regional wage rate and unemployment disparities. But the adjustment process is far too slow to eliminate regional disparities in wages and unemployment. It is in this sense (i.e. that the speed of adjustment is extremely slow) that markets fail.

Why do market forces fail to make a significant rapid impression on regional unemployment disparities? There are two main reasons. First, there are formidable barriers to both capital and labour migration (see chapter 6). Many of the unemployed, for example, live in subsidized housing and do not have the resources to finance a move even if they wanted to move. Firms also exhibit a strong preference for the certainty of their present location rather than the uncertainty and disruption resulting from a move to another region. This geographical inertia is particularly powerful in small firms since their input–output linkages are normally with customers and other firms in their immediate locality. Movement would not be profitable in such cases.

The second reason why market forces fail to reduce regional unemployment disparities is that wages fail to respond to local labour market conditions. Successive British governments between 1979 and 1997 argued that only by reducing wages would the high-unemployment areas be able to win markets and hence jobs. It was argued that the lack of responsiveness of wages to market forces is due to the following factors:

1 Industry-wide collective agreements on wage rates rather than local bargaining.
2 Levels of unemployment benefit and other income support which are 'too high'.
3 Access to unemployment benefit which is 'too easy'.
4 The fixing of minimum wages at levels above the market clearing wage.
5 Inadequate policing of unemployment benefit claims.

The consequence of these factors is that the unemployed are prevented from competing for jobs by offering themselves for low wages in areas of high unemployment.

What should be done to reduce regional unemployment disparities? Two very different approaches can be taken, each one closely associated with a particular political ideology. First, the free market approach views the regional problem as being the result of market inefficiencies, a lack of entrepreneurial 'culture' and excessive state intervention (see table 8.1). The market-based solution to reducing regional unemployment disparities is therefore the removal of constraints on the free operation of market forces. The labour market in particular needs to be 'liberated'. Regional policy, if it exists at all, should be minimal and any financial assistance needed would be selectively provided with tight controls placed on regional policy spending.

The antithesis of the free market approach (referred to by MacKay 1997 as the 'counter-revolutionary approach') is direct state intervention. The latter has also been referred to as *spatial Keynesianism* (Martin 1988; 1989a). At the centre of the interventionist approach is the view that the regional problem is caused by structural weaknesses in the regional economy, coupled with a fundamental deficiency of investment due to a drain of financial capital from poor to rich regions (Martin

Table 8.1   Two opposite approaches to reducing regional economic disparities

Characteristics of the free market approach	Characteristics of the interventionist approach
Political ideology	
Neoclassical economics	Reconstructed Keynesianism
Popular capitalism	Supply-side support for industry and commerce
Deregulation, privatization	State intervention
Small state sector	
Enterprise culture	
Causes of regional economic disparities	
Inefficiency problem in regions due to labour market rigidities	Structural weaknesses
	Low investment
Lack of entrepreneurial 'culture'	Drain of financial capital to rich regions
Excessive state intervention	Inadequate government participation in regional development
Approach to reviving disadvantaged regions	
Deregulation of regional labour markets	Proactive policies at regional and local level
Tax incentives to improve efficiency	Public investment in infrastructure
Regional policy	
Minimal expenditure	Extensive regional aid
Selective assistance	Decentralization of regional regeneration powers to local and regional agencies and authorities

Source: adapted from Martin (1989a)

and Minns 1995). The revival of the problem regions requires supply-side policies in order to rebuild the industrial and commercial base of these areas. This requires government involvement at the local, regional, national and EU levels.

These two opposing approaches to reducing regional unemployment disparities are now discussed in more detail. We turn first to the market-based approach.

Market-based solutions to reducing regional unemployment disparities

Since it is market rigidities which prevent wages from falling to their market clearing levels, the most obvious response is to remove the rigidities. Several policies have been suggested, some relating to the labour market and some to the housing market. We turn first to the labour market. Minford and Stoney (1991) have argued that wage flexibility would be greater if labour unions had less power. The government could achieve this directly through more privatization, further deregulation and more contracting out of public services to private enterprise. In addition, the public sector could improve wage flexibility through the abolition of national wage agreements and by insisting on local bargaining throughout the public sector. Despite rapid progress in this direction in the 1980s and 1990s there is still considerable scope for the extension of this type of policy.

Policies are required to improve labour migration from high-unemployment to low-unemployment areas. Rents for public sector housing could be raised to market levels in order to increase the incentive to move out of high-unemployment areas. The private sector could also be given financial incentives to encourage an increase in the provision of property for rent in low-unemployment areas (Maclennan 1994). Cameron and Muellbauer (1998) argue that such incentives are necessary in order to revive the private rental sector, which in turn would significantly enhance labour migration from high- to low-unemployment areas. This alone, however, would not be enough since high land costs in regions such as the south-east (due to the stringent planning controls) keep the price of property high relative to other regions. More land needs to be made available in order to increase the supply (and reduce the price) of accommodation (Evans 1989). Net migration to the south-east would then increase, particularly if other changes were also made to stimulate migration, such as encouraging more portable pension plans in place of company pension schemes which tie employees to particular firms. The eventual result would be the relief of labour market pressures in the south while simultaneously reducing unemployment in other regions.

Needless to say, this free market approach to reducing regional unemployment disparities has come under heavy fire. The argument that labour unions are responsible for the downward inflexibility of wages in high-unemployment regions through national wage bargaining has been vigorously disputed. Walsh and Brown (1991), for example, show that national wage bargaining has been in decline since the 1950s and this process accelerated during the 1980s. The decline of national wage bargaining, however, has not been the result of a desire by firms to take advantage of local labour market conditions when negotiating wage increases. The shift has been away from national bargaining because multi-regional firms have decentralized their activities to profit centres so that wages are now tied more closely to the profitability of individual production units within the organization. If a unit is highly profitable this will lead to higher wages irrespective of local levels of unemployment.

The proposal to introduce policies to increase the mobility of labour from north to south has also come under attack. Elementary economic theory argues that encouraging labour to move from labour-abundant areas to labour-scarce areas will result in unequivocal economic gains. But this is only the case in elementary demand and supply models, which ignore that fact that in-migrants themselves will create extra demand for the already over-utilized social infrastructure in the south. The wider dynamic implications have also to be considered since encouraging an inflow of people into areas already suffering from congestion only makes matters worse. Moreover, migrants are almost always the younger, more skilled and more active members of a population. Their loss is a great blow to the future growth prospects of the high-unemployment areas.

Instead of introducing policies which make it easier for labour to move into the congested south-east in order to relieve labour market pressure, an alternative policy is to impose higher employment taxes in labour-scarce areas compared with labour-abundant areas. Firms would then be induced to switch to capital-intensive techniques in labour-scarce areas, or to move their operations to labour-abundant areas. A related measure is the imposition of congestion taxes. Any new industrial or commercial development could be taxed by the amount that it increases congestion for others already located in the area. The effect would again be to induce an outward migration of capital (and hence labour demand) to the labour-abundant areas of the north.

The interventionist approach to reducing regional unemployment disparities

Direct government intervention to reduce regional unemployment disparities can take three main forms: (1) inducing inward investment into high-unemployment areas; (2) stimulating indigenous growth in high-unemployment areas; and (3) regenerating high-unemployment areas through public investment in the socio-economic infrastructure.

The policy of inducing manufacturing firms to move from non-assisted areas to assisted areas typifies the interventionist approach. For much of the post-war period, location controls were placed on manufacturing firms in non-assisted areas (especially in the south-east), while investment incentives have been offered to firms moving into the assisted areas. The primary purpose of this carrot-and-stick policy was to achieve a better geographical match between labour demand and labour supply so that unemployment would fall in areas of high unemployment while simultaneously reducing inflationary pressures in the labour-scarce south. Chapter 9 discusses these policies in more detail.

The second strategic approach to reducing regional unemployment disparities is to get the assisted areas to create their own growth. This indigenous growth approach became popular in the 1980s and 1990s for two reasons. First, the previously dominant strategy of encouraging firms to relocate in designated assisted areas had run into problems during the late 1970s due to a lack of mobile investment projects; and, second, the emergence of the enterprise culture fashion in the early 1980s pointed towards stimulating the emergence of new firms and the growth of small firms. The advantages and disadvantages arising from relying upon indigenous growth to reduce regional unemployment disparities are discussed in detail in chapter 10.

The third arm of regional policy is public investment in the social and physical infrastructure of depressed areas. The interventionist approach argues that it is vitally important to improve the stock of social infrastructure in high-unemployment areas in order to improve their competitiveness. Investment in physical infrastructure could include redeveloping derelict sites, improving the transport network, providing better recreational facilities, enhancing the stock of housing and improving the quality of the urban environment more generally. Such improvement to an area's physical and social infrastructure acts as an important signal to the private sector since it demonstrates the government's commitment to reviving depressed areas and acts as a confidence booster for private sector investors. It also helps the depressed areas to retain and attract highly skilled workers who place a premium on their living conditions.

8.3   The historical development of regional policy in Britain

In this section we examine the way in which regional policy in Britain has developed since its origins in 1928. For most of its history, regional policy in Britain has been the virtual monopoly of the *national* government. For this reason we begin with a discussion of the British government's role. This is followed by a brief review of the part played in more recent years by other participants such as the EU and regional and local agencies.

The role of the national government in regional policy in Britain

Regional policy in Britain had an inauspicious start in the inter-war years. The story begins in the late 1920s, when persistent overcapacity and high unemployment in Britain's staple export industries led to unemployment 'black spots' due to the geographical concentration of these industries. The government's response was to set up the Industrial Transference Board: 'for the purpose of facilitating the transfer of workers, and in particular miners, for whom opportunities of employment in their own district or occupation are no longer available' (Ministry of Labour 1928: 1). By 1938, over 200 000 workers had received financial assistance under this scheme. The success of this labour mobility policy in helping the unemployed to move to areas where job opportunities were more favourable was minute, however, compared with the magnitude of the problem that existed in the 1930s. With unemployment approaching 3 million, as it did in 1933, the transfer of 20 000 workers per annum was unlikely to have much impact on regional disparities in the unemployment rate.

The severity of the inter-war slump was both the cause of the emergence of regional policy and, ironically, its great weakness. The enormity of the problem faced by policy makers is vividly illustrated by the unemployment rates given in table 8.2. Although these rates suffer from the fact that the registered unemployed are expressed only as a percentage of *insured* workers (rather than the total workforce), they do nevertheless provide a clear indication of the substantial regional disparities in the unemployment rate that occurred in the depths of the slump. Wales, Scotland, Northern Ireland and northern England suffered particularly high rates of unemployment, and it was the harsh economic and social conditions prevailing in these regions that induced the government to introduce the Special Areas Acts of 1934 and 1937. Unfortunately, government expenditure on aid to industry was pitifully small, with the result that very few jobs were actually created.

Yet this pre-war initiative was important for two reasons. First, it marked the beginning of an approach to regional problems based on the principle of 'taking work to the workers' rather than 'moving workers to the work'. In addition, the objective of reducing regional disparities in unemployment became the guiding principle underlying all subsequent regional policy in Britain.

The turning point in British regional policy came as a result of the publication of the White Paper *Employment Policy* in 1944, which committed post-war

Table 8.2   Unemployment rates in UK regions, January 1933

Region	Unemployment rate (%)[a]
London	14.2
South East	17.0
South West	19.6
Midlands	20.2
North East	29.8
North West	25.7
Wales	37.8
Scotland	30.2
Northern Ireland	28.9
United Kingdom	23.4

[a] % unemployed = (number of insured and uninsured persons registered as unemployed × 100)/ (number of insured employees aged 16 to 64 at mid-year).
Source: Historical Abstract of Labour Statistics, tables 110 and 162, Office for National Statistics, © Crown Copyright

governments to a policy of full employment. The acceptance of Keynesian views on the desirability of government intervention led directly to the belief not only that governments had the power to create jobs, but also that it was their responsibility to do so. The special need to create jobs in areas of traditionally high unemployment had been emphasized in the Barlow Report:

> A beginning must be made in regarding the country as a social and economic unit as well as a political unit. We believe that if it be possible (and we consider that it is possible), by positive action through inducement, advice and direction, to achieve a better balanced industrial development in the areas where excessive specialisation has brought disaster, unemployment will be reduced in these areas without increasing it elsewhere, whilst taking away the urge to locate new industries or to extend old ones in the admittedly congested area around London. (Royal Commission on the Distribution of the Industrial Population 1944: 208–9)

The problem facing the incoming Labour government in 1945 was to construct a policy capable of achieving the objectives set out in the 1944 White Paper. The main thrust of the regional aspects of employment policy was the creation of manufacturing jobs in the newly established Development Areas. A variety of policy instruments were introduced through the Distribution of Industry Act 1945 and its various successors. These included loans and grants to firms, powers to build factories and establish industrial estates, and the provision of basic services for industry. Subsidies were directed towards investment and this emphasis on capital grants persisted for a further two decades. By far the most powerful regional policy instrument in the immediate post-war years, however, was the system of controls imposed on the location of industry. The power of location controls is reflected by the leap in the number of firms moving into assisted areas after 1945, as shown in figure 8.2.

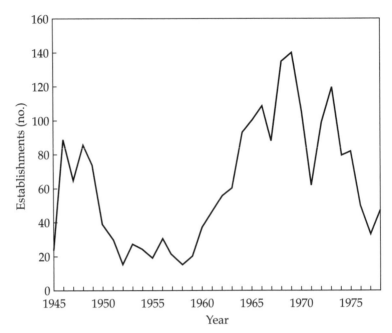

Figure 8.2   The number of manufacturing establishments moving into UK Development Areas, 1945–78.
Source: Moore et al. (1986)

The strict controls on industrial location imposed in the immediate post-war years were of short duration. The government's commitment to regional policy began to wane as early as 1947 in the face of a balance of payments crisis. The lack of commitment accelerated in the 1950s and it was not until the 1958 recession that regional policy was taken seriously again. The decline and subsequent revival of regional policy during the 1950s is clearly indicated in figures 8.3 and 8.4.

The 1958 recession triggered a revival of regional policy since it hit the traditionally disadvantaged regions the hardest, and this revival continued into the 1960s, which witnessed a far more serious and determined attitude by policy makers towards regional problems. The revitalization of regional policy in the early 1960s coincided with a growing interest in two other aspects of economic policy. First, concern was being expressed about Britain's post-war growth performance compared with other industrialized countries. The National Economic Development Council responded to this concern by arguing that: 'the relatively high unemployment rates, and more important still, the relatively low activity rates in these regions also indicate considerable labour reserves. To draw these reserves into employment would make a substantial contribution to national employment and national growth' (1963: 14). Regional policy was therefore to be seen as helping to achieve a faster rate of *national* growth. This contrasted with earlier views which had regarded regional policy merely as a means of reducing regional disparities in economic welfare.

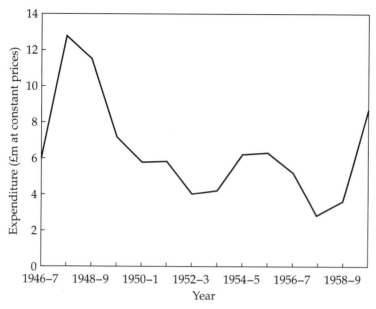

Figure 8.3   Regional policy expenditure under the Distributions of Industry Acts.
Source: Armstrong (1991), figure 10.7. Reproduced with the permission of Taylor & Francis Ltd, London

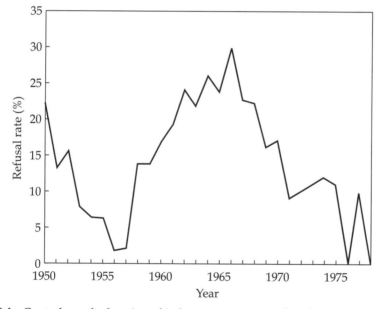

Figure 8.4   Controls on the location of industry: percentage of applications for an Industrial Development Certificate refused, 1950–77.
Source: Department of Trade and Industry; data obtained from P. Tyler, University of Cambridge

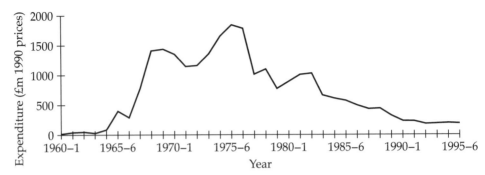

Figure 8.5   Expenditure on regional industrial assistance in the UK, 1960–1 to 1995–6. Expenditure on regional industrial assistance includes initial investment allowances, automatic allowances, automatic investment grants, discretionary grants, loans and labour subsidies assistance (all expressed as grant equivalents): see Wren (1996b: 328) for details.
Source: Taylor and Wren (1997), table 2

Second, concern was being expressed about the problems of excessive growth in Greater London. The externality costs associated with this increasing concentration of population and industry were thought to be sufficiently high to justify a stronger regional policy. The result was a huge expansion of regional policy in the mid 1960s. Expenditure accelerated in the 1960s and a variety of new measures were introduced (see figure 8.5). The main thrust of regional policy, however, remained broadly the same. The aim was to induce manufacturing firms to locate their plant and machinery in the assisted areas and they were encouraged to do this through a mixture of incentives and controls. The emphasis was therefore firmly on inward investment, either from abroad or, more normally, from the more prosperous regions.

Regional policy was strengthened further in 1972 (see figure 8.5), largely in response to a recession which led to a sharp increase in the unemployment rate, particularly in the assisted areas which were suffering their highest levels of unemployment for over 30 years. Reviving regional policy in the mid-1970s proved to be more difficult than had been anticipated, not least because of the severity of the balance of payments crisis and the inflationary problems that beset the British economy. The subsequent deflationary policies led to a sharp fall in investment activity, especially in the manufacturing sector, and this meant that there was a smaller amount of mobile investment which could be induced to move into the assisted areas. The decline of regional policy was therefore well on the way by the time the Conservative Party under Mrs Thatcher regained power in 1979, as figure 8.5 shows. This decline is also clearly reflected by the collapse in the use of location controls at that time (see figure 8.4).

Regional policy was further downgraded in the early 1980s. Location controls were abolished in 1982 and the areas eligible for assistance were drastically cut back. Investment incentives were also reduced as a result of the abolition of the Special Development Areas, which had attracted higher investment grant rates than the Development Areas. An even clearer indication of the rundown of regional policy is provided by the long-term decline in regional policy spending throughout the 1980s. This contrasts starkly with a rapid rise in the UK government's spending on urban policy in the 1980s (Martin 1992). The government was made vividly aware of the intense economic and social problems facing the inner cities in the aftermath of the 1981 riots at Brixton in London and Toxteth in Liverpool. The civil unrest concentrated the attention of policy makers on the need to improve social and economic conditions in the inner cities. Regional policy in the 1980s was therefore steadily downgraded, while urban policy was very much in the ascendancy. This withering away of the *national* government's role in regional policy was mitigated to a limited extent by the emergence of an EU regional policy in the 1970s. The newly created European Regional Development Fund began operations in 1975. It was not, however, until 1989 that EU regional policy began to have a major role in mitigating the effects of the decline in the national government's assistance to the disadvantaged regions.

The severe cuts in regional policy spending during the 1980s were achieved by sharpening up the focus of regional policy. Funds were targeted on a smaller number of assisted areas. In addition, the aim was 'to make the policy much more cost effective in terms of a single guiding objective, that objective being to reduce regional disparities in employment opportunities' (Committee of Public Accounts 1984: 22). There was no question of regional policy being abolished, however, even during the most intense periods of the Thatcher government's drive towards a smaller role for the state. The government remained 'committed to maintaining an effective regional policy to ease the process of change in areas which have been dependent on declining industries and to encourage new business in these areas' (White Paper 1983: 1).

By 1988 the government was contemplating further far-reaching changes. Expenditure cuts included the termination of the automatic investment grants scheme, the Regional Development Grant. Once again, however, regional policy was spared complete abolition, though its role was radically changed. Regional policy was to become part of a government drive to encourage self-help, regional development 'from within', and a renewed commitment to enterprise. This approach marked a significant break from traditional regional policy, as the government reinterpreted the regional problem as one of economic inefficiency due to supply-side rigidities and a deficiency of entrepreneurial activity in the disadvantaged areas (Martin 1989a). The policy response was therefore to help the disadvantaged areas to improve their competitiveness, and to remove supply-side rigidities preventing industry and commerce from generating self-sufficient growth. The key to reducing regional inequalities was therefore believed to be the stimulation of indigenous regional enterprise. The intention was that indigenous development would replace inward investment as the dynamo of regional growth. The White Paper *DTI – The Department for Enterprise* set out the objective succinctly: 'In all our work we will take account of the differing circumstances in the regions . . . to enable those who live there to help themselves' (1988: 29). To try to achieve this objective, government expenditure since 1988 has been switched from automatic to selective investment grants, and help was targeted on schemes such as

Regional Enterprise Grants designed to improve managerial skills, business strategies and innovation. Smaller firms and the encouragement of technological innovation, in particular, were now favoured, as chapter 10 shows. Perhaps the most striking feature of all of the 1980s, however, was the survival of regional policy during a period marked by the most tenacious commitment to free market policies of any government in the post-war period.

By the early 1990s regional policy had become firmly entrenched as a component of the nation's *industry policy*. In particular, emphasis was placed on integrating regional policy into the drive to improve the *competitiveness* of industry in international markets. The focus on indigenous development in the disadvantaged regions was ideally suited to this role of regional policy as one component in a larger national competitiveness strategy. The stimulation of entrepreneurship, small firms and new technology, it was argued, would help to regenerate not only the disadvantaged regions but also the whole national economy.

Concern with the ability of British companies (and their wider EU counterparts) to compete effectively in world markets had grown steadily during the 1980s. By 1988 the Secretary of State for Industry was signalling a move towards a nakedly transparent competitiveness agenda in which: 'Wealth is created through open and competitive markets . . . Government policy is directed at creating a climate which stimulates wealth creation, promotes competition, reduces red tape and encourages enterprise' (White Paper 1988: 1). As a result of the 1988 White Paper, regional policy in the early 1990s swung into action behind a whole raft of national initiatives to strengthen the competitiveness of British industry. This competitiveness strategy threatened to crowd out the other non-economic objectives of regional policy. In 1994, for example, the government was arguing that 'Our living standards and quality of life are not entitlements . . . Success has to be earned through improved competitiveness' (White Paper 1994: 8). This view was very much in line with similar thinking within the EU (Commission of the European Communities 1993). In 1995 the House of Commons Select Committee on Regional Policy argued that 'the principal aim of regional policy should be to increase the competitiveness of the Assisted Areas, both in terms of the suitability as locations for industrial activity and in terms of the competitiveness of the individual firms within them' (House of Commons 1995: xxxi).

A series of White Papers during the 1990s continued to place great emphasis on the need for policies designed to enhance the nation's economic competitiveness (White Paper 1995; 1996). The election of a Labour government in 1997 did little to reduce the enthusiasm for economic competitiveness, for 'The Government's aim is for British business to close the gap with its competitors' (White Paper 1998: 6). Regional policy continued to be seen as playing a supporting role since it involves (a) the 'development of a strategic long-term vision for promoting competitiveness in the region; (b) ensuring national support for competitiveness is tailored to regional and local needs; and (c) providing support for the development of clusters, networks and other partnerships' (1998: 42).

It is clear, therefore, that economic objectives remain at the heart of modern regional policy in Britain and are still at the forefront of government statements of the role which regional policy is expected to play. Gradually, however, as the

1990s progressed, the pendulum once again began to swing away from economic goals (i.e. competitiveness) and back towards social objectives. This process is examined in greater detail in section 8.4.

The emergence of new participants in regional policy in Britain

Britain's accession to the EU in 1973 marked a turning point for regional policy. Prior to 1973 the national government enjoyed an almost complete stranglehold on regional policy spending. The period since 1973 has witnessed the emergence of a series of new participants alongside the national government. Three additional tiers of participants are now involved: the EU, regional-level agencies and local-level organizations. Each will be considered in turn.

EU participation in regional policy

Britain's accession to the EU led immediately to the assisted areas becoming eligible for financial help from a number of existing EU financial instruments. The European Social Fund (ESF) at that time offered grants to part-finance training and worker mobility schemes. The assisted areas, with their high levels of unemployment, were prime candidates for help from the ESF. Britain rapidly became the recipient of no less than one-third of all ESF allocations within the EU and remains a major recipient of this type of help. The European Coal and Steel Community (ECSC) has a separate budget of its own within the EU. British coal and steel areas in 1973 became immediately eligible for financial help from the ECSC. This help takes the form of loans (on attractive terms) for investment and restructuring purposes. In addition, the ECSC offers 'conversion loans' designed to help new industries to set up in the coal and steel areas, and redundant workers also obtain direct help from the ECSC (e.g. for retraining, rehousing and as wage supplements). ECSC assistance remains a valuable type of help in some of Britain's most disadvantaged regions (see chapter 11).

In 1973 the European Investment Bank (EIB) also began to provide loans (on favourable terms) to industrial and infrastructure projects in Britain's depressed regions. The EIB continues to target some three-quarters of its loans on the disadvantaged regions of the EU. Finally, in 1973 Britain's rural areas became eligible for assistance from the Guidance Section of the EU's Agriculture Fund. This provides a wide variety of types of financial help.

In addition to the arrival in 1973 of the various spending funds of the EU, accession soon led to an even more significant event, the creation of a European Regional Development Fund (ERDF) in 1975. The ERDF was designed to complement the British government's regional policy, not to replace it. Assistance was provided in the form of grants and interest rebates towards individual investment projects in industry (including service sector industries) and for small firms. Investment in infrastructure such as roads, industrial estates and telecommunications was also eligible for help.

The ERDF grew slowly at first. Over time, however, as a result of a series of small reforms in the 1980s, the ERDF gradually expanded its activities. The gradual expansion of EU regional policy spending in Britain in the 1980s proved valuable as a means of offsetting some of the decline in spending by the national government. In was the 1990s, however, which witnessed the heyday of EU regional policy. In a response to the strains being imposed on the disadvantaged regions by the introduction of the Single European Market, a root-and-branch reform of EU regional policy was introduced in 1989. Between 1989 and 1993 new EU legislation revamped all aspects of the EU's regional policy and laid the foundations of the EU regional policy which we see today. The ERDF, ESF and Agriculture (Guidance Section) Funds were renamed the Structural Funds and were required to combine their efforts to reduce regional disparities. Help for disadvantaged regions was switched from a piecemeal project-by-project approach to one of co-ordinated multi-annual programmes.

These regional programmes in the 1990s focused EU help on indigenous development rather than inward investment. As such, the activities of the Structural Funds in Britain in the 1990s were very much in harmony with the national government's own efforts. This does not, of course, mean that inward investment was abandoned. Throughout the 1990s, the UK national government continued to use its discretionary regional policy instrument (Regional Selective Assistance) to successfully attract inward investment projects from overseas. The bulk of regional policy help in the 1990s was, however, targeted at indigenous development.

In addition to reinforcing the switch to indigenous development initiatives, the EU Structural Funds in the 1990s had two other main impacts on the manner in which regional policy operated in Britain. First, EU expenditures have expanded rapidly since 1989. The period 1989 to 1993 witnessed a doubling in the size of the Structural Funds (in real terms). A further doubling occurred as a result of a new set of reforms in 1994. A further massive expansion is to be phased in between 2000 and 2006 (see chapter 11).

The result of reforms to EU regional policy in the 1990s has been to make the EU the dominant partner in regional policy in Britain. This is not to belittle the role of the national government. EU regional policy regulations require that the member states must provide *matching funding* alongside the contribution of the Structural Funds on all projects assisted. This matching funding in Britain is drawn from a huge array of sources, most of which in practice are directly or indirectly paid for by the UK Treasury. This process alone ensures that the national government continues to play a vital role in regional policy. It is important, therefore, not to overstate the decline of the role of the national government in British regional policy. The EU, however, is clearly in the driving seat as far as regional policy is concerned.

As well as providing part of the matching funding for EU programmes, the UK government in the 1990s continued to have its own regional policy instruments. As figure 8.6 shows, expenditure on national regional policy initiatives in the 1990s continued to decline (in real terms) until around 1992–3, at which point it stabilized at just under £400 million. It now amounts to approximately 0.05 per cent of national GDP. UK government expenditures now fall well short of EU funding. It is estimated that between 1994 and 2000 the UK will have obtained

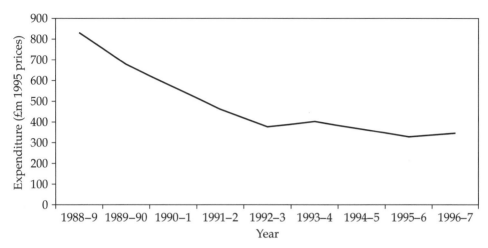

Figure 8.6 Expenditure on regional preferential assistance to industry in Great Britain, 1988–9 to 1996–7.
Source: *Regional Trends*, Office of National Statistics, © Crown Copyright

£9 billion from the Structural Funds (Department of Trade and Industry 1999c). This will rise further in the 2000–6 budget period of the EU.

Regional organizations

The second big impact of the EU Structural Funds in the 1990s was to give a great boost to the role of regional and local participants in regional policy. The EU is committed to a partnership approach to regional policy. This approach is vital where indigenous development is the goal, and has been encouraged by the UK national government too. The 1989 reform of EU regional policy contained measures designed to strengthen the role of regional and local organizations in the delivery of regional policy, and successive reforms to EU regional policy in the 1990s took this process much further.

Regional-level development agencies were first created in Britain in 1976. The Scottish and Welsh Development Agencies, together with the Development Board for Rural Wales, represented a significant step forward for regional policy in Britain. A Scottish equivalent of the Development Board for Rural Wales, the Highlands and Islands Development Board, had existed since 1965 and had pioneered many of the approaches which the new agencies were to adopt. The Scottish and Welsh Development Agencies, however, represented organizations with much greater financial 'clout'.

The regional tier was given a further massive boost in 1998 with the establishment of regional development agencies in the *English* regions, and with the establishment of elected regional governments in Scotland and Wales in 1999 (see chapter 12). Although the powers of the various regional-level agencies in Britain differ significantly from one another, they share a number of important characteristics. They are all non-elected organizations which are financed in a variety of

ways, but with the bulk of the finance in the form of grant-in-aid from the
national government. As the agencies build up a portfolio of income-earning
assets (e.g. land, property, equity in companies and outstanding loans) so the
proportion of their budget financed from own resources tends to slowly increase.
The agencies also seek to increase the financial impact of their operations by acting
as a catalyst and attracting private finance alongside their own investments.

The regional development agencies of Scotland and Wales have proved over
the years to be extremely innovative in the manner in which they have given help.
As well as traditional forms of assistance such as grants, loans and the provision
of business sites and premises, they have expanded into a wide variety of other
measures. These have included the taking of direct shareholdings in firms, the
provision of advisory services to firms (particularly small firms), special schemes
to encourage technological innovation and the redevelopment of derelict land
and environmental improvement schemes. The growing emphasis in the 1980s
and 1990s on indigenous development has led to a flowering of the activities of
the agencies. As regional-level organizations with close links to local authorities
and other local bodies, the regional development agencies have been ideally
placed to operate the new types of regional policy developed in the 1980s and
1990s. Whether the newly established regional development agencies (RDAs) in
the English regions will acquire the status attained by those in Scotland and Wales
remains to be seen. But it is clear that these new RDAs will need to win the confidence not only of the central government but also of the local communities within
the region if they are to play a major role in the region's economic regeneration
and development (Foley 1998).

Local participation in regional policy

The final set of new participants to emerge in the 1980s and 1990s helping to
revitalize the disadvantaged areas of Britain has been at the local level. There are
now hundreds of local development organizations in existence in Britain. There
are two main reasons for the rapid expansion of these local-level development
organizations. First, the gradual fall in the national government's spending on
regional policy has left something of a vacuum. Local authorities and an array of
private and joint private/public organizations stepped into the breach during the
1980s and 1990s. Second, the switch to indigenous development and the enterprise culture created a role for local 'delivery' organizations operating close to
the business sector clients of regional policy. Successful indigenous development
requires the active participation of the local community. Local-level delivery
organizations are crucial if indigenous development policy is to be successful.

Local authorities in Britain have always played a role in granting planning permission and in providing serviced sites and premises for businesses. During the
1980s they greatly expanded their role. By the mid 1980s they were operating over
20 different types of measure to assist firms, particularly small firms (Armstrong
and Fildes 1988; Sellgren 1991). The local councils have now been joined by a
huge array of other local development organizations. Many, such as the Training
and Enterprise Councils, are government sponsored to a large degree. There

are, however, many other *ad hoc* organizations, such as business 'clubs' where business owners can meet and swap information and advice. There are even a number of private sector development agencies seeking to help local communities to overcome the problems of industrial restructuring, such as British Steel (Industry) Ltd.

The emergence in the 1980s and 1990s of so many new participants in the regional policy effort in Britain is both interesting and welcome. As well as helping to fill the gap caused by the partial withdrawal of central government funding, they have also proved to be both enthusiastic and innovative in their methods. There have, however, been problems. The competence of some has been called into question, particularly where they are small and are duplicating the work of others. In addition, there are real fears that the lack of co-ordination between the many participants now involved confuses potential business investors, despite attempts to create 'one-stop shops' such as the Business Links.

8.4 Regional policy: economic efficiency or social inclusion?

Regional policy in Britain has always been bedevilled by two problems. First, successive governments have tended to set *multiple objectives* for regional policy to achieve. Setting multiple objectives is always a risky business since the policy may fall between different stools. Second, there has always been a deep-seated tension between the *economic* and the *social* objectives of regional policy. Economists refer to this tension in terms of the potential for conflict between *efficiency* and *equity goals*. Specialists from other disciplines take a wider view of what constitutes a social objective than merely a more equitable distribution of income, but nevertheless still stress the potential for conflict with economic goals.

The presence of multiple objectives and the tension between economic and social goals are problems which have been present from the earliest days of regional policy. The 1928 Industrial Transference Board saw its role as not only the alleviation of poverty in hard-hit coal mining areas (i.e. a social objective), but also the reallocation of labour to areas of the country where it could be put to productive use (i.e. an economic efficiency objective). The Barlow Report broadened the list of objectives further by adding an environmental objective (i.e. a better balance in the geographical distribution of industry in order to alleviate congestion and overcrowding in London) and a political objective (the dispersion of industry for defensive and strategic purposes). Moreover, the Barlow Report explicitly set regional policy a combination of economic and social objectives by stressing that 'a beginning must be made in regarding the country as a *social* and *economic* unit' (Royal Commission on the Distribution of the Industrial Population 1944: 208, our italics).

As has been shown earlier, by the early 1990s regional policy had come to be seen principally as part of national policy to improve competitiveness and economic efficiency. The switch to an emphasis on indigenous development simply strengthened the economic efficiency objective at the expense of social objectives. However, as Britain gradually pulled out of the recession of the early 1990s,

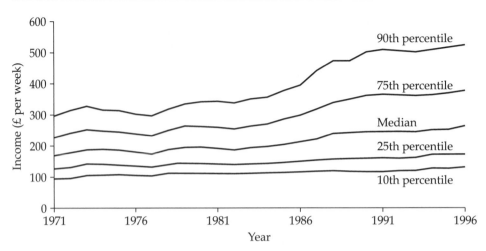

Figure 8.7   Disparities in real household disposable incomes in the UK, 1971–96.
Source: Office for National Statistics, *Social Trends 29*, 1999, the Stationery Office, London, 1999, figure 5.16, Office for National Statistics © Crown Copyright 1999

attention in regional policy began to swing back towards social objectives. This swing took place, as we have seen, against a backdrop of government rhetoric which continued to stress national competitiveness. The growing emphasis on the social objectives of regional policy is, nevertheless, a very real one and rapidly gathered pace in the latter half of the 1990s. Two sets of factors have fuelled pressures to 'bend' regional policy away from its focus on competitiveness to- wards what has come to be known as *social exclusion*.

Growing inequality in the distribution of income

Macroeconomic policy in the 1980s and 1990s was accompanied by an unpreced- ented widening of household income disparities in the UK. Figure 8.7 shows that household disposable incomes have widened dramatically in the period since 1985. For example, between 1980 and 1990 incomes grew by 47 per cent at the 90th percentile, but only 6 per cent at the 10th percentile (i.e. among the lower paid). While the pace at which incomes have diverged stabilized in the 1990s, income inequalities remain historically very wide (Machin 1998). Evidence such as this has resulted in pressure for regional policy to switch emphasis from efficiency to equity.

The growth of multiple deprivation

It would be misleading to think that what occurred in the late 1990s was simply a return to traditional regional policy concerns with an equitable distribution of income. The concept of *social exclusion* is much wider than this. Certain groups within society are heavily concentrated in the lower reaches of the income dis- tribution and these groups appear to find it very difficult to escape the poverty in which they find themselves. For example, in 1996–7, no fewer than 42 per cent of all single parents were located in the bottom fifth of the income distribution, while only 3 per cent found themselves in the top fifth. A number of other groups appear to share the same problem, especially disabled persons, certain ethnic minorities, communities residing in inner cities, those in peripheral social housing estates, the long-term unemployed, and some rural and former coal mining communities.

A common characteristic of many of these social groups is that they face 'multiple deprivation': they must attempt to overcome an array of different barriers to successful reinsertion to the mainstream economy. Many of the unemployed in our inner cities and peripheral housing estates, for example, not only lack appropriate skills, but are also faced with discrimination by employers (e.g. racial or 'postcode' discrimination). In addition, they do not have easy and cheap access to job opportunities, and have been unemployed for so long that they have lost motivation. While great emphasis has been placed on exclusion from the *labour market* (Green 1997; 1999; Martin 1997), many groups are also excluded from housing markets and other parts of the economy and society (McGregor and McConnachie 1995). Concern that these groups in society have become so detached from the mainstream has led to a rapid growth in special initiatives designed to tackle social exclusion.

The growing importance of policies designed to tackle social exclusion has led to an important debate on the issue of whether economic competitiveness or social inclusion should be the prime objective of regional policy. Those who favour the retention of the economic competitiveness objective have pointed to three main arguments.

Social exclusion is concerned with social and political goals which are not properly the concern of regional economic policy

Considerable confusion continues to surround what is meant by social exclusion. One recent definition suggested by the government describes social exclusion as 'broadly covering those people who do not have the means, material or otherwise, to participate in social, economic, political and cultural life' (Brennan et al. 1998: 4). This is an extraordinarily vague concept, but does highlight the importance of social and political objectives. Social exclusion clearly remains 'a slippery concept . . . there has often been little effort systematically to distinguish amongst "social exclusion", "poverty", "deprivation", "polarisation" and "differentiation"' (Lawless 1997: 238). Despite the vagueness of definitions of social exclusion, it is nevertheless clear that the concept does include an *economic* component, even though this is only one part of a much wider agenda. This does, therefore, open up the possibility that regional economic policy can play a role in reducing social exclusion.

Social exclusion is a national problem requiring national rather than regional policy initiatives

This point of view has widespread support among economists, particularly as the objective of an *equitable* distribution of income is seen in the traditional public

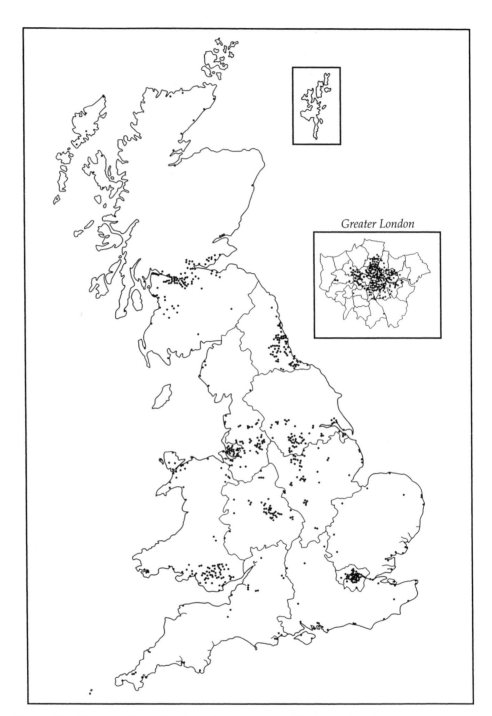

Figure 8.8 Wards in Great Britain suffering extreme labour market disadvantage. Labour market disadvantage is defined here using a combination of indicators of unemployment rates, non-employment and long-term unemployment.
Source: Green (1997), figure 4.4. Reproduced with the permission of The Stationery Office, Norwich

finance literature as a central government responsibility rather than a local or regional authority one. This issue is, in fact, a long-standing one in regional policy. Whether regional policy is a suitable vehicle for helping individuals (or specific groups of individuals) has been debated since the very origins of the policy. It is quite possible, for example, that a regional policy which successfully led to an equalization of *regional* per capita incomes might well have regressive effects on the *personal* distribution of income. This would happen if a region experienced a rise in its per capita income relative to the nation as a whole, but where most of the income gain accrued to high-income households resident in the depressed region. In other words, it is important to distinguish between 'place prosperity' and 'people prosperity'. Even in the poorest of localities, not all those who benefit from regional policies will be low on the welfare scale.

A further twist to the divergence between 'place prosperity' and 'people prosperity' is that owners of capital (and other resources) may not be resident in the same region as the resources they own. Industrial subsidies may increase the earnings of capital owners who are themselves resident in prosperous regions. The debate on what role regional policy should play in reducing social exclusion has reignited 'place prosperity' versus 'people prosperity' arguments. Are policies designed to reduce social exclusion designed to help people or places? Can social exclusion policies really ensure that the help they offer gets through to those who need it, or will the help given, as with many industrial subsidies, end up in the pockets of the already prosperous in affluent areas?

This debate will undoubtedly continue to rage. One fact however is clear: there is a strong regional dimension to social exclusion in Britain. Figure 8.8 shows the distribution of local wards in Britain experiencing severe labour market exclusion problems (Green 1997). Inner areas of London exhibit severe problems, a feature revealed by other measures of social exclusion. Lee (1999), for example, shows that many of the most deprived localities in Britain are in London. Nevertheless, figure 8.8 reveals that labour market exclusion is also very widespread in the disadvantaged regions of the north and west of Britain. While many of these localities are in the larger metropolitan areas, a number are also in rural communities and former coal mining villages. This is an important finding since it suggests that social exclusion is not something which urban policy alone can solve. In Britain, urban policy, particularly in the form of the Single Regeneration Budget, was at the forefront of initiatives to tackle social exclusion in the 1990s. Since the problem arises in areas outside the big cities, urban policy will not be sufficient on its own.

Policies to tackle social exclusion are in direct conflict with policies seeking to enhance economic competitiveness

This too is a debate as old as regional policy itself. Critics of regional policy have long argued that many disadvantaged regions are inherently poor locations for modern industries and that inducing firms to set up there has adverse effects on national competitiveness. Identical arguments have been raised in the debate on social exclusion. Are the localities affected by social exclusion sensible places to encourage firms to set up? Would it not be better for individuals living in socially excluded communities to be encouraged to obtain better skills and move elsewhere for work rather than preserving their failed communities? The issue is critical to the whole debate, and is one to which we return in chapter 9 when the particular policy initiatives used to tackle social exclusion are considered.

Whatever the merits of the case for introducing social inclusion objectives into regional policy, there is no doubt that this process is now well under way. While most of the national government's schemes in Britain remain focused on economic competitiveness, the EU Structural Funds have rapidly incorporated initiatives focused on social exclusion. These have taken the form of special *community economic development* (CED) schemes inserted from 1995 onwards into the 1994–9 Structural Fund programmes (see chapter 11). The Structural Funds programmes have not, however, been completely taken over by social inclusion initiatives. In the UK, most of the EU programmes have continued to run schemes which focus help for small and medium enterprises (SMEs), innovation, inward investment and infrastructure provision for businesses. Nevertheless, CED components in the EU programmes have rapidly been expanded. CED initiatives were allocated between 13 and 25 per cent of total expenditures in the 1997–9 Structural Funds programmes in Britain. In Yorkshire and the Humber, for example, CED initiatives were awarded 17.0 per cent of all allocations between 1994 and 1996, and this was raised to 25.4 per cent for the 1997–9 period (Government Office for Yorkshire and the Humber 1999b). This share is likely to be even higher during budget period 2000–6.

The CED initiatives within existing EU programmes are required to concentrate on employment creation rather than more explicitly social impacts (see chapter 9). In a further development which will enhance the importance of the social exclusion goals of EU regional policy in Britain, the *Agenda 2000* reforms to EU regional policy have introduced a number of *horizontal aims* (European Commission 1997). In future, projects assisted by the EU Structural Funds in Britain, including those with traditional economic and competitiveness aims, will be required to carefully monitor their social exclusion, equal opportunities (i.e. gender) and environmental effects. In other words, the help given by the EU is no longer simply to be judged on whether jobs, income and economic competitiveness are improved. Wider non-economic considerations must now be systematically incorporated.

8.5   Conclusion

Precise specification of objectives is an essential adjunct to regional policy for three distinct reasons:

1   For the purpose of delimiting an appropriate set of policy areas.
2   For the purpose of assembling the most efficient set of policy instruments.
3   For the purpose of evaluating regional policy.

The importance of specifying precise objectives for the selection of policy instruments is obvious: different goals require different types of policies for their achievement. Similarly, it is impossible to estimate how effective regional policies have been, or will be, unless it is clear what they are designed to achieve. Without clarifying the objectives of regional policy, evaluation degenerates into measuring the effects of regional policy rather than measuring the effectiveness – and there is a world of difference between the two.

It is far easier to assess the effectiveness of regional policies if the objectives are expressed in quantitative terms. This means: (1) numerical targets have to be set for each objective; (2) the time period within which the targets are to be achieved should be stated; and (3) weights should be attached to each objective so that priorities can be determined.

For most of the history of regional policy it has proved difficult to get policy makers to specify objectives clearly. Politicians are acutely aware of the dangers of setting targets not subsequently attained. This situation changed dramatically in the 1990s. The setting of detailed targets and performance indicators has become extremely widespread in both EU and UK regional policies (see chapter 13).

One unfortunate feature of the re-emergence of social objectives in the 1990s is that regional policy has again entered one of those periodic phases in which multiple, potentially conflicting objectives are being set for a policy which is inadequately funded to attain any one of them. The late 1990s saw a process of 'policy drift' in which the setting of a single clear economic competitiveness goal became lost. In its place we have witnessed the gradual accretion of social, political and environmental objectives. We have quantified targets a-plenty now. The problem is that there are now far too many for the policy instruments available to achieve them.

Further reading

Green (1997); Lee (1999); MacKay (1997); Martin (1992); McCallum (1979); White Paper *Our Competitive Future* (1998).

Regional policy instruments

contents

Regional policy makers have a wide range of policy options at their disposal. This chapter and the next three investigate these various options and critically examine them. Our concern at this stage is not to evaluate the effectiveness of the individual policy instruments which have actually been used but simply to identify the range of instruments which are available to the policy maker and to examine the economic case for using them.

Policy instruments can be classified in many different ways. As far as regional policy is concerned, however, policy instruments are designed either to influence the location decisions of households and firms or to change the level of income and expenditure in specific regions. This suggests that the traditional distinction between micro-instruments and macro-instruments is a useful one to adopt (see figure 9.1). Micro-policy instruments are concerned with influencing the allocation of labour and capital between industries and between regions, whereas macro-instruments are concerned with changing aggregate regional income and expenditure. It may seem strange that macro-policy instruments could be used for regional policy purposes, yet in practice macro-policies can be expected to

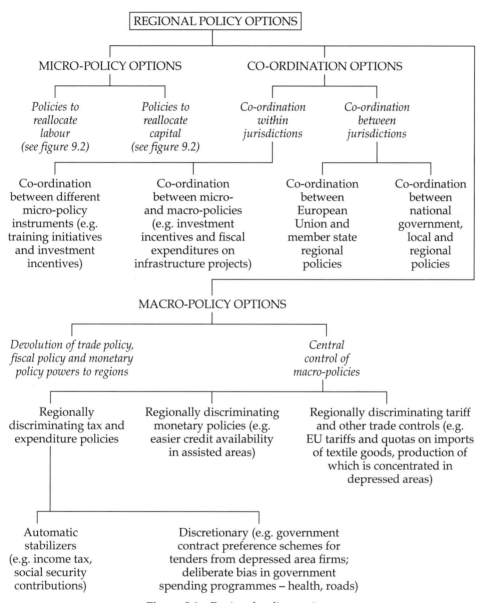

Figure 9.1   Regional policy options.

have different effects in different regions. A depreciation of the exchange rate, for instance, will favour regions which are most dependent on international trade. Similarly, expanding the national economy through fiscal or monetary policies will have different effects on output and employment in different regions. Different types of taxes, for example, are known to have radically differing regional impacts. In principle, it is possible to deliberately introduce a regional dimension into macro-policies so that different changes in output and employment can be induced in different regions. At its most extreme, this could involve adding an entirely new element to macro-policies, namely the devolution of macro-powers to regional agencies or governments. The use of regionally discriminating macro-policies and the pros and cons of devolution are discussed in chapter 12.

Another potentially important set of policy options which are of particular relevance to regional policy are those concerned with the *co-ordination* of government policy. Regional policy needs to be put together very carefully if wasteful duplication is to be avoided. An effective regional policy requires the design and use of careful co-ordination procedures. These fall into two broad types: (1) co-ordination within jurisdictions, and (2) co-ordination between jurisdictions. Taking Britain as an example, we see that regional policy instruments are operated not only by the EU and the UK central government but also by individual regional agencies and local organizations (such as county and district councils and local enterprise agencies). Each of these tiers needs to co-ordinate its various policies with those being used by other tiers.

This chapter concentrates on micro-policy instruments. The use of macro-instruments for regional policy purposes and the need to co-ordinate policy action both within and between different jurisdictions are discussed in chapters 11 and 12. We begin in section 9.1 by describing the wide range of micro-policy instruments available to the policy maker. Section 9.2 examines the thorny issue of whether *administrative controls* are good policy instruments for regional policy. This is followed in section 9.3 by a discussion of the relative merits of capital and labour subsidies in their role as regional policy instruments. This section also compares the case for marginal labour subsidies (i.e. on extra workers employed) with that for general labour subsidies (i.e. on *all* workers in the region). Finally, section 9.4 investigates the case for a radical new group of regional policy initiatives: community economic development (CED) measures. These only really surfaced in regional policy in Britain in 1995, but have rapidly expanded in popularity and look set to expand further in the next decade.

9.1   Micro-policy instruments and regional policy

Regional policy has been dominated by the use of micro-policy instruments to bring about a reallocation of capital and labour. The aim of regional policy is to induce capital and labour to locate in areas which would not normally have been chosen by those making the location decision. This involves not only inducing capital to locate in disadvantaged areas and labour to locate in areas where jobs are available but also inducing disadvantaged areas to produce their own jobs through indigenous development. The various ways in which micro-policy instruments can be used to induce a reallocation of capital and labour are summarized in figure 9.2.

The reallocation of labour

We argued in an earlier chapter that labour does not respond readily to regional differences in either wage rates or unemployment rates (which happen to be only

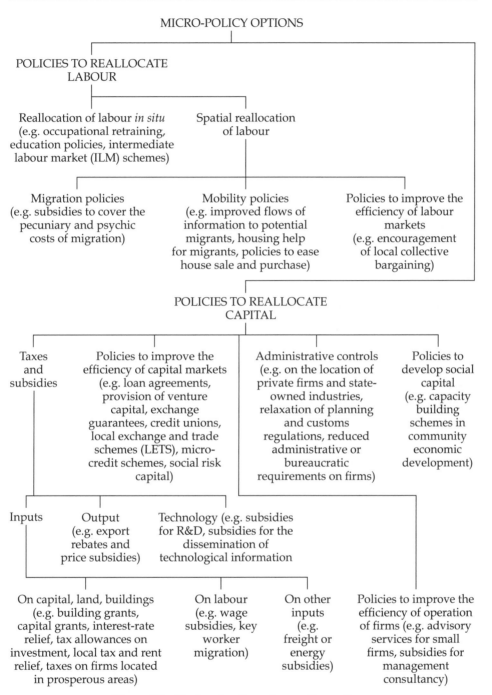

Figure 9.2 Regional policy micro-policy options.

two of the many influences acting upon the geographical movement of workers). Indeed, labour mobility is far from perfect – either between regions or between occupations. Policies designed to stimulate an increase in the geographical mobility of labour, however, have played a relatively minor role in regional policy to date. Much greater emphasis has been placed on policies designed to move capital into areas of high unemployment. This is partly because of the difficulties of removing the impediments to labour migration, but also because of the fear that encouraging out-migration from depressed areas may cause regional problems to worsen as a result of the exodus of highly qualified people.

Ideally, policies to reallocate labour encompass all instruments designed to induce labour to move into those economic activities where its marginal product is highest. Policies designed to stimulate such mobility reap an immediate output gain in terms of increased labour productivity. Expressed in terms of regional policy, this suggests two basic types of policy action: *transfer* policies and *in situ* mobility policies (figure 9.2). Transfer policies are aimed at inducing a shift in the supply of labour between regions; *in situ* mobility policies aim at increasing the occupational and industrial movement of labour at existing locations. *In situ* labour mobility policies (particularly training and retraining schemes) have, unlike transfer policies, always been a very important component of regional policy.

Conceptually, three distinct groups of impediments to labour mobility can be identified. First, earnings differentials between regions, occupations and industries may be unresponsive to corresponding differentials in the marginal product of labour. Second, even if such differentials do occur, labour may not fully perceive them. Third, even if such differentials occur and are perceived, impediments to labour mobility may still persist. This is because mobility is costly for the mover.

One reason for the failure of earnings differentials to reflect differences in the marginal product of labour is the existence of imperfect labour markets. Earnings differentials between regions are unlikely to reflect the efficiency of the marginal worker where collective bargaining is centralized. If occupational or industrial wages are established nationally, there is little scope for regional variations in wage rates for the same type of job (though hourly earnings may still vary between regions due to variations in bonus schemes and other incentive payments).

There are many features of labour markets which make it unlikely that geographical, occupational or industrial wages will even approximate the corresponding variations in the marginal product of labour. To the extent that these economic signals are missing, labour mobility will not occur. The inevitable consequence of such rigidity in the labour market is higher unemployment. Downwardly inflexible wages prevent workers from creating more jobs through bidding down the local wage rate. In addition, government unemployment benefit and other welfare payments play a supportive role in holding wage rates above their equilibrium level. As a result, they also discourage labour mobility.

At least as important as the failure of economic signals to appear in the form of wage rate differentials is the failure of potential migrants to perceive the opportunities open to them. Information flows are crucial to the operation of labour markets. Most decisions either to migrate or to retrain must be made on the basis of limited information. A lack of information causes uncertainty on the part of potential migrants. The latter require not only job information for themselves but also information on behalf of their family: information about housing, schools, social life and recreational and cultural facilities. Such uncertainty may considerably reduce migration. Information can, of course, be obtained but it is not cost-free.

Finally, there is the problem of the cost of geographical migration and the cost of changing occupations. Most obvious of these is the pecuniary cost of migration and retraining, which may be substantial. Of the numerous pecuniary barriers, the liquidity constraint is a serious one for many workers. Lack of financial resources prevents workers from moving to another location or obtaining the necessary skills even though it may well pay off in the long run. The imperfections of the capital market prevent many unemployed workers from obtaining the necessary finance because they lack collateral security. While the pecuniary costs of migration are important, the non-pecuniary costs (or 'psychic costs') of migration are likely to be of even greater significance, as chapter 6 has shown. People are reluctant to leave the location in which they have family and other personal ties.

As with the impediments to labour mobility, government policies designed to reduce these impediments fall into three broad groups. First, the government can encourage local plant-level bargaining rather than national-level bargaining so that wages become responsive to local labour market conditions. Research by Walsh and Brown (1991), however, suggests that such a policy faces formidable problems. National-level pay bargaining has, in fact, become decreasingly important in recent decades and has been replaced by much greater decentralization and local bargaining structures. Pay bargaining within individual companies, for example, has tended to replace national pay bargaining in many sectors. But when firms decide to go it alone in pay determination, they do not 'rush to exploit the competitive conditions prevailing in local labour markets' (1991: 213). When firms decentralize their pay bargaining procedures, they adopt the product division or the profit centre as the pay setting unit and this is independent of the location of production units. The decentralization of pay bargaining which occurred in the 1980s and 1990s was therefore not geographically based but rather organizationally based. It is difficult to see how any government policy could be effective in inducing major new moves towards geographically differentiated payments systems.

The remaining two groups of impediments to geographical and occupational mobility have been the focus of more long-standing policies. The first of these, the failure of households to perceive opportunities in other areas or in other occupations, has been tackled by the creation of an extensive network of government Jobcentres. While the policy of increasing the flow of information in labour markets is important, it is certainly not enough. Central government has been forced to attack the financial impediments to the geographical and occupational mobility of labour in a wide variety of ways. Many private firms operate their own training, retraining and migration schemes. The government helps to finance these programmes. In addition, the government and the EU intervene directly by subsidizing many retraining schemes and by providing grants and allowances to trainees.

In recent years emphasis has switched to schemes such as the introduction of portable private pensions and the reform of the private sector housing market.

Both of these policies are designed to stimulate mobility by reducing the costs of migration. Company pension plans, for example, penalize employees who make a series of career changes during their working life. Portable pension schemes, not tied to a single company, encourage mobility by allowing employees to avoid this financial penalty. Similarly, imperfections in the private housing market (e.g. high legal fees if there is monopoly provision of conveyancing services by solicitors) raise the costs of migration. Several other impediments to labour mobility, such as subsidized rents and rent controls, were discussed in chapter 6.

The non-pecuniary costs of mobility, and particularly the non-pecuniary costs of geographical migration, have proved to be more difficult to deal with. The relatively poor performance of measures such as the Employment Transfer Scheme in Britain, which have met only the pecuniary costs of migration, can be traced to the failure to subsidize the non-pecuniary costs of migration. To overcome these non-pecuniary costs there is a need to provide the right sort of attractions in destination regions. A good example of how non-pecuniary costs can be allevi-ated is the British new towns policy which in the past provided a 'package' of job, home and urban facilities. But the construction of such 'packages' is very expens-ive. Furthermore, some would argue that such non-pecuniary costs should not be subsidized. They are not real resource costs, and if individuals wish to exchange the utility gains from remaining where they are for the utility losses from lower incomes or unemployment, then they should be allowed to do so.

The reallocation of capital

Policies designed to increase the mobility of labour aim at improving the degree of matching between the demand and supply for labour by operating on the supply side of the labour market. The skill structure of labour demand, the geographical pattern of labour demand and the industrial distribution of labour demand are all taken as given. They are exogenous and it is the policy maker's job to match this 'mix' of labour demand by changing the skill structure, the geo-graphical pattern and the industrial distribution of workers by the appropriate labour mobility policies. The complementary policy is to improve the matching between the demand and supply for labour by diverting the demand for labour to areas of high unemployment. In addition to policies designed to transfer indus-trial capacity from one region to another or from overseas (inward investment), capital reallocation policies include policy instruments which induce the growth of investment in indigenous economic activities within regions (indigenous development).

As figure 9.2 shows, policies aimed at reallocating capital towards the dis-advantaged regions take four forms. These are: fiscal incentives (i.e. taxes and subsidies), administrative controls, schemes to improve the access of assisted area firms to sources of finance and to improve the efficiency with which assisted area firms are managed (e.g. advisory services), and schemes to improve social capital. While most regional inducements have been in the form of subsidies on labour and capital inputs, the competitiveness of firms in assisted areas could equally be enhanced by subsidies on other inputs, such as the reduction in transport costs through freight-rate subsidies. Alternatively, as figure 9.2 shows, output could be subsidized, enabling firms to sell at lower prices. Just as inducements can be offered to firms to attract them into specific locations, firms can be discouraged from locating in other regions by imposing taxes on development or by simply restricting expansion.

In the sections that follow, we examine in detail the three main sets of instruments which have been of particular importance in regional policy: administrative controls, labour and capital subsidies, and finally, community economic development initiatives.

9.2   Controls on businesses: location controls or pro-business measures?

The deliberate use of government regulations to influence the regional distribution of industry has a long provenance. In this section we discuss two countervailing opinions. The first is that administrative controls on the location of industry offer a potent weapon to policy makers in their struggle to reduce regional economic disparities. In Britain, administrative controls of this kind have taken two forms. The first has been the use of *land use planning* regulations. These are operated by local authorities in Britain, but under strong central government guidance. Since the land use planning controls in Britain have been operated essentially as instruments of urban and local area policy (i.e. at the sub-regional level) and not as a deliberate part of regional policy, they fall outside the scope of this book.

The second type of administrative controls which have been deliberately used as part of regional policy in Britain have been *industrial location controls*. Success in using central government controls on manufacturing industry in the Second Word War led, after the war in 1947, to the introduction of a system of Industrial Development Certificates (IDCs). This system was differentially applied in a manner designed to restrict manufacturing investment in the south and midlands in the UK, while simultaneously making it easy for firms to set up in the disadvantaged regions. During its period of operation, from 1947 to 1981, firms in the manufacturing sector were required to obtain an IDC before they could build new plant in excess of a specific floor space limit. Similarly, firms in the office sector had to obtain an Office Development Permit if they intended to create new office floor space in areas such as London and Birmingham.

Although location controls were abolished in 1981, their proponents have continued to cite a number of significant advantages. First, controls while they existed were extremely effective in diverting manufacturing establishments to assisted areas in the United Kingdom (Twomey and Taylor 1985). Second, location controls were cost-effective for the government since the only expenditure was on their administration. Third, location controls proved to be a flexible instrument. Permission to expand, for example, could be granted more readily to firms in the export sector than to firms producing for the domestic market; and location controls proved to be easily relaxed during recessions, when national investment was low and needed to be encouraged rather than discouraged. A fourth advantage of location controls proved to be their ability to open up a channel of communication between the government and firms contemplating new investment projects. The need to obtain an IDC had the effect of forcing firms into the arms of government officials who then had the opportunity to inform these firms of the financial incentives available in assisted areas. The value of the 'contact and persuasion' role cannot be quantified, but evidence from surveys at the time that controls were in operation suggests that it was an important factor in inducing firms to move to assisted areas.

Given these advantages, it may seem surprising that IDCs and Office Permits were abolished and that location controls now play no real part in regional policy. The main reason for the abolition of location controls is that they run counter to methods of regulating businesses within modern capitalist systems. One serious disadvantage of controls is that preventing firms from expanding at the location of their choice often has harmful effects on their efficiency by constraining them in their choice of location. In a rapidly globalizing economic system this is a serious problem.

A further damaging effect of location controls is their adverse effect on the aggregate level of investment. If firms are prevented from expanding at the location of their choice, they may well decide not to expand at all. Alternatively, they may move to an assisted area but reduce the scale of the project, or they may even transfer the project to a foreign location. This latter effect was not, it seems, significant in practice at the time IDCs were in operation. Only 1 per cent of those firms refused an IDC actually decided to transfer the project abroad. On the other hand, 13 per cent of those projects refused an IDC were abandoned, while 50 per cent went ahead either in existing premises or by building within the strict limits imposed by location controls (Commission of the European Communities 1981a). It is clear, however, that in the context of the modern EU, with its Single Market for labour and capital and its much freer trading arrangements, IDCs would be much less effective today.

With pressure for industrial location controls having receded, attention has turned instead to the issue of whether the *deliberate relaxation of controls* on businesses might be a better policy for regions seeking to attract investment. In the EU this type of regional policy has not yet been introduced on any significant scale. There are two reasons for this. First, in some of the major EU member states such as Britain, regional governments with the legislative powers to alter business regulations simply do not exist. As chapter 12 will show, a Scottish Parliament with legislative powers was set up in 1999, but no other UK region yet has legislative powers. Second, even in those EU member states which have regional governments with legislative powers there has been neither the will, nor the opportunity, to adopt a far-reaching relaxation of regulations on industry as part of regional policy efforts. In practice, it is very difficult for regional governments to do this in the EU since such controls are increasingly being transferred upwards to the EU under the auspices of the Social Chapter of the 1992 Treaty of Union. Indeed, EU social policy has deliberately taken the route of *increased* business regulation through its burgeoning equal opportunities, health, safety and employment protection directives.

The contrast between the EU and the USA could not be starker. In the USA much greater progress has been made along the path of using the dismantling of controls on businesses as an active arm of regional policy. Here the combination of state governments with wide-ranging legislative powers, together with a wider commitment than in Europe to free market policies, has let to *pro-business policies* becoming very widespread. Precisely what constitutes a pro-business policy remains controversial. The Fantus Index, widely used as a measure of *business climate* in the USA, developed initially in 1975 and regularly updated, contains no fewer than 15 separate indictors of a state's pro-business stance (Weinstein and Firestine 1978). These indicators contain traditional regional policy instruments such as capital subsidies and business tax incentives. Most analysts, however, identify deregulation policies as lying at the heart of pro-business policy. In particular, two sets of measures are thought to be of critical importance. The first is the adoption by a state of much laxer business regulations than is normally the case. These include health and safety regulations, along with environmental, employment protection, equal opportunities and bureaucratic (red-tape) requirements. The second is the adoption of *right-to-work* laws. These are designed to deliberately restrict trade union and collective bargaining rights, and in particular seek to ban the establishment of closed shop arrangements.

The merits or otherwise of adopting pro-business regional policy instruments in Europe have yet to be properly discussed. The debate has been overshadowed by wider discussions on EU social policy. There have been frequent accusations by other EU member states that the UK has effectively sought to develop a *national* pro-business strategy by exercising its opt-out from the Social Chapter of the Treaty of Union. Since the new Labour government of 1997 has unilaterally waived this opt-out these types of claims have receded. In addition, it has never been clear whether it was the UK's pro-business legislation or other advantages (e.g. political stability and the English language) which had been the most important in underpinning the success of the UK's inward investment strategy in the 1980s and 1990s. Evidence from the USA, however, suggests that states operating active pro-business policies have been able to engineer striking changes in the location patterns of manufacturing industries (Moore and Newman 1985; Holmes 1998). In view of this evidence from the USA, it is surprising that this group of policy instruments has not yet attracted much attention in Europe.

9.3   Capital subsidies versus labour subsidies

This section addresses the following question: which type of input subsidy is more appropriate for regions suffering from poor employment opportunities, a labour subsidy or a subsidy on plant and equipment? Investment subsidies have been by far the most popular instrument used by regional policy makers in their attempt to encourage growth in assisted areas. Despite a proliferation of different types of assistance for firms in the 1980s and 1990s, investment subsidies remain a favoured weapon for policy makers.

Table 9.1   Regional industrial assistance spending in Britain,[a] 1946–90

Year	Initial allowances	Investment grants	Discretionary assistance	Labour subsidies: REP and SEP	Other assistance	Total
1960–61	–	1	3	–	–	4
1961–62	–	4	15	–	–	19
1962–63	–	6	18	–	–	24
1963–64	–	5	10	–	–	15
1964–65	12	19	12	–	–	43
1965–66	178	36	7	–	–	221
1966–67	94	51	10	–	–	155
1967–68	15	257	8	139	–	419
1968–69	–	266	15	489	–	770
1969–70	–	283	15	486	–	784
1970–71	–	330	12	393	–	735
1971–72	27	245	12	342	–	626
1972–73	115	208	16	296	–	635
1973–74	47	383	25	287	–	742
1974–75	–	507	37	357	1	902
1975–76	–	567	43	398	2	1 010
1976–77	–	593	32	347	3	975
1977–78	–	495	53	1	3	552
1978–79	–	489	108	–	4	601
1979–80	–	341	76	–	3	420
1980–81	–	434	43	–	5	482
1981–82	–	486	59	–	4	549
1982–83	–	496	66	–	4	566
1983–84	–	306	52	–	6	364
1984–85	–	278	53	–	4	335
1985–86	–	231	75	–	9	315
1986–87	–	182	79	–	11	272
1987–88	–	148	75	–	13	236
1988–89	–	159	76	–	10	245
1989–90	–	107	62	–	8	177
1990–91	–	69	57	–	3	129
Total	488	7 982	1 224	3 535	93	13 322

[a] The expenditure totals are expressed as grant equivalents. See Wren (1996) for method of calculation and a full list of the initiatives included.
Source: Wren (1996), table 2

Consider, for example, the British regional policy schemes operated by the Department of Trade and Industry. Table 9.1 sets out the main components of the UK government's regional assistance to industry from 1960–1 to 1990–1 (Wren 1996a). Investment grants have dominated the expenditures made, except for a brief period between 1967–8 and 1976–7 when labour subsidies in the form of the Regional Employment Premium (REP) and Selective Employment Premium (SEP) were in existence. The first column of table 9.1 (initial allowances) represents investment incentives in the form of tax breaks for investments in buildings, plant and machinery. These are therefore capital subsidies. The second column (investment grants) is dominated by schemes which concluded with the Regional Development Grant (RDG), which ran from 1972 to 1984, and which provided automatic investment grants to firms. The third column (discretionary assistance) largely comprises Regional Selective Assistance (RSA) which, although discretionary in nature, is principally allocated in the form of grants for new investment.

Hence almost all of the central government's main regional policy schemes have historically been dominated by investment subsidies. The precise nature of these has changed from time to time (e.g. tax incentives and loans have dominated in some periods such as 1970–2), but grants have been the mainstay. This continues to be the case. Regional Selective Assistance (RSA) is now the main national policy instrument. Regional Selective Assistance has been used in the past to finance a variety of different types of policy instruments (e.g. the injection of cash into businesses by purchasing the shares of the firm, and the provision of training grants to firms). In practice, however, Regional Selective Assistance is dominated by grants towards the fixed and working capital costs of firms. That is, it has been used essentially as a capital subsidy instrument. In 1997–8 some £267 million was allocated to firms under RSA (House of Commons 1998). This help was almost all allocated by way of investment grants to manufacturing firms in the British assisted areas.

Other DTI schemes have also been dominated by capital subsidies. Regional Enterprise Grants, for example, were targeted on small firms between 1988 and 1996 and took one of two forms. The first, Investment Grants, were a simple capital subsidy. The second, Innovation Grants, were given to small firms to enable them to introduce a new product or a new production process embodying the latest technology. These were not simply capital subsidies since they were designed to meet all of the costs of the new innovation up to the point of commercial production. Part of the Innovation Grant could, however, be spent on capital equipment since much new technology is embodied in new plant and equipment. Finally, it should be noted that expenditures on new factories, managed workshops and business parks, all major components of UK regional policy, are also largely a form of capital subsidy since they are a subsidy on new buildings.

The British government is not alone in relying on capital subsidies as the mainstay of its regional policy effort. The EU's European Regional Development Fund was traditionally used to offer investment grants to meet part of the capital costs of infrastructure projects (e.g. roads, electricity, telecommunications) and private sector industrial projects. Between 1975, when the Fund was created, and 1989 the United Kingdom received over £3 billion in the form of European Regional Development Fund project investment grants, mostly for infrastructure projects. From 1989 onwards the EU deliberately reduced the amount of capital subsidies directed towards large infrastructure projects, but has continued to subsidize *productive investments* heavily (i.e. investment in plant and machinery by private firms) and investment in business premises (especially for small and medium enterprises). The early predominance of investment subsidies in EU regional policy has receded somewhat, and the EU has diversified into many other types of policy instruments (e.g. subsidies towards advice for small and medium firms, and training grants). Nevertheless, spending by the EU Structural

Funds on investment grants has continued to figure prominently in regional development programmes in the 1990s (see chapter 11).

As noted earlier, labour subsidies have also been used in Britain, but for much shorter periods of time. Employment subsidies were paid to manufacturers located in assisted areas during 1967–76. They were abandoned at the end of 1976 because of objections from Britain's partners in the EU. Similarly, between 1984 and 1988 changes to the UK government's major regional subsidy scheme at that time (the Regional Development Grant) were such that it was effectively converted from being purely a subsidy on capital inputs to a partially *marginal* employment subsidy scheme (i.e. providing subsidies on additional units of labour hired). The revised RDG scheme, however, was terminated in 1988. Labour subsidies have not since been reintroduced.

The microeconomics of factor subsidies

In view of the choice faced by policy makers between investment subsidies and labour subsidies, it is important to examine their relative merits so that appropriate and efficient policies can be devised. There has been a continuing debate on the relative merits of investment subsidies and labour subsidies, with powerful arguments being mounted on both sides. Intuitively, labour subsidies appear to have substantial advantages over investment subsidies given that the main aim of regional policy is to create jobs in assisted areas. Intuition, however, is not always a good substitute for careful economic analysis. It may even be misleading and inappropriate to regard investment and labour subsidies as substitutes for each other. In some circumstances, they may be complementary rather than competitive.

This section points to some of the major pitfalls in the investment subsidy versus labour subsidy debate and urges caution in jumping to quick conclusions about the merits of labour subsidies *vis-à-vis* investment subsidies. The remainder of the section focuses on three aspects of the capital subsidies versus labour subsidies debate: the importance of the substitution effect in determining the impact of input subsidies on the demand for those inputs, the output effects of factor subsidies, and the dynamic effects of subsidies on assisted areas (Holden and Swales 1995).

Labour subsidies and the substitution of labour for capital

Much of the intuitive appeal of labour subsidies rests on the argument that lower labour costs will induce firms to substitute labour for capital, thereby creating more jobs. Such substitution effects can be illustrated diagrammatically. Figure 9.3 shows a manufacturing plant before the receipt of a labour subsidy. Its production level is 200 as indicated by isoquant I_{200}, which shows the various alternative combinations of labour and capital which together yield an output of 200. Production costs are minimized when $K = 30$ units of capital and $L = 30$ units of labour are employed. The optimum combination of capital and labour is therefore at X,

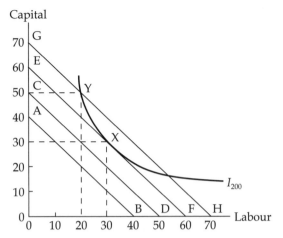

Figure 9.3 The optimum combination of capital and labour inputs. The slope of all isocost lines (AB to GH) is P_L/P_K, where P_L is the price of labour and P_K is the price of capital.

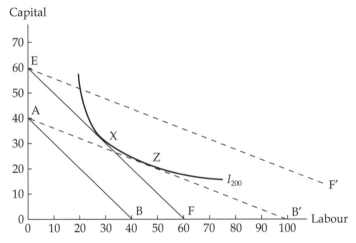

Figure 9.4 The substitution effect of a labour subsidy.

where the plant is operating on its lowest possible isocost line EF. With the price of labour at £5 per unit, and the rental price of capital at £5 per unit, production costs along EF are £300. Any other combination of capital and labour would be more costly.

Figure 9.4 shows the effect of a labour subsidy which reduces the price of labour to the firm from £5 to £2 per unit. The price of capital is unchanged. All isocost lines now swing outwards as a result of the subsidy. Consider the £200 isocost line AB. Which labour and capital at £5 per unit, the firm is restricted to a maximum labour input of 40 units at B, or a maximum capital input of 40 units at A. With the price of labour down to £2, the firm can now hire up to 100 units of labour for £200 (at B'). Since the price of capital is unchanged at £5, the firm's maximum input of capital remains unchanged at 40 given an outlay of £200.

The substitution effect of the labour subsidy can now be shown. We assume that the firm decides to continue producing 200 units of output. The existing combination using $K = 30$ units of capital and $L = 30$ units of labour (at X) is no longer the least-cost technique. At the new (post-subsidy) factor prices, total production costs are:

$$
\begin{aligned}
\text{capital costs} = 30 \times £5 &= £150 \\
\text{labour costs} = 30 \times £2 &= \underline{£60} \\
\text{total cost} &= £210
\end{aligned}
$$

Total costs have fallen from £300 to £210 as a result of the subsidy. The firm can do better than this, however, by substituting 20 extra units of labour for 10 fewer units of capital. This is reflected by a move along the isoquant I_{200} from X to Z:

$$
\begin{aligned}
\text{capital costs} = 20 \times £5 &= £100 \\
\text{labour costs} = 50 \times £2 &= \underline{£100} \\
\text{total cost} &= £200
\end{aligned}
$$

This move from X to Z is the substitution effect of the labour subsidy. It occurs because the price of labour falls relative to the price of capital, as reflected by the flatter isocost line. A capital subsidy, which reduced the price of capital while leaving the price of labour unchanged, would have the opposite effect: capital would be substituted for labour.

At first sight, the existence of the substitution effect is a powerful argument in favour of regional labour subsidies and against capital subsidies. Oversimplification must be avoided, however, for two reasons. First, this substitution effect represents only one of a whole range of effects that subsidies have on regional employment. These other effects are examined later in this section. The critical point is that the overall effect on employment may differ substantially from the simple substitution effect described above. Second, it is important to be precise about what determines the actual number of jobs created or lost as a result of the substitution effects. The number of jobs created or lost will depend upon:

1 The supply elasticities of labour and capital.
2 The shape of the isoquants (i.e. the plant's production function).
3 The size of the subsidy.

The supply elasticities of labour and capital are important because the above example shows only how the firm's demand for labour and capital changes as result of the subsidy. Whether or not this demand is converted into jobs depends upon the responsiveness of labour and capital supplies to the changing demands of the firm. If the supply of labour is restricted, then labour subsidies, by increasing the demand for labour, could result in wages being bid up as firms attempt to translate this additional demand into employment. This can easily occur, for

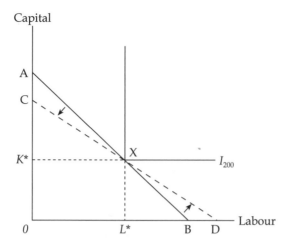

Figure 9.5 Zero substitution between capital and labour.

example, if the labour in demand is highly skilled. The job-creating effect of labour subsidies is therefore by no means a foregone conclusion.

The technical conditions of production are also important in determining the size of the substitution effect. These may be such that the firm is tightly constrained in its use of labour and capital. In the extreme case, the firm has no power to substitute labour for capital when labour subsidies are made available. This is shown by the L-shaped isoquant in figure 9.5. With only one technique of production, there can be no substitution between inputs in response to changes in factor prices when subsidies are made available. The 'shape' of the firm's production function is therefore of critical importance.

Although the slope of the isoquant is often used as a measure of the degree of substitution between inputs, a more useful measure is the price elasticity of substitution σ:

$$\sigma = \frac{\Delta(K/L)/(K/L)}{\Delta(w/r)/(w/r)}$$

where K is the capital stock, L is the employed labour, w is the real wage rate, r is the real rental price of capital and Δ means 'a small change in'. When $\sigma = 1$, a 10 per cent change in relative factor prices causes a 10 per cent change in the firm's desired capital/labour ratio. A value of zero implies that no substitution is possible (the case of the L-shaped isoquant). Values between 0 and 1 indicate that the capital/labour ratio is relatively unresponsive to changes in factor prices, while values greater than 1 indicate the opposite.

Estimates of σ indicate that industries differ considerably in the extent to which labour and capital can be substituted for each other. Moreover, many manufacturing industries appear to have low elasticities of substitution. Values for elasticities of substitution appear to be well below unity in most UK manufacturing industries: weighted averages for each UK region range from 0.23 to 0.88. Northern

Ireland is perhaps the one region where substitution effects are large (Harris 1982; 1991). An obvious implication of these results is that there may be a case for offering subsidies on a selective basis, with labour subsidies only being offered to those few industries with relatively high substitution potential. We need to be cautious with such proposals, however, for several reasons.

First, empirical estimates of the elasticity of substitution are not very reliable. Broad industry groups, as typically used in these studies, encompass large variations in the substitutability of labour for capital among different firms, plants and products. The methods used to derive estimates of the elasticity of substitution also rest on unrealistic assumptions. Cross-checks in the past on the reliability of the estimates for particular individual industries (McDermott 1977; O'Donnell and Swales 1979) have cast doubt on the accuracy of the estimates. Second, the elasticities of substitution only indicate how the demand for inputs changes as a result of subsidies. Effects on the actual employment of inputs also depend on the response from the supply side, which itself depends on the availability of resources. Third, the substitution effect of input subsidies is only one part of a whole range of possible effects on the demand for inputs. One of these other effects is the output effect, which is discussed next.

The output effect of capital and labour subsidies

Returning to our labour subsidy example above, it was observed that the subsidy reduced total production costs as well as causing a substitution of labour for capital. When faced with a fall in production costs, firms are unlikely to continue producing the same level of output. In particular, if this reduction in costs is passed on to consumers in the form of lower prices (either in whole or in part), there will be an expansion in demand for the firm's output. This is known as the *output effect* of a subsidy.

Suppose the firm decides to increase its output from 200 to 400 units as a result of the reduction in total production costs. Figure 9.6 shows the results. The labour subsidy causes the firm to increase its use of labour at the expense of capital due to the substitution effect (shown by the move from X to Z). In addition, the firm expands its output and moves to the higher isoquant I_{400}. Given the post-subsidy isocost lines, the firm minimizes its cost of producing an output of 400 at combination Y. The planned level of employment increases from L_1 to L_3. L_1L_2 is the substitution effect and L_2L_3 is the output effect. Notice that the demand for capital may also increase since a positive output effect may outweigh a negative substitution effect. Whether a positive net effect on the demand for labour would occur in practice depends upon the technical conditions of production in the individual plant or process. In principle, it is even possible for a labour subsidy to result in a fall in the demand for labour (as can be seen by 'sliding' the isoquant I_{400} upwards along the isocost line LM until Y is to the left of X). This is extremely unlikely in practice, however.

The presence of output effects can also mean that a capital subsidy will result in additional employment. This would be the case if a strong output effect outweighed a negative substitution effect. The size of the output effect on the demand for labour, however, will depend on a number of factors:

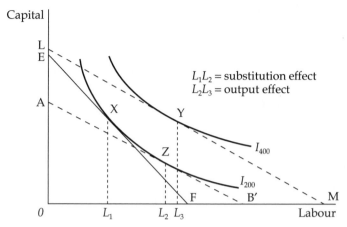

Figure 9.6 The output and substitution effects of a labour subsidy. The firm's new least-cost combination Y does not necessarily mean that total costs are the same as the pre-subsidy combination X. Here the new isocost line LM is drawn such that the firm's total expenditure on inputs is now slightly higher as a result of the subsidy. Allowing the new isocost line to shift its position as well as changing its slope simply means that the producer has more freedom of action that in the case where total costs are held constant.

1   The size of the reduction in production costs resulting from the subsidy.
2   The extent to which the reduction in production costs is passed on to customers in the form of lower product prices.
3   The responsiveness of the demand for the product to a fall in its price.
4   The technical conditions of production (as already explained above).

The size of reduction in production costs to the firm depends on two things: (1) the size of the subsidy in relation to the price of the factor being subsidized; and (2) the relative importance of the factor being subsidized in total production costs. A large subsidy per worker will have only a small effect on production costs in highly capital-intensive firms. The relative importance of the labour factor will vary substantially between industries and between plants within industries due to variations in capital intensity.

    The fact that regional subsidies reduce production costs is not in itself sufficient to lead to an output effect. The stimulus to product demand (and hence output and employment) depends on how much of the cost reduction is passed on to customers. Subsidies may be put to different uses by the firm. They may be used to reduce commodity prices while wages are held constant. Alternatively, workers may bid up wages, leaving product prices unchanged. Finally, labour subsidies may simply be absorbed into profits. Any combination of these potential effects is possible, which means that the output effect resulting from a reduction in production costs is simply not predictable.

    Whether or not an input subsidy is reflected in the product price also depends on the nature of the industry in which the firm is operating. Under either perfect competition or monopoly, subsidies may be passed on (Swales 1981), but in more realistic situations such as oligopoly this may not happen. Oligopolists may be unwilling to risk a price war, especially if the subsidy is small and temporary.

A further factor of some importance in determining the effect of a subsidy on final product prices is the value added to a product by the firm receiving the subsidy. If the value added locally (relative to the final value of the product) is small, the effect of the subsidy on the product price will also be small. The existence of a high degree of interregional trade in intermediate products could result in a situation where input subsidies to assisted areas have little effect on final product prices.

One must therefore be pessimistic about the extent to which input subsidies are likely to reduce the final product price. On the other hand, the demand for the products of any one region is likely to be very responsive to any price reduction which occurs. This is because the price elasticity of demand for the products of any one region is likely to be high as a result of intense interregional competition. Indeed, it has often been argued that input subsidies are equivalent to a regional devaluation in their effects on product demand. The products of assisted areas become more competitive in both national and international markets. Hence, the responsiveness of product demand to price reductions will go some way towards offsetting the fact that only a part of an input subsidy is likely to be passed on to customers in the form of lower product prices.

The reasoning set out above points to the immense complexity involved in trying to estimate the effects on employment of labour and capital subsidies. Estimates must capture much more than simple substitution effects. There are output effects to consider, and these in turn depend on the extent to which subsidies are reflected in more competitive prices for the region's products. Similarly, allowance must be made for responses on the supply side of the labour market.

Indirect and long-term effects of capital and labour subsidies

Any discussion of the relative merits of capital and labour subsidies would be incomplete without some reference to the indirect and long-term effects to which they are likely to give rise. Their potential significance stems from the fact that the indirect and long-term effects may greatly outweigh any substitution and output effects associated with input subsidies.

Isoquant analysis is useful for expositional purposes, but its limitations should be kept firmly in mind. It suffers from at least two serious problems: it is partial and it is static. When the fuller system-wide effects of subsidies are examined and when allowance is made for possible dynamic effects, the choices facing the policy maker become even more complex.

Isoquant analysis of output and substitution effects is partial in that it ignores the indirect employment effects of capital and labour subsidies. At first sight, one may feel that labour subsidies are likely to have greater regional multiplier effects because payments to labour enter the regional economy directly via the household sector. Subsequent rounds of expenditure will have a further local multiplier impact on those firms supplying the regional market since part of the extra household expenditure will remain within the region. With capital subsidies, the immediate multiplier consequences are likely to be smaller since much of the initial capital spending will 'leak out' of the region because of the need to import the required capital goods. This leakage in the initial injection can be substantial and has to be taken into account when calculating the multiplier effects of different types of subsidy.

Consideration must also be given, however, to the inter-industry effects of capital subsidies and to the long-term effects on the competitiveness of the region's economic base. It can be argued that capital subsidies are vital for future competitiveness by allowing manufacturers to modernize their operations. Although this may be highly capital-intensive at the point of investment, there will be employment spinoffs elsewhere in the region when all the indirect and induced effects on other sectors are taken into account.

Finally, in considering the indirect effects of labour and capital subsidies it is necessary to consider the *deadweight* and *displacement* effects of each type of subsidy (Holden and Swales 1995). *Deadweight* refers to a situation where a subsidy is given to a firm but the firm, while accepting the subsidy, would have gone ahead with the resulting employment creation in any event. The subsidy, in other words, simply causes public sector funds to be substituted for private sector investment. *Displacement* is where a subsidy results in new jobs in the recipient firm, but at the cost of jobs in other firms in the assisted area. All types of subsidies have the potential to create deadweight problems and displacement effects, since they effectively allow the subsidized firm to compete more strongly with rivals by cutting its costs. They are not a problem peculiar to either capital or labour subsidies. Indeed, these two effects are so important for regional policy that they form major components of the techniques developed to evaluate regional policy (see chapter 13).

Turning to long-term effects, however, there is a strong case for preferring capital subsidies to labour subsidies. First, fast growing manufacturing industries tend to be capital-intensive. Second, capital subsidies are invariably investment subsidies and as a result they encourage not only the substitution of capital for labour but also the substitution of new, technologically advanced capital for older capital. This is to the advantage of depressed regions. Third, labour subsidies are continuous subsidies and this tends to ossify the existing technologies by keeping older, declining industries going longer than would otherwise have been the case. Investment subsidies, on the other hand, are a once-for-all reward for modernizing the technological base of a region.

In summary, considerable caution needs to be exercised in deciding whether to favour capital or labour subsidies. It is naive to support labour subsidies simply because some substitution of labour for capital is likely to occur. The effects of subsidies on employment are much more complex and more far-reaching than mere substitution effects. The employment effects will vary from firm to firm and from industry to industry, and also over time as industries become more technologically advanced. Each subsidy introduced by policy makers must be taken on its own individual merits.

General or marginal employment subsidies?

In the case of subsidies directed towards capital as a factor of production, there has been little debate on whether such subsidies are best offered to the whole of the existing *capital stock* or to *new capital* (i.e. investment). The advantages of only subsidizing incremental capital are so great that it is investment subsidies which have always predominated.

In the case of labour subsidies, however, there continues to be an animated debate on whether subsidies are best offered to *all workers* in a region (i.e. a general labour subsidy) or only to new workers taken on (i.e. a marginal employment subsidy). The UK has had examples of both types. The Regional Employment Premium which existed from 1967 to 1978 was a general employment subsidy paid to all workers in manufacturing in the assisted areas. The modified Regional Development Grant which existed from 1984 to 1988 was a marginal employment subsidy. The debate on the relative merits of general and marginal employment subsidies has led to the need to consider not only the direct microeconomic effects of subsidies, but also wider general equilibrium and macroeconomic impacts.

An early attempt to providing estimates of the effects of general labour subsidies by drawing on a full regional econometric model (and hence analysing the system-wide effects) is provided by a study of the effects of labour subsidies in Northern Ireland. Roper and O'Shea (1991) use the Northern Ireland Economic Research Centre's full econometric model to analyse the historical effects on jobs and output of labour subsidies in the province. Only full econometric models incorporating equations which pick up both demand-side and supply-side effects are capable of exposing the complete effects of capital and labour subsidies. Interestingly, labour subsidies in Northern Ireland, whilst effective in stimulating jobs, have been shown to have only small effects on unemployment because the success of the subsidies led to a reduction in out-migration.

The more recent development of a new generation of regional econometric models using computable general equilibrium (CGE) techniques has allowed the system-wide impacts of a general labour subsidy to be more accurately estimated. Harrigan et al. (1996) have used just such a model to analyse the effects on Scotland of an hypothetical 3 per cent across-the-board general employment subsidy. The application of this model clearly reveals not only that the various substitution, output and other effects discussed earlier are important in determining the effect on jobs, but also that a general employment subsidy has the capacity to generate additional job gains by way of a *fiscal stimulus*. This arises because the subsidy is paid for by national taxpayers and therefore represents an injection of income into the assisted region. General labour subsidies involve a greater fiscal stimulus to a region than marginal subsidies and hence can be expected to create more jobs in total. How effective the subsidy is in creating jobs turns out to be dependent on how wage levels are set in the region and hence on how quickly wages rise in the region as the demand for labour is boosted.

A strong counter-case can also be made for marginal employment subsidies. The paying of a general labour subsidy does have problems of its own. Taxpayers' money, for example, can easily be wasted. Although lavishing taxpayers' money on a general labour subsidy creates jobs by stimulating regional aggregate demand (the fiscal stimulus mentioned above), it has to be acknowledged that many of the jobs subsidized would have been created in any event. In other words, there is a serious deadweight problem associated with general employment subsidies. Layard and Nickell (1980; 1983) have been among the most persuasive advocates of marginal employment subsidies. Their proposal has been for a weekly labour subsidy paid for each extra job provided by firms. Using macroeconomic models they demonstrate how the subsidy can generate additional employment by way of four mechanisms:

1 *Increased real personal incomes* The subsidy results in lower product prices, thus raising real incomes and stimulating consumer demand. Firms then expand employment in order to meet the demand.
2 *Increased profit* This occurs when only part of the subsidy is passed on as lower prices. Some of the extra profit is spent by shareholders, thereby stimulating consumer demand and employment.
3 *Import substitution* Subsidy-induced price cuts enable local firms to undercut import prices. Local employment is therefore increased.
4 *Increased exports* Subsidized local firms can cut prices and thus increase their share of export markets either abroad or in other regions. Again local employment is increased.

Mechanism 4 is the most interesting one. Firms using marginal cost pricing in export markets, or alternatively being forced to match prevailing world prices in export markets, are very sensitive to cost cuts at the margin. A marginal labour subsidy will allow such firms to cut costs at the margin in export markets, even if average costs fall only slightly.

Under the Layard and Nickell proposals the subsidy triggers a whole series of beneficial effects, including cuts in inflation and an improved balance of payments position. The debate on the merits of a marginal employment subsidy has been a fierce one (Whitley and Wilson 1983; Hart 1989).

Although couched in terms of a subsidy to firms in the whole nation, and with the subsidy being phased out gradually as recovery from high unemployment proceeds, the Layard and Nickell arguments can easily be adapted to support a regionally differentiated employment subsidy. Regions, after all, are equivalent to small open macroeconomies, whose firms are mostly price-takers in export markets, being forced to match 'world' prices (the 'world' being defined to include other regions as well as other countries). Indeed, Canning and Evans (1988) have used this argument to call for a marginal employment subsidy to be adopted by the whole EU as part of its regional policy. They argued that a marginal employment subsidy would be nearly twice as cost-effective in creating new jobs in the disadvantaged regions as a 'global' subsidy paid for all workers employed.

Support for a marginal employment subsidy also grew as a result of retrospective evaluation of the Revised Regional Development Grant (RRDG) scheme which existed in Britain from 1984 to 1988. Retrospective analysis of the RRDG scheme showed that it had been highly cost-effective in terms of government expenditure per job created when compared with other types of subsidy. Moreover, the scheme had the great benefit of allowing firms to calculate accurately the value of the subsidy ahead of receiving it, something not possible with earlier labour subsidy schemes (Wren 1989; Wren and Swales 1991). Government fears of wasting money on subsidizing jobs which would have been created anyway – fears which were exaggerated – and the desire to terminate automatic subsidies in favour of selective assistance, conspired to end this promising experiment in 1988. As a result, the UK has yet to test out properly what is a potentially valuable type of regional subsidy.

9.4   Community economic development initiatives

The fundamental principles of community economic development

The key ideas which underpin community economic development (CED) are not new. Urban policy in Britain has a long history of attempting to regenerate disadvantaged areas within cities using community development approaches. The 1968–78 Community Development Project is an early example of this, as are many of the schemes embodied in the Urban Programme of the 1980s. However, a combination of circumstances in the early 1990s resulted in a major shift in urban policy in Britain, particularly through the City Challenge programme introduced in 1991 and the larger Single Regeneration Budget (SRB) programme starting in 1994.

One reason for the shift was the burgeoning extent of the UK's socially excluded communities, most of which, as the previous chapter has shown, are located in the larger cities. A second factor was the emergence in the 1990s of theories of local and regional development based on the concept of *social capital* – the view that strong community bonds and close local networking can significantly improve an area's economic prospects. The concept of social capital is considered in greater detail in chapter 10. Social capital theory has given proponents of CED an intellectual foundation previously lacking. A third factor in the emergence of CED initiatives in the early 1990s in the UK's urban programme was harsh criticism of the 1980s' approach contained in retrospective evaluations (Audit Commission 1989).

Proponents of CED have argued that the principal reason for failure prior to 1990 lay in the lack of genuine engagement of local communities. It has been argued, for example, that 'whilst the rhetorical commitment to community engagement . . . has remained strong in political circles for over 30 years, in practice regeneration initiatives have tended to be imposed top-down rather than developed bottom-up, from the grassroots' (Haughton 1998: 872). The desire to see local communities genuinely taking the lead is what fundamentally distinguishes modern CED from its predecessors. The importance of community 'empowerment' is most succinctly put in an influential European Commission report: 'Community Economic Development . . . is a policy which begins from a particular premise: that people in local communities, however marginalised, have an

Table 9.2 The proportion of expenditure allocations made to CED priorities in EU Structural Funds
Objective 2 programmes in British regions, 1997–9

Objective 2 region	CED	SME development	Tourism[a]	Technology	Strategic spatial development
East London	24.6	34.7	–	14.5	26.2
East Midlands	25.1	44.1	–	13.7	17.1
Eastern Scotland	15.5	40.9	16.9	25.4	NA
Greater Manchester	23.4	30.0	5.6	13.8	27.2
Industrial South Wales	13.1	26.9	11.9	20.0	26.6
North East England	14.2	35.1	–	17.2	33.5
Plymouth	16.1	45.0	26.5	12.5	–
Thanet	20.4	38.6	24.4	–	–
West Midlands	18.1	41.6	7.7	19.2	13.4
Western Scotland	16.7	36.2	14.9	9.4	22.8
Yorkshire and the Humber	25.4	38.4	–	13.4	22.8
West Cumbria	19.7	43.1	16.6	20.7	–

[a] In the case of tourism, some regions have incorporated the measures into the strategic spatial
development category (hence the spaces in the column).
Source: Government Office for Yorkshire and the Humber (1999b), table 2.2

unrealised capacity to contribute both to their own insertion in the economic
mainstream and to the sum of regional development . . . Critically, it offers to the
residents and businesses of areas of disadvantage the opportunity to formulate
their own requirements for economic and social integration and to devise and
implement their own strategies for insertion into the regional mainstream' (1996b:
18).

The early 1990s witnessed the paradoxical situation of CED taking a rapid grip
on UK urban policy whilst regional policy became more strictly focused on economic competitiveness. This situation changed with dramatic suddenness in 1995.
The catalyst was the 1994–9 EU Structural Funds programme. While the UK's
own regional policy remains focused on the goal of economic competitiveness,
a fundamental shift has occurred in the EU component of regional policy. So
sudden was the shift that in many regions separate CED priorities were inserted
into EU programmes which were already one year into the 1994–9 budget period.
This has had the unfortunate consequence that the CED initiatives have tended
to be largely free-standing within the 1994–9 programmes. In the meantime, the
other spending priorities (e.g. for SMEs, innovation, inward investment and
the like) have happily proceeded along the route of jobs, wealth creation and the
enhancement of economic competitiveness.

As well as representing a switch of unprecedented suddenness, the subsequent
growth of CED initiatives within the EU's regional policy has also been dramatic.
Table 9.2 shows that in some regions over 25 per cent of total funding is currently
being targeted at CED initiatives. Further rapid growth of CED initiatives is being
planned in UK regions for the Structural Funds in 2000–6.

Table 9.3 highlights a number of the key differences between CED and more
traditional regional policy instruments. In addition to the vital role accorded to

Table 9.3   Principles for sustainable regeneration

Principles	Top-down approach	Grassroots approach
Inter-generational equality	Quick-fix approach to attracting investment and jobs; driven by short-term targets and political goals	Long-term approach to local capacity and asset building; emphasis on creating durable jobs
Social justice	Wealth creation ethic, linked to rhetorical attachment to trickle-down; wage reduction seen as acceptable way to create wealth and (arguably) jobs	Emphasis on socially valuable products and services, including rewarding training and jobs, including livable wage
Geographical equity	Competitive ethos, open trade, place marketing and focus on attracting external investment irrespective of effects on other (potentially 'worthier') areas	Attempts to create a localized economy, with fair terms of trade locally and externally; avoidance of zero-sum inter-locality competition
Participation	Corporatist inclusion of large institutional investors, plus some tokenist engagement with community groups to 'buy' legitimacy	Engagement of local community with all stages of regeneration, from design to implementation; links to local democracy
Holistic approaches	From economic development comes social wellbeing and environmental improvement; trickle-down works, though targeted linkage schemes might be acceptable	Virtuous integration of attempts to improve local economic development, social conditions and the environment

Source: Haughton (1998), table 1. Reproduced with permission from Taylor & Francis Ltd., Oxford

participation (i.e. the active involvement of the local community at all stages), four other key differences are identified in table 9.3. The first is the unusually *long-term nature* of CED instruments. The problems of multiple deprivation, it is argued, are so deep-seated that a step-by-step approach over many years will be needed. Indeed, 'CED is conceived as a *process* the end point of which is sustainable development and reconversion in spatially targeted areas. It is, above all, a process based on *capacity building*' (European Commission 1996b: 19–20). Capacity building is a process linked closely to the concept of social capital. It includes not only the development of the capacities of individuals to rejoin the mainstream economy and society (e.g. through training and confidence building policies), but also the institutional capacity of the community as a whole. Also important is the capacity to resolve conflicts within the community, and community 'empowerment' to make sure that local organizations (including those delivering the regional policy instruments) are responsive to local wishes.

Focus on capacity building leads to a broad two-stage process for CED (European Commission 1996b). The first stage (*programme bending*) involves the local community developing sufficient capacity to take control of the full array of policies on offer (e.g. training, education, transport and business development as well as CED) and alter them to their own needs. At the second stage (*community linking*) members of the local community become reinserted into the mainstream economy and society.

The second difference is the explicit *social, political* and *environmental objectives* of CED. In addition to economic regeneration, CED has explicit social goals (i.e. *social justice* in table 9.3). Some also see CED as offering a route by which a whole new radical politics can be developed based on grassroots democracy – a concept reaching beyond even the aim of extending participation set out in table 9.3.

The third difference is the *co-ordination* of all possible policies and sources of assistance. This is what is implied by *programme bending* and by the principle of an *holistic approach* in table 9.3. Proponents of CED argue for highly co-ordinated multi-sectoral responses to what are complex problems (McGregor and McConnachie 1995).

The fourth difference is that CED policies are *area-based* programmes. While the focus of concern is with particular socially excluded *groups* of individuals, the EU Structural Funds have been targeted on precisely defined local geographical *areas*. In the 1994–6 EU programmes in Britain, these target areas for CED ranged from 14 per cent of the population within the Plymouth Objective 2 area to 35 per cent in Merseyside, Yorkshire and the Humber, the West Midlands, and East London and the Lea Valley (European Commission 1996b). In practice, this spatial targeting has proved to be extremely difficult and *ad hoc* methods of drawing boundaries have frequently been used. Area designation has been difficult because the indexes of social exclusion which have been used to assist in the selection of CED areas are both very dated and controversial (Lee 1999). Moreover, there is a serious problem arising from the fact that some localities contain several distinct socially excluded groups, requiring very different policy mixes. Individual inner city areas, for example, often simultaneously have high proportions of lone parents, ethnic minorities and retired persons. In addition, no spatial boundary can ever encompass all of the members of a given socially excluded group. This means that large numbers of persons who are members of any one socially excluded group fall outside the localities designated as CED areas. Spatial targeting is therefore far from perfect.

A critical moment in the process of CED is when capacity building must switch to community linking. Capacity building and the creation of social capital are concerned with the development of *inputs* (since all types of capital – including social capital – are factor inputs), whereas the linking of communities back into the mainstream is the point at which genuine economic *outputs* are attained. While some proponents of CED see social capital as being beneficial in its own right (by improving the quality of life of the community), from an economic perspective it is no such thing. While mainstream linking should result in social, political and environmental outputs, our concern in this book is obviously with the economic outputs of CED. It is at the mainstream linking stage of CED that these types of initiatives once again find themselves in the familiar regional policy realm of job and wealth creation, and the redistribution of income.

Economists well versed in the gains from trade and specialization and the benefits flowing from being able to compete effectively in an increasingly globalized system see mainstream linking as vital. Linking is vital not only to ensure that the regeneration is sustained (in an economic sense), but also so that the national economy can reap the benefits of CED. Proponents of CED, however, have tended to divide into *localist* and *mainstream* (or *building better bridges*) schools of thought (Haughton 1998). The *mainstream* school is in general agreement with the need not to isolate further socially excluded communities. Members of the *localist* school, however, place much greater emphasis on increasing the self-containment of local communities, for example by taking steps to reduce expenditure leakages, thus raising the local multiplier, and by increasing the local ownership of businesses rather than encouraging non-local investors to hold equity. The focus here is on *social entrepreneurship* involving radically new forms of economic activity. Emphasis is often placed on building up a *Third Sector* economy – 'businesses and cooperatives which operate for social or community benefit' (Cooper 1993: 348).

The Third Sector lies somewhere between the public and private sectors, overlapping both and also incorporating some parts of the voluntary sector. It comprises an increasingly distinctive group of organizations ranging from co-operatives and credit unions through community-owned businesses to charitable trading organizations (Social Exclusion Unit 1998; Chanan 1999). Some of these organizations, such as the Church Urban Fund, are surprisingly large (Lawless et al. 1998). While Third Sector organizations are not necessarily focused wholly on serving local community markets and some do indeed trade internationally, in practice most do have a local focus. Proponents of the Third Sector and the *social economy* stress not only the job creation aspects of the organizations involved (see for example Young 1999 on home care schemes), but also their social and environmental advantages (e.g. improving community welfare through voluntary, unpaid work). Others, however, have pointed to the dangers faced by those taking a *localist* approach in becoming distracted from the need to eventually attain mainstream linking and their tendency to evolve into purely revenue-seeking organizations in their pursuit of public funding (Turok 1999).

The policy instruments of community economic development

To what extent can CED be said to have led to the development of new types of regional policy instruments? This is an important question since, as we have seen, CED is defined as a *process* rather than as a particular type of policy instrument, and part of this process involves *programme bending* (i.e. the seizure by the local community) of *all policy instruments* in existence. Scrutiny of the projects funded by the EU Structural Funds suggests that during 1994–9, CED policies have indeed seen the development of genuinely new types of regional policy instruments in two distinct senses.

First, many traditional policy instruments have in practice been applied in dramatically different ways than in the past: so different in fact that they effectively constitute new instruments. Take, for example, the subsidy and encouragement of credit unions and co-operatives. Neither of these is a new policy instrument, and both had a very chequered history in the 1980s. Modern CED policy, however, has used these instruments as vehicles to deliberately draw local people into their design, management, ownership and operation (i.e. in a capacity building role), even where this might be at the expense of job creation or profitability. Credit unions, for example, grow faster and are more likely to become more quickly subsidy-free where they are extended to include more affluent middle class and suburban members. CED policies usually resist this in order to ensure that the credit union is able to develop capacity within the target community.

Similarly, in harnessing the full array of traditional business development instruments (e.g. financial subsidies, advisory services and managed workspace provision) CED can be said to be using traditional policy instruments. However, in practice CED policies attempt to harness these instruments in the first instance to build local community capacity, and for the longer term to stimulate *community businesses*. The concept of a community business remains a rather imprecise one, and these types of enterprise have in the past been few in number and marginal to the wider economy (McArthur 1993). A popular definition is of 'a trading organisation which is owned and controlled by the local community and which aims to create ultimately self-supporting and viable jobs for local people in its area of benefit, and to use profits made from its business activities either to create more employment or to provide local services, or to support local charitable work' (Calouste Gulbenkian Foundation 1982: 4). This definition can, in principle, incorporate a wide array of business types including traditional partnerships and limited companies. Increasingly, however, the emphasis is on more radical types of organization which encompass co-operatives and charities, but also ethical financial companies and community-based local development trusts.

Second, in addition to using traditional regional policy instruments in new ways, CED has seen the introduction of genuinely new *types* of policy instrument. Two excellent examples are local exchange and trading systems (LETS) and intermediate labour market (ILM) initiatives.

LETS are a form of local currency designed to overcome liquidity constraints in low-income communities which prevent unmet local needs being met by unemployed local people. LETS are set up by associations of people who create their own local unit of exchange. Goods and services are then exchanged using the LETS currency units as the medium of exchange. These schemes also often use the LETS currency as a unit of account and a store of value (for goods and services traded within the system). Although no notes and coins are issued, and although only part of the local community are members of each scheme, a local currency has therefore effectively been created. The fundamental concept of a LETS is not new, as anyone knows who has participated in a babysitting circle or who has read the history of 'payment by tokens' in coal mining communities and company towns. Their use in stimulating an active social economy within the community, thus raising local income retention (Williams 1996a), and their function as a capacity building device to provide a first step back to mainstream work for long-term unemployed persons, are however new departures. While many economists are sceptical of the benefits of anything associated with the balkanization of currency areas, there is no doubt that CED has led to a rapid growth in LETS policies (Stott and Hodges 1996; Williams 1996b; North 1998; Pacione 1999). LETS are also part of a wider, and rapidly growing, set of CED financial instruments which include *micro-credit* schemes (loans of small amounts of funding to marginalized groups in order to encourage self-employment and entrepreneurship) and *social risk capital* schemes. These are similar to venture capital initiatives, but with organizations in the social economy being the target (Lloyd and Ramsden 1998).

ILM policies are designed to allow unemployed members of socially excluded communities to take a step-by-step pathway back into paid employment. An ILM initiative 'sits in the space between unemployment and the formal paid labour market, filling the same policy gap as the training system, but offering a job as well as training and personal development support' (Lloyd and Ramsden 1998: 38). While some traditional training schemes in the past have offered a pathway approach of this kind, what is new is the ability of ILM schemes to offer a portfolio of types of help. Their focus is on 'sustainable demand side activity – that is, producing a service or product that in part recovers the costs of its production from those who consume it' (Lloyd and Ramsden 1998: 39). In order that the unemployed person is forced to make the leap back into the mainstream economy, ILM initiatives typically offer employment only for a strictly limited period of time. Moreover, in order to minimize the displacement of jobs from the mainstream economy, many ILM initiatives concentrate on the social economy or trading for purely social purposes (e.g. environmental improvements, care services). A problem for many ILM initiatives is their high cost and tendency in some cases to fail to bring about eventual mainstream linking (Emmerich 1997).

The economic analysis of CED

CED policies pose an exciting challenge for the regional economist. The precipitate emergence of CED at the heart of EU regional policy has taken regional economists by surprise. Policy initiatives have been founded almost entirely on case studies and not on formal economic analysis or evaluation. Even the experience of pre-1990 urban policy has been of little guidance since modern CED, with its emphasis on capacity building, is very different from what went before.

Since virtually all proponents of CED have argued that there are major economic benefits to be enjoyed, both within the local communities themselves and at the national level, a vital role exists for the regional economist in analysing the economic effects of CED initiatives. The real challenge facing economists is to adapt traditional evaluation methods to CED. The principles underpinning traditional regional policy evaluation (see chapter 13) are as valid for CED as for any other type of regional policy. These revolve around the concepts of deadweight (would the jobs and other economic benefits have occurred anyway?), displacement (has a job created by CED displaced a similar job elsewhere in the assisted areas?), and the extent of additional supply chain and multiplier effects spreading out from the CED area. Unfortunately, applying these tried and tested evaluation methods to CED falls foul of two main problems.

First, there is no consensus on how important the economic objectives of CED are (e.g. jobs, wealth creation) relative to the social, political and environmental objectives. This does not matter if all four sets of objectives can be simultaneously achieved, as is often claimed by proponents of CED, but experience tells us that trade-offs between objectives are much more likely. Many of the CED areas, for example, are in inner city areas where very few modern firms would choose to set up. Spending scarce regional policy resources in these localities may well come at a high opportunity cost in terms of jobs and wealth forgone elsewhere. On the other hand, this does not matter if the goals are simply social or political and economic gains are incidental. Until there is greater clarity in what CED is attempting to attain, proper evaluation will be very difficult.

Second, CED policies are, by definition, long term. This means that the economic benefits will be many years in coming and that a prolonged period of capacity building is in prospect. Capacity building itself poses no problems for econometric evaluation. ILM policies, for example, are amenable to longitudinal econometric analysis of the kind used to evaluate training initiatives. However, the period of time needed for capacity building has never been specified; the period itself almost certainly varies widely among the different types of CED initiatives; and insufficient time has elapsed since CED was introduced to regional policy in 1995 for the empirical evidence to accumulate. Under these circumstances economic evaluation can have little to offer. On the other hand, what is exciting is that in the next few years the accumulation of evidence will gradually allow regional economists to put the claims of proponents of CED rigorously to the test.

Nor is it just in the field of evaluation that regional economics has a role to play in the debate on CED initiatives. Economic analysis offers techniques eminently suitable for the examination of many features of CED of interest. These include critical issues such as how effective CED initiatives are in targeting their chosen social groups and local areas. The extreme openness of local economies, for example, suggests that CED will find it extremely difficult to target them effectively. EU evaluation guidelines already assume that 50 per cent of jobs created by CED will be filled by in-commuters, a finding confirmed by recent research (EKOS 1998; Government Office for Yorkshire and the Humber 1999a). Economic analysis can also address other thorny issues such as the relative effectiveness of CED compared with other, competing, uses of public funds. The opportunity cost of CED remains a largely unexplored area.

9.5   Conclusion

The analysis of regional policy instruments has come a long way in the last 30 years or so. So too has the science of the design and implementation of the instruments. Which instruments are most appropriate continues to be an issue attracting much innovative research. Regional economic analysis has a pivotal role in the process of devising, analysing the likely impacts of and undertaking retrospective evaluation of each new generation of regional policy instruments. This role will continue so long as regional policy has economic objectives.

Three more recent developments have posed great challenges for regional economists. The first has been the emergence of more complex multiple objectives for regional policy, including social, political and environmental goals. This has made the disentangling of the economic effects of regional policy a more difficult task. The second has been the switch from the use of simple, single policy instruments (e.g. an investment grant or a location control) to the delivery of complex packages of different types of help, carefully tailored to the needs of the individual recipient. Analysing the likely effects of a portfolio of help is always more difficult than a single instrument. Finally, the presence of so many different organizations involved in the delivery of regional policy instruments also poses challenges for the analyst. It is now much harder to disentangle the impact of the role played by any one organization. Responding to these challenges will not be easy. Nor will it be dull.

Further reading

European Commission (1996b); Harrigan et al. (1996); Harris (1993); Holmes (1998); Lloyd and Ramsden (1998); Williams (1996b).

chapter ten

Indigenous development: small and medium enterprises and technological progress

contents

Traditional regional policy came under sustained attack in the 1980s. One of the most telling criticisms was that British regional policy in the past had relied too heavily on encouraging firms outside the assisted areas to locate their new plant within the assisted areas. With inward investment (from the rest of Britain as well as from overseas) being given the dominant role, traditional regional policy, it was argued, did not pay sufficient attention to indigenous development. In particular, too little attention was paid to stimulating new firm formation, inducing small and medium enterprises (SMEs) to expand, and encouraging firms to develop the latest technology.

It is important not to exaggerate the drawbacks of traditional regional policy. As will be shown in chapter 13, the disadvantaged areas would have been considerably worse off without regional policy in the post-war era. Moreover, the criticisms are not entirely convincing. Traditional financial incentives for new investment were, and still are, available to firms already located in assisted areas as well as firms moving into these areas. Many indigenous firms have taken advantage of traditional types of incentives.

Nor should we fall into the trap of condemning inward investment out of hand. Inward investment can play a vital role, as British experience in the 1980s and 1990s has shown. By 1999 the UK's total stock of inward investment was valued at £49 billion, some 23 per cent of all inward investment in the EU (*Financial Times*, 15 July 1999). Major inward investment projects such as the Nissan car assembly plant at Sunderland in the north-east of England have been invaluable acquisitions. Such plants have not only brought new jobs, but also generated much work for local suppliers. Moreover, they have led to 'demonstration effects' for local firms by exposing them to state-of-the-art technology and management methods, and have contributed greatly to Britain's export performance.

The purpose of the present chapter, however, is not to defend traditional regional policy, though there is much to be said in its favour. The aim is to investigate the role that regional policy can play in stimulating indigenous development – development 'from within'. The chapter focuses on the two key targets of modern regional policy: SMEs and new technology.

10.1   Regional policy and the SME sector

The Government's aim is to create a broadly-based entrepreneurial culture, in which more people of all ages and backgrounds start their own business. (White Paper 1998: 15)

This quotation illustrates clearly how the SME sector has come to occupy a central position in government policy thinking. Five main arguments have been advanced in favour of a regional policy targeting SMEs:

1   Their ability to create large numbers of new jobs.
2   Their ability to create a diversified and flexible industrial base by creating a pool of entrepreneurs willing and able to take risks.
3   Their ability to stimulate intense competition for small and large firms alike, leading to an energetic enterprise culture.
4   Their ability to stimulate innovation.
5   Their ability to improve industrial relations and provide a superior working environment for employees.

These arguments continue to be the subject of great controversy. Even today, two decades on from the initiation of large-scale government support for SMEs in Britain, many have not been properly analysed, and all are the subject of periodic fundamental attack. A common theme, for example, is that while SMEs are good at job creation, the quality of the jobs created may not be as good as is sometimes claimed. Far from being the superior working environment suggested earlier, SMEs are often attacked on their health and safety record (Curran and Burrows 1988; Townroe and Mallalieu 1993). The SME sector is also sometimes criticized for creating more part-time and freelance jobs, paying lower wage rates, working longer hours and offering poorer training and fringe benefits (Scott et al. 1989; Storey 1994). Not everyone would see these as disadvantages. Part-time and freelance work, for example, is often portrayed as essential for modern, flexible labour markets, as is the lower degree of unionization in small firms. There is also evidence that SMEs appear to have a greater degree of workplace harmony, particularly in the service sector. However, the issue of job creation is of particular importance for regional policy, and it is to this we now turn.

Job creation

Of all the arguments advanced in favour of SMEs, job creation represents the acid test. Unless the SME sector can demonstrate an ability to create large numbers of new jobs, its role at the centre of modern regional policy will be questioned. It is not always appreciated just how recent favourable government attitudes to the SME sector actually are. There is evidence that industrial concentration has been the order of the day for much of the twentieth century. In 1935, for example, 35 per cent of manufacturing jobs in Britain were in small firms. By 1968 this had fallen to 21 per cent and governments of the day were actively intervening to encourage takeovers and mergers in the manufacturing sector (Storey 1982). It was only in the 1970s, and then with increasing vigour since the early 1980s, that the revival of the SME sector has occurred.

Improvements in official data collection in the 1990s enabled researchers to assess the job creation process in the SME sector more accurately than before. Table 10.1 compares, for the UK as a whole, the number of businesses, employment and turnover of small firms (under 50 employees), medium-size firms (50–250 employees) and large firms (over 250 employees). As is shown, of the 3.7 million businesses in the UK in 1998, 99.2 per cent contained fewer than 50 employees. These businesses accounted for 44.7 per cent of employment (9.7 million jobs) and 38.0 per cent (£733 billion) of total business turnover. The very smallest of these small businesses (those with under 5 employees – seven out of ten of which are sole proprietorships) comprised 89.2 per cent of all businesses and contained between them 5 million jobs. When medium-size enterprises (i.e. between 50 and 250 employees) are added to small firms, it can be seen that in 1998 in the UK some 99.9 per cent of all businesses and 56.3 per cent of all jobs (12 million jobs) lay within the SME sector as a whole. These are impressive statistics by any standard. It should be noted, however, that while big firms (over 250 employees) may be small in number (0.2 per cent of all businesses), they still managed to account in 1998 for 43.7 per cent of all jobs (over 9 million jobs) and a massive 48.2 per cent of total turnover (£928 billion).

The sheer size of the SME sector suggests that it is simply far too important to be neglected by regional policy. This view is strengthened by international comparisons. Table 10.2 compares the size of the UK SME sector (in terms of employment) with other EU member states. The UK's SME sector is smaller than the EU average, and is also smaller than many of the UK's main competitor countries

Table 10.1   Numbers of businesses, employment and turnover of small, medium and large businesses in the UK, 1998[a]

Size (employees)	Numbers of businesses		Employment[b]		Turnover	
	(000s)	*(%)*	*(000s)*	*(%)*	*(£b)*	*(%)*
Small businesses						
0–4 employees	3 362	89.2	5 105	23.6	302.9	15.7
5–49 employees	364	10.0	4 547	21.1	430.1	22.3
Total under 50 employees	3 626	99.2	9 652	44.7	733.0	38.0
Medium businesses						
50–249 employees	25	0.7	2 508	11.6	265.7	13.8
Large businesses						
Over 250 employees	7	0.2	9 435	43.7	928.3	48.2
All firms	3 658	100.0	21 595	100.0	1 927.0	100.0

[a] Statistics are derived from the Office of National Statistics *Inter-Departmental Business Register* (IDBR). This register provides a snapshot picture of businesses 'live' at the start of a given year. IDBR holds records for all businesses either registered for VAT or operating an Inland Revenue Pay-As-You-Earn (PAYE) scheme. Estimates have been made for the numbers of businesses which do not fall in either of these categories, a process which means that the main inaccuracies lie in the very smallest category of firms – the self-employment group with no employees.
[b] In 1998 the total UK workforce was 26 million persons. The estimate of total employment shown in the table is smaller than this since it excludes central and local government employees, members of HM Forces and persons on government training programmes.
Source: Department of Trade and Industry (1999a), table 3. Reproduced with permission of the Department of Trade and Industry, SME Statistics Division, Sheffield

within the EU, such as France, Spain and Denmark. This is confirmed by other measures of the size of the SME sector, such as the extent of self-employment (Moralee 1998). Other main competitor countries outside the EU, such as Japan and the USA, also have better developed SME sectors than the UK (Organization for Economic Cooperation and Development 1994; Doi and Cowling 1998).

In addition to the large absolute size of the SME sector in the UK and its potential to expand further, supporters of SME policy point to the *employment growth* performance of the sector. Credit for identifying that the SME sector had become a vital source of job growth must go to the influential study by Birch (1979), who argued that two-thirds of the increase in manufacturing employment in the United States between 1969 and 1976 had occurred in firms with fewer than 20 employees. These results stimulated a great controversy (Armington and Odle 1982; Storey and Johnson 1987), together with a series of studies which produced evidence of similar trends in other countries (Commission of the European Communities 1987). A more recent review of the US evidence (Davis et al. 1996) has reawakened the controversy surrounding Birch's original conclusions (Carree and Klomp 1996; Robson 1996; Gallagher and Robson 1995). It has become clear that

Table 10.2   Employment share in enterprises of different sizes, EU member states, 1996

Member state	Percentage of total employment in each size group					
	Very small (0–9)	Small (10–49)	Medium (50–499)	All SMEs (0–499)	Large (over 500)	All
Austria	25	19	21	65	35	100
Belgium	48	14	11	73	27	100
Denmark	30	22	18	70	30	100
Finland	23	16	17	56	44	100
France	32	19	15	66	34	100
Germany	24	20	14	57	43	100
Greece	47	18	14	79	21	100
Ireland	18	16	14	49	51	100
Italy	48	21	11	80	20	100
Luxembourg	19	26	29	71	29	100
Netherlands	26	19	15	60	40	100
Portugal	38	23	18	79	21	100
Spain	47	19	12	79	21	100
Sweden	25	17	16	59	41	100
UK	31	16	12	59	41	100
EU	33	19	14	66	34	100

Source: *The European Observatory for SMEs Fifth Annual Report 1997*, EIM Small Business Research Consultancy, adapted from Bank of England (1998), table 27

some of the claims made in the 1980s for job creation in the SME sector were exaggerated. In addition, there has been a recent welcome recognition that a more balanced view of SMEs and large firms needs to be taken than was the case in the 1980s. It may be, for example, that the productivity gains which have triggered the job losses seen in big manufacturing firms are nevertheless the source of the wealth creation on which so many service sector SMEs depend. In addition, whilst the bigger firms have indeed lost a lot of jobs in recessions, they have continued to show excellent employment growth in business cycle upturns (Storey 1994).

Despite the reservations which surround the claims of the Birch study and others in the 1980s, few now doubt that the SME sector has proved to be a major engine of job creation at a time when the large companies in manufacturing have been engaged in a process of retrenchment. Evidence of the strong role of SMEs in job creation in the UK can be found even in the difficult days of the early 1980s' recession. Between 1979 and 1986, for example, employment in firms with under 50 employees increased from 32 to 43 per cent of total employment in the UK (Bannock and Daly 1990). Employment in the very smallest category (under 5 employees) increased from 12 to 19 per cent of all jobs, the most rapid increase of all. By contrast, firms with over 500 employees saw their share of total employment fall from 43 to 29 per cent between 1979 and 1986 (Griffiths 1991). Many of the larger, multi-location firms have chosen to close plants in the disadvantaged regions, although the processes by which closure decisions are taken are complex (Watts and Kirkham 1997; 1999).

Table 10.3   Changes in employment and turnover in small, medium and large companies, 1994–7

Size of firms (numbers of employees)	Employment (000s)		% of total of employment		Turnover (£ billion)		% of total turnover	
	1994	1997	1994	1997	1994	1997	1994	1997
Small businesses								
0–4	4 528	4 972	21.9	23.6	215	302	5.9	16.8
5–49	4 558	4 446	22.1	21.1	503	407	14.0	22.7
Total under 50	9 086	9 418	44.0	44.7	719	709	19.9	39.5
Medium-size businesses								
50–249	2 862	2 544	13.9	12.1	974	257	27.2	14.2
Large businesses								
Over 250	8 661	9 112	42.1	43.2	1 900	832	52.8	46.3
All businesses	20 609	21 074	100.0	100.0	3 593	1 797	100.0	100.0

Sources: Department of Trade and Industry (1999), table 1; Department of Trade and Industry (1998a), table 1.1. Reproduced with permission of the Department of Trade and Industry, SME Statistics Division, Sheffield

   The SME sector continues to be effective in creating jobs, as table 10.3 shows. Small businesses (i.e. under 50 employees) increased their share of total employment between 1994 and 1997, with growth being concentrated in the smallest firms with under 5 employees.
   The precise mechanisms by which SMEs create new jobs are complex. A valuable way of looking at employment creation in SMEs is provided by *components of change* analysis. This identifies two ways in which SMEs create jobs: through the formation of new businesses (new firm formation) and by way of the expansion of existing ('mature') SMEs. The process, however, is complex because in any one year the number of *net* new jobs created depends partly on the balance between new firms created ('births') and those closing ('deaths'), and partly on the balance between the numbers of jobs in *expanding* and *contracting* SMEs. The overwhelming evidence from components of change studies in the UK is that SMEs have been able to generate net new jobs via both routes simultaneously: an excess of births over deaths and an excess of expanding firms over contracting firms (Daly et al. 1991; Organization for Economic Cooperation and Development 1994). This is in stark contrast to the situation in large firms where it has been the contraction of existing companies which has dominated the picture and accounted for most of the job losses.

Births and deaths of SMEs

Given the limited extent of the SME sector in the UK at the beginning of the 1980s, it is not surprising that most research and government policy making initially concentrated on the new firm formation process rather than mature SMEs. The

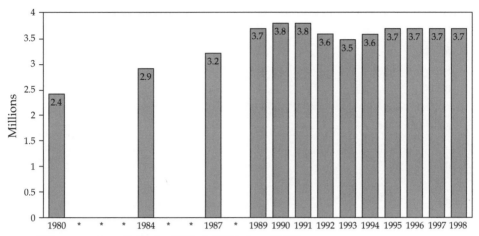

* Figures not available for 1981–3, 1985–6 and 1988.

Figure 10.1   Total numbers of enterprises in the UK, 1980–98.
Source: Department of Trade and Industry (1999a) figure 1. Reproduced with permission of the Department of Trade and Industry, SME Statistics Division, Sheffield

early 1980s were a period of severe recession in the UK. A great concern at that time was that any expansion of the SME sector would be a temporary phenomenon. During economic downturns the SME sector can increase its *share* of total employment simply because total employment is falling faster in big firms than it is among the SMEs. Genuine new jobs are not necessarily being produced in these circumstances.

These misgivings, however, proved to be unfounded, and the SME sector went from strength to strength throughout the 1980s. This is revealed clearly in figure 10.1, which shows the growth in the total number of businesses in the UK between 1980 and 1998. The overwhelming proportion of these businesses are SMEs. Between 1980 and 1998 the total number of businesses in the UK rose from 2.4 million to 3.7 million, a rise of 54 per cent. The pattern of growth over time is particularly revealing. All of the growth took place between 1980 and 1990, and the number of businesses remained stable during the 1990s.

Did the 1980s represent a once-for-all growth in the stock of SMEs in the UK to a new stable ceiling of between 3.6 million and 3.8 million businesses? Only time will tell since, as table 10.2 has shown, the UK still has a smaller SME sector than many other countries. In a review of the major studies of the UK's SME sector, Storey (1994) concludes that government policies to encourage SMEs had only a marginal impact in the 1980s. The rapid growth in the 1980s appears therefore to have resulted in a major structural shift to a larger SME stock, helped by high levels of aggregate demand in the late 1980s and easier access to capital for SMEs.

The issue of the effect of recessions on the SME sector continues to be one of considerable importance. The drop in the number of businesses in 1992 and 1993, revealed by figure 10.1, superficially suggests that recessions have detrimental effects on SMEs. Figure 10.2 throws additional light on the relationship between

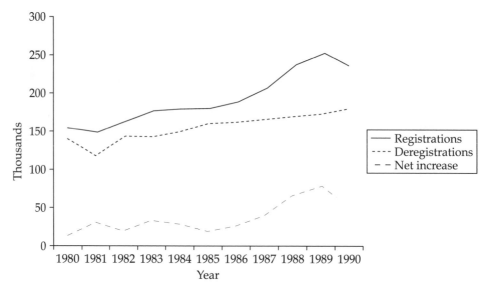

Figure 10.2   Registrations and deregistrations for value-added tax, 1980–91.
Source: Daly (1991), figure 1. Office for National Statistics, © Crown Copyright

new firm formation rates and cyclical downturns. This plots the number of new firms registering for VAT purposes between 1980 and 1990, together with the annual numbers of deregistrations. The annual difference between gross new firm formation (registrations) and gross deaths of firms (deregistrations) is shown on figure 10.2 as the 'net increase'. The sharp recession of the early 1990s can be seen to have led to a fall in the number of new firms being created, together with a rise in deaths. Indeed, as figure 10.1 has shown, net *reductions* in the numbers of businesses were recorded in 1992 and 1993, although changes in the VAT registration data have meant that they cannot be shown on figure 10.2.

Perhaps of greater interest in figure 10.2 is what happened in the deep recession of the early 1980s. Net new firm formation (the difference between births and deaths) fell back somewhat as the recession bit. The contrast, however, between the early 1980s and early 1990s recessions could not be clearer. In the early 1980s the recession appears to have led to only a slight hesitation in what was subsequently to develop into a prolonged expansion of the SME sector. Indeed, between 1980 and 1990 new firm registrations exceeded deregistrations in every single year.

Considerable controversy still surrounds the interpretation of the picture revealed by figure 10.2. Intuitively, one would expect the SME sector to suffer badly during economic downturns. A decline in aggregate demand is very serious for firms which are generally so close to their markets and which are known to suffer more than large firms from cash flow problems, late payment of bills and difficulties of accessing loan finance. On the other hand, there is evidence that during economic downturns a series of *recession-push* factors can lead to a surge in new firm formation rates. Starting one's own business in a recession is a difficult task. Nevertheless, redundancy or the threat of redundancy is a powerful incentive to new small firm creation (Robson 1991). In addition, redundancy lump-sum payoffs and the ready availability of cheap second-hand machinery and premises (freed from bankrupt firms) make the entry of new firms easier than is normally the case. Finally, during recessions many big firms ruthlessly rationalize their operations by closing down peripheral activities (thereby creating market niches for new small firms), or by selling off peripheral activities (often as management buyouts), thus creating new small businesses.

Experience in the early 1980s recession suggests that up to one half of all new small firm owners may have been pushed by the recession into founding their own businesses. This phenomenon also explains the obsession of many SME owners with job security and hence an unwillingness to take risks by expanding rapidly. Nevertheless, it is still unclear whether it is the 'push' of becoming unemployed in a downturn or the 'pull' of market opportunities in an economic upturn which is the main influence on new firm formation. Hence, 'probably the fairest conclusion is that both influences are at work, and that their relative impact will vary sectorally, spatially and temporally. Even so, on balance, it would appear that the weight of evidence is that unemployment generally exerts a positive influence upon new firm formation' (Storey 1994: 77).

Despite the failure of the SME sector in the 1990s to replicate its remarkable growth in the 1980s, almost all of the evidence presented so far suggests that governments have been right to switch their regional policy focus to SMEs. The sector has demonstrated an ability to create jobs via new firm formation even during recessions. This fact, together with the underlying upward trend in the stock of businesses since 1980, bodes well for a regional policy founded on support for SMEs.

There are, however, features of job creation by SMEs which require careful attention by policy makers. The most important of these is the extraordinary volatility exhibited by SMEs, and hence the instability of employment which they offer. This is dramatically revealed by figure 10.2. Annual *net* increases in the stock of new businesses are the outcome of a balance between much larger numbers of gross new births and deaths of firms. As a result, 'the world of small business is . . . exceptionally turbulent, with around one in ten businesses leaving the VAT registers in any one year . . . Within this turbulent world the very smallest firms are six times more likely to leave the register than the rest. Around 60 per cent of those leaving the register each year have, on average, done so because of . . . business failure' (Hughes 1997a: 3). Typically, only 55 per cent of newly created firms survive three years and a mere 35 per cent survive six years (Hughes and Storey 1994; Storey 1994). There is also evidence that the problem of job insecurity is not just confined to *new* small firms facing bankruptcy. Established SMEs also appear to experience greater year-on-year variability in employment size than do large firms (Davis et al. 1996).

Very high death rates are a universal feature of SMEs and represent something which policy makers have had to learn to cope with. There is some evidence that active policy support can mitigate death rates to some degree (Keeble and Walker 1994), but the death rates remain high compared with larger firms whatever is done. It is known that 'the young are more likely to fail than the old, the very

Table 10.4   Growth and death in a sample of UK manufacturing and business service firms, 1990–5

Employment size band 1990	Number of firms 1990	Employment size band 1995							Total firms alive in 1995	Death rate (%)
		0–9	10–19	20–49	50–99	100–199	200–499	499+		
0–9	376	186	51	4	1	1	1	–	244	35.1
10–19	258	43	104	39	2	–	–	–	188	27.1
20–49	281	6	27	137	31	2	–	1	204	27.4
50–99	206	–	2	35	85	27	5	2	156	24.3
100–199	115	–	3	2	18	61	11	1	96	16.5
200–499	93	–	–	–	2	13	56	5	76	18.3
Number of firms 1995	–	235	187	217	139	104	73	9	964	27.5

Source: Hughes (1997a), table 2

small are more likely to fail than their larger counterparts, and that, for young firms, probably the most powerful influence on their survival is whether or not they grow within a short period after tart-up' (Storey 1994: 109). Given the importance to subsequent performance of SMEs 'hitting the ground running', it is not surprising that attention has increasingly shifted away from new firm formation towards the factors which influence the growth of existing firms, and it is to this which we now turn.

Expansion and contraction of existing SMEs

An interesting feature of employment creation in the SME sector is that the most rapid growth in employment is among the very smallest firms of all, particularly among those with under 5 employees. These results highlight an important feature of SMEs. Once established, small firms grow rapidly at first but soon reach a ceiling which they find it difficult to get beyond. This ceiling appears to lie at about 8–10 employees (Dunne and Hughes 1994; Hart and Oulton 1996). Very few firms grow beyond this level: either by choice – preferring to stay small – or for some other reason, they are unable to expand. One widely used classification of SMEs which graphically illustrates this feature of the behaviour of existing firms distinguishes between 'failures', 'trundlers' and 'flyers' (Storey 1994). There are very few 'flyers'.

One effect of the existence of growth ceilings is that only a few of the survivors in today's cohort of new firms will dominate long-term job creation in the SME sector. In the UK, for example, it is thought that over a ten-year period a mere 4 per cent of survivors for a given cohort of new firms account for 50 per cent of all jobs created (Storey 1994). Hence few new firms survive, and even fewer go on to create the new jobs needed in a dynamic economy. This phenomenon is graphically illustrated by table 10.4 (Hughes 1997a). This table plots the movement of individual firms between 1990 and 1995 for a sample of 1329 SMEs with under 500 employees. Almost all firms can be seen to remain within their initial size class (as shown by the large numbers on the principal diagonal of the table). However, among the few firms which did spectacularly break free of their initial size class, nine went on to create over 6000 new jobs between 1990 and 1995. Small firms therefore truly do represent the seedcorn from which future industrial giants will grow. Many will die and few will grow quickly. Those that do grow, however, determine future employment prospects.

There has been considerable recent research on the characteristics which distinguish the 'flyers' from the 'trundlers', although the forces affecting the growth rates of established SMEs are still not yet fully understood. Successful fast growing SMEs appear to have a combination of three sets of factors. First, there is the background of the entrepreneurs (e.g. education and the presence of multiple owners). Second, there are the characteristics of the firm itself, with smaller firms and limited companies doing best. Finally, there is the willingness or otherwise of an SME to take certain key strategic decisions (e.g. sharing of ownership and equity) necessary for growth, within a management and organizational framework designed to encourage growth (Hughes 1998; Storey 1994).

Existing SMEs face many barriers to rapid growth. Government bureaucracy and the taxation system (especially VAT) are often stressed, as are difficulties arising from late payment of bills by big firms and obtaining appropriately skilled labour during economic upturns. A barrier to expansion which has received particular attention is the 'equity gap': the failure of the financial system to provide the relatively small sums of capital necessary for rapid growth by an SME. Most SMEs rely heavily at first on the personal savings of their owner, help from family and friends, and loans based on the collateral security of their family home (Small Business Research Trust 1999). These sources soon become inadequate for a rapidly growing small firm. Not all researchers would agree that there is a genuine case of capital market failure, although it is clear that rapidly growing small firms do have perennial problems with the financial sector (Hughes 1998; Binks and Ennew 1997). One problem is that providing loans to SMEs is inherently a risky business given the high death rates. In these circumstances it is hardly surprising that banks seek good collateral security. Another problem is that many SME owners are extremely reluctant to share equity by selling it to financial institutions. There have been repeated attempts to design new policies to help small firms seeking to grow to access adequate finance at critical moments (Harrison and Mason 1991; Hughes 1997b), and virtually all UK regional policy programmes now include financing initiatives such as venture capital (Mason and Harrison 1994; Buckland and Davis 1996). Finance, however, remains a very difficult problem for SMEs (Lund and Wright 1999).

Despite the instability of the SME sector and the many barriers to growth, there are good reasons to continue backing SMEs. Keeble (1990) suggests that there are five different long-term forces leading to a strengthening of the SME sector in modern economies:

1   *Fragmentation and the externalization of demand*   In an attempt to cut costs, many large firms have chosen, and will continue to choose, to concentrate on their core businesses. In doing this, they are increasingly ready to subcontract work and to buy in outside services which, in the past, they would have undertaken in-house. This process greatly encourages the establishment of specialist SMEs

supplying larger firms. The buying-in of consultancy services is an excellent example of this type of activity.

2   *Changes in market demand*   Rising incomes of consumers have encouraged the demand for specialized, often individually customized, products. This has enabled small firms to survive by serving niche markets in which they have specialist expertise.

3   *Technological change*   Many of the newer 'sunrise' industries such as information technology and biotechnology are dominated by small firms. The rapid pace of current technological change is therefore stimulating the creation of SMEs.

4   *Competition from newly industrialized countries*   This appears to have hit larger firms hardest, particularly those producing relatively standardized products. Smaller firms tend to produce more specialized products and services for niche markets.

5   *Government policy*   The UK government has pioneered new types of help for SMEs and placed great emphasis on encouraging an enterprise culture. So long as this policy stance continues, the SME sector will be encouraged to expand, although perhaps not as fast as was possible in the 1980s where growth was occurring from a very low base.

Job creation: the regional dimension in the UK

Geographical differences in the performance of SMEs are complex. In order to understand how the job creation potential of the SME sector varies from region to region, it is necessary to focus again on the different components of change: the balance between births and deaths, and the balance between expansion and contraction of mature SMEs.

Births and deaths

There are systematic differences between UK regions in the rates at which new firms are formed and die, and hence in the total stock of SMEs which has accumulated in each region. Table 10.5 shows the total stock of SMEs (i.e. firms under 250 employees) in each UK region in 1997. The absolute numbers of these businesses are given in the first column, while the second column expresses the stock as a rate per 10 000 of the adult population. It is immediately apparent from table 10.5 that there are large regional differences in the stock of SMEs per 10 000 adult population. A north–south division is revealed by table 10.5. With the exception of the North West, it is the South East, London, the Eastern region, the South West and the West Midlands which have the biggest stocks of SMEs. The further north and west one goes, the lower the stocks of SMEs, with Merseyside, the North East and Scotland having particularly low stocks.

Similar results emerge when new firm formation rates are examined (the third column of table 10.5). Again it is the south and east of the UK which are revealed as having the highest rates of new firm formation in 1997. London, the South East and the Eastern region all have rates of new firm formation in excess of the UK average for 1997. Merseyside, the North East and Wales have particularly low

Table 10.5   The regional distribution of SMEs[a] in the UK and rates of births and deaths,[b] 1997

Region[c]	Number of businesses with under 250 employees	Number of SMEs per 10 000 adult population	VAT registrations per 10 000 adult population	VAT deregistrations per 10 000 adult population
North East	96 915	465	20	21
North West	322 735	737	34	34
Merseyside	60 525	542	29	23
Yorkshire/Humber	291 060	738	30	31
East Midlands	239 875	662	36	34
West Midlands	306 095	741	33	33
Eastern	378 335	890	43	37
London	566 300	1 006	66	50
South East	612 130	960	47	41
South West	363 100	925	39	37
Wales	156 765	678	27	27
Scotland	243 500	595	30	28
Northern Ireland	84 430	680	31	29
UK	3 701 070	791	39	35

[a] SMEs are defined as firms with under 250 employees.
[b] Stocks of firms and birth and death rates of firms are normally expressed as a proportion of the adult or working population (as here) or, in the case of birth and death rates, as a proportion of the existing stock of businesses. These two methods give slightly different results, but are broadly comparable (Storey 1994: 54). The convention followed by the Department of Trade and Industry in presenting its SME statistics has been followed here.
[c] The regions are those defined for the Government Offices established in 1996.
Sources: adapted from Department of Trade and Industry (1998a), table 4.1; and Department of Trade and Industry (1998b), table 7.1. Reproduced with permission of the Department of Trade and Industry, SME Statistics Division, Sheffield

rates of new firm formation. Comparison of births with deaths again illustrates graphically how fine the balance between annual births and deaths is for SMEs. Typically, the higher the birth rate, the higher too is the death rate. All regions share in the high risks associated with new firm formation.

It is important not to take too simplistic a north–south view of the process of new firm formation. Table 10.5 presents results only for very broad regions of the UK. However, even at this very broad level it can be seen that there are geographical differences which need to be explained. Why, for example, is the Merseyside stock of SMEs so much smaller than the rest of the North West (which includes another large city in the form of nearby Manchester)? Why does London do so well when it contains some extremely disadvantaged inner city areas which would be expected to be hostile environments for new firms? Why has Wales a bigger stock of SMEs (per 10 000 population) than Scotland, but a lower new firm formation rate?

Greater clarity can be brought to the issue by examining new firm formation rates at sub-regional level in the UK. Figure 10.3 shows rates of new firm formation in 1997 for the counties and unitary authorities of the UK. This figure reveals

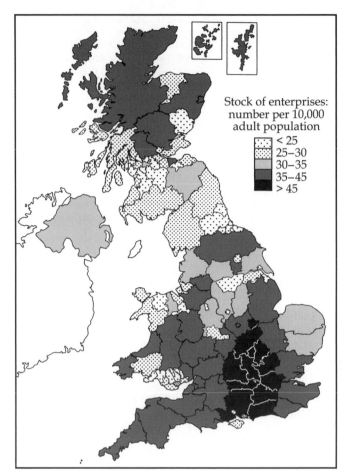

Figure 10.3   Business start-ups: enterprises registering for VAT by area per 10 000 adult population, 1997.
Source: Department of Trade and Industry (1998b), table 7.1. Reproduced with permission of Department of Trade and Industry, SME Statistics Division, Sheffield

that although the geographical pattern is very complex, three broad characteristics are apparent:

1   The broad north–south difference in new firm formation rates revealed by the regional data of table 10.5 is also picked out clearly at sub-regional level. The higher rates of new firm formation in 1997 are generally in counties in the south and east of the UK, with generally lower rates in the north and west.

2   With the exception of London, the large metropolitan areas and older industrial cities of the UK generally have rather low rates of new firm formation. This is clearly shown by the low rates of new firm formation for the conurbations of Merseyside, the West Midlands, South and West Yorkshire, and Tyne and Wear. Cities formerly heavily dependent on manufacturing industries

also have low new firm formation rates (e.g. Middlesborough, Derby, Neath/ Port Talbot and Dundee). Inner city areas away from the central business districts have particularly low rates of new firm formation.

3   Smaller and medium towns, even outside the more prosperous south, appear to do quite well (as, for example, with Bristol in the South West, and Stirling in Scotland). On the other hand, very remote rural areas do not appear to do so well, as is shown by the remoter parts of Scotland and Wales.

It is clearly vital for regional policy purposes to be able to understand the reasons for these geographical variations. The forces at work are long-standing ones. It became apparent at the start of the 1980s that the more prosperous regions in the south of Britain had more active SME sectors than the north (Gould and Keeble 1984; Lloyd and Mason 1984). Even at that time it was clear that the smaller and medium towns in the south were particularly attractive locations for new SMEs (Cross 1981). Traditional industrial heartland areas such as Cleveland were quickly revealed as having a weak SME culture (Storey 1982), one which was incapable of replacing the huge job losses in manufacturing in the early 1980s' recession (Storey 1983).

The early patterns continued to persist throughout the great expansion in the numbers of SMEs in the 1980s. Figure 10.4 shows the geographical pattern of *net* new firm formation between 1980 and 1990 (i.e. allowing for deaths as well as births). The success of the south and east of the country is very apparent, particularly along a broad belt running from Cambridge to Exeter. Certain industries also seem to have been much more successful incubators of new small firms in the 1980s than others. Most successful of all were business services such as finance, property and professional services, which showed a 7.3 per cent growth of new firms, net of closures, from 1980 to 1990 (Daly 1991). Personal services (e.g. hairdressing) also exhibited strong growth (6.8 per cent more firms in 1990 compared with 1980). Manufacturing had only 2.5 per cent more firms in 1990 than 1980, while agriculture and retailing actually lost businesses over the period. Each of these industries has its own distinctive geographical pattern of growth, but with the south generally favoured. For example, the key financial, professional and business service sector, the target of many regional policy initiatives, had a pattern of growth in the 1980s strongly focused on London and nearby areas in the South East. Manufacturing firms had a more dispersed pattern of growth, although still with a southern bias (Keeble and Walker 1994).

The picture is a rather depressing one. The south had a head start in 1980 in that its industry mix was heavily slanted in favour of sectors such as business services which are natural incubators for new small firms. Trends during the 1980s actually strengthened the industry mix advantages of the south, which by the 1990s had a higher proportion of small firm incubator industries than it had in 1980 (Daly 1991). London may have lost much of its manufacturing base, but it has retained its service industries. The rest of the south has gained both new manufacturing and new service firms in their thousands.

Identifying the determinants of geographical differences in new firm formation rates has been the focus of a major research effort (Storey and Johnson 1987;

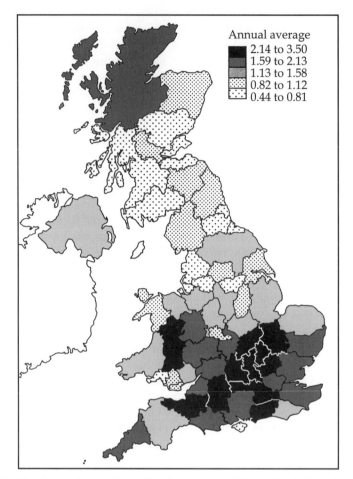

Figure 10.4   Net change in number of businesses per 1000 civilian labour force, 1980–90. *Source*: Keeble and Walker (1994), figure 7. Reproduced with the permission of Taylor & Francis Ltd, Oxford

Keeble and Walker 1994; Ashcroft et al. 1991; Ashcroft and Love 1996; Love 1996; Reynolds et al. 1994; Storey 1994; Westhead and Moyes 1992). The phenomenon is not a simple one. Taking the *birth rates* of small firms first, eight groups of determinants appear to be operating (Storey 1994):

1   *Population and its characteristics*   Rapid population growth in an area has an important effect in stimulating new firm formation. Other less important influences are the proportion of the population aged 25–45 (the age group of new entrepreneurs) and population density (since remoter and sparsely populated rural areas create few new firms).

2   *Industrial structure*   New firm formation is higher where many SMEs already exist since most founders of new firms previously worked in a small firm in the same area. By contrast, areas which are heavily dependent on industries

such as heavy engineering (in which barriers to entry are important) have lower rates of new firm formation.

3   *Wealth*   Those areas which are already wealthy tend to create more new SMEs, partly because of higher disposable income available to be spent on the products of the new firms, and partly because wealth makes raising capital to set up new firms easier.

4   *Owner-occupied housing*   Finance raised using the entrepreneur's home as collateral security is the key method of funding a business start-up. The more owner-occupied housing in an area, and the higher are house prices, the greater the probability that new businesses will be created.

5   *Occupational and educational characteristics*   New firm formation is higher in areas where the workforce contains a high proportion of people with managerial skills, or with high levels of educational attainment (particularly scientific and technical skills).

6   *Unemployment*   The 'push' and 'pull' effects of unemployment on new firm formation have already been discussed. Since unemployment rates exhibit large spatial variations, their effect on new firm formation rates is also important.

7   *Government*   Government expenditure in an area can boost new firm formation by stimulating the local market. The pro- or anti-business political complexion of local government may also be an important factor.

8   *Policy initiatives*   There is some evidence that SME policy initiatives do have an effect on new firm formation (e.g. a 'Welsh effect' arising from the Welsh Development Agency: Keeble and Walker 1994; Ashcroft et al. 1991). Interestingly, however, the policy effects on firm *births* appear to be minor.

The determinants of new firm formation rates are clearly both numerous and complex. The forces at work appear to be similar in many different countries. Scrutiny of the list of determinants quickly reveals that the traditionally depressed areas score badly on most of the above factors, as is shown by Storey's (1982) well-known index of entrepreneurship. These results imply that regional policy based upon measures designed to increase the rate of new firm formation in many disadvantaged areas faces a difficult socio-economic environment (Robson 1998).

Evidence on the determinants of spatial variations in *death rates* for SMEs reveals a rather different picture. The most important cause of a high death rate of SMEs is, paradoxically, the birth rate in an area. Indeed, birth rates and death rates are closely intertwined. The 'entry and exit of businesses is . . . a "revolving door" phenomenon: firms are born, often quickly die, this process in turn leads to further entry and so on' (Love 1996: 449). In addition, high unemployment rates tend to push up death rates (in contrast to the positive 'push' effect of unemployment on birth rates). Big city locations, particularly in the inner city, also result in an increased risk of death. By contrast, regional policy help targeted on small firms does seem to increase the chances of survival (Keeble and Walker 1994).

Expansion and contraction of existing SMEs

There has been less research on geographical variations in the employment growth performance of existing SMEs than on new firm formation, despite a welcome

Table 10.6 Regional[a] variations in SME performance, 1990–5

Performance measure	South-east	Outer southern	Industrial heartland	Periphery
Manufacturing SMEs				
Employment growth (%)	14.5	6.0	18.2	7.9
Turnover growth (%)	13.0	19.8	21.3	8.8
Service SMEs				
Employment growth (%)	64.9	13.2	28.3	−6.2
Turnover growth (%)	18.0	19.3	42.7	19.8
All SMEs				
Employment growth (%)	44.0	8.8	21.6	2.4
Turnover growth (%)	15.4	19.5	25.0	11.3

[a] The regions are defined as follows: south-east (the South East standard region, including London); outer southern (East Anglia, South West and East Midlands); industrial heartland (West Midlands, North West, Yorkshire and the Humber); and periphery (Scotland, North and Wales).
Source: Keeble (1997), table 4. Statistics are from a sample of 1000 firms conducted by the Centre for Business Research at the University of Cambridge: some 698 questionnaires produced usable responses. Reproduced with the permission of Taylor & Francis Ltd, Oxford

increase in studies in the 1990s. Given the importance for overall employment change of the growth performance of existing SMEs, particularly those few which become 'flyers', the issue is a vital one for regional policy.

Perhaps the most important issue is whether employment growth rates for established SMEs exhibit north–south differences of the type seen with new firm formation. Table 10.6 presents the results of a recent survey of the growth performance of 1000 SMEs in the UK between 1990 and 1995 (Keeble 1997). Taking employment growth rates first, it can be seen that the south-east (the South East region including London) had by far the fastest growth in these established SMEs (44.0 per cent growth between 1990 and 1995). By contrast, the periphery (the North, Scotland and Wales) grew most slowly (2.4 per cent). Interestingly, it has been the service sector which has been the main cause of this stark difference. Employment in service sector SMEs grew by a massive 64.9 per cent in the south-east between 1990 and 1995 and actually fell by 6.2 per cent in the periphery. However, the south-east also registered a faster rate of growth of employment in manufacturing SMEs (14.5 per cent) compared with the periphery (7.9 per cent). Much of the overall employment growth in the south-east has taken place in London service sector SMEs.

While comparisons between the south-east and the periphery appear to show clear evidence of a north–south division in growth rates, it is also clear from the evidence in table 10.6 that the picture is nevertheless quite a complex one. The industrial heartland (which contain many of Britain's declining industrial areas) between 1990 and 1995 contained SMEs which grew faster in both employment and turnover terms than the outer southern region (East Anglia, East Midlands and South West). This stands in direct contrast to the evidence for rates of new firm formation.

Most explanations for the better employment performance of established SMEs in the south-east focus on 'resource munificence' arguments. These include industrial structure (particularly the concentration of fast growing service sector firms), the buoyancy of local markets, easier access to labour, capital and other factors of production, and the existence of a supportive network of other small firms in the south-east. However, 'northern regions cannot be crudely categorized as "hostile environments" for successful SME growth . . . because of a good 1990s' employment, turnover and innovation performance by Industrial Heartland SMEs' (Keeble 1997: 291). It is possible, therefore, that significant numbers of SMEs within the 'hostile environment' areas have been able to respond in ways which overcome the problems inherent in their locations (Vaessen and Keeble 1995).

Policy makers must take account of the complexities of the situation. Indeed, there is evidence that in the late 1980s and early 1990s SMEs in many northern and western regions of the UK were able to out-perform their south-east counterparts (Keeble and Bryson 1996; Barkham et al. 1996). The north–south division in SME performance may not therefore be something which occurs in all time periods. The successful performance of established SMEs in the industrial heartland from 1990 to 1995 may also in part reflect a degree of success for policies deigned to help these firms. If so, this suggests that the inherent problems faced by established SMEs in the disadvantaged areas can be tackled by appropriate policies.

Further complexity is added to the situation by the fact that growth rates for established SMEs also differ for local areas *within* the broad regions set out in table 10.6. With the exception of London, most of the bigger urban areas (and particularly the inner city areas) exhibit lower growth rates for their existing SMEs than do more rural parts of the region (Keeble et al. 1992; Storey 1994). This is particularly the case for manufacturing SMEs (North and Smallbone 1995). On the other hand, the most remote rural areas also appear to be rather unfavourable environments for SMEs seeking to grow quickly.

SMEs and regional policy: some dilemmas

The available evidence suggests that harnessing the growth potential of the SME sector in the disadvantaged regions is unlikely to be an easy task for regional policy. Formidable difficulties exist for policy makers, and much research and experimentation remains to be done.

Regional SME policy is now at a crossroads. Its success will depend on a continuation of the national and international trends which encouraged SME expansion in the 1970s and 1980s, but which appear to have been less strong in the 1990s. It will also need to overcome the formidable inherent disadvantages of many of the older industrial areas, inner city areas and remoter rural areas as locations for new businesses. It must, moreover, find solutions to a number of key dilemmas, which currently hinder the creation of an effective regional SME policy. Four dilemmas are of particular importance.

Table 10.7   The regional distribution of loans under the Small Firms Loan Guarantee
Scheme, 1987–94

Region	Loans (No.)	%	Value (£m)	(%)	Average size (£)
North East	1 013	4.7	27.2	4.0	26 881
North West[a]	1 924	8.9	57.1	8.4	29 673
Yorkshire/Humberside	1 557	7.2	47.6	7.0	30 565
West Midlands	1 693	7.8	50.3	7.4	29 716
East Midlands	2 523	11.6	77.5	11.4	30 713
South East[b]	7 393	34.1	252.8	37.1	34 192
South West	3 162	14.6	91.1	13.4	28 808
Scotland	1 091	5.0	50.6	7.4	46 379
Wales	1 198	5.5	38.7	5.7	32 304
Northern Ireland	145	0.7	7.7	1.1	53 172
UK	21 699	100.0	680.6	100.0	31 366

[a] Including Cumbria.
[b] Including East Anglia.
Source: Cowling (1998), table V. Reproduced with kind permission of Kluwer Academic Publishers

A national or a regional SME policy?

Most government policies designed to assist SMEs in the 1980s were made available in all regions. It was only belatedly, in 1988, that the UK government began to build a regional bias into its SME policy with the introduction of the Regional Investment Grant and Regional Innovation Grant schemes designed to provide financial subsidies at higher rates to assisted area SMEs. There grants were suspended in 1996, but the UK has continued to use a combination of national and regional policy schemes to promote the SME sector. The Small Firms Loan Guarantee Scheme (SFLGS), for example, is a typical national scheme. It is designed to offer loan guarantees to established and start-up small firms unable to offer sufficient collateral security to obtain normal private sector finance. Between the start of the SFLGS in 1981 and 1998 the scheme guaranteed loans worth £2.1 billion to 62 000 firms (House of Commons 1998).

A problem with national schemes of this type is that the hostile environment in many disadvantaged areas for SMEs means that non-assisted areas tend to be the principal beneficiaries. Research on the SFLGS has clearly demonstrated that this is the case (Harrison and Mason 1986; Cowling 1998). Table 10.7 presents the results of a regional analysis of loans guaranteed by the SFLGS between 1987 and 1994. As can be seen, the South East obtained 34.1 per cent of all loan guarantees. This was despite the fact that in some of the more disadvantaged regions (e.g. Northern Ireland and Scotland), the average value of each loan guaranteed was higher than in the South East. Hence the SFLGS, although a national scheme, has a built-in bias towards regions which already have a large stock of SMEs, such as the South East. The fact that the regional bias has been gradually reduced over time through careful management of the SFLGS (Cowling 1998) has still not succeeded in eliminating this bias.

Despite being fully aware that *any* national initiative to help SMEs will inevitably help the already successful regions more, the UK government has continued with an active national programme of help. The 1998 Late Payment of Commercial Debts Act, designed to force large firms to speed up their payment of bills for work done for them by SMEs, is a recent example of this programme. One might ask why the bulk of new policies to help SMEs remain national rather than regional policies. The answer is that the government faces a dilemma. The nation as a whole would benefit from a bigger and more successful SME sector, as table 10.2 has shown. The issue is therefore not simply a regional policy one. It is a national policy issue too. Moreover, there is still a large body of opinion, including many SME owners, which is against financial incentives and other interventionist policies and would rather see the government help the SME sector by simply reducing taxes, bureaucracy, regulations and controls. These types of initiatives are inherently national (or EU-wide) in nature and not regionally discriminating.

The essence of the national versus regional policy dilemma is one of limited resources. National policies will tend to help already prosperous regions, but will be more effective in raising the nation's stock of successful SMEs. Regional policies will help to solve the problems of the disadvantaged areas, but given the inherent problems SMEs face in these areas, the nation's stock of successful SMEs will not be increased by as much as would be the case with national SME policies. There are simply not sufficient financial resources available to fund policies which will attain both objectives simultaneously.

This dilemma has not yet been properly confronted. Successive governments have chosen to try to have their cake and eat it by running a number of regionally discriminating SME policies alongside the national schemes. The UK government's important Regional Selective Assistance (RSA) scheme, for example, is made available to SMEs as well as to large firms. In 1998 the government introduced a new set of eligible areas within which SMEs employing up to 250 workers are eligible for new Enterprise Grants (Department of Trade and Industry 1999b). The EU Structural Funds too have been heavily biased towards SMEs in the disadvantaged areas eligible for them (see chapter 11). Regional development agencies and local councils have also been more active in helping small firms in the disadvantaged areas than in more prosperous regions. We are therefore left in a situation in which there is a programme of national assistance and legislation to help SMEs (which inherently favours the more prosperous regions), running alongside a set of regionally discriminating initiatives, neither of which is adequately funded for the massive task which they must confront.

Who to help: new starts or survivors?

As has been shown earlier, starting a new business is a high-risk affair. Death rates for new small firms are extremely high. Moreover, of those which survive the risky early years, only a tiny minority are able or willing to grow. The dilemma is a stark one. Help entrepreneurs to get started and you will be pouring resources into firms of which most will go bust. The trouble with seedcorn is that most of it falls on stony ground. On the other hand, helping only the survivors simply raises new concerns. To do so may result in some projects with excellent long-term prospects simply never getting off the ground. There is also the problem of deciding which survivors to help. Many small firms have no desire to grow. Indeed many of their founders created their own business to get away from big firms. Only a few of those that wish to grow have either the ability or the pro-spects. It would be nice to think that policy makers could home in on small firms in the fast track and help them on their way. But picking winners is hazardous at the best of times and is perilous indeed in the high-risk world of the small business (Storey 1994).

Some authors, for example, have argued for initiatives which target younger SMEs, since these are known to grow fastest in employment terms and may also respond better to subsidies (Wren 1998). Some older firms, however, also exhibit rapid growth potential and cannot therefore be ignored (Smallbone and North 1995). In the 1990s, the UK national government and the EU Commission increas-ingly decentralized decisions on precisely how to target SME policies. Regional and local partnerships charged with delivering EU Structural Funds and national programmes such as the Single Regeneration Budget are allowed great discretion in deciding how to target the many types of help offered to SMEs. In principle, this should allow better policy delivery. Hence some local areas may favour a policy based on helping new business starts, while elsewhere the focus can be on helping mature SMEs to grow, depending on the local circumstances. In practice, however, this process has not solved the policy dilemma since programmes tend to play safe by trying to simultaneously increase both new starts and growth rates of existing SMEs.

Who to help: manufacturing or services?

The most rapid rates of new firm formation have been in certain service indus-tries. Providing regional policy to service sector firms is fraught with difficulties. Many services (e.g. hairdressing, filling stations) serve purely local markets. Help for one firm is therefore counterproductive since it results in the displacement of another local firm. For this reason, most regional policy aid is targeted on services that generate an injection of money from elsewhere (e.g. manufacturing and tourism) or that help to improve the efficiency of local businesses (e.g. finance and consultancy).

One of the great dilemmas facing regional SME policy in the UK is that the less prosperous areas seem to have deep-seated disadvantages for most of the import-ant service sector incubator industries such as financial services. London and the South East have a stranglehold on many business and financial services, and it is hard to see how this can be broken without damaging some of the country's most successful sectors.

If regional small firm policy concentrates on manufacturing, however, it faces further dilemmas. Rates of new firm formation are smaller in manufacturing than in services. In addition, new manufacturing firms tend to favour smaller towns and are less attracted to the old industrial cities, where most of the unemployed live.

Where to provide the help: enterprise nodes or uniform help?

A fourth key dilemma for regional small firm policy concerns the idea of how sharply to target the help. Assistance for SMEs is currently very widely dispersed across the UK. Even if one ignores the national initiatives and focuses on regionally differentiated assistance, help for SMEs is still spread very thinly. All of the major EU Structural Funds programmes in the UK are built around SME policies. So too are most of the UK's urban and inner city policy initiatives.

Should help for SMEs continue to be offered at all places within the assisted areas, or should some attempt be made to spatially target the help given? This dilemma has long been recognized and yet it remains one of the most difficult facing policy makers. Successive governments have struggled to come to terms with this dilemma. The result has been a series of experiments in spatially targeting SME initiatives, whilst at the same time continuing to operate 'blanket' national and regional policies. As early as 1980, the very beginning of the rapid expansion of the SME sector in the UK, the government was experimenting with enterprise zones and freeports. Although not strictly part of regional policy, these experiments were designed to test whether greater freedom from government interference and control in strictly targeted locations leads to faster growth. Their major aim was to help to regenerate British business, particularly in inner city areas. The fact that many of the 31 enterprise zones and six freeports subsequently set up were located in the assisted areas, however, meant that they were effectively instruments of regional policy. Enterprise zones and freeports have been of particular relevance to the analysis of regional policy since they were a radical departure from the interventionist philosophy underlying traditional regional policy. As Hall points out, enterprise zones were meant to be 'an essay in non-plan. Small, selected areas of inner cities would be simply thrown open to all kinds of initiative, with minimal control. In other words, we would aim to recreate the Hong Kong of the 1950s and 1960s inside inner Liverpool and inner Glasgow' (1982: 417).

Three main benefits have accrued to firms located in these zones. First, firms have gained tax concessions, the most important being exemption from industrial and commercial rates. In addition, firms were eligible for 100 per cent tax relief on industrial and commercial buildings. Second, planning procedures were simplified for firms located in enterprise zones. This reduced the gap between investment decisions and the construction of new plant. Third, firms located in enterprise zones have been subject to less bureaucratic intervention. Firms have access to quicker planning decisions, and requests for statistical information are kept to a bare minimum.

Freeports are rather different. A freeport is 'an enclosed zone within or adjacent to a seaport or airport within which goods are treated for customs purposes as being outside of the customs territory of the country' (HM Treasury 1984: 1). Apart from the obvious advantage of localities being able to use the label of a freeport to try to attract new firms, two main benefits have been enjoyed: (1) customs duties, levies and value-added tax payments are paid only when the goods leave the freeport for the rest of the United Kingdom or the EU, the effect being to increase the firm's cash flow; (2) firms benefit from simplified customs procedures and less red tape.

The enterprise zones and freeports have generally been quite successful (PA Cambridge Economic Consultants 1995b; Potter and Moore 2000). Despite this, however, they never succeeded in supplanting 'blanket' national and regional initiatives in the UK. The dilemma of whether to spatially target SME initiatives continues to challenge policy makers. In the 1990s it has reappeared in the form of the debate on how best to encourage industrial clusters and new industrial districts (discussed in detail in section 10.3). In practice, most of the partnerships delivering SME policies in the assisted areas have continued to operate 'blanket' schemes available in all parts of the designated assisted area. Given that SMEs appear to find inner cities and declining industrial areas less attractive locations than smaller and medium towns, and given the advantages claimed for industrial clustering, one must question the wisdom of 'blanket' schemes.

10.2   Regional policy and new technology

The importance of technical progress to a region's economic wellbeing is self-evident. Most of the theories of regional growth and trade discussed earlier place great emphasis on technical progress. Original ideas (i.e. inventions) must be distinguished from their application (i.e. innovations). The innovation process itself divides into two parts: the *first application* and the subsequent *diffusion* to other locations. A futher distinction of primary significance in discussing regional differences in innovations is that between *product* innovations and *process* innovations. Product innovations refer to the introduction of a new commodity (or service) or an improvement of existing commodities. *Original* product innovations (those new not only to the firm but also to the whole industry of which the firm is part) also differ from *continuing* product innovations (Keeble 1997). Process innovations refer to new production techniques for existing commodities, and come in at least three forms:

1   Innovations that reduce production inputs (e.g. labour-saving).
2   Innovations that improve working conditions (e.g. safety).
3   Innovations designed to overcome a technical difficulty in manufacturing or that improve a service.

The traditional view of innovation in the UK is that it is the south (and particularly the South East) which is the nation's 'innovation leader' (Townsend et al. 1981). Table 10.8, for example, presents results from a study of 'significant' innovations for the period 1945–83 (Harris 1988). As can be seen, the South East recorded 38.7 per cent of the innovations over this long period of time, a percentage well

Table 10.8 The regional distribution of 3817 'significant' innovations in manufacturing establishments, 1945–83

Region	Percentage of innovations in each region, 1945–83	Percentage of manufacturing employees in employment, 1981
South East	38.7	27.1
North West	12.9	13.0
West Midlands	10.4	13.0
Yorkshire/Humberside	8.4	9.3
East Midlands	7.7	8.6
South West	5.8	6.4
North	5.6	5.5
Scotland	5.0	8.2
East Anglia	2.7	3.0
Wales	1.9	3.9
Northern Ireland	0.7	2.0
UK	100.0	100.0

Source: Harris (1988), table 1; *Regional Trends*, 1991. Reproduced with the permission of Taylor & Francis Ltd, Oxford

in excess of its 27.1 per cent share of the nation's manufacturing workforce. The other regions have lagged well behind. These results have been supported by other similar studies (Smith et al. 1993; Phelps 1995). An obvious question to ask is whether regional disparities in innovation are explained by corresponding disparities in the industry mix. This does not seem to be the case. Industries in the south have higher innovation rates than similar industries elsewhere (Oakey et al. 1982; Harris 1988; Harris and Trainor 1995).

While there is no doubt that the South East continues to be the lead region for innovation in the UK, more recent research has shown that the picture is more complex than that of a simple north–south divide. The distinction between product and process innovations is a very important one in this respect. The South East has its greatest lead over the other regions in product innovations rather than process innovations (Oakey et al. 1982; Phelps 1995). Indeed, there is evidence not only that process innovations diffuse very quickly among regions, but also that regional subsidies for new investment may have encouraged assisted area firms to buy state-of-the-art machinery embodying the latest in process technology (Oakey et al. 1982; Oakey and O'Farrell 1992).

The tendency of earlier research to focus on manufacturing (excluding innovation in service sector firms), on 'significant' innovations (often rather arbitrarily defined) and on purely technological innovation and technology-intensive firms, has also contributed to a somewhat oversimplified view of a north–south divide. Where wider definitions of an innovation are used, the importance of the South East is confirmed, but a more complex picture is revealed. Table 10.9 presents the results of a survey of innovations in SMEs, as defined by the SMEs themselves, between 1992 and 1995. The south-east (the South East standard region) can be seen to have a clear advantage over the periphery (the North, Scotland and

Table 10.9 Regional[a] variations in innovation rates in small and medium enterprises, 1992–5

Type of innovation	Percentages of respondents initiating an innovation			
	South-east	Outer southern	Industrial heartland	Periphery
Manufacturing				
Product innovations	55.7	58.3	58.9	53.1
Process innovations	42.0	40.7	52.1	45.3
Services				
Product innovations	50.6	47.1	44.1	42.6
Process innovations	44.2	38.6	48.4	42.6
All				
Product innovations	52.7	53.9	53.5	48.3
Process innovations	43.3	39.9	50.8	44.1

[a] The regions utilized are defined as follows: south-east (South East standard region); outer southern (East Anglia, South West and East Midlands); industrial heartland (West Midlands, North West and Yorkshire and the Humber); and periphery (North, Scotland and Wales).
Source: Keeble (1997), table 5. Data are based on a survey of 1000 small and medium enterprises undertaken in 1995 by the Centre for Business Research at the University of Cambridge: some 698 questionnaires produced usable responses. Reproduced with the permission of Taylor & Francis Ltd, Oxford

Wales) for both manufacturing and service *product innovations*. The reverse is the case, however, for *process innovations*. The real surprise is the strong performance of the industrial heartland (West Midlands, North West and Yorkshire and the Humber). These have done well in the 1990s, particularly for manufacturing product and process innovations.

In summary, the evidence for the 1990s suggests that a north–south difference in innovations does still exist. The picture is, however, quite a rather complex one. The periphery appears to do universally badly. The southern regions do well for product innovations, with the south-east strongest in service sector product innovations and the outer southern regions doing best for manufacturing product innovations. The industrial heartland regions are by no means the struggling innovation areas they are sometimes portrayed, at least as far as the manufacturing sector is concerned. These results do not, however, overturn the conventional wisdom of the strength of the south for innovation. Since it is in the service sector that employment growth has been most rapid, the head start of the south is particularly important. Moreover, when the results for manufacturing are considered in greater detail, the south-east is revealed as having a clear lead over the industrial heartland in the vitally important category of *original product innovations* (i.e. those innovations not already in use in the same industry). Some 29.6 per cent of south-east manufacturing firms between 1992 and 1995 introduced an original product innovation, compared with 24.5 per cent of industrial heartland firms. Where the industrial heartland regions have done better is on product innovations already in use elsewhere within the industry (Keeble 1997).

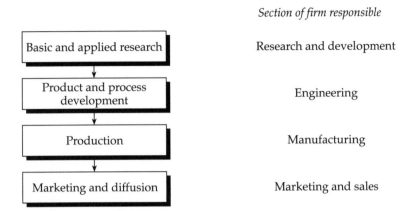

Section of firm responsible

Basic and applied research — Research and development

Product and process development — Engineering

Production — Manufacturing

Marketing and diffusion — Marketing and sales

Figure 10.5   The traditional 'linear' model of technological change.
Source: based on Malecki (1991). © Longman Group UK Limited, 1991

Causes of regional differences in innovation

In order to understand why the south is the 'innovation leader' in the UK, we must examine the process by which firms generate technical innovations. Figure 10.5 sets out the traditional 'linear' model (Malecki 1990; 1991). Although increasingly challenged as a model of the innovation process, the linear model of figure 10.5 does identify the key stages in this process.

Research and development

Private R&D establishments undertake applied research. The basic research on which this is based is undertaken in the UK in universities and government research establishments. Table 10.10 sets out the regional distribution of R&D expenditures (expressed as a percentage of regional GDP) for 1996. Figures are given separately for R&D in private businesses, the government (including local authorities) and higher educational institutions. Universities and other higher educational institutions in Britain are quite widely distributed among the regions as table 10.10 shows and, interestingly, in the past have not attracted clusters of private R&D establishments to their sites (Howells 1986). By contrast, government research establishments, many undertaking defence-related research, are for strategic and historical reasons heavily concentrated in southern England, particularly in the Eastern, South East and South West regions (Heim 1988). The British experience with university-based R&D may not be typical. Evidence from the United States suggests a much closer link between the amount of basic research at a university and industrial research in the local area (Jaffe 1989). This suggests that US universities have in general been able to develop better research links to private industry than their British counterparts. There would appear to be potential for universities in the British depressed regions to play a more important role in the future in stimulating innovation.

Table 10.10   Expenditure on research and development in UK regions, 1996

Region[a]	Private businesses		Government[b]		Higher educational institutions	
	(£m)	(% GDP)	(£m)	(% GDP)	(£m)	(% GDP)
North East	187	0.7	18	0.1	95	0.3
North West	929	1.3	75	0.1	166	0.2
Merseyside	135	1.5	12	0.1	61	0.7
Yorkshire/Humber	275	0.5	59	0.1	216	0.4
East Midlands	710	1.4	69	0.1	146	0.3
West Midlands	628	1.0	188	0.3	154	0.2
Eastern	2057	2.8	268	0.4	203	0.3
London	889	0.8	263	0.2	700	0.6
South East	2207	1.9	640	0.6	416	0.4
South West	726	1.3	260	0.5	124	0.2
Wales	117	0.4	32	0.1	105	0.3
Scotland	357	0.6	163	0.3	348	0.5
Northern Ireland	83	0.5	23	0.1	57	0.3
UK	9301	1.3	2070	0.3	2792	0.4

[a] Regions are those defined for the Government Offices.
[b] Government R&D includes estimates of National Health Service and local authorities' R&D.
Source: *Regional Trends*, 1998, table 13.8. Office of National Statistics, © Crown Copyright

Private R&D activity in the UK, like government R&D, is also heavily concentrated in the southern regions. Interestingly, as table 10.10 shows, London itself now has only limited private sector R&D. It is the rest of the South East, together with the Eastern region (which includes East Anglia), which dominates private R&D. The key to the success of the south in attracting R&D activity is the presence of London. The tendency of R&D to concentrate close to, but not actually in, major cities occurs in many European countries, not just in the UK. The Netherlands, interestingly, seems to be an exception (Kleinknecht and Poot 1992).

Large, diversified cities act as a magnet for R&D establishments because of a complex set of mutually self-reinforcing advantages (Thwaites and Alderman 1990; Malecki and Bradbury 1992). The first of these is *labour market* advantages. R&D relies heavily on highly paid and highly trained professional labour. Such personnel are in short supply and their presence tends to draw R&D establishments towards them. Big cities have a larger pool of such workers and the peripheral areas of big cities offer a combination of a good residential environment together with easy access to a sophisticated urban lifestyle. The new towns close to London have proved to be particularly attractive for R&D employees. Once a locality gains a reputation as an R&D centre (e.g. the Western Crescent of London), R&D establishments and potential employees tend to cluster around it.

The second advantage of the southern areas of the UK lies in *information access*. Interpersonal communications and access to external information are vital to the success of an R&D establishment, often with key staff members ('technological gatekeepers') playing a dominant role. Proximity to a large city has obvious information access advantages (reducing the *cost* of information and increasing *opportunities* to get information). The clustering of R&D establishments also cuts information costs.

The third big advantage of the south of the UK for R&D is *market access*. Large cities typically have the largest and most affluent population of a country and therefore the largest market for new products. London is also an administrative capital, an important factor for R&D establishments seeking contract research funds from government.

Finally, regions close to London also reap the benefit of R&D being tied to features of *corporate organization*. In the UK as elsewhere, R&D is dominated by larger firms. For management and cost reasons, these large firms tend to concentrate their R&D activities at headquarter sites and main plants. These, of course, are predominantly in the south close to or in London. In recent years there has been a certain amount of dispersal of company R&D activity away from London, but the pattern of R&D remains overwhelming dominated by the South East and Eastern regions.

Product development and manufacture

Once a new product becomes established, the locational pull of the south gradually weakens. Mass production of established, standardized products is usually shifted to plants (e.g. in disadvantaged regions or overseas) where labour and other costs are lower than in the south of England. There are, however, a number of important exceptions to this process of farming out mass production to branch plants. Of particular interest are the *high-technology* (or sunrise) industries such as information technology and biotechnology. These are industries where the product lifecycle is very short and where continuous rapid research and new product development is vital for survival. Such industries are dominated by SMEs. High-tech industries are favoured targets for policy makers. The pattern of high-technology jobs closely mirrors that of R&D establishments with which they are closely linked (Begg 1991). The South East has the overwhelming advantage. High-technology firms show a marked propensity to cluster together at particular localities within regions, a phenomeon to which we return in section 10.3. The new towns of South East England have proved to be magnets for high-technology firms. They offer a potent combination of a good infrastructure, a 'clean' image, a vigorous, well-trained workforce and flexible development corporations.

The case for a technology-based regional policy

There is no doubt that encouraging rapid technological progress and attracting high-technology industry are popular goals for regional policy makers. Technology is a key element in regional growth, and high-tech firms both are dynamic and offer high-quality, high-wage jobs for workers (Malecki 1991).

Considerable efforts have been made in many countries to improve innovativeness in disadvantaged regions and to help indigenous firms to upgrade their technology. These efforts have included the setting-up of innovation centres and technology transfer agencies (Hilpert 1991). Most countries use a combination of national and regional policies to stimulate innovation. National policies include the provision of technical education, government support for R&D, technology transfer (e.g. in agriculture), and protection for high-technology industries such as telecommunications. These policies typically help already established innovation-leader regions such as the South East more than other regions. By dominating existing R&D and high-technology industry, the South East is best placed to take advantage of *national* policy initiatives.

Regional policy initiatives to help stimulate innovation in depressed regions show an extraordinary variety. Apart from the technology transfer agencies already mentioned, and investment grants which allow firms to buy in the latest process innovations, other distinctive initiatives include science parks and technopoles (Asheim and Cooke 1998; Castells and Hall 1994), venture capital initiatives (Oakey and Mukhtar 1999) and improved infrastructure provision. Public expenditure can be used to create improved environmental and urban living conditions in order to encourage technology-based industries. The rundown of traditional manufacturing has given policy makers in the disadvantaged regions the opportunity to create conditions more favourable to high-technology firms. Whether all of this will be sufficient is an issue of considerable controversy.

10.3 Industrial districts, innovative milieux and 'learning regions'

In recent years there has been a revolution in thinking on how regional policy should attempt to bring about faster indigenous development. Traditionally, each SME was regarded as an individual client of regional policy and attempts were made to tailor different combinations of policy instruments (e.g. advice, financial help, training etc.) to the needs of the particular firm. This approach was not surprising given that traditional regional policy had dealt with large companies in exactly the same manner.

There has, however, been a renaissance of interest in policies deliberately designed to encourage *geographical clusters* of firms. In some cases these clusters are focused on large firms, as with policies which attempt to cultivate *supply chains* around large inward investment projects. The overwhelming majority of industrial cluster policies, however, are based upon SMEs and new technology. It is for this reason that they are considered in this chapter.

Industrial agglomerations are not, of course, a new phenomenon in regional economic analysis. Indeed, almost all of the current thinking has looked for its inspiration to the work of Marshall (1890) on nineteenth century industrial districts. The new thinking, however, has been bolstered by advances in regional growth and trade theory (see chapters 3, 4 and 5) which have shown clearly that 'geography matters' and that cumulative growth processes leading to industrial agglomeration remain widespread in modern regional economies.

The new thinking on industrial clusters has been very influential in its effects on regional policy, although the debate still has a considerable distance to run and many key issues still have to be resolved. The initial work on *new industrial districts* was largely concerned with manufacturing SMEs, often in traditional industries such as textiles. As the debate has progressed, however, it has become increasingly apparent that technological change lies at the heart of any successful industrial cluster. As a result, attention has moved on to *innovative milieux* and the concept of the *learning region*.

New industrial districts

Research on new industrial districts had its origins in studies from the late 1970s onwards on a number of successful clusters of SMEs in the 'Third Italy' (Bagnasco 1977; Piore and Sabel 1984). By 'Third Italy' is meant the north-eastern and north-central regions of Italy, particularly Emilia–Romagna, Veneto, Trentino and Toscana. These regions are typically contrasted on the one side with the older industrial areas in north-western Italy (e.g. Milan, Turin), and on the other with the lagging south of Italy (Camagni and Capello 1997). The new industrial districts of the Third Italy are dominated by small craft and artisanal firms which have proved themselves to be world leaders in luxury apparel, furniture, machine tools and ceramics.

The term 'industrial district' to describe these new agglomerations was deliberately chosen. There are many similarities between the clusters in the Third Italy and Marshall's nineteenth century industrial districts of England. Both are dominated by SMEs and are clusters of manufacturing firms. It would be a mistake, however, to assume that Marshall's industrial districts are the same as the new industrial districts. The new industrial districts can be defined as comprising (Rabellotti 1998: 244):

1   A cluster of mainly small and medium enterprises, spatially concentrated and sectorally specialized.
2   A strong, relatively homogeneous, cultural and social background linking the economic agents and creating a common and widely accepted behavioural code, sometimes explicit but often implicit.
3   An intense set of backward, forward, horizontal and labour linkages, based on market and non-market exchanges of goods, services, information and people.
4   A network of public and private local institutions supporting the economic agents in the clusters.

These characteristics subsume within them those of the classic Marshallian districts: that is, manufacturing SMEs and a series of external economies arising from a local pool of specialized labour, the presence of subsidiary trades and specialized services, together with the opportunity to efficiently use specialized machinery. The Rabellotti definition, however, also illustrates that new industrial districts have characteristics which go beyond those envisaged by Marshall. These include supportive social and cultural attributes, together with a network of public and private institutions which help the SMEs making up the cluster. New industrial districts also differ from their Marshallian counterparts in one further important respect. They function within a much more highly globalized economic system in which the pace of technological change has quickened dramatically. Consumers within the globalizing economy are demanding an ever-widening choice of differentiated goods and services. The characteristics of a supportive social/cultural system, a network of public and private institutions ('institutional thickness'), and external links to global markets, are what make new industrial districts 'new'.

The literature on new industrial districts attempts to blend Marshall's economic analysis with elements of theory drawn from geography, political science and sociology. In particular, the concept of a new industrial district draws upon ideas from *post-Fordism* and *social capital* theories. Since these theories lie outside the modern discipline of economics they will be only briefly considered here.

Post-Fordism theory has been widely used in the new industrial district literature as a means of examining the implications of globalization and a new world mode of production. Links to the global economy are much more important in new industrial districts than in Marshall's nineteenth century districts. The post-Fordist approach views the world system of capitalism as being subject to recurrent but widely spaced crises. In the 'golden age of Fordism', which lasted from the 1930s to the end of the 1960s, production systems were characterized by assembly-line processes and the large-scale manufacture of highly standardized products. High productivity was bolstered by successful Keynesian demand management policies, new methods of wage determination and successful income redistribution policies.

By the late 1960s and early 1970s this Fordist mode of production had entered a 'double-sided crisis of capitalism' affecting both the aggregate demand and aggregate supply sides of the macroeconomy (Lipietz 1992; Dunford 1993). From this crisis has emerged a new post-Fordist mode of production which is characterized by 'flexible specialization'. As a result of rapid globalization, manufacturing firms can no longer rely on protected local markets. They must instead seek out and actively compete for customers in much wider markets than before. In order to compete effectively in global markets, it is argued, firms must exhibit much greater flexibility. Growing affluence and rapid technological advances have resulted in consumers demanding a wider array of differentiated products with much shorter lifecycles than in the past.

The keys to success in the post-Fordist mode of production are the ability to tailor goods to the varied demands of customers and to respond flexibly to changing tastes and technology. Since it is customer choice which now drives technological change, and since the exploitation of economies of scale through the mass production of standardized products is no longer imperative, 'flexible specialization' favours craft and artisanal SMEs producing highly specialized products for global markets. The new industrial districts of the Third Italy are seen as successful examples of how SMEs can adapt and thrive in the post-Fordist era. While the initial emphasis in the literature was on manufacturing firms in traditional manufacturing industries (e.g. fashion wear), it was quickly realized that many high-technology industrial clusters and some service sectors exhibit similar characteristics.

One important paradox is how a rapidly globalizing economic system can give rise to *local-level* industrial clusters. Globalization and localization appear to have gone hand in hand, despite the fact that reduced transport costs and trade barriers should loosen the spatial ties linking firms. Proponents of new industrial districts have reached back to traditional Marshallian external economies to provide one set of explanations for local clustering. With plant economies of scale less relevant, traditional external economies (Rabellotti's 'intense set of backward, forward, horizontal and labour linkages') assume renewed importance. Vertical disintegration in modern manufacturing has given new life to subcontracting, the buying-in of specialist services from other SMEs, and complex networks of externalized transactions among local firms.

In addition to the traditional Marshallian external economies, however, SMEs within new industrial districts are thought to enjoy two other sets of advantages which reinforce their competitiveness. The first of these is a supportive socio-cultural system. The second is 'institutional thickness' – a strong local network of private and public institutions. Both of these act as further sources of external economies for SMEs within the cluster.

Analysis of the role of social and cultural factors draws heavily on *social capital theory*. This was developed initially by Putnam (1993) to try to explain historical differences in economic development between northern and southern Italy. Social capital theory argues that economic development is in part determined by the cultural characteristics of a local community. Over long periods of time, communities build up durable civic traditions. These may be either supportive of economic development or detrimental to it: social capital can be either good or bad. Once established, however, these civic traditions are very difficult to change. To Putnam, 'social capital . . . refers to features of social organization such as trust, norms and networks, that improve the efficiency of society by facilitating coordinated action' (1993: 167). The new industrial districts of the Third Italy, it is argued, benefit greatly from being located in communities which, as a result of a long history of independent city-states and civic government, have built up a stock of good social capital. Communities in southern Italy, with its history of feudalism and despotic government, have poor social capital.

The key to good social capital is trust. Trust between companies, customers and the labour force reduces costs by removing the need for expensive contracting, monitoring and enforcement. To social capital theorists it is no surprise that the new industrial districts of Italy are composed of networks of SMEs, often with close family ties and large-scale *non-market* exchanges of goods, services, information and labour as well as more formal market transactions. Trust is essential for extensive non-market interrelationships. Trust is itself gradually built up through *norms of reciprocity* and *networks of civic engagement*. Norms of reciprocity are sets of unwritten rules that govern relationships between individuals and firms. These are gradually built up over time in local communities and are reinforced by social sanctions against those who breach them. These norms are partly family-centred and partly established by local communities. Local civic engagement through participation in networks of public and private organizations also helps to establish trust.

Social capital does not figure prominently in traditional analysis of industrial districts, and has only recently begun to be incorporated into formal neoclassical growth theory (Knack and Keefer 1997). Although trade associations were given a role by Marshall, nineteenth century industrial districts were seen to be largely based on free enterprise. New industrial districts are very different. Here local and regional governments are given an important role, as is networking between firms and a whole series of other public and private organizations. Amin and Thrift define 'institutional thickness' as a network of organizations and institutions which support local firms, and which also include 'financial institutions, local chambers of commerce, training agencies, trade associations, local authorities, development agencies, innovation centres, clerical bodies, unions, government agencies providing premises, land and infrastructure, business service organisations, marketing boards and so on' (1995: 103). Amin and Thrift give 'institutional thickness' a key role in economic success and stress that it not only encourages greater trust (as in social capital theory) but also stimulates entrepreneurship and embeds firms more securely in their local cluster.

The concept of a new industrial district remains controversial. Amin and Robins (1990), for example, have stressed that the globalization process continues to reinforce the power of large multinational companies and this means that local freedom and autonomy are in practice very limited. Others have questioned how new the concept is, or how widespread new industrial districts actually are, and have noted that the Italian examples have long historical roots which may be difficult to replicate elsewhere (Amin and Thrift 1992; Harrison 1992; Storper 1995). Moreover, it is clear that the craft-based new industrial districts of the Third Italy are by no means the only type possible. High-technology clusters of SMEs (e.g. Cambridge, Silicon Valley and Bangalore) and clusters based on key large firms (e.g. Baden Württemberg) are alternative types which have been studied and which have very different dynamics of growth (Amin 1994). It has been argued that there are actually four different types of industrial district (Markusen 1996a; 1996b):

1 *The Marshallian industrial district, with its recent 'Italianate variety'.*
2 *The hub-and-spoke district,* where the cluster of SMEs is grouped around one or more large corporations (sometimes inward investors, in other cases established industries).
3 *The satellite industrial platform district,* made up of a cluster of branch plants of absent multinational corporations and characterized by low internal linkages.
4 *The state-anchored industrial district,* where 'a major public or nonprofit entity, be it a military base, a defense plant . . . or a concentration of government offices, is a key anchor tenant in the district' (1996: 306).

As figure 10.6 shows, the internal and external networks of linkages are very different for these different types of districts. So too are their growth paths and the policy measures necessary to encourage them.

Marshallian industrial district

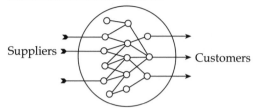

Hub-and-spoke district

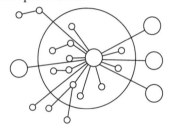

Satellite platform district

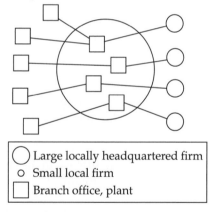

Figure 10.6   Firm size, connections and local embeddedness in different types of industrial district.
Source: Markusen (1996b), figure 1

Innovative milieux and the 'learning region'

Innovation and the development of a strong technical knowledge base has always been important in successful industrial clusters. Marshall himself laid great stress on knowledge accumulation. In the new industrial districts literature, success is dependent upon the need, even in traditional industrial sectors, to respond quickly and flexibly to the rapid pace of technological change. Technological change cannot therefore be separated from industrial clusters and the SMEs inhabiting them.

One type of regional cluster which has attracted particular attention has been that of the high-technology industry. High-technology firms are not necessarily found just in manufacturing since they can include 'firms and industries whose products and services embody new, innovative and advanced technologies developed by the application of scientific and technological expertise' (Keeble and Wilkinson 1999: 296). High-technology industries show a clear tendency to form spatial clusters. Examples which have excited particular research interest have been Silicon Valley (California), Cambridge (England), Grenoble and Sophia–Antipolis (France), Munich (Germany), and Pisa, Piacenza and north-east Milan (Italy), although many other cases of high-technology clusters have been identified.

The particular interest of high-technology clusters and *innovative milieux* lies partly in their attractiveness for policy makers since the jobs created are very high quality and in industries with excellent long-term growth prospects. More importantly, however, policy makers are attracted by the fact that a central role is given to technological change in almost all theories of regional growth. There is a clear logic in focusing policy on firms which are self-evidently so important in the growth process.

While an innovative milieu is a type of industrial district, not all new industrial districts develop into innovative milieux. New industrial districts help to produce the essential preconditions for an innovative milieu. The presence of a closely networked group of SMEs, together with their specialized local labour markets and close co-operative relationships, makes it easier for technical knowledge to flow more freely. At some point a genuine innovative milieu may develop in which the accumulation of a strong local knowledge base and the readily shared nature of technological information become a cumulative process. Keeble et al. (1999) have shown that in the case of the Cambridge high-technology cluster three mechanisms have been of particular importance in promoting technological accumulation and exchange:

1   Close networking between different firms and between the firms and the many other private and public sector organizations promoting technology in Cambridge.
2   The free movement within the local labour market of persons with specialized scientific and management expertise.
3   The spin off of new SMEs from existing firms, higher education institutions and government research institutions, with the University of Cambridge playing an important role.

The role and potential importance of intraregional linkages between high-technology SMEs has also been investigated in Germany. Sternberg (1999) draws on empirical research into innovative linkages in three German regions noted for being innovation leaders. These are the research triangle of Hanover–Brunswick–Göttingen, Saxony and Baden. One of the main conclusions of the German study into innovative linkages between SMEs, and between SMEs and research institutions within these three regions, is that collective learning is easier to develop between actors within a region than between actors located in different regions.

This is particularly true for SMEs since SMEs are more likely to depend upon, and benefit from, intraregional linkages than are larger firms. This is because large firms are more likely to establish linkages with economic actors, such as other large firms located in other regions.

These types of mechanisms form the fundamental building blocks of a virtuous circle in which at some point technological change in a mundane industrial cluster transforms itself into a *collective learning* system. Once established, in a collective learning situation, the SMEs within the *innovative milieu* begin to feed off one another as well as taking advantage of the local knowledge base to produce generation after generation of product and process innovations.

Success is by no means always guaranteed. An industrial district may be successful in its own right but fail to reach the take-off into continuous learning and innovation implied by an innovative milieu. Even the classic industrial districts of Emilia–Romagna may have failed to make the transition fully (Amin 1999). Moreover, previously innovative milieux may ossify since success itself can 'drive the milieu towards an increasingly narrow specificity, and could lock the agents into obsolete, not competitive yet stable technological trajectories' (Capello 1999: 358). Where they are successful, however, innovative milieux can provide a priceless asset for a region by generating wave after wave of product and process innovations.

The realization that technological change lies at the heart of regional growth, and that it may be possible for policy makers in stagnating regions to replicate the conditions found within the best innovative milieux, has stimulated researchers. The focus of the research has been on the learning processes lying at the heart of technological change. These include learning processes with firms, and region-wide *collective learning* processes. The importance of the latter is encapsulated in the concept of the *learning region* (Asheim 1996; Simmie 1997; Morgan 1997) or the *regional innovation system* (Cooke et al. 1997; Cooke and Morgan 1998).

Much of this research is still at an early stage and is dominated by case studies of existing successful technological clusters. It has led, however, to a welcome move away from treating innovating firms as 'black boxes' and from simple 'linear' models of the innovation process towards interactive models. Attention is now being focused on learning processes and the organizational structures best suited to rapid learning and innovation.

Three main sets of concepts are at present being subject to intense research. The first of these is the set of *competences* or *capabilities* needed by firms and other organizations in the local industrial cluster for successful collective learning to be triggered (Lawson 1999). The initial research on *competences* was undertaken from the perspective of individual firms, with 'a "core" competence . . . being defined as what an organisation is able to do better than others, and a "dynamic" capability referring to the ability of a firm to renew, augment and adapt its core competences over time' (Lawson and Lorenz 1999: 306). Learning (and hence technological advance) *within* firms is seen to depend on three basic processes: the *sharing of knowledge* within the firm, the ability of the firm to *combine* many diverse types of knowledge to create an innovation, and the ability to adapt in ways which avoid *organizational inertia* – the inability to make use of new knowledge. It has been argued that these three characteristics are precisely what is needed not only within firms but also among the many firms and organizations within a high-technology cluster – a genuinely *collective* learning system (Lawson and Lorenz 1999). What was initially a theory of the firm has therefore developed into a theory of regional technological change. Distinctions are also made between different types of technological knowledge. Knowledge may be either *codifiable*, in which case it takes on the attributes of a pure public good and is readily shared, or else *tacit*. In the latter case the information is effectively trapped within small groups of firms in the local industrial cluster. It is tacit technological information which is thought to lie at the heart of the reason why high-technology firms become clustered in localized innovative milieux.

In focusing upon collective learning processes within regions, and particularly upon the development and exchange of *tacit* knowledge, recent research has inevitably found itself focusing on social capital. The relationships between the many firms and other organizations which make up a high-technology cluster are vital if collective learning is to occur. Hence 'the ability to form and maintain effective social relations is therefore a key competence' (Keeble and Wilkinson 1999: 299). As we have already seen, social capital of this type is often not part of the formal market system and is what Storper (1995) has called a network of 'untraded interdependencies' which go well beyond market transactions and the formal relationships in a cluster.

The final concept which is the subject of active research interest is that of 'institutional thickness' (Amin and Thrift 1995). Technological change is, as we have seen, not simply confined to private firms. A whole array of other organizations are actively involved, and 'institutional thickness' is thought to be as important for high-technology clusters as it is for other types of industrial districts. Many studies of the *learning region* place great emphasis on local non-firm organizations (public and private) which contribute to technological change and provide an array of important services (Glasmeier 1999). Work on the Cambridge technology cluster suggests that in addition to the University of Cambridge, the development of no fewer than three science parks (Melbourn Science Park, Cambridge Science Park and St John's Innovation Park) and an array of specialist business service providers have contributed to the buildup of 'institutional thickness' locally (Keeble et al. 1999).

The UK government's 1998 White Paper on policies needed to encourage a more innovating, knowledge-driven economy in the UK notes the need to 'support the development of clusters, networks and other regional partnerships' (1998: 42). This statement indicates just how much the concepts of industrial clusters and the *learning region* have now entered mainstream policy thinking.

10.4   Conclusion

Small firms and technology are seen by many as being greatly superior methods of stimulating regional development than traditional regional policies with their emphasis on big firms and inward investment. The resulting potent brew of an aggressive enterprise culture and fierce local competition forces regions to stand on their own feet.

Research in the 1980s and 1990s has slowly led to a more balanced and pragmatic approach to regional policy. Indigenous development remains very much at the heart of modern regional policy, and this undoubtedly will remain the case in the future. However, the merit of a certain amount of inward investment as part of a balanced regional development strategy is now widely accepted. Indeed, many regions now link indigenous development and inward investment together by initiatives designed to 'embed' the inward investor companies within a network of small local suppliers.

The development of clusters of SMEs in the form of industrial districts and innovative milieux is the focus of a lot of current thinking in regional policy. The problems, however, remain formidable. There are currently two main difficulties faced by policy makers in attempting to implement the proposals emerging from recent research. First, it is clear that most of the highly successful industrial districts and innovative milieux are in the already prosperous regions. The prosperous regions appear to be holding most of the best cards for attracting industrial clusters and high-technology firms. It is clear that disadvantaged regions face formidable obstacles in making themselves more attractive for SMEs and new technology. These disadvantages are exacerbated by the fact that policy makers must strive to hit a 'moving target' since globalization is continually undermining the advantages of existing industrial districts (Maskell and Malmberg 1999).

The second and more critical problem facing policy makers is that there is still a gulf between the results of academic research on industrial clusters and the kind of specific advice needed for effective policy formulation. Policy makers are told that a successful industrial cluster or innovative milieu needs to be based upon the development of a set of traditional Marshallian external economies (e.g. dense networks of input–output linkages and specialized local labour markets). They must also encourage an array of mechanisms and interrelationships which together make up social capital. A difficulty here is that the firms must simultaneously develop international networks as well as local ones since industrial clusters and innovative milieux are now much less 'closed' than in the past (Keeble et al. 1998). In addition, regional policy must try to assemble the vast set of organizations constituting 'institutional thickness'. This is an impossible task for policy makers in many disadvantaged regions lacking almost all of these building blocks. Here, the advice which is needed is on how the very limited resources available to the policy maker can be targeted to best effect. Existing research cannot provide advice at this level of precision.

Future research must try to answer the following types of questions. How long does it take a community to develop good social capital? What are the two or three key organizations at the heart of 'institutional thickness'? Which two or three external economies are most important? What is the sequence in which they should be established? At what spatial scale (local, regional or national) is it best to establish a cluster? At present, many policy makers are faced with a 'counsel of perfection', impossible to attain with the resources available. The result is a desperate attempt to attain all of the necessary elements for a successful industrial cluster and a failure to adequately target resources.

Some authors are pessimistic, arguing that 'a scenario of generalised regional regeneration and the substantial elimination of interregional differences in living standards via creating internationally competitive industrial districts of networks of flexibly specialised and co-operative small firms is fundamentally misconceived' (Hudson 1997: 475). Some will win and some will lose in the modern global economy. Others take a rosier view, arguing that neoclassical convergence forces can be combined with small firm policies and high-technology initiatives to gradually reduce the gaps.

Further reading

Amin and Thrift (1995); Cooke and Morgan (1998); Hudson (1999); Hughes (1997b); Keeble (1997); Putnam (1992); Storey (1994); White Paper (1998).

Regional policy and the European Union

contents

The present chapter and the next are concerned with the question of where economic power should lie. Should economic power be more centralized or should it be more decentralized? This chapter examines the case for greater centralization of economic power within the European Union (EU). The next chapter discusses the case for greater decentralization of economic power to regional authorities. Since this book is concerned with regional policy, we intend to discuss only the *regional* implications of the centralization and decentralization of economic power. We are not concerned here with the broader issues of whether UK entry into the EU was worthwhile, whether further economic and political integration is desirable, or whether or not the establishment of elected assemblies in the regions is a good thing. We are concerned with the more limited question of whether *regional policy powers* should be reassigned away from the national government.

What effect does economic integration (such as that occurring in the EU) have on regional problems? Should regional policy be designed for the EU as a whole rather than for each member state independently? Does the devolution of economic power to regional authorities help individual regions to solve their own particular problems? There are no easy answers to these questions, but it is nevertheless important to raise them since regional policy issues now figure prominently in the EU.

The present chapter concentrates on the question of the extent to which regional policy powers should be reassigned from national governments to a centralized European authority. It begins by considering existing regional problems in the EU and the potential effects of further economic integration. This is followed by a discussion of the merits of EU regional policy and the case for strengthening it further. The final section describes and evaluates the regional policy as it has emerged at EU level.

11.1   Regional problems in the European Union

This section is concerned with the effect of economic integration on regional economic disparities. In particular, we aim to investigate the extent to which the creation and development of the EU has affected, and is likely to continue to affect, regional economic disparities within the EU. Before discussing these disparities, however, it is useful to examine the meaning of the term 'economic integration'. Five main types can be identified:

1 *Preferential tariff areas*   Member states set lower tariffs on imports from one another than they do on imports from non-members.
2 *Free trade areas*   Free trade is established between member states but each state retains its own independent trade policies with non-member states.
3 *Customs unions*   These are free trade areas which operate a common external policy for trade with non-members.
4 *Common markets*   These are customs unions within which capital and labour move freely.
5 *Economic and monetary unions*   These are identical to common markets except that fiscal and monetary policy is dominated by a central authority rather than by the individual member states. There may also be a common currency.

The EU is engaged in a determined effort to put in place the final steps in the process of economic integration. Three processes are taking place simultaneously. First, the EU is slowly but inexorably removing the remaining non-tariff barriers continuing to hinder free trade, capital mobility and labour mobility among member states. The Single Europe Act of 1986 launched this process. It will, however, be many years before this legislation fully achieves its aim of creating a genuine Single European Market (SEM) in which there is unhindered exchange of goods, services, capital and labour. Part of the reason for this is that it takes time for such profound changes to affect the behaviour of firms and consumers in Europe. There have also been delays in fully implementing the SEM legislation. The EU therefore cannot yet be properly described as a common market. It is, however, well on the way.

A second process of integration in which the Community is involved is the steady widening of the boundaries to incorporate countries not previously members. Spain and Portugal joined the EU in 1986 (the Third Enlargement). The collapse of communism brought East Germany into the EU in 1990. In 1996 the

Fourth Enlargement saw the accession of Austria, Finland and Sweden. A long line of other countries are now awaiting the chance to enter, most in Central and Eastern Europe. With accession negotiations under way with six potential new entrants, the Fifth or Eastern Enlargement (likely to occur from 2002 onwards) is posing a new set of challenges for the EU which have particularly far-reaching implications for regional policy.

The third process of integration under way is the conversion of the EU from a common market to a full economic and monetary union (EMU). In January 1999, 11 of the 15 EU member states formally created a single currency (the 'Euro'). This will begin freely circulating as notes and coin in 2002.

It needs to be stressed at the outset that ascertaining the effect of greater economic integration on regional economic disparities is not a simple task. Economic integration occurs automatically (even in the absence of deliberate political and economic structures such as the EU) as a result of falling transport costs and increasing 'globalization'. It is consequently difficult to distinguish between the regional disparities that have been affected by the emergence and development of the EU, and those that would have occurred anyway as a result of general European or worldwide economic integration.

Whatever the underlying causes of regional economic disparities in the EU may be, there is no doubt that these disparities are considerable and constitute a major challenge to policy makers. In 1996, GDP per capita ranged from 193 per cent of the EU average in Hamburg (Germany) to only 44 per cent in Ipeiros (Greece) (see figure 11.1). Similar disparities are also revealed when other types of regional disadvantage are examined, such as unemployment rates. In 1997, unemployment rates ranged from a massive 32.0 per cent in Andalusia (Spain) to a mere 2.5 per cent in Luxembourg.

A wide variety of different types of depressed area exist in the EU. These include depressed industrial areas, areas of severe urban poverty and decline, border areas which have suffered as a result of the dismantling of frontier controls, and depressed rural communities which include amongst their number the poorest regions in the EU. There is also a distinct tendency for the poorest regions to be located on the geographical periphery of the EU (especially southern Italy, Spain, Portugal, East Germany and Greece) and for the most prosperous regions to be centrally located, as is clear from figure 11.1.

The emergence and development of the EU since its origins in 1958 has had substantial effects on individual regions. More recent developments are merely continuing a long process of integration. The forces unleashed are having profound effects on the pattern of regional disparities in the EU. The three changes which at the present time are of particular importance (the SEM, EMU and Eastern Enlargement) will each be considered in turn.

The Single European Market

In the past, national governments often deliberately used their tariff and other protectionist policies to assist their domestic economies as a whole, or to help key

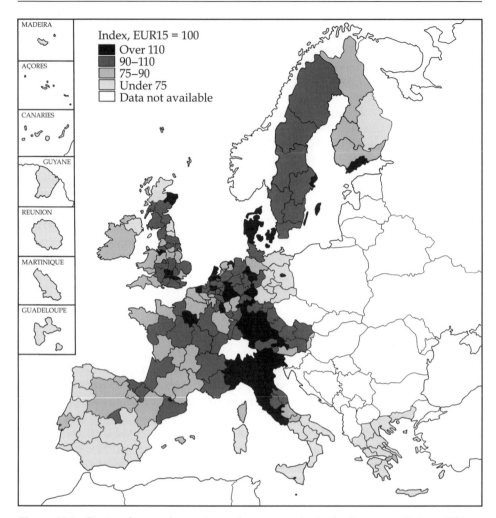

Figure 11.1   Regional gross domestic product per capita in the European Union, 1996. GDP per capita values have been adjusted for purchasing power parities using Eurostat's PPS system of adjustments. Data are in index form, with the EUR15 average GDP per capita value set at 100.
Source: European Commission (1999a), map 1

industries in specific regions. Trade protection policies can be of two types. Traditionally *tariffs* (and to a lesser extent *quotas* on imports) have been widely used. In addition, *non-tariff barriers* (NTBs) have also been widely used. The EU was quick to abolish tariffs and quotas, and at each subsequent round in the enlargement process new member states have had to do the same.

Non-tariff barriers have proved to be much more intractable. They are many and varied. Some, it must be admitted, such as transport costs and language barriers, are unlikely ever to be completely eliminated. The SEM process is designed to sweep away as many of the remaining NTBs as possible. The SEM legislation has concentrated on three main groups of the NTBs:

1   *Cost-increasing barriers*   These are barriers raising the costs to firms wishing to trade with other member states. Examples are the red tape and delays experienced at customs posts (now mostly eliminated), and the costs of having to meet different product, technical and safety standards in different member states.

2   *Market-entry barriers*   These are where member states prevent firms from other member states entering and competing freely in the domestic market. Governments themselves are often the worst culprits by deliberately placing their own contracts with local firms. Opening up 'public procurement' contracts to genuinely free tender would eliminate a major barrier to free trade.

3   *Market-distorting practices*   Many EU member states still operate price controls and differential taxes and subsidies on goods, all of which prevent a genuinely Single Market in the EU for products. VAT rates and excise duties, for example, have still not been harmonized across member states despite the SEM. The Dover–Calais 'booze run' has its counterparts in many other parts of the EU. Governments also continue to allow collusion among local firms which keeps out foreign competitors.

The majority of the 300 pieces of legislation implementing the SEM were introduced between 1989 and 1992. As a result, the citizens of the EU have been able to witness a gradual unwinding of the three types of NTBs discussed above. This process still has a considerable distance to run. The EU continues to carefully monitor the SEM process and has a rolling action plan designed to keep the pressure on the member states to fully implement the legislation.

Research has shown that the eventual full implementation of the SEM could generate benefits (mostly in the form of lower prices of goods for consumers) equivalent to between 4.5 and 6.5 per cent of the combined GDP of the EU (Emerson et al. 1988; Cecchini 1988; Pelkmans and Winters 1988). There will also be gains in the form of lower inflation, up to 5 million more jobs, an improved balance of payments for the EU as a whole, and lower member state public sector deficits. These are massive benefits. It should be stressed, however, that in order to achieve them the EU must be prepared to accept significant structural change in the decades ahead. The SEM process has already led to industrial decline in some regions, as competition from other parts of the EU has increased. In compensation, other industries in these same regions have expanded. Tremendous reallocation of capital and labour between industries and between regions has already occurred and more will be necessary if the full benefits of SEM are to be reaped.

The SEM represents a massive new step towards full integration of EU member states. It has been grafted onto the existing *customs union* which the United Kingdom entered in 1973, and which was expanded as new countries joined the EU in the 1980s and 1990s. The full effects of the customs union are themselves still working their way through the economic system.

The effects of the SEM are complex and profound. Each new round of integration has its own distinctive effects. Prior to its entry into the EU customs union in 1973, the United Kingdom had developed a set of national tariffs which tended to protect manufactured goods rather than primary or service sector products (Oulton 1973). It is likely that regions heavily dependent upon manufacturing industries, such as the North West and West Midlands, were the principal beneficiaries from the protection offered by national tariff policies in the United Kingdom prior to entry into the EU, and hence the principal losers once these were removed.

Entry into the EU had a significant impact on the United Kingdom as a whole and its individual regions. The SEM will eventually have equally far-reaching effects. The forces set in motion by the SEM (and indeed all other rounds in the integration process) are of two broad types: allocation effects and accumulation effects.

Allocation effects of integration can be subdivided into a series of different types (Baldwin et al. 1997). The most well known of these are trade creation and trade diversion effects. Trade creation occurs because freedom of trade encourages regions to specialize in those commodities they can most competitively produce. Expensive domestic production is therefore replaced by cheaper imports. Trade diversion, on the other hand, occurs when imports from the rest of the world are restricted by tariff walls around the customs union. This is the case with many foodstuffs previously imported into the United Kingdom from the Commonwealth and other countries. The United Kingdom after entry in 1973 had to switch from cheap food imports from outside the EU to more expensive imports from within the EU. Trade creation and trade diversion effects have been very substantial for the United Kingdom. Exports and imports have grown far more rapidly with the EU than with other parts of the world since entry to the EU in 1973.

Alongside the trade creation and trade diversion effects of European integration there are a number of other allocation effects. The first of these takes the form of the elimination of *trade rents*. Prior to the EU, member states were able to enjoy extensive revenues from customs duties (a type of trade rent). These are no longer collected since the tariffs have come down. Moreover, there are grounds for believing that a number of longer-term allocation effects are also set in motion by integration. One of these is the exploitation of *economies of scale* by firms able to sell commodities to the full EU market, an effect which is often linked to external (agglomeration) economies and other polarization effects which help central core regions of the EU. Another important allocation effect is the lower costs resulting from increased competition among firms in the increasingly integrated markets of the EU (sometimes known as the pure profit effect). The final allocation effect is the benefit which consumers reap in the form of greater choice from a wider *variety of commodities* as European integration allows consumers in one member state easier access to the goods and services from all of the other member states.

All of the various allocation effects listed above arise from the same basic process: the shifting of resources from one activity to another within the EU. To these must be added the *accumulation effects* of EU integration. These arise because the EU encourages the growth of the total stock of factors of production. In particular, the EU encourages a growth in the capital stock through increased investment. The wider investment opportunities available to firms in a bigger EU means that higher rates of return to investment are available and a corresponding increase in investment can be expected. In addition, the *risk levels* facing investors are also falling. Reduced risk stimulates more investment. More investment and a growing capital stock mean higher incomes and growth rates for all.

As can be seen, the effects of EU integration are both complex and far-reaching. There is no reason to expect the benefits and costs of economic integration to fall evenly across all regions. As far as the EU is concerned, some of the benefits have been enjoyed disproportionately by the central regions, one reason for this being market access. Regions at the geographical centre of the EU are able to exploit their natural positional advantage of being closest to the main population centres. In addition, this positional advantage may be being reinforced by advantages flowing from the economies of scale which have resulted from the increase in market size. Firms at the geographical centre of the EU are well placed to serve the whole EU market and therefore exploit additional economies of scale.

Other economic processes may also favour the central regions of the EU. The central regions contain the majority of the major urban concentrations as well as the financial and administrative capital cities. A whole series of agglomeration economies and external economies favour the further concentration of firms and industries in these central regions. The major cities, for example, have better transport and telecommunications facilities. They have access to large and well-qualified labour forces. They also benefit from proximity to the centres of political power, a major advantage when public sector contracts are being awarded. The cities of these areas are therefore ideally placed to attract economic growth stimulated by the EU. Moreover, it must be remembered that the EU is not just a customs union; it is a common market with relatively free capital and labour mobility. It is sometimes argued that the central regions may become the principal beneficiaries of a process of cumulative growth as capital and labour are attracted into these areas from the periphery. This process is reinforced by the selective nature of migration. The central regions, it is argued, tend to drain the peripheral regions of the younger, better educated and more economically active members of their population.

Arguments have also been advanced, by those who take a global view of the regional problems of the EU, that the peripheral regions are characterized by small uncompetitive *microeconomic firms*, which are simply unable to compete with the large multinational firms located in central regions. The freer trading conditions of the EU pose a severe threat to the backward economies of the peripheral regions. There is evidence that many of the peripheral regions of the EU do indeed suffer serious difficulties in matching the competitiveness of firms in the more prosperous core regions (Commission of the European Communities 1990; European Commission 1999: part 2). The major problems seem to be related to poor location, inadequate infrastructure, low-skill labour forces and local financing and taxation difficulties (IFO Institute for Economic Research 1991).

The structural changes set in motion by EU integration are clearly very complex in their effects on different regions although, as we have seen, central regions are often favoured. Greater complexity still is added by the fact that no two acts of

European integration are ever the same in their impact on different regions. The SEM is an excellent example of this. The SEM process has borne most heavily on those 40 or so sectors which had previously enjoyed the protection of the main non-tariff barriers (e.g. telecommunications equipment, automobiles, financial services). The impact the SEM has on a region depends first on the particular mix of industries in the region. Regions, for example, heavily dependent on an industry strongly affected by the SEM, such as financial services, will face the need to make deep-seated structural changes (Begg 1995). Second, how hard a region is hit by the SEM depends on how competitive the local companies are, and hence on their ability to respond to the challenges of structural change and greater competition. Research on the *geographical footprint* of the SEM has shown that it is the vulnerable regions of the EU, particularly those in the disadvantaged Mediterranean areas, which face the greatest challenges (Quévit 1995).

Economic and monetary union

Economic and monetary union (EMU) should, as with the SEM, eventually generate significant benefits. The Euro will eliminate a significant barrier to trade – the cost of exchanging different currencies. It is estimated that exchange costs alone amount to 0.5 per cent of combined GDP of EU member states each year. Trade will also be enhanced by greater price stability and lower interest rates as member state inflation rates converge, and as member states running large budget deficits are reined in (Emerson et al. 1991).

The stimulus to trade and investment following EMU will trigger the same broad types of allocation effects and accumulation effects already considered. Once again, it can be expected that the central regions of the EU will enjoy some inherent advantages in exploiting the situation when compared with the more peripheral regions. As always, however, no two acts of EU integration ever have the same *geographical footprint*. Full monetary union will strip participating member states of monetary and exchange rate powers which they can use, at present, to protect their economies from competition from the other EU members. Tighter central control of public spending (with a system of fines for profligate member states) will also reduce the discretion of member states to use fiscal policy to help disadvantaged regions. Weaker member states containing a high proportion of depressed peripheral regions have frequently resorted to exchange rate devaluations and public spending to boost their flagging economies. Under EMU this will no longer be possible.

The precise pattern of regional impacts of EMU is not yet known. The first wave of 11 participating member states established a set of locked exchange rates only in January 1999. The full introduction of the Euro will not occur until 2002. Until some experience has been gained in how the Euro currency area responds to outside pressures (and particularly external shocks which affect some EU regions more than others), the effects on disadvantaged regions will not be clear. The European Commission is upbeat, arguing that 'neither economic theory nor the current experiences of the least favoured and geographically peripheral regions . . .

point to a bias in the sense that these regions might systematically profit either more or less from EMU than the average. While the economic centre of the Community benefits from economies of scale advantages, it is not evident that these relative advantages are destined to grow. The least favoured regions still have other advantages' (Emerson et al. 1991: 27). This remains to be seen. Even if this is true in the longer term, it should be noted that the shorter-term effects of the loss of the power to use protective exchange rate devaluations could be serious. So too is the squeeze on public spending by member states (on which so many of the weaker regions depend) as countries have struggled to meet the convergence criteria of the EMU process.

Central and Eastern European Enlargement

The third major act of integration confronting the EU is Eastern Enlargement. The sudden collapse of communism in the early 1990s took the EU by surprise. An immediate impact was the reunion of Germany, an act which brought into the EU a swathe of highly disadvantaged regions in the form of the East German *Länder*. The brunt of the cost of integrating East Germany has largely fallen on West German taxpayers. The EU response was first to offer a special programme of regional assistance to the East German *Länder*, and then to integrate them into the existing regional policy of the EU by designating them as regions eligible for the highest rates of assistance.

East Germany is just the start. The EU has committed itself to a major new enlargement to incorporate a series of Central and Eastern European countries from 2002 onwards. This was a radical decision at a time of great change, with the the SEM and EMU coming on stream. One reason for this radical decision was the desire to help these countries to recover from the economic and social disruption which occurred as a result of the collapse of the communist trading system. Other reasons were to do with self-interest. Eastern Enlargement offers the opportunity for yet another major act of economic integration. The market to the east is a huge one. Eastern Enlargement offers the opportunity to exploit the various allocation effects and accumulation effects discussed earlier. The subsequent boost to trade and investment should be to the benefit of east and west alike (Baldwin et al. 1997).

The first steps in the process of Eastern Enlargement have already occurred. Accession negotiations are in progress with the first wave of six countries (Cyprus, the Czech Republic, Estonia, Hungary, Poland and Slovenia). Other Central and Eastern European countries such as Bulgaria and Romania will eventually form a second wave. It may seem curious to consider the regional effects of Eastern Enlargement at a time when it has not yet occurred. It must be borne in mind, however, that the removal of the Iron Curtain has already led to the rapid reorientation of trade for the acceding countries away from Russia and towards the EU. Integration is therefore already well under way, hindered only by the widespread economic dislocation which accompanied the collapse of communism. This integration, like all other types of integration, is already having its own distinctive geographical footprint within the EU. Moreover, the EU has introduced policies in the form of trade association agreements and *pre-accession assistance* to help the countries of Central and Eastern Europe to prepare for future accession. The pre-accession assistance has taken the form of special programmes of financial help and also aid in the form of regional policy and agricultural policy help. EU regional policy is therefore already engaged with the first wave of new entrants.

There is a further reason to take Eastern Enlargement seriously. As shall be shown later, the need to cope with Eastern Enlargement has triggered a major new reform of EU regional policy. The sheer scale of Eastern Enlargement, and the extent of the structural change which will be needed to cope with countries emerging from the shadow of communism, pose enormous challenges for EU regional policy. Some idea of the extent of these challenges can be seen from table 11.1 which sets out the population, GNP per capita and share of agriculture in GDP of key countries of Central and Eastern Europe. For comparison, similar statistics are given for the 15 existing member states of the EU (EUR15). Cyprus and Malta apart, the countries of Central and Eastern Europe set out in the lower part of table 11.1 can be seen to have very low GNP per capita. The first wave of new entrants are relatively more prosperous than the others such as Bulgaria and Romania. Their GNP per capita levels, however, remain well below those of the existing member states of the EU. Moreover, the Eastern Enlargement will also bring in states which are both populous and have large agricultural sectors. Table 11.1 shows that the first wave of new entrants have a combined population of 63 million persons, and that they are more heavily dependent on agriculture than the existing EU member states.

Eastern Enlargement is therefore posing two fundamental challenges for EU regional policy. These are, first, its impact on the regions of the existing EUR15 member states, and second, the problem of how to finance the demands on the EU budget arising from the accession of countries as poor as those in Central and Eastern Europe. Each of these will be considered in turn.

The geographical footprint of Eastern Enlargement

The opening up of Central and Eastern Europe to trade with the EU is likely to affect some regions of the EU much more than others. As always with the integration process a complex set of allocation and accumulation effects have been initiated. Precisely how these will impact on the different regions of the EU is extremely difficult to ascertain. The sheer size of the economies of the new entrants means that the regional impacts are likely to be very large. Moreover, the fact that the whole centre of gravity of the EU is being shifted eastwards means that the impacts are unlikely to take the form of simple core–periphery effects.

Estimates of the impact of Eastern Enlargement are, inevitably at this stage, highly speculative. Part of the geographical impact depends on which member states gain most from the boost to trade and investment that will follow Eastern Enlargement. The bulk of these gains are likely to be enjoyed by the new entrants themselves rather than the existing EUR15 countries of Western Europe, since it is the new entrants which have the most ground to make up. It is thought that the

Table 11.1 A comparison of key economic characteristics of EUR15 member states and Central and Eastern European countries, 1997

	Population (m)	GNP per capital (US$)	Agriculture as % of GDP[b]
EUR15 member states			
Austria	8	27 980	2
Belgium	10	26 420	1
Denmark	5	32 500	4
Finland	5	24 080	6
France	59	26 050	2
Germany	82	28 260	1
Greece	11	12 010	21
Ireland	4	18 280	3
Italy	57	20 120	3
Luxembourg	0.4	45 330	2
Netherlands	16	25 820	3
Portugal	10	10 450	3
Spain	39	14 510	3
Sweden	9	26 220	2
United Kingdom	59	20 710	2
Selected countries in Central and Eastern Europe			
Bulgaria	8	1 140	10
Czech Rep.[a]	10	5 200	6
Cyprus[a]	0.7	14 930	NA
Estonia[a]	1	3 300	7
Hungary[a]	10	4 430	7
Latvia	2	2 430	9
Lithuania	4	2 230	13
Malta	0.4	8 630	NA
Poland[a]	39	3 590	6
Romania	23	1 420	21
Slovak Rep.	5	3 700	5
Slovenia[a]	2	9 680	5
Turkey	64	3 130	17

[a] The countries of the Czech Republic, Cyprus, Estonia, Hungary, Poland and Slovenia are those which will form the first group of entrants from Central and Eastern Europe.
[b] The final column is agricultural value added as a percentage of GDP. Figures are for 1997 except for Denmark, Finland, Greece, Ireland, Luxembourg, Netherlands, Spain, Sweden, UK, and Czech Republic (all 1995).
Source: World Bank, *World Development Reports 1997 and 1998/99*, Oxford University Press, Oxford, 1999, tables 1, 1a and 12. Reproduced with the permission of Oxford University Press

new entrants could experience gains of up to 20 per cent on their existing GDP levels following accession. By contrast, the Western European countries can expect perhaps an extra 0.25 per cent on their combined GDP. However, two-thirds of the Western European gains in income and jobs will accrue to just three countries – Germany, France and the UK. Germany alone will enjoy one-third of the gains (Baldwin et al. 1997). Hence it is the relatively more prosperous northern parts of the EU which are likely to gain the most, rather than the weaker Mediterranean areas.

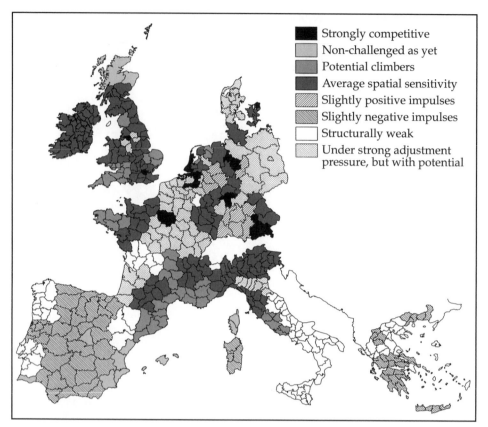

Figure 11.2   The regional impact of the opening up of Central and Eastern Europe.
Source: European Commission (1996a)

Identifying which regions are likely to be affected most *within* each member state is an extremely difficult task. Figure 11.2 presents the results of analysis by the European Commission (1996a) of the likely regional impact of the opening up of Central and Eastern Europe. Despite its complexity, figure 11.2 shows that most of the gaining regions are indeed in France, Germany and the UK (together with northern Italy), while it is the already weak Mediterranean regions, together with the East German *Länder*, which face the greatest pressures.

The budgetary implications of Eastern Enlargement

In addition to the regional impact effects of Eastern Enlargement, the regions of the existing EU member states are faced with a further challenge: how to pay for Eastern Enlargement. On the basis of the existing per capita incomes shown in table 11.1, virtually all of the regions in the six states which have entered accession negotiations will be eligible for the highest rates of assistance under the EU regional policy's Structural Funds. Moreover, as table 11.1 also shows, countries

Table 11.2 Estimates of the likely additional EU budget costs of Eastern Enlargement

	ecu (billion)
Regional policy (Structural Funds)	
At 400 ecu per capita	26.6
At 5% of GDP	12.8
Common Agricultural Policy	
Anderson and Tyers (1995) estimates	37.0
Most recent consensus estimates	10.0
'Best estimates'	
Structural Funds	13.0
Common Agricultural Policy	10.0
New member state contributions	−4.0
Net cost to EU budget	19.0

Sources: Baldwin et al. (1997); Anderson and Tyers (1995). Reproduced with permission

such as Poland and Hungary have large farming sectors producing many of the agricultural products (such as cereals and dairy products) which attract the highest Common Agricultural Policy (CAP) subsidies. This means that under existing regulations the new member states will be eligible for very large amounts of CAP money. Since the Structural Funds and CAP are by far the largest two items in the EU budget, the demands facing this budget in the years ahead will be huge.

An estimate of the likely scale of these demands on the EU budget is provided in table 11.2. If we consider the Structural Funds first, estimates of likely costs vary from 12.8 billion to 26.6 billion ecu. The upper value is based on the assumption that the new member states would obtain an amount per capita from the Structural Funds equivalent to what Portugal (the poorest of the existing member states) obtained in 1999. The lower value is based on the assumption that the new member states could not effectively absorb more than 5 per cent of their GDP in the form of an inflow of Structural Funds money. There is also a wide variation in the likely costs to the CAP budget – from 10 billion to 37 billion ecu. 'Best estimates' of the likely budget costs are shown at the bottom of table 11.2. These indicate a *net* additional cost of 19 billion ecu.

How to fund these huge additional costs has proved to be a major headache for the EU in planning its budget for the 2000–6 period. The EU has therefore taken the decision to cut back regional spending in the disadvantaged areas of the existing EUR15 in order to free up money for Eastern Europe. Table 11.3 shows the budget settlement that has been reached (European Council 1999). As can be seen from table 11.3, regional policy spending in EUR15 countries ('structural operations' in the table) is scheduled to fall from 32.0 billion Euros in 2000 (34.8 per cent of the full budget of the EU) to 29.2 billion Euros in 2006 (27.3 per cent of the full budget). By contrast, spending on regional policy in the new entrant countries is projected to rise from 3.8 billion Euros in 2002 to 12.1 billion Euros in 2006. In

Table 11.3   EU budget commitments, 2000–6 budget period

	Commitment appropriations,[a] in billion Euros at 1999 prices[b]						
	2000	2001	2002	2003	2004	2005	2006
Structural operations of the EUR15 states							
Structural Funds	29.430	28.840	28.250	27.670	27.080	27.080	26.660
Cohesion Fund	2.615	2.615	2.615	2.615	2.515	2.515	2.510
Total	32.045	31.455	39.865	30.285	29.595	29.595	29.170
Agriculture of the EUR15 states							
CAP expenditure	36.620	38.840	39.570	39.430	38.410	37.570	37.290
Rural development	4.300	4.320	4.330	4.340	4.350	4.360	4.370
Total	40.920	42.800	43.900	43.770	42.760	41.930	41.660
Other internal policies of the EUR15 states	5.900	5.950	6.000	6.050	6.100	6.150	6.200
External actions of the EUR15 states	4.550	4.560	4.570	4.580	4.590	4.600	4.610
Administration and reserves	5.460	5.500	5.350	5.200	5.100	5.400	5.500
Pre-accession aid for acceding states							
Agriculture	0.520	0.520	0.520	0.520	0.520	0.520	0.520
Structural operations	1.040	1.040	1.040	1.040	1.040	1.040	1.040
PHARE	1.560	1.560	1.560	1.560	1.560	1.560	1.560
Total	3.120	3.120	3.120	3.120	3.120	3.120	3.120
Post-accession expenditure							
Agriculture			1.600	2.030	2.450	2.930	3.400
Structural operations			3.750	5.830	7.920	10.000	12.080
Internal policies			0.730	0.760	0.790	0.820	0.850
External action			0.370	0.410	0.450	0.450	0.450
Total			6.450	9.030	11.620	14.200	16.780
Total commitments	91.995	93.385	100.255	102.035	103.075	104.995	107.040

[a] Figures refer to commitments and not to actual payments which will be made. Payments lag commitments as the various programmes incur expenditure.
[b] Euro is approximately £0.70.
Source: European Council (1999), annexes 1 and 2

other words, disadvantaged regions in Western Europe are being asked to give up some of their EU regional policy aid in order to help the new entrants.

Taking the SEM, EMU and Eastern Enlargement together, it is clear that many of the forces at work would appear to broadly favour the northern and central regions of the EU at the expense of the weaker southern and peripheral regions. It must be borne in mind, however, that the whole purpose of the EU is to bring about an expansion in the total level of income of the member states. If successful, the EU will be a more prosperous place for all and growth will be faster than before. In such circumstances the peripheral areas can expect benefits to trickle down to them from the more prosperous central regions, even if they themselves are not the principal beneficiaries. Europhiles would also point once again to the neoclassical adjustment mechanisms of trade and factor mobility. As we saw in chapter 5, free trade of the type envisaged in the EU can be a powerful force reducing regional differences in incomes and unemployment. The EU is also likely to result in larger flows of migrants from peripheral to central regions (in search of higher wages and job opportunities), and capital flows in the opposite direction (in search of cheap, plentiful labour supplies). This too may tend to reduce regional disparities in incomes and unemployment over the very long run.

Adverse regional effects of EU policies

In addition to the regional impacts of different stages in the integration process, there are a number of EU policies that have their own distinctive regional impacts, some of which are adverse. Three deserve special mention.

First, the EU obtains its revenue from member states by imposing a precept on value-added tax, and from customs and excise duties and levies. Each of these has its own distinctive regional incidence. VAT, for example, has regionally regressive effects since the burden is greatest in low-income regions (Commission of the European Communities 1979).

Second, EU agricultural policy operates with a distinct regional bias. It discriminates against regions with little agriculture of their own and whose residents would prefer to purchase food from non-EU countries at lower world prices. Moreover, because of the types of crops which receive the greatest support (principally cereals, dairy products, beef and sugar beet), and because large farms receive greater financial assistance than small farms, the already prosperous agricultural regions of northern Europe have been the principal beneficiaries. This contrasts with the poorer farmers of the Mediterranean and hill farm regions who benefit the least (Commission of the European Communities 1991b; Deutsches Institut für Wirtschaftsforschung 1991; European Commission 1996b).

Third, EU competition policy imposes a series of controls and regulations on the regional policies operated by the individual member states. This restricts their ability to tackle their own regional problems. Competition policy, for example, has imposed constraints on the levels of state aid in more prosperous regions and on certain types of help such as continuing labour subsidies (Wishlade 1998; European Commission 1998a).

Does integration lead to regional convergence or divergence?

The crucial question raised by our discussion of the forces unleashed by EU economic integration is whether the result is convergence or divergence of regional disparities, once the immediate effects of the SEM, EMU and enlargement have passed through the system. Opinions are sharply divided on this issue. The

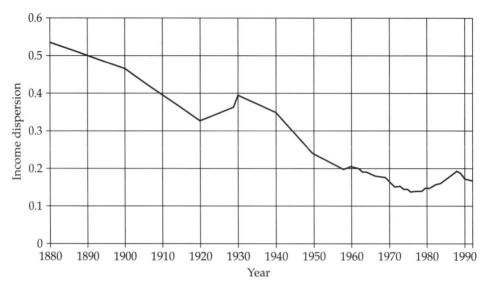

Figure 11.3   Standard deviation of personal incomes per capita across US states, 1880–1992.
Source: Sala-i-Martin (1996), figure 2. Reproduced with the permission of Elsevier Science

effect of EU integration on regional disparities can best be regarded as the out-come of a series of countervailing forces.

Traditional economic analysis is quite reassuring about the effects of integra-tion on regional disparities in income and employment. As we have noted earlier, free trade and factor mobility should set in motion a series of equilibrating forces.

The forces leading to convergence cannot be expected to act instantaneously. As we saw in chapter 6, labour migration in particular is a slow and faltering adjustment mechanism. The full effects of trade and capital mobility take gen-erations to make themselves felt. Nevertheless, there is some evidence that over very long periods of time regional income differentials gradually narrow as integration proceeds and as countries develop. This tendency has long been known (Williamson 1965). Figure 11.3 shows that income differences per capita between US states have been narrowing almost continuously since at least 1880, at a rate of approximately 2 per cent per annum. The same researchers (Barro and Sala-i-Martin 1991; 1992; Sala-i-Martin 1996a) have found evidence that regional differ-ences in GDP per capita among EU regions may have been narrowing at roughly the same rate since 1950. The United States, of course, has had a clear head start, in that the states have been an effective economic and monetary union since the country was established. The US states also have a common language and culture whereas the EU does not. We should not, therefore, be surprised to find that regional disparities within the EU are over twice those of the United States (Euro-pean Commission 1996a). There is evidence that slow convergence of regional per capita incomes also appears to have occurred *within* individual EU member states as well as within many other countries around the world, such as Japan, Canada,

Australia and India (Armstrong 1995; Mas et al. 1995; Abler and Das 1998; Kangasharju 1998).

The finding of what appears to be a long-term process of regional convergence is important. On the other hand, the research findings have also provoked a fierce debate, with attacks on both the economic theory and research methods of those who have found evidence of convergence (Fingleton and McCombie 1998). Some researchers, for example, have found evidence of divergence or persistence of regional disparities in the EU (Dunford 1996; Cheshire and Carbonaro 1996; Magrini 1999; Baddeley et al. 1998b).

Long-term convergence of EU regional disparities must not therefore be regarded as a foregone conclusion. Part of the reason for the wide differences in research results arises because different periods of time or different groupings of regions have been considered. As figure 11.3 has shown, it is quite possible for there to be convergence for some periods of time, but divergence in others (Dewhurst 1998; Fagerberg and Verspagen 1996; Neven and Gouyette 1995). Moreover, some individual regions and countries may be converging in the EU in any one period, while others are not (Quah 1996).

Taking the evidence as a whole, regional convergence in the EU was strong in the 1950s and 1960s but came to a halt in the mid 1970s, and disparities may actually have widened between 1975 and 1985. Moreover, they have shown little tendency to narrow again since 1985 (European Commission 1996b; 1999).

Irrespective of whether or not economic integration does eventually result in a narrowing of regional disparities, there is no doubt that a period of rapid structural change can occur when a customs union is formed or as a consequence of further integration, such as Eastern Enlargement. The allocation and accumulation effects trigger major structural dislocation in *all* regions. Some industries decline and other industries expand. Major reallocation of labour and capital must occur if the benefits of integration are to be realized. We should not be surprised to find regional disparities widening temporarily under those circumstances. One thing we can be certain about is that the forces of convergence need all the help they can get. An EU regional policy would seem to be an obvious ally, and it is to this that we now turn.

11.2   Regional policy in the European Union

The case for an EU regional policy

As the previous section has shown, the creation and development of the EU has given rise to a number of serious regional problems. Those who cause problems, however, are not necessarily best able to solve them. The fact that European economic integration has led to regional problems does not in itself justify the involvement of the EU in the provision of regional policy. It may be better to leave it to individual member states, which have developed their own particular brands of regional policy in order to solve their own particular regional problems. Those who argue in favour of an EU regional policy must show that this approach is likely to be more effective than if regional policy were controlled by the member states themselves.

Arguments can be presented both for and against the establishment of an EU regional policy. We turn first to the major arguments in favour of a role for the EU.

The EU can ensure that regional policy spending by member states is more closely matched to the severity of the problem faced

Some member states of the EU face more severe regional problems than others. Moreover, regional problems tend to be worse in countries that can least afford to fund a regional policy. This is true, for instance, of countries such as Greece and Portugal, and to a lesser extent Italy and the United Kingdom.

There is therefore a mismatch between the severity of regional problems in the EU and the ability of individual countries to deal with these problems. The situation is made worse by member states using their regional subsidies to bid against each other for mobile investment projects. The richer member states can afford to offer higher regional grants with the result that the countries with the most severe regional problems lose out in attracting new investment into their problem regions. This mismatch between the severity of a country's regional problems and its ability to fund them suggests a distinctive role for the EU. Only the EU can ensure that the bulk of the funds available are directed to the most disadvantaged regions.

Much more controversial is the form that the EU involvement should take. One approach is for the EU to generate a set of *financial transfers* from rich to poor member states for regional policy purposes. This would simultaneously improve the funding of regional policy in the more disadvantaged areas and enable the poorer regions to compete more effectively with richer member states for mobile investment. An alternative solution is for the EU to institute a set of *legal controls* on the regional policy expenditures of member states. Tight controls on regional spending in the richer member states and lax controls on regional spending in the poorer member states would improve the matching between expenditure and the severity of regional problems and could also prevent richer member states out-bidding the poorer ones for mobile investment.

Interestingly, the existing EU regional policy is in fact a mixture of both financial transfers and controls. Neither, however, has been sufficient to prevent either mismatching or competitive bidding for mobile investment. Suggestions for tighter controls (Deacon 1982) have the advantage of being inexpensive and practicable at times of financial stringency. Suggestions for greater financial transfers have the advantage of increasing the overall volume of spending on regional policy and of enabling member states to retain considerable freedom to pursue solutions to their own problems in their own way.

The EU can greatly improve the co-ordination of regional policy

When individual nations decide to have a regional policy, very little thought (if any) is given to the consequences of that policy on other nations. Similarly, when

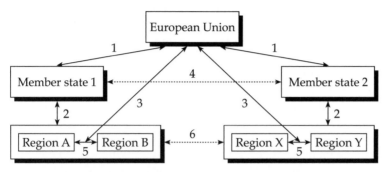

Figure 11.4 Co-ordination of regional policy in the European Union.

individual local or regional authorities decide to have their own industrial development policies, rarely will much thought be given to the effects of those policies on other local or regional authorities even within the same nation.

The complexity of regional policy is illustrated in figure 11.4. It is not simply a question of getting member states to co-ordinate their different regional policies or getting local authorities to co-operate with each other. Since all three levels of government – EU, member state and regional/local authorities – are now involved in regional policy, these too must somehow be persuaded to harmonize their policy actions.

In addition to the need to get governments to co-ordinate their regional policies, there is also a need for each government to co-ordinate its regional policy with other policies which have significant regional impacts. EU agriculture policy is a case in point. It has major regional effects and should consequently be closely co-ordinated with EU regional policy. A similar case can be made for all other policies that have differential regional impacts.

While there is a clear need to ensure that regional policy is closely co-ordinated, exactly what role the EU should play is less obvious. There is a stronger case for EU involvement in some types of policy co-ordination than in others. Member states have shown little interest in co-operating with each other on regional policy and the EU has an important role to play here. The EU is also responsible for ensuring that its own regional policy is closely co-ordinated with the regional policies of its member states. In addition, it must ensure that its regional policy is co-ordinated with other EU policies such as agriculture or trade policy. The case for EU involvement at lower levels, such as co-ordinating local authority schemes, is much weaker.

> An EU regional policy offers a means by which any one
> member state can legitimately become involved in solving
> the regional problems of other member states

Member states of the EU have a legitimate interest not only in their own regional problems but also in the regional problems of other member states. This interest of member states in the regional problems of other member states arises because of the existence of EU-wide effects. Regional policies designed to correct the problems of one member state frequently lead to benefits which spill over to other member states: hence the legitimate interest and concern of the latter. In a highly integrated EU, for example, high levels of unemployment in one region mean a lower demand for the goods produced by other member states. It is therefore in everyone's interest to solve the regional problem. Without EU-level involvement in regional policy, it is virtually impossible for member states to become involved in solving each other's regional problems. This represents a powerful argument for EU involvement.

There are in fact various ways in which the benefits of regional policy can spread to other member states. First, there are equity benefits. The redistribution of income through regional policy can be expected to yield utility gains for individuals in non-assisted areas as well as in the assisted areas themselves. Concern for the welfare of others extends well beyond national boundaries as the various international aid programmes testify. The use of regional policy to assist the inhabitants of severely disadvantaged regions is therefore likely to yield utility gains right across the EU.

Second, the openness of regional economies means that any increases in output and income resulting from regional policy quickly leak across to other regions. Nations too are open economies. The effects of regional policy on output and income will therefore rapidly spill over into the regions of other member states.

Third, regional policy can normally be expected to involve fiscal transfers in one form or another. Taxpayers as a whole pay for regional policy programmes, whereas the initial benefits will occur in the region receiving the regional assistance. Fiscal clawbacks occur when regional policies lead to a fall in unemployment and an increase in income. Payments to the unemployed fall and tax payments to governments increase. In some circumstances the benefits of regional policy to taxpayers – in assisted areas and non-assisted areas alike – may be substantial. Normally it would be mainly taxpayers within the member states who eventually benefit from reduced unemployment in the depressed areas. The EU itself, however, obtains some of its revenues from taxes and also makes payments through a variety of schemes to unemployed persons. A successful regional policy in any one member state will therefore eventually yield some benefits to taxpayers in other member states.

Finally, social and cultural benefits may accrue to the entire EU from, for example, the preservation of minority communities such as those in the Scottish Highlands and Islands. Regional policy may also yield environmental and strategic benefits to the extent that one of its objectives is to prevent the over-concentration of industry and population.

EU regional policy is necessary if further integration is to be sustained

There is a strong presumption that regional policy is desirable not only because of the benefits that regional policy itself brings but also because it will permit greater economic integration in the EU. Hence regional policy 'is not only desirable, it is . . . one of the conditions for continuing European integration' (Commission of the European Communities 1977: 4). In other words, if the benefits of further integration in the EU are to be obtained, it will be necessary to find ways of alleviating the adverse regional effects of integration. This is probably one of the weaker arguments for EU involvement in regional policy. There is little evidence that regional problems have prevented member states from agreeing to further development of the EU.

Centralization versus decentralization: Should EU regional policy replace the regional policies of member states?

Although a strong case can be made for establishing and strengthening EU regional policy, this does not mean that regional policy should be controlled entirely from the centre and that member states should give up their own regional policies. None of the arguments presented above implies that the EU should wholly replace member states in the provision of regional policy. The argument, for example, that the EU can help to ensure that the poorer member states can adequately fund their regional policy efforts implies a degree of EU involvement but not complete control. Individual member states must be expected to provide the greater part of the resources necessary to finance their own regional policies.

The EU-wide benefit argument is also open to criticism. It was noted earlier that member states have a legitimate interest in the regional policy of other member states because some of the benefits accrue to the whole Union. Valid though the argument is, it must be borne in mind that only a fraction of the benefits of regional policy are likely to accrue to other member states. This fraction is sufficiently large to justify an EU regional policy but not to justify an EU takeover of regional policy from the individual member states.

There are strong reasons for resisting the over-centralization of regional policy in the EU. One of these is the danger of a uniform approach to solving problems which by their very nature differ from one region to another. The substantial advantages of local knowledge and experience in designing particular regional policy programmes for specific geographical areas mean that member states must be expected to retain substantial control over regional policy. Over-centralization is also likely to stifle innovation in the development of policy instruments. Decentralization allows for greater diversity and experimentation in the construction of policies, thus helping policy makers to discover which policies are likely to be the most effective. Finally, decentralization encourages greater local participation and makes policy makers more accountable to those they serve.

In conclusion, while powerful arguments can be advanced for an EU regional policy, there is nothing in those arguments implying that member states have no role to play. Indeed, a strong case can be made against complete centralization of regional policy. In principle, there is no reason why regional policy powers should not be divided between the EU and member states. The EU has its own distinctive role to play, in particular in generating financial transfers to the member states with the worst regional problems, and in helping to co-ordinate regional policy across the Union. Member states, however, have a major role to play in financing and implementing their own distinctive regional policies. The resulting diversity of regional policy in Europe should be seen as a strength, not a weakness.

11.3   Existing EU regional policy

EU regional policy has had a short history. The principal elements of the policy came into existence in 1975 with the establishment of the European Regional Development Fund (ERDF), though only after a long debate and in a form that differed substantially from the Commission's initial and far more ambitious proposals. The policy has been reformed on five separate occasions since its initial establishment in 1975.

Reforms in 1989 were by far the most important (Commission of the European Communities 1989). They were triggered by the SEM process, which as we have seen, is posing serious challenges for the disadvantaged regions of the EU. As a result, the reforms were phased in over the period 1989–93 in a process designed to run alongside the introduction of the SEM legislation. The 1989 reforms are notable in the following respects.

First, the ERDF was brought together with two other pre-existing EU financial instruments to form the *Structural Funds*. These two other instruments were the European Social Fund (ESF) and the Guidance Section of the European Agricultural Guidance and Guarantee Fund (EAGGF). The ESF is a fund designed to finance training, retraining, migration, anti-discrimination and other labour market policies. The Guidance Section of EAGGF is used to encourage the restructuring of farming in the EU and a diversification into non-farming activities such as tourism and manufacturing in rural areas. The Guidance Section is distinct from the much larger Guarantee Section of EAGGF, which is used to finance the price support element of the Common Agricultural Policy. Since 1989, the Structural Funds have been expanded to include a fourth component: the Financial Instrument for Fisheries Guidance (FIFG). This is a specific instrument designed to help fishing communities facing difficulties as a result of the operation of the Common Fisheries Policy.

Second, the period 1989–93 saw a doubling of the size (in real terms) of the financial allocations to the Structural Funds. This occurred because the EU realized that the SEM process would pose serious challenges to the weaker regions and that significant extra sums of money would be needed for regional policy.

Third, the 1989 reforms established a radical new system for the delivery of regional policy within the EU. This revolutionized the manner in which regional policy is implemented in countries such as the UK. The EU delivery system is based around a number of key principles: concentration of assistance, co-ordination, partnership, subsidiarity, programming and additionality. These are considered in greater detail below.

The 1989 reforms have stood the test of time. Experience in the 1989–93 budget period led to minor changes to the system in a new set of reforms introduced in 1994 (European Commission 1996c). The delivery system set up in 1989 was retained for the 1994–9 budget period in all of its important aspects. It has also been retained as the basis of the EU's regional policy for the 2000–6 budget period.

Its survival is even more remarkable in the light of the upheavals of the 1990s. The reunification of Germany in 1990 brought the highly disadvantaged East German *Länder* into the EU. These were accommodated by increasing the budget and by designating these regions as eligible for the highest rates of assistance from the Structural Funds. The Fourth Enlargement of 1996 brought with it new challenges in the form of the peripheral Arctic and sub-Arctic regions of Finland and Sweden. These were accommodated by a further increase in the Structural Funds budget and by the creation of a new category of assistance specifically designed to help them. Lastly, and most importantly of all, the commitment to EMU in the Maastricht Treaty of 1992 posed a whole new set of challenges for the disadvantaged regions. It was quickly realized that it would be unreasonable to ask the disadvantaged regions of the EU to cope simultaneously with both the SEM process and monetary union without extra help. Simply delaying monetary union to 2002 did not solve the problem. Member states were to join a stage-by-stage process towards monetary union under which a whole series of strict convergence criteria were to be met (e.g. on inflation, public sector deficits and interest rates). Monetary union, therefore, posed new challenges for the disadvantaged regions in the 1990s. Since EMU was posing its own distinctive set of challenges for the disadvantaged regions, it was decided to double once again (in real terms) the financial resources available to the Structural Funds in the 1994–9 budget period. By 1999, the EU's regional policy had come to command 36 per cent of the full EU budget.

In addition, in recognition of the fact that joining the monetary union poses particular problems for some of the weaker member states, the EU introduced a wholly new financial instrument, the *Cohesion Fund*, in 1994. Although not strictly one of the Structural Funds, the Cohesion Fund does effectively operate as an arm of EU regional policy. It was used in the 1994–9 budget period to provide grant assistance for transport and environmental projects in Greece, Ireland, Portugal and Spain. Its purpose is to help weaker member states to prepare for EMU by integrating their economies more closely with the rest of the EU.

EU regional policy, 1994–9

EU regional policy is constructed around six key principles, as described in the following sections.

Concentration of assistance

The concentration of Structural Funds on the most disadvantaged regions is a requirement of any regional policy. In the case of the EU's Structural Funds there are two further reasons for concentration. First, as noted earlier, a key justification of an EU role in regional policy lies in its ability to switch funds from richer member states towards those with a heavier burden of disadvantaged regions.

Table 11.4   Priority objectives, 1994–6 Structural Funds

Priority objective	Funds committed[a]	Regional or non-regional?[b]
Objective 1: Promoting the development and structural adjustment of regions whose development is lagging behind ('lagging regions')	ERDF, ESF, EAGGF (Gu), FIFG	Regional
Objective 2: Converting regions seriously affected by industrial decline ('regions in industrial decline')	ERDF, ESF	Regional
Objective 3: Combating long-term unemployment and facilitating the integration into working life of young people and persons excluded from the labour market	ESF	Non-regional
Objective 4: Facilitating the adaptation of workers to industrial changes and changes in production systems	ESF	Non-regional
Objective 5a: Speeding up the adjustment of agricultural structures in the framework of the reform of the Common Agricultural Policy and promoting the modernization and structural adjustment of the fisheries sector in the framework of the reform of the Common Fisheries Policy	EAGGF (Gu), FIFG	Non-regional
Objective 5b: Facilitating the development and structural adjustment of rural areas ('rural areas')	ERDF, ESF, EAGGF (Gu)	Regional
Objective 6: Promoting the development of regions with an extremely low population density ('low-population-density regions')	ERDF, ESF, EAGGF (Gu), FIFG	Regional

[a] ERDF = European Regional Development Fund; ESF = European Social Fund; EAGGF (Gu) = Guidance Section of the European Agricultural Guidance and Guarantee Fund; FIFG = Financial Instrument for Fisheries Guidance.
[b] The term 'regional' refers to those objectives where a distinction is drawn between regions eligible for help and those ineligible. 'Non-regional' objectives are available in all regions of the EU.
Source: European Commission

Second, the EU lacks a system of large-scale fiscal transfers to weaker regions via a federal government. This means that the Structural Funds alone must bear the burden. Focusing the limited financial resources available is therefore vital.

Concentration is achieved by focusing the Structural Funds on a limited number of priority objectives. During the 1994–9 period there were six objectives. As table 11.4 shows, only four of the six objectives were actually regional policy objectives. These were: Objective 1, lagging regions (regions with GDP per capita under 75 per cent of the EU average); Objective 2, declining industrial regions (designated on the basis of unemployment rates, employment decline and industrial structure); Objective 5b, rural areas (designated on the basis of farm employment, low incomes and population decline); and Objective 6, low-population-density regions. The remaining objectives (3, 4 and 5a) were not strictly regional policy

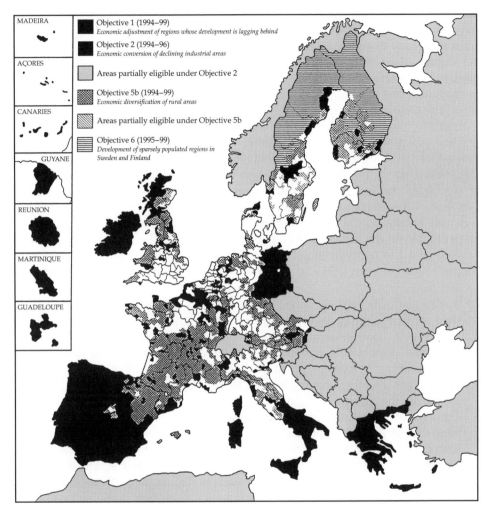

Figure 11.5   Regions eligible for Structural Funds assistance, 1994–9.
Source: European Commission

objectives, their primary concern being with labour markets and agriculture. In reality, however, even the 'non-regional' objectives tend to spend more money in disadvantaged regions than elsewhere, given their bias towards helping the unemployed.

By retaining control over which regions are eligible for the various priority objectives, the EU has been able to concentrate assistance on the most disadvantaged regions to some degree. Figure 11.5 shows the regions eligible for Structural Funds between 1994 and 1999. As can be seen, the most severely disadvantaged Objective 1 regions were concentrated in the Mediterranean south of the EU, in Ireland and in East Germany. In all, 94 million people lived in the Objective 1 regions (25 per cent of the EU population). Within the UK only Merseyside,

Northern Ireland and the Scottish Highland and Islands enjoyed Objective 1 status during 1994–9 (6 per cent of the UK population). The declining industrial areas (Objective 2) encompassed over 60 million people in 1994–9 (16 per cent of the EU population). However, in the UK, 31 per cent of the population were covered by Objective 2 status. The other two regional objectives are less important in absolute terms (although furnishing very high per capita aid for their inhabitants). The Objective 5b areas in 1994–9 covered 9 per cent of the EU population (almost 32 million people), including 5 per cent of the UK population. Objective 6 regions, as figure 11.5 shows, were confined to the Arctic and sub-Arctic areas of Finland and Sweden and contained only 0.4 per cent of the total EU population. The limited extent to which concentration was attained in the 1994–9 period can be seen from the fact that the four 'regional' objectives between them covered over half of the whole EU population (51 per cent).

Simply totting up the percentage of the EU population to be found in the regions eligible for the Structural Funds understates the real extent to which the EU has succeeded in concentrating the funds where they are most needed. Further concentration between 1994 and 1999 was attained through three other devices:

1   Some two-thirds of the Structural Funds were earmarked solely for the Objective 1 regions (lagging regions) for the 1994–9 period.
2   The EU operates a system of *indicative allocations* for each *member state* (based on eligible populations, national and regional prosperity and the relative seriousness of their problems, particularly as indicated by unemployment rates). These act as a further check to ensure that the poorest parts of the EU get the most from the Structural Funds.
3   The EU 'top-slices' part of the Structural Funds (9 per cent of the Structural Funds in 1994–9) which it uses for *Community Initiatives* (CIs). There were 13 such CIs in the 1994–9 period. Their purpose was to focus Structural Funds assistance on highly specific problems that span member state boundaries. These ranged from sectoral initiatives such as Rechar (coal mining areas) and Resider (steel areas) to highly specific CIs such as Horizon (disabled workers) and Konver (areas affected by defence industry cuts).

Co-ordination

The EU has always taken its co-ordination role seriously. The use of competition policy regulations to prevent individual member states from using their state aids (which include regional subsidies) to compete aggressively for inward investment and distort competition has already been commented upon. Regulations of this kind are a form of co-ordination. The 1989 reforms also greatly strengthened the co-ordination role of the EU by bringing together the various disparate Structural Funds within a common policy framework.

This long-overdue process of pulling together the EU's own financial instruments was not confined solely to the four Structural Funds. The 1989 reforms also established procedures to ensure that the *European Investment Bank* (EIB) and the *European Coal and Steel Community* (ECSC) would carefully tailor their activities with the Structural Funds. Since 1994 the Cohesion Fund too has been required to carefully co-ordinate its activities with the Structural Funds.

The EIB is a substantial contributor to EC regional policy. Using capital subscribed by member states and borrowed from international capital markets, the Bank provides loans and loan guarantees for investment projects. Loans for regional development purposes are only one of the Bank's functions, but this is a prominent one. In 1997 EIB loans to the disadvantaged regions comprised 70 per cent (14.7 billion ecu) of all internal loans made (European Investment Bank 1998). Although the Bank makes loans rather than grants, the loans are usually on attractive terms and it is willing to take greater risks than commercial banks.

By the very nature of the industries involved, the ECSC is also inevitably a part of EU regional policy. Substantial loans are made to coal, iron and steel and associated industries for investment purposes. In addition, the ECSC provides 'conversion' loans to industries other than coal and steel in order to create jobs and absorb redundant coal and steel workers. The ECSC also provides grants for retraining and resettling redundant coal and steel workers.

Partnership

Perhaps the most valuable contribution of all towards co-ordination made by the 1989 reforms was the increased importance attached to partnership. Partnership is seen by many as being of fundamental importance to the success of EU regional policy. There are three main reasons for this. First, there is simply no logical case to be made for the EU to take over regional policy from the member states. Since the member states should, and have, continued to operate their own powerful regional policies, it is inevitable that the EU and member states must work in close partnership with one another. Second, the EU is not a federal system. In particular, it lacks the large tax-raising powers and budget of a true federal government. In the EU, for example, the European Commission has command over only 3 per cent of the total taxation collected each year, the remainder accruing to the member states. What this means is that the EU simply does not have the financial clout to run a regional policy on its own. It must operate in partnership with the more powerful member states. This point is reinforced by the fact that the European Commission does not have a system of strong member state and regional offices through which it can implement policies. It must rely on the bureaucracies of each member state government. The final reason for a partnership approach lies in the changing system of 'governance' in the EU, with a much greater role being played by regional and local economic development organizations. This is partly the result of the EU's commitment to subsidiarity, to which we now turn.

Subsidiarity

EU regional policy lays great emphasis on procedures to encourage subsidiarity: the decentralization of power to the lowest tier of government compatible with efficient policy delivery. Although the principle of subsidiarity really only explicitly appeared in the Maastricht Treaty of 1992, the 1989 reforms to the Structural

Funds had already foreshadowed its rise to prominence. Indeed, the Structural Funds are now regarded as the best example of the application of subsidiarity within the EU. There has been considerable controversy associated with the concept of subsidiarity. Some have seen it as the process of shifting powers back to the member states from the EU. In the case of regional policy, however, it is seen as the process of empowering regional and local partners (both governments and non-elected organizations). The 1989 reforms brought regional and local partners actively into EU regional policy for the first time. Subsequent reforms in the 1990s have continued this trend. The principal mechanism for bringing about subsidiarity, and also the encouragement of both co-ordination and partnership, has been the development of the *programming* method of delivering the Structural Funds.

Programming

The programming approach to regional policy stands in stark contrast to the traditional manner in which regional policy has been delivered in the UK, where project-by-project assistance was offered to individual investment projects. Since 1989, however, the bulk of assistance from the EU's Structural Funds has been spent by way of programmes of assistance. A programme is essentially a multi-annual, multi-project, multi-partner contract which is designed as a co-ordinated attack on the problems of a region. For the main categories of regions helped by the EU in the budget period 1994–9, the programmes were designed to be six-year strategies spanning the full period 1994–9. In the case of Objective 2 (declining industrial) regions, two separate three-year programmes were adopted (i.e. 1994–6 and 1997–9).

The actual programmes themselves are called either *Community Support Frameworks* (CSFs) or *Single Programming Documents* (SPDs). The latter are drawn up using simpler procedures and were used for Objective 2 and 5b programmes. The CSFs are implemented on the ground through a series of *Operational Programmes* (OPs). Between 1994 and 1999 some 500 OPs and SPDs were produced for regions eligible for Structural Funds assistance. The CSF/SPD documents are written to a common format which must include an economic and social analysis of the region, a clear strategy, a set of targets for the strategy, and an environmental impact assessment of the strategy. The strategy is broken down into priorities for action, together with detailed sets of measures to show how the priorities are to be attained. Above all, the CSF/SPD sets out how the Structural Funds will be combined with financial assistance pledged by the member state, regional and local partners.

Although the CSF and SPD documents can be thought of as a form of regional economic planning, the whole process is essentially a highly decentralized one. The planning process is driven by the regions, who submit the initial development plans which form the basis of the CSF/SPD to the Commission. The Commission plays an active role but does not dominate the process. The 1990s have witnessed something of a revival of ideas of EU-wide regional planning, as is shown by documents such as *Europe 2000* (European Commission 1994a), but these have not affected the more decentralized system in operation for the Structural Funds (Hague 1996).

Table 11.5 The 1997–9 Yorkshire and the Humber Objective 2 Programme

Description of priorities and measures	Million ecu	
	ERDF/ESF	Total
Priority 1: improving SME competitiveness		
Measure 1.1: access to finance (ERDF)	10.0	24.7
Measure 1.2: developing quality approaches (ERDF)	8.1	44.5
Measure 1.3: access to new markets and customers (ERDF)	17.0	43.1
Measure 1.4: human resources for SME competitiveness (ESF)	37.6	107.3
Total priority 1	82.7	219.6
Priority 2: new employment opportunities		
Measure 2.5: the information society (ERDF)	12.1	29.0
Measure 2.6: sectoral initiatives (ERDF)	19.7	48.2
Measure 2.7: specialized business space and facilities (ERDF)	21.2	51.9
Measure 2.8: human resources for new employment opportunities (ESF)	15.1	43.5
Total priority 2	68.1	172.6
Priority 3: delivering the Regional Innovation Strategy		
Measure 3.9: new products and processes (ERDF)	14.6	35.8
Measure 3.10: technology transfer activities for SMEs (ERDF)	13.6	33.3
Measure 3.11: developing 'green' ways of working (ERDF)	9.1	22.5
Measure 3.12: people for the 21st century (ESF)	15.1	45.4
Total priority 3	52.4	137.2
Priority 4: targeted strategic development		
Measure 4.13: strategic development sites (ERDF)	40.9	117.0
Measure 4.14: developing tourism poles (ERDF)	28.7	71.8
Measure 4.15: capturing local benefit (ERDF)	10.0	25.5
Measure 4.16: local investment in people (ESF)	10.0	26.7
Total priority 4	89.6	241.0
Priority 5: community economic development		
Measure 5.17: Helping communities to help themselves (ERDF)	62.5	125.1
Measure 5.18: access to work (ERDF)	10.1	40.3
Measure 5.19: getting communities into work (ESF)	27.1	59.9
Total priority 5	99.7	225.3
Technical assistance	8.2	16.4
Programme total	400.7	1012.1

Source: Government Office for Yorkshire and the Humber, *Single Programming Document
1997–9: Yorkshire and the Humber Objective 2 Area*, Leeds, 1997

The Yorkshire and Humber Objective 2 SPD for 1997–9 is a typical example of programming in action. Table 11.5 sets out the key priorities and measures through which the programme was designed to operate. This three-year programme envisages spending over 1 billion ecu (approximately £700 million). Of this, some

40 per cent is committed from the Structural Funds (i.e. the ERDF and ESF: as an Objective 2 declining industrial area there are no EAGGF or FIFG funds committed). The remainder is made up of 45 per cent from various member state public sector sources and 15 per cent from the private sector (mostly as part contributions for business services and advice). The Yorkshire and Humber Objective 2 SPD is typical of most UK programmes in that the emphasis is very much on indigenous development policies, in particular help for small and medium enterprises (priorities 1 and 2 in table 11.5) and innovation (priority 3). Some inward investment is supported in priority 4 (targeted strategic development), but even in this priority much of the help is for local firms through help for tourism (measure 4.14, developing tourism poles) and by encouraging local supply chains to established firms (measure 4.15, capturing local benefit). Priority 5 in table 11.5 (community economic development) is a more recent innovation in Structural Funds assistance. This priority helps to finance a diverse array of policies designed to help socially and economically excluded communities, mostly inner city and coalfield communities. These policies are designed to help members of excluded communities back into employment through step-by-step procedures and by stimulating new local businesses (Lloyd 1996; Lloyd and Ramsden 1998).

Additionality

The final key principle underpinning EU regional policy is additionality: the use of Structural Funds in a genuinely complementary manner alongside the public expenditure of each member state. This principle has proved one of the most difficult of all to attain. Many member states have seen the advent of the Structural Funds as an excellent opportunity to cut back their own domestic regional policy commitments. The issue is a vital one. The extra pressures placed on the regions through the combination of the SEM, EMU and Eastern Enlargement are severe. The EU simply cannot afford to see the impact of its Structural Funds frittered away as a result of cutbacks in the financial contributions made by the member states. The reluctance of many member states to honour the principle of additionality has led the EU to steadily expand its monitoring procedures for the Structural Funds. The EU is also careful to build additionality into the CSFs and SPDs. Programmes must be jointly financed by the member states. Strict co-financing rates are laid down to limit the proportion of spending within a programme financed by the EU. At the level of individual projects there are also strict regulations for matched funding from the public sector alongside Structural Fund commitments. Despite all of these efforts, additionality remains a difficult problem for the EU.

EU regional policy, 2000–6

The challenges to the disadvantaged regions posed by Eastern Enlargement have, as has already been shown, triggered large-scale changes in the funding of the EU Structural Funds (table 11.3). Additional funding has been set aside for the six acceding states from Central and Eastern Europe for the budget period 2000–6. This additional funding has been partially at the expense of regions eligible for Structural Funds within the pre-existing 15 member states of the EU.

The closeness of Eastern Enlargement, combined with the onset of a new (seven-year) budget period, has provided an opportunity for a new reform package of the Structural Funds. This has been done under the auspices of the *Agenda 2000* discussions (European Commission 1997; 1998b; European Council 1999). These reforms are not as far-reaching as the 1989 reforms, but are nevertheless very significant. In addition to the major funding changes set out in table 11.3, the 1999 reforms envisage the following.

Cutting back of areas eligible for assistance

This is necessary to free up money for the new member states, all of which will be eligible for Objective 1 status. Some redrawing of eligible area boundaries was needed anyway (e.g. with areas such as Ireland rising out of Objective 1 status). The opportunity for a simpler system and more concentrated assistance has been taken too. The first part of this process has involved the cutting back of the number of priority objectives from six to three:

- *New Objective 1 (lagging regions)* These are to continue to be denominated as regions with GDP per capita under 75 per cent of the EU average, but with the former Objective 6 regions (low population density regions) of Sweden and Finland given the concession of Objective 1 status for 2000–6. Some very remote parts of the EU (i.e. Canary Islands, Azores and French overseas territories) are also awarded Objective 1 status. The population covered by Objective 1 will fall from 25 per cent of the EU population (1994–9) to 20 per cent (2000–6).
- *New Objective 2: economic and social conversion of regions in structural crisis* It is among the regions previously eligible for Objective 2 (industrial decline) and 5b (rural areas) that the biggest cuts in eligibility will occur. The new Objective 2 for the period 2000–6 will encompass both of the previous objectives. The eligible areas will, however, be cut back from the 25 per cent of the EU population covered in 1994–9 to only 18 per cent in 2000–6. Moreover, as well as the formerly eligible industrial and rural areas, now urban areas and areas dependent on services and fisheries are also eligible under the new Objective 2. Apart from setting broad overall limits on the industrial/services areas (10 per cen of the EU population), rural areas (5 per cent), urban areas (2 per cent) and fisheries areas (1 per cent), and setting strict limits for each member state, the EU has left the precise designation of new Objective 2 areas to the member states themselves.
- *New Objective 3: development of human resources* This new ESF objective has effectively been transformed into a 'regional' objective since it is for *all regions outside the new Objectives 1 and 2*. As before, however, the ESF will focus on training and other labour market initiatives (including initiatives to tackle social exclusion and discrimination).

To soften the blow for areas losing eligibility status, the EU has instituted a system of safety nets and transitional funding designed to ensure that regions losing out have their Structural Funds progressively withdrawn over the 2000–6 period. However, many areas within the pre-existing 15 EU member states face further cuts in structural funding as a result of the decision to drastically reduce the number of Community Initiatives. These will be reduced from 13 to a mere three (cross-border co-operation, rural development and anti-discrimination). CI funding will also be cut from 9 to 5 per cent of the Structural Funds budget.

Strengthening subsidiarity and a clearer division of responsibilities

The 1999 reforms envisage a stronger role for regional and local partners, and the drawing into the programming process of new partners such as local voluntary groups, non-governmental bodies and trades unions. As part of this process, the Commission has taken steps to clarify its own role relative to regional and local partners. The Commission has strengthened its role at the stage of designing strategic programmes for each region, and in financial control, evaluation and monitoring. It has, however, decentralized more power to the regions to actually spend the money and take their own decisions in implementing the programmes. To encourage regions to take more responsibility and to learn from best practice elsewhere, a 10 per cent *performance reserve* has been set aside to reward the most effective regions from 2003 to 2006.

Simpler procedures and more flexibility for the regions

Finally, the 1999 reforms attempted to simplify the regulations and also to free up some of the restrictive features of the Structural Funds. From 2000 onwards, for example, a wider range of types of financial assistance in the form of venture capital holdings, loan guarantees, interest rate subsidies and other types of *financial engineering* will be allowed for the first time.

11.4   Conclusion

Regional differences in living standards within individual nations are sometimes considerable. When nations join together in an economic union, regional disparities within such unions of nations are likely to be very wide indeed. Moreover, one of the consequences of economic integration is to cause major dislocation in depressed regions – unless policy markers take action to prevent this from happening.

The entry of the UK into the EU and its participation in subsequent developments have not only had implications for regional disparities in living standards but also thrown open the whole question of who should control regional policy. The emergence of a distinctive EU regional policy effectively ended the UK government's virtual monopoly of regional policy within its borders. The reforms to EU regional policy since 1989 have been welcome steps towards a stronger EU regional policy. Welcome though many of these reforms have been, we must not lose sight of just how serious the regional problem remains within the EU. Regional disparities have barely narrowed in the EU since 1975. Moreover, in allowing the accession of six new member states from Central and Eastern Europe, the EU is effectively taking on a whole raft of new regional problems. This is occurring at a time when the SEM and EMU are themselves posing new regional challenges.

The division of regional policy responsibilities between the EU and the individual member states remains a contentious issue. Considerable disagreement exists over the role that each party should have. The arguments presented in this chapter imply that there are sound reasons for creating and strengthening EU regional policies. This does not mean, however, that the EU should be solely responsible for regional policy within the Union. The individual member states and regional and local partners also have an important part to play and this role needs to be protected since there are considerable dangers in over-centralizing policy powers.

The centralizing forces of European integration are closely related to the decentralizing forces of devolution. The latter are considered in the chapter which follows, and it is no surprise to find that many of the issues which have emerged in the present chapter have parallels in the devolution debate to which we now turn.

Further reading

Armstrong (1998); Bachtler and Turok (1997); Baldwin et al. (1997); European Commission (1997); Quévit (1995); Sala-i-Martin (1996a; 1996b).

chapter twelve

Regional policy and devolution

contents

In the previous chapter, attention was focused on the regional effects of economic integration in Europe. We showed how the centralization of economic powers within the European Union could have profound effects on regional problems. The central question under discussion was how far regional policy powers should be concentrated in the hands of the European Union rather than leaving the individual member states to devise their own regional policies. In the present chapter, the spotlight is turned on the decentralization of economic policy functions. To what extent should economic policy be in the hands of regional or local authorities rather than in the hands of the central government?

The extent to which economic powers are devolved varies tremendously between nations. In the UK, for example, the major levers of economic power – fiscal policy, monetary policy and trade policy – are still extremely centralized. This is true despite the creation of a Scottish Parliament and a Welsh Assembly in 1999. At the opposite end of the spectrum are countries such as Canada, Germany and the United States. These operate highly decentralized systems with powerful state and provincial governments. Countries also differ in the manner in which powers are decentralized. In Germany, for example, all of the regional *Länder* governments have identical powers. By contrast, countries such as Spain and the UK have opted for 'variable geometry' solutions in which some regions are given greater economic powers than others.

Devolution is a complex issue and there is a need for some simplification in order to highlight the most important economic aspects of it. Our concern here is with the *regional implications* of devolution. Broader issues, such as whether more devolution is preferable to less devolution or whether some optimum degree of devolution exists, are beyond the scope of this book.

This chapter begins by setting the UK devolution debate within the context of the rapidly changing system of *regional governance* within the European Union (section 12.1). Having set the scene, attention is then turned to the economic arguments for and against greater decentralization of regional policy powers. In order to clarify the issues involved, three quite different 'states of the world' are considered in this chapter. First, we consider a situation in which fiscal policy, monetary policy and trade policy powers are controlled almost entirely by the central government (section 12.2). This resembles the UK case, at least as far as the English regions are concerned. Regional and local governments exist, but they are assumed to have only minor powers. Two key questions arise. Should the national government alone control regional policy or should local and regional authorities also be given a role? How best can the national government manipulate its fiscal, monetary and trade policy powers in order to help disadvantaged areas?

Section 12.3 considers a situation of partial devolution. Regional authorities are assumed to have some fiscal policy powers, but monetary policy and trade policy remain under the control of central government. Most federal countries operate this kind of system with state governments being given powers to levy taxes and spend the proceeds. Scotland and Wales have also now moved into this position within the UK. This type of devolution again raises two key questions. Would devolving more tax and spending powers help or hinder the attainment of regional policy objectives? Could the disadvantaged areas operate their own fiscal policies in order to raise output and employment?

Finally, we consider the extreme case of a situation in which fiscal, monetary and trade policy powers are completely devolved to regional authorities. Section 12.4 therefore considers whether such a dramatic step, giving enormous freedom of action to regional authorities in the disadvantaged areas, would allow regional governments to make a better job than the national government of stimulating output and employment in disadvantaged areas.

12.1 The changing system of regional governance

This chapter is concerned with the devolution of *economic* policy powers rather than *political* powers. Nevertheless, no discussion of devolution would be complete without considering the rapidly evolving *regional governance* system. Traditional economic theory for the analysis of regional devolution (especially the

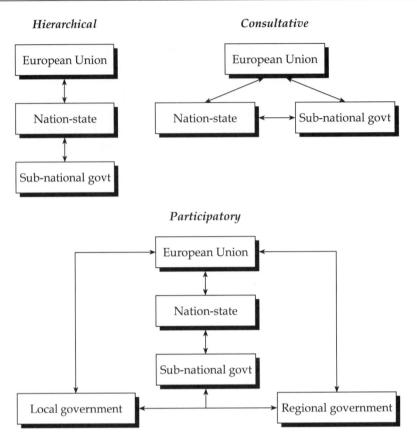

Figure 12.1   Different forms of regional governance.
Source: Rhodes (1996), reproduced in Haynes et al. (1997), figure 1

theory of *fiscal federalism*) takes as its basis the hierarchical division of responsibilities existing between federal, state and local tiers of government (Breton and Scott
1978; King 1984). Typically in these systems there is a clear division of responsibilities between the different tiers of government. The federal government, for
example, will have certain functions, including the provision of public goods such
as defence, together with the fiscal policy powers needed to bring about macroeconomic stabilization and income redistribution. By contrast, regional and local
governments will have other powers, including the provision of public goods
such as refuse collection and policing. In these systems there is a close coincidence
between *territorial space* – the area under the jurisdiction of a particular elected
government – and *functional space* – the particular policy responsibilities of each
jurisdiction. Moreover, there is a clear hierarchy, with higher-order governments
being more powerful than lower-order governments. The hierarchical system is
shown as the first of three possible regional governance systems in figure 12.1.

The traditional hierarchical view of the world has always only been an approximation of reality when it comes to regional policy. Close consultation between

the different tiers of government has always occurred, even where the national government has retained the ultimate policy powers (the 'consultative system' shown in figure 12.1). However, as has been shown in chapter 8, even in a highly centralized nation-state such as the UK, regional policy was never simply just a consultative model. Local authorities have played an active role in regional policy since the early decades of the twentieth century by providing both land and serviced sites for businesses. Moreover, the UK government has long chosen to operate its regional policies with the help of the regional offices of the various ministries and, from the mid 1970s onwards, through non-elected regional development agencies in Scotland, Wales and Northern Ireland. Regional policy powers have always, therefore, been shared to some degree between national and local government in the UK, and between elected and non-elected organizations.

The 1980s and 1990s witnessed an extraordinary flowering of regional and local organizations participating in regional policy delivery. This is true not only for the UK, but also for virtually every other EU member state. It is no coincidence that this explosion of regional and local participation has coincided with the rapid expansion of the EU's own regional policy. As chapter 11 has shown, large amounts of EU Structural Funds money has been given to regional and local organizations since 1989. The commitment of the EU to the principle of *subsidiarity* (the devolution of regional policy powers to the lowest tier compatible with efficient policy delivery) and to the concept of a *Europe of the Regions* has also driven this process along. The governance system is now very much of the 'participatory' type shown in figure 12.1. Typically, in the UK there are now no fewer than five jurisdictional levels involved in the delivery of regional policy (i.e. the EU itself, the national tier, and regional, county and local tiers). Within these five tiers there are literally hundreds of individual organizations actively participating as part of regional policy partnerships. Some of these organizations are elected bodies, others are wholly non-elected public sector bodies, and some are in the private sector.

Opinions differ sharply on why the rapid change in regional governance from hierarchical to participatory systems has occurred. There are a number of possible exlanations for the rapid growth of regional and local involvement in regional policy delivery:

1   *Radical reforms in the management of all aspects of modern government functions, including regional policy*   These have mirrored changes in the manner in which private corporations are managed. Changes in *corporate governance* have set fashions which have been adopted in the public sector. These are a key element in what has come to be known as the 'hollowing out of the state' (Rhodes 1996). The process has included extensive privatization of government functions and the deliberate limiting of the scope and types of state intervention. Greater deregulation of the economy has also taken place. In addition, central and local governments have opted for arm's-length delivery through semi-autonomous agencies as a means of limiting the role of the state. The use of agencies has been particularly widespread in regional policy.
2   *EU regional policy*   The emergence since 1989 of a powerful EU regional policy has strengthened the role of the regional and local tiers at the expense of the

nation-states. The motives here have been the EU's commitment to subsidiarity, partnership and a Europe of the regions (Tömmel 1998).

3 *Changes in the basic nature of regional policy*   Changes in the nature of regional policy since the mid 1970s have also encouraged the greater participation of regional and local tiers. Policies designed to stimulate indigenous development (e.g. through the encouragement of small firms, new technology and community economic development) simply cannot be run from the centre. Active regional and local participation is needed if they are to be successful.

4 *The distinctive role of regional and local organizations*   The distinctive advantages of the regional and local tiers are discussed later in this chapter. There has been a growing realization that regional policy simply cannot be parachuted in from above. The enthusiastic participation of regional and local partners can greatly enhance policy effectiveness.

5 *Political motives and the desire to improve democratic accountability*   Attempts to move government closer to the people have also strengthened the regional and local tiers.

An obvious question concerning the changing system of regional governance is how much further the process has to run. Opinions differ sharply. What is occurring with regional policy can best be seen as part of the wider debate on the power of nation-states. There is a long-standing controversy surrounding the extent of the erosion of the power of the nation-states both in Europe and in the wider international community. On one side are those who take an *intergovernmentalist* view and argue that it is the national governments that continue to determine precisely which powers are to be devolved, and which are shifted upwards to supranational organizations such as the EU. By acting as 'gatekeepers' between the EU and the regional organizations, nation-states such as the UK can also control the pace at which devolution occurs (Hoffman 1982). This *state-centrist* view of the world continues to have its adherents (Moravcsik 1993; Pollack 1995). Some more recent analyses portray the nation-states as *flexible gatekeepers* which are indeed seeing their powers erode, but which can step in from time to time to change the pace of the devolution process (Bache 1998).

On the other side are those who take a *neofunctionalist* view. Here the argument is that with regional policy, as with other economic policy powers, there is an inexorable process at work in which nation-states find themselves increasingly stripped of powers both upwards (to the EU) and downwards (to regional and local organizations). This process, it is argued, is both long-standing and one which will continue because of ever-increasing integration in Europe (Lindberg 1963; Caporaso and Keeler 1995). More modern *multi-level governance* variants of this view reach less stark conclusions on the decline of the nation-state (Marks 1993; Marks et al. 1996). Here the nation-states continue to have an important role to play in regional policy, but their powers are being continually weakened over time. Their influence must be brought to bear through partnerships and collective decision making in which regional, local and EU partners are also actively involved. Analysis of the many kaleidoscope policy networks which now exist in European regional policy has become a major focus of research (Rhodes 1997; Peterson 1995).

Understanding the system of governance within which regional devolution is occurring is extremely important for understanding the issue of 'who does what' in regional policy. Research on regional governance has been valuable in disentangling the networks and partnerships which have proliferated in regional policy. It is also clear that future steps towards greater devolution in countries such as the UK are likely to be driven as much by wider trends in political governance fashions as by economic realities. Nevertheless, even in a world of partnerships and collective decision-making processes, hard economic realities must still be faced. It is perfectly feasible to have a regional policy partnership that includes the EU, the national government, and a host of regional and local organizations. This is, after all, how the EU Structural Funds are now delivered. But partnerships are rarely made up of equal partners. The issue of which of the partners (i.e. EU, national, regional or local) *should have* the greater powers, and over precisely which elements of regional policy, remains a fundamental one which is not addressed in the governance literature. It is this issue which forms the focus of the remainder of this chapter. The approach adopted is to examine different 'states of the world' in which economic powers range from highly centralized to highly devolved levels of control. We begin with the most highly centralized state of the world possible.

12.2   The regional implications of centralized control

This section assumes that the state of the world is one of almost complete centralization of fiscal policy, monetary policy and trade policy. Regional and local authorities and non-elected organizations are assumed to have little, if any, economic power. This is an extreme case. Even the UK, with its long history of highly centralized government, has always allowed local authorities certain fiscal powers – such as raising revenue through imposing taxes on domestic property (e.g. the Council Tax) or through borrowing.

Where the levers of economic power are centrally held, two issues with profound regional implications arise. The first concerns regional policy itself. Should the all-powerful national government keep a firm grip on regional policy or should it provide regional authorities with a role to play? The second concerns fiscal, monetary and trade policy powers. Can these be manipulated by the central government in such a way that they help to solve the problems of the depressed areas? It is to these two issues that we now turn.

Should the central government alone control regional policy?

Complete centralization of regional policy would be an extreme situation. Even in the English regions of the UK, where there is a long tradition of centralized government control, local authorities are allowed to encourage industrial development within their own boundaries. In addition, various *ad hoc* regional organizations (such as the regional development agencies in the English regions) exist for the same purpose, and a number of government departments operate with decentralized administrations and regional offices. In England, for example, there are 10 separate Government Offices in the regions. These have been created to integrate the functions of three national ministries (i.e. the Department for Education and Employment, the Department for Environment, Transport and the Regions, and the Department for Trade and Industry).

Control over regional policy powers nevertheless remains very firmly with the central government as far as the English regions within the UK are concerned. This contrasts with the situation in some other countries such as the United States and Germany, where the federal structure allows local and state authorities considerably more latitude to mould their own regional development policies.

The case for strong central control over regional policy rests on four main arguments, as follows.

The central government has a legitimate interest in seeking solutions to regional problems

Regional policy does not exist solely for the benefit of the inhabitants of the assisted regions. Residents of non-assisted regions who do not benefit directly from regional policy may nevertheless benefit indirectly. If extra jobs are created in the assisted areas, there will be spillover effects into the non-assisted areas. This is because regional economies are very open, with input–output linkages and multiplier effects rapidly ensuring that economic effects leak away. Furthermore, the creation of extra jobs will increase tax revenue as more income is earned and will reduce government expenditure if fewer people are unemployed. In addition, a more balanced geographical development of the nation's industrial population may have social and environmental benefits, as well as helping to stimulate growth in regions otherwise facing persistent decline. Taxpayers in prosperous regions may well be willing to fund regional policy as a means of redistributing income to their fellow citizens (i.e. equity spillovers).

Since the benefits of regional policy spill over into non-assisted areas, there is a strong case for national government involvement in the development and implementation of regional policy (Armstrong 1997; Kervenoael and Armstrong 2000). The full benefits of regional policy are unlikely to be obtained if each region is left to work out its own regional policy independently.

Central government control is necessary in order to ensure that regional policy is adequately funded in the regions of greatest need

If regional policy were funded entirely by each separate regional authority, there would be little chance that regional disparities in economic welfare would be reduced. Disadvantaged regions would simply be unable to compete for mobile investment if the more prosperous regions decided to develop similar policies. Nor would they be able to adequately fund policies designed to help their indigenous industries to develop. The central government therefore has an essential role to play in controlling the pattern of regional policy spending. Its role is to ensure that public funds for regional policy are concentrated in the most disadvantaged regions. There are three main ways in which this can be achieved.

First, the central government can establish its *own regional policy*. This would be financed by the central government which would also control how, where and to whom expenditures are made. Regional and local governments are largely by-passed under this approach. Much of UK regional policy was traditionally of this type from its origins in 1928 through until approximately 1975.

Second, the central government can, if it wishes, allow regional and local author-ities a greater role in regional policy and yet still retain control of the pattern of expenditure by making intergovernmental grants to regional and local author-ities. Under this system the total amount of regional policy expenditure in each region is determined by the central government. Many countries with federal structures operate such a system, the prime advantage being that detailed deci-sions on how the money is spent and which development initiatives are pursued are left in local hands. Something resembling this system is to be seen in the block grants made by the UK central government to the Scottish Parliament and Welsh Assembly as well as to the various English government offices and regional development agencies (Spencer and Mawson 1998).

Third, the central government could use legal controls to prevent more pros-perous regional authorities outbidding and outspending the authorities of the disadvantaged regions. This is directly analogous to controls imposed by the European Union (through its Competition Policy) on the regional incentives offered by individual member states. The problem with controls is that they do not solve the fundamental problem of chronic lack of finance in disadvantaged regions. They tend to hold down the general level of spending on regional develop-ment initiatives.

Central government involvement is necessary to ensure the effective co-ordination of regional policy

Regional development policies are undertaken by national, regional and local agencies. It is necessary for the policies operated by these various authorities to be efficiently co-ordinated in order to avoid wasteful overlap and unnecessary con-flicts. Central governments are well placed to do the co-ordinating.

More importantly, the central government must ensure that the fiscal, monet-ary, industrial and trade policies under its control are closely co-ordinated with regional policy. Co-ordinating regional and non-regional policy effectively means that the regional implications of all policy changes need to be estimated so that these regional effects can be taken into account explicitly in deciding which policy changes are most desirable. If taxes are to be cut in order to stimulate the demand for goods and services, one type of tax cut may have more favourable effects on disadvantaged areas than another type of tax cut. Other things being equal, the tax cut more favourable to the disadvantaged areas would be the most appropriate.

Central provision of a regional policy instrument is sometimes more efficient

In some cases a strong argument can be made for central control of a regional policy instrument because it is simply more efficient to operate it centrally. Take, for example, the case of a regional policy which seeks to create jobs in disadvantaged regions by attracting more foreign tourists. Promoting the attractions of the disadvantaged regions in *overseas* tourism markets is very expensive and needs staff with highly specialized tourism marketing skills. There are clear *economies of scale* arguments here for having a single centrally controlled overseas marketing effort. Moreover, many regional and local organizations simply do not have the necessary critical mass of staff with the appropriate skills to run the policy effectively, or may not have the capacity to do the extensive research necessary to ensure that the policy is effective.

The arguments for national involvement in regional policy are powerful ones. Regional and local authorities, however, can muster convincing arguments to justify their involvement in the regional policy effort. Local knowledge and local experience are invaluable assets in constructing appropriate regional development programmes for specific areas. Encouraging local and regional involvement in constructing development programmes also provides opportunities for experimentation with different approaches as well as encouraging greater local participation. This has the additional advantage of enhancing the accountability of policy makers to the people they represent.

This section has suggested that central governments have a distinct role to play in devising and controlling regional policy powers. Complete centralization, however, would be a mistake. Local and regional authorities have detailed knowledge of their own areas and the problems faced by these areas and it is of utmost importance to utilize this knowledge to the full. Local input into the policy process is particularly important where regional policy is seeking to stimulate indigenous development by, for example, providing assistance to small firms. Despite a rapid growth in local authority involvement in economic development initiatives in the 1980s (Armstrong and Fildes 1988), together with the growth of regional participation examined in section 12.1, the full potential for local and regional organizations in UK regional policy has yet to be realized.

Can the central government manipulate its macroeconomic policy powers for the benefit of the disadvantaged regions?

Ideally, regional policy should be closely co-ordinated with other government policies, though in practice this occurs only rarely. It is already achieved to a certain extent through the co-ordination of regional and industrial policy in the United Kingdom: investment incentives are provided in order to stimulate national investment, but these incentives vary according to whether the region is an assisted area or a non-assisted area. Two objectives are being achieved simultaneously as a result of policy co-ordination.

The possibility of achieving greater co-ordination between regional policy and other major areas of economic policy must also be considered. The potential for utilizing fiscal, monetary and trade policies for regional policy purposes, for example, should always be carefully investigated since they are three very powerful areas of economic policy. UK membership of the European Union and the rapid evolution towards economic union and a single EU currency mean that there will in future be little scope for the use of monetary and trade policies by individual member states for regional policy purposes. This does not, however, preclude the EU itself from using monetary and trade policies for regional development purposes.

Fiscal policy: regional aspects of government expenditure and taxation

Fiscal policy instruments take two forms: automatic stabilizers and discretionary action. Many taxes and transfer payments are designed so that they will automatically stabilize employment and income by preventing large cyclical swings in business activity. Progressive income tax rates, for example, lead to an automatic increase in tax revenue as income rises, which is the required effect if cyclical fluctuations are to be minimized. A similar role is played by unemployment benefits on the expenditure side of budgetary policy. Benefit payments rise in recessions and so help to maintain expenditure at exactly the time they are required. Automatic stabilizers, however, have not proved adequate *per se* to avert serious recessions or bouts of inflation, and governments have consequently developed a wide array of discretionary instruments which can be used if and when required. The most important discretionary instruments on the revenue side are income and expenditure taxes. The yield from income tax can be altered by adjusting tax rates, or by adjusting the tax base of income earners. Taxes on goods and services can be similarly adjusted. The role of government expenditure as a discretionary instrument is obvious and needs no elaboration.

Extensive fiscal policy powers are available for controlling the level of demand in the economy as a whole. This raises the possibility that fiscal policy should be designed so that it deliberately discriminates in favour of disadvantaged regions in its effect on economic activity. Instead of an across-the-board expansion of aggregate demand, any required contraction or expansion of demand could be allocated between regions with a built-in bias favouring those most heavily disadvantaged. A regional bias in fiscal policy does, in fact, already exist: automatic stabilizers raise demand in low-income regions and reduce demand in high-income regions. This occurs, on the one hand, as transfer payments such as unemployment benefits flow into areas of high unemployment (Disney 1984), while, on the other hand, progressive income tax rates exert a restraining effect on regions experiencing a high level of income and employment.

The built-in regional bias of automatic stabilizers has long been known. Income tax, National Insurance contributions and social security payments all result in a narrowing of regional per capita income disparities. By contrast, taxes on expenditure such as VAT and excise duties have a perverse effect on regional disparities since they are regressive (Commission of the European Communities 1979). It is worth noting that the extent to which taxes are regionally progressive varies substantially from country to country, thus indicating considerable scope for changing the structure of taxes in order to achieve regional policy objectives.

It is usually the case that progressive taxes also tend to reduce regional income disparities, while regressive taxes tend to widen disparities. The introduction of a poll tax, the Community Charge, in England between 1990 and 1993 vividly

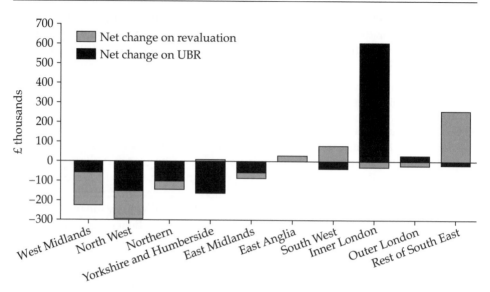

Figure 12.2 Changes to business property tax (rates) bills: the impact of the 1990 reforms in England.
Source: Denny and Ridge (1991), figure 1. Reproduced by permission of the Institute for Fiscal Studies

illustrated this principle. Poll taxes are extremely regressive taxes. The property tax which the Community Charge replaced was much less regressive. The result was a switch in the tax burden away from more prosperous regions with high property resources such as the South East and West Midlands towards less prosperous regions such as the North and North West (Barnett et al. 1990).

The regional impact of changes in taxation policy are rarely as clear as the poll tax. Every tax change is different, and the details of the new tax regulations can greatly influence the precise impact it has on each region. The introduction of the Community Charge in 1990, for example, was accompanied in England by a switch from a *locally* set property tax on businesses (Business Rates) to a *nationally* set tax (Uniform Business Rates). The impact of this major tax change on the different regions has proved to be complex. Extra complexity, however, was added by the fact that the government took the opportunity of the Uniform Business Rates to undertake a long-overdue revaluation of business properties to produce values on which the tax is calculated. Figure 12.2 shows the resulting regional impact of the combined tax/revaluation policy change. The two regions most badly affected, Inner London and the rest of the South East, can be seen to have been hit for different reasons. In Inner London, it was the switch from a locally set property tax to one set by central government which led to the biggest increases in taxation. In the rest of the South East it was the revaluation of properties which had the major impact (Denny and Ridge 1991).

Great care must be taken in analysing the regional impact of taxation policy. The regional impact of the removal of one tax and the introduction of another (as occurred in 1990 with the Uniform Business Rates) can be very different from the effect of *subsequent changes* to that same tax. In the case of Uniform Business Rates, for example, it has been shown that 'tax shifting' has occurred in the years since 1990. In regions such as Inner London, part of the extra burden imposed by the new system of Uniform Business Rates was subsequently passed on to the property owners (rather than renters) through the lower rents that the landlords were able to charge their tenants. The *effective incidence* of the tax therefore falls only partly on the business tenants and the remainder on the landlords. Attempts to ease the burden on businesses in areas such as Inner London by *cutting* the level of Business Rates can therefore be only partially successful since landlords will respond to the tax cut by pushing rentals up. With many Inner London landlords actually residing in other regions of the UK or overseas, it can be seen that the regional impacts of Business Rate changes are extremely complex (Bond et al. 1996).

A further way in which the government already operates a regionally discriminating fiscal policy is through its role as a purchaser of goods and services. Governments can affect the level of employment in particular regions by taking the geographical distribution of purchases into account when drawing up their spending plans. The food processing, engineering and vehicle industries, for instance, supply state-owned enterprises and government departments with a vast array of goods, and these linkages represent only the tip of the iceberg. The government has also in the past provided extensive subsidies to industries such as coal mining, which tend to be concentrated in the most disadvantaged regions.

Finally, the government is an employer in its own right. It therefore has the ability to create jobs in assisted areas directly. The Hardman Report (1973) suggested that over 30,000 civil service jobs could be dispersed from London to the provinces and considerable success in this direction has subsequently been achieved, particularly since 1979 (Jefferson and Trainor 1996; Marshall et al. 1997). Figure 12.3 shows that London and the rest of the South East of England have lost a significant share of overall civil service employment since 1976, while the South West, West Midlands, North West and Yorkshire and Humberside have been the principal beneficiaries of the relocation policy. It should be noted, however, that the relocation policy has taken place against a backdrop of persistent cuts in the numbers of civil servants in total (down by 38 per cent from the peak year total of 573,000 in 1976). The government continues to be keen that civil service departments should seek out lower-cost locations away from London.

Although the government does exercise some regional discrimination in its fiscal policies in the United Kingdom, the extent of this discrimination falls far short of the systematic planning that is required if regional policy objectives are to be achieved. The three main functional requirements for systematic planning are:

1   A continuing and detailed analysis of the regional impact of all major tax and spending programmes and of any changes planned for these programmes.
2   A mechanism for ensuring that the government considers the regional effects of fiscal policy changes before the changes are implemented.
3   Close co-ordination between fiscal policy and regional policy. This is needed if the undesirable regional effects of fiscal action are to be offset by regional policy measures.

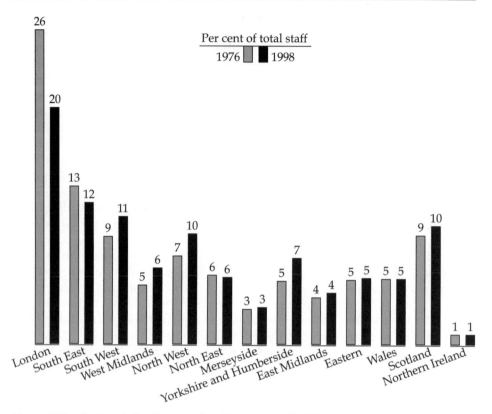

Figure 12.3   Regional distribution of civil service staff, 1976–98.
Source: Cabinet Office (1998), figure 9. Office of National Statistics © Crown Copyright 1998

A necessary preliminary to co-ordinating fiscal and regional policies is an under-standing of the regional impact of government expenditure and tax policies. It has long been known that *all* tax and spending programmes have their own distinct-ive regional bias (Short 1981). This is borne out by table 12.1 (HM Treasury 1999). The Treasury's analysis reveals marked differences between regions. Scotland, Wales, Northern Ireland and (within England) the North and London all benefit from the regional bias in total expenditure, with the East Midlands, the South East and the South West being well below the national average. As might be expected, the regional distribution of public expenditure within individual programmes reveals even greater regional disparities than when all programmes are taken together. The wide regional disparity in expenditure on trade, industry, energy and employment (see table 12.1) is exactly as expected since this programme is designed to be regionally discriminating.

The reasons for the regional pattern of expenditure in many of the other pro-grammes, however, are complex and varied. Sometimes the pattern reflects dif-ferences in regional preferences for public services. This is the case, for example, for housing in Scotland and Northern Ireland where local authority and social housing provision remains widespread. In other cases the needs and costs of

Table 12.1 Identifiable general government expenditure,[a,b] by region and function, 1996–7 (£ per capita)[c]

	North East	North West	Yorks/ Humber	East Midlands	West Midlands	South West	Eastern	London	South East	England	Scotland	Wales	Northern Ireland	UK
Agriculture, fisheries and food	28	27	27	26	25	26	25	24	30	62	198	115	251	81
Trade, industry, energy and employment	72	56	49	46	51	43	39	48	33	96	179	139	302	112
Roads and transport	87	130	100	93	113	97	87	245	107	163	202	188	116	167
Housing	49	66	55	45	29	42	20	157	40	61	120	96	147	70
Other environmental services	206	154	138	134	146	117	102	201	124	153	155	250	177	159
Law, order and protective services	214	198	186	166	183	166	153	367	157	267	265	230	632	275
Education	571	565	562	531	567	504	529	678	513	586	780	622	867	613
Culture, media and sport	42	33	34	30	29	31	29	39	32	49	57	33	23	48
Health and personal social services	828	809	800	718	762	766	694	974	726	831	1047	968	944	860
Social security	1778	1721	1538	1428	1515	1499	1373	1508	1368	1593	1719	1885	1907	1627
Miscellaneous	–	–	–	–	–	–	–	–	–	–	34	28	42	6
Total	3875	3757	3488	3217	3420	3291	3050	4241	3130	3860	4756	4553	5408	4017

[a] The analysis divides expenditures into 'identifiable expenditure' (expenditure which can be identified from the official records as having been incurred on behalf of the population of the region) and 'non-identifiable expenditure' (expenditure incurred on behalf of the UK as a whole such as defence and overseas aid or where 'who benefits' is not clear).

[b] 'Identifiable expenditure' attributable to the territorial units (i.e. England, Scotland, Wales and Northern Ireland) comprises 87 per cent of all expenditure, the remainder being mainly defence spending. Only part of the figure for England can, however, be disaggregated among the individual English regions (some 91 per cent the English total).

[c] Columns may not sum precisely because of rounding.

Source: HM Treasury (1999), tables 8.5b and 8.10. Office of National Statistics © Crown Copyright 1999

Table 12.2   The regional deployment of defence personnel (service and civilian), together with employment dependent on equipment spending (thousands of full-time equivalent jobs)

Region	Defence personnel 1980	Defence personnel 1997	Change in personnel 1980–97	Jobs dependent on equipment spending 1996–7
North	7.5	2.6	−4.9	5
Yorkshire/Humberside	23.9	14.0	−9.9	5
East Midlands	23.0	10.4	−12.6	3
East Anglia	16.6	16.0	−0.6	1
South East	189.4	96.2	−93.2	27
South West	100.9	68.1	−32.8	18
West Midlands	20.7	13.4	−7.3	5
North West	14.7	4.0	−10.7	8
England	396.7	224.6	−172.1	71
Wales	16.4	8.2	−8.2	0
Scotland	40.0	23.7	−16.3	7
N. Ireland	15.1	14.6	−0.5	0
UK	469.3	271.3	−198.0	79

Source: Defence Analytical Services Agency (1999), tables 1.12 and 2.4. Office for National Statistics © Crown Copyright 1999

some regions are greater in certain policy areas (such as roads or law and order in London). All too often, however, policy makers are simply not sufficiently aware of the regional effects of their decisions.

The key implication of the regional allocation of central government expenditure is that all government spending programmes have their own distinctive regional impacts. This is true even for defence and overseas aid, the two major categories omitted from table 12.1 because their benefits are enjoyed by everyone in the United Kingdom. Table 12.2, for example, shows the regional distribution of defence personnel in the United Kingdom, together with the regional distribution of private sector jobs dependent on defence equipment spending. As can be seen, in 1997 the South East and South West regions were the main beneficiaries from the injection of wage incomes associated with defence personnel, a major spending item in the UK government's budget. Spending on defence equipment has also led to jobs which are highly concentrated in the South East and South West (some 57 per cent of the total in 1997). The third column of table 12.2 reveals the regional incidence of cuts to defence personnel associated with the *peace dividend* arising from the ending of the Cold War. The dominance of the South East and South West as locations for defence personnel has meant that these regions have also suffered most from recent cuts in spending (Oakey 1991; Oakey et al. 1998). The sheer size of the UK defence budget, despite the peace dividend cuts, means that the existing regional distribution of spending does little to redress regional disparities (Lovering 1991).

Overseas aid, the other main category of expenditure excluded from table 12.1, also has a differential impact in different UK regions. This occurs because much UK overseas aid leads directly to orders for goods and services being placed with

UK firms. The North and Yorkshire/Humberside together with the East Midlands do particularly well out of orders for manufactured products, while the South East did best for service contracts (May and Malek 1990).

The frequently unexpected regional incidence of expenditure and taxes indicates a need for closer co-ordination between fiscal policy and regional policy. This co-ordination should be extended to all types of taxation and to all government expenditure programmes. The co-ordination should take two distinct forms. First, fiscal policy should where possible be regionalized. Tax and expenditure policies need to be systematically examined and changed in order to render greater assistance to the depressed regions. There are, of course, limits to how far this can be taken. Individual fiscal programmes must be designed to achieve their own objectives and these cannot be sacrificed in order to achieve regional policy objectives. Where the limits to regionalizing a fiscal programme have been reached, the second form of co-ordination should be brought into play. Regional policies should be introduced which counter any adverse regional effects of fiscal policies.

There has been a tendency to exaggerate the difficulties of 'regionalizing' fiscal policy. Two considerations, however, need to be kept in mind. First, the enormous magnitude of non-regional fiscal spending and of tax yields greatly exceeds spending on regional policy itself. Even the most modest of changes to the regional impact of government spending and taxation has the potential to dwarf the effect of regional policy. Second, wherever the regional effects of fiscal policy have been carefully measured, considerable scope has been discovered for changing their regional incidence. This is certainly the implication to be drawn from the indices of the regional incidence of government expenditure given in table 12.1.

Regional aspects of monetary policy

Even prior to entry into the EU, the use of monetary policy by the UK central government for regional policy purposes was strictly limited. Monetary policy instruments can be used to expand the economy during periods of high national unemployment in order to create jobs in those regions where unemployment is particularly high. But, as with fiscal policy, any expansion of aggregate demand by means of monetary policy will be limited by the effect this has on inflation and the balance of payments.

In principle, monetary policy such as the provision of easier credit facilities to firms and households located in depressed areas could be used in a regionally discriminating manner. Severe problems, however, would inevitably arise. A large proportion of the increase in demand will leak away into other regions as imports into the depressed regions expand in response to the higher level of spending. This problem is common to regionally discriminating fiscal policy and indeed to all regional policy measures. Attempts to regionalize monetary policy face even more formidable obstacles, however, because of the highly integrated nature of the monetary system. It nevertheless remains a possibility that certain aspects of monetary policy could be adapted in order to make expenditure in depressed areas more attractive, as for instance by providing firms with favourable borrowing terms when investing in new plant and buildings in assisted areas. The rapid process of monetary integration now under way in the EU is, however, greatly reducing the ability of either the EU itself or the UK government to use monetary policy to help depressed regions.

Regional aspects of trade policy

Trade policies, particularly the use of tariffs and quotas to control imports, have been widely used in the past to divert demand to home-produced goods. This was done either to give the domestic industry time to increase its efficiency so that it could compete with foreign suppliers, or to slow down the pace of decline so that resources (particularly labour) could be transferred to other industries.

These kinds of import controls tended to automatically favour some regions more than others as a result of regional specialization. The protection given to the UK textile industry in the immediate post-war years conferred benefits on those districts relying heavily on textile production. Most tariffs and import controls, however, were not designed specifically for regional policy purposes (Oulton 1973).

Regionally discriminating trade controls are now almost never used, for one simple but very important reason: all protectionist policies impose costs. Protection denies countries the chance to exploit the gains from specialization and trade. There are now, as a result, very strict limits on this type of policy imposed by the EU and by international agreements such as the World Trade Organization (WTO). Despite the loss of control of trade policy powers from nation-states to the EU, it is important to realize that the issue of the regional impact of trade policies has not gone away. EU protection of the farming industry against cheaper overseas imports, for example, has long been known to have adverse regional impacts within Europe (European Commission 1996).

12.3   Partial devolution: allocating fiscal policy powers to regional authorities

We have so far considered the central government's role in regional policy only in a situation where macroeconomic policy powers are controlled from the centre. A new dimension is added when macro-policy powers can be evolved to regional authorities.

The full devolution debate is outside the scope of this book. Indeed, the debate extends well beyond economic issues alone. In writing about the Canadian case, Scott and Breton argue that 'traditional ties to particular lands, language differences, historical enmities, race and sheer inertia combine in the rejection of complete unification', and the economic costs of devolution have 'little or no significance given the overwhelming political and cultural motives' (1975: 247). Our concern here is not whether devolution is itself desirable, or whether there is some optimum system of devolved government. We intend only to investigate whether devolution of economic policy powers can help to alleviate regional economic disparities.

Devolution exists along a spectrum. It ranges from complete centralization of economic power at one extreme to economic separatism at the other. This section examines situations of partial devolution. Only fiscal policy powers are devolved in this case. Monetary policy and trade policy remain the prerogative of the central government.

Regional government, as distinct from local government, has existed in the UK in the past only in Northern Ireland. Devolution proposals by the Royal Commission on the Constitution (1973) and the Scotland and Wales Bills of 1978 envisaged the creation of elected assemblies for Scotland and Wales which would have had limited expenditure powers. Up to 30 public services were identified as being suitable for control by regional assemblies. The proposals by the Royal Commission, however, did not envisage regional governments having any significant tax powers. Block grants from the UK government were the preferred method of finance (Heald 1983).

After many years of little progress, the devolution debate in the UK was dramatically revived in the 1990s (Scottish Constitutional Convention 1989; 1995; Scottish Office 1993). Following White Papers in 1997 (Scottish Office 1997b; Welsh Office 1997), and referendums in 1998, a Scottish Parliament and a Welsh Assembly were created in 1999. In addition, English regions have been encouraged to establish non-elected assemblies and have been allocated regional development agencies (Bradbury and Mawson 1997; Lynch 1999). These are potentially the first steps towards elected English regional assemblies. Attention here will be concentrated on the Scottish and Welsh cases since they conform most closely to the 'partial devolution' scenario which is the subject matter of this section. The English assemblies remain largely consultative bodies with almost no economic powers.

Table 12.3 sets out the main expenditure functions which have been devolved to Scotland and Wales, together with the position on revenue powers (i.e. taxation and intergovernmental grants). As can be seen, the UK has opted for a devolution process in which the different territorial units involved have been given different powers – a 'variable geometry' system of devolution. The Scottish Parliament has a wider array of functions than the Welsh Assembly. The Welsh Assembly in turn has more powers than the English regions. 'Variable geometry' will almost certainly continue to be the case should devolution to elected English regional assemblies ever be introduced. The English regional assemblies are most unlikely to either seek, or be awarded, economic policy powers on the same scale as Scotland and Wales.

Consideration of table 12.3 shows that the 1999 devolution measures for Scotland and Wales are limited and fall well within the 'partial devolution' scenario of interest in this section. The economic functions devolved are wholly fiscal policy functions (i.e. taxation and expenditure).

Focusing on the fiscal policy powers devolved, table 12.3 reveals that here too the extent of devolution is limited. Wales has been given no new separate taxation powers and must rely upon a block grant from the UK government. This differs very little from the pre-devolution system in which the Welsh Office of the UK

Table 12.3   Powers devolved to the Scottish Parliament and the Welsh Assembly

Scotland	*Wales*
Functions devolved	
All *except* specified 'reserve matters' comprising:	Functions previously exercised by the Secretary of State for Wales, comprising:
• foreign policy	• economic development
• UK constitution	• agriculture, forestry, fisheries and food
• defence	• industry and training
• border controls	• education
• macroeconomic stabilization policy	• local government
• common markets for goods and services	• health and personal social services
• regulation of employment, social security, professions	• housing
• transport safety and regulation	• environment
	• planning
	• transport and roads
	• arts, culture and the Welsh language
	• built heritage
	• sport and recreation
Legislative powers	
Yes	No
Revenue powers	
'Assigned budget' and limited income tax powers:	Block grant from the UK government utilizing the existing 'Barnett formula' approach
• assigned budget: a block grant from the UK government based on a population-weighted formula approach (the 'Barnett formula': House of Commons 1997)	
• power to raise or decrease income tax by a maximum of 3p in the pound: based on place of residence of taxpayers	
Size of budget under devolved control	
Block grant worth approx. £15b per annum (equivalent to around 30% of Scottish GDP). Max. income tax yield of around £400m (2.6% of the devolved budget and 0.8% of Scottish GDP)	Block grant worth approx. £6.6b per annum – half of all public expenditure in Wales
Relations with EU	
UK responsibility	UK responsibility
Relations with local government	
Legislative and policy responsibility (including funding of) local government in Scotland	Oversight of and funding of local government in Wales

Sources: Scottish Office (1997b); Welsh Office (1997)

government (with its own minister) was funded through a block grant. Scotland too continues to rely on an annual transfer from the national government, but has been granted some limited discretion to vary its income tax rate. No other tax powers are devolved to Scotland.

Despite the very small extent of devolution of revenue powers, the devolution of expenditure powers is still very substantial. The new elected bodies in Scotland and Wales will have substantial budgets and discretion over spending decisions for a wide array of programmes. Crucially for this chapter, the expenditure discretion covers all of the main programmes which underpin economic development policy, such as industry policy, training, transport infrastructure, education and agriculture.

The Scottish and Welsh assemblies are therefore excellent examples of the partial devolution scenario in which only fiscal policy powers are devolved. In line with traditional public finance theory, the central government has retained control of macroeconomic stabilization policy and also the main powers (through its retention of the main tax instruments) over income redistribution policy. Traditional public finance theory has always maintained that these functions can only be effectively provided by the central government.

By devolving fiscal spending powers the central government has ensured that the assemblies will focus on *allocation* decisions. It is the power to influence the provision of public goods and services which offers the opportunity to attain one of the most important benefits of devolution identified by public finance theory. This benefit is the ability of regional and local governments to provide a 'basket' of public goods and services which more closely reflects the wishes of the local community. The resulting diversity in the bundles of public services provided in different areas is an advantage because there exist substantial regional differences in tastes. Citizens in some areas prefer higher taxes and more public services to lower taxes and fewer public services. Citizens in other areas prefer the reverse. In addition, the preferred mix of public services differs between regions and localities. With decentralized provision of public services, citizens can increase their welfare by choosing a location which gives them their preferred combination of taxes and services.

As might be expected, there are difficulties even with this limited form of devolution, but the advantages of devolved provision greatly outweigh the disadvantages. One problem is that different public services have different catchment areas. Problems arise where the boundaries of tax jurisdictions do not coincide with the catchment area within which the benefits of these public services are reaped. Commuters into urban areas, for example, use and benefit from urban facilities financed by city dwellers while they themselves live in rural areas and pay lower rural taxes. Here, the tax jurisdiction (i.e. the city) is smaller than the benefit catchment area (i.e. the travel-to-work area). Compensatory transfer payments from one authority to another are therefore needed and this requires the co-ordinated action of adjacent authorities or the intervention of regional government to settle any disputes. Another problem is that the existence of too many jurisdictions can increase the costs of providing public services. These problems are, however, more important for local authorities than for large regional bodies such as those in Scotland and Wales.

In addition to the benefits from devolution in the form of a more efficient allocation of resources to different public goods and services, the devolution of fiscal powers to regional authorities poses two important questions of interest in this chapter.

Does the devolution of fiscal policy powers help or hinder regional policy?

The post-1999 system in Scotland and Wales is based on the premise that the central government will continue to control the total expenditure of the two assemblies. However, the assemblies have been given extensive powers over the allocation of their block grant between competing public sector expenditures. Such a system has several implications for regional policy. First, devolving expenditure powers to assemblies allows individual regions to develop their own economic development policies. This has the advantage of drawing directly on local knowledge and exploiting local initiative rather than relying on central government officials.

There are other advantages too. With each region developing its own distinctive policy, more innovative types of regional policy can be tried. Those providing regional policy would also be more directly accountable to the people they serve. A complete free-for-all, of course, is not desirable and has not been allowed in the UK. The central government continues to exercise control over the overall geographical pattern of regional policy expenditure through its control of block grants. There is also a need to co-ordinate the activities of the various regional assemblies and agencies to prevent conflicts of interest.

Concentrating on Scotland and Wales, we can examine further the important issue of whether devolution will lead to a more effective regional policy. One obvious point is that the newly elected assemblies in Scotland and Wales have very little in the way of *additional* devolved power over regional policy. By and large, with the exception of the income tax powers for the Scottish Parliament, the newly elected assemblies have simply inherited both the budget and the regional policy powers of the former non-elected Scottish and Welsh Offices and their respective regional development agencies. The fact that most regional policy powers in the English regions, as well as in Scotland and Wales, had already been devolved (to non-elected organizations) is the reason why some have argued that the case for elected assemblies is essentially a political one (Armstrong 1997; Newlands 1997).

The issue of whether devolution of spending powers can enhance regional policy is, however, still a very important one. We have noted already that tapping into local knowledge and expertise is important, particularly where regional policy is based on indigenous development rather than inward investment. Much more important is the fact that modern growth theory places much greater emphasis on *supply-side* policies than traditional Keynesian theory with its emphasis on taxation, spending and demand. By giving regional assemblies control over the key functions which can be used to drive supply-side policies, devolution offers the opportunity for a much more effective regional policy than one run by the central government.

Most economists who have analysed Scottish and Welsh devolution see the boost to supply-side policies and long-term growth as the key argument in support of devolution (McGregor et al. 1997; Newlands 1997). Whether these hopes are realized remains to be seen. By their very nature these benefits will be long term. Many require complex social and political changes, such as the building up of networks of co-operation and new norms of behaviour. These processes might work in some European regions, but may prove difficult to relocate to UK regions (Ashcroft 1998; Newlands 1997). A good example of the kind of innovation on the supply side which is possible, but which will require fundamental change to bring to fruition, is the creation of a virtuous circle of investment, borrowing and growth (Bell and Dow 1995; Dow 1997).

In addition to supply-side policy, the existence of regional assemblies gives the regions the chance to develop a more powerful voice in national and EU decision making. Individual regional assemblies, for example, can monitor the implications for their own region of any proposed changes in national and EU policy. Any expected adverse effects can quickly be made known to the central government. Finally, the existence of regional assemblies provides an opportunity for improving the co-ordination of development initiatives at local authority level.

It should be noted that the devolution of regional policy powers is not without problems of its own, particularly where a 'variable geometry' system is adopted as in the UK. Modern regional policy continues to place emphasis on attracting inward investment. Scotland and Wales have been particularly successful in this respect. There are dangers here in the kind of competitive bidding for inward investment seen among EU member states spreading to regions within the EU's member states. With the power to offer inducements to firms in regional hands, competitive bidding and the creation of a zero-sum game situation for inward investment projects is an ever-present threat. There is a case here for nation-states to follow the lead of the EU and use competition policy regulations to control the extent of this competitive bidding. In 'variable geometry' situations, such as that which now applies in the UK, there is also the danger that regions with fewer devolved powers, such as Wales and the English regions, will actively seek to boost their own regional policy powers. This may be necessary in order to compete with Scotland and Northern Ireland for inward investment, thereby triggering a zero-sum game.

The devolution of tax powers to Scotland represents a significant further step in fiscal policy devolution. Taxation is actively used as an instrument in regional policy, and giving regional assemblies a greater say in determining tax policies could be problematic. The issue of precisely which taxes are suitable for devolving to local and regional authorities has received a good deal of attention (Layfield Report 1976; Blow et al. 1996). Several considerations need to be kept in mind. Regionally controlled taxes should ideally be capable of generating sufficient revenue to cover intended expenditure. They must be easy to understand, fair, and efficient to administer and collect. Their yields must be capable of rapid adjustment as circumstances change. Changes in tax yield must be predictable when changes are made to tax rates; and they should have no significantly adverse effects on the rest of the tax system. These criteria suggest that income and sales taxes are the most appropriate taxes for devolving to regional authorities.

*Can fiscal policy be used by regional governments to stimulate
the demand side of the regional economy?*

The ultimate step in the devolution of fiscal policy powers to regional governments is when the central government relinquishes its control over each region's
total spending. As has been shown, this has not yet occurred in the UK. Disadvantaged regions would then be expected to use their tax and expenditure powers to
boost demand in their own regions. Such a policy, however, faces very severe
limitations. The most serious problem is that the central government would lose
control of fiscal policy. National public spending and national taxation would be
determined by the combined expenditure and taxation decisions of the regional
authorities. This would have serious consequences for macroeconomic stabilization
policy.

   Moreover, depressed regions cannot spend their way to greater prosperity for
two reasons. First, regional economies are open, with the result that a large proportion of any increase in regional expenditure would be spent on imports. The
expansionary effects would therefore leak away into other regions. This means that
any attempt to rely on the multiplier effects of public finance expenditures would
be doomed to failure. Second, the weak financial position of disadvantaged regions,
due to low income levels, would reduce the ability of regional governments to
raise the necessary finance for a substantial expansion of regional spending.

   If extensive fiscal policy powers were devolved to depressed regions, most
would face chronic budget deficits, which would greatly restrict their room for
manoeuvre (King 1973; Short 1984). Disadvantaged regions tend to have a weak
tax base and heavy spending burdens (e.g. unemployment benefits and infrastructure renewal). This gives them chronic budget deficit problems. Interestingly, this situation applies even in Scotland which, alone within the UK, could
count on significant tax revenues from offshore oil production. While Scotland
would have run a public sector surplus in the 1980s had it been able to access oil
taxes, by the 1990s falling oil prices have meant that annual public sector deficits
of between £6 billion and £8 billion have been recorded (McGregor et al. 1997).
The normal solution in federal countries to the chronic budget deficits faced
by disadvantaged regions is an intergovernment grant from the federal to the
regional government. This is a vital accompaniment to devolution, and is of
course precisely what has happened in the UK. Any attempt by a disadvantaged
region, left to fend for itself, to use taxes to meet a deficit would cause severe
problems. The depressed region would have to raise taxes substantially and this
would have detrimental effects on migration as well as reducing private expenditure in the region.

   Does borrowing offer a way out for regional governments which cannot finance
their expenditures through tax policies? The answer is negative. Any debts will
have to be serviced and eventually repaid. This means that the region's future
taxpayers would be heavily burdened unless the gamble of stimulating development within the region (with the borrowed funds) actually pays off. Higher
future regional incomes can then be used to repay the debt.

The problems highlighted here show just how restricted modern regions are in their use of devolved fiscal powers to stimulate the demand side of a region's economy. This is why so much emphasis is now placed on supply-side policies by regional governments. There is, however, one limited mechanism by which a region with extensive tax and spending policies can attempt to stimulate demand: the balanced budget multiplier. It has long been known that a region can run a balanced budget and still stimulate demand by raising taxes and spending simultaneously in equal amounts. Switching from private to public consumption leads to a small boost in aggregate demand. The decision to devolve income tax powers to Scotland has stimulated research interest in the possibility of triggering a balanced budget multiplier. General equilibrium modelling of the Scottish economy has shown that this effect is indeed a possibility, provided that Scottish taxpayers would be willing to pay the extra tax without trying to obtain additional wage increases to compensate; and provided that the subsequent boost to the economy does not run into major capacity and supply constraints (McGregor et al. 1996b; Newlands 1997). The boost to demand will, however, be small unless much bigger increases in tax and spending than are currently allowed take place. Even if the rules are relaxed, however, the prevailing wisdom is that most taxpayers would not agree to the kind of 'big government' which balanced budget multipliers need.

12.4   The complete devolution of fiscal, monetary and trade policy powers

Devolving fiscal powers to regional authorities is only the first of several steps that could be made towards the full-scale devolution of macroeconomic policy powers. Monetary and trade policy could both in principle be devolved to regional governments. This would open up further possibilities for providing regions with the means to cope with their own economic problems.

One immediate possibility which arises from devolving fiscal powers, monetary powers and trade controls simultaneously is that fiscal deficits can be at least partially met by an expansion of the money supply. If regional government securities, for example, find few buyers, the region's central bank could step in and purchase the securities, thereby increasing the region's money supply. This, however, would create both inflation and balance of payments problems for the region. One response to the balance of payments problem would be to restrict trade with other regions. Unfortunately, the consequent fall in trade would cause losses all round, since trade benefits all trading partners. Hence, even adding monetary powers and trade controls would do little to assist the depressed regions.

Devolving monetary policy powers to regional authorities opens up further possibilities. Specifically, each region could have its own currency. Such Balkanization of national currency areas has the advantage that it allows individual regions to compete more effectively in world trade by allowing their exchange rate to adjust in response to market forces. Effectively, the introduction of regional currencies allows individual regions to adjust more rapidly to changes in consumption patterns and production techniques. A decline in the demand for a region's exports would lead to depreciation of its currency and a consequent improvement in its competitive position. Export demand would recover as a direct result of the fall in the price paid by foreigners for the region's exports. The internal effect of the currency depreciation is quite straightforward. The rise in import prices (because of the depreciation) will reduce the real wage of workers in the region. This is the only way that the region can regain its former competitive position in the short run. Thus, by having their own fluctuating exchange rate, individual regions may be able to protect their competitive position, just as nations do.

All this seems to be a rosy state of affairs at first sight. In practice the problems facing separate regional currencies are overwhelming since beneficial trade and capital mobility are choked off by exchange rate volatility, and large fluctuations in incomes and price levels are also triggered. As a result, the case for separate regional currencies is now almost never advocated, and the EU has refused ever to countenance such a step.

Separate regional currencies have not, therefore, been seriously considered as a means of assisting disadvantaged regions. But even if separate regional currency and exchange rate powers are not used, there still remains the possibility of devolving powers to restrict interregional trade and interregional factor movements by means of controls. Such a policy would avoid some of the problems already discussed. The restriction of trade would raise the regional multiplier by reducing expenditure leakages through imports. This would enhance the effectiveness of regional fiscal or monetary policies, but the costs would be enormous. One of the greatest attributes of regional systems is the free movement of goods and factors of production. It is interesting to note that even the most ardent devolutionists within the UK have avoided advocating such controls and have sought devolution within the EU which precludes the sue of trade controls by regional governments. The costs of restricting interregional trade and factor movements would be so high for all concerned that this policy is not viable.

12.5   Conclusion

This chapter has ended on a pessimistic note. The full-scale devolution of fiscal, monetary and trade policy powers to regional authorities offers little hope of a solution to regional economic disparities. The rejection of what amounts to virtual economic separation does not, however, mean that centralization is the best policy. There are many different types of devolution lying between complete centralization on the one hand and economic separatism on the other. Our analysis in this chapter suggests two main conclusions.

First, there is a strong case for allowing regional governments greater freedom to develop their own regional policy strategies. It is through the manipulation of supply-side initiatives that devolution offers the greatest potential for growth. The strategies would, of course, need to be closely co-ordinated by the national government just as the regional government itself would need to co-ordinate initiatives between different local authorities. Second, the devolution of some fiscal policy powers, though not those allowing regional governments to expand their economies by operating major budget deficits, could have substantial advantages for depressed regions.

It is wrong to think that regional authorities in the disadvantaged regions can spend their way to prosperity. The realities of budget financing would prevent this. Their depressed condition makes it difficult for them to raise tax revenues, and borrowing on a large scale is simply not possible. Disadvantaged regions will continue to rely on transfers from the central government or the EU even if fiscal powers are substantially devolved. Since the central government will have control over these fiscal transfers, fears that devolving fiscal powers will threaten stabilization policy are greatly exaggerated. The danger is not that the disadvantaged regions will go on a wild spending spree, but rather that the central government will starve them of the fiscal transfers they so desperately need.

Finally, it should be noted that many countries (particularly those with a federal system of government) do seem to have found it possible to give regional authorities substantial powers over taxation and spending without this having significantly adverse effects on their control over the macroeconomy. This fiscal freedom in countries with federal governments may well help to point the way towards future developments in regional policy in countries with more centralized political systems, such as the UK. Some further relaxation of the rigid central control of fiscal policy than has occurred in the 1999 devolution legislation in the UK could stimulate the attack on regional problems from within the disadvantaged regions themselves.

Further reading

Ashcroft (1998); Blow et al. (1996); Kervenoael and Armstrong (2000); McGregor et al. (1997b); Newlands (1997).

chapter thirteen
The evaluation of
regional policy

contents

If government policies are to be efficient and effective, it is essential to evaluate each policy thoroughly and comprehensively. This is why so much effort is devoted to developing and improving evaluation techniques. Although much progress has been made during the past two decades, this does not mean that policy evaluation is now 'cut and dried'. Rather, it means that the evaluation of regional policy is now taken far more seriously and that more resources are being devoted to monitoring and evaluating the effects of government policies than ever before. Regional policy evaluation consequently took on a new dimension during the 1990s as a result of the need for methods of evaluating a wide variety of publicly funded regional development projects and programmes.

Given the very broad regional development responsibilities of the EU, it is not surprising that the EU's economic agencies have been at the forefront of developing a more comprehensive methodology for evaluating a wide range of regional development expenditures in different regions and different countries. At the same time, agencies within regions have been developing their own methodological frameworks in order to improve the quality of the evaluation process. The Output Measurement Framework (OMF) introduced by Scottish Enterprise, for example, has imposed a consistent approach to assessing the performance of publicly funded projects and programmes on the entire network of regional development organizations in Scotland (Scottish Enterprise 1997).

This research by economists into developing better methods of evaluating regional policy has been driven by the need to assess whether regional policy has been worthwhile. Policy makers therefore need answers to questions such as:

- What is regional policy expected to achieve?
- What effects is regional policy likely to have and what methods are available for estimating these effects?
- Which policy instruments are the most effective for achieving the objectives of regional policy?
- Does past experience provide any useful guidance about which policy instruments are likely to be efficient and effective?

Policy makers also need answers to rather more specific questions, such as:

- Are capital subsidies an appropriate policy instrument for creating jobs in areas of high unemployment?
- Should regional financial incentives be biased in favour of small firms and medium firms rather than large firms?
- To what extent are foreign inward investors influenced in their choice of location by the availability of regional financial incentives?
- How should regional development expenditure be allocated between alternative policies such as training schemes, business advice for small firms, and the provision of business premises to encourage new firm formation in depressed areas?

Answers to such questions are critically important if regional policy is to achieve its objectives. The first step in policy evaluation is therefore to be clear about the objectives of the policy. We need to know what policy makers hope to achieve if the merits of their policies are to be accurately assessed. This takes us to the first section of this chapter, which provides an outline of the evaluation process. The remainder of the chapter reviews the various methods that have been used, particularly in the UK, for evaluating regional policy.

13.1   The evaluation process

A policy must have objectives, and if policy makers are to be provided with estimates of the extent to which these objectives are being achieved, the objectives must be stated as clearly as possible. Ideally, they should be expressed quantitatively. For example, one of the major objectives of regional policy is to increase employment in the assisted areas. It is only possible to estimate the extent to which this objective is being achieved, however, if a target number of jobs is specified, and if the time period within which the target is to be reached is clearly stated. It is also crucial to spell out the extent to which the jobs created are full-time or part-time, and how long they are expected to last. Information may also be needed about the quality of the jobs created and at whom the jobs are targeted. Are the jobs, for example, aimed at the unemployed in well-defined target areas? Does it matter whether the newly created jobs are taken by in-migrants or by commuters?

In addition to specifying the policy objectives as precisely as possible, the policy maker needs to spell out the range of policy options available. We need to know (1) whether there are alternative ways of achieving the same objectives and (2) the relative costs associated with these alternative policies. The list of alternative policies should include any plausible *new* policy options as well as existing policy options and should include having no policy at all.

Having decided on the policy objectives and on the various policies available for achieving these objectives, the next step is to forecast the effects of each possible course of action on the target variables so that the various policy options can be evaluated. Only when the various policy options have been evaluated will it then be possible to select the 'best' policy option.

Finally, it needs to be recognized that evaluation is not a once-and-for-all event undertaken after a project has been completed, but is a process which occurs before, during and after a project's completion. In other words, evaluation involves three main stages, each of which is crucial to the evaluation process. These are as follows.

Ex ante appraisal

Appraisal is required before the decision to go ahead with a project is taken in order to assess whether it is likely to achieve its goals and at what cost to the exchequer. The aim is to answer questions such as:

- What are the chances of success?
- Are the benefits of the project likely to be worth the public expenditure incurred?
- Are there cheaper ways of achieving the same objectives?

Ongoing monitoring

Continuous monitoring is required in order to measure the effects of a project as they occur. This allows policy makers to adjust policy in the light of events as they unfold. Monitoring involves the collection and analysis of information which is essential not only in assessing the effects of projects as they occur, but also in the final evaluation phase of the project (which will require quantitative and qualitative information relating to the effects of the project). Monitoring is also required in order to check on whether public money has been used appropriately.

Ex post evaluation

At some stage after the completion of a project, it is necessary to make an assessment about whether public expenditure on a project has been economically and socially worthwhile. An *ex post* evaluation is needed to see whether the planned outcomes have been achieved so that lessons can be learned for informing future policy. In principle, *ex post* evaluation should be undertaken in a cost–benefit framework so that the net social worth of all public expenditures can be estimated. In practice, policy makers have to fall back on less rigorous methods of project evaluation, as will become clearer as this chapter progresses.

Policy evaluation is therefore a continuous interactive process. It may, for example, be necessary to revise individual policy instruments after gaining experience of their effectiveness. This interactive approach emphasizes the need to regard evaluation as an ongoing process. Policies have to be continuously appraised in the light of changing circumstances and changing needs. An illustration of the evaluation process is provided in figure 13.1.

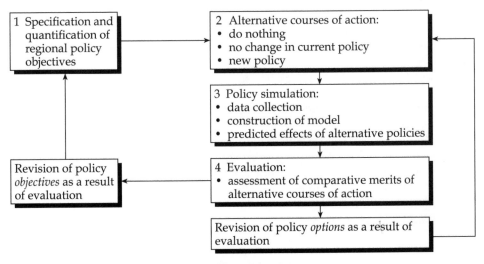

Figure 13.1 The evaluation process.

An example of the evaluation process: the guidelines set by Scottish Enterprise

A more precise statement of how the evaluation process works in practice is provided by the evaluation framework set up by Scottish Enterprise, which is the government agency with responsibility for regional economic development in Scotland. The evaluation methodology adopted by Scottish Enterprise is interesting because this agency has been at the forefront of adopting and implementing a clear set of rules for evaluating regional policy. The role of Scottish Enterprise is to stimulate economic development in Scotland through a wide range of policies. These include:

- promoting the formation of new firms
- encouraging the growth of small and medium firms
- encouraging inward investment
- enhancing the skill level of Scottish workers
- improving job prospects for Scottish workers
- improving the physical environment
- increasing the attractiveness of Scotland to tourists
- improving Scotland's export performance by raising competitiveness

The crucial role that Scottish Enterprise has played in Scotland's economic development policy has meant that it has acquired considerable experience in policy evaluation. Scottish Enterprise is also the focal point of a network of local economic development agencies (i.e. Local Enterprise Companies) and has developed a set of guidelines for evaluating economic development policies for the entire network. All local development agencies under the umbrella of Scottish Enterprise are required to use these *Output Measurement Framework Guidelines* (or *OMF Guidelines* for short: Scottish Enterprise 1997). They show the objectives of Scottish Enterprise, the range of policy instruments available and the range of variables used in the evaluation process. They are essentially a strategic tool designed to achieve a high level of cost-effectiveness in the allocation of scarce resources (Jackson 1998).

The Scottish Enterprise network has several functions. These include:

- setting the broad strategies for the network
- formulating policies
- deciding on the policy instruments to be used
- constructing and implementing economic development programmes
- appraising the programmes *ex ante*
- monitoring the programmes
- estimating the impact of the programmes
- evaluating the programmes *ex post*

The actual process of evaluation used by Scottish Enterprise is summarized in figure 13.2. The main purpose of the *OMF Guidelines* is to encourage consistency

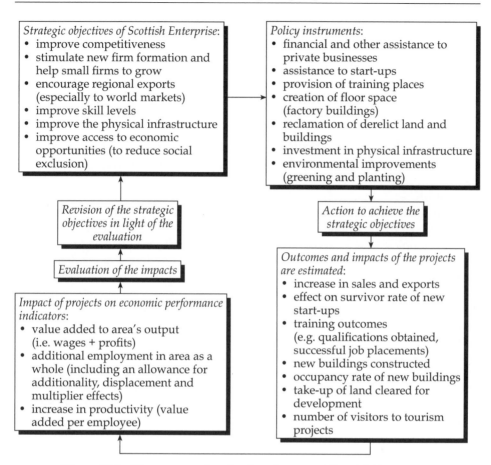

Figure 13.2 The process of evaluation: the case of Scottish Enterprise.

across the entire network of local economic development organizations in the evaluation process. These guidelines impose a common 'language' on all network members so that:

- partner organizations acquire expertise and evidence that can be used by all members of the network
- the evaluation of programmes and projects can be compared across the entire network
- funds can be allocated optimally between competing programmes
- the impact of all economic development expenditure can be summed across the network as a whole in order to provide an overall assessment of 'value for money'

The ultimate purpose of the OMF is therefore to help to improve the effectiveness of economic development expenditure throughout the entire system of local economic development organizations in Scotland. Learning from each other about which programmes and projects have been the most worthwhile will play a central role in this process.

We now turn to the many different ways that have been used to evaluate regional policy. The first focuses on the overall effect of regional policy on employment levels in the assisted areas as a whole.

13.2   Aggregate studies of the effect of regional policy on employment trends in the assisted areas

The earliest attempt to estimate the effect of regional policy on employment in the assisted areas was by Moore and Rhodes (1973). They estimated the impact of regional policy as a whole by comparing actual employment in the assisted areas with the employment level that would have occurred if the policy had not existed. This counterfactual approach assumes that trends in employment are determined primarily by a region's industry mix, but may change direction if a 'shock' such as regional policy is introduced. Trends discerned during a policy-off period are then used to estimate the counterfactual position during a subsequent policy-on period.

The importance of this early attempt at policy evaluation was that it induced researchers to construct economic models designed to explain the time path of employment rather than relying simply on the extrapolation of trends from policy-off periods into policy-on periods. These subsequent studies were also based on time-series data and used regression analysis to estimate the effect of several potential explanatory variables on employment changes over time, including the effect of regional policy. The dependent variable in these models is the annual change in regional employment. This variable is regressed on a number of explanatory variables including indicators of the strength of regional policy. As already noted, a variable likely to be of key importance is a region's industry mix. Its influence can be taken into account by calculating the growth in employment that would have occurred if all industries in the region had grown at national growth rates per industry. In other words, each industry in the assisted area is assumed to grow at the same rate as its national counterpart. The expected employment in each industry is then summed across all industries to give the employment level that would have occurred if each industry had grown at national growth rates per industry (e^*). Finally, a range of other possible influences on a region's employment growth are added to the model, which is specified as follows:

$$\Delta e_t = f(\Delta e_t^*, RP_t, X_t)$$

where Δe is the annual change in employment in industries eligible for assistance in the assisted areas, Δe^* is the expected annual change in employment in industries eligible for assistance in the assisted areas, RP represents regional policy instruments, X is the other possible determinants of employment growth (e.g.

wage costs relative to other areas, labour availability, access to finance) and t is time (in years).

In one of these studies, Moore et al. (1986) estimate the effect of capital and labour subsidies on employment trends in the UK's assisted areas during 1950–81. Their model is as follows:

$$\Delta e_t = f(\Delta e_t^*, INVEST_t, GRANTEXP_t, LSUBSIDY_t)$$

where Δe is the annual change in manufacturing employment in the assisted areas, Δe^* is the expected annual change in employment in the assisted areas, $INVEST$ is the present value of automatic Regional Development Grants per £100 expenditure, $GRANTEXP$ is the total annual expenditure on Regional Selective Assistance at constant prices (discretionary investment grants) and $LSUBSIDY$ is the total annual expenditure on the Regional Employment Premium at constant prices. It was found that the three regional policy instruments had a substantial effect during 1950–81 on employment growth in the assisted areas.

A potentially serious problem with such highly aggregated studies of the effect of regional policy on changes in employment is that they may conceal trends which can only be revealed in more disaggregated studies. For example, the effect of policy instruments on employment trends is likely to vary between industries and between regions. In some cases, regional incentives were designed to modernize older industries by making them more capital-intensive, thus resulting in a decline in employment, whereas in other cases the incentives were intended to induce entirely new industries to move into the assisted areas. In view of these criticisms, Wren and Taylor (1999) estimate a model disaggregated by industry and by region. This model allows for employment trends to be affected by a range of other variables, such as the growth in demand for each regional industry's output, in addition to regional financial incentives.

The findings of this study were somewhat mixed. Automatic investment grants were found to cause a decline in employment levels, the explanation being that the RDG has been used to improve efficiency and productivity, thereby reducing the capital/labour ratio. By contrast, labour subsidies (REP) led to an increase in employment, while discretionary grants (RSA) had mixed effects on employment.

The purpose of these regional-level studies of regional policy is to estimate the effect of each specific regional policy instrument on employment in the assisted areas. They suffer, however, from two defiencies. First, they fail to focus on those firms which have actually received financial assistance. The dependent variable in these aggregate studies is the sum of many different decisions reached by many different firms, the vast majority of which have not received regional financial assistance. Researchers have attempted to overcome this problem by estimating the effects of regional policy on the firms actually receiving government assistance. The second problem with these aggregative studies is that they do not allow for the wider effects of financial incentives on the competitiveness of the regional economy as a whole. These two criticisms indicate a need for more disaggregated approaches to estimating the effects of regional policy.

13.3   Estimating the effect of regional policy on inward investment into the assisted areas

During its heyday in the 1960s and 1970s, UK regional policy relied heavily on steering manufacturing industry into the assisted areas. The main policy instruments were location controls, capital subsidies and labour subsidies. Numerous studies have attempted to estimate the effect of specific regional policy instruments on inward investment into the assisted areas. Two main approaches have been taken: (1) attempts have been made to explain why the *aggregate* movement of industry into the assisted areas had fluctuated over time; (2) cross-sectional models have been constructed to explain the movement of industry between regions during specific periods of time.

Time-series models of industrial movement

The time-series approach to estimating the effect of regional policy on the movement of industry attempts to explain why the movement of industry into the assisted areas has fluctuated so markedly over time. Moore and Rhodes (1976), for example, argue that the movement of industry into the assisted areas has been influenced by four main variables:

- the pressure of demand in the economy as a whole
- investment incentives
- labour subsidies
- controls on the location of industry in non-assisted areas

The pressure of demand variable is included to allow for the fact that investment is higher during booms than in recessions. The potential effect of each regional policy instrument in determining industrial movement is self-evident. All three regional policy variables are expected to have a positive effect on the aggregate movement of industry.

   The effect of regional policy instruments on the movement of industry is estimated by first regressing the number of establishments moving into the assisted areas on the four explanatory variables. The regression equation is then used to estimate the effect of each policy instrument on the movement of industry. The method is very simple: once the equation has been estimated, each policy instrument is 'switched off' in turn in order to obtain an estimate of the movement of industry that *would* have occurred if that particular instrument had not been in existence. According to Moore et al. (1986), all three policy instruments identified above had a substantial effect on industrial movement: nearly 2000 manufacturing establishments are estimated to have moved into the assisted areas as a direct result of regional policy during 1960–81.

   An alternative approach to modelling the movement of industry was taken by Ashcroft and Taylor (1977; 1979). They argued that the movement of industry is

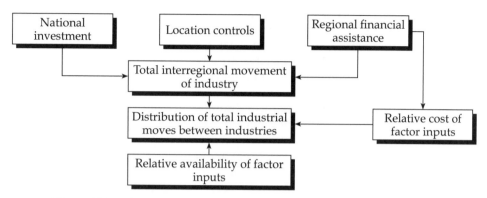

Figure 13.3   The generation–distribution model of industrial movement.

best treated as a two-stage process (see figure 13.3). In stage 1, the total movement of industry to all regions is assumed to be determined primarily by the national level of investment. In addition, total industrial movement may be affected by regional policy variables since location controls in non-assisted areas and the availability of capital and labour subsidies in assisted areas may be expected to induce more industrial movement than would otherwise have occurred. In stage 2, the spatial distribution of industrial movement is explained by factors which reflect the economic attractiveness of alternative locations. These factors include regional policy instruments. The Ashcroft–Taylor approach is therefore based upon the notion that industrial movement is first generated at national level and is then distributed between regions. This two-stage model is as follows:

$$M_t = f(INV_t, LC_t, GRANTS_t)$$

$$\frac{M_{at}}{M_t} = g\left(\frac{W_{at}}{W_t}, \frac{U_{at}}{U_t}, LC_t, GRANTS_t\right)$$

where M is the number of firms moving between all regions, INV is the national level of investment, LC is the strength of location controls in non-assisted areas, $GRANTS$ is the value of investment incentives to firms in assisted areas, M_a is the movement of industry into assisted areas, W_a is the wage rate in assisted areas, W is the national wage rate, U_a is the unemployment rate in assisted areas and U is the national unemployment rate. This two-stage generation–distribution model is therefore based on the idea that industrial movement is first generated at national level and is then distributed between regions according to their relative economic pulling power. This approach indicates that over 50 per cent of the industrial movement during 1960–71 was a direct result of regional policy.

Research on the movement of industry in the United Kingdom has concentrated on estimating the effect of regional policy on the number of establishments moving into assisted areas. Del Monte and de Luzenberger (1989) proceed one step further in their investigation of the movement of industry into southern Italy.

Their aim is to discover whether the inflow of firms into southern Italy from other regions had a positive or a negative impact on locally based industries. Two conflicting hypotheses are investigated. First, it has been argued that the inflow of firms into depressed areas will have an adverse effect on local firms since the latter will lose customers if the immigrant firms displace existing firms by producing competing products for the local market. In addition, potential entrepreneurs may be attracted to work for the immigrant firms rather than setting up on their own since the higher wages will reduce the expected rewards from creating a new firm.

The second (and completely opposite) hypothesis is that immigrant firms have beneficial effects on the growth of local firms through local supply chains and local multiplier effects. These may occur for several reasons. Immigrant firms may establish production links with local firms. Forward linkages will be established where immigrant firms relieve production bottlenecks and provide cheaper inputs to local firms. Backward linkages will occur when the expansion of output by immigrant firms results in local purchases of inputs. Another possible benefit to local firms is the transfer of technology that may occur as the immigrant firms bring in new techniques of production from other regions. Finally, the birth rate of local entrepreneurs may increase since the inflow of new firms from other regions may stem the out-migration of talented workers. The immigrant firms may also provide an appropriate training ground for potential entrepreneurs.

It is these two hypotheses that del Monte and de Luzenberger (1989) investigate in their study of the link between the inflow of firms into southern Italy and new firm formation during 1951–81. Their two-equation model (ignoring time subscripts) is as follows:

$$M_j = f(GNP, RP_j)$$

$$B_j = g(GRP_j, RP_j, M_j)$$

where M_j is the number of establishments moving into southern Italy (j), B_j is the birth rate of new firms in southern Italy, GNP is the gross national product, RP_j is the annual expenditure on regional policy in southern Italy and GRP_j is the gross regional product of southern Italy. The first equation argues that the inward movement of firms into southern Italy is determined by two factors: national GNP and regional policy. Both variables are found to have a significant positive effect on the movement of industry into southern Italy. The second equation argues that the birth rate of local firms in a region is determined by three factors: regional GNP, regional policy and the inflow of new firms into a region. Empirical tests indicate that the birth rate of local firms in southern Italy was significantly (positively) related to the inflow of new firms but not to the other two explanatory variables. Regional policy therefore appears to have had a positive effect on the inflow of firms into southern Italy, which in turn has had a positive effect on the birth rate of entirely new firms.

Cross-sectional models of the interregional movement of industry

Cross-sectional data provide an alternative empirical framework for modelling the interregional movement of industry. Twomey and Taylor (1985), for example, argue that the movement of industry between regions will depend upon three main factors:

- the size of the origin region and the destination region (since larger regions are likely to generate more moves than smaller regions and larger regions may be expected to attract more moves than smaller regions because of the existence of scale economies and larger markets)
- the distance between regions (since firms will normally prefer short-distance moves to long-distance moves in order to maintain close contact with existing manufacturing operations and existing suppliers)
- the relative economic attractiveness of each region (including the effect of regional policy on economic attractiveness)

The inclusion of the size of the origin and destination regions in the interregional movement model, together with the distance between regions, is based on the gravity model. This model can now be applied to industrial movement. It is argued that the movement of industry between any two regions (i and j) is positively related to the stock of plants in both i and j, and negatively related to the distance between i and j. The model can be extended to incorporate variables which measure differences in the relative economic attractiveness of the origin and destination regions. The model to be estimated is as follows:

$$M_{ij} = f(P_i, P_j, DIST_{ij}, ATTRACT_{ij})$$

where M_{ij} is the number of establishments moving from region i to region j, P_i is the number of plants in region i, P_j is the number of plants in region j, $DIST_{ij}$ is the distance between region i and region j, and $ATTRACT_{ij}$ is the relative economic attractiveness of regions i and j (e.g. wage rate in j *minus* wage rate in i).

According to surveys of industrial movement, a wide range of factors is likely to determine the relative economic attractiveness of each region. These suggest that location decisions are influenced by factors such as: financial incentives, the availability of labour, controls on the location of industry, transport links, access to markets, and the availability of industrial sites and industrial buildings (Munday 1990). In an investigation of over 900 firms moving into new establishments in the Strathclyde region in Scotland during 1981–91, for example, accessibilities to markets, suppliers, support services and staff were all found to have a significant effect on the location decision (McQuaid et al. 1996). It was also found, however, that large firms were far more likely to be influenced by access to markets and to relevant staff than are small firms. Furthermore, firms moving into Strathclyde from outside the area were more likely to be influenced by access to suppliers in deciding upon a suitable location. Different types of firms are therefore influenced in different ways by the same set of location factors. Ideally, this means that the statistical analysis of industrial movement should be undertaken with micro-level (firm-level) data, but this requires far more data than are often available in practice. Researchers have therefore had to fall back on more aggregrative approaches such as the one discussed in this section.

Once the variables likely to influence the spatial pattern of industrial movement have been identified, multiple regression techniques can then be employed to estimate the effect of each variable on the movement of industry between each pair of regions (M_{ij}). Once the effect of the various determinants of M_{ij} have been identified and measured, it is then possible to provide estimates of the effect of individual regional policy instruments on M_{ij}. This is done by simulating a policy-off situation. Thus, to estimate the overall effect of regional policy on M_{ij}, the policy instruments are simply 'switched off' in order to provide an estimate of what M_{ij} would have been in the absence of regional policy. The results of this exercise indicated that about 42 per cent of all manufacturing industry moves in Great Britain during 1960–77 were due to location controls (29 per cent) and investment incentives (13 per cent). In addition, the three main assisted areas (Scotland, Wales and the North) were estimated to have benefited substantially from regional policy. Analyses at county level produce similar results (Taylor and Twomey 1988).

Despite the relative success of these various investigations of the effect of regional policy on the movement of industry into the UK's assisted areas, this approach has not been followed up in subsequent research work. There are three main reasons for this. First, regional policy has switched away from encouraging firms to move from non-assisted areas to assisted areas since this job diversion was thought to be too costly for the regional and national benefits likely to be gained. Second, regional policy has been refocused towards stimulating indigenous growth in the assisted areas themselves. Third, increasing emphasis has been placed on attracting foreign investors into the assisted areas since this means that the economy as a whole will gain rather than there simply being a geographical redistribution of jobs.

13.4   Regional policy and foreign inward investment

Foreign direct investment (FDI) has played a substantial part in the economic development plans of many countries, particularly in developing economies. It has also played an important part in the regional development policies of the industrialized world, particularly during the past two decades. The importance of FDI varies considerably, however, between countries. For example, the USA and Europe are both leading importers of FDI as well as being leading exporters of FDI, while Japan is a leading exporter of FDI but imports very little FDI.

The UK has been particularly attractive to FDI originating in the USA and Japan over recent decades, having attracted over 40 per cent of total FDI flowing into Europe from these two major sources (see table 13.1). The popularity of the UK to US investors is probably explained as much by the long-term historical

Table 13.1   The distribution of foreign direct investment in the European Union, 1983–96

Destination country	GDP as a % of EU's GDP, 1996	Origin of foreign inward investment: % of total 1983–96	
		USA	Japan
UK	16.4	43	41
Germany	24.4	17	9
Netherlands	4.4	9	24
France	17.9	11	8
Italy	15.0	6	0
Other	21.9	14	18
Total	100	100	100

Source: Christodoulou (1996: 41)

Table 13.2   Reasons for foreign-owned firms locating their plant in the UK

Reason given for locating in UK	% of firms replying 'very important'
Capturing new markets in:	
UK	70
EU	50
Elsewhere in world	17
Strengthening existing market share in:	
UK	57
EU	57
Elsewhere in world	17
Growth of firm	40
Need for physical presence near market	40
Global strategy of company	30
Lower labour costs	13
English language	13
Access to skills	10
Government policy stance	7

Source: PA Cambridge Economic Consultants (1995a)

relationship between these two countries as by any other factor. It has also been extensively argued that the UK's 'welcoming attitude' to foreign inward investors over many decades and its key position as a bridgehead to the Single European Market has also played a major role in attracting FDI from the USA and Japan (see table 13.2).

The sheer magnitude of FDI across the world economy has meant that individual countries have seen this as a potentially effective method of stimulating economic development in lagging regions. In the USA, for example, individual states have attempted to attract FDI though tax incentives, investment subsidies, provision of industrial sites and infrastructure, and by being proactive in enticing

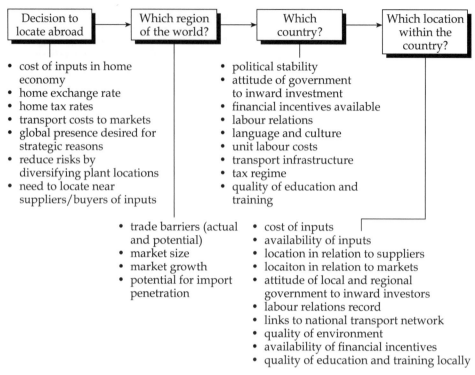

Figure 13.4 The location decision: potential determinants.

foreign firms to invest within their borders. Similar policies have been used in the UK and other member states of the EU.

It is not therefore surprising to find that several studies have attempted to estimate the impact of regional policy incentives on the location decisions of foreign inward investors. The general framework underlying these studies is based on the idea that the location decision of foreign investors divides into three stages. First, foreign firms have to decide that they wish to locate abroad. There may be several reasons for this, such as a desire to locate nearer to major markets or because production costs are too high at home. Several other reasons for this desire to set up plants abroad are given in figure 13.4. Second, having decided to set up new plants abroad, foreign firms then have to decide in which country to locate. Again, a wide range of factors will come into play. These will include: language, culture, attitude of the government towards inward investment, political stability, production costs, quality of the workforce, and the availability of financial and other incentives. Finally, foreign firms have to select a location within the country of their choice and this will be determined by the relative economic attractiveness of alternative sites.

This framework has been used as a basis for several empirical investigations, predominantly in the USA and the UK. The aim has been to identify the main factors influencing the locational choice of foreign investors. US studies have

Table 13.3   Reasons for the choice of a particular locality

Reason given for actual choice of location in UK	% of firms replying 'very important'
Site/premises availability	53
Availability of labour	33
Presence of pre-existing company	33
Availability of skilled labour	30
Low-cost labour	20
Financial incentives	20
Utilities available (water/energy)	20
Road/rail connections	13
Proximity to customers	13
Air connections	10
Training provision	7
Good industrial relations	7
Proximity to suppliers	7
Image of location	3

Source: PA Cambridge Economic Consultants (1995a)

found a range of factors to be statistically significant in determining the locational choice of inward investors' plant (Friedman et al. 1992; Coughlin et al. 1991). These include the following, where + denotes a positive effect and – denotes a negative effect:

1   Access to markets:
  - access to road, rail and air links (+)
  - access to a port (+)
  - access to the US market (+)
2   Labour market conditions:
  - labour costs (–)
  - labour availability (+)
  - labour productivity (+)
  - unionization of the labour force (+)
3   Promotional activities of the state:
  - state expenditure on economic development (+)
4   State taxes (–).
5   Access to land (+).
6   Industrial structure at the new location:
  - manufacturing employment density (+)

It is clear from US studies that regional development policy designed to attract inward investment into particular states is only one of many influences on the location decision. Similar results have been obtained for the UK. There is strong evidence, for example, that the availability of a suitable site and the availability of labour have both been influential in determining the geographical pattern of Japanese inward investment in the UK (see table 13.3). Regional financial incentives

Table 13.4 The regional distribution of manufacturing employment in foreign-owned firms in the UK, 1963 and 1994

Region	Employment in foreign-owned firms			
	1963		1994	
	(000s)	*(%)*	*(000s)*	*(%)*
South East	277.7	51.4	205.1	26.0
East Anglia	17.3	3.2	28.4	3.6
South West	4.3	0.8	46.6	5.9
East Midlands	20.3	3.4	28.4	6.5
West Midlands	45.9	8.5	113.6	14.4
Yorkshire/Humberside	20.5	3.8	57.6	7.3
North West	70.8	13.1	50.7	11.5
North	8.6	1.6	52.1	6.6
Wales	23.8	4.4	52.1	6.6
Scotland	45.9	8.5	71.0	9.0
Northern Ireland	7.0	1.3	20.5	2.6
UK	540.3	100	789.0	100

Source: Business Monitor, PA 1002

also appear to have had a powerful effect. The UK's assisted areas have attracted far more Japanese plants, for example, than would have been expected on the basis of their relative size (Taylor 1993). Some assisted area locations, however, have been far more successful in attracting Japanese plants than others, one possible reason for this being that 'success breeds success'. Once an area is successful in attracting FDI, it is easier to attract further FDI in the future.

There is, in fact, substantial evidence that inward investors are attracted to locations where there is already a concentration of firms in the same industry. According to US research, this pull of existing firms in the same industry on new plants is due to the presence of agglomeration economies which arise as a direct consequence of the clustering of industries in particular geographical areas (O'Huallachian and Reid 1997). This is supported by the high level of clustering of Japanese plants in the same industry in particular locations in the UK. This clustering of foreign investment has direct implications for regional policy makers since it suggests that once the initial breakthrough of attracting a major inward investor has been made, it will then be easier to attract further foreign investors into the area in the future.

The crucial importance of inward investment to the UK's assisted areas is widely recognized (Hill and Munday 1994; Stone and Peck 1996). Moreover, there has been a substantial increase in the relative importance of foreign-owned firms in the UK's assisted areas during the past two decades. Table 13.4 shows that there has been a considerable shift of employment in foreign-owned companies away from the South East and towards regions on the geographical periphery of the UK during 1963–94. These long-term trends continued through the 1990s.

Table 13.5   Foreign direct investment in UK regions, 1981–90 and 1991–7

Region	Estimated jobs associated with inward investment, 1981–90	Number of inward investors, 1991–7			
	Manufacturing (%)	Manufacturing		Non-manufacturing	
		(no.)	(%)	(no.)	(%)
South East	9.0[a]	86	5.4	161	24.7
East Anglia		29	1.8	76	11.7
South West	3.5	79	5.0	20	3.1
East Midlands	4.4	68	4.3	46	7.1
West Midlands	17.4	255	16.0	91	14.0
Yorkshire/Humber	4.8	122	7.7	43	6.6
North West[b]	11.6	176	11.0	68	10.4
North	8.7	179	11.2	48	7.3
Wales	13.6	242	15.2	42	6.5
Scotland	17.6	269	16.9	85	13.1
Northern Ireland	9.3	88	5.5	11	1.7
UK	100	1593	100	651	100

[a] Includes East Anglia.
[b] North West includes Cumbria for the number of moves.
Source: Regional Trends, 33, 1998, p. 158

Table 13.5 shows that the peripheral regions were very successful in attracting inward investors during the 1990s, particularly in manufacturing. These areas have varied considerably, however, in their ability to attract foreign investment, with Wales and the North having been highly successful (relative to their size) in the interregional competition for FDI. The importance of regional assistance in causing this geographical shift of foreign-owned companies towards the assisted areas is indicated by the fact that over 40 per cent of regional financial assistance has gone to foreign firms in recent years (Taylor and Wren 1997).

Finally, the location decisions of foreign inward investors into the emerging economies of South East Asia have been influenced by a range of factors similar to those identified as being of importance in the USA and the EU. Inward investment into China, for example, has increased phenomenally during the 1990s and investigations of its geographical distribution between provinces indicate that several factors have been influential in the location decision (Wei et al. 2000a). The coastal areas have proved to be particularly attractive because of:

- their location in relation to international trade routes
- their experience in exporting to other countries
- the geographical concentration of workers
- a workforce with experience in the manufacturing sector
- their preferential treatment by the government in the provision of infrastructure

Perhaps it should not be so surprising that inward investors have located in the most economically advanced areas along the coast, especially if the government has actually encouraged this to happen, as seems to have been the case in China. The next step, however, should be to make it more attractive for inward investors to locate in the poorer regions of the interior in order to redress the growing regional imbalance in productive capacity and economic efficiency. But this will require the government to lay the foundations by improving transport networks and investing in the economic infrastructure of these remoter regions.

The impact of foreign inward investors on domestic firms

Although the primary purpose of encouraging inward investment is to create jobs, income and wealth for the recipient region or country, especially in areas of high unemployment, there is ample evidence from several studies that inward investment may have very diverse impacts. The impact on the local economy will vary, for example, depending upon the types of linkages that emerge between the inward investor and local firms. These potential linkage effects have been carefully investigated by Turok (1993), who identifies two distinct sets of outcomes, which are referred to as *developmental* outcomes and *dependency* outcomes respectively. The aim of this theoretical exercise is to show that the consequences of inward investment for the local economy will be determined by the strategies of the inward investors.

In the *developmental* case, the linkages established within the local economy are characterized by collaborative activities based on sharing technology and knowledge between the inward investor and local firms. Linkages are developed in order to maximize the benefits of networking and the aim is to build up long-term relationships with local firms. The linkages within the local economy therefore become deeply embedded and local firms are encouraged to become involved in product development in order to increase competitiveness in world markets. The various potential outcomes are shown in table 13.6.

The predicted outcomes for the local economy are very different for the *dependency* case, which is characterized by inward investors whose primary aim is to minimize production costs in order to be price competitive. The relationship with local firms is therefore hierarchical rather than collaborative and the strength of the linkages is dominated by short-term cost considerations. The ties of inward investors to the local economy are therefore weakly embedded compared with the developmental case.

This distinction between developmental outcomes and dependency outcomes will not be as clear cut in practice as suggested in table 13.6 since individual inward investors may well have developmental relationships with some local firms and dependency relationships with others (Young et al. 1994). Moreover, the depth of embeddedness achieved by inward investors will depend on the extent to which the local economy is willing and able to invest in new technology, education, research and development, and in public investment in the economic infrastructure needed to support the emerging industrial cluster. The distinction

Table 13.6 The potential effects of inward investors on the local economy: the developmental case and the dependency case compared

	Developmental	Dependency
Type of local linkages	Collaborative Technological Trust	Unequal trading relationship Subcontracting to local firms Emphasis on minimizing costs
Duration of linkages	Long-term partnership	Short-term contracts
Degree of flexibility	Close relationship with local suppliers to facilitate product development	Weak commitment to local firms
Ties of inward investor to local economy	Deeply embedded Management functions highly decentralized to facilitate local control over operations	Weakly embedded Branch plant controlled from elsewhere in organization
Benefits for local firms	Transfer of technology and expertise to local firms Local firms involved in product development	Local firms contracted to make low-tech components
Quality of jobs created	Diverse range of jobs including high skill	Low skill
Growth prospects for local economy	Self-sustained growth through expansion based upon the new industrial cluster	Growth dependent on strategic decisions made outside the region by the multinational firms

Source: adapted from Turok (1993)

between these two very different potential outcomes, however, is nevertheless a useful one since it indicates that the consequences of inward investment for the local economy may be extremely diverse.

Surveys of inward investors indicate that domestic firms have benefited in several ways from contact with these newly established foreign firms (see figure 13.5). First, inward investors bring new management practices which domestic firms may observe and imitate. Second, domestic firms supplying inputs to the inward investors may have to work to higher standards and introduce new practices to win new business. Third, inward investors sometimes acquire domestic firms and will impose new management practices on new acquisitions. Fourth, domestic firms in competition with inward investors may have to revise their practices in order to maintain market share.

The impact of inward investors on UK firms has been investigated by PA Cambridge Economic Consultants (1995a). Three main types of impact are identified.

Impact on suppliers

A majority of inward investors were found to have an explicit strategy for developing supply networks in the UK. They are keen that domestic suppliers have appropriate quality assurance systems and product development activities. Many inward investors have taken the view that domestic suppliers have responded

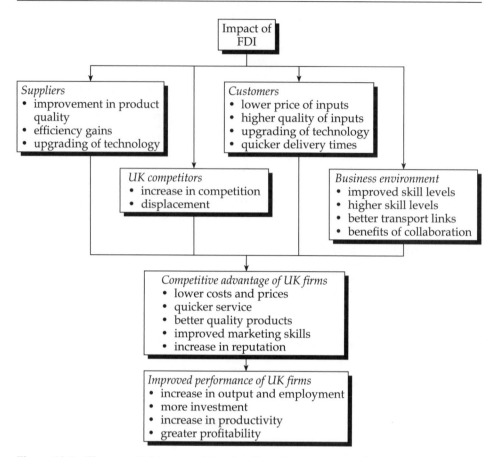

Figure 13.5 The potential impact of foreign direct investment on the performance of UK firms.

to the challenge by improving product quality while simultaneously reducing production costs, thereby improving their competitiveness. Similar views were expressed by the suppliers themselves, many of whom claimed to have changed their practices to meet the expectations and requirements of the inward investors. Many domestic suppliers stated that their association with inward investors had resulted in higher sales, higher employment and higher profits and there was very little evidence of any negative impacts.

Impact on competitors

Views about the impact of inward investment on their UK competitors diverged considerably between the inward investors and their major competitors. While the inward investors believed that their presence had beneficial effects on product quality, product design and production costs, the competitors themselves claimed that many of these improvements would have occurred anyway. On balance, however, domestic competitors agreed that the impact of inward investors had been positive and not negative.

Impact on the local economy

The impact of inward investors has obviously been highly visible in some local-ities simply because of the sheer size of some plants and the number of inward investors locating in relatively small local economies. The 'knock-on' effects of the direct impact through local supply chains vary from area to area, however, and depend upon the responsiveness of the local supply network. The largest quant-itative impact was found to be on business services; and the smallest impact has been on capital goods that are imported not just into the locality but also into the UK from the inward investor's country of origin. On average over all the firms investigated, it was found that for every 100 direct jobs created by the inward investor, about 30 additional jobs were created in the UK as a whole. In addition to this impact on jobs, the areas in which inward investors have located have benefited from increased market visibility and a general improvement in their image. This has helped to attract further inward investment into the successful localities. Local development agencies have also reported an improvement in labour force quality as a result of increased investment in education and training through the local further education system.

This detailed survey of a sample of inward investors in the UK therefore indicates that there are wider benefits to the economy more generally in addition to the jobs created in the localities in which they locate. Both suppliers and competitors appear to have gained from the inflow of foreign direct investment and there can be little doubt that successive UK governments have been correct to encourage overseas firms to locate their plant in Britain.

13.5   Surveys of assisted firms

Numerous attempts have been made to estimate the effectiveness of regional policy through collecting information directly from the recipients of regional aid themselves. The information collected is both quantitative and qualitative, the ultimate purpose of such surveys being to provide sufficient information to judge whether or not regional incentives have been worthwhile. Asking firms whether they have been affected, and in what way, by regional incentives has one distinct advantage over other methods: the firms receiving the incentives are asked for their views about the effect of these incentives on their own operations. A poten-tially serious drawback of such surveys is that so many factors affect a firm's operations that they may not know themselves what effect regional incentives have had. Furthermore, the recipients may be 'economical with the truth' if they believe that their answers could have an effect on the future availability of gov-ernment aid. Despite these problems, direct surveys of firms are thought to pro-vide useful information for the evaluation process.

Industrial surveys of the effectiveness of regional investment incentives have focused upon three main questions:

1   To what extent has regional aid affected a recipient firm's level of investment, output, employment and productivity?
2   Would the investment have occurred if regional aid had not been available?
3   What is the cost per job of regional aid?

An early example of the use of detailed firm-by-firm enquiries into the effectiveness of regional financial incentives is provided by Robinson et al. (1997), who surveyed 201 manufacturing establishments located in north-east England which had received some form of investment incentive. Using the results of this survey, Wren (1987) compared the relative impact of three types of grant: automatic grants awarded by central government available to all qualifying firms, discretionary grants awarded by central government, and grants provided by local authorities. Automatic capital grants and local authority financial assistance were both found to have greater effects on profitability, productivity and output than discretionary grants, but discretionary grants were found to be more effective in helping firms to develop new products and new processes. None of the three financial incentives had a significant effect on a firm's exports or on its R&D spending.

Deadweight, displacement and multiplier effects

The most important question to be answered in assessing the effectiveness of regional incentives is how many extra jobs are created in an assisted area as a consequence of such assistance. Information is required about:

*   whether the project would have gone ahead without government assistance (to identify the extent of *deadweight* spending)
*   whether the increase in employment is at the expense of other firms in the same local economy (i.e. are there *displacement* effects?)
*   whether there are any impacts on other firms in the locality through the *supply chain*
*   whether there are any *multiplier* effects on local economic activity through increases in household income
*   whether the additional jobs go to local residents or to commuters from neighbouring localities

These issues need to be investigated carefully if the jobs resulting from regional assistance are to be accurately estimated. Figure 13.6 explains the sequence of the analysis that needs to be undertaken.

To calculate the expected impact of regional incentives on jobs, it is necessary to calculate deadweight, displacement and local multiplier effects. Deadweight is not simply the probability that a project takes place as a direct result of regional

Assumption: a firm located in an assisted area expands its employment level and simultaneously receives financial assistance for a specific project

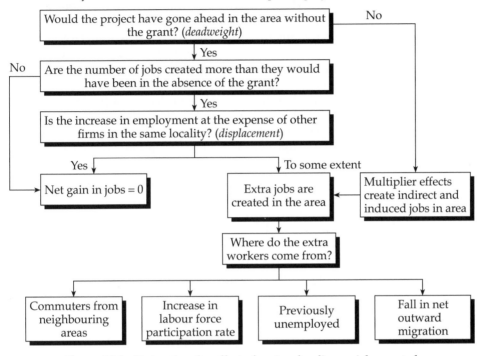

Figure 13.6   Estimating the effect of regional policy on jobs created.

assistance, but also takes into account the extent to which a project is larger than it otherwise would have been or occurs sooner than it otherwise would have done. If a project would have gone ahead without assistance, then no additional jobs are created. Displacement is the extent to which the project displaces jobs in other firms in the same region due to taking away market share from existing firms in the same locality. Finally, the multiplier effects of the project on the local economy are calculated from information about the supply linkages of the firm receiving the grant and from estimates of the household expenditure effects in the local economy.

The degree of deadweight is likely to vary considerably from project to project. A primary influence is likely to be the nature of the project itself. On average, deadweight has been estimated to be about 50 per cent of the direct jobs created (PA Cambridge Economic Consultants 1993). Not surprisingly, however, the amount of deadweight in assisted projects varies according to type of assistance. For example, Wren (1987; 1988) finds that deadweight spending is far higher for local authority financial assistance and for automatic investment grants than for discretionary investment grants linked to the number of jobs created. Deadweight spending was also found to be higher for new start-ups than for existing firms, which is not surprising since start-ups have a high death rate. The lower percentage of deadweight spending for discretionary grants is due to the fact that firms that qualify for assistance have to establish that they cannot obtain finance from elsewhere. The scrutiny of projects by government officials helps to weed out some of the deadweight projects.

An alternative way of estimating the job creation effects of regional assistance is to compare the employment trends of assisted firms with non-assisted firms. A control group is established by selecting firms which have similar characteristics to the assisted firms. The employment trends of the assisted firms are then compared with the control group in order to obtain an estimate of the impact of the assistance. The comparison with the control group allows the deadweight loss to be estimated since the experience of the control group is assumed to indicate what would have happened to the assisted firms in the absence of regional assistance. Hart and Scott (1994) use this method for assessing the employment impact of financial assistance given to small firms in Northern Ireland.

Despite its obvious attraction in producing estimates of what would have happened in the absence of regional aid, the control group approach suffers from a major drawback: the non-assisted firms may not be a reliable control group (Storey 1990). It may be extremely difficult to find a control group that possesses similar characteristics to the assisted firms. One obvious way in which assisted firms differ from the control group of non-assisted firms is that the firms in the control group did not apply for (or obtain) regional assistance. This may be because they did not desire to expand their activities whereas the assisted firms clearly did intend to expand their operations in some way. Ideally, we need a model capable of predicting what would have happened to the assisted firms if they had not received assistance.

Econometric techniques have also been used to estimate the impact of financial assistance on the employment level of firms. An example of the econometric modelling approach based on data obtained from assisted firms is the study by Wren and Waterson (1991). Data were first obtained from a sample of around 200 firms located in the north-east of England and this was then used to estimate the effect of several different types of financial assistance on employment trends. Since data were available describing the characteristics of each firm (such as industry group, firm size and employment level), these characteristics could be included as control variables in the regression model. This was then used to estimate the employment impact of financial assistance in order to obtain estimates of the cost per direct job created by each form of financial assistance. The relative efficiency of different forms of financial assistance could then be compared.

The cost per job of regional incentives: is the taxpayer getting value for money?

One simple device for estimating whether government expenditure on regional incentives offers value for money is to calculate the direct cost to the exchequer of the jobs created as a result of the grants awarded. This means calculating the *gross* costs per *direct* job created. The cost per job estimates can then be used not only to

Table 13.7 Net jobs created as a percentage of gross jobs created or safeguarded

Policy measure	Net jobs as a % of gross jobs created or safeguarded[a]
Action to support SMEs	
Venture capital	0.42
Advice to SMEs	0.42
Construction of business premises	0.20
Action to support mature SMEs	
Help with development and growth	0.53
Creation of partnerships and supply chains	0.14
Development of new technologies	
Support for innovations	0.87
Support for technology transfer	0.53
Support for advanced telematics	0.45
Measures to support new industries	
Construction of sites and premises	0.20
Improvements to transportation systems	0.09
Development of tourism	
Measures to attract more tourists	0.30
Improvements to town centres	0.14
Support for cultural activities	0.24

[a] Net jobs created = gross jobs created – deadweight – displacement + multiplier effects.
Source: 1997 Programme Wide Appraisal, PACEC, Cambridge

compare the cost per job of different types of regional aid but also to compare the effectiveness of regional incentives for different types of firms (Wren 1989).

This measure of cost per job based on the gross costs per direct job created has two potentially severe disadvantages. First, *gross* exchequer costs may differ from the *net* costs to the exchequer. If regional incentives create entirely new jobs, for example, the exchequer will benefit not only from tax clawbacks due to more people having jobs but also from reduced expenditure on unemployment and related benefits. Second, the *gross* jobs created may differ substantially from the *net* jobs created because of deadweight, displacement and multiplier effects. In fact, the difference between the gross and the net jobs created has been shown to vary substantially between different kinds of regional assistance. This is evident from table 13.7, which shows that support for tourism has a smaller net/gross jobs ratio than support for new technologies. What is needed, then, is an estimate of the *net* exchequer costs per *net* job created.

One of the first studies to attempt to estimate *net* costs per *net* job created was undertaken by King (1990), who calculated this revised cost per job measure in order to evaluate the effectiveness of the UK's Regional Selective Assistance policy during the 1980s. Estimating the net jobs created or safeguarded in RSA-supported projects is not, however, the end of the story. It is also essential to estimate how long the jobs will last. King makes the simple (but plausible) assumption that the jobs will last as long as the capital assets are in use. The estimated lifetime of the capital assets is therefore used to approximate the duration of the jobs. It is then possible to express this time stream of employment in terms of the total *job years* of employment which the project generates. It is estimated that expenditure on grants generated 1.1 million job years (i.e. 110 000 jobs per year for ten years). The equivalent number of *permanent* jobs associated with these 1.1 million job years is then estimated as follows (using the present value formula for a perpetual annuity):

permanent jobs = total jobs years × real rate of interest

Letting the real interest rate be 5 per cent (0.05), the permanent jobs equivalent of 1.1 million job years is 55 000 (i.e. 0.05 × 1.1 million). The estimated net cost per net job year was under £600 (at 1988 prices), which is an excellent return compared with paying out unemployment and related benefits. The main finding of King's study is that 'RSA did indeed have the effect of raising the level of employment in the Assisted Areas – and by substantial amounts' (1990: 85).

The purpose of King's study was also to discover whether the gross cost per direct job created could be used as a performance indicator for individual projects. On investigating the differences between projects, it was discovered that there was little correlation between the gross costs per direct job created and the net costs per net job created. Gross costs per gross job created cannot therefore be used with any confidence as an indicator of net costs per net job created. *Gross cost per job* was higher for foreign firms, for example, than for domestic firms, yet the *net* cost per job was very similar for these two groups of firms. The more favourable *net* cost per job for foreign firms is the result of smaller displacement effects for foreign firms, many of which would not have located in an assisted area without financial assistance. Indeed, some foreign firms would not have located in the UK without financial assistance.

13.6   *Ex ante* evaluation of regional incentives using the cost–benefit approach

Although policy makers need to evaluate regional assistance *ex post*, they also have to make judgements about the worthiness of projects *ex ante* in order to decide whether or not awards should be made. The most comprehensive approach to *ex ante* evaluation, though certainly not the only approach, is cost–benefit analysis. In a world of full information, the evaluation of regional policy would weigh all the social costs against all the social benefits so that its *net* social worth could be assessed. The centrepiece of the cost–benefit approach is the net present value (*NPV*) formula, which takes society's preference for consumption today rather than consumption tomorrow into account by discounting all future costs and benefits:

$$NPV = \frac{B_1 - C_1}{(1 + r)^1} + \frac{B_2 - C_2}{(1 + r)^2} + \ldots + \frac{B_t - C_t}{(1 + r)^t} + \ldots + \frac{B_n - C_n}{(1 + r)^n} - C_0$$

where B_t is the social benefit in year t, C_t is the social cost in year t, and n is the number of years over which the benefits and costs are expected to accrue. Benefits and costs are expressed at constant (base year) prices in order to remove the effects of any price changes that occur over time. A discount rate r is used to express future benefits and costs as present values. Provided that NPV is positive, the policy is judged to be worthwhile. The problem is to estimate B and C for all future years up to year n.

Regional policy is an amalgam of subsidies, training schemes and infrastructure projects. Its effects reach far beyond the firms receiving assistance and the direct jobs created by these firms. They include, for instance, the effects which spill over into other regions as a consequence of interregional trade flows as well as to firms not receiving policy assistance. The effects also include improvements in the stock of human capital and in the quality of the physical environment. The cost–benefit approach attempts to quantify the full range of effects and to translate them into measurable costs and benefits so that the net benefits of policy action to society as a whole can be estimated.

The wider costs and benefits of regional policy: beyond job creation

Increased output is the most obvious social benefit of regional policy and forgone output is the most obvious social cost. There are, however, a number of other benefits and costs which need to be considered. These are identified in table 13.8.

Table 13.8 The social benefits and social costs of regional policy

Social benefits	Social costs
Additional output arising from increased economic activity	Output forgone as a result of productive resources being transferred from elsewhere in the economy
Lower public spending on infrastructure due to less migration from high-unemployment to low-unemployment areas	Costs to firms of moving to a new location
Avoidance of migration costs to people who do not have to move out of the assisted areas to get a job	Resource costs of constructing new factories
Reduced congestion costs resulting from excessive growth of low-unemployment areas	Environmental costs of constructing new factories
Benefits of a more equitable spatial distribution of job opportunities	Infrastructure costs of regional policy
Non-economic benefits (political, social and environmental)	Administrative costs of regional policy

On the benefit side, reduced migration from assisted to non-assisted areas will lead to cost savings not only for those who do not have to migrate once jobs become available in their own areas but also for the government. This is because there will now be no need to provide extra infrastructure and public services in the non-assisted areas. A further benefit of regional policy is the reduction in external diseconomies such as congestion in the heavily urbanized parts of the non-assisted regions. This ought to lead to a reduction in congestion and pollution. Such externalities, however, are virtually impossible to quantify with any degree of accuracy and no one has yet provided estimates of the effect of regional policy on urban diseconomies. These particular benefits of regional policy are therefore very uncertain.

Since regional policy also aims to achieve greater equity in the regional distribution of job opportunities, it has been proposed that the cost–benefit method should be amended to take these distributional benefits into account. In principle, this can be done by attaching different weights to the costs and benefits falling on different groups of people. In order to favour policies which redistribute income from rich to poor, the weights attached to the costs and benefits are such that the weight for low-income groups would exceed unity and the weight for high-income groups would be less than unity.

There may also be political benefits accruing from regional policy. Needless to say, these cannot easily be incorporated into the cost–benefit equation. Regional policy may be used, for example, as a means of alleviating social and political tensions which arise in high-unemployment regions. This is undoubtedly a major driving force behind regional policy in many parts of the world. Yet these beneficial effects cannot be quantitatively measured and cannot therefore be included in the cost–benefit equation, even though they may be politically important.

On the cost side of the equation, the major item is the output forgone as a result of resources being used up by regional policy which would otherwise have been used to produce other types of output. Additional losses will be incurred if a firm's productivity is adversely affected by having to locate in an inferior location, or if firms decide to invest overseas rather than invest in an assisted area. Other costs include those arising as a result of the move itself and the costs of settling in after the move has been made. There are also the resource costs of factory construction, though these will only be included if they involve the use of resources which would not otherwise have been idle. Finally, there are the administrative costs.

The task of evaluating regional policy is made even more complicated when the macroeconomic implications are considered. Regional policy has to be financed in some way. The government can raise the finance needed for regional policy in one of four ways: it can raise taxes, cut other government expenditure, print more money or borrow from private investors. Each of these methods will have different distributional and macroeconomic effects on the economy. Such complications raise immense problems for the application of cost–benefit methods to policy evaluation.

Table 13.9 The overall impact of the Scottish Enterprise network

Impact	Estimated impact, 1991–6
Total expenditure by Scottish Enterprise network	£354 million
Private sector leverage per £1 expenditure by Scottish Enterprise	2.63
Estimated gross impact on employment in Scotland	78 180
Estimated net impact on employment in Scotland	25 200
Implied gross cost per net job created in Scotland	£14 050

Source: Jackson (1998)

Adapting the cost–benefit decision rule

Not surprisingly, the cost–benefit approach to policy evaluation is not used by policy makers for evaluating government subsidies due to its complexity and the lack of relevant data. The UK government has preferred to use a much simpler approach based upon an assessment of value for money, one such indicator being the exchequer costs per job created. It has been shown, however, that the cost–benefit approach can be modified in order to produce a more consistent and more reliable decision rule than one based simply on value for money indicators (Swales 1997a; 1997b). In particular, a decision rule based upon a simple value for money indicator can be derived directly from the cost–benefit decision rule and is therefore entirely consistent with this fundamental rule. In other words, if policy makers used this new decision rule devised by Swales, they would be implicitly using the cost–benefit approach. It is important to realize, however, that this new decision rule does not attempt to incorporate the wide range of potential costs and benefits associated with regional policy. A strictly limited definition of costs and benefits is used.

The UK Treasury requires government agencies to use the gross cost per net job created to evaluate applications for selective financial assistance. It is assumed that regional incentives do not lead to any positive macroeconomic effects and so it is the *gross* costs of a project which are appropriate, not the *net* costs. The Treasury takes the view that jobs are simply 'diverted' and not 'created', unless they would otherwise have gone to another country. This would be the case, for example, if foreign inward investors decided to choose another country for the location of their plant unless regional incentives were adequate. This is likely to be a major factor explaining the larger grant per job obtained by foreign-owned firms compared with domestic firms in the UK (Raines 1998; Raines and Wishlade 1997). The purpose of estimating the *gross* cost per *net* job created for individual projects is to assess whether or not the taxpayer is getting 'value for money'. An example of the use of this measure of gross cost per net job created is provided by Scottish Enterprise, which calculates this statistic for its entire expenditure each year. The estimates for 1995–6 are provided in table 13.9, which also shows the extra private sector expenditure estimated to have been induced by public sector expenditure (referred to as leverage).

The problem with this value for money indicator is that it does not provide the policy maker with a clear cut decision rule. In its present form, its use is limited to comparing the value for money indicator across projects. In addition, it fails to take into account the lower real costs to the economy of creating jobs in the assisted areas. It is consequently possible for a project to be rejected even though it may have a positive net present value to the economy as a whole. Swales (1997a; 1997b), however, shows that this value for money indicator can be converted into a decision rule which can be used for identifying all projects which have a positive net present value. An important feature of this decision rule is that it takes into account the real resource cost of each individual project. Specifically, it takes into account the extent to which a project results in unemployed labour being brought into use as a consequence of the project going ahead.

The great advantage of Swales's decision rule is that it is firmly embedded in cost–benefit analysis, which argues that a project is worthwhile provided that its social benefits outweigh its social costs. A simplified version of how Swales derives this decision rule is shown below. Swales begins by defining the net present value of a project as follows:

| net present value of project | = | value added by project | − | costs of applying for and administering the project | − | subsidy |

The value added V by the project to the assisted area is defined as follows:

$$V = R_n \alpha L (1 - d)(1 + m)(w - w^*)$$

where R_n is the present value of a £1 income stream discounted over n years, α is the additional employment as a proportion of direct jobs created by the project $(0 < \alpha < 1)$, L is the direct jobs created by the project, d is the displacement of other jobs in the locality $(0 < d < 1)$, m is the additional jobs created in the locality through supply chain and household income multiplier effects, w is the average market wage in the locality for the type of workers employed by the project, and w^* is the shadow wage (an estimate of the opportunity cost of employing extra workers in the locality).

This formula estimates the value added by a project by taking into account the deadweight, displacement and multiplier effects discussed in the previous section. The direct employment L created by the project is therefore multiplied by three factors, α, $1 - d$ and $1 + m$, in order to estimate the net jobs created in the locality. This estimate of the net jobs created is then converted into a monetary value by multiplying it by the difference between the local wage and the 'shadow' wage, $w - w^*$. The shadow wage has to be subtracted from the actual wage to allow for the fact that the extra workers employed in the region may have been producing some output even if they were unemployed. The assumption that the shadow wage is greater than zero therefore prevents the value added by the project from being overestimated. The higher the shadow wage, the lower the value added by the project.

The following decision rule is then obtained by substituting the equation for V into the net present value formula:

$$\frac{\text{cost per job}}{\text{wage}} = \frac{\text{subsidy}/L(1-d)}{w} = \frac{R_n[\alpha(1-\lambda)(1+m)]}{\alpha + c}$$

where λ is the ratio of the shadow wage to the market wage and c is the administration-costs/subsidy ratio. The left-hand side of this equation is simply the exchequer cost per net job created (allowing for displacement effects) divided by the wage. This equation gives the *maximum* cost-per-job/wage ratio consistent with the net present value being positive (as required for the project to be worthwhile). Provided that the ratio of the cost per job to the market wage is less than the numerical value of the right-hand side of the equation, the subsidy will result in positive net benefits and the project will be worthwhile.

Using plausible values for the parameters of the above equation, Swales estimates that the cost-per-job/wage ratio must not exceed 2.3 for a project to be worthwhile. For example, with a real interest rate of 6 per cent, R_n is 7.8. Assuming an additionality factor α of 0.5, a ratio of the shadow wage to the actual wage of 0.7, a multiplier of 1.3 and a value for c of 0.15, gives a value of 2.3, which indicates that the cost-per-job/wage ratio would have to be less than 2.3 for the subsidy to be worthwhile. This decision rule is very sensitive, however, to small variations in the shadow-wage/market-wage ratio λ and to the number of years the project is expected to last (and hence R_n), but it is relatively insensitive to small changes in the other parameters. This indicates that the maximum value of the cost-per-job/wage ratio will vary (perhaps substantially) between projects and between assisted areas, since the parameters themselves will vary between projects and between assisted areas.

The two primary advantages of Swales's decision rule are worth restating. First, it is directly related to the cost–benefit decision rule, which is the optimal approach to evaluating public expenditures. Second, it is relatively easy to use in practice.

13.7 Using large-scale regional models to estimate policy impacts

The use of large-scale models of the regional economy to estimate the impact of policy instruments on variables such as output, household income and employment has become increasingly popular in recent years. A prime example is provided by the annual updating of the Scottish input–output tables in order to provide policy makers with a tool for estimating the impacts of their policies (Alexander and Whyte 1995; Alexander and Martin 1997). The great advantage of input–output models is that they are able to provide detailed estimates of the impact on all industries of exogenous shocks to the regional economy, such as an expansion of output due to inward investment or the prospective closure of a large employer in a particular region.

   A problem with input–output models, however, is that they are based upon
unrealistic assumptions of how the regional economy operates and may consequently give poor predictions, especially when used for estimating impacts over
short periods of time. Input–output models, for example, assume that the regional
economy has an unlimited supply of labour at the going market wage, and that
the market wage is unaffected by any change in the demand for labour in the
region. More complex models have been constructed, however, which are able
to provide detailed predictions of impacts, but which also allow more realistic
assumptions to be made about the behaviour of the labour market in the regional
economy. Giesecke and Madden (1997), for example, use a large-scale econometric
model of the Australian economy to estimate the impact of various regional fiscal
policies on the Tasmanian economy. This model is used to simulate the potential
effects of increasing government expenditure and reducing a range of taxes in the
region. A different type of model is used by Harrigan et al. (1991; 1996), who
construct a computable general equilibrium (CGE) model of the Scottish economy.
This model allows the researchers to make different assumptions about how the
local economy operates, thereby producing different estimates of the effect of
exogenous shocks on the regional economy depending upon the assumptions
made. An example is the assumption that the regional labour supply is not perfectly elastic, as assumed by input–output models, but responds to market forces.
This allows the researchers to produce more realistic estimates of the impact of
regional policy on the Scottish economy.
   The way in which the CGE model takes into account the response of the labour
and product markets to a demand injection is shown in figure 13.7. The amount of
'additionality' provided by the project is first estimated. This involves estimating
the deadweight loss and any initial displacement of jobs due to increased competition resulting from the expansion of the assisted firm. The additional jobs
provided by the assisted firm will now have multiplier effects in the assisted area
due to supply chain effects and through increases in household income, which
in turn results in an increased demand for non-traded goods. At this point the
labour market effects 'kick in'. The CGE model allows for wages (and hence
prices) to increase as a result of the increased demand for labour. Firms in the
traded goods sector lose some of their competitiveness as a result of the wage
increases and this results in job losses. The net employment effects on the regional
economy of regional assistance are therefore somewhat less than they otherwise
would have been if wages had been set nationally and were unrelated to conditions in the local labour market.
   The estimated effects of regional assistance have been shown to vary substantially according to the assumptions made about the responsiveness of the regional
labour market to an increase in demand for labour (Gillespie et al. 1998). The
negative feedback from increased wages can substantially reduce the net effect of
financial incentives on employment in the long run, even allowing for the fact that
an increase in labour demand will induce net in-migration and an increase in the
regional participation rate (thereby relieving the labour shortage). For example,
the estimated impact of regional selective assistance on Scotland's employment

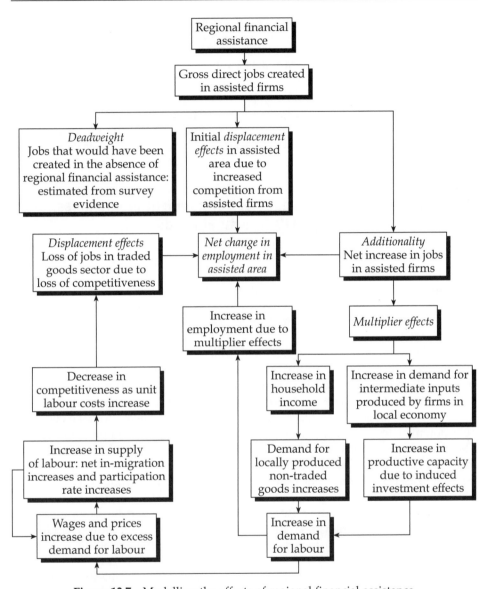

Figure 13.7 Modelling the effects of regional financial assistance.

level differs considerably between (1) an input–output model and (2) a CGE model in which wages are determined in the Scottish labour market. The simulation shows that the ultimate employment level after ten years estimated by the CGE model is 77 per cent of the employment level predicted by the input–output model (see table 13.10).

Table 13.10   The estimated effect of Regional Selective Assistance on jobs created in Scotland

Model	Estimated number of jobs created after ten years	Present value of job years[a]
Input–output model	9260	59 400
CGE model	7140	37 200

[a] The present value of job years (*PVJY*) is calculated by summing the number of *net* jobs created over a ten-year period, discounted at an annual rate of 6 per cent as follows: $PVJY = \sum_{t=1}^{10}[E_t/(1.06)^t]$.
Source: Gillespie et al. (1998)

13.8   Evaluation of regional development programmes: the EU's Structural Funds

The increasing financial commitment of the EU to regional policy during the 1990s led to demands for more thorough methods of evaluating this expenditure. Is the money being spent efficiently and effectively? Are there more efficient ways of achieving the same policy objectives? Answers to such questions are needed if confidence in an EU-wide regional policy is to be strengthened (Bachtler and Mitchie 1997).

One of the major aims of EU regional policy during the 1990s was to stimulate the growth of small and medium enterprises (SMEs). This aim is typically pursued through wide-ranging regional development programmes designed to correct 'structural weaknesses', such as the decline of a region's manufacturing industries. SMEs have been targeted because they are believed to have considerable potential for revitalizing the economic performance of depressed regions. The increased emphasis on SMEs stems from two factors. First, there was a switch in policy during the early 1980s from relying on diverting industry from non-assisted to assisted areas to one based upon stimulating indigenous growth within the assisted areas themselves. Second, the balance of EU regional policy has switched away from funding infrastructure projects towards providing more support for business enterprise. Regional development programmes funded by the EU have consequently focused increasingly on supporting SMEs located in the assisted areas (Turok 1997).

In view of the increased expenditure on regional policy in the EU during the past decade, the European Commission has recognized the need for improving the process of evaluation. This is indicated by the creation of a common set of guidelines for monitoring and evaluating these expenditures on regional assistance (Bachtler and Mitchie 1995). In addition to monitoring committees being set up in each region receiving EU regional aid and the submission of annual reports to the European Commission, all programmes are subject to both *ex ante* and *ex post* evaluation. Attempts have also been made to impose a common framework for evaluating regional development programmes. For example, a research programme (Methods for Evaluating Actions of a Structural Nature, or MEANS for short) was established in 1993 to develop common evaluation methods and to improve the quality of the techniques used to evaluate the Structural Funds.

An important feature of the MEANS methodology is that it urges those evaluating the Structural Funds to use a range of evaluation methods. Hence, top-down approaches based upon econometric, input–output and computable general equilibrium models can be used for estimating the aggregate effects of regional policies (as explained in the previous section), while 'bottom-up' approaches can be used based on surveys of individual recipients of regional aid. Not only does this dual approach provide a means of cross-checking the estimated effects, it also provides different kinds of information which results in a more comprehensive evaluation of regional aid.

It needs to be emphasized, however, that policy evaluation still faces many difficult problems. These include the following:

- programmes have many different objectives
- many different organizations are usually involved in any single programme
- a wide range of different policy instruments are used to achieve the objectives of a programme
- the outcomes of the programme are affected by many factors and it is difficult to isolate the effects of the programme from the influence of these other factors
- adequate and appropriate data are often not available for undertaking a comprehensive evaluation

These difficulties of evaluating regional development programmes have led to evaluations being dominated by a tendency simply to measure what is easily measurable. For example, targets such as the number of firms contacted, the number of businesses receiving some form of assistance, or the number of training places taken up are all easy to measure and have therefore been used as indicators of a programme's degree of activity. An example is provided in table 13.11, which shows the quantitative targets set and the numbers actually achieved in a recent evaluation of an EU programme to help small businesses in the Yorkshire and Humber region. But such quantitative measures fall a long way short of what is needed. A major problem with the target-setting approach to policy evaluation is that the targets are often defined too vaguely. An example is provided by the target set for the number of firms assisted without specifying exactly what 'assistance' means or how substantial the assistance has to be before being regarded as worthy of recording. In the Yorkshire and Humber programme, assistance to firms included *any* assistance at all, no matter how trivial.

Another problem with quantitative targets is that there is no indication of the quality of the outputs attained. This is evident from the quantitative measures of land improvements, the provision of business floor space and investment in other infrastructure. This inadequacy is also evident from the job creation targets, which say nothing about the quality of the jobs, who gets the jobs, how long the jobs are expected to last, or whether the jobs are part-time or full-time.

Table 13.11   Output targets and estimated attainment levels of the Yorkshire and the Humber Objective 2 Programme

Type of project	Quantitative target output	Estimated attainment levels
Number of firms assisted	20 700	58 450
Permanent jobs created	18 200	24 760
Jobs safeguarded	5 000	9 320
Jobs created indirectly (in other firms in region)	2 500	4 850
New firm start-ups	100	1 079
Improvements to land, industrial sites (ha)	400	769
Floor space constructed (m^2)	65 500	164 350
Access roads constructed (km)	16	22
Transport networks improved	8	103
New tourist attractions	15	106
Town centres improved	20	55

Source: table 4.1 in *Final Evaluation of the Yorkshire and the Humber Objective 2 1994–6 Programme*, Yorkshire and the Humber Universities Association; Millburn, Trinnaman La Court; EKOS Limited, May 1999

An even more fundamental criticism of the target-setting approach is that the targets could have detrimental effects on the underlying goals of the regional development programme. The programme managers may allocate resources to achieving the set targets even though experience with the programme indicates that the resources could be better used in other ways, such as achieving objectives which are not as easy to quantify. Devoting more resources to improving technology transfer within a region, for example, may well be a better way of helping a region's long-term growth prospects than trying to help a large number of SMEs. This is the case even though improving technology transfer inevitably means that far fewer jobs are created in the short to medium term.

For evaluation to be a useful guide to the development of future policy, it is necessary to obtain information about the effects of the policies on the recipients themselves and on the local economy in which the policy is operating. The aim should be to find out more about *how* the policies work since this is crucial for designing future policies. Some policies will work better in some local economic environments than others and this diversity of local environment needs to be taken into account in the evaluation process.

Given the difficulties of evaluating entire regional development programmes, Turok (1997) argues that it would be more fruitful to concentrate on evaluating clearly defined components of programmes. This would make it easier to compare the effectiveness of specific policy instruments across programmes. An example provided by Turok is the evaluation of business development projects designed to stimulate indigenous growth in two Scottish regions which received financial support under Objective 2 of the EU's Structural Funds during 1989–93. The purpose of this evaluation is to assess the quality of the way the projects were planned and implemented, and to estimate the economic effects of the projects on

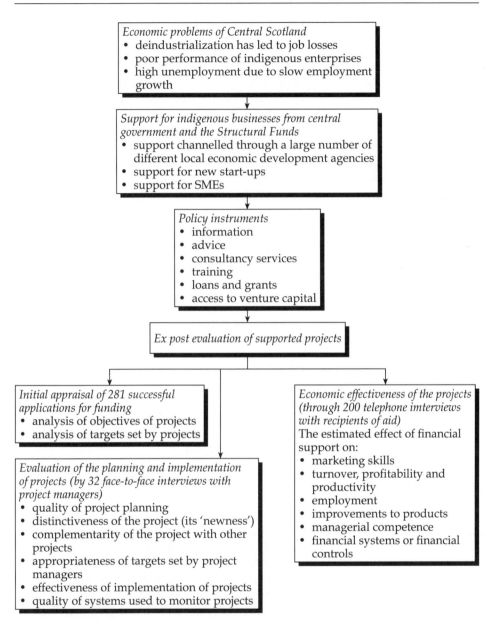

Figure 13.8 *Ex post* evaluation of business development projects supported by the EU's Structural Funds: a case study of Scotland.

the performance of individual businesses. The evaluation is done in three stages, as shown in figure 13.8.

- *Stage 1* The initial applications for funding were appraised in order to obtain an overall picture of the types of projects receiving assistance. What were the objectives of the projects? What targets were set? How many jobs were expected to be created or safeguarded?

- *Stage 2* Information was then obtained from the project managers in order to assess the quality of the planning and implementation of the projects. Were the targets realistic and appropriate? Were the projects distinctive? How effective were the project managers in implementing the projects? Were the projects well planned? Was the funding from the EU necessary for the projects to go ahead?
- *Stage 3* The effect of the financial and other support on the businesses themselves was estimated by collecting information from the businesses receiving support. To what extent did the support received by firms affect their profitability, turnover, marketing activities, productivity and the competence of the firm's management?

This example of an evaluation of regional development policy supported by the EU's Structural Funds is a clear demonstration of the qualitative approach to evaluation. Much of the evaluation relies heavily upon the subjective judgement of the evaluator, with the consequent danger that the results of the evaluation will be subject to wide variation depending upon who does the evaluating. This potentially damaging criticism is particularly relevant for evaluations which rely heavily on extracting qualitative information from managers, especially since the latter may have an incentive to give a favourable impression about the value of financial and other support to their businesses. Managers may believe that the best way to secure further support for their businesses is to report favourably on the effects of earlier support.

13.9 Conclusion

The evaluation of regional policy is a complex and difficult task. It involves far more than simply estimating the effect of regional policy on variables such as the number of jobs created and the increase in investment in the assisted areas. The estimation of such effects is an important first step in the process of evaluation. But if regional policy is to be properly evaluated, a much broader view needs to be taken of the consequences of regional development policies. Ideally, the full social costs and benefits resulting from regional policy should be estimated. In practice, this is not possible since the information needed for a comprehensive cost–benefit analysis simply does not exist. We have to be satisfied with second-best solutions, which effectively means that evaluation is limited to measuring the effects of regional policy.

Looking on the brighter side, there have been several significant developments in evaluating regional economic development policies since the mid 1980s with the result that regional policy evaluation is now in much better shape. Significant developments in regional policy evaluation have occurred in two areas. First, the application of econometric techniques has yielded some extremely useful information about the effects of regional policy on variables such as employment and investment in the assisted areas. As more quantitative data become available, increasing use will be made of econometric models, particularly for forecasting economic impacts of regional development policies. Second, the industrial survey approach has produced much needed data at the level of the individual firm and these surveys have resulted in improved methods of discovering the effect of incentives on the economic performance of recipient firms. These micro-level data have made it possible to obtain more accurate estimates of the effects of policy action in the local economies in which the recipients of regional assistance are located.

Surveys of firms have been particularly useful in providing information relating to the critical distinction between direct jobs created and total net jobs created. Clarification of issues such as deadweight spending, displacement, additionality and cost per job has helped to improve the methodology of regional policy evaluation considerably. This should not only improve the efficient allocation of scarce resources between different types of regional policy instrument, but also be helpful in establishing the appropriate share of national resources to devote to regional policy compared with other areas of government policy.

Finally, substantial improvements have been made to policy evaluation by imposing a common evaluation methodology on government-financed local economic development agencies, such as the Local Enterprise Companies in Scotland and the regions receiving EU financial assistance. Nevertheless, there is still much work to be done in the development of an appropriate and efficient methodology for evaluating regional policy. No doubt further significant strides will be made in the next decade.

Further reading

Del Monte and de Luzenberger (1989); Fisher and Peters (1998); Foley (1992); Friedman et al. (1992); Gillespie et al. (1998); Hill and Munday (1994); Schofield (1989a); Storey (1990); Swales (1997b); Turok (1989; 1997); Twomey and Taylor (1985); Wren (1989).

References and bibliography

Abler, D. G. and Das, J. (1998) 'The determinants of the speed of convergence: the case of India', *Applied Economics*, 30, 1595–602.

Alexander, C. and Barrow, M. (1994) 'Seasonality and cointegration of regional house prices in the UK', *Urban Studies*, 31, 1667–89.

Alexander, J. M. and Martin, S. (1997) '1994 Scottish input–output tables', *Scottish Economic Bulletin*, no. 55, 45–50.

Alexander, J. M. and Whyte, T. R. (1995) 'Output, income and employment multipliers for Scotland', *Scottish Economic Bulletin*, no. 50, 25–40.

Amin, A. (1994) 'The difficult transition from informal economy to Marshallian industrial district', *Area*, 26, 13–24.

Amin, A. (1999) 'The Emilian model: institutional challenges', *European Planning Studies*, 7, 389–405.

Amin, A. and Robins, K. (1990) 'The re-emergence of regional economies? The mythical geography of flexible specialisation', *Environment and Planning D: Society and Space*, 8, 7–34.

Amin, A. and Thrift, N. (1992) 'Neo-Marshallian nodes in global networks', *International Journal of Urban and Regional Research*, 16, 571–87.

Amin, A. and Thrift, N. (1995) 'Globalisation, institutional "thickness" and the local economy', in P. Healey, S. Cameron, S. Davoudi, S. Graham and A. Madani-Pour (eds), *Managing Cities: The New Urban Context*, Wiley, Chichester, 92–108.

Amiti, M. (1998) 'New trade theories and industrial location in the EU: a survey of the evidence', *Oxford Review of Economic Policy*, 14, 45–53.

Anderson, J. (1979) 'A theoretical foundation for the gravity equation', *American Economic Review*, 69, 106–16.

Anderson, K. and Tyers, R. (1995) 'Implications of the EC expansion for European agricultural policies', in R. Baldwin, P. Haaparanta and J. Kiander (eds), *Expanding Membership of the European Union*, Cambridge University Press, Cambridge, 209–39.

Antolin, P. and Bover, O. (1997) 'Regional migration in Spain: the effect of personal characteristics and of unemployment, wage and house price differentials using pooled cross-sections', *Oxford Bulletin of Economics and Statistics*, 59, 215–35.

Archibald, G. C. (1967) 'Regional multiplier effects in the UK', *Oxford Economic Papers*, 19, 22–45.

Armington, C. and Odle, M. (1982) 'Small business – how many jobs?', *Brookings Review*, Winter, 14–17.

Armstrong, D. (1999) 'Hidden male unemployment in Northern Ireland', *Regional Studies*, 33, 499–512.

Armstrong, H. W. (1988) 'Variations in the local impact of district council assisted small manufacturing firms', *Local Government Studies*, May/June, 21–33.

Armstrong, H. W. (1991) 'Regional problems and policies', in N. F. R. Crafts and N. Woodward (eds), *The British Economy Since 1945*, Clarendon, Oxford, 291–334.

Armstrong, H. W. (1993) 'The local income and employment impact of Lancaster University,' *Urban Studies*, 30, 1653–68.

Armstrong, H. W. (1995) 'Convergence among regions of the European Union, 1950–90', *Papers in Regional Science*, 74, 143–52.

Armstrong, H. W. (1997) 'Regional level jurisdictions and economic regeneration', in M. Danson (ed.), *Regional Governance and Economic Development*, European Research in Regional Science no. 7, Pion, London, 26–46.

Armstrong, H. W. (1998) 'European Union regional policy', in A. M. El-Agraa (ed.), *The Economics of the European Community*, 5th edn, Routledge, London, 363–88.

Armstrong, H. W. and Fildes, J. (1988) 'Industrial development initiatives in England and Wales: the role of the district councils', *Progress in Planning*, 30, 85–156.

Armstrong, H. W. and Taylor, J. (1981) 'The measurement of different types of unemployment', in J. Creedy (ed.), *The Economics of Unemployment in Britain*, Butterworth, London.

Ashcroft, B. (1998) 'The economic possibilities for a Scottish Parliament', *Regional Studies*, 32, 175–80.

Ashcroft, B. and Love, J. (1996) 'Firm births and employment change in the British counties, 1981–9', *Papers in Regional Science*, 75, 483–500.

Ashcroft, B. and Taylor, J. (1977) 'The movement of manufacturing industry and the effect of regional policy', *Oxford Economic Papers*, 29, 84–101.

Ashcroft, B. and Taylor, J. (1979) 'The effect of regional policy on the movement of manufacturing industry in Great Britain', in D. Maclennan and J. Parr (eds), *Regional Policy: Past Experience and New Directions*, Martin Robertson, Oxford.

Ashcroft, B., Love, J. H. and Malloy, E. (1991) 'New firm formation in the UK counties, with special reference to Scotland', *Regional Studies*, 25, 395–409.

Asheim, B. T. (1996) 'Industrial districts as "learning regions": a condition for prosperity?', *European Planning Studies*, 4, 379–400.

Asheim, B. T. and Cooke, P. (1998) 'Localised innovation networks in a global economy: a comparative analysis of endogenous and exogenous regional development approaches', *Comparative Social Research*, 17, 199–240.

Ashworth, J. and Parker, S. C. (1997) 'Modelling regional house prices in the UK', *Scottish Journal of Political Economy*, 44, 225–46.

Aturupane, C., Djankov, S. and Hoekman, B. (1999) 'Horizontal and vertical intra-industry trade between Eastern Europe and the European Union', *Weltwirtschaftliches Archiv*, 135, 62–81.

Audretsch, D. B. (1998) 'Agglomeration and the location of economic activity', *Oxford Review of Economic Policy*, 14, 18–29.

Bache, I. (1998) *The Politics of European Union Regional Policy*, Sheffield Academic Press, Sheffield.

Bachtler, J. and Mitchie, R. (1995) 'A new era of regional policy evaluation? The appraisal of the Structural Funds', *Regional Studies*, 29, 745–51.

Bachtler, J. and Mitchie, R. (1997) 'The interim evaluation of EU regional development programmes: experiences from Objective 2 regions', *Regional Studies*, 31, 849–58.

Bachtler, J. and Turok, I. (1997) *The Coherence of European Union Regional Policy*, Regional Studies Association/Jessica Kingsley, London.

Baddeley, M., Martin, R. and Tyler, P. (1998a) 'European regional unemployment disparities', *European Urban and Regional Studies*, 5, 195–215.

Baddeley, M., Martin, R. and Tyler, P. (1998b) 'Regional wage rigidity: the European Union
and United States compared', Department of Land Economy, University of Cambridge
(mimeo).

Bagnasco, A. (1977) *Tre Italie: La Problematica Territoriale dello Sviluppo Italiano*, Il Mulino,
Bologna.

Bairam, E. (1988) 'Balance of payments, the Harrod foreign trade multiplier and economic
growth: the European and North American experience 1970–85', *Applied Economics*, 20,
1635–42.

Baldwin, R. E., Francois, J. F. and Portes, R. (1997) 'The costs and benefits of Eastern
Enlargement: the impact on the European Union and Central Europe', *Economic Policy: A
European Forum*, 24, 127–76.

Bannock, G. and Daly, M. (1990) 'Size distribution of UK firms', *Employment Gazette*, May,
255–8.

Barkham, R., Gudgin, G., Hart, M. and Hanvey, E. (1996) *The Determinants of Small Firm
Growth: An Inter-Regional Study in the UK 1986–90*, Jessica Kingsley/Regional Studies
Association, London.

Barnett, R. R., Levaggi, R. and Smith, P. (1990) 'An assessment of the regional impact of the
introduction of the Community Charge (Poll Tax) in England', *Regional Studies*, 24, 289–97.

Barro, R. (1991) 'Economic growth in a cross-section of countries', *Quarterly Journal of
Economics*, 106, 407–43.

Barro, R. and Sala-i-Martin, X. (1991) 'Convergence across states and regions', *Brookings
Papers*, 1, 107–82.

Barro, R. and Sala-i-Martin, X. (1992) 'Convergence', *Journal of Political Economy*, 100, 223–51.

Barro, R. and Sala-i-Martin, X. (1995) *Economic Growth*. McGraw-Hill, Boston.

Batey, P. and Madden, M. (1998) 'Socio-economic impact assessment: meeting client requirements', Department of Civic Design, University of Liverpool.

Batey, P., Madden, M. and Scholefield, G. (1993) 'Socio-economic impact assessment of
large-scale projects using input–output analysis: a case study of an airport', *Regional
Studies*, 27, 179–92.

Bayoumi, T. A. and Masson, P. R. (1995) 'Fiscal flows in the United States and Canada:
lessons for monetary union in Europe', *European Economic Review*, 39, 253–74.

Bayoumi, T. A. and Rose, A. K. (1993) 'Domestic savings and intra-national capital flows',
European Economic Review, 37, 1197–202.

Bean, C. R. (1994) 'European unemployment: a survey', *Journal of Economic Literature*, 32,
573–619.

Beatty, C. and Fothergill, S. (1998) 'Registered and hidden unemployment in the UK
coalfields', chapter 5 in P. Lawless, R. Martin and S. Hardy (eds), *Unemployment and
Social Exclusion: Landscapes of Labour Inequality*, Regional Policy and Development 13,
Jessica Kingsley, London.

Beatty, C., Fothergill, S., Gore, T. and Herrington, A. (1997) 'The real level of unemployment', Centre for Regional and Social Research, Sheffield Hallam University.

Begg, I. (1991) 'High technology location and the urban areas of Great Britain', *Urban
Studies*, 28, 961–81.

Begg, I. (1995) 'The impact on regions of competition of the EC Single Market in financial
services', in S. Hardy, M. Hart, L. Albrechts and A. Katos (eds), *An Enlarged Europe:
Regions in Competition?*, Jessica Kingsley, London, 145–58.

Bell, D. and Dow, S. C. (1995) 'Economic policy options for a Scottish Parliament', *Scottish
Affairs*, 13, 42–67.

Bell, D. N. F. and Kirwan, F. X. (1979) 'Return migration in a Scottish context', *Regional Studies*, 13, 101–11.

Bentolila, S. (1997) 'Sticky labour in Spanish regions', *European Economic Review*, 41, 591–8.

Binks, M. R. and Ennew, C. T. (1997) 'The relationship between UK banks and their small business customers', *Small Business Economics*, 9, 167–78.

Birch, D. L. (1979) *The Job Generation Process*, MIT Program on Neighbourhood and Regional Change, Cambridge, Massachusetts.

Blackaby, D. H. and Manning, D. N. (1990) 'Earnings, unemployment and the regional employment structure in Britain', *Regional Studies*, 24, 529–35.

Blackaby, D. H. and Manning, D. N. (1992) 'Regional earnings and unemployment: a simultaneous equation approach', *Oxford Bulletin of Economic Statistics*, 54, 481–501.

Blanchard, O. and Katz, L. (1992) 'Regional evolutions', *Brookings Papers in Economic Activity*, 1, 1–75.

Bleaney, M. F., Binks, M. R., Greenaway, D., Reed, G. V. and Whymes, D. K. (1992) 'What does a university add to its local economy?', *Applied Economics*, 24, 305–11.

Blow, L., Hall, J. and Smith, S. (1996) 'Financing regional government in the UK: some issues', *Fiscal Studies*, 17, 99–120.

Bond, S., Denny, K., Hall, J. and McCluskey, W. (1996) 'Who pays Business Rates?', *Fiscal Studies*, 17, 19–35.

Borts, G. H. and Stein, J. L. (1964) *Economic Growth in a Free Market*, Columbia University Press, New York.

Boulier, B. I. (1984) 'What lies behind Verdoorn's Law?', *Oxford Economic Papers*, 36, 259–67.

Bover, O., Muellbauer, J. and Murphy, A. (1989) 'Housing, wages and UK labour markets', *Oxford Bulletin of Economics and Statistics*, 51, 97–136.

Bowen, H. P., Leamer, E. E. and Sveikauskas, L. (1987) 'Multicountry, multifactor tests of the factor abundance theory', *American Economic Review*, 77, 791–809.

Boyle, P., Halfacree, K. and Robinson, V. (1998) *Exploring Contemporary Migration*, Longman, Harlow.

Bradbury, J. and Mawson, J. (1997) *British Regionalism and Devolution: The Challenges of State Reform and European Integration*, Pion, London.

Bradley, J., O'Donnell, N., Sheridan, J. and Whelan, K. (1995) *Regional Aid and Convergence: Evaluating the Impact of the European Funds on the European Periphery*, Avebury, Aldershot.

Bradley, S. and Taylor, J. (1996) 'Human capital formation and local economic performance', *Regional Studies*, 30, 1–14.

Brennan, A., Rhodes, J. and Tyler, P. (1998) 'New findings on the nature of economic and social exclusion in England and the implications for new policy initiatives', Discussion Paper 101, Department of Land Economy, University of Cambridge, Cambridge.

Brennan, M. J. (1967) 'A more general theory of resource migration', in M. J. Brennan (ed.), *Patterns of Market Behaviour*, Brown University Press, Providence, RI, 45–64.

Breton, A. and Scott, A. (1978) 'The assignment problem in federal structures', in M. S. Feldstein and R. P. Inman (eds), *The Economics of Public Services*, Macmillan, London.

Brown, S. and Sessions, J. G. (1997) 'A profile of UK unemployment: regional versus demographic influences', *Regional Studies*, 31, 351–66.

Brownrigg, M. (1971) 'The regional income multiplier: an attempt to complete the model', *Scottish Journal of Political Economy*, 18, 281–97.

Brownrigg, M. (1973) 'The economic impact of a new university', *Scottish Journal of Political Economy*, 20, 123–39.

Buckland, R. and Davis, E. W. (1996) *Finance for Growing Enterprises*, Routledge, London.

Butler, F. (1993) 'The European Community's common agriculture policy', in J. Lodge (ed.), *The European Community and the Challenge of the Future*, 2nd edn, Pinter, London, 112–30.

Büttner, T. (1999) *Agglomeration, Growth and Adjustment*, Centre for European Economic Research, Mannheim, Germany; Physica, New York.

Calouste Gulbenkian Foundation (1982) *Community Business Works*, Calouste Gulbenkian Foundation, London.

Camagni, R. and Capello, R. (1997) 'Innovation and performance of SMEs in Italy: the relevance of spatial aspects', Working Paper WP60, ESRC Centre for Business Research, University of Cambridge, Cambridge.

Cameron, G. and Muellbauer, J. (1998) 'The housing market and regional commuting and migration choices', *Scottish Journal of Political Economy*, 45, 420–46.

Cameron, G. and Muellbauer, J. (1999) 'Earnings, unemployment and housing: evidence from a panel of British regions', Nuffield College, Oxford.

Canning, D. and Evans, R. (1988) 'Regional policy in the European Community: the case for employment subsidies', Discussion Paper, London School of Economics, London.

Capello, R. (1999) 'Spatial transfer of knowledge in high technology milieux', *Regional Studies*, 33, 353–65.

Caporaso, J. A. and Keeler, J. T. S. (1995) 'The European Union and regional integration theory', in C. Rhodes and S. Mazey (eds), *The State of the European Union III: Building a European Polity*, Longman, Harlow, 29–62.

Carlsen, F. (2000) 'Testing equilibrium models of regional disparities', *Scottish Journal of Political Economy*, 47.

Carree, M. and Klomp, L. (1996) 'Small business and job creation: a comment', *Small Business Economics*, 8, 317–22.

Castells, M. and Hall, P. (1994) *Technopoles of the World*, Routledge, London.

Castro, E. A. and Jensen-Butler, C. (1999) 'Regional economic inequality, growth theory and technological change', Discussion Paper 9903, Department of Economics, University of St Andrews, Scotland.

Cecchini, P. (1988) *The European Challenge: 1992: The Benefits of the Single Market*, Wildwood House, Aldershot.

Chanan, G. (1999) 'Employment policy and the social economy: promise and misconceptions', *Local Economy*, 14, 361–8.

Cheshire, P. and Carbonaro, G. (1996) 'Urban economic growth in Europe: testing theory and policy prescriptions', *Urban Studies*, 33, 1111–28.

Christodoulou, P. (1996) *Inward Investment: An Overview and Guide to the Literature*, British Library Board, London.

Coles, M. G. and Smith, E. (1996) 'Cross-section estimation of the matching function: evidence from England and Wales', *Economica*, 63, 589–97.

Collis, C. and Roberts, P. (1992) 'Foreign direct investment in the West Midlands: an analysis and evaluation', *Local Economy*, 7, 114–30.

Confederation of British Industry (1995) *Moving Forward – A Business Strategy for Transport*, CBI, London.

Cooke, P. M. and Morgan, K. (1998) *The Associational Economy: Firms, Regions and Innovation*, Oxford University Press, Oxford.

Cooke, P. M., Uranga, G. and Etxebarria, G. (1997) 'Regional innovation systems: institutional and organisational dimensions', *Research Policy*, 26, 475–91.

Cooke, T. J. and Bailey, A. J. (1996) 'Family migration and the employment of married women and men', *Economic Geography*, 72, 38–48.

Cooper, M. (1999) 'The development of the third sector economy in Bristol', *Local Economy*, 14, 348–59.

Coughlin, C. C. and Fabel, O. (1988) 'State factor endowments and exports: an alternative to cross-sectional studies', *Review of Economics and Statistics*, 70, 696–701.

Coughlin, C. C., Terza, J. V. and Arromdee, V. (1991) 'State characteristics and the location of foreign direct investment within the United States', *Review of Economics and Statistics*, 73, 675–83.

Cowling, M. (1998) 'Regional determinants of small firm loans under the UK Loan Guarantee Scheme', *Small Business Economics*, 11, 155–67.

Creedy, J. (1974) 'Interregional mobility: a cross-section analysis', *Scottish Journal of Political Economy*, 21, 41–53.

Cross, M. (1981) *New Firm Formation and Regional Development*, Gower, Aldershot.

Curran, J. and Burrows, R. (1988) *Enterprise in Britain: A National Profile of Small Business Owners and the Self-Employed*, Small Business Research Trust, London.

Cushing, B. J. (1987) 'A note on the specification of climatic variables in models of population migration', *Journal of Regional Science*, 27, 641–50.

Da Vanzo, J. (1983) 'Repeat migration in the US: who moves back and who moves on?', *Review of Economics and Statistics*, 60, 504–14.

Daly, M. (1991) 'VAT registrations and de-registrations in 1990', *Employment Gazette*, November, 579–88.

Daly, M., Campbell, M., Robson, G. and Gallagher, C. (1991) 'Job creation 1987–98: the contribution of small and large firms', *Employment Gazette*, November, 589–96.

Danson, M. W. (1996) *Small Firm Formation and Regional Economic Development*, Routledge, London.

Davis, D. R. and Weinstein, D. E. (1999) 'Economic geography and regional production structure: an empirical investigation', *European Economic Review*, 43, 379–407.

Davis, D. R., Weinstein, D. E., Bradford, S. and Shimpo, K. (1997) 'Using international and Japanese regional data to determine when the factor abundance theory of trade works', *American Economic Review*, 87.

Davis, S., Haltiwanger, J. and Schuh, S. (1996) 'Small business and job creation: dissecting the myth and reassessing the facts', *Small Business Economics*, 8, 297–315.

Deacon, D. (1982) 'Competition policy in the common market: its links with regional policy', *Regional Studies*, 16, 53–63.

Deardorff, A. V. (1979) 'Weak links in the chain of comparative advantage', *Journal of International Economics*, 9, 197–209.

Decressin, J. and Fatás, A. (1995) 'Regional labor market dynamics in Europe', *European Economic Review*, 39, 1627–55.

Del Monte, A. and de Luzenberger, R. (1989) 'The effect of regional policy on new firm formation in Southern Italy', *Regional Studies*, 28, 231–40.

Denny, K. and Ridge, M. (1991) 'The implications of a switch to non-locally varying business rates', *Fiscal Studies*, 13, 22–37.

Dewhurst, J. (1992) 'Using the RAS technique as a test of hybrid methods of regional input–output table updating', *Regional Studies*, 26, 81–92.

Dewhurst, J. (1998) 'Convergence and divergence in regional household incomes per head in the United Kingdom 1984–93', *Applied Economics*, 30, 31–5.

Disney, R. (1984) 'The regional impact of unemployment insurance in the United Kingdom', *Oxford Bulletin of Economics and Statistics*, 46, 241–54.

Dixon, R. J. (1973) 'Regional specialisation and trade in the UK', *Scottish Journal of Political Economy*, 20, 159–69.

Dixon, R. J. and Thirlwall, A. P. (1975) 'A model of regional growth rate differentials along Kaldorian lines', *Oxford Economic Papers*, 27, 201–14.

Doi, N. and Cowling, M. (1998) 'The evolution of firm size and employment share distribution in Japanese and UK manufacturing: a study of small business presence', *Small Business Economics*, 10, 283–92.

Dow, S. C. (1986) 'The capital account and regional balance of payments problems', *Urban Studies*, 23, 173–84.

Dow, S. C. (1987) 'The treatment of money in regional economics', *Journal of Regional Science*, 27, 13–24.

Dow, S. C. (1997) 'Scottish devolution and the financial sector', in M. Danson (ed.), *Regional Governance and Economic Development*, Pion, London, 229–41.

Dow, S. C. and Rodriguez-Fuentes, C. J. (1997) 'Regional finance: a survey', *Regional Studies*, 31, 903–20.

Doyle, M. F. (1990) 'Regional policy and European economic integration', in Committee for the Study of Economic and Monetary Union, *Report on Economic and Monetary Union in the European Community (Delors Report). Volume II: Collection of Papers*, Office for the Publication of Official Publications of the European Communities, Brussels, 69–79.

Dunford, M. (1993) 'Regional disparities in the European Community: evidence from the REGIO databank', *Regional Studies*, 27, 727–44.

Dunford, M. (1996) 'Disparities in employment, productivity and output in the EU: the roles of labour market governance and welfare regimes', *Regional Studies*, 30, 339–58.

Dunne, P. and Hughes, A. (1994) 'Age, size, growth and survival: UK companies in the 1980s', *Journal of Industrial Economics*, 42, 115–40.

EKOS Ltd (1998) *Baselines and the Quantification of the UK's Objective 2 Programmes. Volume II: Priority Indicators, Baselines and Benchmarks*, Report for the European Commission, Brussels.

Emerson, M., Aujean, M., Catinat, M., Goybet, P. and Jaquemin, A. (1988) *The Economics of 1992*, Oxford University Press, Oxford.

Emerson, M., Gros, D., Italianer, A., Pisani-Ferry, T. and Reichenbach, H. (1991) *One Market, One Money: An Evaluation of the Potential Benefits and Costs of Forming an Economic and Monetary Union*, Oxford University Press, Oxford.

Emmerich, M. (1997) 'Making a virtue of necessity? The role of intermediate labour markets', *Local Economy*, 12, 98–103.

Estle, E. (1967) 'A more conclusive regional test of the Heckscher–Ohlin hypothesis', *Journal of Political Economy*, 75, 886–8.

Ethier, W. (1982) 'National and international returns to scale in the modern theory of international trade', *American Economic Review*, 72, 389–405.

Evans, A. W. (1989) 'South East England in the eighties: explanations for a house price explosion', in M. Breheny and P. Congdon (eds), *Growth and Change in a Core Region*, Pion, London, 130–49.

Fagerberg, J. (1996) Technology and competitiveness, *Oxford Review of Economic Policy*, 12, 39–51.

Fagerberg, J. and Verspagen, B. (1996) 'Heading for divergence? Regional growth in Europe reconsidered', *Journal of Common Market Studies*, 34, 431–48.

Faini, R., Galli, G., Gennari, P. and Rossi, F. (1997) 'An empirical puzzle: falling migration and growing unemployment differentials among Italian regions', *European Economic Review*, 41, 571–9.

Fatás, A. (1997) 'EMU: countries or regions? Lessons from EMS experience', *European Economic Review*, 41, 743–51.

Felsenstein, D. (1996) 'The university in the metropolitan area: impacts and public policy implications', *Urban Studies*, 33 (9), 1565–80.

Fingleton, B. and McCombie, J. S. L. (1998) 'Increasing returns and economic growth: some evidence for manufacturing from the European Union regions', *Oxford Economic Papers*, 50, 89–105.

Fisher, P. S. and Peters, A. H. (1998) 'Industrial incentives: competition among American states and cities', W. J. Upjohn Institute for Employment Research, Kalamazoo, MI.

Foley, P. (1992) 'Local economic policy and job creation: a review of evaluation studies', *Urban Studies*, 29, 557–98.

Foley, P. (1998) 'The impact of the Regional Development Agency and Regional Chamber in the East Midlands', *Regional Studies*, 32, 777–82.

Fothergill, S. and Gudgin, G. (1982) *Unequal Growth: Urban and Regional Employment Change in the UK*, Heinemann, London.

Friedman, J., Gerlowski, D. A. and Silberman, J. (1992) 'What attracts foreign multinational corporations? Evidence from branch plant location in the United States', *Journal of Regional Science*, 32, 403–18.

Gallagher, C. and Robson, G. (1995) 'Small business and job creation: an even further dissection of the Davis, Haltiwanger and Schuh paper', *International Small Business Journal*, 13, 64–7.

Ghali, M. A., Akiyama, M. and Fujiwara, J. (1981) 'Models of regional growth: an empirical evaluation', *Regional Science and Urban Economics*, 11, 175–90.

Gibson, H., Riddington, G., Whigham, D. and Whyte, J. (1997) *Caledonian Blue Book 1997: National Accounts for Scotland 1951–96*, Cogent Strategies Ltd/Glasgow Caledonian University, Glasgow.

Giesecke, J. A. D. and Madden, J. R. (1997) 'Regional government economic policy', *Australasian Journal of Regional Studies*, 3, 3–18.

Gillespie, G., McGregor, P. Swales, K. and Ya Ping Yin (1997) 'The regional impact of inward investment: product market displacement, labour market effects and efficiency spillovers', Discussion Paper 97/2, Department of Economics, University of Strathclyde.

Gillespie, G., McGregor, P., Swales, K. and Ya Ping Yin (1998) 'The displacement and multiplier effects of Regional Selective Assistance: a computable general equilibrium analysis', Discussion Paper 98/3, Department of Economics, University of Strathclyde.

Glasmeier, A. (1999) 'Territory-based regional development policy and planning in a learning economy: the case of "real service centres" in industrial districts', *European Urban and Regional Studies*, 6, 73–84.

Glasson, J., van Der Wee, D. and Barrett, B. (1988) 'A local income and employment multiplier analysis of a proposed nuclear power station development at Hinckley Point in Somerset', *Urban Studies*.

Gordon, I. (1985) 'The cyclical interaction between regional migration, employment and unemployment: a time series analysis for Scotland', *Scottish Journal of Political Economy*, 32, 135–58.

Gordon, I. and Vickerman, R. (1982) 'Opportunity, preference and constraint: an approach to the analysis of metropolitan migration', *Urban Studies*, 19, 247–62.

Goss, E. and Paul, C. (1990) 'The impact of unemployment insurance benefits on the probability of migration of the unemployed', *Journal of Regional Science*, 30, 349–58.

Gould, A. and Keeble, D. (1984) 'New firms and rural industrialisation in East Anglia', *Regional Studies*, 18, 189–202.

Grant, K. E. and Vanderkamp, J. (1976) *The Economic Causes and Effects of Migration 1961–71*, Economic Council of Canada, Ottawa.

Grant, K. E. and Vanderkamp, J. (1980) 'The effects of migration on income: a micro-study with Canadian data', *Canadian Journal of Economics*, 13, 375–406.

Graves, P. E. (1983) 'Migration with a composite amenity: the role of rents', *Journal of Regional Science*, 23, 541–6.

Green, A. (1997) 'A question of compromise: case study evidence of the location and mobility strategies of dual career households', *Regional Studies*, 31, 641–57.

Green, A. (1998) 'The changing geography of non-employment in Britain,' chapter 4 in P. Lawless, R. Martin and S. Hardy (eds), *Unemployment and Social Exclusion: Landscapes of Labour Inequality*, Regional Policy and Development 13, Jessica Kingsley, London.

Green, A. (1999) 'Insights into unemployment and non-employment in Europe using alternative measures', *Regional Studies*, 33, 453–64.

Green, A., Hogarth, T. and Shackleton, R. E. (1999) 'Longer distance commuting as a substitute for migration in Britain: a review of trends and implications', *International Journal of Population Geography*, 5, 49–67.

Green, G., Gregg, P. and Wadsworth, J. (1998) 'Regional unemployment changes in Britain,' chapter 3 in P. Lawless, R. Martin and S. Hardy (eds), *Unemployment and Social Exclusion: Landscapes of Labour Inequality*, Regional Policy and Development 13, Jessica Kingsley, London.

Greenaway, D. and Milner, C. (1986) *The Economics of Intra-Industry Trade*, Blackwell, Oxford.

Greenaway, D., Hine, R. and Milner, C. (1995) 'Vertical and horizontal intra-industry trade: a cross-industry analysis for the United Kingdom', *Economic Journal*, 105, 1505–18.

Greenwood, M. J. (1985) 'Human migration: theory, models and empirical studies', *Journal of Regional Science*, 25, 521–44.

Greenwood, M. J., Hunt, G. L., Rickman, D. S. and Treyz, G. I. (1991) 'Migration, regional equilibrium and the estimation of compensating differentials', *American Economic Review*, 81, 1382–90.

Griffiths, A. (1991) 'The small firm', *British Economic Survey*, 20, 38–42.

Groenewold, N. (1997) 'Does migration equalise regional unemployment rates? Evidence from Australia', *Papers in Regional Science*, 76, 1–20.

Grubel, H. G. and Lloyd, P. J. (1973) *Intra-industry Trade*, Macmillan, Basingstoke.

Guerrero, D. C. and Seró, M. A. (1997) 'Spatial distribution of patents in Spain: determining factors and consequences on regional development', *Regional Studies*, 31, 381–90.

Hague, C. (1996) 'Spatial planning in Europe: the issues for planning in Britain', *Town Planning Review*, 67, iii–vii.

Hall, P. (1982) 'Enterprise zones: a justification', *International Journal of Urban and Regional Research*, 6, 416–21.

Hanson, G. H. (1998) 'North American economic integration and industry location,' *Oxford Review of Economic Policy*, 14, 30–44.

Harrigan, F. J. (1982) 'Revealed comparative advantage and regional industrial specialisation: the case of Scotland', Discussion Paper 22, The Fraser of Allander Institute, University of Strathclyde, Glasgow.

Harrigan, F. J. (1983) *On Regional Industrial Structure and Trade: Some Tests of Alternative Theories*, Research Report, The Fraser of Allander Institute, University of Strathclyde, Glasgow.

Harrigan, F. J., McGregor, P., Dourmashkin, N., Perman, R., Swales, K. and Yin, Y. P. (1991) 'AMOS: a macro–micro model of Scotland', *Journal of Economic Modelling*, 8, 424–79.

Harrigan, F. J., McGregor, P. G. and Swales, J. K. (1996) 'The system-wide impact on the recipient region of a regional labour subsidy', *Oxford Economic Papers*, 48, 105–33.

Harris, R. I. D. (1982) 'Estimates of inter-regional differences in production in the United Kingdom', *Oxford Bulletin of Economics and Statistics*, 44, 241–60.

Harris, R. I. D. (1988) 'Technological change and regional development in the UK: evidence from the SPRU database on innovations', *Regional Studies*, 22, 361–86.

Harris, R. I. D. (1991) 'The employment creation effects of factor subsidies: some estimates for Northern Ireland manufacturing industry 1955–83', *Journal of Regional Science*, 31, 49–64.

Harris, R. I. D. (1993) 'Retreat from policy: the rationale and effectiveness of automatic investment grants', in R. T. Harrison and M. Hart (eds), *Spatial Policy in a Divided Nation*, Jessica Kingsley/Regional Studies Association, London, 64–84.

Harris, R. I. D. (1997) 'The impact of the University of Portsmouth on the local economy', *Urban Studies*, 34 (4), 605–26.

Harris, R. I. D. and Lau, E. (1998) 'Verdoorn's law and increasing returns to scale in the UK regions, 1968–91: some new estimates based on the cointegration approach', *Oxford Economic Papers*, 50, 201–19.

Harris, R. I. D. and Liu, A. (1998) 'Input–output modelling of the urban and regional economy: the importance of external trade', *Regional Studies*, 32, 827–38.

Harris, R. I. D. and Trainor, M. (1995) 'Innovations and R&D in Northern Ireland manufacturing: a Schumpeterian approach', *Regional Studies*, 29, 593–604.

Harris, R. I. D. and Trainor, M. (1997) 'Productivity growth in the UK regions, 1968–91', *Oxford Bulletin of Economics and Statistics*, 59, 485–510.

Harrison, B. (1992) 'Industrial districts: old wine in new bottles', *Regional Studies*, 26, 469–83.

Harrison, R. and Mason, C. M. (1986) 'The regional impact of the Small Firms Loan Guarantee Scheme in the United Kingdom', *Regional Studies*, 20, 535–50.

Harrison, R. and Mason, C. M. (1991) 'Informal investment networks: a case study from the United Kingdom', *Entrepreneurship and Regional Development*, 3, 269–79.

Hart, M. and Scott, R. (1994) 'Measuring the effectiveness of small firm policy: some lessons from Northern Ireland', *Regional Studies*, 28, 849–58.

Hart, P. E. and Oulton, N. (1996) 'Growth and size of firm', *Economic Journal*, 106, 1242–52.

Hart, R. A. (1989) 'The employment and hours effects of a marginal employment subsidy', *Scottish Journal of Political Economy*, 36, 385–95.

Hartman, L. M. and Seckler, D. (1967) 'Towards an application of dynamic growth theory to regions', *Journal of Regional Science*, 7, 167–74.

Hasluck, C. (1987) *Urban Unemployment*, Longman, Harlow.

Haughton, G. (1998) 'Principles and practice of community economic development', *Regional Studies*, 32, 872–8.

Haynes, K. E., Maas, G. C., Stough, R. R. and Riggle, J. D. (1997) 'Regional governance and economic development: lessons from federal states', in M. Danson (ed.), *Regional Governance and Economic Development*, Pion, London, 68–84.

Head, K., Ries, J. and Swenson, D. (1995) 'Agglomeration benefits and location choice: evidence from Japanese manufacturing investments in the United States', *Journal of International Economics*, 38, 223–47.

Heald, D. (1983) *Public Expenditure: Its Defence and Reform*, Martin Robertson, Oxford.

Heim, C. E. (1988) 'Government research establishments, state capacity and the distribution of industry policy in Britain', *Regional Studies*, 22, 375–86.

Helpman, E. (1998) 'Explaining the structure of foreign trade: where do we stand?', *Weltwirtschaftliches Archiv*, 134, 573–89.

Helpman, E. and Krugman, P. R. (1985) *Market Structure and Foreign Trade*, Wheatsheaf, Brighton.

Henderson, D. S. (1984) *Scottish Input–Output Tables for 1979: Introduction and Summary Tables*, ESU, Industry Department for Scotland, Edinburgh.

Henley, A. (1998) 'Residential mobility, housing equity and the labour market', *Economic Journal*, 108, 414–27.

Herzog, H. W. and Schlottmann, A. M. (1983) 'Migrant information, job search and the remigration decision', *Southern Economic Journal*, 9, 43–56.

Hill, S. and Munday, M. (1994) *The Regional Distribution of Foreign Manufacturing Investment in the UK*, Macmillan, London.

Hill, S., Roberts, A. and Strong, C. (1998) 'The export earnings of Welsh higher education institutions and their impact on the Welsh economy', Welsh Economy Research Unit, Cardiff Business School.

Hilpert, U. (1991) *Regional Innovation and Decentralisation*, Routledge, London.

Hirschman, A. O. (1958) *The Strategy of Economic Development*, Yale University Press, New Haven, CT.

Hofer, H. and Wörgötter, A. (1997) 'Regional per capita income convergence in Austria', *Regional Studies*, 31, 1–12.

Hoffman, S. (1982) 'Reflections on the nation-state in Western Europe today', *Journal of Common Market Studies*, 21, 21–37.

Holden, D. R. and Swales, K. (1995) 'The additionality, displacement and substitution effects of factor subsidies', *Scottish Journal of Political Economy*, 42, 113–26.

Holmes, T. J. (1998) 'The effect of state policies on the location of manufacturing: evidence from state borders', *Journal of Political Economy*, 106, 667–705.

Horiba, Y. and Kirkpatrick, R. C. (1981) 'Factor endowments, factor proportions and the allocative efficiency of US interregional trade', *Review of Economics and Statistics*, 63, 178–87.

Howells, J. (1986) 'Industry–academic links in research and innovation: a national and regional development perspective', *Regional Studies*, 20, 472–6.

Hudson, R. (1997) 'Regional futures: industrial restructuring, new high volume production concepts and spatial development strategies in Europe', *Regional Studies*, 31, 467–78.

Hudson, R. (1999) 'The "learning economy", the learning firms and the learning region', *European Urban and Regional Studies*, 6, 59–72.

Hughes, A. (1997a) 'Small firms and employment', Working Paper WP71, ESRC Centre for Business Research, University of Cambridge, Cambridge.

Hughes, A. (1997b) 'Finance for SMEs: a UK perspective', *Small Business Economics*, 9, 151–66.

Hughes, A. (1998) 'Growth constraints on small and medium-sized firms', Working Paper WP107, ESRC Centre for Business Research, University of Cambridge, Cambridge.

Hughes, A. and Storey, D. J. (1994) *Finance and the Small Firm*, Routledge, London.

Hughes, G. and McCormick, B. (1981) 'Do council house policies reduce migration between regions?', *Economic Journal*, 91, 919–37.

Hughes, G. and McCormick, B. (1987) 'Housing markets, unemployment and labour market flexibility in the UK', *European Economic Review*, 31, 615–45.

Hughes, G. and McCormick, B. (1990) 'Does migration reduce differentials in regional unemployment rates?', in J. Van Dijk, H. Folmer, H. W. Herzay and A. M. Schlottman (eds), *Migration and Labour Market Adjustment*, Kluwer, Holland.

Hughes, G. and McCormick, B. (1994) 'Did migration in the 1980s narrow the North–South divide?', *Economica*, 61, 509–27.

Hughes, J. (1998) 'The role of development agencies in regional policy: an academic and practitioner's approach', *Urban Studies*, 35, 615–26.

Hulten, C. R. and Schwab, R. M. (1984) 'Regional productivity growth in US manufacturing: 1951–78', *American Economic Review*, 74, 152–62.

Hyclak, T. and Johnes, G. (1987) 'On the determinants of full employment unemployment rates in local labour markets', *Applied Economics*, 19, 191–200.

Hyclak, T. and Johnes, G. (1992a) 'Wage flexibility and unemployment dynamics in regional labour markets', W. E. Upjohn Institute for Employment Research, Kalamazoo, MI.

Hyclak, T. and Johnes, G. (1992b) Wage flexibility and unemployment dynamics in Great Britain', *Scottish Journal of Political Economy*, 39, 188–200.

Innis, H. (1920) *The Fur Trade in Canada*, Yale University Press, New Haven, CT.

Jackman, R. and Savouri, S. (1992a) 'Regional migration in Britain: an analysis of gross flows using NHS Central Register data', *Economic Journal*, 102, 1433–50.

Jackman, R. and Savouri, S. (1992b) 'Regional migration versus regional commuting: the identification of housing and employment flows', *Scottish Journal of Political Economy*, 39, 272–87.

Jackman, R., Pissarides, C. and Savouri, S. (1990) 'Labour market policies and unemployment in the OECD', *Economic Policy*, 11, 450–90.

Jackson, T. (1998) 'Determining the impact of discretionary development assistance: the Scottish Enterprise Output Measurement Framework', *Regional Studies*, 32, 559–65.

Jaffe, A. B. (1989) 'Real effects of academic research', *American Economic Review*, 79, 957–70.

Jefferson, C. W. and Trainor, M. (1996) 'Regional development and mobile public sector employment', *Urban Studies*, 33, 37–48.

Jensen, R. C. (1980) 'The concept of accuracy in regional input–output models', *International Regional Science Review*.

Johnes, G. and Hyclak, T. (1994) 'House prices, migration and regional labour markets', *Journal of Housing Economics*, 3, 312–29.

Johnes, G. and Hyclak, T. (1995) 'The determinants of real wage flexibility', *Labour Economics*, 2, 175–85.

Jones, C. I. (1998) *Introduction to Economic Growth*. Norton, London.

Jones, D. R. and Manning, D. N. (1992) 'Long-term unemployment, hysteresis and the u–v relation: a regional analysis', *Regional Studies*, 26, 17–30.

Kaldor, N. (1970) 'The case for regional policies', *Scottish Journal of Political Economy*, 18, 337–48.

Kangasharju, A. (1998) 'Beta convergence in Finland: regional differences in the speed of convergence', *Applied Economics*, 30, 679–87.

Kay, J. (1996) *The Business of Economics*, Oxford University Press, Oxford.

Keeble, D. (1990) *Small Firms, New Firms and Uneven Regional Development*, Working Paper WP2, Small Business Research Centre, University of Cambridge, Cambridge.

Keeble, D. (1997) 'Small firms, innovation and regional development in the 1990s', *Regional Studies*, 31, 281–93.

Keeble, D. and Bryson, J. (1996) 'Small-firm creation and growth, regional development and the North–South divide in Britain', *Environment and Planning A*, 28, 909–34.

Keeble, D. and Walker, S. (1994) 'New firms, small firms and dead firms: spatial patterns and determinants in the United Kingdom', *Regional Studies*, 28, 411–27.

Keeble, D. and Wilkinson, F. (1999) 'Collective learning in regionally clustered high technology SMEs in Europe', *Regional Studies*, 33, 295–303.

Keeble, D., Tyler, P., Broom, G. and Lewis, J. (1992) *Business Success in the Countryside: The Performance of Rural Enterprise*, HMSO, London.

Keeble, D., Lawson, C., Smith, H. L., Moore, B. and Wilkinson, F. (1998) 'Internationalisation processes, networking and local embeddedness in technology-intensive small firms', *Small Business Economics*, 11, 327–42.

Keeble, D., Lawson, C., Moore, B. and Wilkinson, F. (1999) 'Collective learning processes, networking and "institutional thickness" in the Cambridge region', *Regional Studies*, 33, 319–32.

Kervenoael, R. J. and Armstrong, H. W. (2000) 'An economic perspective on the assignment of policy powers: the case of tourism policy', *Regional and Federal Studies*, forthcoming.

Kim, S. (1995) 'Expansion of markets and the geographic distribution of economic activities: the trends in U.S. regional manufacturing structure, 1860–1987', *Quarterly Journal of
Economics*, 110, 881–908.

Kim, S. (1999) 'Regions, resources and economic geography: sources of U.S. regional comparative advantage, 1880–1987', *Regional Science and Urban Economics*, 29, 1–32.

King, D. N. (1973) 'Financial and economic aspects of regionalism and federalism', Research Paper 10, Royal Commission on the Constitution, HMSO, London.

King, D. N. (1984) *Fiscal Tiers*, Allen and Unwin, London.

King, J. (1990) *Regional Selective Assistance 1980–84*, HMSO, London.

King, R., Warnes, A. M. and Williams, A. (1998) 'International retirement migration in
Europe', *International Journal of Population Geography*, 4, 91–111.

Kitching, R. (1990) 'Migration behaviour among the unemployed and low skilled', in
J. H. Johnson and J. Salt (eds), *Labour Migration*, David Fulton, London, 172–90.

Klaasen, T. A. (1973) 'Regional comparative advantage in the United States', *Journal of
Regional Science*, 13, 97–105.

Kleinknecht, A. and Poot, T. P. (1992) 'Do regions matter for R&D', *Regional Studies*, 26,
221–32.

Knack, S. and Keefer, P. (1997) 'Does social capital have an economic payoff? A cross-
country investigation', *Quarterly Journal of Economics*, 112, 1251–88.

Kohler, J.-P. (1997) 'The effect of hedonic migration decisions and region-specific amenities
on industrial location: could Silicon Valley be in South Dakota?', *Journal of Regional
Science*, 37, 379–94.

Krauss, M. B. and Johnson, H. G. (1974) *General Equilibrium Analysis: A Micro-Economic
Text*, Allen and Unwin, London.

Krugman, P. (1979) 'Increasing returns, monopolistic competition, and international trade',
Journal of International Economics, 21, 173–81.

Krugman, P. (1980) 'Scale economies, product differentiation and the pattern of trade',
American Economic Review, 70, 950–9.

Krugman, P. (1989) 'Differences in income elasticities and trends in real exchange rates',
European Economic Review, 33, 1031–54.

Krugman, P. (1991a) 'Increasing returns and economic geography', *Journal of Political
Economy*, 99, 483–99.

Krugman, P. (1991b) *Geography and Trade*, MIT Press, Cambridge, MA.

Krugman, P. (1998) 'What's new about the new economic geography?', *Oxford Review of
Economic Policy*, 14, 7–17.

Krugman, P. and Elizondo, R. L. (1996) 'Trade policy and the Third World metropolis',
Journal of Development Economics, 49, 137–50.

Krugman, P. and Venables, A. (1995) 'Globalisation and the inequality of nations', *Quarterly Journal of Economics*, 110, 857–80.

Krugman, P. and Venables, A. (1996) 'Integration, specialisation, and adjustment', *European Economic Review*, 40, 959–67.

Lawless, P. (1997) 'The policy challenge', in P. Lawless, R. Martin and S. Hardy (eds),
Unemployment and Social Exclusion: Landscapes of Labour Inequality, Jessica Kingsley/Re-
gional Studies Association, London, 235–48.

Lawless, P., Else, P., Farnell, R., Furbey, R., Lund, S. and Wishart, B. (1998) 'Community based
initiatives and state urban policy: the Church Urban Fund', *Regional Studies*, 32, 161–74.

Lawson, C. (1999) 'Towards a competence theory of the region', *Cambridge Journal of Economics*, 23, 151–66.

Lawson, C. and Lorenz, E. (1999) 'Collective learning, tacit knowledge and regional innovative capacity', *Regional Studies*, 33, 305–18.

Layard, P. R. S. and Nickell, S. J. (1980) 'The case for subsidising extra jobs', *Economic Journal*, 90, 51–73.

Layard, P. R. S. and Nickell, S. J. (1983) 'Marginal employment subsidies again: a brief response to Whitley and Wilson', *Economic Journal*, 93, 881–2.

Lee, P. (1999) 'Where are the socially excluded? Continuing debates in the identification of poor neighbourhoods', *Regional Studies*, 33, 483–6.

Leontief, W. (1953) 'Domestic production and foreign trade: the American capital position re-examined', *Proceedings of the American Philosophical Society*, 97, 332–49.

Leontief, W. (1956) 'Factor proportions and the structure of American trade: further theoretical and empirical analysis', *Review of Economics and Statistics*, 38, 386–407.

Lindberg, C. (1963) *The Political Dynamics of European Economic Integration*, Stanford University Press, Stanford, CA.

Lipietz, A. (1992) 'The regulation approach and capitalist crises: an alternative compromise for the 1990s?', in M. Dunford and G. Kafkalis (eds), *Cities and Regions in the New Europe*, Belhaven, London, 309–34.

Lloyd, P. (1996) *Social and Economic Inclusion through Regional Development: The Community Economic Development Priority in European Structural Funds Programmes in Great Britain*, Study for European Commission (DGXVI), Brussels.

Lloyd, P. and Mason, C. M. (1984) 'Spatial variations in new firm formation in the UK', *Regional Studies*, 18, 207–20.

Lloyd, P. and Ramsden, P. (1998) *Local Enterprises and Enterprising Localities: Area Based Employment Initiatives in the UK*, Report for the European Commission, Brussels.

Love, J. H. (1996) 'Entry and exit: a county-level analysis', *Applied Economics*, 28, 441–51.

Love, J. H. and McNicoll, I. H. (1988) 'The regional economic impact of overseas students in the UK: a case study of three Scottish Universities', *Regional Studies*, 22, 1–10.

Lovering, J. (1991) 'The changing geography of the military industry in Britain', *Regional Studies*, 25, 279–93.

Luger, M. I. and Goldstein, H. A. (1996) 'What is the role of public universities in regional economic development?', in R. D. Bingham and R. Mier (eds), *Dilemmas in Urban Development: Issues in Theory and Practice*, Urban Affairs Annual Reviews 47, Sage, London.

Lund, M. and Wright, M. (1999) 'The financing of small firms in the United Kingdom', *Bank of England Quarterly Review*, 39, 195–210.

Lynch, P. (1999) 'New Labour and the English regional development agencies: devolution as evolution', *Regional Studies*, 33, 73–8.

MacDonald, R. and Taylor, M. P. (1993) 'Regional house prices in Britain: long-run relationships and short-run dynamics', *Scottish Journal of Political Economy*, 40, 43–55.

Machin, S. (1998) 'Recent shifts in wage inequality and the wage returns to education in Britain', *National Institute Economic Review*, 166, 87–96.

MacKay, R. R. (1997) 'Unemployment as exclusion', in P. Lawless, R. Martin and S. Hardy (eds), *Unemployment and Social Exclusion: Landscapes of Labour Inequality*, Jessica Kingsley/ Regional Studies Association, London, 49–68.

Maclennan, D. (1994) *A Comparative UK Economy: The Challenges for Housing Policy*, Joseph Rowntree Foundation, York.

Magrini, S. (1999) 'The evolution of income disparities among the regions of the European Union', *Regional Science and Urban Economics*, 29, 257–81.

Maier, G. (1985) 'Cumulative causation and selectivity in labour market-orientated migration caused by imperfect competition', *Regional Studies*, 19, 231–41.

Malecki, E. J. (1990) 'Technological innovation and paths to regional economic growth', in J. Schmandt and R. W. Wilson (eds), *Growth Policy in the Age of High Technology*, Unwin Hyman, London, 97–126.

Malecki, E. J. (1991) *Technology and Economic Development*, Longman, Harlow.

Malecki, E. J. and Bradbury, S. L. (1992) 'R&D facilities and professional labour: labour force dynamics in high technology', *Regional Studies*, 26, 123–36.

Manning, N. (1995) 'Earnings, unemployment and house prices: some results for British counties', *Scottish Journal of Political Economy*, 42, 428–42.

Marks, G. (1993) 'Structural policy and multilevel governance in the EC', in A. Cafruny and G. Rosenthal (eds), *The State of the European Community II: The Maastricht Debates and Beyond*, Longman, Harlow.

Marks, G., Hooghe, L. and Blank, K. (1996) 'European integration from the 1980s: state-centric v. multi-level governance', *Journal of Common Market Studies*, 34, 341–78.

Markusen, A. (1996a) 'Interaction between regional and industrial policies: evidence from four countries', *International Regional Science Review*, 19, 49–78.

Markusen, A. (1996b) 'Sticky places in slippery space: a typology of industrial districts', *Economic Geography*, 72, 293–313.

Marshall, A. (1890) *Principles of Economics*, 8th edn 1986, Macmillan, Basingstoke.

Marshall, A. (1920) *Principles of Economics*, Macmillan, London.

Marshall, J. N., Hopkins, W. J. and Richardson, R. (1997) 'The civil service and the regions: geographical perspectives on civil service restructuring', *Regional Studies*, 31, 607–13.

Marston, S. (1985) 'Two views about the geographic distribution of unemployment', *Quarterly Journal of Economics*, 100, 57–79.

Martin, R. (1988) 'The political economy in Britain's north–south divide', *Transactions of the Institute of British Geographers*, 13, 389–418.

Martin, R. (1989a) 'The new economics and politics of regional restructuring: the British experience', in L. Albrechts, F. Moulaert, P. Roberts and E. Swyngedouw (eds), *Regional Policy at the Crossroads*, Jessica Kingsley, London, 27–51.

Martin, R. (1989b) 'The growth and anatomy of venture capitalism in the United Kingdom', *Regional Studies*, 23, 389–403.

Martin, R. (1992) 'Reviving the economic case for regional policy', in M. Hart and R. Harrison (eds), *Spatial Policy in a Divided Nation*, Jessica Kingsley, London, 270–90.

Martin, R. (1997) 'Regional dimensions of Europe's unemployment crisis', in P. Lawless, R. Martin and S. Hardy (eds), *Unemployment and Social Exclusion: Landscapes of Labour Inequality*, Jessica Kingsley/Regional Studies Association, London, 11–48.

Martin, R. and Minns, R. (1995) 'Undermining the financial basis of regions: the spatial structure and implications of the UK pension fund system', *Regional Studies*, 29 (2), 125–44.

Mas, M., Maudos, J., Pérez, F. and Uriel, E. (1995) 'Public capital and convergence in the Spanish regions', *Entrepreneurship and Regional Development*, 7, 309–27.

Maskell, P. and Malmberg, A. (1999) 'Localised learning and industrial competitiveness', *Cambridge Journal of Economics*, 23, 167–85.

Mason, C. M. and Harrison, R. H. (1994) 'Informal venture capital in the UK', in A. Hughes and D. J. Storey (eds), *Finance and the Small Firm*, Routledge, London, 64–111.

May, R. S. and Malek, M. M. H. (1990) 'The regional impact within the UK of the overseas development aid programme', *Regional Studies*, 24, 299–310.

McArthur, A. A. (1993) 'Community businesses and urban regeneration', *Urban Studies*, 30, 849–73.

McCallum, J. D. (1979) 'The development of British regional policy', in D. Maclennan and J. B. Parr (eds), *Regional Policy: Past Experience and New Directions*, Martin Robertson, Oxford, 3–42.

McCombie, J. (1982) 'How important is the spatial diffusion of innovations in explaining regional growth rate disparities'?, *Urban Studies*, 19, 377–82.

McCombie, J. (1988a) 'A synoptic view of regional growth and unemployment. I: Neoclassical theory', *Urban Studies*, 25, 267–81.

McCombie, J. (1988b) 'A synoptic view of regional growth and unemployment. II: The post Keynesian theory', *Urban Studies*, 25, 399–417.

McCombie, J. (1992) 'Thirlwall's Law and balance of payments constrained growth: more on the debate', *Applied Economics*, 24, 493–512.

McCombie, J. and De Ridder, J. (1984) 'The Verdoorn Law controversy; some new empirical evidence using USA state data', *Oxford Economic Papers*, 36, 268–84.

McCombie, J. and Thirlwall, A. P. (1997) 'The dynamic Harrod foreign trade multiplier and the demand-oriented approach to economic growth and evaluation', *International Review of Applied Economics*, 11, 5–26.

McCormick, B. (1991) 'Migration and regional policy', in A. Bowen and K. Mayhew (eds), *Reducing Regional Inequalities*, Kogan Page, London.

McCormick, B. (1997) 'Regional unemployment and labour mobility in the UK', *European Economic Review*, 41, 581–9.

McCrone, G. (1969) *Regional Policy in Britain*, Allen and Unwin, London.

McDermott, P. J. (1977) 'Capital subsidies and unemployed labour: a comment on the regional production function approach', *Regional Studies*, 11, 203–10.

McGilvray, J. (1965) 'Treatment of imports in an input–output model', *Journal of the Statistical and Social Inquiry of Ireland*.

McGregor, A. and McConnachie, M. (1995) 'Social exclusion, urban regeneration and economic reintegration', *Urban Studies*, 32, 1587–1600.

McGregor, P. G. and McNicoll, I. (1992) 'The impact of forestry on output in the UK and its member counties', *Regional Studies*, 26, 69–80.

McGregor, P. G. and Swales, J. K. (1983) 'Professor Thirlwall and balance of payments constrained growth', *Applied Economics*, 17, 17–32.

McGregor, P. G., Swales, K. and Yin, Y. P. (1996a) 'A long-run interpretation of regional input–output analysis', *Journal of Regional Science*, 36, 479–501.

McGregor, P. G., Swales, J. K., Yin, Y. P. and Stevens, J. (1996b) 'Fiscal federalism in the UK context: a general equilibrium analysis of the "tartan tax" under imperfect competition', paper to a Regional Science Association Conference at York University (mimeo).

McGregor, P. G., Swales, K. and Yin, Y. P. (1997a) 'Spillover and feedback effects in general equilibrium interregional models of the national economy: a requiem for interregional input–output', Discussion Paper 97/8, Department of Economics, University of Strathclyde.

McGregor, P. G., Stevens, J., Swales, K. and Yin, Y. P. (1997b) 'The economics of the tartan tax', *Fraser of Allander Institute Quarterly Economic Review*, 22, 72–85.

McGregor, P. G., Stevens, J., Swales, J. K. and Yin, Y. P. (1997c) 'Some simple macroeconomics of Scottish devolution', in M. Danson (ed.), *Regional Governance and Economic Development*, Pion, London, 187–209.

McGregor, P. G., Swales, K. and Yin, Y. P. (1998) 'EMU: the UK regional context', in J. Bradley (ed.), *Regional Economic and Policy Impacts of EMU: The Case of Northern Ireland*, Northern Ireland Economic Council, Belfast.

McGuire, A. (1983) 'The regional income and employment impacts of nuclear power stations', *Scottish Journal of Political Economy*, 30, 264–74.

McKay, D. (1998) 'The economic impact of the overseas student industry: special reference to the Wollongong economy', *Australian Journal of Regional Studies*, 4, 239–52.

McNicoll, I. H. (1984) *The Shetland Industrial Study 1982/83*, Report 7, Fraser of Allander Institute, University of Strathclyde.

McNicoll, I. H. (1991) 'The Western Isles Input–Output Study for 1988/89', *Scottish Economic Bulletin*, June.

McQuaid, R. W., Leitham, S. and Nelson, J. D. (1996) 'Accessibility and location decisions in a peripheral region of Europe: a logit analysis', *Regional Studies*, 30, 579–88.

Miernyk, W. H. (1965) *Elements of Input–Output Economics*, Random House, New York.

Mincer, J. (1978) 'Family migration decisions', *Journal of Political Economy*, 86, 749–73.

Minford, P. and Stoney, P. (1991) 'Regional policy and market forces: a model and an assessment', in A. Bowen and K. Mayhew (eds), *Reducing Regional Inequalities*, National Economic Development Office, Kogan Page, London, 109–84.

Molho, I. (1986) 'Theories of migration: a review', *Scottish Journal of Political Economy*, 33, 396–419.

Molho, I. (1995) 'Migrant inertia, accessibility and local unemployment', *Economica*, 62, 123–32.

Molho, I. and Elias, P. (1984) 'A study of regional trends in the labour force participation of married women in the UK, 1968–77', *Applied Economics*, 16, 163–74.

Moore, B. and Rhodes, J. (1973) 'Evaluating the effects of British regional policy', *Economic Journal*, 83, 87–110.

Moore, B. and Rhodes, J. (1976) 'Regional economic policy and the movement of manufacturing industry to Development Areas', *Economica*, 43, 17–31.

Moore, B., Rhodes, J. and Tyler, P. (1986) *The Effect of Government Regional Economic Policy*, HMSO, London.

Moore, W. J. and Newman, R. J. (1985) 'The effects of right-to-work laws: a review of the literature', *Industrial and Labor Relations Review*, 38, 571–85.

Moralee, L. (1998) 'Self-employment in the 1990s', *Labour Market Trends*, March 1998, 121–30.

Moravcsik, A. (1993) 'Preferences and power in the European Community: a liberal-intergovernmental approach', *Journal of Common Market Studies*, 31, 473–524.

Morgan, K. (1997) 'The learning region: institutions, innovation and regional renewal', *Regional Studies*, 31, 491–503.

Moroney, J. R. and Walker, J. M. (1966) 'A regional test of the Heckscher–Ohlin theorem', *Journal of Political Economy*, 74, 573–86.

Munday, M. (1990) *Japanese Manufacturing Investment in Wales*, University of Wales Press, Cardiff.

Munday, M., Morris, J. and Wilkinson, B. (1995) 'Factories or warehouses? A Welsh perspective on Japanese transplant manufacturing', *Regional Studies*, 29, 1–17.

Muth, R. F. (1971) 'Migration: chicken or egg?', *Southern Economic Journal*, 37, 295–306.

Myrdal, G. (1957) *Economic Theory and Underdeveloped Regions*, Duckworth, London.

Needleman, L. and Scott, B. (1964) 'Regional problems and location of industry policy in Britain', *Urban Studies*, 1, 153–73.

Neven, D. (1990) 'EEC integration towards 1992: some distributional aspects', *Economic Policy: A European Forum*, 10, 13–62.

Neven, D. and Gouyette, C. (1995) 'Regional convergence in the European Community', *Journal of Common Market Studies*, 33, 47–65.

Newlands, D. (1997) 'The economic powers and potential of a devolved Scottish Parliament: lessons from economic theory and European experience', in M. Danson (ed.), *Regional Governance and Economic Development*, Pion, London, 109–27.

Nickell, S. (1997) 'Unemployment and labor market rigidities: Europe versus North America', *Journal of Economic Perspectives*, 11, 55–74.

North, D. and Smallbone, D. (1995) 'The employment generation potential of mature SMEs in different geographical environments', *Urban Studies*, 32, 1517–34.

North, D. C. (1955) 'Location theory and regional economic growth', *Journal of Political Economy*, 63, 243–58.

North, P. (1998) 'LETS, "hours" and the Swiss "business ring"', *Local Economy*, 13, 114–32.

O'Donnell, A. T. and Swales, J. K. (1979) 'Factor substitution, the CES production function and UK regional economies', *Oxford Economic Papers*, 31, 460–76.

Oakey, R. P. (1991) 'High technology industry and the peace dividend: a comment on national and regional industrial policy', *Regional Studies*, 25, 83–6.

Oakey, R. P. and Mukhtar, S.-M. (1999) 'United Kingdom small firms in theory and practice: a review of recent trends', *International Small Business Journal*, 17, 48–64.

Oakey, R. P. and O'Farrell, P. N. (1992) 'The regional extent of computer numerically controlled (CNC) machine tool adoption and post-adoption success in small British engineering firms', *Regional Studies*, 26, 163–75.

Oakey, R. P., Thwaites, A. and Nash, P. A. (1982) 'Technological change and regional development: some evidence on regional variations in product and process innovations', *Environment and Planning A*, 14, 1073–86.

Oakey, R. P., James, A. and Watts, T. (1998) 'Regional sub-contract suppliers to prime defence contractors: evidence of their performance in response to recent changes in demand', *Regional Studies*, 32, 17–30.

Odland, J. and Ellis, M. (1998) 'Variations in the labour force participation of women across large metropolitan areas in the United States', *Regional Studies*, 32, 333–48.

Ogilvy, A. A. (1982) 'Population migration between regions of Great Britain, 1971–9', *Regional Studies*, 16, 65–73.

O'Huallachian, B. and Reid, N. (1997) 'Acquisition versus greenfield investment: the location and growth of Japanese manufacturers in the United States', *Regional Studies*, 31, 403–16.

Oulton, W. N. (1973) 'Tariffs, taxes and trade: the effective protection approach', Government Economic Service Occasional Paper 6, HMSO, London.

PA Cambridge Economic Consultants (1990) *Cambridge Economic Review: The Outlook for the Regions and Counties of the UK in the 1990s*, Cambridge.

PA Cambridge Economic Consultants (1993) *Regional Selection Assistance 1985–8*, HMSO, London.

PA Cambridge Economic Consultants (1995a) *Assessment of the Wider Effects of Foreign Direct Investment in Manufacturing in the UK*, Department of Trade and Industry, London.

PA Cambridge Economic Consultants (1995b) *Final Evaluation of the Enterprise Zones*, Report for the Department of the Environment, The Stationery Office, London.

Pacione, M. (1999) 'The other side of the coin: local currency as a response to the globalisation of capital', *Regional Studies*, 33, 63–72.

Partridge, M. D. and Rickman, D. S. (1997) 'The dispersion of US unemployment rates: the role of market and non-market equilibrium factors', *Regional Studies*, 31 (6), 593–606.

Pehkonen, J. and Tervo, H. (1998) 'Persistence and turnover in regional unemployment disparities', *Regional Studies*, 32, 445–58.

Pelkmans, J. and Winters, A. (1988) *Europe's Domestic Market*, Routledge, London.

Perroux, F. (1950) 'Economic space: theory and applications', *Quarterly Journal of Economics*, 65.

Persson, J. (1997) 'Convergence across the Swedish counties, 1911–93', *European Economic Review*, 41, 1835–52.

Peterson, J. (1995) 'Decision-making in the European Union: towards a framework for analysis', *Journal of European Public Policy*, 2, 69–93.

Phelps, N. (1995) 'Regional variations in rates and sources of innovation: evidence from the electronics industry in South Wales and Hampshire-Berkshire', *Area*, 27, 347–57.

Phelps, N. (1997) *Multinationals and European Integration: Trade Investment and Regional Development*, Jessica Kingsley, London.

Phillips, A. W. (1958) 'The relationship between unemployment and the rate of change of money wage rates in the United Kingdom, 1861–1957', *Economica*, 25, 283–99.

Pickles, A. and Rogerson, P. (1984) 'Wage distributions and spatial preferences in competitive job search and migration', *Regional Studies*, 18, 131–42.

Piore, M. and Sabel, C. (1984) *The Second Industrial Divide: Possibilities for Prosperity*, Basic Books, New York.

Pissarides, C. and McMaster, I. (1990) 'Regional migration, wages and employment: empirical evidence and implications for policy', *Oxford Economic Papers*, 42, 812–31.

Pissarides, C. and Wadsworth, J. (1989) 'Unemployment and the interregional mobility of labour', *Economic Journal*, 99, 739–55.

Pollack, M. (1995) 'Regional actors in the intergovernmental play: the making and implementation of EC structural policy', in C. Rhodes and S. Mazey (eds), *The State of the European Union III: Building a European Polity?*, Longman, Harlow, 361–90.

Porter, M. E. (1990) *The Competitive Advantage of Nations*, Macmillan, London.

Potter, J. and Moore, B. (2000) 'United Kingdom Enterprise Zones and the attraction of inward investment', *Urban Studies* (forthcoming).

Putnam, R. (1993) *Making Democracy Work*, Princeton University Press, Princeton, NJ.

Quah, D. (1996) 'Regional convergence clusters across Europe', *European Economic Review*, 40, 951–8.

Quévit, M. (1992) 'The regional impact of the internal market: a comparative analysis of traditional industrial and lagging regions', *Regional Studies*, 26, 349–69.

Quévit, M. (1995) 'The regional impact of the Internal Market: a comparative analysis of traditional industrial and declining regions', in S. Hardy, M. Hart, L. Albrechts and A. Katos (eds), *An Enlarged Europe: Regions in Competition?*, Jessica Kingsley, London, 55–69.

Rabellotti, R. (1998) 'Collective effects in Italian and Mexican footwear industrial clusters', *Small Business Economics*, 10, 243–62.

Raines, P. (1998) 'Regions in competition: institutional autonomy, inward investment and regional variation in the use of incentives', European Policies Research Centre, University of Strathclyde, Glasgow.

Raines, P. and Wishlade, F. (1997) 'Cross-regional perspectives in the use of incentives to attract foreign investment', in M. Danson, S. Hill and G. Lloyd (eds), *Regional Governance and Economic Development*, Pion, London.

Rauch, J. E. (1993) 'Productivity gains from geographic concentration of human capital: evidence from the cities', *Journal of Urban Economics*, 34, 380–400.

Rey, S. and Montouri, B. D. (1999) 'US regional income convergence: a spatial econometric perspective', *Regional Studies*, 33, 143–56.

Reynolds, P., Storey, D. J. and Westhead, P. (1994) 'Cross-national comparisons of the variation in new firm formation rates', *Regional studies*, 28, 443–56.

Rhodes, R. A. W. (1996) 'The new governance: governing without government', *Political Studies*, XLIV, 652–67.

Rhodes, R. A. W. (1997) *Understanding Governance: Policy Networks, Reflexivity and Accountability*, Open University Press, Buckingham.

Richardson, H. W. (1978) *Regional and Urban Economics*, Penguin, London.

Robinson, F., Wren, C. and Goddard, J. B. (1987) *Economic Development Policies: An Evaluative Study of the Newcastle Metropolitan Region*, Clarendon Press, Oxford.

Robson, G. B. (1996) 'Unravelling the facts about job generation', *Small Business Economics*, 8, 409–17.

Robson, M. T. (1991) 'Self-employment and new firm formation', *Scottish Journal of Political Economy*, 38, 352–68.

Robson, M. T. (1998) 'Self-employment in the UK regions', *Applied Economics*, 30, 313–22.

Rogerson, P. (1982) 'Spatial models of search', *Geographical Analysis*, 14, 217–28.

Romer, P. M. (1986) 'Increasing returns and long-run growth', *Journal of Political Economy*, 94, 1002–37.

Romer, P. M. (1990) 'Endogenous technological change', *Journal of Political Economy*, 98 (October), S71–S102.

Roper, S. and O'Shea, G. (1991) 'The effects of labour subsidies in Northern Ireland 1967–79: a simulation analysis', *Scottish Journal of Political Economy*, 38, 273–92.

Rosenbaum, M. and Bailey, J. (1991) 'Movement within England and Wales during the 1980s as measured by the NHS Central Register', *Population Trends*, 65, 24–34.

Rossi, P. (1980) *Why Families Move*, Sage, New York.

Sala-i-Martin, X. (1996a) 'The classical approach to convergence analysis', *Economic Journal*, 106, 1019–36.

Sali-i-Martin, X. (1996b) 'Regional cohesion: evidence and theories of regional growth and convergence', *European Economic Review*, 40, 1325–52.

Salt, J. (1990) 'Organisational labour migration: theory and practice in the UK', in J. H. Johnson and J. Salt (eds), *Labour Migration*, David Fulton, London, 53–69.

Schachter, J. and Althaus, P. G. (1989) 'An equilibrium model of gross migration', *Journal of Regional Science*, 29, 143–59.

Schofield, J. A. (1976) 'Economic efficiency and regional policy', *Urban Studies*, 13, 181–92.

Schofield, J. A. (1989a) *Cost–Benefit Analysis in Urban and Regional Planning*, Unwin Hyman, London.

Schofield, J. A. (1989b) 'Federal regional development policies in Canada: employment impact in Quebec and the Atlantic Provinces', *Review of Urban and Regional Development Studies*, 1, 65–79.

Scott, A. and Breton, A. (1975) *The Theory of the Structure of the Public Sector*, University of British Columbia Press, Vancouver.

Scott, M., Roberts, I., Holroyd, G. and Sawbridge, G. (1989) *Management and Industrial Relations in Small Firms*, Research Paper 70, Department of Employment, London.

Scottish Constitutional Convention (1989) *Towards a Scottish Parliament*, Scottish Constitutional Convention, Edinburgh.

Scottish Constitutional Convention (1995) *Scotland's Parliament; Scotland's Right*, Scottish Constitutional Convention, Edinburgh.

Selden, J. (1998) 'Small and medium enterprises: their role in the economy', *Labour Market Trends, October 1998*, Government Statistical Service, London, 511–17.

Sell, R. E. (1990) 'Migration and job transfers in the United States', in J. H. Johnson and J. Salt (eds), *Labour Migration*, David Fulton, London, 17–52.

Sellgren, J. (1991) 'The changing nature of economic development activities: a longitudinal analysis of local authorities in Great Britain 1981–7', *Environment and Planning C: Government and Policy*, 9, 341–62.

Sheppard, E. S. (1978) 'Theoretical underpinnings of the gravity hypothesis', *Geographical Analysis*, 10, 386–401.

Short, J. (1981) *Public Expenditure and Taxation in UK Regions*, Gower, Aldershot.

Short, J. (1984) 'Public finance and devolution: money flows between government and regions in the United Kingdom', *Scottish Journal of Political Economy*, 31, 114–30.

Simmie, J. (1997) *Innovation, Networks and Learning Regions?*, Jessica Kingsley, London.

Sinclair, M. T. and Sutcliffe, C. M. S. (1978) 'The first round and the Keynesian regional income multiplier', *Scottish Journal of Political Economy*, 25, 177–86.

Sinclair, M. T. and Sutcliffe, C. M. S. (1984) 'Keynesian income multipliers and first and second round effects: an application to tourist expenditures', *Oxford Bulletin of Economics and Statistics*, 44, 321–38.

Sinclair, M. T. and Sutcliffe, C. M. S. (1989) 'Truncated income multipliers and local income generation over time', *Applied Economics*, 21, 1621–46.

Siriopoulos, C. and Asteriou, D. (1998) 'Testing for convergence across the Greek regions', *Regional Studies*, 32, 537–46.

Sjaastad, L. A. (1962) 'The costs and returns of human migration', *Journal of Political Economy*, Supplement, LXX, 80–93.

Small Business Research Trust (1999) 'Business finance', *NatWest SBRT Quarterly Survey of Small Business in Britain*, 15, 17–22.

Smallbone, D. and North, D. (1995) 'Targeting established SMEs: does their age matter?', *International Small Business Journal*, 13, 47–64. Smith, B. (1975) 'Regional specialisation and trade in the UK', *Scottish Journal of Political Economy*, 22, 39–56.

Smith, I. J., Tether, B., Thwaites, A., Townsend, J. and Wynarczyk, P. (1993) 'The performance of innovative small firms: a regional issue', in P. Swann (ed.), *New Technologies and the Firm*, Routledge, London, 54–82.

Snaith, J. (1990) 'Migration and dual career households', in J. H. Johnson and J. Salt (eds), *Labour Mobility*, David Fulton, London, 155–71.

Social Exclusion Unit (1998) *Bringing Britain Together: A National Strategy for Neighbourhood Renewal*, Cabinet Office, The Stationery Office, London.

Solow, R. M. (1956) 'A contribution to the theory of economic growth', *Quarterly Journal of Economics*, 70, 65–94.

Solow, R. M. (1957) 'Technical change and the aggregate production function', *Review of Economics and Statistics'*, 39, 312–20.

Spencer, K. and Mawson, J. (1998) 'Government offices and policy coordination in the English regions', *Local Governance*, 24, 101–9.

Staiger, R. W. (1987) 'Heckscher–Ohlin theory in the presence of market power', *European Economic Review*, 31, 97–102.

Sternberg, R. (1999) 'Innovative linkages and proximity: empirical results from small and medium sized firms in German regions', *Regional Studies*, 33, 529–40.

Stillwell, J., Duke-Williams, O. and Rees, P. (1995) 'Time series migration in Britain: the context for 1991 Census analysis', *Papers in Regional Science*, 74, 341–59.

Stone, I. and Peck, F. (1996) 'The foreign-owned manufacturing sector in UK peripheral regions, 1978–93: restructuring and comparative performance', *Regional Studies*, 30 (1), 55–68.

Storey, D. J. (1982) *Entrepreneurship and the New Firm*, Croom Helm, London.

Storey, D. J. (1983) *The Small Firm: An International Survey*, Croom Helm/St Martin's Press, London.

Storey, D. J. (1990) 'Evaluation of policies and measures to create local employment', *Urban Studies*, 27, 669–84.

Storey, D. J. (1994) *Understanding the Small Business Sector*, Routledge, London.

Storey, D. J. and Johnson, S. (1987) 'Regional variations in entrepreneurship in the United Kingdom', *Scottish Journal of Political Economy*, 34, 161–73.

Storper, M. (1995) 'The resurgence of regional economies, ten years later: the region as a nexus of untraded interdependencies', *European Urban and Regional Studies*, 2, 191–221.

Stott, M. and Hodges, J. (1996) 'Local exchange and trading schemes', *Local Economy*, 11, 266–8.

Suarez-Villa, L. (1993) 'The dynamics of regional invention and innovation: innovative capacity and regional change in the twentieth century', *Geographical Analysis*, 25, 147–64.

Suarez-Villa, L. (1999) 'Policies or market incentives? Major changes in the geographical sources of technology in the United States, 1945–94', Department of Urban and Regional Planning, University of California, Irvine, CA.

Sun, H. (1995) 'Foreign investment and regional economic development in China', *Australasin Journal of Regional Studies*, 1, 133–48.

Sun, H. (1998) 'Economic growth and regional disparity in China: 1979–96', Working Paper Series 9812, Department of Economics, Deakin University, Australia.

Swales, J. K. (1979) 'Relative factor prices and regional specialisation in the United Kingdom', *Scottish Journal of Political Economy*, 26, 127–46.

Swales, J. K. (1981) 'The employment effects of a regional capital subsidy', *Regional Studies*, 15, 263–73.

Swales, J. K. (1983) 'A Kaldorian model of cumulative causation: regional growth with induced technical change', in A. Gillespie (ed.), *Technological Change and Regional Development*, Price, London.

Swales, J. K. (1989) 'Are discretionary regional subsidies cost-effective?', *Regional Studies*, 23, 361–8.

Swales, J. K. (1997a) 'The *ex post* evaluation of Regional Selective Assistance', *Regional Studies*, 31, 859–66.

Swales, J. K. (1997b) 'The cost–benefit approach to the evaluation of Regional Selective Assistance', *Fiscal Studies*, 18 (1), 73–85.

Taylor, J. (1993) 'An analysis of the factors determining the geographical distribution of Japanese manufacturing investment in the UK, 1984–91', *Urban Studies*, 30, 1209–24.

Taylor, J. and Bradley, S. (1983) 'The analysis of spatial variations in the unemployment rate', *Regional Studies*, 17, 113–24.

Taylor, J. and Bradley, S. (1994) 'Spatial disparities in the impact of the 1990–2 recession: an analysis of UK counties', *Oxford Bulletin of Economics and Statistics*, 56, 367–82.

Taylor, J. and Bradley, S. (1997) 'Unemployment in Europe: a comparative analysis of regional disparities in Germany, Italy and the UK', *Kyklos*, 50, 221–45.

Taylor, J. and Twomey, J. (1998) 'The movement of manufacturing industry in Great Britain: an inter-county analysis', *Urban Studies*, 25, 228–42.

Taylor, J. and Wren, C. (1997) 'UK regional policy: an evaluation', *Regional Studies*, 31 (9), 835–48.

Thirlwall, A. P. (1969) 'Types of unemployment with special reference to non-deficient-demand unemployment in Great Britain', *Scottish Journal of Political Economy*, 16, 20–49.

Thirlwall, A. P. (1974) 'Types of unemployment in the regions of Great Britain', *Manchester School*, 42, 325–39.

Thirlwall, A. P. (1980) 'Regional problems are balance of payments problems', *Regional Studies*, 14, 419–26.

Thirlwall, A. P. (1983) 'A plain man's guide to Kaldor's Laws', *Journal of Post-Keynesian Economics*.

Thwaites, A. T. and Alderman, N. (1990) 'The location of R&D: retrospect and prospect', in R. Capellin and P. Nijkamp (eds), *The Spatial Context of Technological Development*, Avebury, Aldershot, 17–42.

Tömmell, I. (1998) 'Transformation of governance: the European Commission's strategy for creating a "Europe of the Regions"', *Regional and Federal Studies*, 8, 52–80.

Townroe, P. and Mallalieu, K. (1993) 'Founding a new business in the countryside', in J. Curran and D. J. Storey (eds), *Small Firms in Urban and Rural Locations*, Routledge, London, 17–53.

Townsend, J., Henwood, F., Thomas, F., Pavitt, K. and Wyatt, S. (1981) 'Science and technology indicators for the UK: innovations since 1945', Occasional Paper 16, Science Policy Research Unit, University of Sussex, Brighton.

Trelfer, D. (1995) 'The case of missing trade and other mysteries', *American Economic Review*, 85, 1029–46.

Treyz, G. I., Rickman, D. S., Hunt, G. L. and Greenwood, M. J. (1993) 'The dynamics of US internal migration', *Review of Economics and Statistics*, 75, 209–14.

Turok, I. (1989) 'Evaluation and understanding in local economic policy', *Urban Studies*, 26, 587–600.

Turok, I. (1993) 'Inward investment and local linkages: how deeply embedded is "Silicon Glen"?', *Regional Studies*, 27, 401–17.

Turok, I. (1997) 'Evaluating European support for business development: evidence from the structural funds in Scotland', *Entrepreneurship & Regional Development*, 9, 335–52.

Turok, I. (1999) 'Localisation or mainstream bending in urban regeneration', *Local Economy*, 14, 72–86.

Twomey, J. and Taylor, J. (1985) 'Regional policy and the interregional movement of manufacturing industry in Great Britain', *Scottish Journal of Political Economy*, 32, 257–77.

Vaessen, P. and Keeble, D. (1995) 'Growth-oriented SMEs in unfavourable regional environments', *Regional Studies*, 29, 489–505.

Van Dijk, J., Folmer, H., Herzoy, H. W. and Schlottmann, A. M. (1989) *Migration and Labour Market Adjustment*, Kluwer, Amsterdam.

Vanderkamp, J. (1971) 'Migration flows, their determination and the effects of return migration', *Journal of Political Economy*, 79, 1012–31.

Vanderkamp, J. (1989) 'Regional adjustment and migration flows in Canada, 1971–81', *Papers of the Regional Science Association*, 67, 103–19.

Venables, A. J. (1996) 'Equilibrium location with vertically-linked industries', *International Economic Review*, 37, 341–59.

Venables, A. J. (1998) 'The assessment: trade and location', *Oxford Review of Economic Policy*, 14, 1–5.

Verdoorn, P. J. (1949) 'Fattori che regolano lo sviluppo della producttivita del lavaro', *L'Industria*.

Vickers, L. (1998) 'Trends in migration in the UK', *Population Trends*, Winter, 25–34.

Walsh, J. and Brown, W. (1991) 'Regional earnings and pay flexibility', in A. Bowen and K. Mayhew (eds), *Reducing Regional Inequalities*, Kogan Page, London, 185–215.

Warr, P. B. (1987) *Work, Unemployment and Mental Health*, Clarendon, Oxford.

Watts, H. D. and Kirkham, J. (1997) 'The influence of plant profitability on plant closures in multi-locational firms', *Growth and Change*, 28, 459–74.

Watts, H. D. and Kirkham, J. (1999) 'Plant closures by multi-locational firms: a comparative perspective', *Regional Studies*, 33, 413–24.

Wei, Y., Liu, X., Parker, D. and Vidya, K. (1999) 'The regional distribution of foreign direct investment in China', *Regional Studies*, 33, 857–67.

Wei, Y., Liu, X., Song, H. and Romilly, P. (2000b) 'Endogenous innovation growth theory and regional income convergence in China', *Journal of International Development*, forthcoming.

Weinstein, B. L. and Firestine, R. E. (1978) *Regional Growth and Decline in the United States: The Rise of the Sunbelt and the Decline of the Northeast*, Praeger, New York.

West, G. (1991) 'A Queensland input–output econometric model: an overview', *Australian Economic Papers*, December, 30, 221–40.

Westhead, P. and Moyes, A. (1992) 'Reflections on Thatcher's Britain: evidence for new production firm registrations 1980–8', *Entrepreneurship and Regional Development*, 4, 21–56.

Whitley, J. D. and Wilson, R. A. (1983) 'The macroeconomic merits of a marginal employment subsidy', *Economic Journal*, 93, 862–80.

Williams, C. C. (1996a) 'Local purchasing schemes and rural development: an evaluation of Local Exchange and Trading Systems (LETS)', *Journal of Rural Studies*, 12, 231–44.

Williams, C. C. (1996b) 'An appraisal of local exchange and trading systems in the United Kingdom', *Local Economy*, 11, 259–66.

Williamson, J. (1965) 'Regional inequality and the process of national development: a description of patterns', *Economic Development and Cultural Change*, 13, 3–45.

Wishlade, F. (1998) 'EC competition policy: the poor relation of EC regional policy?', *European Planning Studies*, 6, 573–97.

Wisniewski, M. (1996) *Introductory Mathematical Methods in Economics*, McGraw-Hill, London.

Woodward, D. P. (1992) 'Locational determinants of Japanese manufacturing start-ups in the United States', *Southern Economic Journal*, 58, 690–708.

Wren, C. (1987) 'The relative effects of local authority financial assistance policies', *Urban Studies*, 24, 268–78.

Wren, C. (1988) 'Closure rates for assisted and non-assisted establishments', *Regional Studies*, 22, 107–19.

Wren, C. (1989a) 'Factors underlying the employment effects of financial assistance policies', *Applied Economics*, 21, 497–513.

Wren, C. (1989b) 'The revised Regional Development Grant scheme: a case study in Cleveland County of a marginal employment subsidy', *Regional Studies*, 23, 127–38.

Wren, C. (1996a) *Industrial Subsidies: The UK Experience*, Macmillan, Basingstoke.

Wren, C. (1996b) 'Grant equivalent expenditure on investment subsidies in the post-war United Kingdom', *Oxford Bulletin of Economics and Statistics*, 58, 317–53.

Wren, C. (1996c) 'Gross expenditure on UK industrial assistance: a research note', *Scottish Journal of Political Economy*, 43 (1), 113–26.

Wren, C. (1998) 'Subsidies for job creation: is small best?', *Small Business Economics*, 10, 273–81.

Wren, C. and Swales, J. K. (1991) 'An economic analysis of the revised Regional Development Grant scheme', *Scottish Journal of Political Economy*, 38, 256–72.

Wren, C. and Taylor, J. (1999) 'Industrial restructuring and regional policy', *Oxford Economic Papers*, 51.

Wren, C. and Waterson, M. (1991) 'The direct employment effects of financial assistance to industry', *Oxford Economic Papers*, 43, 116–38.

Yan, C. (1969) *Introduction to Input–Output Economics*, Holt, Rinehart and Winston, New York.

Young, R. (1999) 'Prospecting for new jobs to combat social exclusion: the example of home care services', *European Urban and Regional Studies*, 6, 99–113.

Young, S., Hood, N. and Peters, E. (1994) 'Multinational enterprises and regional economic development', *Regional Studies*, 28, 657–77.

Government publications

Audit Commission (1989) *Urban Regeneration and Economic Development: The Local Government Dimension*, HMSO, London.

Bank of England (1998) *Quarterly Report on Small Business Statistics, December 1998*, Business Finance Division, London.

Cabinet Office (1998) *Civil Service Statistics 1998*, The Government Statistical Service, London.

Commission of the European Communities (1977) *Guidelines for Community Regional Policy*, Commission Communication COM (77) 195 final, Brussels.

Commission of the European Communities (1979) *Report of the Study Group on the Role of Public Finance in European Integration (McDougall Report)*, vols I and II, Office for Official Publications of the European Communities Brussels/Luxembourg.

Commission of the European Communities (1981a) *Deglomeration Policies in the European Community: A Comparative Study*, Regional Policy Series 18, Office for Official Publications of the European Communities, Brussels/Luxembourg.

Commission of the European Communities (1981b) *Study of the Regional Impact of the Common Agricultural Policy*, Regional Policy Series 21, Office for Official Publications of the European Communities, Brussels/Luxembourg.

Commission of the European Communities (1987) *Job Creation in Small and Medium Sized Companies*, vols I and II, Office for Official Publications of the European Communities, Brussels/Luxembourg.

Commission of the European Communities (1989) *Guide to the Reform of the Community's Structural Funds*, Office for Official Publications of the European Communities, Brussels/Luxembourg.

Commission of the European Communities (1990) *The Regions in the 1990s: Fourth Periodic Report on the Social and Economic Situation and Development of the Regions of the Community*, Office for Official Publications of the European Communities, Brussels/Luxembourg.

Commission of the European Communities (1993) 'Growth, competitiveness, employment: the challenges and ways forward into the 21st century: White Paper', *Bulletin of the European Communities*, Supplement 6/93, Office for Official Publications of the European Communities, Brussels/Luxembourg.

Committee of Public Accounts (1984) *Regional Industrial Incentives*, House of Commons, Session 1983–4, House of Commons Papers 378, HMSO, London.

Defence Analytical Services Agency (1999) *UK Defence Statistics, 1998*, The Stationery Office, London.

Department of the Environment, Transport and the Regions (1997) *Building Partnerships for Prosperity: Sustainable Growth, Competitiveness and Employment in the English Regions*, Cm 3814, The Stationery Office, Norwich.

Department of Trade and Industry (1995) *Regional Industrial Policy*, Cm 2910, HMSO, London.

Department of Trade and Industry (1996) *Small Firms in Britain Report 1996*, DTI, London.

Department of Trade and Industry (1998a) *Small and Medium Enterprise (SME) Statistics for the United Kingdom, 1997*, Statistical Report URN 98/92, SME Statistics Unit, Sheffield.

Department of Trade and Industry (1998b) *Business Start-ups and Closures: VAT Registrations and De-registrations 1980–97*, Statistical Report URN 98/111, SME Statistics Unit, Sheffield.

Department of Trade and Industry (1999a) *Small and Medium Enterprise (SME) Statistics for the United Kingdom, 1998*, Statistical Report URN 99/92, SME Statistics Unit, Sheffield.

Department of Trade and Industry (1999b) *The Government's Proposals for New Assisted Areas*, DTI, London.

Department of Trade and Industry (1999c) *Trade and Industry: The Government's Expenditure Plans 1999/2000–2001/2002*, Cm 4211, The Stationery Office, London.

Deutsches Institut für Wirtschaftsforschung (1991) *The Regional Impact of Community Policies*, European Parliament, Directorate-General for Research, Regional Policy and Transport Series Paper 17, Brussels/Luxembourg.

European Commission (1994a) *Europe 2000: Co-operation for European Territorial Development*, Office for Official Publications of the European Communities, Brussels/Luxembourg.

European Commission (1994b) *Competitiveness and Cohesion: Fifth Periodic Report on the Social and Economic Situation of the Regions in the Community*, Office for Official Publications of the European Communities, Brussels/Luxembourg.

European Commission (1996a) *First Cohesion Report*, Office for Official Publications of the European Communities, Brussels/Luxembourg.

European Commission (1996b) *Social and Economic Inclusion through Regional Development: The Community Economic Development Priority in European Structural Funds Programmes in Great Britain*, Report for the European Commission, Brussels.

European Commission (1996d) *The Impact of the Development of the Countries of Central and Eastern Europe on the Community Territories*, Regional Development Studies Series 16, Office for Official Publications of the European Communities, Brussels/Luxembourg.

European Commission (1996c) *The Structural Funds and Cohesion Fund 1994–9: Regulations and Commentary*, Office for Official Publications of the European Communities, Brussels/Luxembourg.

European Commission (1997) *Agenda 2000: For a Stronger and Wider Union*, Office for Official Publications of the European Communities, Brussels/Luxembourg.

European Commission (1998a) 'Guidelines on national regional aid', *Official Journal of the European Communities*, 41, C74 of 10 March 1998, 9–30.

European Commission (1998b) *Proposed Regulations and Explanatory Memorandum Covering the Reform of the Structural Funds 2000–6*, Directorate-General for Regional Policy (DGXVI), Brussels.

European Commission (1999) *Sixth Periodic Report on the Social and Economic Situation of the Regions in the Community*, Office for Official Publications of the European Communities, Brussels/Luxembourg.

European Council (1999) *Presidency Conclusions: Berlin European Council, 24–5 March*, Brussels.

European Investment Bank (1998) *Annual Report 1997*, European Investment Bank, Luxembourg.

Government Office for Yorkshire and the Humber (1997) *Single Programming Document 1997–9: Yorkshire and the Humber Objective 2 Area*, Leeds.

Government Office for Yorkshire and the Humber (1999a) *Ex Post Evaluation of the 1994–6 Yorkshire and Humber Objective 2 Programme*, Government Office, Leeds.

Government Office for Yorkshire and the Humber (1999b) *Interim Evaluation of the Yorkshire and Humber Objective 2 1997–9 Programme*, Government Office, Leeds.

Hardman Report (1973) *The Dispersal of Government Work from London*, Cmnd 5322, HMSO, London.

HM Treasury (1984) *Memorandum: Freeports in the United Kingdom: Guidance for Potential Operators*, HM Treasury, London.

HM Treasury (1991) *Economic Appraisal in Central Government: A Technical Guide for Government Departments*, HMSO, London.

HM Treasury (1995) *A Framework for the Evaluation of Regeneration Projects and Programmes*, HMSO, London.

HM Treasury (1999) *Public Expenditure: Statistical Analyses 1999–2000*, HM Treasury, London.

House of Commons (1995) *Regional Policy*, Fourth Report of the Trade and Industry Committee, Session 1994–5, HC 356, I and II, HMSO, London.

House of Commons (1997) *The Barnett Formula*, Treasury Committee, Second Report, House of Commons Papers Session 1997/98, The Stationery Office, London.

House of Commons (1998) *The Industrial Development Act 1982: Annual Report for 1998*, House of Commons Papers 1069, Session 1997/98, The Stationery Office, London.

IFO Institute for Economic Research (1991) *An Empirical Assessment of the Factors Shaping Regional Competitiveness in Problem Regions*, Study for the Commission of the European Communities, Brussels.

Layfield Report (1976) *Committee of Enquiry into Local Government Finance: Report*, HMSO, London.

Ministry of Labour (1928) *Report of the Industrial Transference Board*, Cm 3156, HMSO, London.

National Economic Development Council (1963) *Conditions Favourable to Faster Growth*, HMSO, London.

Organization for Economic Cooperation and Development (1994) 'Job gains and losses in firms', *Employment Outlook*, July, 103–35.

Royal Commission on the Constitution (1973) *Volume I: Report*, HMSO, London.

Royal Commission on the Distribution of the Industrial Population (1940) *Report*, Cm 6153, HMSO, London.

Scottish Enterprise (1997) *Output Measurement Framework Guidelines*, Scottish Enterprise, Glasgow.

Scottish Office (1993) *Scotland in the Union: A Partnership for Good*, Cm 2225, HMSO, London.

Scottish Office (1997a) *Input–Output Tables and Mutipliers for Scotland 1994*, Education and Industry Department, Scottish Office.

Scottish Office (1997b) *Scotland's Parliament*, Cm 3658, The Stationery Office, Edinburgh.

Welsh Office (1997) *A Voice for Wales: The Government's Proposals for a Welsh Assembly*, Cm 3718, The Stationery Office, London.

White Paper (1944) *Employment Policy*, Cm 6527, HMSO, London.

White Paper (1983) *Regional Industrial Policy*, Cm 9111, HMSO, London.

White Paper (1988) *DTI – The Department for Enterprise*, Cm 278, HMSO, London.

White Paper (1994) *Competitiveness: Helping Business to Win*, Cm 2563, HMSO, London.

White Paper (1995) *Competitiveness: Forging Ahead*, Cm 2867, HMSO, London.

White Paper (1996) *Competitiveness: Creating the Enterprise Centre of Europe*, Cm 3300, HMSO, London.

White Paper (1998) *Our Competitive Future: Building the Knowledge Driven Economy*, Cm 4176, The Stationery Office, London.

World Bank (1999) *World Development Reports 1997 and 1998/99*, Oxford University Press, Oxford, tables 1, 1a and 12.

Index